Understanding the Nature of Autism
A Practical Guide

Janice E. Janzen, M.S.

with Foreword by
June Groden, Ph.D.

Illustrations completed under contract by Dian Moore

Therapy Skill Builders™
a division of
The Psychological Corporation

555 Academic Court
San Antonio, Texas 78204-2498
1-800-228-0752

Reproducing Pages from this Book

As described below, some of the pages in this book may be reproduced for instructional or administrative use (not for resale). To protect your book, make a photocopy of each reproducible page. Then use that copy as a master for photocopying.

Published by

Therapy Skill Builders™ ®
a division of
The Psychological Corporation

555 Academic Court
San Antonio, Texas 78204-2498
1-800-228-0752

The author grateful acknowledges permission to reprint the following copyrighted material:

"Understand," "Youth So Sober," "Talk," "Happy Feelings," "Lonely Boy," and "In My Mind" by David Eastham, from *UNDERSTAND: Fifty Memowriter Poems.* Copyright © 1985 by Oliver-Pate. Reprinted by permission of the publisher.

"A Lovely Day," "Fiddlesticks," and "Upsets" by David Eastham, from *Silent Words and Forever Friends.* Copyright © 1990 by Oliver-Pate. Reprinted by permission of the publisher.

Excerpts from "Bridging the Gaps: An Inside-out View of Autism (Or, Do You Know What I Don't Know?)" by Jim Sinclair, in *High-Functioning Individuals with Autism,* edited by E. Schopler and G. B. Mesibov. Copyright © 1992 by Plenum Press. Reprinted by permission of the publisher.

Figures 6.1 and 6.2; and forms 6.3, 6.4, 6.8, 11.1: Developed for Project QUEST, a project funded in part by the U.S. Department of Education, Office of Special Education and Rehabilitation Services, Grant #G00873042688. Adapted with permission from *Project QUEST Inservice Manual* by R. Falco, J. Janzen, J. Arick, K. Wilgus, and M. DeBoer (1990).

Figure 13.1; and forms 6.2 and 6.6: Adapted with permission from *Judevine® Training System* by Lois Blackwell (1978).

Forms 6.5, 6.7, 25.1, 25.2, 25.3, 25.4, and 25.5: Adapted with permission from Oregon Regional Autism Services.

ISBN 0761643796

10 9 8 7 6 5 4 3 2 1

Printed in the United States of America

About the Author

Janice E. Janzen has been involved in the field of autism since 1972, first as a teacher in early childhood classes in a private treatment center and in the public school system in Anchorage, Alaska. Later, as an Autism Specialist for the Oregon Department of Education, she was instrumental in developing services for students with autism across the state. While at the Department, Ms. Janzen had statewide responsibility to support the Regional Autism Specialists, to consult in difficult situations, to develop training materials, and to conduct workshops for educators and parents.

Janice Janzen received the B.S. degree in Elementary/Early Childhood Education from the University of Oregon; and the M.S. degree in Special Education/Learning Disabilities from the University of Alaska. Her initial autism training at the Judevine Center in St. Louis, Missouri, occurred simultaneously with her master's program. During this period, she began to develop her unique understanding of the autism learning style.

Ms. Janzen has a special interest and concern with the problems of families, and emphasizes the need for families and educators to work collaboratively. She is a cofounder of the Autism Council of Oregon, an organization for parents and professionals.

She has written numerous technical assistance and special topics papers on autism for distribution by the Oregon Department of Education. Her RAPSOURCE papers on autism, prepared for the Head Start Training Office, Resource Access Project at Portland State University, have received wide distribution.

Currently, Janice Janzen is in private practice, consulting, writing, and teaching.

Contents

Figures

Reproducible Forms

Foreword

Janice E. Janzen has undertaken a formidable task in writing this book. She has covered the spectrum of autism by first discussing the definition of autism and then reviewing learning styles, communication, placement and program decisions, the development of programs, management of behavioral problems, and assessment. It can be considered a primer in autism and is an excellent resource for training parents, teachers, and program personnel.

The book is admirable in many respects. It is written so that people of all reading levels can understand and apply the concepts. The strength of the book lies in the many relevant examples that appear throughout the chapters. They show how the principles that are discussed can be applied to actual cases of people with autism, thereby continuously clarifying the information. Although there is a growing body of literature in the field of autism, this book has a number of special features that differentiate it from the others.

The concept of an autism specialist as an interpreter brings new light to the role. Jan Janzen describes the autism specialist as a person who can organize information, give guidance to parents, teachers, and therapists, and design tools to help people with autism function more independently in the community. As an interpreter, the autism specialist has a pervasive role which includes numerous settings—inclusive and special classrooms, private programs, vocational and community settings, and at home—and numerous types of programs—communication, academic, social skills, physical education, and others. The role of the autism specialist as a regular and important member of the support team is also emphasized. I feel this often makes the difference between a successful and unsuccessful program for a person with autism.

Throughout the book there are figures that include descriptions of deficits and strengths of people with autism, and numerous checklists for assessment and evaluation. These figures can be used independently as a helpful resource and a quick reference in all settings. They also can be part of a teacher- or therapist-training packet that can be carried along, left in classrooms, or posted.

The section on the use of visual supports, including the importance of calendars and schedules, is admirable. It underscores the fact that autism still is not understood and that there is a need for these visual systems for both verbal and nonverbal learners.

The case study provided at the end of the book has considerable merit. The study synthesizes all the material and is an excellent summary. It allows the reader to follow one case and shows the sequence from assessment to program design. The steps that lead to goal setting and the description of the actual goals are well done. The information imparted to the reader can make a difference in the daily functioning of the person with autism. The personal accounts from families are very moving and help the reader to gain perspective on how autism affects the lives of parents.

The reference list is so extensive and complete that it can be used as a reading list for a course in autism or for further study for those who want to broaden their knowledge in the field. Other helpful resources include lists of organizations, training centers, resource centers, and publications that specialize in autism services.

This book will be appreciated by those who train teachers, parents, and other professionals in the field of autism. It is a comprehensive and concise book and a welcome addition to the literature in the field. It is apparent from reading this book that Janice E. Janzen has worked "hands on" for many years, and she is able to combine her knowledge of research and theory with applied practices. She is like a master chef who gives all the ingredients to make a recipe successful. Those who read this book will come away with useful information and the ability to put into practice the information they have gleaned.

June Groden, Ph.D.
The Groden Center, Providence, Rhode Island

Preface

Never in my wildest dreams did I ever expect to write a book, but my life holds many surprises and opportunities. Many people provided insights and support to help me develop the philosophy and strategies presented here. I will take this opportunity to acknowledge some of them. Many other friends and colleagues, who are unmentioned, were also influential, supportive, and highly appreciated. I hope they will know that they were remembered as well.

I must begin by acknowledging the influence of my husband, Marvin. Without his love, encouragement, and support I would never have become a teacher or written this book. When the youngest of our four children (Sandy, Tom, Ron, and Becci) was 12 years old and I was 40, Marv prodded me to return to college.

My bachelor's degree from the University of Oregon is in education with an emphasis in early childhood education. Experience with my mentor, Mildred Robeck, triggered my interest in brain development and the neurology of learning. In 1972, when my husband's work took us to Anchorage, my first teaching position was at the Alaska Treatment Center, where I taught preschool children with communication disorders.

It was at this Center where I met my first child with autism, and where I learned to value multidisciplinary teams. Inadvertently I had become a special education teacher without the credentials, and so my husband again encouraged me to work toward a master's degree in special education with an emphasis in learning disabilities. Marilyn Johnson, my graduate supervisor at the University of Alaska, became my mentor and friend. She added to my understanding of the learning process and learning style. I was teaching several children with autism and began to compare and contrast their learning style and that of children with severe learning disabilities. Marilyn helped me articulate the autism learning style.

As I got to know the families of my students with autism in Anchorage, I began to understand the strength and power of parents. Through parent advocacy, the Anchorage School district discovered the cost effectiveness of developing its own autism services. Margaret Lowe, director of Whaley Center, offered me the opportunity to be part of a team to develop these autism services.

In 1974, I completed the three-week Competency Based Training Program at the Judevine Center in St. Louis. Lois Blackwell, founder and director of the Judevine Center, became my next mentor. At a time when behaviorism dominated the field of autism, I learned the value of social learning theory, and that behavior modification could be applied sensitively and respectfully to teach new skills. Through a federal replication grant, staff members at Judevine came to Anchorage several times to provide technical assistance as the autism services developed. After this training, I taught demonstration classes and provided consultation and training to teachers in Anchorage and surrounding areas.

During the next three years of intense work with children ages 2½ to 16, I became fascinated with autism. I was constantly amazed by the unexpected confusion and stress, the amazingly literal perspective, and the surprising memory and speed of learning. I became convinced that teaching those with autism was the most creative, challenging, and rewarding job there could be.

The next turn in my education occurred when we returned to Oregon in 1978. Specialized autism services were available to only a few students who lived near the universities in Portland and Eugene. I was employed by the Marion County Education Service District (MESD) to provide itinerant consultative services in rural areas to students with severe emotional disturbances. I discovered a few students who had autism that was never diagnosed. At the same time, a colleague at the MESD, Karen Brazeau, who supervised the classrooms for those with severe and multiple disabilities, was concerned about the few students with autism in her programs who were having little success and exhibiting serious behavior problems. Consequently, Karen and I developed a collaborative relationship to establish autism services in Oregon. Our first ventures were to organize a parent support group, to sponsor a conference, and to write a grant proposal to replicate the Judevine Teacher Training Model.

The grant was funded to cover the costs of basic training in St. Louis for a team from Oregon and advanced training for me. With technical assistance from Judevine, three of us began to offer evening, weekend, and summer training for teachers and parents. Oregon's first autism conference was a resounding success. The keynote speaker was Lorna Wing, an international leader in the field. Professionally, Dr. Wing is a psychiatrist; her personal experience with autism is from the perspective of a parent. The conference attracted major interest from parents and professionals alike.

The parent group was established, and it grew and evolved into the Autism Council of Oregon. The ACO parents successfully lobbied the state legislature to fund autism services through the Department of Education's existing Regional Services Model for those with low-incidence disabilities. In 1983, Oregon's Regional Autism Services became a reality. Karen and I were employed by the Department to develop a service model that could be implemented in public schools. In this role, we had the unique opportunity to visit some of the major autism centers in the country. Thus began the development of an eclectic service model that integrated the work of those at Judevine, Division TEACCH in North Carolina, the Groden Center in Rhode Island, and other nationally recognized contributors to the field of autism.

Until my retirement in 1992, I coordinated Oregon's Regional Autism Services, training and supporting the Regional Autism Specialists and providing consultation and training for parents and teachers throughout the state. While driving the byways and back roads of Oregon with the Regional Autism Specialists, I developed close friendships as we shared and solved many of the problems that are unique in this field. I particularly want to recognize a few of the first specialists who did so much to challenge and expand my understanding of autism over the years: Hedi Bayliss, Judy Fryor, Colleen Nyberg, Annette Skowron-Gooch, and Joyce Stratton.

In the years that I worked with Oregon's Regional Autism Services, Gene Stubbs, M.D., an associate professor of psychiatry at the Oregon Health Sciences University, inspired me with his quiet dedication to those with autism and their families. As he searched for the causes of autism, he supported the development of the Regional Autism Services and was always available to help me understand some of the medical issues.

While many parents shared stories, anecdotes, and experiences and provided support to me, I want to recognize three who became friends as well. Mary Anne Seaton, Diana Lett, and Elaine Piper-Vardas were committed to sharing their child's experiences so others could understand the problems of their children and others with autism.

Some of the leaders in the fields of autism and special education who indirectly influenced the content and philosophy of this book also must be acknowledged. The findings from the neurobiological research of Eric Courchesne and colleagues, integrated with Barry Prizant's descriptions of the gestalt learning process, triggered my understanding of the autism learning style. Gary Mesibov influenced my understanding of structure as a positive behavior-management and teaching tool. The scheduling strategies and use of contingencies to increase flexibility and tolerance were adapted from the Judevine Competency Based Training. Lyle Chastain, Geraldine Dawson, and James MacDonald influenced the development of chapter 20, concerning strategies for teaching early social interaction skills. Gary LaVigna, Louanna Meyer, and Robert Horner and his colleagues contributed to the development of the material on functional analysis of behavior and positive, proactive, behavior strategies. The development of the systematic and precise use of cues, prompts, and correction procedures described in chapter 17 was influenced by Anne Donnellan, Gary LaVigna, and the Judevine training. The discussion of teaching concepts and teaching for generalization was influenced by the work of Robert Horner, Robert Koegel, Edward Carr, and others. The material on relaxation, self-control, and imagery procedures was drawn from the work of June Groden. The material on functional assessment and programming, especially that related to teaching in the context of natural routines, was developed with Ruth Falco and Joel Arick at Portland State University as part of the federally funded Project QUEST (Quality Educational Services and Training).

More direct assistance was provided by Allyson Goodwyn-Craine, speech-language pathologist in private practice. She generously provided current reference material and the benefit of her experience as I wrote some of the sections on communication, especially that related to facilitated communication. Hedi Bayliss, former autism specialist, provided hours of stimulating and challenging discussions and semantic maps to analyze and clarify the organization of the book and the presentation of concepts. My husband was my first and most honest editor; he read every word. Without his feedback and support, this book would never have been finished.

I especially want to thank the following colleagues and friends who waded through the drafts of this book to help clarify the content. Carol Christ, an autism specialist and a detail person, not only reviewed for clarity of ideas but critiqued the punctuation and sentence structure. (One chapter was returned with the following note: "Jan, I simply cannot tolerate more than three *ands* in a single sentence!") Nancy Marshall, a school counselor and trusted friend, reviewed the material from the perspective of a regular school teacher. Her ideas and emotional support were highly valued. Finally, thanks to my editor, Ricky Bourque, who was trained to condense. We had many negotiations and laughs because I was trained to tell the audience what you will say, say it, then tell them what you said. I hope our collaboration was successful.

Ultimately, it was the comments of parents, teachers, and teachers in training who participated in my classes and workshops that really stimulated this book. One said it best: "I wish you would write it all down so I could review it. . . . Then I could really understand and use it." With the help and support of my friends and my family, this book is a reality. To all of those mentioned and to those unmentioned whose influence and support are remembered and valued, I thank you.

Introduction

UNDERSTAND

I WANT PEOPLE TO UNDERSTAND
I KNOW ITS HARD TO DO
I THINK THEY CAN, IF THEY TRY
UNDERSTAND WON'T YOU?

UNDERSTANDING IS SO HARD
I LONG TO SEE IT REAL
I JUST HOPE, REALLY HOPE
IT'S NOT A LOST IDEAL

—David Eastham

In 1985, I read a small book of poems, *UNDERSTAND: Fifty Memowriter Poems,* written by David Eastham. David could not write or speak and was unable to express his thoughts until he learned to communicate on a small computer when he was 19 years old. The eloquence of his poetry (which I quote throughout this book) convinced me that one must be continually aware that there is a sensitive person inside everyone with autism and that the limit of any person's potential is never certain. David's plea to UNDERSTAND represents what I hope to accomplish in this book. (For David's life story and more poetry, read *Silent Words and Forever Friends* by M. W. and David Eastham.)

Understanding the Nature of Autism is a very personal work, written with the encouragement of parents who want others to understand the way their children think, and of dedicated teachers who are too busy to search the literature and apply the research—teachers who have said they wish they had known these things sooner.

A common problem for teachers and others who support those with autism is that much of the literature on autism is in the form of research reviews or recipes to resolve single problems or a narrow range of issues. It is difficult for the practitioner faced with everyday challenges to unravel and apply this information in a flexible way to address the specific and changing needs of the whole child.

- In Part 1, the foundation is established for understanding autism and the impact of autism on learning and thinking.

- In Part 2, some assessment and evaluation issues are addressed. Strategies are provided for solving common assessment problems to elicit the best possible information.

- In Part 3, guidelines are provided for making the many decisions that are required for planning educational programs and support systems that will most likely lead to more positive outcomes.

- In Part 4, a foundation is provided for planning all interventions. A set of basic strategies is introduced to address the deficits and problems most commonly associated with autism.

- In Part 5, the information from previous chapters is integrated and applied to the process for teaching a broad range of new skills.

- Part 6 serves as a summary of the processes and strategies while addressing some potentially serious problems.

The book will be most valuable if initially read from beginning to end to get the full perspective. Then reread the book, reviewing sections that have particular relevance. Study the guidelines for implementing specific strategies. The basic foundation for intervention is developed in parts 1 and 4. The basic concepts and strategies presented there are applied in different ways throughout the book to address a range of problems. To avoid duplication, references guide the reader from the introduction of a concept to the various applications.

Notes on Style

- All information and strategies are applicable to address the needs of those with autism of any age or level of ability. An example of a situation that occurred at home or at school will also apply to work or community settings.

- The words *unable, inability, do not,* or *cannot* simply mean that those with autism do not automatically understand or learn certain types of information or skills, or they are less able to do them efficiently and effectively. It does not imply that they cannot be *taught to compensate* for these deficits in some way.

- Most of the behavioral examples were selected from personal experiences. Others were shared by parents, service providers, and specialists in autism. Names used in the examples were assigned to represent many different individuals with similar levels of ability. For example, Jose represents many different individuals with severe but classic autism who echo, are compulsive, literal, and have limited verbal abilities. The examples assigned to Jose represent situations from early childhood to young adulthood.

- Ponder the poetry of David Eastham that is interspersed throughout the book. These particular poems were selected to provide eloquent insights that are intended to keep your attention focused on the reason for this book.

- Five mothers agreed to contribute some of their personal experiences and thoughts. Some quotations from their stories are placed in the text and in the appendix. Teachers will find some measure of understanding of the trials and the rewards that come as a result of living with autism. These stories also will provide a balance and perspective to other parents.

While the process and procedures outlined in this book may seem overwhelming at first, with practice they become automatic. Teachers will find that the strategies are basic and will benefit all. It is my hope that through your understanding of autism and use of these strategies, an increasing number of students will become more independent and lead more interesting and rewarding lives. I also hope that as teachers increase their understanding of the nature and perspective of those with autism, they will feel increasingly confident, creative, and rewarded.

1
The Nature of Autism

A LOVELY DAY

A LOVELY DAY
TO JUMP INTO
THE POOL OF LIFE,
BUT LIFE ILLNESS
IS DAMN SAD

YEARS FALL FROM SKY
TASK WAS HARD
I AGED IN MY MIND QUIETLY
LOVE WAS ALL AROUND
BUT YOUTH* HAD NO
MEANS TO OPEN QUEST
FOR LOVE
IT WAS LIKE A PAIN
FOR SEVENTEEN YEARS

WATCHED PEOPLE
AND LEARNED BEAUTY
OF LIFE
HEART DAMN LONELY
A PERSON SOMEDAY
WOULD SEE FALSE WALL
AND BE A PAL

I HAD A FANTASY
LAST NIGHT AND
I WALKED OUT OF
MYSELF
I WENT SO FAR AWAY
AND SAW MANY THINGS

—David Eastham
In *Silent Words and Forever Friends*

---

*David sometimes called himself *Youth*.

Answers to Commonly Asked Questions

A review of fairy tales, myths, and old medical records indicates that throughout history there have been people with autism. Superstitions were developed to explain the unexpected and the unusual. Individuals with such distinctive features seemed to be "possessed" by devils or sometimes by angels. They were often referred to as idiots, witches, wild people, fools, and sometimes prophets.

The condition received little attention until Leo Kanner, a psychiatrist at Johns Hopkins Medical Center, noted that 11 of his young patients had remarkably similar symptoms. In 1943, Kanner's detailed observations were published in a paper that described the symptoms of the condition which he labeled *early infantile autism* (Kanner 1943). This paper triggered considerable interest and marked the beginning of serious study and research. *Autism* is from the Greek word *autos,* meaning *self,* implying a narrowing of relationships to people and the outside world.

The study of autism is relatively new. Many of the early theories and associated treatments of autism have been refuted. The knowledge base and understanding of autism continues to expand as research progresses; there is yet much to learn.

Most people have had little or no experience with autism, even though more individuals are affected by it than by blindness. Some people have an impression of autism derived from movies such as *Rain Man*, from news reports, or from psychology classes. But it is not until a parent or a teacher first has responsibility for a child with autism that the complexity of the condition becomes evident.

Some of the most frequently asked questions about autism are addressed in this overview. The answers are based on the best information available at this time. New information continually modifies our understanding, so some of the questions could be answered differently in the future.

Commonly Asked Questions

What is autism?

Autism is a neurobiological disorder of development that causes discrepancies or differences in the way information is processed. This information-processing difference affects the ability to:

- Understand and use language to interact and communicate with people
- Understand and relate in typical ways to people, events, and objects in the environment
- Understand and respond to sensory stimuli—pain, hearing, taste, etc.
- Learn and think in the same way as normally developing children

The effects of autism on learning and functioning can range from mild to severe. These learning and thinking differences cause confusion, frustration, and anxiety that is expressed in a variety of unexpected ways, such as withdrawing, engaging in unusual repetitive behaviors, and occasionally in extreme situations by aggression and/or self-injury.

The learning and thinking style exhibited in autism is unique but predictable, and different from the problems caused by other developmental disabilities. The learning style common to those with autism is described in chapter 2.

What causes autism?

Autism is a *syndrome,* or condition, with many possible causes. Anything that makes the central nervous system (CNS) develop abnormally can cause autism. The CNS functions as the computer for the body. Messages from the CNS control all aspects of learning, thinking, and movement that allow us to learn about and function in the world.

The major CNS structures—the brain, spinal cord, and related systems—begin to develop very early in gestation. Intricate nerve systems are refined after birth and continue to develop throughout life as learning occurs. Any interruption or change in the early development of the system will affect continuing development of the system and result in a developmental disability.

The event that initially triggers these developmental differences could occur during fetal development, during birth, or after birth. While it is not always possible to identify the exact cause of the damage, the following conditions have been implicated (Gillberg 1990; Gillberg and Coleman 1992):

- Viral infections such as encephalitis or congenital rubella
- Metabolic imbalances such as phenylketonuria
- Exposure to alcohol and drugs such as in cocaine-addicted babies
- Exposure to environmental chemicals such as lead
- Genetic/chromosomal factors such as in Down syndrome, the Fragile-X syndrome, and others
- Oxygen deprivation

Recent autism research is very exciting. With the advances in medical technology and brain-imaging procedures, differences in both brain formation and brain function have been documented. (For further information, read Courchesne et al. 1994; Minshew 1992; and Peschel 1994.)

In searching for the cause of autism, it is important to know that:

- Autism and other neurobiological disorders *are not caused by lack of love or inadequate parenting skills*
- Anything that affects the functioning of the central nervous system can trigger the symptoms of autism
- Knowing the cause is important for medical research and to help parents get appropriate genetic and medical information

Parents need to know that early intervention and effective educational programs do not depend on pinpointing the exact cause.

How many people have autism?

Autism has been found throughout the world in families of all racial, ethnic, and social backgrounds. It is four times more common in males. Although autism is considered a low-incidence condition, it is not as rare as once believed.

Early definitions of "classic" autism, or Kanner's syndrome, led to prevalence projections suggesting that 4 or 5 individuals in 10,000 births would have autism. Many professionals now believe that Kanner's group represents those with autism who have no other developmental problems.

The current definition of autism, reflecting a better understanding of the condition, predicts that 15 to 20 individuals in every 10,000 births will develop autism. This newer definition recognizes that:

- Autism can occur with or without other disabilities

  Many other conditions or disabilities frequently occur with autism; for example, Down syndrome, tuberous sclerosis, seizure disorders, retinopathy of prematurity (ROP), neurofibromatosis, fetal alcohol syndrome, and cerebral palsy. Some individuals with autism also are blind and/or deaf.

- The symptoms and the effects of autism can range from mild to severe

- Those affected with autism have intellectual abilities ranging from gifted to severely intellectually impaired

The combined effects of autism and other conditions is greater than if any of the conditions occurred independently. Those with autism who also have retardation learn very differently from those who are affected by retardation alone. Therefore, whether or not it occurs with other conditions, the learning style common in autism must be given major consideration when planning educational interventions.

What are the symptoms of autism?

At this time, there are no medical or psychological tests to diagnose autism, so a diagnosis is based on the presence of a cluster of behavioral characteristics or indicators that signal the common developmental discrepancies. The behavioral indicators most commonly found in infants and young children are summarized in figure 1.1 (pages 8-9). It is important to understand that:

- No single behavior is indicative of autism, nor will a child show all the behaviors listed

  The significant factor is a pattern of behaviors from each of the four areas.

- Some of the behavioral indicators may be intense, while others may be relatively mild

- Some of the behaviors that indicate autism are typically seen at specific stages of normal development

  The significant difference in autism is the intensity of the behavior and the persistence of the behavior beyond the normal developmental stage.

Uta Frith, a research scientist at London's Medical Research Council, Cognitive Development Unit, says that in autism, "a disorder that affects all of mental development, symptoms will . . . look very different at different ages. Certain features will not become apparent until later; others disappear with time" (Frith 1989, 1).

For the most commonly accepted diagnostic criteria for autism, see *Diagnostic and Statistical Manual of Mental Disorders, Fourth Edition (DSM-IV)* (American Psychiatric Association 1994). The APA publishes this manual to standardize the diagnostic criteria for mental and emotional disorders and to improve the reliability of diagnostic judgment and research. Every few years, the manual is revised to incorporate new information. See page 65 for an explanation of the procedures for determining a diagnosis.

Figure 1.1. Behavioral indicators of autism in the young child

No single behavior is indicative of autism, nor will any child show all the behaviors listed; it is the pattern of indicators from each category that is significant. Some indicators may be intense, others more mild.

Language/Communication

Has flat or limited facial expressions
Does not use gestures
Rarely initiates communication
Fails to imitate actions or sounds
May have little or no speech, or may be quite verbal
Repeats or echoes words and phrases
Uses unusual vocal intonation/rhythm
Seems not to understand word meanings
Understands and uses words literally

Relating

To people:

Is unresponsive
Has no social smile
Does not communicate with the eyes
Eye contact is limited/fleeting
Seems content when left alone
Seeks social contact in unusual ways
Does not play turn-taking games
Uses adult's hand as a tool

To the environment:

Play is repetitive
Is upset by or resists changes
Develops rigid routines
Drifts aimlessly about
Exhibits strong and inflexible interests

Responses to Sensory Stimuli

Sometimes seems deaf
Exhibits panic related to specific sounds
Is oversensitive to sound
Plays with light and reflections
Flicks fingers before eyes
Pulls away when touched
Strongly avoids certain clothes, foods, etc.
Is attracted to specific patterns/textures/odors
Is very inactive or very active
May whirl, spin, bang head, bite wrist
May jump up and down and/or flap hands
Exhibits unusual or no response to pain

(continued)

Figure 1.1. (continued)

Developmental Discrepancies

Skills are either very good or very delayed

Learns skills out of normal sequence; for example:

    Reads, but does not understand meaning

    Draws detailed pictures, but cannot button coat

    Is very good with puzzles, pegs, etc., but is very poor at following directions

    Walks at normal age, but cannot communicate

    Echoed speech is fluent, while self-generated speech is dysfluent

    Can do things sometimes, but not at other times

At what age can autism be identified?

In many cases, the condition that results in autism is likely to be present at birth. Based on their experiences with other children, parents report that their child with autism developed differently from the beginning. But the indicators of autism are generally not obvious until there is a failure to develop some of the early social and communication skills such as eye contact.

- Some children appear to develop normally for a period of time, then begin to lose early communication and social skills; or they fail to develop more advanced language and social skills. In these cases, the indicators are generally the most clear and apparent between 2 and 3 years of age.

- Pediatricians or language/communication pathologists who see many young children in clinical settings sometimes can detect the indicators as early as 12 to 18 months of age.

- Some more capable and quite verbal young children show few, or only mild, characteristics until they are 8 to 10 years of age, when the demand for higher-level thinking skills, social judgments, and time pressures make the indicators more obvious.

- Occasionally, the indicators of autism appear later after a severe illness or accident such as encephalitis or traumatic brain injury (Gillberg 1986).

In a 12-month follow-up study of 2-year-old children referred for possible autism, Lord (1991) reported that over 80% who received a diagnosis of autism at age 2 continued to receive this diagnosis at age 3; and 28% of children who did not receive a diagnosis of autism at age 2 did receive this diagnosis at age 3.

What is high-functioning autism?

The term *high-functioning* is not clearly understood or defined. Other terms such as *more able* (Moreno 1992), *near normal* (Dewey and Everard 1974), *mildly autistic* (Everard 1976), and *Asperger's syndrome* (Frith 1991) also have been used to describe this group of individuals who have slightly different problems and needs than the majority of those with autism.

The term *high-functioning* suggests that the effects of autism occur on a continuum from high to low. In general, the term is used to describe those who show near-normal social and communication abilities and near-normal cognitive development with intellectual abilities at or above the normal range—IQ scores above 60 or 70 (Levy 1988; Tsai 1992). Approximately 20%, or perhaps more, of those with autism would be included in this group.

While the above description suggests that in many ways these individuals are near-normal, Levy says, "I have yet to encounter (higher-functioning persons with autism) who are near normal in how they cope with the more subtle and ever-changing demands of living in this world of people. . . . It is misleading to use this term (near-normal) without further qualifications, because to do so sets up unrealistic expectations and leads to endless disappointments" (Levy 1988, 2). Levy also notes that "high-functioning persons usually not only look normal, but may act quite normal much of the time. Yet in spite of this normal appearance on the surface, the effect of autism can be every bit as debilitating in any situation which requires social knowledge or skills. The more subtle the skill that is required, the more debilitating the effect" (ibid., 1).

Dewey (1992) also documents the eccentricities and thinking problems in this group.

Other important points:

For discussion of treatment needs and prognosis, see pages 11-13.

- Higher-functioning autism is often confused with learning disabilities and emotional disturbances. While there are common features, there also are many important differences. The most important differences relate to treatment needs and outcome or prognosis.

- Those with autism who are high-functioning often have as many problems in educational achievement, competitive employment, and social life as their lower-functioning peers with autism and mental retardation.

- When compared with normally developing peers, it is instantly obvious how different these individuals are and the amount of effort they must make to conform to expectations in a world that makes few concessions.

Mesibov (1992) discusses treatment issues related to this higher-functioning group.

For additional information about this higher-functioning group, see Fullerton 1994; Grandin 1990; Grandin 1992; Moreno 1991; Schopler and Mesibov 1992; Shea and Mesibov 1985; Sinclair 1992; Tsai 1992; Van Bourgondien and Mesibov 1987; Vicker 1988; Williams 1992; Williams 1994a; Wing 1992.

In summary, the term *high-functioning* is misleading; it provides an illusion that the problems are mild and little support will be needed. In reality, those who are higher-functioning have problems and needs that are similar to those who are lower-functioning, but at a higher level. To complicate the situation, it is difficult to obtain a valid IQ score when testing those with autism. (See pages 95-100.)

What is pervasive developmental disability?

Pervasive developmental disability (PDD) is a term used in the *Diagnostic and Statistical Manual of Mental Disorders (DSM)* to describe a group of severe, early-developmental disorders characterized by delays and distortions in multiple areas of development, including social skills, cognition, and communication. A diagnosis of PDD indicates the presence of autism or a related neurobiological disorder. See also the discussions of autism spectrum disorders by Peschel (1994) and the syndromes of autism and atypical development by Wing (1992) and Attwood (1993).

The category of PDD outlined in the *DSM-IV* published in 1994 includes autistic disorder, Asperger's syndrome, pervasive developmental disorder not otherwise specified (PDDNOS), Rett's disorder, and disintegrative disorders. A diagnosis of PDDNOS indicates that many but not all the symptoms of autism are present.

Rett's disorder is also a disintegrative disorder that usually begins within the first or second year of life after a period of normal development. One of the first most noticeable symptoms is a loss of purposeful hand skills and the beginning of stereotyped hand-wringing or hand-washing movements. Other characteristics involve diminishing interest in social interactions, problems in coordination of movements, and severe language/communication impairment. Rett's disorder is most common in girls.

Asperger's syndrome was described in Germany at about the same time as Kanner's description of autism was published in the United States. It is not yet clear whether this is a separate condition or a mild form of high-functioning autism. It is included in the *DSM-IV* as a pervasive developmental disorder, but more research is needed to determine if it is indeed a separate condition.

In summary, a diagnosis of PDD implies that the condition has an impact on or pervades all parts of development to some degree. For example:

- Those with mental retardation have a more *general developmental disability,* with learning and development progressing at a slow but even rate across developmental areas.

- Those with *specific developmental disabilities* (that is, learning disabilities, or LD) show discrepancies—an uneven pattern of information processing strengths and deficits—across developmental areas. Each person with a learning disability has a unique learning style that affects development in one or several *specific* ways, such as difficulty learning to read, do math, spell, or write.

- In autism, there are discrepancies and distortions of development—a common or predictable pattern of learning strengths and deficits that affects development in a much more *pervasive* way—with more pervasive social and communication problems that have an impact on the ability to understand and manage the world of people.

As research reveals more about the related pervasive developmental disorders, the terminology and diagnostic criteria likely will change.

Why are these children with autism all so different?

All of those with autism share a common symptom cluster, a common learning style, and predictable problems that affect their ability to communicate, socialize, and function in the world. Yet each individual's personality, interests, and responses to problems are conditioned by a variety of factors:

- The interrelationship of the severity of the autism and intellectual ability

- The impact of additional disabilities

- Inherited traits, family culture, family interests, family problems and resources, the child's position in the family (only child, eldest child), and the roles and relationships developed within the family

- Past educational and community experiences

All of these factors will influence personality, preferences, interests, and behavior to make each individual unique.

How is autism treated?

At this time there is no cure for autism and it is highly unlikely that anything will be found in the near future that can totally reverse the effects of a developmental process (Frith 1989). A highly structured and specific educational program that addresses the predictable deficits of autism remains the most effective treatment to date. The ability to learn new skills to compensate for deficits continues throughout life.

There is no other treatment that will benefit every individual with autism; however, there are treatments that may relieve some of the symptoms of autism for some individuals. For example, some individuals with autism have responded positively to the following treatments:

- Auditory integration training (page 112), sensory integration therapy (page 113), megavitamin therapies, and nutritional approaches to address allergy-related symptoms (Rimland 1991). Also see Coleman (1990) for a discussion of nondrug biological strategies. A treatment resource book was published by Gerlach (1993).

- Medical research has expanded in recent years and is yielding promising information that may lead to more effective and safer drug treatments. Until then, consider drugs with caution, and avoid using them whenever possible because of potentially negative effects. However, in some cases medications have been helpful (Grandin 1990). (For additional information read Coleman 1990; Gillberg 1990; Gillberg and Coleman 1992; Harty 1990; and Tsai 1994).

Coordination of educational, medical, and nontraditional treatments is important for optimum outcome.

What is the potential for those with autism?

It is just as difficult to predict the potential of a child with autism as it is to predict the potential of a normally developing child. Some young children initially may be severely affected by the autism and seem extremely low-functioning, and then make amazing gains and learn to cope quite well. Others seen initially as "high-functioning" or having mild autism can be more seriously affected and be more limited in adolescence and adulthood. Some live and work independently in the community with minimal support. Most live with their families or in group homes and are supported in regular employment or in sheltered settings (Datlow-Smith 1990).

Although there is still no cure for autism, we know that:

- Limited predictions of potential result in lower expectations and fewer opportunities for the child to learn. Expectations that are too high may lead people to minimize the effects of autism and fail to provide the appropriate education and support to help the child reach potential and to live and work independently.

- Adults with autism generally are very good workers, excelling in jobs that require precision and accuracy rather than speed and judgment. They are employed in offices, hospitals, medical labs, libraries, high-technology sites, universities, food services, retail stores, and other businesses where their special skills and interests are valued and where they have a mentor (Grandin 1990). Some have completed academic high school programs, and a few have acquired advanced degrees with careers in highly specialized fields related to their intense interests.

- Some have learned to communicate by talking, typing, or writing after a lifetime when they were thought to be severely retarded and incapable of communication.

- Most individuals will continue to need some level of support all their lives. This support might range from a mentor to provide periodic assistance to solve social, financial, and practical daily problems, to the more intense support of a personal assistant.

- The amount and nature of support must be continually reevaluated, because illness, family traumas, the loss of a job, or other life problems will raise anxiety levels and decrease the ability to function independently.

Conventional wisdom indicates that autism is a lifelong disorder. Some individuals may show remarkable improvement, but at least some of the problems of autism will remain. However, there are a few reports of recovery, near recovery, or partial recovery. While some would say that the initial diagnoses must have been wrong, in at least some cases the diagnosis cannot be faulted (Rimland 1994). There is much about autism that is not clearly understood. For example, there is some evidence that internal cognitive processes contrast sharply with overt social and communicative behavior (Quill 1993).

Why is there so much conflicting information about autism?

To put this question into perspective, remember that there is little in the world that is certain. Contradictory and conflicting ideas are the rule in education, child rearing, medicine, politics, religion, economics, and almost any other field. Theories are developed to explain complex issues. People become emotionally involved in the support or rejection of one theory or another. Books are written, the media report bits and pieces of research and opinions. Libraries purchase and keep this material with no system for discarding—or labeling—material that has been refuted.

Several factors add to the contradictions and conflicting theories in the field. An overview will clarify a few of the factors and give some guidance for evaluating information.

- Autism is a very complex disorder with a short history of documentation. It takes a long time to research a subject, publish theory, and have it verified or discredited. It takes even longer to put research into practice. Sometimes a child has to grow up before the value of a theory can be substantiated or refuted. In the meantime, teachers, pediatricians, psychologists, and other professionals are trained with the most current information.

  Perhaps the most damaging theory that achieved considerable attention and acceptance prior to 1970 was the idea that autism was caused by parental rejection. One of the most prominent proponents of this theory stated in one of his books that the severity of autism was directly related to the degree that the child was rejected by the parents, even before birth. Those who espoused this theory were prolific writers. This theory, since refuted, continues to have an influence because these books are often the only ones about autism in many libraries and because many professionals were trained under their influence.

- The low incidence of the disorder limits professional experience. Busy professionals who have never treated or taught a person with autism would have little reason to keep abreast of new information. Therefore, they might not recognize autism in one who does not fit the limited picture presented in their earlier training. Their decisions also might be based on discredited theories and practices.

- Diagnostic criteria and labels have changed over the years. Each of the four revisions of the *DSM* reflects the knowledge base at the time of publication and uses different terminology. Some of the labels used in reference to autism over the years include *early infantile autism, infantile autism, Kanner's syndrome, classic autism, childhood schizophrenia, symbiotic psychosis, atypical developmental disorder, atypical autism, residual autism, retardation with autistic characteristics, pervasive developmental disorder (PDD), pervasive developmental disorder not otherwise specified (PDDNOS),* and *autistic disorder. Asperger's syndrome* is the newest label for a subgroup of those with autism.

  It is important to be aware of the implications of these different labels when reviewing the records of older individuals who exhibit symptoms of autism but have never received a diagnosis of autism.

- Professional jargon complicates understanding. While professional jargon helps those within a field to communicate, it impedes the process of communication across fields and with the general public. *The language used in the educational criteria may be different from that used in the DSM-IV.*

For an interesting perspective of the history of autism, read Donnellan (1985).

Is it important to identify autism? If so, why? Who needs to know?

Yes, it is important to identify or diagnose autism. Diagnostic labels carry information and provide access to information. Think about the person found lying unconscious on the street. The police or medics must consider several options. Is the person drunk? If so, the person is taken either to the hospital or to jail and left to sleep it off. Has the person received a head injury? Does the person have diabetes? If either is true, the person needs immediate medical care. An appropriate decision cannot be made until the reason for the problem is known. If the person has a MedAlert bracelet signifying diabetes, the medic understands the implications of the label and can act quickly. *This is the situation for those with autism. Effective decisions can be made only when the proper diagnosis (label) is made and people understand the implications of the label.*

There are several very important reasons for identifying autism:

- The child needs *appropriate* early intervention. Public Law 101-476 requires the public school system to identify students who have autism and to serve them appropriately. In order for the intervention to be appropriate, it must be based on the realities of autism. Those with autism have a right to services based on an accurate diagnosis.

- Parents need to have their concerns resolved. Frequently, parents first learn about autism from watching a TV show, from reading about autism, or from talking to another parent who has a child with autism. If their child has attended a program with other children who have developmental delays, it will be obvious that their child is different from the others. Therefore, they are often the first to recognize the symptoms in their child. Until parents get a diagnosis that fits their child's symptoms, they will continue to worry and to search for answers (Akerley 1984). When the identification is made, they are sad and upset, but usually relieved. One mother said, "Finally, someone else has seen a child like mine. Now I can find out what to do."

> Mary Anne Seaton reported, "I remember clearly the day [I first heard that my son had autism]. I even remember what I was wearing, the room that we went to, and my first opportunity to see a child who displayed characteristics similar to my child's. I remember how very kind and gentle [the professionals] were. But most important, I remember [them] saying, 'There is no cure, but if you work very hard, you can make a difference for your child.' Those words and [their] caring attitude toward me were the beginning of turning my life around and setting the direction for [my son] and our family." (See page 431 for Mary Anne Seaton's story.)

- The child and the parents need access to appropriate medical services. Parents must be prepared to attend to the symptoms of several medical conditions that are quite common in autism. For example, many children have allergies, metabolic abnormalities, and seizure disorders that affect their ability to function. These children also respond differently to drugs. A standard dose of a drug that is effective for other children may cause a major behavioral outburst, severe lethargy, or extreme activity in a child with autism. Finally, families may have a need for genetic counseling.

- Parents, teachers, and other service providers need access to information and training. Parents need as much information—perhaps more—than teachers and other service providers simply because the child spends more time at home. Also, parents must be lifelong advocates for their child, and they must be prepared to make many complex decisions that will have lifelong effects.

> Parent Christine Marshall said, "Charlie was not diagnosed as autistic until he was 8 years old. I knew he was unique in the first year. . . . [Getting the diagnosis of autism] was a very positive step for everyone. Teachers who felt he was weird had more patience, adults around him were more accepting of his odd behavior, and his parents now had articles to read about his uniqueness. . . . [The diagnosis helped us get autism services.] . . . In spite of the services available, [we] need to constantly communicate with [the] schools. . . . I continue to be Charlie's most reliable advocate." (See pages 432-433 for Christine Marshall's story.)

Both the parent and service providers need to understand how autism affects learning and behavior. *Many treatments and strategies that are generally effective for those without autism can cause major disruptions in behavior and learning in this population.* With a common understanding of autism, parents and teachers can work cooperatively to develop appropriate programs and support systems to teach important skills and prevent many of the secondary behavior problems.

- Both the parents and the teacher need emotional support. Parents need the opportunity to meet with other parents and professionals who understand autism and the reality of their lives. The parents' skills and their emotional condition are frequently misunderstood by those who don't understand autism.

> The autism support group, including parents and a few professionals, started their meetings with a family sharing time. At one of the first meetings Mary attended, she said, "I never worry that my child will be kidnapped. They would bring him right back." She quickly covered her mouth and looked around to see how her remark was received. Then she began to cry as she said, "This is the first time I've been able to joke about my child. Other people would think, 'No wonder my child had such terrible problems, with a mother like that.'"

Service providers need support from the child's parents and others who truly understand the complex issues related to autism and the physical and emotional demands that must be faced every day. Well-meaning, sensitive, and highly skilled colleagues are often not able to provide appropriate support or assistance unless they have had specific training or direct experience with autism.

Isn't it stigmatizing to give a child the label of autism?

A label is stigmatizing only if it is inaccurate and misunderstood or if it is used to isolate a person and limit that person's options. Autism has lost its stigma, now that more people understand the nature of this severe learning disorder and understand that it is not the result of faulty parenting. The word *autism* should be no more stigmatizing than the words *diabetes, cerebral palsy, arthritis,* or *Down syndrome.*

It is unethical to withhold information or avoid using a label that provides access to important information. A child has a legal right to services based on an accurate diagnosis. Parents can begin to accept and deal more confidently with their child's disability when professionals explain the disorder and use the label in a calm and accepting manner.

What evaluation resources are available?

When autism is suspected, the individual needs two different evaluations. The first evaluation is provided by a licensed physician (pediatrician, family doctor, or psychiatrist) or psychologist who determines a diagnosis based on the *DSM-IV* criteria. It is important to have this diagnosis by a licensed physician or psychologist because:

- Most medical insurance programs require this diagnosis

- It gives the family assistance in identifying the possible cause of the child's autism and access to accurate genetic information

- It provides a base for identifying associated medical problems (seizure disorders, metabolic problems) and general ongoing medical care based on the current autism research (Gillberg 1990)

- In some states, this diagnosis may be required as part of the school evaluation

A family physician who has little or no experience with autism can refer the family to a local child-study center associated with a local university or hospital.

For information to prepare parents for both evaluations, see pages 59-65.

The second evaluation is that offered through the school system to determine whether the child meets the autism eligibility criteria for early intervention and special education services. This determination provides the *only* access to free public educational services.

What services are available through the schools?

The mandates of the Individuals with Disabilities Education Act (IDEA), Public Law 101-476, place five requirements upon local school districts as they serve those with disabilities from ages 3 through 21:

1. Free and Appropriate Public Education (FAPE)

   Each local public school district must provide a Free and Appropriate Public Education (FAPE) to all its students, regardless of the nature and severity of any disability. This includes special education and related services (such as speech/language therapy, physical and occupational therapy, psychological services, and transportation), which are provided at no expense to parents.

2. Assessment

   Assessment services must be nondiscriminatory; that is, they must be conducted in the child's primary language and have no cultural or racial bias. Educational decisions must be based on a number of assessments and cannot be made on the basis of a single test score.

3. Individualized Education Program (IEP)

   An educational program outlined in an Individualized Education Program (IEP) must be developed by a team that includes the child's parent(s). The IEP must be reviewed and updated annually.

4. Due Process

   School districts must follow specific Due Process procedures to ensure the rights of the child and the parents. These procedures are designed to protect the individual from improper classification, labeling, and placement.

5. Least Restrictive Environment (LRE)

A continuum of service delivery options must be made available, so that students are educated in the Least Restrictive Environment (LRE). Students with special needs must be educated with more typically developing students to the maximum extent that is appropriate.

The 1986 Amendments known as Public Law 99-457 not only mandated FAPE for children with disabilities ages 3 through 5 years, but also established a framework which made it permissible for states to establish special education services for children from birth through age 2. Infants and toddlers identified as having developmental delays, or who are at risk for such delays, can access services through the use of an Individual Family Service Plan (IFSP) that addresses the family's concerns, priorities, and resources along with the needs of the child. The IFSP can be extended for children ages 3 through 5 years if the family chooses to use a family plan rather than an IEP.

It is important that parents understand the provisions of IDEA. Copies of the federal law and the state's administrative rules are available from the special education department of each local school district or from the state education agency or department.

Summary

Frith (1989, 15) provides a summary of the developmental nature of autism and indicates that all of development from infancy onward will be affected. An early-onset developmental difference affects ". . . the very process of building up experiences." She notes that it is unlikely that the impact of any developmental difference can be totally reversed—to leave no trace. In autism it is easy to get caught up or sidetracked by the bizarre, unexpected, and colorful details. Frith urges us to attend to the details only as clues to understanding the whole picture of autism. If we understand the nature of autism, we will be able to provide the support that will help those with autism have a brighter future.

The Learning Style Common in Autism

There are no outward physical signs of autism. Unless there are complicating physical disabilities, individuals with autism not only look like others, they are like their normally developing peers in many ways. For example, they:

- Can do some things better than other things
- Have happy moods and sad moods
- Have unique likes and dislikes
- Have a need for nurturing and support in order to learn

It is the intact and normal appearance that is so confusing. When an individual can do some things so well, people assume that the person should be able to do everything just as well. When a child has intense tantrums, withdraws, runs away, or behaves in unexpected ways, people do not understand. When that child cannot explain or defend himself, he is seen as spoiled or deliberately manipulative, disruptive, or noncompliant. Consequently, parents and teachers become frustrated and angry when their efforts to teach and discipline the child are not successful.

The following examples of seemingly disrespectful and disruptive behavior highlight one of the most basic needs of those with autism: *The reasons for their actions need to be understood.*

> The teacher of the early elementary class gave directions to the children, saying, "Keep your eyes on me." Amy got up and placed her face (eyes) against the teacher's body. Amy's attempt to follow the teacher's directions literally was interpreted as disruptive and inappropriate attention-seeking behavior.
>
> _____
>
> After music class, while children were visiting, putting away the instruments, and moving their chairs, the teacher gave directions for the next activity. Gabriel scrambled up to stand on top of his desk and shouted, "Mrs. Brown, this is no laughing matter!" Gabriel's echoed speech, triggered by sensory overload and confusion, was interpreted as disrespect. Interestingly, the words were those used by his mother when she had reached the end of her patience with him. This is an example of delayed echolalia.

In an effort to cope with the demands of a very confusing world, those with autism behave in unexpected and sometimes unacceptable ways. Interventions will be ineffective and often will make matters worse unless others understand why these children learn and behave the way they do.

Lorna Wing, a London psychiatrist and parent of a daughter with autism, is a highly respected pioneer in the field of autism. She has conducted research and written many articles and books. Her conference presentations and her work to further the understanding of autism have had a major worldwide impact. Some years ago, Dr. Wing wrote, "An autistic child can be helped only if a serious attempt is made to see the world from his point of view, so that the adaptive function of much of his peculiar behavior can be understood in the context of his handicaps" (Wing 1980, xi).

To understand the world from the perspective of individuals with autism, it is necessary to know how they take in and process information, how they think, and how they are likely to respond to certain situations. When one understands the nature of autism, it is possible to identify the cause of many learning and behavior problems. When the cause of the problem is identified, it is possible to respond with more effective strategies.

The Brain as a Computer—An Analogy

The central nervous system (CNS) functions as the computer for the body. Unlike a personal computer that can do only one thing at a time, the brain is designed with numerous interconnected systems that do many things simultaneously. Messages travel back and forth between the systems to take in, analyze, store, and use information.

Some things, like breathing and walking, are done automatically without thinking. Other actions require decisions. The CNS automatically triggers the nerves and muscles to act on those decisions. This masterpiece of design and function is ignored and taken for granted until it doesn't work.

To understand the learning and thinking differences in autism, the function of three computer-operated pieces of equipment will expand the analogy of the brain as a computer.

1. The input system

    A video camera represents the sensory input system that takes in and records information from the environment.

2. The information-processing system

    A video editor represents the information-processing system that derives meaning from the information.

3. The integration and output system

    The computer in a modern automobile represents the integration and output system that uses the information to accomplish specific purposes.

The Input System

We learn about our environment through our sensory system by seeing, hearing, smelling, tasting, touching, and moving (*sensory channels.*) Think about the sensory input system as a specialized video camera. This camera records everything within the range of its lens (*visual channel*) and microphone (*auditory channel*). It also has sensors to record all the odors, the tastes, and the feel of things in the environment. Just as a standard video camera has volume controls and filters to regulate sound, our special camera has automatic filters that modulate the intensity of input from each of its sensors. If the camera is on, everything automatically goes in and is recorded on a tape. If the camera is off, nothing goes in.

Most people have control of the camera, and it works with few glitches. Most of us can automatically:

- Scan the environment and direct the camera toward important events

- Turn the camera on when something important begins and turn it off when those events end
- Adjust the volume and the filters to screen out background noise or clutter—the unimportant stimulation

Those with autism have little control of the camera, and it has many glitches. These glitches interfere with the smooth and automatic function of the system and make it difficult or impossible to instantaneously:

- Scan the environment and focus the camera on important events

  Sometimes the lens is set on wide angle to take in the *whole* picture. At other times, it is focused on some small detail of particular interest to the individual (for example, a light bulb, the sound of a fan, the pressure of an elastic waistband, or the odors from the kitchen). *When the focus is on small details, important events and information occurring in the larger setting may go unrecorded.*

- Turn the camera, or the input system, on or off at the correct time

  Sometimes a glitch in the camera makes it flutter on and off very quickly, *so bits of information may be stored as short units (like a series of snapshots) and there will be gaps in the recorded information.* Or the camera is not turned on and off at the exact beginning or end of an event, so *a tape can contain bits and pieces of unrelated information or events.*

- Adjust the filters to screen out irrelevant background stimulation

  Both relevant information and irrelevant clutter are quickly and permanently recorded on the tape and stored as snapshots or sequences (routines). *Everything that happens in the environment at any one time is recorded together and is given equal value.*

- Adjust or modulate the volume or intensity of the input

  The volume or intensity of the input from one or all of the sensors (sensory channels) may be so overwhelming that *the camera automatically turns off and stops recording, or it narrows its focus and records only the most familiar and least confusing information while leaving other information unrecorded.*

The Information-Processing System

Think about the information-processing system as a computerized videotape editor. This editing device has special features for analyzing and preparing the information for use. It scans the tapes and removes all the background clutter. While it sorts and categorizes the information, it notes relevant information. The editor relates and integrates information from this tape (the new experiences) to information from other edited tapes (past experiences). Finally, the information is labeled for meaning and stored with an efficient cross-referenced system for immediate retrieval and use.

Most people have a wonderfully fast and automatic editing machine to analyze information on their tapes. It allows them to:

- Instantaneously focus on relevant, meaningful information
- Retrieve meaningful information with the clutter removed
- Retrieve information in a sequential order
- Manipulate information, to relate and integrate information from one experience to another
- Review information for accuracy, completeness, and clarity

In autism, the tape bypasses the editor, or the editor is defective. Consequently, information is stored by event without analysis for meaning. The tapes are stored with both the important information and the clutter interwoven. The important information, such as an object and its label, would have as much value as the clutter (for example, the holes in the ceiling tile, the reflections in eyes and eyeglasses, or the odor of garlic on a peer's breath). Storage of unedited information without meaning attached makes it difficult or impossible to:

- Instantaneously focus on relevant and meaningful events
- Retrieve meaningful information with the clutter removed
- Retrieve information in a sequential order to learn cause/effect relationships, predict future events based on past events, and learn from the consequences of errors
- Manipulate or integrate information from one event or experience to another, to organize information in different ways and to expand and modify information
- Review information for accuracy, completeness, and clarity, to evaluate one's own behavior and to make inferences, judgments, and decisions

The Integration and Output System

Think of the automotive computer as the information integration and output system. The car computer works quietly, quickly, and automatically. The driver is aware of it only when it doesn't work, when the car doesn't move, doesn't stop, or lurches along. This device is preprogrammed with information that causes the car to function in a predictable way. When it works as designed, it anticipates the driver's needs in order to make decisions, and sends that information to the gauges and dials on the dash. The computer receives and interprets the driver's commands (decisions) and integrates the command with the relevant information in storage. Finally, it sends messages to the appropriate mechanical system to carry out the command most efficiently.

Most people, like the car with a working computer, can make the decisions that trigger their output system. This allows them to automatically:

- Anticipate and recognize problems and information needs
- Retrieve relevant, clutter-free information voluntarily
- Record decisions that act to trigger motor actions, and then initiate and carry out the actions fluently

Those with autism, like the car with a defective computer, have little control over their integration and output systems. The glitches in their systems make it difficult to automatically:

- Anticipate problems and information needs
- Retrieve relevant clutter-free information at will and hold several pieces of information together at one time in order to think about them and mull them over; to generate new ideas and alternatives to make choices, solve problems, and make decisions
- Record decisions in order to initiate and carry out actions fluently

The Analogy Summarized

The functioning of computerized equipment was used to explain the learning and thinking differences in autism. Although the learning process was explained sequentially, in reality it is a continuous, interactive operation. Information from one system is instantaneously analyzed and edited for meaning, and messages based on that meaning are instantaneously and automatically sent to alter or influence the functioning of other systems. At the same time, the information from a new experience is organized and integrated with relevant information from past experiences until larger, meaningful units or concepts are formed.

For example, normally developing children have many experiences with balls. They see, touch, and hear descriptions of the various kinds of balls—baseballs and beach balls, big and little balls, red and blue balls. At some point, all that information is integrated, it comes together; they see the whole, the gestalt of balls, and they think, "Ah-h! These are all balls. Even though they are all different, they are all the same in some ways."

Uncluttered information is organized meaningfully and stored for later retrieval and use. Thus, most people automatically learn their language fully; they learn about their culture, and they think and behave in ways that others in their culture can predict and understand.

Children with autism also have many experiences with balls, but the gestalt of each experience will be recorded and stored on separate tapes. That gestalt includes not the meaning, but all the co-occurring relevant and irrelevant sensory elements of the experience. Since they cannot identify the important elements of their experiences with balls, these children might have focused more intently on the stitching of the baseball, the stripes on the beach ball, or the texture of the grass on their bare feet as they played with the tennis ball. The intensity of the wind noise or the airplane overhead may have blocked out verbal descriptions of the events. Thus, children with autism are less likely to automatically or independently learn the complete concept or gestalt of *ball*.

When these processing systems cannot interact and function instantaneously and automatically, as is the situation in autism, the language and the cultural rules are learned incompletely, out of context, and with distortions. This distorted and incomplete learning results in behavior that is understood only when the learning style is understood.

Effects of the Autism Learning Style

The predictable effects of the information-processing irregularities include both deficits and strengths. The effects are described below under four headings:

1. Reception and processing problems
2. Response problems
3. Attributes
4. Learning strengths

As with all things in autism, there is a range of effects; not all individuals will experience the problems to the same degree or in the same way. The pervasive effect of this learning style on the development of language, communication, and social skills is described in more detail in chapter 3. The relationship of the learning style to behavior is discussed in chapter 4.

Reception and Processing Problems

Problem 1. The individual is unable to modulate and process or integrate sensory stimulation

Overwhelming sensory stimulation is often painful and disorienting, leading to withdrawal and attempts to avoid or escape the pain and confusion. Temple Grandin, a young professional woman with autism, has eloquently described her sensory problems. She notes that her ears were like an open mike or a hearing aid with the volume set on high. She was unable to filter out irrelevant background noise (Grandin and Scariano 1986). Others with autism have noted that they knew something was being received but could not tell if it was sound, light, or other stimulation (Cesaroni and Garber 1991). In the examples below, some situations are described that offer a broader perspective on distracting and overwhelming stimulation. Also read the books by Stehli (1991) and Ornitz (1987).

Some of the most relevant psychobiological research, summarized by Klinger and Dawson (1992), sheds more light on the reception and processing problems seen in autism. First, children with autism fail to orient, process, and respond to new and unpredictable stimuli or events in the same way as their normally developing peers. Klinger and Dawson propose that this "abnormal orienting response may be related to difficulties in arousal regulation" (ibid., 164). They "hypothesize that children with autism have an unusually narrow range of optimal stimulation" (ibid., 165), ranging from a lower level that allows the child to orient, attend, and respond adaptively; to an upper level that would cause overarousal, confusion, and aversion or avoidance.

Assuming that these findings and hypothesis are correct, in the natural course of events the individual with autism is in an almost constant state of overarousal, bombarded by the vast array of intense stimulation present in new, changing, and unpredictable situations. Stress from this overwhelming stimulation leads to defensive actions—the sensory system shuts down, the individual moves away to avoid the stress, or behaves in disorganized and unproductive ways that lead to failure and lowered self-esteem. The learner with autism avoids these situations because they are not only confusing and stressful but highly punishing.

To learn to communicate, interact, and function more effectively, one must be in contact with people and must try new things. For this to occur, the stimulation must be regulated to provide just enough (or the right kind of) stimulation to maintain arousal and attention but not so much as to be aversive and avoided. Maintaining a balance between new and unpredictable stimulation and that which is familiar and predictable is a critical part of planning new instruction and for teaching new skills to those with autism. Read the material by Courchesne and colleagues (1994) for more information about this research.

> Unable to focus on his work, Gabriel kept looking over his shoulder. Finally, he said, "There's a cricket in here." Others in the area were unaware of any noise or cricket chirping. Gabriel was obviously too distracted to work, so the teacher told him to find the cricket. He went directly to a small bookcase, pulled it out, and picked up a cricket. After putting it outside, he settled immediately to work.
>
> ———
>
> Tony could hear a train coming long before anyone else. He would cover his ears, fuss, and lose focus until well after the train had passed by.
>
> ———
>
> Teachers had worked for some time to teach Jason to walk down the right side of the high school hall. However, he continued to walk at

strange angles, back and forth across the hall. One day as his teacher followed him, she noticed that he walked along the edges of the shadows cast by the sun through the windows. Jason could not ignore those visual patterns even when he knew he should walk in a straight line.

Jose screamed and covered his ears when the teaspoon clinked against the side of the cup as his mother stirred her tea.

Matt was very sensitive to the feel of fabrics on his skin. When he reached his tolerance level and could stand it no longer, he would strip off his clothes.

Problem 2. The individual has decreased ability to scan an area or environment to identify and focus consistently on the important elements or events

Research suggests that there is an impaired ability to control the direction of attention, and that those with autism have a striking ability to concentrate attention in one narrow spatial location while being unaware of sensory events at other locations. These two processing differences interfere with effective learning that depends to a considerable degree on the ability to continuously, selectively, and smoothly shift attention to follow the rapid ebb and flow of objects, actions, sounds, words, gestures, vocal inflexions, facial expressions, internal feelings, memories, and a myriad of other subtle details of the environment. Therefore, "disconnected fragments of information would lack context and temporal continuity" (Courchesne et al. 1994, 20).

Those with autism have unexpected information gaps because bits and pieces or whole strings of important information are missed while they focus intently on some irrelevant detail. For example, all or part of the directions, the rules, and expectations for an upcoming field trip could be missed either because attention was focused on other competing sensory stimulation, or another event seemed more relevant at that time.

When looking at a chalkboard or bulletin board, Jose concentrated on the edges of the board instead of the information on the board.

Problem 3a. Chunks of information that occur simultaneously or very close together in time are quickly associated and remembered

This has been called gestalt, holistic, or one-trial learning.

Problem 3b. Information is not automatically or independently organized or analyzed to eliminate the clutter, to elicit the meaning, or to determine the relationship of new information to that from past experience

The synergistic effects of these two problems include:

- Unexpected associations or superstitious learning occurs. For example, the light fixture in the classroom dropped to the floor just as one young man bent to take a drink from the water fountain. It was a long time before he would use a drinking fountain again.

- Exploratory or trial-and-error experiences often result in random learning, erroneous associations, and nonproductive rituals and routines.

- Repetitious teaching strategies that elicit quick rote responses lead to meaningless and inflexible learning.

During free time, Jose sat in the teacher's chair in the circle area and echoed the total language lesson, including the cues, prompts, correction procedures, and reinforcement. While he had memorized the total lesson, he could not initiate a request for a drink of water or ask for help.

Tony had been taught to comply to the teacher's requests to stand up, sit down, come here, and other directives. One day he left his desk and walked toward his teacher. As he reached the middle of the room, his teacher said, "Tony, sit down." He immediately sat down on the floor. This very compliant young man did what he was told, but had not understood that the teacher meant to sit at his desk.

- Routines are learned quickly and firmly, but without understanding their purpose or function. Those with autism are highly motivated to repeat memorized routines even when they are meaningless. It is difficult for them to omit a part of a routine even if it includes random or stereotypic actions that are irrelevant to the purpose of the routine.

Gabriel developed a recess routine that was repeated over and over until the bell rang, every day, all through the school year. The routine consisted of this sequence: He walked down the path to the curb, down the curb to the steps, and down the steps, where he paused to look at his reflection in the window of the basement door. He walked up a different flight of steps, gave a hop at the top, then returned to the path. This is typical of routines developed independently to fill unstructured time.

Maria was a capable adolescent who could do many things independently. When she was learning to dress herself, her mother always laid her clothing on the bed in a specific way and prompted her to put them on in a specific order. Now, several years later, despite Mom's many efforts to fade herself out of this task, Maria does not dress herself unless her mother is there to perform her part of the routine. This is an example of an individual who learned quickly that her mother's presence, the cues, and the prompts, all were part of the routine. Maria did not understand that dressing is ultimately an independent task. This kind of prompt dependence is very resistant to change.

Amy enjoyed blowing bubbles with her mother. However, she insisted that it always be done exactly as her mother did it the first time. She had sat on the footstool with both feet flat on the floor; and before she blew the bubbles, Mother had said, "Here they come." Now, if her mother crosses her legs, Amy pushes her knee to uncross them. If her mother does not say the correct words at the correct time, Amy jumps up and down, flapping her hands in agitation as she insists, "Say, 'Here they come'" until her mother says the words. Amy learned the original routine without learning the critical purpose of the routine, which was to enjoy watching the bubbles floating through the air.

For Tim to tell his mother when he needed to use the toilet, he was taught to touch a picture of the bathroom that had been hung on the kitchen door. He learned to do this quickly. To test his understanding, the picture was removed. Tim continued to touch the spot on the door where the picture had been before going to the bathroom. The instructional routine had emphasized touching the card without clarifying the purpose—to communicate with his mother.

Jose's speech therapist was teaching him to look at people when they called his name. The strategy was to say, "Jose" as she took his chin and turned his head toward her. Jose quickly learned to grab his own chin and to turn his head whenever he heard his name. However, he didn't look at the speaker; he simply turned his head. Jason had learned a motor routine that included the consistently delivered cues and prompts without learning the purpose of the routine.

Because of the inability to analyze and organize information, those with autism will have less ability to automatically or independently:

- Identify critical elements or meanings, but focus on the details and learn the routine
- Evaluate information for accuracy or completeness, edit or modify information, or know when more information is needed
- Retrieve meaningful information at the appropriate time
- Relate information from one experience to another to develop more complex or higher-level meanings
- Manipulate information flexibly to generate new ideas, to pretend, imagine, or create
- Apply and adapt rules to fit changing situations or subtle social or cultural norms
- Understand analogies, inferences, and other higher-level thinking skills
- Think about things, solve problems, and make choices and decisions

In summary, the ability to learn quickly and to remember information is a real strength if events and experiences are organized to highlight important elements and relationships. Without this assistance, the wrong lessons are learned or the learning is incomplete but firm and time-consuming to correct.

Problem 4. Information is not retrieved in the correct sequence

When information is stored without meaning in unrelated fragments or chunks, it is difficult or impossible to automatically or independently:

- Learn cause/effect and means/ends relationships
- Learn from experience and from the consequences of one's actions
- Explain or relate events and experiences or answer "Why?"
- Predict and prepare for coming events

Problem 5. Time concepts and the perception of passing time are impaired

Although the abstract quality of time is difficult for many children to learn, eventually they figure it out. But the problem in autism is more pervasive and may be the cause of confusion and anxiety-based behavior outbursts. Charlie Hart has spent a lifetime trying to understand why his brother and son, who both have autism, do the things they do. In his book, *Without Reason*, he describes his son's confusion about time. At age 15, his son thought that he would be a child again and be able to do the things he used to do. He could not understand that time flows like a stream, in one direction, irreversibly. If something happens at one moment, it cannot be undone; it will not come back (Hart 1989).

This impaired sense of time, coupled with the inability to sequence events in the correct order and to predict events, results in the following kinds of problems:

- Random drifting from one thing or place to another with little idea of the beginning or ending of events or the passing of time. For example, one might stand up in the middle of a meal or conversation and simply wander off.

- Compulsive clock watching and/or repetitive questions about time. Those with autism compensate for these problems by remembering the specific times for events and by learning to read time on the clock. But even this does not entirely solve the problem and can cause additional confusion and anxiety. For example, if an event is scheduled to begin at 2:00, one of the following things is likely to occur: The individual may:

—Refuse to stop looking at the clock until the clock registers 2:00

—Become very upset if the event does not begin at the exact time

—Become confused if the exact time occurred while the individual wasn't watching, and may insist on waiting until it occurs again in 12 hours

—Persist in asking, "When will it be time to . . ." or "Is it time yet?"

- Anxiety related to nonspecific amounts of time and the nebulous language of time. For example, how long is a minute? Five minutes? How long should you wait before asking for help? How can you save or make up time? Words such as *later, too late, not yet, already, faster, sooner, before, sometimes, pretty soon, in a minute*, and *tomorrow* are extremely confusing to those with autism. The one word that Hart's son understood was *never*, because it was specific, clear, and required no qualitative judgment.

Problem 6. Language is understood and used literally

Even the most capable and verbal children and adults with autism are very concrete and literal in their understanding and use of language. Confusion caused by this literalness is one of the major causes of unexpected learning and behavior problems. Literal interpretation is so common and has such a pervasive effect on the way these individuals function that it is important to periodically review the more complete description of this tendency. (See chapter 3, pages 37-39.)

> When the teacher directed the class to "Turn over your books; it's time for the test," Jeff put his book on the floor and tried to turn his body over the book. This literal interpretation and honest effort to follow the teacher's directions was interpreted as disruptive and attention-seeking behavior.
>
> ———
>
> The PE teacher was trying to teach Jose to dribble the basketball. She had demonstrated and explained what he was to do. However, Jose continued to stand still without making any effort to follow her direction. Finally, in exasperation, she said with great emphasis, "Jose, dribble the ball!" Jose stood very still as tears rolled down his cheeks and a wet spot appeared on the front of his pants. Jose's mother had worked hard to teach him not to dribble urine. Jose had only one very literal meaning for the word *dribble*, and although it was against Mother's rules, he complied with the teacher's request.

Problem 7. Auditory information is not processed efficiently or reliably

Traditionally, most instruction is provided verbally. Information, directions, rules, correction procedures, prompts, and reinforcement are for the most part verbal. This is not a problem for most people, but those with autism have difficulty processing auditory information reliably. This auditory-processing deficit has such important implications for providing instruction and for interpreting behavior and learning problems that it is important to review the elements of this issue periodically.

One of the common symptoms of autism is the intermittent perception of deafness. In most cases, those with autism can hear. There is evidence that those with autism receive, record, and store verbal information.

- After learning to speak, they repeat or echo the things they hear.
- After learning to communicate, they can talk about information that was not specifically taught.
- They sometimes act on conversations or information directed to others nearby or down the hall.

Other aspects of this auditory processing problem include:

- The overwhelming or painful quality of certain kinds of auditory stimulation
- The transience of the spoken word; it comes and it is gone, leaving no record for later reference
- Delays and discrepancies in analyzing and retrieving auditory information

  There is often a significant delay between a verbal request and the generation and production of a meaningful verbal response or motor action. Sometimes this delay is as much as 30 to 45 seconds, sometimes longer. If rushed to respond or if the request is rephrased or changed too soon, confusion and anxiety will increase and result in a behavioral outburst or a lack of response that is often misinterpreted as noncompliance.

- Long chains of auditory information recorded without meaning or without the typical meaning
- A tendency to become dependent on verbal cues and/or prompts*
- A tendency for verbal reinforcement ("Good working"; "Good talking") to distract the learner from the natural and meaningful outcome of actions to delay effective learning*

In summary, auditory stimulation can be overwhelming, and its transient nature leaves no permanent record for later reference. *Because attention is inconsistent and does not always follow the ebb and flow of auditory information, chunks of information can be missed. Parents or teachers are not aware that the information was unrecorded or not understood; and the person with autism does not know that information is missing.*

> When Kim understood the directions, he carried them out quickly and precisely, but with many emotional outbursts. An assessment of the problem revealed that he was trying to follow all the directions he heard, even those intended for others in the room. For example, when the teacher directed the students to move their chairs to the group meeting area, Kim was the first student to carry out the direction. As the teacher repeated the direction for some who had not complied, Kim stood up,

---

*For discussion, see chapter 15, pages 228-243.

looked around, frowned, and threw his chair across the room as he dropped to the floor screaming. He was unable to evaluate his own behavior and know that the directions must be for someone else. This inability to screen out irrelevant directions is fairly common in autism.

When Tony became upset and began to rock and hyperventilate, four people rushed to him, each talking, soothing, or giving directions. After a few minutes of this, he lunged through the circle of people, knocking a lamp off a nearby table as he ran from the room. The confusion and overwhelming stimulation of people too close and talking excitedly while giving contradictory information led to his behavioral outburst.

Jeff was sitting on the floor pushing a toy truck back and forth. His mother said, "Pick up the toys; it's time for lunch." Jeff continued to push the truck. After about 10 seconds, Mother said, "Come on, put all your toys in the box." He stopped pushing his truck but continued to sit on the floor. Within the next few minutes, his frustrated mother rephrased the direction four more times, each time a bit louder than before. After the third direction, Jeff put his hands over his ears and closed his eyes tightly. Finally, with his eyes shut and his ears still covered, he began to scream and kick. Jeff needed time to process the demand and to switch (transition) from one action to another. The additional requests made with different words increased the confusion.

Robert, a teenager who is also blind, enjoyed working with his tape recorder and listening to music. After learning to play the tapes backward, he began to sing the songs both forward and backward with equal enjoyment. This is an example of the ability to record long chains of auditory information without meaning.

Problem 8. Meaning is not automatically attached to visual information

Although those with autism have a remarkable ability to remember and manipulate the things they see and an incredible ability to quickly take in chunks of visual information, often meaning is not attached to the things they see or the words and numbers they can read.

There are reports that some individuals have photographic memories—the ability to read a page from a book or memorize the arrangement of objects in a room almost instantaneously. One young man could read just as easily when the page was placed upside down, diagonally, or in the typical position (Hart 1989).

When information is organized and presented in a clear and permanent visual format to highlight the critical elements, sequences, and relationships, those with autism can learn to use it meaningfully. (See Learning Strengths, page 32.)

Jeff began to read the *TV Guide* over and over again when he was 4 years old. While he could talk about the schedule, he never used the information to select favorite TV shows. Reading without meaning and purpose is common in autism.

Jose began reading the dictionary when he was 3 years old. When given an IQ test at age 9, he could recite the definition of every word included in the test; but he could not use those words in meaningful sentences, nor could he use them to communicate or solve problems.

Gabriel watched from the corners of his eyes as the teacher gave him directions. She verbalized the directions while printing the sequence of steps in a checklist format. After she left him, he studied the list briefly, then calmly began to work. Occasionally he referred to the checklist. The teacher sometimes gave him oral directions without the visuals. At those times, Gabriel appeared confused and tense. He would hunch his shoulders and echo part of the directions. When the teacher turned away, he would just sit, doing nothing. If the teacher pressed him verbally to start, he screamed and covered his ears with his hands.

Temple Grandin has said that she could never think about or relate two things unless they were written down. If she could *see* the two things together, she could visualize their meaning.

Response Problems

Problem 9. The individual is unable to solve problems and generate new or alternative solutions to fit varied or changing situations

Problem solving and the ability to generate alternative responses requires the ability to manipulate meaningful information creatively to reason, evaluate, and make judgments.

Problem 10. The individual is unable to totally and automatically control motor (and verbal) responses

Even though motor skills seemed to be intact and least affected by autism, motor problems were described by Kanner (1943) in his first descriptions of the syndrome. Attwood (1993) summarized some of the early research by saying that those with autism display movements similar to those found in Parkinson's disease. Other movement problems described were poverty of movement, delay in initiation of movement, delay in stopping or changing movements, and rapid fatigue with prolonged tasks.

Some individuals with autism have described the extraordinary concentration and effort it takes to control repetitive and compulsive motor behaviors. "Stereotyped movements aren't things I decide to do for a reason; they're things that happen by themselves when I'm not paying attention to my body. . . . As a general rule, . . . the more 'normal' [my] behavior appears, the more guarded and anxious [I] am" (Cesaroni and Garber 1991, 309).

While more research is needed to understand the effects of motor problems on motor responses, many parents and professionals are aware of the following response problems:

- Delays in initiating verbal and motor actions

  This particularly relates to learning new motor responses. Familiar/meaningful and rote/meaningless responses are more likely to be initiated quickly and fluently.

- Inability to move fluently through an action from beginning to end and to stop one action and switch to another response or action

  Many responses are repetitive, dysfluent, and/or perseverative. For example, a response or action may be repeated over and over in exactly the same way even when the outcome is painful or unproductive.

The door that Gabriel usually used to enter the school was locked. He struggled briefly to open it, but quickly became frustrated and resorted to banging his head on the door until his assistant arrived to stop him. Not only was Gabriel unable to generate a solution to his problem, he was left with a reflexive action of frustration which he was unable to terminate independently.

Maria often "got stuck" as she walked through a door. She would step across the threshold, then rock back and forth from one foot to the other until someone interrupted her.

One day when Jose asked for a drink, his mother gave him a glass of water. As soon as he finished drinking, he asked for another drink. This time he pushed the glass away. He continued to ask for a drink even though he pushed the glass away each time his frustrated mother handed it to him. After a considerable time, this overwrought child made the sign for *music.* His mother quickly gave him the audiotapes. He calmed down immediately as he listened to the music. The inability to switch responses or to recall the correct word or appropriate response is a major problem for many.

- Inability to inhibit compulsive thoughts and actions

Compulsive actions tend to become more problematic when stress is high and during adolescence. Many compulsions are related to:

—Intense interests or fears

—A specific routine or way of doing things

—Neatness and perfectionist tendencies

—Time

Maria, whose limited speech was unreliable, had recently learned to communicate by typing with physical support. Each time she walked past the fire alarm, she pulled the handle to trigger the alarm. After behavior programs failed to solve this problem, the behavior specialist was called in. During the assessment, the specialist asked Maria, "Why do you pull the fire alarm?" She typed, "It's the only thing in my head when I'm in the hall." Maria was unable to inhibit actions triggered by this compulsive thought even to earn rewards.

Jose needed to have materials neatly organized and lined up. The hangers on the coat rack were particularly bothersome to him. Whenever a hanger was the least bit out of line, he insisted on straightening and pushing all the hangers to the right side of the rack. It made no difference what he was doing or how intensely he was focused on an activity; when he sensed an errant hanger, he would dash across the room to put it in its proper place.

- Responses and actions that do not match intentions

Sometimes individuals with autism have little control over their bodies. This is a fairly new theory developed from the use of facilitated communication. The theory might help to explain some of the unexpected things these individuals do and do not do.

> After a period of hard work, Maria, the young woman who had learned to communicate by typing, was restless and fidgety. Her teacher asked, "Do you want a break?" Maria shouted, "No, no, no!" The teacher was surprised by the response because it did not fit the situation, so she repeated her question. As Maria continued to shout, "No, no, no," she took the teacher to the typewriter and typed, "Yes." Later that day, Maria typed, "Listen to what I write, not what I say."

Predictable Attributes

It is important to know that those with autism have endearing and positive attributes. Generally, they are:

- Known for their innocence, honesty, and guilelessness; they are not easily socialized to cover their naiveté

- Not adept at deceiving, nor do they try to impress others

- Not likely to defend or explain themselves even though their actions and their motivation are frequently misunderstood

- Compliant—perhaps overly compliant—when expectations are truly understood

- Perfectionists who are highly motivated to complete familiar routines perfectly and precisely

These predictable attributes provide information that signals a problem and a need for support. For example, whenever a person with autism is thought to be noncompliant, it is most likely that something is misunderstood or interpreted literally or incorrectly, or that some small, seemingly insignificant piece of information is missing.

Predictable Learning Strengths

Six very important abilities provide direction for structuring interventions and solving problems for those with autism. These are the ability to:

- Take in chunks of information quickly

- Remember information for a long time

- Use visual information meaningfully

- Learn long routines and the motivation to repeat familiar routines

- Understand and use concrete, context-free information and rules

- Concentrate on topics of specific interest

Summary

Parents and teachers are often overwhelmed as they begin to understand the problems faced by those with autism. It is especially intimidating to realize that these children are so dependent upon their caregivers, teachers, and mentors to interpret the world for them. Those with autism are also dependent upon interpreters to help others understand them.

Think how difficult it would be to raise a blind child without knowing he was blind. How confusing it would be to use your best efforts to teach and guide the child who kept bumping into things, spilling things, losing things, and breaking things. Without the information about blindness, how disheartening and frustrating it would be.

Similarly, parents and teachers of those with autism are frustrated and confused when their best efforts never seem good enough, when their child seems so unpredictable. The information on learning style and predictable patterns and problems contained in this and the next two chapters provides the foundation for understanding the child with autism. These are the three most important chapters in this manual. When the individual with autism begins to seem unpredictable, review chapters 2, 3, and 4 again and again for a new look at the problem.

It is sometimes difficult for parents and teachers to keep a level of perspective as they guide their child toward independence. Be aware that:

1. The one constant in autism is the inconsistencies. There seems to be no middle ground. Things are too easy or too hard, thinking and actions are too fast or too slow, there are amazing learning strengths and amazing learning deficits. Those with autism have some unexpectedly advanced information and skills, yet have unexpected and surprising knowledge gaps. Things that severely affect the rest of us have little impact on those with autism; yet seemingly insignificant, subtle things can disrupt them significantly. In fact, there is some evidence that internal cognitive processes contrast sharply with overt social and communication behavior (Quill 1993).

2. Variable performance is the rule rather than the exception. What can be done or tolerated at one time may be impossible to do or tolerate at a different time. Expect both progress and regressions. Regressions are often surprising and discouraging, but they are normal in autism. As long as the person's world is structured to clarify information and provide support, skills and abilities will be regained and expanded.

3. Autism is a lifelong problem, but learning is also a lifelong process. The goal is not to make the child normal or to cure autism. That kind of goal wastes valuable time and energy. Rather, the goal is to capitalize on the information-processing strengths to compensate on the deficits common in autism.

Chapters 8 through 23 contain information for capitalizing on strengths and attributes, for individualizing instruction, and for developing intervention strategies that will compensate for the deficits and support learning and effective behavior in this diverse group of individuals.

It is true that those with autism present major challenges for parents, teachers, and mentors. Yet they also provide major rewards for anyone who takes the opportunity to develop a close relationship with them. The ability to understand and deal effectively with their challenges forces us to be creative and flexible. Those who live with and support the person with autism will never stop learning!

Effects of Autism on Language, Communication, and Social Development

The defining characteristics or symptoms of autism are primarily related to the pervasive differences in the development of language, communication, and social skills. This chapter provides an overview, a very brief summary of normal development, and the most typical developmental differences in autism. With this information, it is easier to see the world from the perspective of those with autism. The information provides a foundation for assessing learning and behavior problems and for developing interventions.

Typical Development

Early Skills—The First Year

Most babies have an innate drive to learn language and to socialize. This drive is so strong that when the learning systems are intact, children acquire these skills automatically without being taught. Development of these skills begins at or before birth and depends on trial-and-error learning from experiences in the natural environment.

There is evidence that infants begin to listen to voices before birth and that they show a preference for their parents' voices soon after birth. From the moment of birth, infants are bombarded by new stimulation—sights, sounds, the pressure and texture of clothing, temperature changes, and odors. When babies open their eyes, people begin talking to them, labeling and describing the people, objects, and events in their world. They can adjust or modulate the amount of social stimulation they receive by withdrawing their gaze or closing their eyes. When they withdraw or shut their eyes, people pull back and lower their voices. When they open their eyes, people provide more stimulation.

Within a very short time, as the sensory system matures, infants learn to shut out extraneous background stimulation, showing a predisposition or preference for *social stimuli*. They begin to watch people more intently, following their movements and engaging their caregivers with a powerful eye gaze. At a very early age, infants have the ability to continuously and selectively shift attention to follow rapidly changing social scenes and to identify, analyze, and make sense of very subtle expressions, emotions, gestures, and words. This is the foundation for language and social development.

From the beginning, infants turn their heads toward the source of sound. They cry and make random sounds that get attention from others. These reflexive, nonintentional communications take on meaning for both the infants and their caregivers, and the infants' needs are met.

At some time within the first six months of life as they develop more control over their facial muscles and their bodies, normally developing infants begin to explore objects and establish two-way social exchanges with their caregivers through imitation of facial expressions and vocalizations. Infants and caregivers expand their mutual interest and pleasure in each other by smiling and vocalizing. No longer are infants simply imitating, but actually generating their own responses to keep their caregivers engaged. They begin to signal that they enjoy and want to continue a tickle game by smiling, chuckling, wiggling, and waiting for a response. These actions represent the beginnings of intentional communication.

These simple communicative exchanges are expanded gradually by coordinating attention between the caregiver and an object of mutual interest (*joint attention*). This mutual sharing of feelings and emotional engagement is a very important step toward feelings of social competence and the ability to communicate. Soon infants begin to point, the first nonverbal gesture to indicate an object of interest. They are persistent in efforts to engage the caregiver to solve a problem.

> After dropping a toy, the infant cries. When mother comes, the baby shifts attention from mother to the toy and back while pointing to the toy on the floor. Mother understands this message quickly and returns the toy. This is an example of a deliberate and intentional behavior used to engage a communication partner and express a need with a conventional signal (looking and pointing) that anyone could understand.

Before the first birthday, infants have developed an awareness that "People (including themselves) have different orientations toward a shared world . . . that people are subjects of experience" (Hobson 1992, 175). Sometime within the first 12 to 15 months of age, infants have learned the value of people and the power of communication. They also have learned the most critical and basic concepts:

- The rules of social exchanges—the basic cause/effect relationship:

  —I do something, you do something. We take turns.

  —I can direct people's attention to my needs and interests.

  —I am competent; people are basically predictable.

- That people and things have names and labels; that they respond to their own names and the names of many familiar objects, people, pets, and actions
- To understand and respond to simple questions and directions
- To make a variety of sounds that increasingly sound like real words

The Second and Third Years

Infants and very young children work intently at play, rehearsing and mastering new skills. The second and third years of life bring an explosion of language learning. By the end of the third year, they have virtually mastered the basics of their native language. They have learned:

- That words have multiple meanings and things have multiple labels

  Mother has various names: Mom, Mother, Mary, my wife, and others. They have learned that words such as *shoe, ball,* and *animal* refer to many different kinds of shoes, balls, and animals. They are not confused between words that sound the same (for example, the color *blue* and the fact that they *blew* out their birthday candles).

- That word meanings are dependent upon context, intonation, and inflection

  Most 3-year-old children are beginning to use pronouns flexibly. They understand words related to space and time even though the meaning of those words changes depending on who is speaking and the perspective of the speaker (for example, *here, there, behind, up, later, in a minute, soon*). At 3 years, children are beginning to tease with words and become aware that words take on different meaning when used in the context of humor, jokes, idioms, and slang.

- To talk in sentences that give information, to ask questions to get information, and to tell others what to do

It is usually safe to assume that normally developing children understand the language they hear at or above the level they can speak; that is, generally they understand the meaning of most words they use to communicate.

Continuing Development

Most children progress naturally, by trial and error, to become competent social members of their culture and their community. The intrinsic interest in people and their actions, coupled with the drive to interact and play, provides many experiences and opportunities to practice communication and social skills. The ability to continuously and selectively shift attention to follow rapidly changing social scenes and to identify, analyze, and make sense of very subtle expressions, gestures, and feelings provides a social perspective that is a foundation for making social judgments.

The intuitive sense of the perspective of others and an awareness of self from that perspective gradually expands to an understanding of perspective that involves knowing:

- What I see; what others see
- What I know; what others know
- What I feel; what others feel
- What I believe; what others believe
- What other people know that other people know
- What the group thinks or feels, based on conventional intuition

This perspective of others shapes behavior and actions. Feelings of embarrassment and the desire to be accepted by the group have a profound effect on social development within a culture. The subtleties of social and cultural rules are fine and require the ability to modify and adapt behavior to match the requirements of different situations. To apply rules flexibly depends on the understanding of perspective, the ability to predict the effects of one's own actions, and the ability to make judgments.

In summary, the innate drive to learn the language and become an interactive member of a culture is supported by an efficient information-processing system and a myriad of positive experiences. Individual differences within the population as a whole depend on inherited tendencies and past experiences. Some people are introverts, and others are extroverts; some are highly sensitive to social blunders, and others are almost oblivious.

Developmental Differences in Autism

Learning the language and learning to socialize typically proceeds so smoothly that the process is rarely thought about unless something goes wrong, as it does in autism. Those with autism have little ability to attend to people and to the rapidly changing action in the natural environment. In fact, each of the requirements for effective trial-and-error learning presents problems for those with autism who are overwhelmed with novel stimulation, who concentrate on very narrow elements of the environment, and who have trouble shifting attention and deriving coherent meaning from sensory input (Courchesne et al. 1994; Klinger and Dawson 1992; Hobson 1992).

There are fewer opportunities to hear the language and to practice complex interactive communication skills because interactions and new experiences are often avoided. Even play does not seem to be intrinsically motivating for these children. Given the learning style common in autism, it is not surprising that their perspective differs from that of most other people. In fact, it is dangerous to assume that any concept, rule, or skill is clearly or completely understood without instruction.

Jim Sinclair, a young man with autism, has written, "Being autistic does not mean being unable to learn. . . . It does mean there are differences in *how* learning happens. . . . But what . . . I think is even more basic and [most] frequently overlooked, is that autism involves differences in what is known *without* learning. . . . [There are] gaps between what is expected to be learned and what is assumed to be already understood" (Sinclair 1992, 295). In the following section, some of those differences are summarized.

Differences in Development of Language

Young children with autism neither watch people intently nor consistently turn their heads toward sound. It cannot be assumed that all the complexities of the language will be learned automatically, without instruction, because they have difficulty deriving meaning from their experiences automatically or independently. It is not that these children do not learn any language, but the learning is incomplete and specific to their frame of reference, which is different from others'. Major differences are seen in both the meaning of words and the use of language.

Differences in Learning the Meaning of Words

There are differences in the way most children with autism learn the meaning of words. They do not always learn that:

1. Everything and everybody has a name or label. When one 11-year-old made this amazing discovery, he walked around the room, pointing to inquire the name of each thing—wall, curtain, window frame, window, table. Once he understood the concept, he was highly motivated to learn other labels.

2. Things can have multiple labels (for example, garbage/trash, bag/sack, woman/girl/mother).

3. Words can have multiple meanings. This fact leads to a tendency to interpret and use the language literally.

   - A single word can label objects, feelings, ideas, and actions. The word *feel* refers to emotions and sensations as well as the action of touching; *sack* as a noun refers to various kinds of bags, or as a verb *to sack* objects or be relieved of a job.

   - Context changes the meaning of many words. The meaning of pronouns and words related to space, location, size, shape, and time depend on nonspecific, subtle relationships and perspective (*here, there, up, behind, later, in a minute, bigger, long, you, I*, and so on).

   - Intonation and inflection, as in humor and sarcasm, change meaning. For example, *stop it* and *no* can be said playfully or sharply with serious intent. The meaning of words changes when used in the context of idioms and slang expressions.

Often, those with autism associate an unusual or erroneous meaning to a word or phrase. The following examples illustrate problems that can occur when an overly compliant individual makes an unusual association and interprets language literally.

At recess time, Amy's teacher said, "It's time for recess; get on your coat." Amy quickly threw her coat to the floor and stood on it. This literal interpretation of *get on* and the effort to comply was initially interpreted as disruptive or attention-seeking behavior.

As the refrigerator door swung open, the bottle of salad dressing fell to the floor. Tony, 5 years old, said, "Oh, pants down." At school, Tony had learned that *dressing* means *pants up* or *pants down*. A single meaning was associated with a word that had multiple meanings. If Tony had been asked whether he knew the meaning of the word *dressing,* he likely would have said, "Yes." He did know a single meaning for it; but without instruction, he would not have known that there could be additional meanings.

Jose's father said, "Keep your eye on the ball." Jose picked up the ball and pressed it to his eye.

Jose was learning about the color yellow. His teacher showed him many different yellow objects—a toy truck, block, ball, crayon, pencil—as she said, "This is yellow." Later, she asked Jose to get the pencil. Jose made no effort to respond even though he knew what a pencil was and had responded correctly to similar requests before. After repeating the request several times with no response, she said, "Give me the yellow pencil." Jose handed her the pencil. Since the teacher had just called that specific pencil yellow, to Jose it was no longer simply a pencil.

To reinforce Lee's persistence and hard work, the teacher said, "You're really going to town!" Lee looked up soberly and said, "No, I'm sitting right here." On another day when Lee was tired and moving slowly, the teacher said, "Come on, Lee, shake a leg!" He stood up and shook his leg.

Jason had lost the privilege of going on the field trip and had to stay at the school. After his class had left, he insisted on standing directly behind Mary, a teacher who remained at the school. Later, as his teacher and Mary were trying to understand this unusual behavior, his teacher remembered that she had said, "You have to stay behind with Mary."

Gabriel worried about disasters. One evening he became upset and agitated about the starving children he had just seen on the TV news. When efforts to help him understand the situation had failed, his exasperated sister finally said, with a sarcastic inflection, "You might just as well go bang your head right now," so Gabriel did. Later, as he explained the situation to his mother, he said, "Lisa told me to bang my head, so I did—but I didn't want to." The inability to understand that sarcasm changes meaning, coupled with an overly compliant nature, makes those with autism extremely vulnerable.

When Tony's family stopped at a motel, Tony's brother opened the cat's cage and the cat ran out of the room. Someone yelled, "The cat jumped off the balcony!" Now, Tony shouts, "The cat jumped off the balcony" whenever people around him get very excited. This is an example of an association error and delayed echolalia.

Differences in Use of Language

Children with autism do not automatically learn how to put words together to generate or form their own sentences, questions, or directions to clearly express their message. They rarely initiate a question to ask for information or to clarify a situation. Rather, they often use repetitive or unusual sentence forms that must be interpreted by their listener. Echolalia, metaphorical language, and repetitive questions and sentence forms are common in autism.

Echolalia is the act of repeating or echoing words or sentences that others have said. These "borrowed" words are generally well articulated and repeated with the same emphasis and vocal quality by the original speaker. This ability to echo so precisely is confusing because it makes the individual sound so capable and knowledgeable. However, these words and phrases were recorded and stored "in chunks" without analysis for meaning (Prizant 1983). Parents or teachers cannot assume that echoed words carry the typical or expected meaning. It is more likely that the echoed words are triggered by some element of the current situation that is similar to the situation in which they were first heard.

Echolalia is used for a variety of functional reasons (Prizant 1988). Most likely, when an individual needs to say something and cannot retrieve or generate creative responses, that person uses another person's words from a similar situation—a TV commercial, a rule, a question, a statement, or swear words that were originally made with great emphasis. Some echolalia is not too different from the strategy used by most people when they repeat a word or statement to indicate confusion and a need for clarification. This is a strategy often used when learning a foreign language.

Even though an individual can echo or repeat chunks of words and sentences fluently, *that person's self-generated words and sentences are often expressed in unusual ways and are delivered slowly, laboriously, and with little expression.*

See chapter 21, pages 307-311, for strategies for dealing with echolalia.

Three types of echolalia are used in autism: immediate echolalia, delayed echolalia, and mitigated echolalia, a form of either immediate or delayed echolalia that reflects some change from its original form.

Immediate echolalia
Mother asks, "Do you want a cookie?" The child replies, "Do you want a cookie?" Mother says, "No, do *you* want a cookie?" Child responds, "No, do *you* want a cookie?" This classic example of immediate echolalia can go on and on until Mother simply stops the exchange in frustration.

Delayed echolalia
Whenever Maria had problems with friends, she hit them. Soon the other children began avoiding her. Maria's teacher explained, "The rule is, don't hit; use words. Tell me the rule." Maria responded very precisely, "The rule is, don't hit; use words." A few moments later, as another problem arose, Maria hit the other child as she said, "The rule is, don't hit; use words." The ability to repeat a rule is no guarantee that the rule is understood, that the individual has an appropriate alternative response to the problem, or that behavior will change.

Metaphorical language also is common in autism. Unusual and sometimes poetic-sounding sentence forms or patterns are used that do not clearly state the message. The listener is left to interpret the meaning by asking a sequence of questions.

> One day Gabriel approached his teacher and said, in a flat, emotionless voice, "Guess what?" He waited for the teacher to say, "What? I can't guess." "There's a wallet on the playground," he said, then waited passively. His teacher paused and thought about Gabriel's style of communication, then asked, "Is the wallet yours?" Gabriel replied, "Yes." The teacher asked, "Did you lose your wallet?" He replied, "Yes." The teacher asked, "Do you want help to find your wallet?" He answered, "Yes." Gabriel could not deliver a message in a clear and straightforward way. With thoughtful questioning, the teacher was able to elicit his message.
>
> ────────────
>
> Gabriel opened the refrigerator door and asked his mother, "Is the candy Tom's?" (Tom was his brother.) His mother interpreted his message as she asked, "Do you want the candy?" Gabriel replied, "Yes."

See chapter 21, pages 311-314, for strategies for dealing with repetitive questions.

Repetitive questions and sentence forms are generally used when information is desperately needed, but an effective question or statement cannot be generated. Therefore, questions or statements that are sometimes unrelated to the real need are repeated in the same way, over and over (as in the example of Jose, who wanted music but kept asking for a drink; see page 31). The following situation provides another example of repetitive questioning. The anxiety in these situations often erupts in major behavioral outbursts, especially if the questions are ignored.

> One young man enjoyed conversations with his family and the school staff. Sometimes those conversations were frustrating because seemingly logical or literal answers to his questions failed to satisfy him. One day, he became more and more agitated as he repeated a question over and over, "Is it time to go swimming?" When he didn't get the information he needed, he finally lunged from his chair and raced across the room, bumping people and furniture in his way. He grabbed a magazine, flipped the pages, and pointed to a McDonald's ad as he asked, "Is it time to go to McDonald's?" This is an example of the inability to retrieve the right words to modify a question without seeing the word.

It is difficult to know what individuals with autism truly understand because of their unexpected and surprising gaps and variability. For example, those who are verbal often echo words and phrases that are well beyond their comprehension level. To complicate matters, some of their language is understood at a very high level when it is related to an intense interest (such as weather, flags, light bulbs, or architecture). Therefore, the abilities of these individuals are often overestimated, leading to unrealistically high expectations with less support. These conditions trigger frustration and failure.

It is just as difficult to understand the real ability of those who do not speak. Some parents and teachers who assume that those who do not speak do not or cannot learn to understand language may stop providing verbal information. This underestimation of ability results in understimulation and fewer opportunities to get information and learn higher-level concepts.

Those with autism become confused when they do not understand the spoken word. When they cannot express themselves freely, they become anxious and frustrated. Nearly every learning and behavior problem is, in some way, related to misunderstanding the language and the inability to express oneself effectively.

Until research shows otherwise, it is assumed that those who cannot speak learn and respond to language in a way similar to those with autism who can speak.

> One young man who did not use speech to communicate until he was 12 years old explained, "I simply didn't know that was what talking was for." After he began to talk, expectations were raised significantly. Then, "people [became] impatient when I [didn't] understand things they [thought I was] 'smart enough' to know already or to figure out for myself. . . . [People assumed] that I fail to perform as expected out of deliberate spite or unconscious hostility" (Sinclair 1992, 295-296).

Differences in Early Interaction and Communication Skills

The predisposition and preference for social stimuli that is critical to social learning is lacking or very weak. Social development is not automatic in these young children. "What makes autistic children 'autistic' is the quality of their (relative) engagement with others" (Hobson 1992, 165). Hobson says that even the awareness of others is missing in some of these children.

> During Amy's early years, she showed little or no awareness of others. She paced about the crowded classroom with a small smile as if at some inner amusement, looking into the distance, but never at people. Arms folded across her chest as if to make herself small, she moved among her peers, never ever touching.
>
> ———————
>
> After years of being taught social responses, Gabriel is still not particularly interested in people. When he is with his mother, he will greet family friends and respond to interactions that others initiate. Without his mother's presence, he never recognizes those old friends. It is as if he doesn't see them.

The inability to modulate and adapt to the abundance of stimulation provided by people and unstructured social situations is overwhelming, painful, and disorienting to most of these children whose sensory system is disrupted.

> Jeff's mother was very confused by her new baby, who was very fussy. When she picked him up to comfort him, he stiffened his body and screamed. The more she tried to comfort him, the more upset he became. Her inclination was to leave him alone.

Some babies appear to develop normally for two or three years, then begin to lose their early interactive skills until their social development is similar to those whose autism was obvious at an earlier age. Infants and young children who are later found to have autism do not:

- Use the normal patterns of eye gaze that are the beginnings of communication

  These babies look at others as often, but they do not maintain their eye contact as long as a normally developing child. They do not appear to follow people's movements, nor do they engage people with their eyes in the same way as other infants.

- Become involved in the mutual sharing of feelings and emotional engagement; thus, other people are not reinforced for continuing interactions
- Engage in the early imitative, turn-taking exchanges; use gaze as a means of sharing attention with others
- Signal the desire to continue an enjoyable activity or to direct the adults' attention to objects by shifting gaze, pointing, and vocalizing
- Actively and persistently engage people to provide assistance
- Convey a clear message

Some individuals can enlist a partner, but have difficulty expressing a message clearly, leaving the partner to interpret the message. Refer to the two examples relating to Gabriel (page 40). These examples show the close relationship of language and communication.

Children with autism skip one of the most fundamental stages of social development as they attempt to solve their own problems, seemingly unaware that they could engage someone to help. When efforts to solve the problems are not successful, they may wander aimlessly about or resort to self-abuse or tantrums simply as a reflexive response to frustration.

At 30 months, Amy was emotionally and socially isolated but very observant; she knew that the candy was kept in the cupboard above the refrigerator. When she wanted candy, she would slide a chair to the counter, climb to the top of the refrigerator, try to open the cupboard, then scream and bang her head on the wall when the door didn't open. It never occurred to her that her mother, who was standing nearby, could make it easier.

When Kim had a problem, he would express his need very softly, but people were generally not near enough to hear. He never repeated his need; nor did he move nearer or try to attract the attention of his parents or teacher. Rather, he would pace about and eventually slap his head with his hand. This behavior is often interpreted as unpredictable, unprovoked self-abuse rather than an inability to locate a communication partner or to persist until the partner attends.

Amy needed a drink. Her teacher was sitting on the floor working with a group of other children. Amy took an empty glass from the counter and wandered about the room. As she approached her teacher, Amy backed up and sat down on her lap as if it were a pillow on the floor—she simply sat passively with no words or sounds. Since the busy teacher didn't notice the glass, she put her arm about Amy and continued to work with the other children. Amy finally got up and wandered away. A less passive child would have had a tantrum.

Tony loved to go to the burger shop down the street. He had learned to order his lunch by pointing to the pictures on the menu, pay for his meal, carry the tray, eat appropriately, and empty the trash into the trash can. However, at that point Tony sat on the floor in front of the trash can and refused to move. He became more agitated as his interpreter and other staff members tried to get him to stand up and leave the shop. Finally they removed him physically. After this happened a few times, staff was ready to terminate community outings. In assessing the situation, the behavior specialist hypothesized that perhaps Tony refused to get up because he didn't know what was to happen next and didn't realize that he could ask for information. After staff prepared and presented Tony with a basic picture sequence of the total event, including what was to happen next, he moved through the sequence with no more problems.

The ability to speak, sign, or label and point to pictures does not ensure that communication will occur. In general, communication does not develop automatically; it must be taught. Many individuals with autism can learn to communicate spontaneously, intentionally, and quite proficiently. They can learn:

- To understand and value interactions between people

- That words and signals have power

- A method or system for sending messages, such as gestures, speaking, or pointing to words or symbols

See chapter 20 for strategies for teaching early communication and social skills. For a summary of the research in this area, read Facilitating Early Social and Communicative Development in Children with Autism *(Klinger and Dawson 1992).*

While these skills can be taught, often they are not used fluently, flexibly, or reliably. Learning to communicate and to interact with others is very difficult for those with autism. It rarely comes naturally or easily.

Differences in Development of Advanced Social and Communication Skills

Those with autism have considerable potential. Most individuals can learn to manage their daily care with varying levels of assistance. They are good workers and can have success in jobs or vocations that match their interests and abilities when mentors and support are available. However, it is the lack of social judgment and acceptable social skills that most often prevents independent participation in the community.

Not all individuals with autism are withdrawn, lack emotion and empathy, or want to avoid social situations. Many feel intense emotions and want to be social, but they do not understand how to express feelings or manage and understand social situations. The current studies of social development in autism provides important information to clarify the nature of these problems. Four factors in particular are closely associated with social deficits, the inability to automatically:

1. Understand the perspective of others and the self from the perspective of others

2. Identify and make sense of social information (gestures, facial expressions, nuances of the language, etc.)

3. Generate or formulate an appropriate response to match the varied and rapidly changing demands of different situations

4. Exhibit social judgment

The effects of these deficits include the following:

- Social rules are learned rigidly and inflexibly, with little understanding that there is a range of acceptable behavior. If told what to do, they will do it exactly, every time, forever. This inflexibility makes it difficult to adapt to changes and to blend smoothly into the social world no matter how hard they try.

The language test of prepositions required the student to indicate the answer by pointing to the appropriate picture. George was asked, "Show me *behind.*" He responded, "That's not appropriate." To George, the word *behind* had a single and very literal meaning, and George had learned the rule, "Do not show people your behind; it is not appropriate." In autism, rules are fairly easy to learn, but not easy to modify or apply flexibly.

- Public behavior tends to be the same as private behavior. Without an understanding of the perspective of others in a culture, one would not feel embarrassed or automatically learn social and cultural rules and taboos.

> One young man, who lived with his grandmother, liked to go to the grocery store in the evening to play video games. One evening, his grandmother wanted him to stay home after dinner because she was too tired to go with him to supervise. To solve the problem, she hid his clothes. After his grandmother went to bed, the young man went to the store in his underwear. He had no concept of social conventions.

- Behavior will seem incongruent or startling. Those with autism may see conventional behavior as inappropriate, and unconventional behavior as normal or reasonable, because they do not share a common social perspective or intuitive viewpoint (Dewey 1991).

- They are unable to organize and manage themselves appropriately in loosely structured situations at parties, during free time, breaks, weekends, and vacations.

> Robert, who lived alone, worked for a major electronics firm, enjoyed his job, and was good at it. His life was fine as long as he maintained his workday routines. However, his supervisor made him take the weekends and holidays off—and worse, he had to take vacations. Robert didn't know what to do with his free time. He became bored and anxious, and the time seemed endless. The inability to manage leisure or unstructured time is a serious but common problem.

> One young man paced about the staff room cleaning up the area during breaks. He checked and moved things about in the refrigerator, cupboards, and counter with no regard for ownership. One day, he smelled each lunch bag in the refrigerator and threw away those he didn't like. While he was good at his job, he almost lost it because he was driving the staff crazy. This is an example of the inability to fill unstructured time appropriately and the lack of awareness of the effect of one's behavior on others.

- Those with autism have difficulty initiating interactions, entering into ongoing interactions, or negotiating conversations. They cannot read the subtle body language or cues indicating that others are bored or embarrassed and have a desire to change the subject or end an interaction.

> At recess time, Kim would run to the kids swinging on the bars, grab their legs, and pull them down. The children tried to avoid him because they sometimes got hurt. When the children understood that Kim wanted to play and he was taught how to get involved in their play, the children lost their fear of him and helped him out. While this behavior was initially interpreted as intentional aggression, it illustrates the behavior of a young man who wants to interact but doesn't know how to get involved. This example also highlights the importance of providing information to peers.

- They are unable to focus on the relevant information when engaged in a group activity in order to have a common experience to review and share.

> After Jeff returned from his first experience at the races with friends, Jeff's dad asked, "How did you like it?" Jeff replied, "It was amazing! There were 20 sections in the bleachers, with 20 rows of 25 chairs. There were 47 flags around the track—17 were red and white, 15 were blue and yellow, and 15 were green and white." With his attention on the details, he will have little ability to share the race experience in a meaningful way with others.

- Friendly social overtures, humor, and jokes are misunderstood.

> In an effort to establish a relationship with Gabriel, a new friend said, "Tell me about your family." Gabriel immediately responded, "What is 81 times 81?" When unable to respond to a broad open-ended question, Gabriel compensated with a question about numbers—a topic he understood.
>
> ---
>
> As Gabriel was depositing his paycheck, the attractive teller said, "Hi! How are you today?" At home that night, he told his mother that the teller was his girlfriend and that probably he would marry her. The misinterpretation of casual social greetings is a common problem and can have unfortunate consequences. One young man innocently followed a girl to her home after a casual comment.

Even the most capable adults with autism have difficulty expressing and interpreting the range of emotion and subtle social and cultural rules that others learn automatically. The social and emotional skills they are able to use have been learned from sensitive instruction and long-term intervention. While those with autism can learn to compensate for some of their social problems, their social interactions are rarely natural and fluent, but instead are out-of-step and inappropriate in many ways. They are often dependent on others for organizing and interpreting social situations and for keeping conversations going.

Their natural innocence, honesty, guilelessness, and their lack of social judgment make them vulnerable to exploitation. They are often misunderstood and easily hurt when they are corrected or teased.

Summary

Wing has suggested that individuals with autism can be grouped into three groups just by the way they handle themselves in social situations (Wing and Attwood 1987). Those in the first group are observed on the edges of a social situation, either watching other people socialize or randomly exploring the environment, seemingly oblivious to the interactions going on about them. They appear to be aloof, cut off, and withdrawn. They are particularly sensitive to the noise, touch, and movement of people. Some of those in this group enjoy a measure of physical contact when they can initiate it themselves and can end it at will. They generally have few reliable communication and social skills, so they are dependent on others to read their limited signals.

For more information about social development and social perception in autism, read Baron-Cohen 1988; Courchesne et al. 1994; Dawson and Fernald 1987; Dewey 1991, 1992; Dewey and Everard 1974; Eastham and Eastham 1990; Frith 1989, 1991; Hobson 1992; Kasari et al. 1990; Sinclair 1992; Williams 1992, 1994a; Wing 1992; Yirmiya et al. 1992.

For discussion of intervention and teaching strategies to address the social problems, see chapters 20, 22, and 23.

Those who are fairly passive make up a second group. These individuals also watch interactions, but make few social approaches. However, they willingly respond if others initiate an approach, and they are easily led into activities. They often try to fit in by imitating others, but they do not really understand the complexities of the situation. Although they want to have friends, they misinterpret casual social remarks and are easily hurt by rebuffs and being left out.

Those in the third group are actively involved in social situations, blithely unaware of the effect of their behavior on others. These individuals often pursue their intense interests, unaware that their reluctant partners are trying to extricate themselves from one-sided conversations, recitations of facts, or repetitive questions. They appear to know more than they can demonstrate, and their abilities are frequently overestimated because they have some reasonably good social and communication skills. These individuals are easily upset and sometimes aggressive if confused or misunderstood.

The profound effect of the learning-style differences in autism cannot be overemphasized. These differences have an incredibly pervasive effect on the ability to interpret the social world and respond to typical situations. Most individuals with autism are unable to tell us when or why they are confused or frustrated. Because they are unable to derive coherent meaning from their experiences and operate from such a different perspective, they are dependent upon us, their parents, teachers, and mentors, to help them make sense of things.

People who are deaf or blind are dependent on others to interpret their world, to organize information, and to give them the tools to function in their world. While those with autism may be able to see and hear, they have difficulty processing and making sense of the things they see and hear. They, too, need interpreters who can organize information, give them guidance, and design the tools to help them function more independently in the community.

Behavior and the Effects of Autism on Behavior

Our understanding of a situation influences or determines our actions. Different perspectives of autism result in different treatments. When autism was seen as an emotional disorder caused by parents, the treatment was psychotherapy for both the parents and the child. Parents were counseled to place their child in an institution to receive good physical care when autism was viewed as a hopeless condition.

When it was discovered that those with autism could learn—that they did respond to instruction based on behavioral principles—the focus of treatment changed. The treatment of choice was behavior modification. Behavior could be changed, appropriate behaviors could be taught, and inappropriate behaviors could be eliminated. During this period, behavior was defined narrowly; it was observable, learned, and purposeful, either appropriate or inappropriate.

After several years, it was noted that there was a significant number of people whose behavior did not improve as expected—whose behavior became more severe and intense. These individuals required more restricted environments—treatment that involved drugs, restraints, and more severe consequences. Many of the individuals in this situation had autism and related disorders.

The human rights movement stimulated a change in the direction of behavioral research and practice, to view behavior in a broader context and to focus more positively on prevention and instruction. This new behavioral technology, coupled with the current knowledge of the learning style common to those with autism, is likely to help these individuals lead more independent and enjoyable lives now and in the future.

In this chapter we expand the concepts presented in the previous two chapters, integrate the new information, and provide a perspective for understanding the behavior that has been so puzzling. Once problems are understood in the context of the disability, they can be prevented—or at least not made worse.

Understanding Behavior

What Is Behavior?

An understanding of behavior includes the following four concepts:

1. Behavior is communication—a logical response to a current situation and an effort to regulate conditions that do not match needs. For example, a hungry infant cries—a reflexive (nonintentional) act. Parents instinctively review a mental checklist to interpret the infant's problem: Is it pain? discomfort? loneliness? hunger? When they identify the purpose or reason for the crying, they can meet their baby's need. In this situation, a reflexive behavior signals a need. The need must be interpreted by others.

Every so often and for no apparent reason, Jason would slug a vocational or group-home staff member in the stomach. An autism consultant who was assessing the problem observed one incident that occurred while several of the residents were boarding the van to go shopping. Just as Jason started to step into the van, he suddenly stopped and turned to leave. A staff member took him firmly by the arm to assist him back onto the van. At that point Jason slugged him in the stomach and ran back to the house. The consultant followed him to his room and observed the following sequence of actions: Jason stood on his bed, removed the ceiling tile, took his belt from the opening, and put it on. Quietly, with no assistance, he returned to the van, got in, sat down, and fastened his seat belt as if nothing had happened. In reviewing this information with parents, the consultant discovered that as a boy, Jason had been taught the rule: You must wear a belt before going outside. In his panic to follow the rule, he had to break away to get his belt. This reflexive (nonintentional) panic response certainly signaled a need, but the unconventional nature of the signal made it difficult for anyone to interpret.

2. Behavior is a logical response to the environment in which the behavior was first learned. But in those with autism, the history of the behavior gets lost. The intervention is likely to be misdirected without the history that provides clues to the meaning and purpose of the behavior.

During periods of free time, Jose ran from wall to wall slamming into the windows with both fists and forearms. After several behavior interventions had failed to eliminate this potentially dangerous behavior, a consultant was called in to conduct a functional assessment. From Jose's file, it was learned that this behavior began several years earlier when Jason lived in the state institution. During that period, he began to watch ice hockey on TV. When Jose had nothing else to do, he pretended to play hockey, running from wall to wall and banging on the windows like the professional players bumped or hit the glass walls around the ice rink.

Thus it was discovered that the behavior itself was not inappropriate; the problem was that it occurred in the wrong place. When it was understood that the purpose of the behavior was to fill unstructured leisure time and that there was nothing wrong in pretending to play hockey, staff members capitalized on Jose's interest. For example, he could be allowed to take free time in the gym, he could watch hockey on TV, and he could be encouraged to save his money to buy videotapes and magazines about hockey or to buy tickets and attend games.

See chapters 14 and 15 for discussion of visual strategies.

What is most important is that staff used a variety of visual strategies to teach Jose:

—Why it is dangerous to hit windows

—When and where he could pretend to play hockey, and

—What he could and could not do for free time in various locations.

See chapter 23, pages 363-364, for strategies for dealing with repetitive and stereotypic behaviors.

The effects of negative reinforcement on R/S behavior are described in chapter 17, page 239. Also see the example in problem 5, page 55.

3. Behavior is an attempt of the brain to keep itself stimulated or in equilibrium. Repetitive and stereotypic (R/S) movements are an example of this situation. Behaviors such as rocking, arm and hand flapping, and finger flicking appear to serve as a release of tension and energy. They are more intense versions of our own nervous habits and reflect the individual's emotional state. When asked why they rock, flip their hands, or hop up and down, many individuals with autism say that it makes them feel better or more relaxed. Others indicate that R/S behavior occurs automatically "when (I am) not paying attention to my body" (Cesaroni and Garber 1991, 309).

   Repetitive and stereotypic behaviors occur more frequently and intensely during periods of either very high or very low levels of stimulation—when bored, overly excited, frustrated, confused, or very tired. The meaning of these unconventional signals is difficult to interpret without knowing the individual very well.

4. Behavior is an outward expression of an inward state. Illness, worries, fears, fatigue, and anxiety have a significant effect on tolerance and control. Initially, the behavioral signals of these internal states are reflexive actions that can be incredibly difficult to interpret.

   Medical problems and medications cause many behavior problems and sudden changes in the pattern of an individual's behavior, including unusual behavior, self-injury, and behavioral outbursts. There are many examples of problems that did not respond to behavior modification that were corrected when the underlying medical condition was treated. (See figure 24.1, page 381.)

This broader perspective of behavior removes much of the stigma from those with autism who learn and communicate differently. *The person is no longer the problem.* Rather, those with autism have problems with logical solutions:

Problem: An environment that does not make sense
Solution: Environments can be modified to make more sense.

Problem: A lack of skills (social/self-management, communication, and others)
Solution: Skills can be taught.

Problem: A medical problem
Solution: Medical problems can be treated.

Behavior problems can generally be solved when they are understood as logical and predictable responses to a person's situation.

Stress and Behavior

Daily life is complex for everyone. Many demands and stressors affect a person's ability to be productive and lead a satisfactory life. Life is even more stressful for those with autism, who cannot always make sense of and adapt to the demands of daily life. Groden discussed the impact of stress and anxiety on those with autism (Groden et al. 1994). Hardy (1985) discussed anxiety and panic disorder in those with autism.

Suppose that everyone drew a line to reflect the intensity of frustration and anxiety that ebbs and flows throughout a day, a month, a year. Most of the lines—even those of individuals with autism—would be similar, with ups and downs and stretches of calm equilibrium. Some of the lines would show sharper or higher highs and deeper or longer lows. Some lines would have many highs and lows, while others would show long stretches of stable, even temperament and fewer variations.

When a section of each person's line is enlarged to study the sequence and the intensity of stress and behavior that occurs before, during, and after a severe behavioral outburst, a predictable profile is evident. (See figure 4.1.) When a problem occurs, stress increases; and as stress increases, the intensity of the behavior increases until there is a peak or crisis. Once the crisis is past, the stress drops to a level of equilibrium—an optimum level of stress at which a person can function productively.

Awareness of the ebb and flow of stress is the foundation for intervening positively in the problems of those with autism. The intensity of stress is reflected by the intensity of behavior. Since the individual's need is different at each stage, the intervention goal is different at each stage. Strategies that would be effective at one stage might exacerbate the problem at a different stage. With this understanding, intervention strategies are flexible and designed to match the individual need at any specific point in a given situation.

Figure 4.1. Profile: The fluctuating levels of stress

An illustration of the varying levels of stress that ebb and flow over time
The enlarged area highlights the changing levels of stress that occur before, during, and after a crisis.

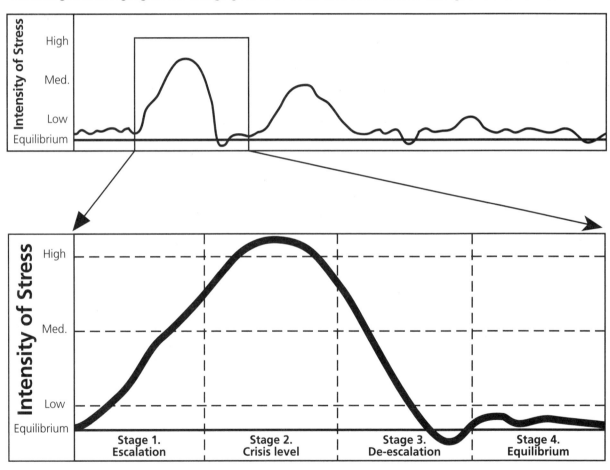

The Message Behind the Behavior

Communication is difficult at best. Even people who are considered to be good communicators can miscommunicate. Body language can alter the conventional meaning of words, and much is left to the interpretation of the listener.

The interpretation of messages is easier when people share a common language—signals and signs (body language and words) with culturally determined meanings and rules for use. Then everyone in the culture knows that a smile generally means that a person is friendly and happy or sees some humor in a situation. Everyone would also understand that a smile could have other meanings depending on the situation, the tone of voice, and the facial expression of the speaker.

Because those with autism do not automatically learn the culturally accepted rules and meanings of body language and words, it is difficult—but not impossible—to interpret their behavioral signals. We must look for clues for understanding the function or the message behind behavior.

Chains of Behavior

Intense and severe behavior problems generally start with small behavioral signals. Most people, including those with autism, begin to show irritation, boredom, fatigue, and confusion in a variety of subtle ways—yawning, stretching, restless movements, frowning, a raised eyebrow, or a questioning facial expression. If the situation does not change or if pressures are added, the feelings are likely to intensify; the individuals may raise their voices, become flushed, breathe harder, or pound on the table.

Most people have learned not to show intense feelings in public. They know how to manage these emotional and stressful situations. They can communicate in an attempt to effect change, they can leave, or they can talk themselves through the situation. Those with autism have little control over their lives and in many cases must depend on others to identify their feelings and needs and make changes in the environment. *If the first small signals of a problem are ignored or not interpreted in a way to help resolve the problem, a chain of increasingly intense and severe behaviors is likely to develop.* As stress increases, the behavioral signals intensify. This escalating chain of behavioral signals is illustrated in the profile of stress, figure 4.2.

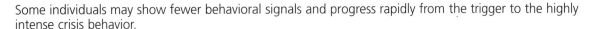

Figure 4.2. Profile of stress: The sequence of an increasingly intense chain of behavior

Some individuals may show fewer behavioral signals and progress rapidly from the trigger to the highly intense crisis behavior.

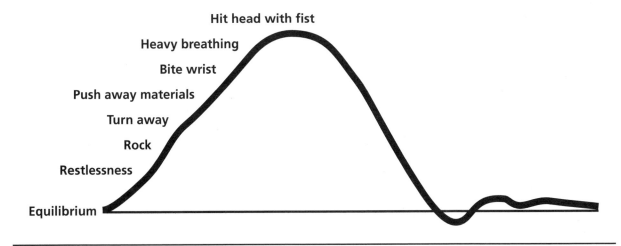

Signals Have Multiple Meanings

Communication serves many functions. It is used to request help, food, a social interaction, or an object; to reject, avoid, or protest a situation; to express feelings; to seek clarification or affection. It is easy to interpret the function of a behavior when a person intentionally uses a conventional signal (for example, stating a message and pointing to a picture or an object to direct the listener's attention to the need). It is more difficult to be certain of a message when the signal is reflexive or nonconventional, when it could have a variety of meanings.

Consider a woman sitting in an audience, tapping and swinging her foot. It would be hard to know why she is making those movements. She might be bored, impatient, or excited. She might also have an itchy foot, a nervous habit, or a need to go to the bathroom. She may be thinking about something that occurred at another time and place. In order to interpret the exact meaning of that behavior in that specific context, her habits, likes, worries, and past experiences must be known.

Most people can generate a variety of solutions for a single problem. (See figure 4.3a.) Those with autism, however, have few alternatives for solving the many problems encountered each day. Therefore, a single behavior may be triggered by many different problems. (See figure 4.3b.) For example, a scream could mean, "I need a drink"; "Look at me"; "I don't want to"; "That hurts"; "Let's play"; "I have to get out of here"; or "You haven't heard me, and I don't know what else to do."

Interpreting the meaning of a nonconventional signal at any given time depends on knowledge of the individual and knowledge of the various elements of the situation. Interpretation of the meaning of a communication need or effort is easier with an awareness of situations commonly associated with problems.

Figure 4.3. Problems and solutions

The first circle (a) illustrates that most people can generate a multitude of solutions for a single problem, while (b) illustrates that those with autism have limited solutions or alternatives for dealing with a multitude of problems. If an ineffective (or inappropriate) solution is eliminated (punished) without teaching a new solution, the individual is left with no solutions.

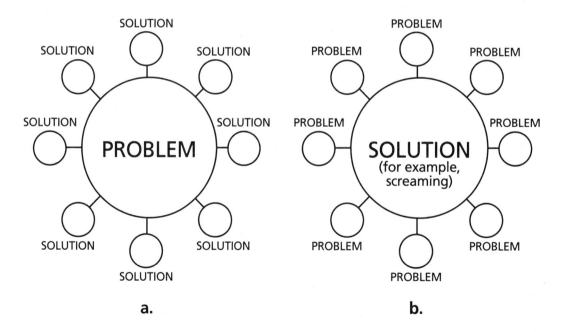

a.

b.

Situations Associated with Problems

The following situations are commonly associated with problem behaviors. These situations are even more likely to cause an outburst when the person's tolerance is low because of illness, fatigue, worries, or fears. A review of the learning and thinking problems associated with autism may provide insights for interpreting the individual's perspective to target the exact problem when confronted with:

- Boredom—having nothing to do, having to do or repeat meaningless things, or having to endure a long period of time with no attention

- Demands to do difficult or nonpreferred activities, having to work on these tasks for too long a period, being rushed to move faster or do more

- Repeated demands, especially if they are made in a louder or harsher voice or if the speaker moves closer and closer

- Making repeated mistakes, especially when followed by negatively stated corrections made in a loud or harsh voice

- Physical management—being pulled, pushed, tugged, or physically restrained

- Transitions from one activity to the next or from one setting or situation to the next

- New or unfamiliar situations, settings, activities, clothing, food, or people

- Sensory overload—noise and confusion of crowded situations, a flickering light, the texture of clothing, and other distractions

  (Frequently the sensory stimulation is so subtle that it would seem irrelevant or go unnoticed by most people.)

- Interruptions or unexpected changes in schedules, routines, activities, room arrangements, travel routes, and other changes

> Gabriel frequently went to meetings with his mother. On one occasion the meeting was in an unfamiliar restaurant. He had taken a foreign language workbook and electronic equipment catalogs to work with during the meeting. Shortly after he had spread his work out on the table, the light bulb over his table burned out. It was too dark to read. He began to hyperventilate and rock back and forth. His mother suggested some alternative activities and moved a candle to the table. He stared at the wavering light of the candle and began flicking his fingers close to his eyes. The intensity and noise of his breathing and rocking began to increase. His mother could predict that a major outburst was imminent, and she took him home. The unfamiliar setting, sudden change of plans, and the sensory stimulation of the low, flickering light combined to overwhelm him.

- Misunderstandings or misinterpretations of a situation

> Jeff, who loved movie projectors, was quite verbal. He was scheduled to set up the projector so the class could view a movie after the math lesson. While Jeff was sitting across the table from his teacher as they worked on math, another teacher entered the room and asked to use the projector later in the afternoon. When his teacher confirmed the request, Jeff jumped to his feet, leaned across the table, placed his hands around the teacher's throat, and, breathing heavily, brought his face close to

hers. Calmly and without moving, his teacher said, "Jeff, first do your math. Second, set up the projector and see the movie. And third, take the projector to Mrs. Peters' room." Immediately Jeff sat down and continued working as if nothing unusual had occurred. His panic and reflexive, nonconventional behavior were triggered by his fear that he had lost a favorite activity—a misunderstanding of the discussion and the sequence of events. In his panic, he was unable to use verbal communication skills to ask for clarification. The situation was saved by an understanding teacher who quickly interpreted the function of the nonconventional signal and provided the needed information to defuse the situation and prevent escalation.

Unique Interpretation Problems

Parents and teachers must be prepared to identify, interpret, and respond appropriately to the subtle and not-so-subtle problems and messages of those with autism. This requires vigilance and extreme sensitivity. The stakes are high; if they fail, a behavioral outburst is likely to occur. The need to be constantly alert is tiring; it is frustrating when messages are hidden. There are at least six interpretation problems that cause confusion, frustration, and even anger.

Problem 1. People are confused when conventional signals are used unconventionally—when words and gestures that look familiar are used with different, unusual, and unexpected meanings

This is a frequent problem in autism. Individuals may smile when they are in pain or when sad or confused. They may echo words without understanding their meaning or associate unusual meanings to words. Sometimes these signals seem so appropriate to the situation that their meanings are not questioned. This often occurs with higher-functioning individuals who insert echoed phrases into conversations. At other times, the echoed statement or phrase makes no sense in the specific situation. Recall the young man who shouted, "The cat jumped off the balcony"; or Jose, who kept repeating, "Drink" when he meant music; and Maria, who said, "No" when she meant "Yes."

For an in-depth discussion and strategies for dealing with these interpretation problems, see chapter 10, pages 137-151.

Interpretation in these situations is difficult and dependent upon an understanding of the individual, the common learning style, the types of communication problems, and the situations that are likely to trigger confusion and problems.

Problem 2. People get angry when they think behavior is deliberate

When people assume that the behavior of those with autism is deliberate and purposeful, they tend to feel paranoid—that the individual is deliberately trying to make life miserable, to disrupt, to hurt, to avoid. When frustration and anger persist, it is natural to want to punish and to avoid. These reactions are likely to make the situation worse. In most cases, individuals with autism are doing the best they can in a very confusing world.

In some cases, the behavior is intentional; but in many other situations, the behavior is reflexive, a quick reaction to confusion, frustration, and anxiety when the individual has no other alternative. There are clues to help determine whether the behavior is intentional or reflexive.

- Intentional behavior depends on a clear understanding that a specific signal will achieve a specific goal, and a persistent effort is made to engage a listener and to send the specific message.

- Nonintentional or reflexive behavioral signals are reactions or habitual responses to the stimulation and feelings of the situation or the moment. They are not planned or deliberate, but reactive; and they will occur whether or not there is a listener. In some situations, these reactive behaviors are intense versions of primitive and instinctive fight-or-flight responses (such as that shown by Gabriel when he said, "Mrs. Brown, this is no laughing matter").

- Reflexive, reactive responses are usually quick, rote, and often smooth and fluent. For example, echolalic verbal messages are delivered quickly; they are well articulated, grammatically correct, and fluent, with expressive vocal quality.

- Intentional verbal responses are often less fluent, generally delivered more slowly, with a flat vocal quality and little change of expression. Words are often used in unusual combinations, or speech may be excessively formal.

Problem 3. People are confused when someone who can talk or communicate sometimes does not talk or communicate all the time

Most people communicate and behave in both intentional and reflexive ways. Most of the time, communicative behavior is thoughtful and deliberate to accomplish a specific purpose. However, when startled, surprised, or frustrated by a situation, behavior becomes more reflexive and unpredictable. The higher the anxiety, the less rational, deliberate, and effective the behavior and the communication.

This is also true in autism. Communication is not a natural and automatic process for those with autism. Those who can speak and communicate in other ways under normal and familiar situations forget or are unable to use those skills when they are startled and anxious. As a rule, in stressful situations, communicative behavior is more frequently nonintentional, reflexive, and reactive. *Even though a behavior is reactive and nonintentional, it still has communicative value. It reflects a message about a person's emotional state and about his or her problems. It is up to caregivers and friends to identify, interpret, and help solve the problem.*

See chapter 21, pages 311-314, for strategies for dealing with repetitive questions.

Problem 4. People get tired of answering the same questions over and over

Sometimes the signal is a question repeated again and again. Many times these questions are seen as meaningless and are ignored. Sometimes the exact question is answered over and over as the individual gets more and more upset. In these situations, the question is used intentionally and has a legitimate message that must be interpreted by others.

See chapter 17, pages 225-246, for strategies to avoid teaching erroneous concepts.

Problem 5. People are confused because the same behavior sometimes is a reflexive response and sometimes is used intentionally

A reflexive, reactive signal can take on meaning if it is consistently and predictably followed by a certain reaction. For example, a person who is consistently sent to time-out when head-banging may head-bang to signal, "I need a break"— especially if the person has no better or more efficient alternative.

In this way, a nonconventional signal, such as R/S behavior, may be used intentionally to avoid or escape from an unpleasant situation, when initially it was used reflexively in response to a boring, painful, or overwhelming situation. The problem of interpretation is now more complex.

See chapter 10, pages 148-149, for strategies for dealing with this problem.

Problem 6. Sometimes the words and the message are understood, but people cannot or do not want to acknowledge the message

Parents and teachers often want to ignore a message when it does not fit their agenda. For example, when the individual with autism says, "All done" or "Outside" when the schedule says there is more work to be done, what is a person to do? If the goal is for that person to communicate spontaneously, the person must find out that communication pays off. Therefore, messages must be acknowledged so the power of communication is evident.

Summary

Just as most people have many small and large problems (needs and wants), the person with autism has many problems, needs, and wants. While most people have many alternative ways to solve each of their problems, those with autism have limited alternatives and solutions. If information cannot be manipulated to generate and evaluate alternatives and if communication is difficult or unreliable, solutions are likely to be both inappropriate and ineffective. If interventions are simply directed to eliminate the inappropriate behaviors, the individual is left with no solutions. The learning and thinking problems in autism are such that effective support and intervention must be based on accurate interpretations of behavior. The following chapters provide information and guidance to support those with autism in a positive and productive way.

2

Assessment

YOUTH SO SOBER

YOUTH NEED HELP
FROM EVERY SOURCE
HELP US FIND A WAY
SEE OUR NEEDS
HOPE YOU WILL STAY
HELP US FIND A WAY

BE THERE FOR US
GET TO KNOW US
SEE WHO WE ARE

TALK

HOW I ONLY WANT TO TALK
GOD GRANT ME THAT DREAM
YOUTH NEEDS TO WONDER
WHY HIM?
UNUSUAL ROW TO HOE
IT SEEMS

UNDERSTAND THE SILENCE
ROARS IN MY HEAD
TOO ROTTEN YOUTH SAID
PERHAPS IT WILL END

—David Eastham
In *UNDERSTAND: Fifty Memowriter Poems*

Issues Related to Diagnosis and Eligibility for Special Educational Services

Once a child is suspected of having autism, those suspicions must be confirmed or denied. Parents are understandably anxious and frustrated at this time, not only because they are worried about their child's future, but for a variety of other reasons.

- Parents probably have known—or at least suspected—for some time that their child was not developing normally. Now, they are relieved yet fearful that they will soon have some answers. If their fears are confirmed, they must deal with an unknown future. If their fears are denied, they must continue to seek answers.

- Parents are tired. Their child has required constant day and night supervision for quite some time.

- Parents are confused. They probably have received conflicting information from various professionals and from reading about autism. Part of this confusion comes from not having enough information; parents don't know where to have their child evaluated or what the evaluation will involve. Once they get into a system, there seems to be duplication and delay, as if professionals are incompetent or trying to avoid responsibility. This delay is particularly frustrating if parents have been told that their child's best hope is early intervention.

- Parents also may be confused because they want to trust the professionals, but they have heard from some other parents that professionals cannot be trusted.

These fears and concerns are valid and must be acknowledged by professionals. In many parts of the country, it is difficult to find medical or educational professionals who have extensive experience with autism. There are at least two reasons for this. First, until quite recently, there was never a mandate to identify or diagnose autism. Consequently, the need for specific services went unrecognized. Because the need was not recognized, there was never a major demand for specialized training and little opportunity to get experience.

A second reason for the limited number of experienced professionals is that training in autism is not easy to obtain. Several major universities, medical schools, and private autism centers offer excellent training; but the training is accessible only to those who live nearby or who have the resources to travel and pay for it.

The situation is changing. In 1990, enactment of the Individuals with Disabilities Education Act (IDEA) required public school systems to identify their students with autism and serve them appropriately. With this mandate, autism resources and services in public schools have expanded. As the numbers of identified students grow, more professionals in many fields receive specialized training and gain experience. Administrators and service providers from other agencies also are becoming aware of the need for specialized training and services that match the needs of those with autism.

The purpose of this chapter is to provide information that will guide and support parents through the evaluation process. If parents and professionals have access to this same information, it can help to establish trusting and cooperative working relationships that can benefit the children.

Parent/Professional Relationships—
Assumptions and Considerations

Parents and professionals are individuals with their own sets of past experiences that affect their attitudes. Parents cannot judge a specific professional from their experiences with another professional; nor can they always make judgments about professional competence on the basis of another parent's report. Furthermore, professionals cannot judge parents by their experiences with other parents. Each relationship is new and has the potential to be positive.

Because autism is such a complex problem, the ideal situation is for the parent and the professional to build a sharing and problem-solving relationship or partnership. This type of relationship is supportive and productive for all. Each member of the parent/professional partnership plays a unique role.

- Parents have a responsibility to be advocates for their children. They have a wealth of critical information to share, based on their child's history. In many cases, parents will have lifelong responsibility as caregivers. Therefore, they must become experts in autism. It is reasonable for parents to check a professional's training and experience; and professionals must not feel threatened by parents who have a broad knowledge of autism or who ask about credentials. Rather, parents can be engaged as valuable resources.

- Professionals are skilled and experienced in their own fields and have much to offer both the parents and the child. An effective professional continually seeks information about autism, consults with experts, and encourages a sharing relationship with parents.

- Those involved in the education system do some things because of federal, state, and local laws and administrative requirements. The requirements protect the rights of the child and family, to ensure unbiased and appropriate services. Some requirements also protect the school and school staff. "Paper trails" prove that the correct procedures were followed. Schools are monitored by state and federal education agencies to see that they follow the requirements of the law. If a school system does not comply with the law, it loses federal money and could be open to lawsuits.

Educators can become defensive because they feel helpless in the face of parents' frustration. Often, professionals are caught in a bind between their concern for the child and family, overwhelming caseloads, or a system that sometimes seems rigid.

Issues related to the evaluation process and the outcome of the evaluation also may be confusing for parents.

- Parents must assume that evaluators are caring people who are qualified to evaluate their child. Evaluators must assume that parents are loving, responsible, and capable. In general, both assumptions are true. If either assumption is later found to be wrong, there are procedures to follow to remedy the situation.

- Sometimes the interview questions seem irrelevant to the issue of diagnosing autism. Parents must feel free to ask about the purpose of such questions. They have a right to challenge and refuse to answer any question or statement that suggests they caused their child's autism. The myth that autism is caused by parental rejection or lack of love must not intrude into current practice.

- Children with autism behave differently in different settings, on different days, and under different conditions. Therefore, to be valid, a diagnosis must be based on observations and reports of the child's behavior and development under various conditions, in various settings, and at various times. Information from parents and others who know the child well is critical and must be solicited and given adequate weight.

- An evaluation must identify *all* the conditions that affect the child's development and learning. Sometimes parents are discouraged if the list of coexisting problems begins to grow. Some professionals who are opposed to labels avoid other than generic labels (such as mildly, moderately, or severely disabled) to establish eligibility. However, to ensure that the most effective educational plan is developed to address a child's specific needs, parents and professionals need all the information possible.

- Even when a child has a diagnosis of autism from a physician, psychologist, or child-study center, the school must conduct an evaluation based on federal and state regulations and requirements in order for the child to be eligible for special educational services. In most cases, earlier diagnostic reports are given serious consideration. Unless there are reasons to believe that the report is inaccurate, the same procedures would not need to be repeated. However, school personnel generally need to complete a comprehensive assessment to identify the child's specific educational needs. See chapter 6 for information about this assessment.

- Occasionally, a physician or a psychologist will determine that a child does not have autism. However, in some states, the child still may be eligible for autism services through the school. This happens because the educational criteria may be similar but not identical to the criteria specified in the *Diagnostic and Statistical Manual (DSM-IV)* of the American Psychiatric Association.

- In some cases, parents or a teacher will identify subtle but very real indicators of autism in a child who is quite verbal and who functions quite well. These signs may not be apparent to the evaluator, or they may be so mild that they are seen as individual idiosyncrasies not relevant to the child's future development. Consequently, it may be determined that the child does not qualify for autism services. In these cases, the parents and the teacher have several options. They can:

  1. Ask that the evaluation data be reviewed when they can provide additional information or correct any information that may have been misinterpreted

  2. Continue to document the subtle signs; and when the indicators are more apparent, ask for another evaluation

  3. Ask for an independent evaluation by someone outside the system

     The law has provisions for independent evaluations.

- Parents must direct their questions to the appropriate professional. A teacher is not qualified to discuss (except in the most general way) the causes of autism, related medical problems, or medications. A physician is not qualified to suggest educational programs or strategies. If questions are directed to the wrong person, the answers may be inaccurate, incomplete, and misleading. However, when the teacher, the physician, and the parent share information, the child benefits.

- It is rarely helpful to ask medical or educational professionals to predict a child's potential. There are simply too many variables to make a prediction with any degree of certainty. The outcome for those with autism is very different today from what it was before appropriate early intervention and special education were available.

For additional information and strategies for forming more collaborative and effective parent/professional relationships, see Turnbull and Turnbull 1990.

See pages 436–439 for information and resources for advocates.

The Evaluation Process

Prepare for the Evaluations

Parents or teachers who are not already familiar with autism need basic information such as that presented in chapter 1. They must know why autism is suspected and why it is important to recognize the autism if it is present. Other basic information may be available from the special education office. An autism specialist may be available to provide additional information and answer more specific questions.

Both the parents and the teacher have important information to contribute to the evaluators. The parents have knowledge of their child's earliest development and behavior in a variety of situations. The child's teacher, who has experience with many children, can compare this child's behavior with that of typically developing children in similar situations. Together or separately, parents and teachers can prepare lists or anecdotal descriptions of the child's responses and behavior in different situations, as in Figure 5.1. This written information either can be sent to the evaluator prior to the appointment or can be left at the conclusion of the interview.

There are several reasons for writing down the information.

- Sometimes it is difficult to think of important information in a stressful situation. Also, the evaluator may not ask the questions in a way that triggers some of the significant information.

- The child may not show the behaviors of concern during the observations.

Figure 5.1. Sample: Anecdotal description of behaviors

The italicized labels are added to show significance. An actual description would not include these labels.

- Tommy does not seem to hear some loud noises (trucks going by on the street or a door banging), but frantically covers his ears and runs to hide under the table when a specific song is played or when a spoon clinks against a cup (*sensory responses*). He has never answered or come to me when I call his name (*language; lack of meaning*). When he wants something in the cupboard, he gets a chair and climbs up on the counter. If he can't get the door open, he will scream and have a tantrum rather than ask for help (*communication*).

- Whenever he sees a number, he jumps up and down and flaps his hands (*sensory responses*) and begins to count. I have heard him count to 1,000, then quickly count backward to 1. He can label any number he sees (*developmental discrepancy*). The only time we have heard him talk is when he counts or labels numbers (*communication; developmental discrepancy*). The only time he smiles and interacts with us is when we have blocks, cards, or puzzles with numbers on them (*relating to people*).

- When he is alone, he lines up the blocks or cards in a specific order and gets very upset when we stop him (*relating to environment; resisting change*). Frequently he will walk with his head close to walls, fences, or large pieces of furniture so he can "sight" (*sensory responses*). When we have guests who try to hug him, he pushes them away and runs to hide (*relating to people; sensory responses*). . . .

- A teacher's description of differences between a particular child's responses and those of the child's age mates has special significance. The teacher's list is most helpful if it includes statements such as, "When . . . happens, most of the children do . . .; but this child does . . . instead."

- A written list provides a broad sample of the child's behavioral symptoms for follow-up questions or reference while summarizing the evaluation data.

Parents must be prepared to answer questions about:

- Family history—information regarding family members with developmental problems, health of parents, the course of the pregnancy and delivery, and similar questions

  This information specifically relates to identifying factors that may have caused the child's developmental problems. These questions generally are not asked during the educational evaluation.

- Developmental milestones

  At what age did the child first roll over? sit up? walk? smile? say first words? Often it is helpful to have a baby book or medical records available for reference during interviews.

The evaluator will want information about behavior related to language, communication, social, emotional, and sensory issues from both the parents and the teachers. The following questions can serve as an outline to prepare for the interview.

1. What does this child do when alone? when with other children? with toys? when stressed? when things get noisy? when routines are changed? when given a gift? when shopping or at the mall? during a family visit or reunion? when touched or hugged? at mealtime? at bedtime?

2. What things does this child do too seldom? too intensely? too often?

3. What things are done very well? What things are very difficult?

4. Describe specific repetitive behaviors or routines (motor movements, verbal routines, compulsive routines, intense interests, and others).

5. How does this child show pain? happiness? sadness? excitement? anxiety? fear? a need for comfort? a desire for an activity, food, or object? a desire for something to end? a lack of interest? protest?

6. How can this child be comforted? calmed? corrected? taught something new?

7. Does the child have intense likes and dislikes in foods? objects? activities? situations? other areas?

8. Describe the child's responses to any specific odors, textures, noises, movements, patterns, or lights.

9. Describe any unusual or different responses when hugged by parents or relatives, when in familiar settings with familiar people, and when in a new place or with new people.

Evaluation to Determine Eligibility for Special Educational Services

The evaluation to determine eligibility for special educational services is available at no cost through the public school system. This evaluation process is based on the federal law (IDEA) and is governed by administrative rules. The process will differ somewhat from state to state, but the law stipulates the following common elements:

- Parents must be notified of their rights under the law
- Parents must be informed about the evaluation process
- Parents must sign a form giving permission for the evaluation
- A multidisciplinary team (MDT) must conduct the evaluation and determine eligibility

The Multidisciplinary Team (MDT)

The goal of the team is to determine whether the child meets the autism criteria for special educational services. This criteria is based on the definition of autism in IDEA, but the wording of this criteria may differ somewhat from state to state.

Membership of the MDT must include at least two individuals, one of whom is a specialist in the education of students with the suspected disability. An appropriate team for a child suspected of having autism would include the child's teacher, a speech-language pathologist, an occupational therapist, a school psychologist, and a specialist with current and extensive training and experience in the education of *many* children who have autism. If additional complicating factors are present, other members are included on the MDT (for example, the school counselor or a teacher of the deaf).

The Evaluation Process

The administrative rules require the MDT to do certain things to document the presence of the indicators defined in the criteria. Again, there will be variations from state to state. Most likely the evaluation will include some or all of the following activities:

- Interview parents and/or review records to document the presence of the indicators of autism during early development
- Observe the child in different settings on different days

   Observations are described in chapter 6, pages 67-68.

- Interview the teacher to identify how the child's behavior differs from the behavior of others
- Conduct a speech and language assessment

   This assessment is likely to involve interviews with parents and teachers.

- Conduct a standardized intelligence test
- Conduct an evaluation of sensorimotor integration and development
- Perform a hearing test
- Complete a standardized autism rating scale or checklist

   Because autism behavior looks different under different situations, it is critical that this checklist be completed by or with information from one or more people (parents, teachers, and others) who know the child very well and have knowledge of the child's behavior in different situations.

- Obtain a physician's statement indicating whether any physical factors are contributing to the child's learning problems
- Many states require a physician's diagnosis based on the *DSM-IV* criteria

At the conclusion of this evaluation, the team has information to determine eligibility as well as some important information for developing a child's educational plan.

Evaluation to Determine a Diagnosis

Evaluation can occur in a child-evaluation center attached to a university, medical center, or hospital. The school staff or family physician can help the family locate an appropriate assessment site. This evaluation also can occur in the private office of a physician or psychologist.

A psychologist in private practice may use the *DSM-IV* to confirm a diagnosis of autism. In some cases, this diagnosis might satisfy health insurance requirements, but it would not provide access to genetic and medical information that is important to families; nor would it necessarily provide access to free special educational services.

The Evaluation Process

If the evaluation occurs in an assessment center, the procedures are likely to be similar to those used in the school system. The major difference is that in the assessment center, usually a physician, psychologist, physical therapist, occupational therapist, social worker, and sometimes an educator all will be involved in the evaluation. The parents are interviewed in detail by several of the evaluators. The purpose of the questions is to identify the possible cause and the onset or development of the child's problems. The evaluation may be scheduled for one day, but sometimes these evaluations require several days. The longer evaluation offers opportunities for the child to be observed with other children in a play or classroom setting.

If the evaluation occurs in the physician's office, the process generally involves an extensive interview with parents to elicit details of family history, the pregnancy and birth, the child's early development, and current functioning. Additional information is obtained as the physician observes the child's behavior during the interview. There may be one or several appointments.

Summary

The importance of identifying autism and providing appropriate services cannot be overemphasized. The parents play an important role in both evaluations, to determine a diagnosis and to determine eligibility for special education services that address the unique needs of those with autism. While parents are often highly stressed during this period of uncertainty, the evaluation process provides a prime opportunity to establish trusting and cooperative parent/professional relationships that are of major importance for the child.

Assessment for Program Development

To obtain useful assessment information, an evaluator must understand the implications of autism on learning and thinking, communication, and behavior. With this understanding, appropriate assessment tools and procedures can be selected and behavioral responses can be interpreted accurately.

A comprehensive assessment for the individual with autism includes both functional and standardized procedures. Since the goals are selected and integrated from the following three sources, each area must be assessed:

1. The goals that address the learning and thinking differences and deficits common in autism, which impact every minute of life

2. The chronological, age-appropriate developmental skills such as language, social, motor, or reading readiness skills

3. The functional skills needed for independence in the home, school, and community

Parents are the prime source of information about their child's development and functioning. They and the child's teachers provide the examiner with information to make the assessment session more productive. Often they are enlisted to observe the testing session or a videotape of the session, or to review behavioral notes to interpret specific responses. Having parents or a teacher verify the interpretations avoids the possibility that some seemingly irrelevant detail, a subtle sensory problem, or motivation issue does not affect the outcome.

> While being observed in the play area, Amy was busily engaged at the doll house, placing the tiny furniture and talking to the dolls. The play looked creative. However, her mother reported that Amy did and said exactly the same things each time she played with the doll house. Without mother's knowledge of Amy's play, this highly repetitive routine would have been interpreted as creative play by the examiner.

> As Tony watched, the examiner placed a piece of candy under one of three cups on the table, moved the cups about on the table, and directed Tony to "Find the candy." Tony continued to rock back and forth in his chair. After several attempts to get a response, Tony's father suggested that the candy be replaced by the strings that Tony flipped repetitively. As this was done, the child immediately became alert, watched the cups intently, and located the cup to find his strings. Like most children with autism, Tony was not motivated by typical reinforcers.

The Functional Assessment

Procedures

The purpose of the functional assessment is to find out how a person actually operates in the natural environment. (What does he do, and how does he do it?) There are two basic procedures for getting this information: interviews and observations.

Interviews

Interviews with parents and teachers are important to find out exactly how the individual performs under a broad range of conditions. Information from interviews is more complete and useful when:

- The parents and teachers have an opportunity to see the questions and make notes before the interview

  These notes are used to jog memories during the interview. Since the notes may contain important information and examples that were not addressed during the interview, they are left for the evaluator to examine later.

- The evaluator asks open-ended questions to expand and clarify responses (for example, "Can you tell me more about that?"; "What exactly did Juan do?"; "What did that tantrum look like?"; "What happened first?")

In some situations, a group interview is both productive and efficient. When parents, teachers, and others have an opportunity to share together, one person's example often triggers another person's memory. It is also an excellent way to identify the things the individual does in one setting but not another.

Observations

Observations in various natural settings allow the evaluator to see how the individual functions and the impact of environmental conditions on the ability to function. To see the performance variability from day to day and in various situations, observe the learner on at least two or three different days and in several different settings. It is as important to observe the performance in settings where problems *do not* occur as it is to observe the settings where problems *do* occur. With multiple observations, it is possible to establish reasonable expectations, to understand what conditions are necessary for optimal performance, and to determine the conditions that disrupt effective functioning.

The procedures described below elicit the types of details needed to develop the instructional and behavioral support plan for those with autism; that is:

- Identify priority goals and routines
- Assess priority routines and student skills
- Assess sensory and instructional demands of routines
- Assess functional communication
- Assess social skills
- Identify preferences and interests
- Assess daily life activities
- Monitor instructional progress and problems

Several of the procedures and forms included in this chapter were developed by Falco and associates (1990) for Project QUEST (Quality Educational Services Training Project), Portland State University, Portland, Oregon. Other forms were developed and used by the author and other autism specialists in Oregon's Regional Autism Services program. Other resources for developing individual curricula include Gray (1992) and Neel (1989).

These are only a sampling of possible forms and procedures for conducting a functional assessment. Those included have some unique features that are especially helpful for eliciting the kinds of detailed information needed to develop effective programs for those with autism.

Identify Priority Goals and Routines

Priorities are identified by analyzing the routines that make up a day in the life of the family and peers in the classroom, determining how the individual currently participates, and targeting those routines that would increase the individual's involvement and independence.

See figure 6.1, *Sample (partial form): Family Priorities: Weekday Schedule.* This QUEST format provides a logical method for identifying and prioritizing functional goals and natural routines that will allow the learner to participate more actively in the life of the family. The form can be used to guide an interview with parents as they list their family's daily schedule from the time their child gets out of bed in the morning until bedtime. The next steps are to identify whether and how the child participates in those activities, the level and type of participation, and how much assistance is provided. Finally, the parents decide which of the activities should be targeted for instruction. (Which would make life more interesting for their child, easier for the family, or would lead to greater independence?) Figure 6.1 is an illustration of part of this form.

Teachers complete a similar form that covers the school day.

After these lists are prioritized, it is relatively easy to identify realistic functional goals that relate directly to specific family and school situations. Parents and teachers have reported that this process is extremely helpful and worth the one to two hours of interview time. In succeeding years, the time is reduced considerably; when they become familiar with the process, parents can update the forms independently. Once the forms are completed, the meeting to clarify and integrate the information is relatively short.

Other checklists are available for use in situations where parents might feel uncomfortable having school staff review their daily schedules.

Assess Priority Routines and Student Skills

The natural components or steps of a routine are identified by observing how peers of the same age do the things they do. Natural cues are discovered by observing how people know when and where to do things. A realistic criterion for mastery is identified by observing how well peers do the routine. Potential problems, natural prompts, and the possible need for adaptations are identified by observing the amount and kinds of help others receive and the type of assistance needed by the individual being assessed.

See chapters 11 and 18 for a more complete description of the process for developing the instructional plans to teach functional routines.

See figure 6.2, *Sample: Functional Routines: Assessment of Student Skills.* This sample illustrates the QUEST format for analyzing the components of priority routines, the student's performance within the routine, and the need for adaptations.

The importance of identifying the natural components of the routine cannot be overestimated when planning instruction for those who learn routines exactly as taught. Integrating these naturally occurring elements into the instructional plan will help the individual become more independent.

Figure 6.1. Sample (partial form): Family priorities: Weekday schedule

Adapted with permission from *Project QUEST Inservice Manual* (Falco et al. 1990)

Student: _____ Dean _____   **Age:** _17_   **Date:** _____ 5/10 _____

Directions: Ask family members to describe what the student does or is helped to do at home (from getting up, going to school; and from arriving home until going to bed). Identify routines that are age-appropriate and those that are family priorities, to be included in the student's IEP.

Approximate Time	Routine	Environment/Area	How does this happen now? How much help is needed?	Age Appropriate? Y/N	Priority? Y/N	Comments
6:00 a.m.	Getting up	Dean's bedroom at foster home	Mom goes to his room. He is usually awake and in bed. He is wet (wears diaper at night).	Y (not diaper)	Y	Night toilet training is a priority.
6:05 a.m.	Undressing	Bathroom	Undresses when told to. Takes off pajamas and diaper. Drops them on floor.	Y (not diaper)	N	
6:10 a.m.	Showering/Bathing	Bathroom	Does not like shower. Requires much physical assistance to use shower. Will sit in bath when it has been prepared. Will rub chest, arms, face with cloth. Will get out of tub when requested.	Y	Y?	Not sure this is a high priority right now.
6:25 a.m.	Drying after shower or bath	Bathroom	Requires physical assistance to dry body.	Y	Y?	
6:30 a.m.	Get dressed	Bedroom	If each item is handed to him with repeated reminders, he can dress; but usually he is assisted with all items. (It takes too long without assistance.)	Y	Y	Mom knows she should work on this, but worries about time.
6:45 a.m.	Free time	Bedroom	Gets out "wrestling" figure and plays with it, or looks at magazine, or watches TV in his room.	N Y Y	N	Mom satisfied with his ability to occupy himself.
7:00 a.m.	Breakfast	Kitchen	Mom gives him prepared food at the table. He eats adequately without assistance. He will carry dishes to sink if reminded and assisted (but usually Mom does it).	Y	Y?	Mom thinks he may be able to prepare a bowl of cereal and put dishes in sink.
7:15 a.m.	Prepare for school bus	Hall closet, bedroom, kitchen	Mom assists him to get his coat and put it on and get his communication notebook. He sits in kitchen and watches for bus.	Y	Y?	Mom is unsure whether he could put on coat and get notebook independently.

Figure 6.2. Sample: Functional routines: Assessment of student skills

Adapted with permission from *Project QUEST Inservice Manual* (Falco et al. 1990)

Student: _____ **Environment:** Home, school _____

Routine: _Occupy Free Time_ _____

Component	Natural Cues	Skills	+/o	Quality/Tempo	Y/N	Need Assist/Errors	What To Do
INITIATE	Time free of tasks/chores/ expectations	Have a repertoire of free-time activities available.					
PREPARE	Choices of free time are accessible.	Make a decision of what to do with free time.					
PERFORM	Choice made.	Get materials together to do free-time activity.					
	Activity does not require anyone else.	Independently engage in the activity.					
	Activity requires other people to participate.	Find someone to do the activity with.					
	Finished with chosen activity.	Put materials away.					
	More free time left.	Make another choice.					
		(Repeat the steps.)					
TERMINATE	Available free time is gone.	Go to next activity/task/scheduled routine.					

(continued)

Figure 6.2. (continued)

Adapted from *Project QUEST Inservice Manual* (Falco et al. 1990)

Student: _____ **Environment:** Home, school

Routine: Occupy Free Time

Component	Natural Cues	Skills	+/o	Quality/Tempo	Y/N	Need Assist/Errors	What To Do
PROBLEM SOLVE	Can't think of anything to do.	Ask parent/teacher for suggestions of things to do.					
	Materials are missing or broken.	Ask someone to help find or repair/replace items.					
ENRICHMENT: SOCIAL	Tired of doing same things.	Try new activities					
	Often do solitary activities	Make friends. Do things with others.					
	Expectations	Use materials correctly. Keep area clean. Maintain acceptable noise levels					
COMMUNI-CATION	Other persons are available.	Ask someone to engage in free time with you.					
	Can't find or reach materials	Ask someone for help. Get a step stool.					
CHOICE	Variety of free-time choices	Choose desired free-time activities.					
	Peers/family available	Choose whom you wish to spend free time with.					

Assess Sensory and Instructional Demands of Routines

If the individual with autism is ultimately expected to participate independently in natural activities, it is necessary to identify potential sensory and instructional problems and either adapt the environment, adapt the activity, or develop visual support systems. To determine the potential need for modifications or adaptations, observe:

- The sensory demands of the environment—the light, noise, crowding, temperature, odors, and other factors

- The instructional demands—teacher's language level, use of visual supports or requirement for listening, waiting, making judgments, or for cooperative work

- The response demands—verbal responses, written work, homework, and others

Form 6.1, *Checklist for Assessing Environmental Demands* (page 75), represents a method for accomplishing the tasks listed above. When completing this assessment, the individual's specific abilities, preferences, and sensitivities must be considered.

Form 6.2, *What Happened (Flow Chart)* (page 76), is an observation tool adapted from one developed at the Judevine Center (Blackwell 1978). It is used to record the flow of environmental demands and the responses of the individual. It represents a simple, objective method of recording the flow of an event or social exchange—the antecedents, the response, and the reciprocation or consequences. This is a useful way to identify instructional and environmental conditions that require modification. With experience, the evaluator can record frequency, duration, and intensity data.

Assess Functional Communication

While standardized tests can measure many facets of language and communication development, a natural environment is needed for assessing a person's actual communication. An examiner can observe the individual in the natural environment or can set up situations that require communication (for example, putting favorite things in sight but out of reach). However, these procedures are time consuming and limited in scope.

Form 6.3, *Functional Communication Assessment: Informant Interview* (pages 77-86), is used to guide interviews with parents and teachers who know how the individual actually communicates in many situations and under many conditions.

The question, "How do you know when your child . . .?" is used to discover how the individual requests, rejects, protests, expresses feelings, comments, responds to questions, and acknowledges others. Parents and teachers need time to study the items and make notes about the full range of the child's communicative behavior prior to the interview. During the interview, the examiner (a special education teacher, a speech-language pathologist, or autism specialist) can help them expand their examples of communicative behavior. The information is summarized on a form-and-function matrix, a highly visual summary of the individual's communication skills and major skill deficits.

This tool not only identifies effective communication effort, it also identifies the accelerating chains of behavior that occur when communication breaks down and stress increases. This is a particularly valuable tool for assessing the communication of those with severe behavior problems—*those who are highly verbal as well as those who are nonverbal.*

Other Communication Assessment Tools

Milieu Communication Project: Pragmatic Protocol (Pruitting and Kirchner 1987) is a practical and easy-to-use tool for assessing language use. Thirty aspects of language use are rated as appropriate, inappropriate, or not observed.

Communication and Symbolic Behavior Scales (CSBS) (Wetherby and Prizant 1993) is another useful tool for assessing the communication of young children with autism. With this tool, structured opportunities and unstructured play can be examined within natural contexts while the child is engaged with the caregiver. *CSBS* provides information about the child's ability to persist and repair if communicative attempts are not successful. It also notes the hierarchy of verbal and gestural cues used during the structured opportunities to elicit initiations and responses. In this scale, 22 communication and symbolic behaviors are rated on a five-point scale to derive seven cluster scores:

1. Communicative functions
2. Gestural communicative means
3. Vocal communicative means
4. Verbal communicative means
5. Reciprocity
6. Social/affective signaling (use of gaze shifts, etc.)
7. Symbolic behavior

Speech-language pathologists will know of other tools to assess functional communication and the pragmatic aspects of language.

Assess Social Skills

Form 6.4, *Social Skills Assessment: Informant Interview* (pages 87-90), another form created by QUEST, provides an interesting format for assessing ten functional social skills across eight different situations or contexts.

Form 6.5, *Social Interaction Checklist* (page 91), is an informal tool for assessing and monitoring 15 social interaction behaviors that are important to success in integrated classroom settings. This rating scale was created by Oregon's Regional Autism Specialists. Several times a year, classroom teachers are asked to rate students' interactions, using a five-point scale. In this way, progress is noted and problems are identified and addressed in a timely manner.

Other Social-Skills Assessment Tools

The Transdisciplinary Play-Based Assessment: A Functional Approach to Working with Young Children, Revised Edition (Lindner 1993) can be used to assess the cognitive, social-emotional, communication/language, and sensory motor skills in the context of natural play situations. Designed for use with children functioning between 6-month to 6-year levels, it is useful for developing the child's program plan.

The Social Strategy Rating Scale: An Approach to Evaluating Social Competence (Beckman and Lieber 1994) is developed to provide a relatively simple method of measuring social competence in young children with disabilities across multiple contexts.

Identify Preferences and Interests

Form 6.6, *Preference Survey* (page 92), created at the Judevine Center (Blackwell 1978), is used in the assessment of those with strong and sometimes unusual likes and dislikes and who have difficulty organizing information, expressing feelings, requesting, protesting, or rejecting. When completed in detail, this tool identifies people, activities, events, objects, foods, or other factors that trigger positive, negative, or neutral feelings. This survey can be completed by parents, teachers, or others who know the individual well, and it can be integrated and expanded during an individual or group meeting.

The information elicited with this form is used to develop daily schedules and contingencies at home, school, work or in the community. This survey also is used to assess the relationship of activities and activity schedules to problem behaviors.

For completed samples of the Preference Survey, see page 172; and Case Study, page 423.

Assess Daily Life Activities

Form 6.7, *Assessment of Daily Life Activities: Informant Interview* (page 93), is used to identify the relationships of various environmental conditions to a serious behavior problem, and to organize critical information for modifying an existing program to ensure a balanced and positive daily schedule of events to support appropriate behavior.

Monitor Instructional Progress and Problems

Evaluation and refinement is a continuous process if maximum progress is to occur. Form 6.8, *Routine Data* (page 94) can be used to monitor instructional support and progress when teaching functional routines. See page 254 for a discussion of ways to modify this form for monitoring the variations required for generalization.

Student: _____ **Environment:** _____ **Date:** _____

Use this checklist to identify and determine which adaptations may be necessary. Match the learner's sensitivities and deficits to: (1) the level of environmental stimulation and (2) the demands of the activity. Note examples.

1. **Nature and level of the activity and environmental stimuli**
   (Consider the intensity, frequency, and duration of stimuli.)

   ☐ Noise—Subtle (echoes, fans, lights, halls, street), people (talking, singing, shuffling feet or paper)

   ☐ Noise—Intense (whistles, bells, trains, loudspeakers, machinery)

   ☐ Visual—Objects (pictures, mobiles, lights and shadows, bulletin boards, materials on open shelves), surfaces (wood grain, reflecting, or patterned), people (glasses, jewelry, movement)

   ☐ Odors—People, materials (perfumes, glues, paint, paper), cafeteria, cleaning supplies, nearby businesses (bakery, factory, service station)

   ☐ Touch—People (crowding, touching, holding hands, physical assistance or touch for reinforcement), materials (textures of fabrics, furniture, sticky or rough materials)

   ☐ Movement (Vestibular)—Demand for getting up and down, reaching, stooping, moving about, moving up or down inclines, sitting or standing in one place

   ☐ Taste—Meals and snack foods, exploratory tasting activities for young children

2. **Demands of the event (work or activity)**

   ☐ Complexity of the language used in directions

   ☐ Requirement for written work, oral communication

   ☐ Time pressures

   ☐ Need to keep several thoughts together in a sequence

   ☐ Need for generating new motor and/or verbal responses

   ☐ Requirement for solving problems, using judgment, making decisions

   ☐ Clarity of the beginning and end of the activity or routine

   ☐ Waiting requirements—(for bus, before/after transitions, for help, in line)

   ☐ Participation with others (cooperative teams, assembly lines, competitive activities, partners, large or small groups)

3. **New or unfamiliar elements**

   Activity: ☐ New   ☐ Familiar

   Materials: ☐ New   ☐ Familiar

   Location: ☐ New   ☐ Familiar

   Staff members: ☐ New   ☐ Familiar

   Peers: ☐ New   ☐ Familiar

   Other new: _____

Adapted with permission from *Judevine® Training System* (Blackwell 1978)

Student:_____**Interpreter:**_____

Setting:_____**Date:**_____**Consultant:**_____

Directions: Record the flow of events that occur during the observation period. Include sensory conditions, activity demands, and responses. Note the time every few minutes. Also note the type of activity/materials as they change. Record 1:1 interactions in script format. Code to speed recording: T=teacher, S=student, SR=repetitive behavior, etc. When the action is faster than the ability to write, add a dash to note a break in the flow; then simply move on. At end of observation, review the notes and add missed details, clarify abbreviations, highlight critical elements, and pull out specific data.

Time/Activity/Materials	What Happened

Adapted with permission from *Project QUEST Inservice Manual* (Falco et al. 1990)

Child's name: _____ **Age:** _____

Date: _____ **Interviewer:** _____

Informant: _____ **Relationship:** _____

Directions: The following questions are designed to obtain information about the ways your child communicates. The information will be used to develop the most appropriate communication program for your child.

Please answer each question thoroughly. Add information wherever you want. It is most helpful to get as many examples as possible and to add details, such as, "He is just starting to do this"; "He used to do it"; or, "He does it only when I tell him to do it." Add information to describe how often and how hard your child tries to communicate and how difficult it is to understand. Also note whether your child looks at you when trying to communicate.

EXPRESSING FEELINGS

How do you know when your child:

1. Likes an activity, food, or other? _____

_____

_____

2. Does not like an activity, food, or other? _____

_____

_____

3. Feels good or happy? _____

_____

_____

4. Feels ill or in pain? _____

_____

_____

5. Is hungry? _____

_____

_____

6. Is uncomfortable? _____

_____

_____

7. Is anxious or afraid? _____

_____

(continued)

REQUESTING

How do you know when your child:

8. Wants attention? _____

_____

9. Wants more of something? _____

_____

10. Wants you to continue an activity (for example, playing a game or rocking)? _____

_____

11. Wants you to stop an activity? _____

_____

12. Wants you to start a familiar routine (for example, fixing a snack or playing peek-a-boo)? _____

_____

13. Wants help? _____

_____

14a. Wants something to eat? _____

_____

14b. Wants something to drink? _____

_____

15. Wants a certain object? _____

_____

16. Wants to do something? _____

_____

17. Wants to use the bathroom? _____

_____

18. Wants affection? _____

_____

(continued)

REQUESTING (continued)

19. Does your child make a choice between several objects when the objects are presented or in view? _____

    Describe. _____

    _____

20. Does your child make a choice among several activities? _____ Describe. _____

    _____

    _____

21. Does your child make a choice of an object or activity when the possible selections are not presented or in view?

    _____ Describe. _____

    _____

22. How do you know when your child does not understand something that someone has said? _____

    Does your child ask for clarification by saying, "What?" or "I don't understand" or by doing something like

    self-biting? _____ Describe. _____

    _____

23a. Does your child ask for information (for example, where someone is, where someone lives, or when a birthday

    or holiday will occur)? _____ Describe. _____

    _____

23b. Does your child ask the same questions repeatedly? _____

    _____

23c. Does your child ask for one thing but appear to want something different? _____ Describe. _____

    _____

    _____

PROTESTING

How do you know when your child:

24. Does not want to do something or wants to stop doing something? Describe. _____

    _____

    _____

(continued)

PROTESTING (continued)

25. Does not want a specific object or food? Describe. _____

_____

_____

_____

What does your child do when:

26. Not allowed to do or have something desired? Describe. _____

_____

_____

_____

27. A desired object is taken away? Describe. _____

_____

_____

28. The environment or routine is changed? Describe. _____

_____

_____

RESPONDING

Describe your child's response to each of the following:

29. Verbal directions _____

_____

_____

30. Questions that begin with *what, who, where, when, how,* or *why* _____

_____

_____

31. Questions that call for a *yes* or *no* answer _____

_____

_____

(continued)

ACKNOWLEDGING OTHERS

32. How does your child greet you or others without direction? _____

_____

_____

33. How does your child respond when greeted by others? _____

_____

_____

34. Does your child use polite words (such as "Thank you," "Please," and "Excuse me") appropriately? _____

Without prompting? _____

Describe. _____

_____

35. If another child asks for a turn or a toy, will your child acknowledge the request? _____

_____

_____

COMMENTING
Does your child:

36. Comment about himself and his own activity? Describe. _____

_____

_____

_____

37. Comment about other people or their actions? Describe. _____

_____

_____

_____

38. Comment about objects or events when the object is present or the event is occurring? Describe. _____

_____

_____

_____

(continued)

COMMENTING (continued)

39. Comment about objects or events when the object is not present or the event is not currently occurring?

    Describe. _____

    _____

40. Talk about events that happened in the past or will happen in the future? Describe. _____

    _____

    _____

NONCOMMUNICATIVE LANGUAGE

41. Does your child say the names of objects or people for no apparent reason, without looking at you or relating

    to you? _____ Describe. _____

    _____

42. Does your child talk to himself about what he is doing, is going to do (for example, "Sit down" as he sits down),

    or is not supposed to do (for example, "Don't touch" when beginning to touch something that is off limits), as

    if repeating a rule? Describe. _____

    _____

    _____

43. Does your child talk to himself about things that don't appear to be related to the current situation? Describe.

    _____

    _____

VOCABULARY

44. If your child has a limited vocabulary (25 words or so), please list the words and describe any words that are

    used in specific or unusual ways or situations. _____

    _____

    _____

    _____

    _____

(continued)

CURRENT NEEDS

45. What functions, concepts, vocabulary, or forms of communication do you feel are most important for your child

to learn this year? _____

_____

_____

_____

_____

_____

_____

_____

_____

_____

_____

_____

_____

_____

_____

_____

_____

_____

_____

_____

_____

_____

_____

(continued)

Functional Communication Assessment: Summary

Adapted with permission from *Project QUEST Inservice Manual* (Falco et al. 1990)

Child:_____

Date: _____

Code: / = Uses sometimes

    + = Uses consistently

    (Use a different color ink for each
    assessment or setting.)

Forms of Language and Communication		A. FEELINGS							B. REQUESTING				
		1. Likes	2. Dislikes	3. Feels good	4. Pain	5. Hungry	6. Discomfort	7. Afraid	8. Attention	9. More	10. Continue	11. Stop	12. Start
Speech:	a. One word												
	b. Two or three words												
	c. Complex utterance												
Sign:	d. One word												
	e. Two or three words												
	f. Complex utterance												
Combined forms:	g. One word												
	h. Two or three words												
	i. Complex utterance												
Echolalia:	j. Immediate: Exact												
	k. Immediate: Mitigated												
	l. Delayed												
Nonverbal behavior:	m. Gesture/Pointing												
	n. Manipulation of other												
	o. Vocalizations												
	p. Cries												
	q. Gaze												
	r. Gaze shift												
	s. Proximity: Moves closer												
	t. Proximity: Moves away												
	u. Facial expression												
	v. Head nod												
	w. Bodily contact												
	x. Action (grab, reach, give, other)												
	y. Self-injurious behavior												
	z. Aggressive behavior												
	aa. Tantrum behavior												
	bb. Other:												
Total Forms per Function													

(continued)

	B. REQUESTING (continued)											C. PROTESTING					D. RESP.			E. ACKNOW.			
	13. Help	14. Eat/Drink	15. Object	16. To Do Action	17. Bathroom	18. Affection	19. Choose object	20. Choose action	21. Choose without seeing	22. Clarity	23. Information	24. Activity	25. Object/Food	26. Not allowed	27. Taken object	28. Change	29. Directions	30. WH questions	31. Yes/No questions	32. Greeting	33. Response to greeting	34. Polite words	35. Take turns
a.																							
b.																							
c.																							
d.																							
e.																							
f.																							
g.																							
h.																							
i.																							
j.																							
k.																							
l.																							
m.																							
n.																							
o.																							
p.																							
q.																							
r.																							
s.																							
t.																							
u.																							
v.																							
w.																							
x.																							
y.																							
z.																							
aa.																							
bb.																							

(continued)

	F. COMMENT					G. NON-COM.		
	36. On self	37. On others	38. Object/Action	39. Not present	40. Past/Future	41. Say labels	42. Direct self	43. Unrelated
a.								
b.								
c.								
d.								
e.								
f.								
g.								
h.								
i.								
j.								
k.								
l.								
m.								
n.								
o.								
p.								
q.								
r.								
s.								
t.								
u.								
v.								
w.								
x.								
y.								
z.								
aa.								
bb.								

Assessments:

1. Informant: _____

   Date: _____ Color code: _____

   Total functions: _____ Forms: _____

   Total forms per each function: _____

2. Informant: _____

   Date: _____ Color code: _____

   Total functions: _____ Forms: _____

   Total forms per each function: _____

3. Informant: _____

   Date: _____ Color code: _____

   Total functions: _____ Forms: _____

   Total forms per each function: _____

4. Informant: _____

   Date: _____ Color code: _____

   Total functions: _____ Forms: _____

   Total forms per each function: _____

5. Informant: _____

   Date: _____ Color code: _____

   Total functions: _____ Forms: _____

   Total forms per each function: _____

6. Informant: _____

   Date: _____ Color code: _____

   Total functions: _____ Forms: _____

   Total forms per each function: _____

Adapted with permission from *Project QUEST Inservice Manual* (Falco et al. 1990)

Student: _____

Date: _____

Informant: _____

Rating code:
0 = No opportunity to do it, or never observed
2 = Gets it done, but does it inappropriately
3 = Does it occasionally or if prompted
4 = Does it consistently and appropriately in a variety of situations
NA = Not applicable

Directions: Read the definitions for Social Skills 1–10 (page 4 of this form). For each situation below, rate your child's performance in each social skill. Give examples of what your child does in each situation.

SITUATIONS	1. Initiate interactions	2. Respond to greetings or initiations	3. Take/ manage/ relinquish turns; share	4. Self-manage	5. Solve problems	6. Provide feedback indicating pleasure or displeasure	7. Offer/ provide/ obtain/ accept assistance	8. Indicate preference/ make choice	9. Follow social rules/ norms/ manners	10. Terminate interaction/ activity
1. Private Independence When alone, how does your child: • Entertain self? (Play video game, listen to music, play cards, . . .)										
• Carry out responsibilities? (Fold clothes, do math, complete a job, . . .)										
2. Friendship Interactions When with a friend, how does your child: • Play or hang out? (Play games, play with toys, listen to music, . . .)										
• Work? (Set table, rake leaves, prepare snack, . . .)										
3. Homogenous Small Group When with 3 or 4 same-age friends, how does your child: • Play? (Structured games, pretend games, other)										

(continued)

SITUATIONS	1. Initiate interactions	2. Respond to greetings or initiations	3. Take/manage/relinquish turns; share	4. Self-manage	5. Solve problems	6. Provide feedback indicating pleasure or displeasure	7. Offer/provide/obtain/accept assistance	8. Indicate preference/make choice	9. Follow social rules/norms/manners	10. Terminate interaction/activity
• Socialize? (Hang out, listen to music, go for a snack, . . .)										
• Work? (Plan an outing, cook a meal, . . .)										
4. Heterogeneous Small Group With family or groups of adults and children, how does your child: • Play? (Games, . . .)										
• Socialize (Visit, go for a snack, go to a movie, . . .)										
• Work? (Clean up the yard, cook a meal, fix a bike, . . .)										
5. Active, Goal-Oriented Group How does your child participate in a small structured work or play group? (Sports team, job crew, reading group, Scout troop, church group, . . .)										
6. Passive, Goal-Oriented Group How does your child participate as part of an audience with family or friends? (Attending ball game, movie, concert, church, . . .)										

(continued)

SITUATIONS	1. Initiate interactions	2. Respond to greetings or initiations	3. Take/manage/relinquish turns; share	4. Self-manage	5. Solve problems	6. Provide feedback indicating pleasure or displeasure	7. Offer/provide/obtain/accept assistance	8. Indicate preference/make choice	9. Follow social rules/norms/manners	10. Terminate interaction/activity
7. Interactions with Stranger in Public Place In a public place (without supervision), how does your child: • Socialize or refrain from socializing with an unfamiliar person? (Help small child or older person, comment to another while waiting in line; avoid making or responding to inappropriate advances, . . .)										
• Tolerate unexpected behavior of strangers? (Being bumped while in an elevator, ignoring loud shouting from person in the street, . . .)										
• Engage an appropriate person for help to accomplish a goal? (Asking a clerk for help in locating an item, help in locating a restroom or telephone, . . .)										
8. Public Independence In a public place (without supervision), how does your child: • Engage in a free-time activity? (Jogging on a trail, playing video games in an arcade, . . .)										
• Accomplish a specific goal? (Buying groceries in a supermarket, riding the school bus, waiting in the airport, . . .)										

(continued)

	MAJOR SOCIAL SKILLS	DEFINITION
1.	Initiate interactions	Gain access to interaction, either to initiate an interaction or enter one already underway; begin an event or exchange
2.	Respond to greetings or initiations	Acknowledge others' greetings or initiations and either join an interaction/activity or decline to participate
3.	Take/maintain/relinquish turns; share	Engage in reciprocal interaction by filling turns and waiting for responses
4.	Self-manage	Follow serial-order routines; respond to expectations in absence of teacher/adult prompts, including the inhibition of responses (self-control) in certain situations
5.	Solve problems	Exhibit alternative strategy to complete a task, or seek alternative interaction/activity when previous effort resulted in a negative consequence or difficulty in effecting needs or intent
6.	Provide feedback indicating pleasure or displeasure	Provide others with positive feedback rewarding to them; provide others with feedback to indicate that their behavior was inappropriate or unpleasant (with the intent to extinguish or reduce that behavior)
7.	Offer/provide/obtain/accept assistance	Is alert to others' need for assistance and spontaneously provides help; recognizes when he needs help and knows who and how to ask; accepts help/information from others when it is offered
8.	Indicate preference/make choice	Makes a choice/decision from among alternatives available or presented by others
9.	Follow social rules/norms/manners	Adheres to culturally accepted rules and body language, body contact, personal space, and social amenities
10.	Terminate interaction/activity	Withdraws from or terminates an interaction, ceasing participation in an activity as desired or appropriate

Adapted with permission from Oregon Regional Autism Services

Student: _____ **Teacher:** _____

School Year: _____ **Class:** _____

Directions: Use the space provided below to summarize teacher reports. Highlight 4s and 5s to indicate trends. Use a heavy line to separate reporting periods.

Code for rating frequency of each behavior and intensity of the problem:

1 = Consistently uses / No problem
2 = Often uses / Mild problem
3 = Sometimes uses / Moderate problem
4 = Seldom uses / Increasing problem
5 = Never uses / Major problem

Teacher:																										
Date:																										
BEHAVIOR																										
1. Plays with peers during breaks																										
2. Responds to questions of peers																										
3. Participates in games with other children in the classroom																										
4. Participates in games with other children at breaks																										
5. Has particular peers with whom this child interacts																										
6. Participates in group activities in the classroom																										
7. Appears to enjoy time spent in group activities																										
8. Responds to teacher questions during whole-group instruction																										
9. Talks with other children in the classroom at appropriate times																										
10. Helps other children with tasks																										
11. Shares materials with other children																										
12. Shows concern (verbal or nonverbal) for the problems of other students																										
13. Shares feelings at appropriate times																										
14. Interactions with adults seem to be of a positive nature																										
15. Interactions with children seem to be of a positive nature																										

Adapted with permission from *Judevine® Training System* (Blackwell 1978)

Student: _____ **Date:** _____

LIKES What people, objects, or activities are liked a lot or selected during free time?	TOLERATES What is done when asked, but never done if not asked?	DISLIKES What people, objects, or activities are resisted, avoided or rejected?
People	People	People
Activities	Activities	Activities
Sensory	sensory	sensory
Foods	Foods	Foods
other	other	other

Assessment of Daily Life Activities: Informant Interview

Adapted with permission from Oregon Regional Autism Services

Student: _____   **Date:** _____

Directions: This form is used to structure an interview to determine the relationship of various conditions to problem behavior. First, parents and/or staff members make notes on a copy of the form prior to the interview. The interviewer then structures questions to clarify the details and to enlarge on the examples. When making comments, give details such as: types of problems, environmental conditions when problems occur, types of assistance, consequences, types of directions, and the possible perspective of the student when problems occur.

Time (from/to)	Activity Location/Supervisor and Group Size	Is this activity:			Does the individual have:		Comments Give details
		Age-appropriate?	Meaningful?	Liked?	Choice? Control?	Problems?	

Adapted with permission from *Project QUEST Inservice Manual* (Falco et al. 1990)

Student: _____ **Routine:** _____

Setting(s): _____

Natural Cues	Correct Response	Date										%
24.												
23.												
22.												
21.												
20.												
19.												
18.												
17.												
16.												
15.												
14.												
13.												
12.												
11.												
10.												
9.												
8.												
7.												
6.												
5.												
4.												
3.												
2.												
1.												
Data Code:	Total Independent:											

Standardized Testing

Problems with Standardized Procedures

The results of standardized procedures are often of questionable value because the tests were not standardized for use with those who have autism. The reliability of the scores is also affected because those with autism:

- Display wide discrepancies between visual/motor tasks and those with auditory and verbal demands; between concrete, factual, and rule-based requirements and those that require abstract reasoning and judgment

- Display variable ability to perform from day to day or at different times during a day

- May not understand the language specified in the standardized procedures, may interpret the language literally, or may be unable to communicate responses effectively

- May become anxious and unable to perform in situations involving unfamiliar people, settings, materials, and schedule changes

- May show little motivation to complete tasks and may attempt to avoid the situation or leave the area

- May become distracted, disorganized, and lose concentration between tasks

Planning the Assessment

With foresight, a highly skilled examiner can increase the likelihood of obtaining useful results.

1. Talk with parents and teachers before the testing sessions to obtain information about reinforcers, the nature of processing delays, and potential triggers for tantrums and out-of-control behavior; and to understand unique language and communication issues. For example, it is important to know:

    - Whether the individual can reliably use *yes* and *no* to answer questions

    - Whether gestures, pictures, or sign language help the individual understand directions

    - Whether any words or phrases have unexpected meaning for the individual (for example, '*bye* meaning *all done* or *no*)

    - How the individual indicates a need for a drink or to go to the bathroom

2. Arrange for parents or a teacher to observe the assessment session in order to verify the results. Otherwise, prepare to videotape the session and review the performance with parents or teachers later.

3. To prevent fatigue and maintain an optimal level of performance, schedule several short testing sessions rather than one long session.

4. Develop a relationship with the individual before testing. Visit the classroom for an introduction, and invite the student to the evaluation room prior to the testing date. Otherwise, make certain that the teacher prepares the student for this change before test time, and allow some time for exploration of the room before testing begins.

To prepare Jeff for an unexpected testing session, his teacher said, "Jeff, there is a change. At 10:00 you will go to Mr. Brown's office and work with him. When you finish that work, you will come back to class and work with the math flash cards." (Working with the flash cards is a well-liked activity.) As she talked, the teacher printed the new information on a small sticky-note and pasted it on his calendar over the previously planned activities. The note read:

1. Work with Mr. Brown

2. Math flash cards

At 10:00, the teacher gave Jeff the sticky-note and walked with him to Mr. Brown's room.

Mr. Brown quickly introduced himself and showed Jeff the things in the room. Jeff watched as Mr. Brown printed out and explained the work schedule, with breaks interspersed with test tasks. The last item on the list was: *Math flash cards.* As tasks were completed, Jeff crossed them off the list. When all tasks were crossed out, he returned to class with his sticky-note and independently started working with the flash cards.

5. Select tests that provide separate measures of language and nonlanguage skills, or use a battery of tests that contains both language- and nonlanguage-based tasks.

6. Present a broad range of tasks, and begin testing at a point well below the individual's chronological age in order to ensure success and avoid frustration on initial test items. Continue testing beyond the standardization criteria to identify more advanced skills.

7. Have extra paper or 3"x5" cards available for preparing quick visual supports.

8. Place a box or similar container on the floor within reach. As each task is finished, allow the individual to place the materials in the *Finished* box.

9. Break from the standardized procedures to probe, to determine the type or level of support needed for the individual to respond correctly.

10. During the testing session, be alert to subtle, nonverbal signs of fatigue, frustration, or confusion. Respond by altering or adapting the situation in some way to keep the performance at an optimal level and to prevent possible behavioral outbursts.

Strategies for Managing Specific Problems

Problem: Apparent lack of motivation to complete tasks

1. If some parts of the directions are unclear, the individual often does nothing.

   - Direct the student's attention to the task with nonverbal cues before giving a direction (for example, shift the material or tap the table near the material). Do not require eye contact; this distracts attention from the materials, and the individual may not be able to shift attention back to them.

   - Use gestures to clarify directions.

   - Give the directions nonverbally. Model, draw a diagram, or list the sequence or steps required to follow the directions.

- Use only important words when giving directions. Omit unnecessary words and polite forms. Use specific language (for example, "Put your hands on the table," or "Give me the *picture* of the cow").
- Clarify the response mode. Is the student to point, give, draw a circle around, or tell you the answer?

2. If the individual has a processing delay, there may be as much as 30 to 60 seconds between a verbal request and a response.
   - Pause after giving a request to allow time for processing the request and generating a response.
   - Provide a visual reference when restating or rephrasing the directions. Then wait.

3. If the individual has difficulty initiating and carrying out a motor action (to point or to give a verbal response), the lack of response may appear to be lack of motivation or noncompliance.
   - Provide firm but passive physical support to the hand, wrist, or arm. This type of support can help some individuals focus and initiate a motor response. This support is like that used in facilitated communication. It is *not* the same as the more traditional and directive or forceful physical prompting or physical guidance procedures.

4. If the task is too easy or without meaning to the individual or the reinforcer is not valued, the lack of response may appear to be laziness or lethargy.
   - A few individuals respond positively to the evaluator's acknowledgment that some of the tasks may be too easy or seem silly.
   - Identify real reinforcers before the session begins. Make sure that these reinforcers can be seen clearly.
   - Use contingency statements to direct attention to the expectation. ("Two more, then it's time for a break.")

A test of receptive language requires the examiner to set out three picture cards and say, "Give me the picture of _____." If there is no response or if there is an error, the examiner makes the task easier (removes one of the cards). When this task was presented, Tony sat quietly and stared out the window. When Mr. Brown removed a card and repeated the request, Tony continued to stare out the window. At this point, Tony's teacher, who was observing the session, suggested that the examiner spread all the cards on the table. As Mr. Brown spread the cards, Tony sat up and scanned them. When the examiner repeated the same request again, Tony quickly picked up the correct card. Tony saw no reason to attend to a boring task with no challenge.

5. If the task is too hard, lack of response may appear to be lack of motivation.
   - If the above strategies are not effective, ask, "Do you know the answer?" or "Do you know how to do this?" The verbal individual may simply say, "No." If speech is unreliable, prepare a visual response card so the individual can answer the question by pointing to either *yes* or *no*.

6. Some types of seizure activity can result in a lack of response, giving an appearance of laziness or lack of motivation.
   - Before the evaluation, check on presence of seizures. During the evaluation, make note of subtle behaviors.

Problem: Apparent avoidance; attempts to end a task or leave the area

1. An individual who puts hands over the ears, covers the eyes, puts the head down, or tries to get under the table may be bothered or fatigued by some subtle sensory element in the room—too much talking, a squeaky fan, or flickering fluorescent lights.

   - Reflect the individual's need and offer a change or a break. ("You look tired. Let's go for a walk, and then we'll come back and finish the work.") As you talk, mark the task list so the next task is clear.

2. If several difficult or new tasks are presented in a sequence and the failure rate is high, frustration and anxiety will build.

   - Adapt the session schedule to alternate difficult with familiar or easy tasks and breaks.

   - Adapt the tasks. Provide a visual reference, decrease the difficulty, or provide assistance until a correct response is achieved.

3. If directions are repeated too many times or too loudly when the individual does not understand what to do, anxiety increases and efforts to escape or stop the situation may lead to out-of-control behavior.

   - Speak softly, and avoid repeated demands. If a direction must be repeated, use the strategies described above for dealing with apparent lack of motivation.

   - Identify and respond quickly to subtle, nonverbal signs of fatigue, frustration, or anxiety. ("You want to stop? Do one more then we will take a break.") It is better to end a session positively than to push the individual into a major behavioral breakdown.

Problem: Distraction, disorganization, or disorientation between tasks

1. If unable to track the passage of time and unsure about the end of the session, the individual may appear distracted and disorganized and may try to leave the area.

   - Develop a task list to clarify the amount of work. The opportunity to cross off the tasks as completed is a concrete way of marking the passage of time. It is highly motivating for most individuals and keeps attention focused in the testing area.

   - Use contingency statements to highlight the relationship of the completed work to the reinforcer.

   - Involve the individual in putting materials away. Moving the materials to a *Finished* box is a concrete way to mark progress and keep the focus in the area.

2. An inability to scan an area to select and focus on important information, coupled with anxiety about unfamiliar materials and tasks, can cause disorientation and distraction.

   - Quietly describe and label materials as they are placed on the table. This not only keeps the individual focused on the work area, but makes the task and the materials more familiar.

   - To ease the transition from a table task to a task that requires standing or movement, clarify the directions (with a visual reference) while the individual is still sitting at the table. A marker to indicate where to stand may help the individual become organized in space.

Interpretation of Test Results

It is difficult to determine exactly what individuals with autism really know. Those who have learned to communicate by spelling words with physical facilitation are able to read, spell, and communicate at a level much higher than was expected from previous performance on standardized tests. Thus, use caution when interpreting and viewing standardized test results in this population.

As a general rule, those with autism are not deliberately manipulative, negative, or resistant. A clearly understood request will generally receive a correct response, but there are many reasons for no response or an incorrect response. Therefore, when interpreting scores on these standardized tools, keep these points in mind:

- If testing did not cover a broad enough range of skills, scores may suggest either unrealistically high or unrealistically low expectations.

- Reliance on full-scale or average scores masks the true nature of the individual's abilities. Analysis of performance on each task or subtest and of the overall profile of scores pinpoints learning strengths and difficulties—information that is important when developing instruction and adaptations.

- Modification of standardized procedures will negate the meaning of standardized scores. However, modifications are likely to produce the most valid and useful information.

Tests Standardized for Those with Autism

While there are many good standardized tests for a variety of purposes, there are only a handful designed and standardized specifically for those with autism. Both of the following tools were developed at the Division for the Treatment and Education of Autistic and Related Communication Handicapped Children (Division TEACCH), University of North Carolina School of Medicine, Chapel Hill. A trained and experienced examiner can elicit a broad range of useful information and practical recommendations from these two tests.

- *Psychoeducational Profile—Revised (PEP-R)* (Schopler et al. 1990). This is a diagnostic and developmental assessment tool for children with autism up to 12 years of age who are functioning in some areas at a preschool level. It is a useful tool for assessing those thought to be untestable. It employs a flexible administration format, allowing the examiner to structure the testing session to the student's needs, and it contains many materials that are interesting to those with autism. Items are organized in seven developmental areas and a separate Pathology Scale. Results provide practical information for educational programming geared to capitalize on the student's strengths to compensate for deficits.

- *Adolescent and Adult Psychoeducational Profile (AAPEP)* (Mesibov et al. 1988). This is a tool for assessing severely disabled adolescents and adults. It is designed to identify levels of functional development and individual instructional needs. It includes three different scales—a Direct Assessment Scale, a Home Scale, and a School/Work Scale. The AAPEP provides valuable information that identifies functional programming priorities, the impact of various sensory conditions on performance, and the individual's learning style.

Summary

Functional assessment procedures are helpful in identifying the types of skills and strategies the student uses in actual situations and those that are not used. A major question remains: Why is the skill not used? Is some small piece of information missing that prevents use? Could the individual perform the skill with an adaptation? Could it be that for some reason the individual cannot perform the motor movements to use the skill? There is some evidence that "internal cognitive processes contrast sharply with overt social and communicative behaviors" (Quill 1993, 99). Therefore, it is well not to limit an individual's options for learning by the IQ scores of standardized tests. More useful information is achieved when standardized procedures are modified to obtain information about the individual's approach to tasks and the type of assistance needed to accomplish a task.

3

Program Decisions

HAPPY FEELINGS

TODAY I FEEL
HAPPY
TEACH ME JOKE
TEACH ME LOVE
AND GREATNESS
TEACH ME FUN
AND TEACH ME
SOME
OF EVERYTHING
YOU
POSSESS

—David Eastham
In *UNDERSTAND: Fifty Memowriter Poems*

Placement and Support Decisions

Supported education is a term used to describe a program that provides the support necessary to ensure that educational goals are met. The term generally applies to those with disabilities served in integrated or inclusive settings (for example, a regular classroom in the neighborhood school). The concept of supported education is important to those with autism, whether they are served in self-contained special classes or are partially or fully integrated into regular classes. To profit from any educational setting or program, students with autism must rely on others to provide support—to organize the environment, design instruction, and interpret the meaning of events. When all elements of a program match individual needs, motivation is high, the learning rate is increased, and behavior is stable.

When critical supports are missing, those with autism become confused and anxious. Increasing anxiety leads to behavior problems that can disrupt learning for everyone in the classroom. Disruptions often result in staff burnout, parent frustration, and transfers to more restrictive settings. Perhaps the most costly effect of inappropriate settings and inadequate support is that students with autism acquire a reputation for being noncompliant, disruptive, and destructive, when by nature they are generally compliant, naive, and gentle.

Some of the most successful educational programs for those with autism are implemented in regular, integrated settings. The major issue is not "readiness" for integration in terms of appropriate behavior, but how the setting can support learning and productive behavior. The one common element in every successful program is an active and committed support team whose members include parents, teachers, and others who are directly involved in providing services.

Making Decisions

Basic guidelines for making educational decisions are provided in the federal law. Public Law (PL) 94-142, as amended by PL 99-457, provides a standard for educational services to those with disabilities. PL 101-476 reauthorized the law and renamed it the Individuals with Disabilities Education Act (IDEA). These laws include the requirements for individual service plans and team decision making. Copies of these laws are available from state educational agencies, special education offices of local school districts, and advocacy organizations.

A team approach to the decision-making process brings together those who know the individual best and those with training and experience in educating and supporting others with similar conditions and problems. If this decision-making team operates with a common goal and with common basic principles for selecting alternatives, their decisions are most likely to produce the desired outcome.

Principles for Making Decisions

In *The Criterion of the Least Dangerous Assumption,* Anne Donnellan, Ph.D., suggested the following standard for making educational decisions. "The criterion of the least dangerous assumption holds that in the absence of conclusive evidence, decisions ought to be based on assumptions which, *if incorrect*, will have the least dangerous effect on the likelihood that students will be able to function independently as adults" (Donnellan 1984, 141).

When the common goal of an educational program is to enable students to function independently and productively in the community as adults, then Donnellan's criterion and the following eight principles can guide the team's decisions.

1. The learning style (strengths and deficits) common in autism provides the foundation for understanding problems and selecting program options. The critical goals that address the deficits of autism provide the basis for setting priorities. (See figure 7.1.)

2. Teach useful and meaningful skills in natural, chronological, age-appropriate settings, so students learn when and where to use the skills and the purpose or reason for using them.

3. Teaching strategies and instructional materials must be as natural as possible. They must highlight and capitalize on the *natural cues, prompts,* and *reinforcers* commonly available in the community, so the student does not become dependent on another person for cues, prompts, and reinforcement.

4. Integrate all therapies and services to support the total program, to avoid confusion and the learning of unrelated splinter skills.

5. Adaptations and individualized support systems must be available and used as needed, to support learning and independence in all settings.

6. Strengths and interests are developed and used to compensate for deficits and increase motivation.

7. A balanced program that includes a broad range of experiences in many settings and situations is most likely to have a positive and lasting outcome.

8. Expectations and support must be flexible and at a level to ensure success. Success is an essential ingredient for continuing effort and effective learning.

These eight principles apply to all decision making in autism. However, unique interests, strengths, past experiences, and patterns of development will demand highly individualized options and applications.

> Both Tomas and Leah are 4 years old, and both have autism. They have similar and predictable learning and behavior problems (for example, they find noise and crowding painful, and they show confusion during transitions and in new situations). Tomas can communicate and socialize at a 6-month level; yet he is fascinated by numbers and letters. He can count to 1,000 and read words at the fourth grade level. He has advanced visual-motor skills for blocks, pegs, and puzzles, and he can print letters, numbers, and some words. His attention span for most fine motor, reading, or math tasks is almost endless, and he gets very upset when these activities are completed. He is afraid to climb, trips and falls when he runs, has no interest in balls, and cannot put on his coat or carry a chair to the music circle.
>
> Leah communicates and socializes much like a 2-year-old, watching and playing beside the other children. She is agile and can run and climb, throw and catch balls, and she is fascinated with video equipment and computers. Leah's attention span and ability to manipulate this equipment

Figure 7.1. Critical goals that address the deficits of autism

1. **To value people, interact, and communicate intentionally**
   To learn:
   a. That people can provide information, assistance, pleasure, and comfort
   b. To tolerate the closeness of people
   c. To intentionally seek out and spontaneously initiate interactions
   d. To stay in interactions with people; to persist in efforts to communicate
   e. That people have a common but different experience or perspective

2. **To learn the language and to communicate effectively**
   To learn:
   a. That everything has a label (sometimes multiple labels)
   b. That some words have multiple meanings
   c. That words, toys, and pictures are symbols for real things
   d. That words can be spoken and written down
   e. That objects and actions have a purpose that can be labeled
   f. That words can label and define concepts and relationships
   g. To use gestures, objects, and words to communicate meaningfully
   h. To understand the language spoken by others

3. **To tolerate change and accept new experiences; to be more flexible**
   To learn:
   a. That materials, schedules, and settings can be used and arranged flexibly
   b. That there are alternative ways and times to do things
   c. That change is okay and new things can be interesting

4. **To focus on and participate in instruction**
   To learn:
   a. The language of instruction
   b. To watch others for information
   c. To focus on relevant and screen out irrelevant information
   d. To be actively engaged; to try, and to persist
   e. To work independently, in 1:1 situations and in small and large groups

5. **To do things independently, without constant verbal direction**
   To learn:
   a. To follow visual information systems
   b. Effective routines for doing purposeful things

6. **To monitor and manage stress**
   To learn:
   a. To identify stress in self
   b. To ask for and take a break
   c. To relax and then to reengage in the ongoing activity
   d. To accept correction
   e. To solve problems or ask for assistance

is no less than amazing for a 4-year-old. However, she finds work with puzzles, pegs, blocks, pencils, and crayons extremely frustrating. She does not look at books, numbers, or letters.

Both children need similar adaptations to address the sensory problems, and both need a visual schedule to organize time and help them tolerate transitions and changing activities. However, each program will be designed and implemented very differently.

The Support Team

With some exceptions, the support team members are the same as those on the assessment and the IEP (Individualized Education Program) or IFSP (Individualized Family Service Plan) teams. At least four people are needed to make effective educational decisions: parents and/or caregivers, building principal or supervisor, teacher (or teachers), and a specialist in autism. Others who provide related services also participate, either on a regular basis or as needed to resolve specific problems.

1. Parents must be integrally involved in the planning and problems solving process because they:

    - Have information from a lifetime with their child in many situations that is essential for understanding the total picture

    - Have responsibility to advocate and provide for their child

    - Must live day-to-day for a lifetime with the results of all decisions

2. The role of the building principal and/or program supervisor is to inform the team of school policy and procedures and to make timely decisions about things that might impact those procedures and the budget. When actively involved with the support team, the principal—who is ultimately responsible for everything that happens in the school building—will always be informed and prepared to respond effectively:

    - To participate in and support behavior or disciplinary decisions

    - To answer the questions of other parents, students, and staff members

    - To support the efforts of hard-working school staff

    - To deal with placement and staffing issues

3. The teacher has legal responsibility for the student's total program. When a student is integrated in a regular class, both the regular classroom teacher and a special education teacher or integration specialist serves on the team.

4. Specialists in autism are an important resource because of their specialized training and experience with the education of many individuals with autism. Because of that experience, they can interpret the world of autism to the team just as the staff interprets the world to the student. The autism specialist provides balance, perspective, and an objective view to those who are physically and emotionally involved in day-to-day instruction and support. Perhaps their most important role is to help team members adapt strategies and materials to match the common learning style. In addition, the autism specialist provides:

    - Training, feedback, and support to staff

    - Assistance in assessing, predicting, and preventing learning and behavior problems

- Assistance in the ongoing problem-solving process to refine and adapt program components and support systems
- Knowledge of resources for parents and professionals

An autism specialist is most helpful as a regular member of the support team with an opportunity to develop a collaborative, trusting, and supportive relationship with team members; and observe and work with the individual students to understand their unique characteristics.

> The second grade class started each school day by reciting the pledge of allegiance. Gabriel did not like to do this activity because it held little meaning for him and he wanted to read the *TV Guide*. As soon as the children began the pledge, he would drop to the floor screaming. The teacher said, "Gabriel, as soon as the pledge is over, you can read your *TV Guide*." Immediately, he stopped screaming and stood up and finished the pledge with the others. This routine was repeated for several days, until the autism specialist visited and suggested that the teacher reverse the situation: before Gabriel drops to the floor, let him know that he will get the *TV Guide*. The next morning as class was beginning, the teacher said, "Gabriel, as soon as the pledge is finished, you can have the *TV Guide*." He immediately recited the pledge with the group and got his reward without first doing something inappropriate.
>
> It is important to have an objective observer who understands autism and knows how a teacher can be drawn into an unproductive and disruptive routine.
>
> ———————
>
> Two 4-year-old boys in the Head Start class were deaf. A teacher for the deaf was assigned to interpret and supplement the regular teaching program. One child was alert and social, continually watching the other children and the regular teacher for information. He also kept his eyes on the interpreter and was rapidly learning to sign. The other child, whose scores on nonverbal tests were in the gifted range, wandered aimlessly about. He did not attend to his peers, the regular teacher, or the teacher who was signing to him. He was not learning to sign. When it was discovered that autism was affecting his ability to learn, an autism consultant was engaged to provide staff training and to work with the team to make program adaptations. This child began to make progress and to attend to peers and staff.

Team Responsibilities

The team has five major responsibilities:

1. Conduct formal and informal assessments and incorporate information to develop and implement the educational program

2. Collaborate to integrate therapies and services into the total program

3. Collect important data and keep anecdotal records to identify and interpret potential problems, and then make program adaptations in a timely manner

4. Assist in the design, construction, and modification of adaptations, schedules, and other visual support systems

5. Support the classroom staff

The Support Team
Members included:
1. Parents and/or caregivers
2. School principal
3. Teacher(s)
4. Autism specialist
5. Speech-language pathologist
6. Occupational therapist
7. Other

Team Process:
1. Plan developed for establishing and maintaining team rapport and process.
2. On-site case manager assigned.
3. Recorder assigned.
4. Regular meeting times established (every 2 or 3 weeks).
5. Plan established for communicating student's priorities to all staff.
6. Plan developed for collecting and reviewing data.
7. Construction materials manager assigned.

The Instructional Setting
1. Is natural and includes age-appropriate peers who are both verbal and social
2. Is organized visually to prevent confusion
3. Has a quiet area for relief from sensory overload
4. Has well-defined work and leisure areas
5. Reflects individual safety considerations

The Instructional Staff
1. Receives ongoing training and support
2. Accommodates student's learning style
3. Identifies and interprets the student's nonconventional communication
4. Gives the student quick and positive feedback
5. Communicates effectively with the student
6. Organizes information visually and concretely to highlight meaning
7. Capitalizes on naturally occurring events and teachable moments
8. Prepares the student for new or changing events
9. Organizes transitions to prevent confusion
10. Predicts and defuses behavioral outbursts
11. Knows how to keep people safe in a crisis

The Program
1. Activities are adapted to address the critical goals for those with autism. (See figure 7.1.)
2. The program includes both cognitive/concept development and functional applications.
3. The daily/weekly schedule is balanced to incorporate a broad range of activities. (See chapter 8, page 122.)
4. Instruction emphasizes meaning and function vs. rote memorization.
5. Expectations match variations in student's tolerance and functioning level.
6. Strengths and interests are used to compensate for the student's deficits.
7. Teaching strategies include natural cues, prompts, consequences, and reinforcers.
8. Visual strategies are used to clarify meaning and increase student's independence.
9. Related services are integrated into the natural activities and routines of the day.

Effective team members understand the impact of autism on learning and behavior. They are flexible, nondefensive, and able to brainstorm; they are willing to creatively modify any program or strategy that is not promoting meaningful progress.

Strategies for Effective Teams

An effective team collaborates and shares information and expertise. For this to occur, members must establish a supportive, nonthreatening relationship for open discussion, solving problems, and providing positive feedback. Active involvement with such a team provides many opportunities for personal and professional growth.

Teams that include both professionals and nonprofessional family members often need more time to develop nondefensive and trusting relationships. While there are many resources for facilitating the understanding of feelings and roles between parents and professionals, Raaz (1982) specifically addresses the issues of autism. (Also refer to Turnbull and Turnbull 1990.) The books written by parents who have children with autism are particularly helpful in understanding the problems these families encounter and the contributions parents can make. (See Dewey 1991; Eastham and Eastham 1990; Hart 1989; Bristol and Schopler 1983; DeMyer and Goldberg 1983; and the family stories on pages 429–435.)

Unexpected and complex problems occur that can either escalate or become habitual unless program adaptations are implemented in a timely manner. Therefore, busy team members must organize to meet often and function efficiently. The following strategies can lead to an efficient and effective team that operates proactively.

- Develop rapport and a good working relationship. At the beginning of the school year or whenever a new member joins the team, take the time to establish trust and an open and supportive relationship for discussion and effective decision making.

- Assign an on-site team manager. The manager may or may not be the teacher. The team manager who is easily accessed by regular and support staff calls the team together, keeps it focused on the issues, and monitors communications and follow-through.

- Assign a recorder to keep track of the meeting agenda, major discussion points, and decisions. Notes recorded on a chalkboard or chart during the meeting are easy to review and clarify, ensuring that all members leave the meeting with a common understanding. Later, distribute copies of the meeting notes. These notes provide a good history of problems, strategies, adaptations, and progress.

- Meet regularly and frequently. A team that meets regularly can develop very efficient working relationships and ultimately save time. The members are in a position to review progress, identify and deal with potential problems, and make program revisions before problems escalate. When the team meets frequently—every two or three weeks—the members can maintain a common direction and provide encouragement to those working most closely with the student. It is easier to schedule short, regular meetings early in the year. It is more disruptive and time consuming to pull team members together to deal with emergencies when the problems are severe and staff may be fatigued, worried, or defensive. If things are going well, team members are in a position to reinforce each other and meetings can be brief.

- Assign one member to bring construction materials to the meeting. The team can construct or refine the student's visual adaptations as quickly as decisions are made. This policy ensures that modifications are made before problems escalate. It also relieves the pressure on the teacher and teaching assistant.

Efficient strategies for making visual adaptations are discussed more fully in chapters 12, 14, and 15.

- Take advantage of each member's area of expertise, strengths, and interests. Team members will have many complementary skills; for example, one team member's ability to organize and sequence details can complement and support another team member's ability to see the big picture, the gestalt. One team member's interest and experience in arts and crafts provides guidance and support for other team members as they design and construct the essential visual materials.

In summary, a good working relationship between team members and frequent but brief regular meetings are the keys to effective decision making.

Staffing

Teachers in the regular classroom are exceedingly busy meeting the needs of 20 to 30 students, many with special needs. A full classroom includes a lot of action, stimulation, and information. Special classroom teachers are also busy. While they have fewer students, each one takes specialized attention. When one of the students in either setting has autism, a teacher will most likely need extra assistance if all students are to have a positive educational experience. There is a need for additional classroom assistance, for someone must always be available to:

1. Identify and respond quickly to the student's nontypical efforts to communicate

2. Restructure activities to capitalize on natural teaching opportunities with peers

3. Model and coach effective communication and social behavior in natural situations

Additional staff assistance can be provided in a variety of ways. The most common way is to hire, train, and assign an assistant either to the special student or to the classroom teacher. While the distinction is fine, there is the potential for several problems when an assistant is specifically trained and assigned to the student with autism.

- The assistant, who is generally not a certified teacher, is perceived to have expertise and is often left with full responsibility to make decisions that could have legal implications. The teacher, who is legally responsible for the student and the program, is at a disadvantage without the training and information to effectively supervise and provide feedback and support to the assistant.

- The teacher has little opportunity to establish a competent and confident teaching relationship with the student, a disadvantage when the assistant is absent or leaves.

- The student can become isolated from peers and overly dependent on a single adult. A conscientious assistant who focuses all day on a single student becomes highly sensitive to that individual's needs and feelings. Without objective and informed feedback, it is easy to become overly protective, smoothing the way to avoid any stress instead of providing assistance to deal with stress.

The teacher must develop a close and trusting relationship with the student and feel confident and competent in this relationship. A teacher also must maintain full responsibility for the student. This is more likely to occur when the assistant is assigned to the teacher. Then the classroom staff can work cooperatively, switching roles, solving problems creatively, and structuring opportunities for social interactions. This practice has many advantages for students with autism. It provides more opportunities to:

- Learn to work alone and to share attention as the assistant helps other students
- Be included in small-group activities
- Be seen by peers as more capable and independent
- Become more flexible and able to work with more adults
- Have more people interpret and provide support in more settings

During free-play periods when peers were busy with toys, Matt routinely gathered all the long, narrow blocks, set them precisely side by side, tensed his shoulders, and grimaced and flapped his hands excitedly as he watched them. When staff was available to structure his play and model more creative and interactive play, he played with a larger selection of toys and had more opportunities to interact with peers.

Heidi had just moved from the local Head Start class to a special, self-contained classroom in a regular elementary school. Her classmates were children who had various severe disabilities. None could speak more than a brief word or phrase. Several children in wheelchairs had classroom assistants to attend to their special needs.

Heidi was very alert and followed basic classroom directions quickly. She had excellent motor skills. Although Heidi was unable to speak, she tried to communicate by shifting her gaze from the teacher to objects and by touching or pointing to things. However, she had not learned to attract the teacher's attention first.

Each day, Heidi's behavior disintegrated. By the end of the first week of school, she screamed, bit her wrist, and banged her head many times a day. Her behavior was so disruptive to peers in adjoining rooms that she was in danger of being moved to an even more restrictive setting.

An autism consultant assessed the situation and found that Heidi's screaming and subsequent self-injury occurred in two situations: immediately after an unacknowledged attempt to communicate, and after she had complied with a direction but had to wait for peers. For example, when the teacher said, "Line up at the door; it's time for library," Heidi went directly to the door, waited briefly, pointed to the door as she turned toward the teacher, frowned, and eventually screamed and bit her wrist. The teacher, who was trying to get peers to the door, did not see Heidi's compliance and attempt to communicate.

When the principal and staff understood that Heidi needed someone who could attend quickly to her communication and that she needed the stimulation of verbal and social peers, a full-time assistant was hired and Heidi was integrated into a regular classroom. While the plan called for gradual integration, her behavior improved so dramatically that by the end of the second week of school, Heidi was fully integrated into the regular first grade classroom.

Staff Support

Teaching and supporting those with autism is demanding. Constant vigilance and quick thinking are required. While it is a creative challenge, it can be emotionally and often physically draining. For staff to feel competent and be successful—to prevent burnout—they need:

1. Training to understand autism and positive behavior support

   Training is most effective when provided in units over a period of time and when there are opportunities to practice new skills with feedback

2. Time to plan

   A consistent, flexible, and productive program is possible only when the teacher and the assistant have time to review the data and make program adaptations together.

3. Feedback and support

   Just as the staff shapes the student's behavior, the student shapes staff behavior. Without feedback from someone who understands this phenomenon, problems can occur as staff inadvertently become involved in ineffective routines.

Related Services

Services provided to compensate for problems and deficits related to or associated with the disability are called *related services* or *related support services*. These services ensure that the student benefits from instruction and makes appropriate progress toward goals. Related service needs are determined as the team reviews the assessment information.

The local public school or education agency is responsible for providing a Free and Appropriate Educational Program (FAPE), including the related support services, to all eligible students in the district through the age of 21. An appropriate program is a very individual matter, since it must reflect the goals, learning style, and support needs of a single student. Sometimes it is hard for the team to agree on the kinds and the amount of services needed. While a student might benefit from more intense and comprehensive services, the public school is obligated to provide only appropriate services—not the *most* appropriate services (Board of Education of the Hendrick Hudson Central School District *vs* Rowley 1982).

Auditory Integration Training (AIT) is an example of a treatment or therapy that many parents want for their child, but that schools often feel is outside their responsibility. AIT is a relatively new and little understood procedure that seems to have helped many individuals with autism who have highly sensitive hearing. The training involves listening to individually adapted music twice a day for a period of two weeks. It is not yet clear why this training helps some individuals or which individuals may benefit. For a perspective of AIT, refer to Rimland and Edelson 1994; Amenta 1994; and Stehli 1991.

Commonly Needed Services

The related services most often needed by the student with autism are those that address severe:

- Language and communication problems
- Sensory and motor problems

- Social and behavior problems

- Attention and information-processing problems

The services most commonly needed to address those problems are listed below with basic information about the delivery of the service.

- A *speech-language pathologist* (SLP) is an essential and regular member of the support team. The student needs SLP services in 1:1 sessions, when new skills and concepts are introduced, and/or with a small group of peers to provide a context for learning interaction skills. Perhaps the most important role of the SLP is to show families and school personnel how to teach and support language and communication all day, every day, and in every situation.

- An *augmentative or alternative communication specialist* (AAC) is trained to provide technical assistance to select and adapt electronic communication devices to match a student's need. The AAC also may provide training to parents and staff who support the student's use of the device. The AAC is a resource to the support team, and generally participates only as needed.

For more information on facilitated communication, see pages 326-333.

- A *communication facilitator* may be a necessary related-service provider if the team decides that the student would benefit from facilitated communication (FC). FC is a method or form of communication that initially requires a person to provide physical support to assist the individual to spell or write messages either on paper, by pointing to letters on an alphabet board, or by using a typewriter or computer. The facilitation is generally provided by a teaching assistant, the teacher, parents, or friends.

- *Specialized communication equipment* is often needed. Some students need low-tech communication systems—systems that use concrete objects, picture or word boards, notebooks, and other materials—that are developed and constructed by staff. With advances in technology, specialized typewriters, computers, and electronic communication boards with voice output may be recommended.

For more information about therapy to address sensory processing issues, see Ayres 1979; Bissell et al. 1988; Blanche et al. 1995; Coling 1991; and Fisher et al. 1991.

- An *occupational therapist* (OT) is a valuable resource because autism is characterized as a major sensorimotor and sensory-processing problem. An OT understands the neurology of sensory processing and motor functioning. The OT is particularly helpful in assessing problems related to sensory overload, attention, stereotypic behavior, and self-injury. An OT may provide individual therapy and also show parents and teachers how to adapt natural, age-appropriate activities so appropriate sensory stimulation and motor practice are provided throughout the day. An occupational therapist should be a regular member of the support team during early development and when severe and challenging attention or behavior problems occur during later development.

- *Extra classroom staff* is generally needed for at least some part of each day. A younger child most often needs assistance (or an interpreter) full time. The older, more capable student may need assistance for 15 or 20 minutes at the beginning and end of the day for help in organizing schedules, homework, and materials, or to clarify and resolve interpersonal problems.

The need for assistance varies from time to time. More assistance is needed when there are disruptions at home (for example, a family illness, a new baby) or at school (a substitute teacher, preparation for holidays). Medical problems also affect tolerance for confusion, frustration, and ability to function. At certain seasons, allergies may create the need for more assistance.

- Other related services may be required from time to time. A *specialist in learning disabilities, school counselor*, and a *school nurse* are excellent resources to address specific problems. A *special education teacher* and an *integration specialist* provide important related services for students in regular classrooms.

Program Decisions

Placements

The federal law, IDEA, stipulates that placement decisions should be made after all the goals and support needs are identified. The law specifies that a child be placed or served in the most normal environment possible. The most normal setting is that attended by the neighborhood children of the same age. If the team determines that the support cannot be provided in the setting attended by neighborhood peers, that decision must be justified.

Setting Requirements

Since those with autism do not automatically transfer learning from one setting or situation to another, it is dangerous to assume that skills learned in isolated settings will transfer to the real world. It is also dangerous to assume that placements outside the local school will result in friendships and supportive relationships with those in the neighborhood. Therefore, the most appropriate settings for those with autism of any age are generally where neighborhood peers are found *and* where the necessary support services and systems are in place.

For the infant and toddler, that natural setting is in the home with perhaps several hours a week in a local play group. The natural settings for older children and adolescents are the neighborhood schools, parks, recreation centers, stores, churches, and malls. Regardless of age, those with autism need to be in settings where:

1. Others of the same age model effective communication and social skills and provide natural opportunities for active social engagements and interactions

2. Same-age peers learn to understand and accept the problems, provide support, and serve as mentors or advocates in the school, neighborhood, and community

3. Materials and activities are appropriate to the student's chronological age

4. Safe and quiet areas are provided for periodic relief from stimulation

5. Staff members are trained to understand autism, to structure and clarify instruction, to prevent or quickly identify problems, and to respond flexibly with effective strategies

6. Appropriate support services and systems, as defined in the IEP, are provided and used

Contrary to earlier beliefs, *readiness for mainstreaming or inclusion is not dependent on "appropriate" behavior.* Inappropriate or problem behaviors are an indicator of inadequate or inappropriate support. They also indicate that some element of the environment, even in a special class, does not match the individual's need.

At age 15, Tony was still served in the special class for young elementary and preschool children. This decision was justified because he was unable to speak, had not mastered readiness skills, had periodical violent outbursts, and was socially immature and vulnerable. When observed in that elementary setting during a free-time period, this adolescent was lying on the rug in the play area randomly manipulating preschool toys. While his new teacher was trying to teach him some functional skills, he was passive and resisted most instruction. Smaller peers and some staff were afraid of him because occasionally he pushed or hit them when they got too close. At the end of that school year, it was decided that he must transfer to the special class in the high school.

After six weeks in the new setting, Tony was much more alert and stood tall. He had a job in the library, and he carried books as he walked in the halls, just like his peers. He continued to need a great deal of assistance, but he seemed comfortable in the setting with same-age peers, where there were real and meaningful things to do. His parents reported a much happier son who began to show interest in family activities.

It is important to emphasize that placement in a regular classroom does not ensure success. Without the appropriate staff training, services, and support systems, learning may have little meaning and usefulness. Students with autism can become:

- Isolated, ignored, and devalued
- Overstimulated and confused; they can lose control
- Dependent on others for verbal directions and physical support

The key to a successful placement in any setting is an appropriate system to support effective learning and positive behavior. Services are currently provided successfully in a variety of natural settings such as in neighborhood schools and churches, Head Start programs, neighborhood cooperatives, and community colleges.

The criterion of the least dangerous assumption would suggest that when team members determine the need for a more sheltered or isolated placement, a target date for full inclusion should be set and a plan developed to keep the student in contact with normally developing peers and natural settings, and to transition smoothly between settings.

In making the final placement decision, consider the criterion of the least dangerous assumption, and ask, which setting is most likely to lead to independence in the community as an adult? Once that question is answered, the appropriate support systems and services can be put into place.

Safety Considerations

Those with autism are generally unaware of potentially dangerous situations. At the same time, they have some unique abilities and disabilities that can cause harm to themselves or others. Since parents are aware of their child's specific needs, they must see that specific safety issues are addressed in the student's individual program. Typical safety problems are related to the following issues:

- Some individuals have an unusual ability to open locks and childproof bottles. They may smell, taste, and even eat unsafe material—cigarette butts, things from the garbage, things found on the ground or floor, leaves from plants, pieces of glass, small tacks. Care must be taken in storing cleaning and medical supplies and other potentially dangerous chemicals. Sometimes special instruction is needed to address these problems (for example, the proper way to dispose of garbage, to discriminate between edible and nonedible items, and so on). The occupational therapist is a resource for problems that appear to be related to sensory issues, such as the odor, taste, or texture of specific items.

- Some individuals will respond unpredictably in an emergency. For example, they may run and hide at the sound of alarms or sirens. Specific staff must be assigned to be certain the student is escorted to safety whenever an emergency may occur. These individuals need many opportunities to practice safety drills in all settings.

- Others may be attracted to windows, lights, fans, or high places. Screens over fans, unbreakable glass in windows, and other safety precautions may be needed.

Summary

Specifically designed adaptations and instruction are always needed to ensure that instruction is understood and that new skills will be applied and used effectively in a variety of real situations. Specific strategies and adaptations are discussed in Part 4 of this book.

Develop a Balanced Program

There are many considerations for developing an effective Individualized Education Program (IEP). The IEP is actually an intervention and support plan—a document that lists prioritized goals and objectives and the support required to achieve the goals.

An intervention and support plan is much like a travel plan. It specifies the starting place (current level of functioning), a final destination (goals), and the hotels, restaurants, fuel, and repair services needed along the way (related services, adaptations, and teaching strategies). Travel plans vary from person to person. Some people who are flexible and have few needs require plans with a minimum amount of detail. Others who have many needs and feel insecure in strange places require a highly detailed plan with little left to chance. A skilled travel agent (the support team) carefully assesses the client's needs before developing the travel plan.

Those with autism need travel plans with considerable detail because they are unable to organize information or communicate reliably to cope with unexpected situations. The support team that prepares the plan must know a lot about the individual—the person's moods, abilities, tolerances, and preferences. The team must be prepared to assess and modify the plan regularly to reflect unexpected situations and the changing needs of the client, who is continually learning.

Develop the IEP

Some of the issues and considerations for developing an effective and balanced intervention and support plan—one that will cause the least damage if the decisions are wrong or inadequate—are discussed below.

Identify the Destination: Select Goals and Priorities

Teachers and parents sometimes dedicate their efforts to cure autism—to make the individual with autism look and act "normal." Such a goal is not only limiting, but frustrating and demoralizing. It is simply the nature of autism to interpret the world differently; therefore, no matter how hard parents and teachers work, some problems are inevitable and behavior will continue to look somewhat different. One father indicated that life might have been better for his son, now a young adult, if the effort spent on trying to make him look appropriate had been spent in teaching him to be more independent and to have fun.

Types of Goals

Three types of goals are considered in this section: the critical goals, traditional developmental goals, and functional goals.

- *Critical goals* are those based on the deficits of autism. (See figure 7.1, page 105.) These goals are given the highest priority and provide the basis for selecting other goals, developing the support system, and adapting activities. The six critical goals have implications throughout the life span for those with autism, but the emphasis will be different during different ages and stages of development, with more emphasis during initial intervention and during periods of high stress. These goals are addressed within the context of ongoing natural activities.

- *Traditional developmental goals* are based on the orderly, step-by-step sequence of skills learned during the normal development of cognitive, language, social, readiness, and motor skills. The developmental approach is the basis for teaching most academic subjects. Movement to a higher step of the sequence depends on mastery of the previous step, and independence is achieved with mastery of all the steps. Traditional special education was based on this approach—to identify the deficits and remediate until the skills are mastered.

Because those with autism learn in a holistic rather than a step-by-step sequential mode, rigid adherence to the goals of this traditional approach leads to:

—Acquisition of rote, isolated, and inflexible splinter skills that are difficult to generalize or transfer to natural contexts

—Decreasing motivation to work on skills that have little apparent meaning to them

—Fewer opportunities to learn how to perform basic life skills, thus limiting options and independence in adulthood

- *Functional goals* address important life routines and activities that occur in specific natural environments—home, work, community, school. The functional curriculum approach teaches students how to participate in meaningful routines that have a highly motivating outcome. Broadly stated, functional goals specify the important life routines the student will learn to perform and the environment where the routine will be taught. An example of an integrated functional goal is: Given assistance to start the equipment, Amy will play computer games during her leisure time in the classroom and at home. . . .

The developmental goals are integrated and taught in the context of the important life routines such as dressing, preparing meals, and participating in community leisure activities. These integrated goals provide a framework for teaching numerous subskills such as moving, reaching, requesting, and counting. Because important life routines (dressing, shopping, and others) are repeated every day or on a regular basis, there are frequent opportunities to practice, master, and maintain the skills into adulthood.

This functional approach was developed to meet the needs of those with disabilities who are unable to master all the individual developmental steps, and thus as adults never learn to function effectively in the community. The functional approach that teaches skills in the context of meaningful life routines is important for those with autism, who learn routines relatively quickly. Functional programming results in greater independence *when the appropriate supports are in place.*

Positive, Proactive Goals

IEP goals can be negative and focus on eliminating or decreasing inappropriate behaviors. Such goals are limiting and give little direction for positive growth and increasing independence. While problem behaviors should be addressed in the IEP, goals are most productive when stated positively to specify what the individual will

Refer to Chapter 23 for a discussion of self-control procedures and Chapters 24 and 25 for a broader discussion of behavior problems and strategies to address them.

learn. For example: In stressful situations that occur in the context of natural routines, the student will learn to use a self-controled relaxation response and ask for assistance. . . . One measure of goal achievement could be a decrease in head banging, hitting, or running away.

Prioritize Important Life Routines

The number of possible goals is practically unlimited. Prioritizing to select the most important and timely routines is difficult. Following a comprehensive assessment, the support team members collaborate to make the best decisions. The importance of any potential routine can be determined or weighted by asking:

1. Is this goal a family or caregiver priority? Often, the family's highest priority is to resolve the eating, sleeping, toileting, and behavior problems that dominate family life. Families are also concerned that their children learn to dress and care for themselves, communicate basic needs, participate in family social activities, manage leisure time, help with chores, and manage a job.

2. Is this goal important and essential? Will it lead to greater independence and increased self-esteem now and in the future? Does this skill have immediate relevance to solve or prevent recurrence of specific problems at home, school, work, or community environments? Will this skill prevent a serious problem in the future? Will mastery of the goal increase options and increase peer respect and acceptance? For example, the ability to dress independently is important now and in the future. It increases the options to use the community gym and swimming pool and to stay overnight with friends. Learning to dress oneself leads to increased self-esteem and respect from peers.

3. Is the goal related to the student's special interest or strength? Has the student expressed interest in this specific job, leisure activity, or course of academic study?

4. Is it a priority for the support team? Is it age-appropriate? The different members of the support team see the student in various settings, and they may identify important routines that parents may not have considered. The team must consider the balance of goals and include routines for self-care, leisure, work, home, school, and community.

One note of caution: A rigid adherence to a functional curriculum approach can limit opportunities for those with autism to gain basic information and general knowledge about the world and to engage in advanced study in areas of particular interest and aptitude. Opportunities to learn academic skills and gain knowledge of the world are motivating for many with autism and should be a part of a balanced program. *It is nearly impossible to accurately predict the learning potential of those with autism, especially during the early years. Options should remain open.*

Identify the Starting Place: The Assessment

An IEP, like a travel plan, cannot be developed without understanding the starting place—the current level of functioning in the home and community.

Assessment Goals

An assessment for a person with autism is similar to that for an individual of the same age who has any other disability; but it is different in that much more emphasis must be given to the details. For example, the basic assessment questions for all individuals with disabilities are:

1. What does this person do now, and what support is currently provided?

2. What do we wish this person could do, and what support will be needed for this person to learn and continue to perform the new skills?

An assessment of those with disabilities must address their ability to function in various environments and their level of development in all areas affected by the disability. In autism, the assessment must identify more specific details including, but not limited to:

- Interests, preferences, dislikes
- Sensory problems and tolerance levels
- Reactions to change and new experiences
- Ability to relate and communicate with people
- Level of independence in various situations
- Specific pattern of learning strengths and deficits
- Specific discrepancies in skill development
- Gaps in understanding and use of language
- Gaps in understanding and use of social rules
- Ability to focus on meaningful information in various situations
- Ability to manage anxiety—to relax

Types of Assessment

Because of the nature of the autism disability, it is difficult to obtain valid and reliable information from traditional assessment procedures. For this reason, a comprehensive assessment must include two different types of procedures: functional assessment procedures and standardized testing.

- Functional assessment

  The purpose of the functional assessment is to find out how the person actually operates or functions in the natural environment. There are two basic procedures for getting this information:

  1. Interviews with parents and teachers

  2. Observations in various natural settings

  There are many ways to structure observations and interviews to obtain the detailed information needed for selecting high-priority goals and personalizing needed adaptations and teaching strategies. See chapter 6 for examples of strategies for:

  —Identifying priority goals and routines

  —Assessing priority routines and student skills

  —Assessing sensory and instructional demands

  —Assessing functional communication

  —Assessing social skills

  —Identifying preferences and interests

  —Identifying daily life activities

  —Monitoring instructional progress and problems

- Standardized testing

Standardized tests and checklists are designed to compare the performance of the person being tested with the performance of many others of the same age and with a similar background. Scores on these tests are valid only when the standardized procedures are followed during the assessment and when those in the standardization group are similar to that of the individual being tested.

Standardized procedures provide an opportunity to examine a broad range of learning processes and skills in a relatively short time. Yet when used to test those with autism, the scores of standardized procedures are often of questionable value because very few tests are standardized for this population. The reliability of the scores also is affected because of a variety of problems common to those with autism. See chapter 6, pages 95-99, for discussion of these problems and strategies for obtaining more reliable and useful information.

Develop the Daily Plan

Referring again to the analogy of the travel plan: The travel agent develops a daily plan or itinerary after establishing the client's needs and interests, point of departure, and final destination. The itinerary specifies the stops, the points of interest, the information centers, and key services. While the IEP is a guide—an outline of goals and objectives that *give direction* to the daily instructional program—it does not specify exactly what happens each day.

Teachers are responsible for implementing the IEP—developing the daily activities and schedules that provide the opportunities for achieving the goals. This is a demanding and time-consuming task. While there are numerous curriculum products and resources on the market to provide ideas and strategies, virtually all curricular approaches and products need adaptations to match the individual needs of those with autism.

See chapter 11 for strategies for structuring activities and routines.

Essentially, the age-appropriate developmental materials and activities that naturally occur in typical school and community settings and within the ongoing life of the family provide the foundation and structure for achieving the goals. The skillful teacher schedules and structures the natural routines and activities of the day to address the critical, autism-specific goals (see figure 7.1, page 105) and the important developmental and functional goals. With sufficient planning, many things can be taught in the context of a single situation or activity.

Amy screams and throws materials when she wants to stop working. She bites her wrist and closes her eyes when peers bump or brush against her. One of her functional goals is to participate in small-group activities that occur in her Head Start class. Two of her critical goals are to increase the amount of time she can tolerate sitting and working beside peers; and to communicate "All done" by pointing to a picture in her communication book.

When her peers work with puzzles, pegs, and other manipulative toys to improve their fine motor skills, Amy works beside them. A teaching assistant working nearby is alert for signs of stress so she can cue Amy to communicate "All done" before she throws materials or bites her wrist. As soon as Amy points to the picture (with some gestural prompting), the assistant acknowledges her message and quickly helps her put the materials away. Other less stressful individual activities that address other goals are prepared for Amy to do while her peers continue with puzzles. In the context of this single activity, Amy is strengthening her fine motor skills, increasing tolerance for working beside peers, and learning to communicate; and screaming and throwing behaviors are decreasing.

Matt's functional goals include a job at the library, managing his money, travel in the community, and preparing his meals at home. He is taking science and home economics classes at high school. His critical goals relate to increasing independence, flexibility, and ability to communicate when stressed. To accomplish these goals, he is learning to use a small appointment/reference book (a visual support system) to help him communicate when stressed, to manage his flexible schedule, and to organize his homework and other chores. As he gains competence in using his support system, he is less dependent on others for verbal directions. Thus Matt is working to accomplish functional, academic, and critical goals each day.

Balanced Daily Plans and Schedules

Just as the most effective IEPs are balanced to address the range of important life routines, the most effective daily plans and schedules are balanced to provide many opportunities. A balanced approach is more likely to lead to success in the community than overemphasizing any one skill, strategy, or approach. A balanced program with a variety of activities, settings, and people leads to greater flexibility and increases options and motivation of students and staff. A balanced plan includes opportunities for:

- Learning developmental, academic, creative, and functional skills
- Work, play, and leisure—seriousness and silliness
- Work and play in various locations and group sizes (alone and in small and large groups)
- Student-directed and adult-directed experiences
- Active involvement and quiet recovery time
- Work and leisure that involve movement and quiet sitting
- Helping and receiving help from peers
- New situations balanced with familiar situations
- Difficult and disliked tasks balanced with easier and preferred activities
- Interactions with those of different ages, interests, and abilities
- Instruction and practice in both natural and simulated settings
- Developing special interests and aptitudes

Activities that are scheduled and structured to include this balance are most likely to achieve the IEP goals, while at the same time achieving other goals that may have had a lower priority. Learning to play and enjoy leisure activities is as important as learning to work and manage self-care. In the midst of serious work, those with autism and those who support them occasionally need to relax and be a little silly together to relieve the pressure. In other words, those with autism need a broad range of opportunities just as those without disabilities need varied experiences.

Strategies for organizing and structuring time are described in chapter 13.

Special Interests and Academic Studies

Many of those with autism are highly motivated to learn about areas of special interest. Others are capable of advanced study in highly specialized areas. Development of special interests and aptitudes leads to:

- Increased motivation and feelings of satisfaction and competence
- Increased leisure and vocational options
- Increased respect and peer acceptance
- Opportunities for making friends with similar interests

Academic skills can be taught and strengthened in the context of learning about these special interests and fixations. One young woman with autism was motivated by her high school science teacher to do research and pursue her interest in cattle squeeze chutes. This encouragement and assistance led her to a doctoral degree in animal psychology and an international reputation for excellence in designing cattle-handling equipment for stockyards and major meat-packing firms (Grandin 1992). Not every student with autism would have such strong abilities, but many are more capable than IQ scores would suggest.

There are several issues to consider when making decisions about academic goals and curriculum:

1. Basic academic instruction begins in early childhood through a language- and print-rich environment. (See chapters 15 and 19.)

2. Capitalize on individual interests and fixations. (See chapter 17, page 242.)

3. Teachers, parents, tutors, and mentors organize and interpret the content meaningfully to ensure functional applications and generalization. (See chapters 9, 10, and 19.)

4. Selection of curriculum and strategies is based on learning style. (See chapters 2 and 9.)

Maria was interested in letters. When she and her peers learned letter names and sounds, she memorized them quickly and wanted to "do letters" all day. However, she wanted to use the letters only in a certain order with a certain deck of cards and with people who would repeat the scripts. When the teacher tried to move her to the next step, to blend the letter sounds to make words, Maria screamed, kicked, and fell to the floor.

Because she had developed such a rigid routine with the letters, Maria's program was changed in two ways:

1. Her daily schedule provided two times a day to "do letters" as a reinforcing activity following a period of other work.

2. Maria and her assistant developed written labels for the things she did and the objects she used. They planned class activities on charts and made lists for the things Maria needed to remember. As the class reviewed the activities of the day, her assistant wrote out a simple experience story for Maria to take home to show her parents.

When Maria discovered that words had meaning and that the spoken word could be written down, she quickly learned to read from this visual, holistic approach. This modified language experience approach was productive in several ways. As she learned new language, it facilitated her recall of events in sequential order; and it prevented behavior problems by preparing her for changes and new activities.

Academic instruction is only one part of a balanced program. Problems are likely to occur when academic goals are overemphasized—when the primary goal is to graduate from high school with peers.

> Without specific instruction, Gabriel had learned to read by the time he was 3 years old. Although he was severely affected by autism, he made good progress in school and was in the regular academic program. He had an assistant who interpreted for him, helped him with his academic studies, and developed a peer network to support him. His parents helped him every night with his homework. With a great deal of effort, Gabriel graduated from high school with a regular diploma at age 18.
>
> His friends planned to go on to college, get jobs, and move away from home, and Gabriel wanted to do these things, too. However, he did not know how to make a phone call, manage money, find his way to the grocery store or the doctor, buy food or clothing, or do laundry. It was hard for him to accept that his high school diploma did not ensure that he had the skills to live away from home. He returned to high school and enrolled in a program for older students with disabilities. He worked hard until he was 21, learning to work, to take care of his basic needs, to manage his anxiety, and to fill his leisure time. At 25, he had a part-time job in an office and lived in an apartment with a friend/mentor. Gabriel has taken some classes at a local community college. His family continues to advocate and provide support whenever needed.

Contexts for Instruction

The information in chapters 11 and 12 that provide strategies for organizing events and environments applies to individual and small-group contexts as well as to natural contexts.

Most new information and skills are introduced and rehearsed in both individual and small-group settings where the learner has the support to think and understand the meaning and purpose. Instruction is transferred almost immediately to natural settings where new skills are practiced within the context of functional routines. Instruction in the natural setting is critical to ensure that the learner attends to the natural cues, is guided by natural prompts, and is motivated by natural reinforcers.

Success in natural settings depends to a large extent on the support and instruction that occurs in individual and group instructional contexts.

Individual Instruction

Individual instruction, as described here, is quite different from traditional one-to-one direct instruction based on behavioral theories or the therapy based on psychoanalytic theory. Rather, cognitive and behavioral theories support the organization of instruction to compensate for the information-processing differences and involves the learner in thinking about the meaning and purpose of skills. This process involves the learner in preparation, rehearsal, evaluation, and feedback. These instructional practices avoid rote responses, repetitive practice, and high-criterion levels for advancement.

An individual instructional context is important for those with autism of any age because it offers:

1. Reduced stimulation that allows the learner to focus on relevant cues

2. A familiar, stress-free setting and structure for introducing new information and for preparing the learner for changes

Chapter 20 includes information for teaching attending and early interaction skills in 1:1 sessions. See chapter 22 for strategies for addressing sensitive issues in 1:1 sessions.

3. A supportive and sensitive environment for providing guidance, practical feedback, and an opportunity to practice new skills for coping with everyday problems or personal, confidential issues

Informal one-to-one support and problem-solving sessions occur throughout the day when the learner needs more information, a previously developed skill needs refinement, or when an unexpected problem occurs.

Small-Group Instruction

Many of the critical goals, especially those involving language concepts, social interactions, and cooperative skills, are more naturally introduced and practiced with peers. To provide a supportive context and more opportunities to practice these subtle skills, it is generally necessary to bring together a small group of peers on a regular basis—at least once a week. The purpose of these groups is to encourage interaction, group cooperation, and support while involved in natural play or work situations. A successful interactive group is structured so that natural interactions are possible and everyone enjoys the experience and wants to return. Four types of groups are particularly helpful for learners with autism: play groups, social skill groups, cooperative work groups (such as academic work groups, scout or church groups, and special interest groups), and social support groups for adults.

Small-group instructional issues are expanded in chapter 22.

Five elements of successful group instruction require thoughtful planning: membership, rules, routines, leadership, and generalization.

Monitor Progress

Formal data and informal notes and anecdotal records provide important information for making decisions and for showing progress toward goal achievement. Because initial instruction is designed to prevent errors, the student will nearly always perform a task or a step of the routine correctly. Progress is shown by changes in the level of motivation, independence, or assistance required. Consider the following issues when developing a monitoring plan:

- When a new routine or skill is presented, teachers need their hands free to manage materials, to prompt and prevent errors, and to refine or modify the instruction as soon as a problem is identified. For this reason, delay formal data collection for a day or two. Instead, make notes immediately following instruction. Describe problems, modifications, the level of assistance required, and the student's general attitude.

- Take probe data at least once a week to monitor progress and identify problems on the steps of each priority routine and the subskills listed on the IEP.

Present the anecdotal records and formal data to the support team at least once a month for analysis and recommendations. Because minor modifications are made as the need is identified, progress is continuous and the learner maintains a positive attitude and does not develop unproductive routines or practice errors.

Summary

More detailed planning is required to ensure that an intervention program will match the needs of those with autism. The effective program depends on:

1. A comprehensive assessment to elicit the myriad details to understand the individual's unique needs

2. Integrated functional goals

3. A balanced daily plan that capitalizes on the important natural routines of life at home, school, and community

The time spent in initial planning is time well spent because the learning rate is increased and behavior problems are decreased. Teachers find that the clarity of instruction required for those with autism also will increase the learning rate of other students in a class—those with auditory processing difficulties, learning disabilities, attention deficits, other neurological problems, and communication disorders. Those who are learning English as a second language and those with stress- and anxiety-related emotional problems also find these strategies beneficial.

Life is a continuing challenge, often overwhelming and frustrating for those with autism and for those who support them. Parents and teachers feel pressure to accomplish goals quickly. Life then becomes increasingly serious, filled with hard work and effort. While it is necessary to focus on goals and structure to make life more comfortable and productive, it is also important to have fun. A well-balanced program includes both work and play, seriousness laced with fun.

Humor breaks down barriers and resistance; it reduces stress and makes life worth living. Humor and fun renew the energy for continued effort. David Eastham illustrated the importance of keeping a sense of humor and balance in the following poem. (David sometimes referred to himself as "youth.")

LONELY BOY

JOKES HELP LONELY PEOPLE
THE WORLD DOESN'T SEEM SO BAD
HUMOUR JUST EASES PAIN
YOUTH NEEDS IT TO FORGET THE SAD

KIND PEOPLE GOOD TO KNOW
KILLING BOREDOM OF LIFE
NO ONE UNDERSTANDS
JOKES GOD'S SALVE ON LIFE

NO ONE YOUTH'S LOVER
GOD HAS SEEN TO THAT
JOKES PREVENT CLOSENESS
HOPE TO REMEDY THAT

HOPE GOD HAS A PLAN
HOPE PEOPLE KIND TO KNOW
BOTHERED BY IT GREATLY
LOOKING TO FIND OUT HOW

—David Eastham
In *UNDERSTAND: Fifty Memowriter Poems*

4

Intervention

FIDDLESTICKS

LOONEY EASTHAM
TRYING SO HARD
FIDDLESTICKS
JUMPING OUT IN
THE YARD
FIDDLESTICKS

ROTTEN YOUTH WASTED
ON ME
FIDDLESTICKS
GOD HAS IMITATED A
TREE

I REACH UP,
CANNOT TOUCH
FIDDLESTICKS
WANT TO MOVE AROUND
SO MUCH
FIDDLESTICKS

GUTS ARE NEEDED IN
A TREE
FIDDLESTICKS
HOPELESS TO TRY, ME
AND THE TREE

—David Eastham
In *Silent Words and Forever Friends*

Intervention Planning— A Proactive Approach

One mother said, "I thought that child-rearing would allow me to put into practice all the wonderful knowledge I'd gleaned while getting my master's degree in education and during numerous years of teaching elementary school. I am having a difficult time finding examples of anything in my training or experience that prepared me for coping with a child who did not respond the way those children in the textbooks and classes responded." Read the rest of Christine Marshall's story on pages 432-433.

Parents and teachers are often confused by the sometimes contradictory array of intervention strategies suggested in the literature of autism. Strategies that teachers and parents find effective with most students must be modified for those who learn and see the world differently. Teachers and parents need some process to focus and guide their intervention efforts because they do not have the time to interpret and apply research findings to the needs of individual students.

Figure 9.1. Typical teaching strategies

These strategies are effective for most students, but must be modified for effective use
for students with autism.

- Verbal instruction
- Social rewards
- Role play
- Rigid behavioral programs
- Exploratory and incidental learning
- Logical/natural consequences
- Repetitive practice for retention
- Mastery or criteria skill-based training
- Large-group instruction
- Commercially produced curriculum materials

If effective intervention and support can be developed from an understanding of the perspective of those with autism, what might day-to-day life be to one with such a disability? Daily life might be like living in a dream world where people and events fade in and out randomly without any familiar context, where problems have no solutions even when extreme effort is applied. Every day might be like the first day in a foreign country. Imagine the overwhelming and disorienting stimulation of the unfamiliar sounds of the language. How confusing and stressful to be unable to find anything familiar in the printed signs or social customs. How frustrating to be unable to ask for assistance. Perhaps life is just as disorienting day after day for those who have difficulty making sense of their social/cultural world, who find it difficult to elicit meaning from their experiences, and who have difficulty understanding and using language to communicate.

Using the above analogy, consider having a guest from a very different culture in your home, classroom, or community. This guest uses language with some similar or familiar-sounding words, but the words, gestures, and facial expressions are used in different contexts and with different meanings. This guest expresses emotions in unexpected ways that are difficult to interpret. What would this guest need to feel comfortable and to manage effectively in this new situation?

If no language interpreter is available, the host must serve as both interpreter and guide to devise ways to transmit information from one to the other. It certainly would not be helpful for a host to talk more or to talk louder. To help the guest relax and be comfortable in this new place and to enjoy new experiences, a thoughtful host would most likely:

- Learn about the guest's language and cultural background so as to anticipate potentially confusing situations

- Use gestures and draw pictures to convey clear and concise information and to give meaning to the spoken words

- Orient the guest to the physical world—the location of things

- Develop some familiar routines and prepare the guest for changes to those routines with pictures and gestures

- Help the guest communicate needs, questions, thoughts, and feelings—again with the support of gestures and pictures

Above all, the thoughtful host would assume that this guest had feelings, legitimate needs, and the intelligence to learn and solve problems together.

These are the very strategies that are helpful and necessary for making the person with autism more comfortable and more able to participate with some degree of confidence in this confusing world. The principles and processes for making the guest with autism more comfortable, competent, and confident are outlined in the following sections.

An Intervention Planning Process

Learning and behavior are influenced not only by the antecedents and the consequences surrounding a situation, but also by the interpretations, thoughts, and feelings about the situation. In autism, these interpretations, thoughts, and feelings are influenced by the learning or cognitive processing style. Therefore, traditional behavioral principles and cognitive strategies are integrated as instructional and support plans are developed. Two basic rules guide this planning:

1. Capitalize on learning strengths (see figure 9.2) and individual interests to compensate for predictable learning problems. (See figure 9.3.)

2. The autism learning style guides the integration of cognitive strategies and behavioral technology.

Intervention strategies most likely to ensure competence and independence are based on both rules. An understanding of the learning style gives insight into the perspective of individuals with autism and is essential for predicting potential problems, for interpreting assessment results, and for developing adaptations and support systems. An understanding of behavior principles is also important as learning and behavior problems are assessed and instructional sequences are developed and delivered with clarity. Cognitive strategies provide a broader range of alternatives to ensure that learning is meaningful and more flexible. Reliance on either rule, to the exclusion of the other, has costly and sometimes paradoxical effects.

- Important and meaningful skills are not learned or generalized.
- Unintended and unexpected things are learned.
- The learner becomes overly dependent on the instructor.
- The above problems are highly resistant to change.

Figure 9.2. Learning strengths and personality traits common in autism

The ability to:
1. Take in chunks of information quickly—the whole thing
2. Remember information for a long time
3. Learn to use visual information meaningfully
4. Learn and repeat long routines
5. Understand and use concrete, context-free information and rules
6. Concentrate on narrow topics of specific interest

Predictable Personality Traits
- Perfectionism; honest, naive, and overly compliant

Figure 9.3. Learning deficits of those with autism

An inability or decreased ability to automatically, consistently, and/or independently:
- Modulate and process or integrate sensory stimulation
- Control attention, scan to identify, and focus on important information (overfocuses on irrelevant details)
- Analyze, organize, and integrate information to derive meaning (memorizes details, rote responses, and rules rather than concepts)
- Retrieve information in sequential order (interferes with learning cause/effect relationships and ability to predict and prepare for future events)
- Perceive and organize events in time and understand language related to time (leads to confusion and time-related anxiety)
- Understand the complex and changing meanings and nuances of the language (understands and uses the language literally)
- Integrate auditory information efficiently (leads to delays in response time and information gaps)
- Generate alternatives or solve problems that involve hypothesis testing and social judgment (often repeats the same responses over and over)
- Modify or generalize information from one situation to another (learns and uses concepts and skills exactly as taught)
- Control thoughts, movements, and responses (perseverates and gets stuck in motor and verbal routines or responses; may seem driven and compulsive)
- Adjust to new or novel information and events (leads to extreme anxiety associated with change and trying new things)
- Initiate communication to ask for assistance or clarification (leads to confusion, frustration, anxiety, and ineffective behavioral responses)
- Perceive social/cultural rules and the perspective of others (leads to confusion, misunderstandings, and unexpected and ineffective responses)

In summary, those with autism are unable to integrate bits and pieces of information to make meaning, to expand, or to use flexibly.

Strengths and Deficits

There are both positive and paradoxical effects of the six learning-style strengths typical in autism.

Strength 1. The ability to take in chunks of information quickly—the whole thing

Gestalt processing, holistic learning, and *one-trial learning* are terms often used to identify this processing style.

Positive effect. With prior organization of the information to highlight relevant details, relationships, and meaning, the learning rate is accelerated.

Paradoxical effect. Without prior organization and editing for relevance and meaning, the chunks of information are cluttered with irrelevant background details and unrelated information. For example, cues, prompts, and reinforcement are learned and have as much relevance as the critical details.

Strength 2. The ability to remember information for a long time

Positive effect. When information is organized for clarity of meaning prior to presentation, information is stored meaningfully, remembered, and available for meaningful use.

Paradoxical effect. Unanalyzed and cluttered information is stored firmly without meaning, thus is unavailable for integration and effective use.

Strength 3. The ability to use visual information meaningfully

Positive effect. When information is organized and presented visually, it is available for later reference and compensates for the attention, auditory processing, and sequential memory deficits. The ability to use visual information leads to greater independence from constant verbal cues and prompts.

Paradoxical effect. Visual details can overwhelm or block attention to relevant information and meaning. For example, the detail of wood grain on a table or reflections in a mirror can totally override important visual details. Unless the relevant visual details are organized and highlighted, they will not automatically lead to an understanding of the big picture—the major concepts.

Strength 4. The ability to learn and repeat long routines

Refer to the guidelines for planning and teaching routines in chapter 18, pages 247-268.

Positive effect. When the steps and skills of an important routine are tied together in an integrated sequence with a clear beginning and end and taught fluently without errors, the total routine is recorded together on the same tape. In this way, many functional and meaningful skills are taught and generalized within a fairly short period of time. The opportunity to complete a familiar routine to accomplish an important goal is highly motivating and reduces the need for artificial reinforcers.

Paradoxical effect. Independently developed routines often include extraneous and irrelevant steps that prevent the accomplishment of a meaningful purpose. A familiar routine is likely to be repeated over and over again without modification or useful outcome simply because it provides highly reinforcing predictability and comfort. Severe behavior problems often occur when these rigid routines are interrupted.

Strength 5. The ability to understand and use concrete, context-free information and rules

(For example, math rules are concrete; social rules change depending on the context.)

Positive effect. When concepts and rules are clearly defined and presented visually to show the range of applications, it is more likely that they can be applied to different situations and that they will be applied more flexibly.

Paradoxical effect. Without specifically designed instruction, rules and concepts will not be modified to apply appropriately in different situations but *will be used rigidly and exactly as taught* in similar situations.

Strength 6. The ability to concentrate on narrow topics of specific interest

Positive effect. With thoughtful and creative planning and support, topics of specific interest serve as important reinforcers for learning a broad range of concepts and skills, for increasing flexibility, esteem, and peer respect. Special interests are an important vehicle for establishing friendships and they have potential leisure and vocational value.

Paradoxical effect. Without concerted effort and organization to broaden the focus and expand the interests, rigidity and inflexibility frequently lead to severe problem behaviors, potential isolation, and limited skills.

When both learning style and behavioral principles guide interventions, learning rate, flexibility, self-esteem, and independence are increased while learning errors and behavior problems related to confusion and failure are decreased.

Three Basic Intervention Processes

To maintain an optimum level of stimulation for effective learning and behavior, intervention involves and revolves around three major processes:

1. *Evaluate* problem situations *and refine* the structure of environments and elements of the teaching/support plan to clarify the situation, solve problems quickly, and prevent reoccurrence.

   Small and seemingly insignificant elements or factors have a profound effect on the ability to focus, learn, and function effectively. Similarly, small and seemingly insignificant adjustments or refinements in the environment or the intervention and instructional plan can make a significant difference. These immediate refinements or modifications prevent anxiety and support an optimal learning environment.

2. *Organize and structure* space, time, and events (including instruction) to compensate for the deficits of autism.

   Those who have difficulty processing sensory information must rely on others to provide external structure that reduces distractions, highlights relevant information, clarifies meaning and purpose, and supports independent action.

3. *Teach new skills* to develop and expand competence and independence.

   Those whose early learning and development were disrupted by the autism learning style lack many of the subtle but basic understandings and skills that peers learn automatically from simply living in the culture. Many problems of those with autism are related to concept and skill deficits.

These three very general processes are dynamic and constantly evolving. Each action, or procedure, is a part of an interrelated, creative problem-solving process that guides and provides a focus for intervention and support efforts. With experience, this process can be applied to match the ever-changing needs of those with autism of various ages, in varied situations and with varied problems. The driving force behind these three procedures is the presence of a knowledgeable and sensitive interpreter and guide.

For an in-depth description of the effects of the autism learning style, review chapter 2. Refer to chapter 17 for an overview of behavior principles and rules for applying those principles precisely to achieve positive results and prevent costly learning errors. Cognitive strategies are described throughout the remaining chapters.

Figure 9.4. Three basic intervention processes

These three dynamic and interrelated processes drive the intervention:
- Evaluate and refine.
- Organize and structure.
- Teach new skills.

The Interpreter/Guide

Who interprets and guides? Family members, teachers, and educational, vocational, or residential assistants are logical interpreters; not only do they have the responsibility to provide support, but they are most available. To provide broader experiences and opportunities for their child, families sometimes hire a person to serve as an interpreter (companion) on weekends or evenings. Often peers, family friends, coworkers, or community service providers can be enlisted. For example, when the waitress at a favorite restaurant, a store clerk, an athletic club attendant, or a neighborhood police officer establishes a relationship with the individual, that person generally is more than willing to interpret and provide support and understand what to expect and how to help. When interpreters have basic training and support, these helping relationships can expand into long-term friendships that provide meaning for both parties.

Qualities of an Effective Interpreter

An effective interpreter must be able to predict the things that can happen and know why they might happen. This ability to predict potential problems allows the interpreter to be proactive—to intervene in ways to prevent many of those problems.

Without the foundation to predict problems, to understand why they occur, and to act proactively, everyone is left with a feeling of being constantly out of control, constantly reacting to seemingly unpredictable and unexpected situations and problems. Reactive responses tend to make a situation worse, they lead to cycles of out-of-control behavior for the person with autism as well as for those who provide support, and they result in feelings of inadequacy and incompetence.

The ability to understand why a problem occurs helps the interpreter respond more effectively to those that do occur. The preplanning and the support that is a part of this proactive approach helps the individual feel and function more competently and comfortably. The interpreter feels more capable and confident as the learner becomes more relaxed and independent.

The effective interpreter serves as the key that expands the world for those with autism. The interpreter sets the stage for expanding relationships and increasing opportunities. To be effective, the interpreter:

- Is alert and sensitive to the things occurring in the environment; is quick to identify the signals of confusion and frustration and identify the cause of that confusion and frustration

- Provides information to clarify the situation so others in the setting do not become alarmed or negative and so the individual can relax and understand what to do

Therefore, the interpreter must have some understanding of:

- The learning strengths and deficits common in autism
- Basic behavioral principles
- Basic strategies for clarifying information and providing assistance to solve problems

The interpreter must also know the individual very well:

- What activities are difficult and what are easy?
- What types of things are confusing or often misunderstood?
- What things are liked or disliked?
- What is overstimulating or disorienting?
- What is calming and comforting?
- What is boring or frightening?
- What communication strategies are used under normal conditions?
- What are the early behavioral signals or signs of stress that highlight a problem?

Develop a Relationship

The following strategies can help an individual with autism establish a trusting relationship with a new interpreter.

- Prepare the individual with autism prior to the introduction.
  - —Provide the new person's name, hobbies, and interests.
  - —Clarify the relationship, describing what this new person will do and where the new person will be involved.
  - —Clarify the expectation for the first visit (for example, when, where, and what will happen).
  - —Highlight the critical information with visual references—printed words or line drawings.

See chapters 14 and 15 for strategies for developing visual references.

- Introduce the new person in a familiar setting, with a familiar and liked activity and by a familiar and trusted person. Make the first visit short. For example, the new person may be introduced at a favorite ice-cream store. The visit would end when the dish of ice cream is finished.
- Plan one or two brief visits to simply hang out. Bring some small thing related to a special interest—a magazine, a picture, or a toy. Share a favorite snack, go for a walk or watch a TV show together. Have fun!
- Do not force conversation or ask too many questions. Be comfortable with quiet sharing. Answer questions.

A new interpreter who maintains an open, friendly and nondemanding attitude, speaks calmly and clearly but not too much, neither too softly or too loudly, during initial visits will be accepted. With such a beginning, generally the relationship will flourish. If there is not time for this extended lead-in, do as much as is possible.

Summary

An effective intervention plan to address the critical needs and goals of those with autism is based on cognitive/behavioral strategies and guided by the common learning style. Intervention efforts are based on three strategies:

1. Evaluate and refine. (See chapter 10.)

2. Organize and structure events, space, and time. (See chapters 11 through 16.)

3. Teach new skills. (See chapters 17 through 23.)

The presence of an interpreter who has the ability to predict and clarify situations to prevent problems is the first and perhaps the most important element in providing support for the guest from another culture—the individual with autism who has difficulty learning the language and rules of the native culture.

In the remainder of this book, the word *interpreter* is used to refer to a parent, teacher, or other person who is responsible for providing support at the moment. The word *learner* is used to indicate the individual with autism.

10 Evaluate and Refine to Support Effective Learning and Behavior

The interpreter's primary role is to help the learner with autism understand and function at an optimal level. To do this successfully, the interpreter must continually evaluate, think quickly, and make immediate decisions in order to resolve problems on the spot.

When stress or behavior problems increase or the learner has difficulty learning a new concept or skill, it usually means that some part of the teaching sequence or some element of the environment is confusing or interfering. At these times, the naive interpreter can step in to fix the problem, end the activity, or ignore the problem and continue to push on in the hope that the emotional/behavioral expressions (and the problem) will go away.

Fixing the problem can lead to dependency, ending the problem can reinforce inappropriate behavior, and ignoring the problem rarely makes it go away. Repetition of a confusing sequence and errors is not likely to induce effective learning. To push on and ignore the learner's needs is disrespectful and punishing for both the learner and the interpreter, for neither is successful.

If one ignores the behavior that signals a problem, the emotional expressions will most likely accelerate because the problem still exists. While repetition of an unmodified instructional sequence may be useful for those who learn slowly, it is not useful for those with autism, who take in and remember chunks of information at one time and who learn effective skills quickly when the presentation is clear. Nor is it useful for those who learn things exactly as taught (including errors and correction procedures) and miss the important meaning and intent of the situation. When failure and lack of success continues, motivation decreases and the frequency and intensity of behavior problems increase.

Evaluation is an ongoing process, and refinements must be made as soon as a problem is identified rather than to wait a week or a month to see what will happen. It is more efficient to maintain an ongoing diagnostic/prescriptive policy. When problems are allowed to continue, the environment and the plan generally require major changes and significant time to repair the damage.

Effective intervention that conserves time and energy depends on identifying and analyzing the ebb and flow of stress to find clues for deciding when and how to intervene. The profile of stress illustrated in figure 10.1 is a key for matching intervention efforts to the changing needs of those with autism.

Stress is a normal part of life. A certain amount of stress provides motivation; but without adequate resources, too much stress is defeating. The variations in stress depend on such things as physical condition, competence, feelings of self-esteem, trauma (for example, losses, grief, worries, and excitement), and the level of available support. Most of the time, people function best at a level of equilibrium, when the level of stress is balanced by an equal level of competence, confidence, and support.

Variations in the level of stress are identified by subtle and not-so-subtle variations of behavior (for example, from frowning to screaming). Thus the interpreter constantly evaluates the learner's subtle behavioral signals and the context of those

Figure 10.1. Profile of stress: Basis for matching interventions to needs

To identify the points or stages of the emotional sequence when specific kinds of interventions are not only critical but most effective

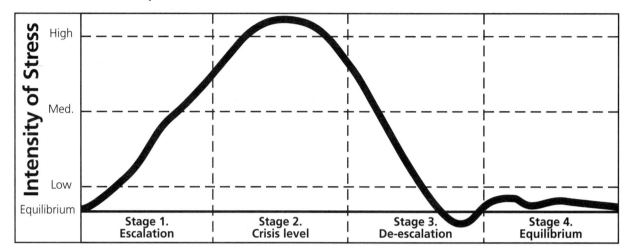

Behavior:

1a. Increasing agitation

1b. More intense agitation

Intervention goals:

- Solve problem
- Defuse stress and return to equilibrium
- Capitalize on natural problem to teach new skill

Behavior:

2c. High tension/highly vulnerable; on the edge

2d. Out of control, panic—reflexive; unthinking

2e. High tension with signs of calming/highly vulnerable

Intervention goals:

2c. Solve the problem quickly to prevent escalation to crisis

2d. Keep people safe

2e. Support de-escalation and relaxation

Behavior:

Increasingly calm, highly vulnerable to re-escalation

3f. Quiescent, fatigue

Intervention goals:

- Support and reinforce relaxation and self-control
- Re-engage in productive activity

Behavior:

Stable, under control

Intervention goals:

- Evaluate and refine situation to prevent recurrence
- Organize and structure to clarify expectations
- Teach new skills

variations for clues to guide intervention decisions; that is, to identify the points or stages of the emotional sequence when specific kinds of intervention are not only critical but most effective.

The primary purpose for this ongoing evaluation and refinement process is to defuse stress and maintain positive and purposeful efforts directed to increased learning and effectiveness in the community now and in the future.

Evaluate and Refine: The E/R Process

The evaluation process occurs throughout the day and in every setting. The process includes four steps:

1. Identify the subtle behavior that signals a problem.

2. Analyze to determine the cause or reason for the problem.

3. Determine intervention priority, clarify, and adapt to resolve the problem.

4. Make adaptations and teach new skills to prevent recurring problems.

Step 1. Identify the behavior that signals a problem

A problem is any question or matter involving doubt, uncertainty, or difficulty that needs a solution or causes confusion and frustration. Many things are problematic for those who have difficulty organizing information, generating effective solutions, and asking for clarification or assistance in reliable and understandable ways. There are three important rules for identifying problems:

1. Be familiar with the learner's subtle patterns of behavior.

2. Stay attuned to the subtle variations of attention, emotion, and behavior that highlight increasing levels of stress, frustration, and confusion.

3. Identify small behavioral signals before they reach the crisis stage.

Predictable Warning Signals or Signs of a Problem

Whether able to speak or not, a learner still communicates, but it is left to the interpreter to recognize the message. The following list begins with the earliest and most subtle communication signals.

1. Physical signs of confusion, frustration, anxiety, or stress—a flushed face, yawning, stretching, changes in breathing patterns, or hyperventilation

2. Repetitive or stereotypic verbal or motor actions—rocking, pacing, finger flicking, or repetitive questions

3. Disorganized behavior that is random, frantic, or compulsive

4. Signs of apathy, lack of motivation, or withdrawal—covering ears with hands, closing eyes, placing head down on table, limpness or falling limply to the floor, turning away, hiding under a table or behind a couch

5. Signs of resistance (apparent noncompliance)—dropping to the floor, active resistance, pulling away, pushing away or throwing materials, running away

6. Emotional outbursts that do not fit the situation—giggling and laughing when someone is hurt, or standing on the table and shouting

7. Self injury—biting the wrist, slapping or banging the face or head, poking at the eyes

8. Apparent aggression—pinching, scratching, squeezing the interpreter's hand or arm, biting, kicking, hitting, or threats to pinch, scratch, bite, kick, or hit

When confused, Tony simply held his hand over his teacher's hand and waited. If the subtle signal was ignored and demands continued, he pinched the teacher's hand. He had no other way to say, "Wait a minute, what does this mean?" or "Stop, I've about had it."

When confused and in need of assistance, Amy made throaty noises, then began running about the room, kicking at the teacher each time she passed.

These signals may or may not be delivered intentionally or persistently. Some are reflexive reactions or emotional responses to a situation. Even when the behavioral reactions or responses are inappropriate or unacceptable, they do convey a message: "I have a problem."

Step 2. Analyze to determine the cause of the problem

Once a problem is signaled, it is left to the interpreter to identify the cause of the problem. The interpreter must be aware of the situations that cause problems and constantly sensitive to the context of the problem: what is happening near the learner, in other parts of the room, or outside the immediate area?

Situations that Typically Cause Problems

The following four situations are likely to increase stress and reduce effective learning and behavior:

1. Situations involving people. These are troublesome because of difficulty with or inability to:

   - Ignore or tolerate the abundance of sensory stimulation: talking, laughing, touching, odors, patterns of fabrics or jewelry, changing facial expressions

   - Understand what other people know, their points of view, their emotions, their social customs and cultural rules

UNDERSTANDING THE NATURE OF AUTISM

See chapter 3 for a review of these problems and illustrations of the kinds of communication problems that can occur.

- Understand and become involved in the quick and ever-changing interactions, games, and activities
- Understand the communication
- Initiate and communicate effectively, especially under stress

2. Over- or understimulation. These trigger many problems:

- The inability to ignore, modulate, or organize sensory information, causing confusion, disorganization, and fear
- Time pressures, too many choices or options, and worries about health, family matters, or world situations that are often overwhelming
- Boredom and lack of interesting activities and variety

> The calendar, the bulletin board, the pictures, and other writing on the chalkboard distracted Jose so much that he was unable to copy the spelling words onto his paper. He copied the list quickly after the teacher highlighted his word list with a strip of red crepe paper.

> Matt, who loved to be outside, suddenly refused to go out. After several days, his frustrated teacher discovered that he could not tolerate the odor of blooming sage and never went outside during the blooming period.

> The additional materials for Kim's new job were arranged on a shelf near his work table. This placement required him to stand up, move to the shelf, and return to his space with the materials. Each time Kim stood up to get more materials, he became disorganized and started to rock back and forth, sit down, stand up and leave the area, seeming to forget what he was to do.

3. Changes—both big changes and seemingly insignificant ones—frequently trigger confusion, anxiety, and problems:

- Staff changes—substitute teachers, volunteers, peer tutors, a new person to deliver a message, or *the absence of a familiar person*

> When Maria's interpreter left the room without warning, Maria became frantic, visually searching about the room, biting her wrist, and hyperventilating. When the interpreter stepped back inside the door a few moments later, Maria calmly returned to her work as if nothing had happened.

> Maria is quite verbal and knew how to ask for clarification and assistance; but in this unexpected, stressful situation, she was unable to use those skills.

- Changes in rules, schedules, or arrangement of objects and materials

> Each day when Ben returns home from school, he is agitated and cannot relax until he has returned everything in the house to its specific familiar location. He moves and adjusts everything—even the things on the kitchen counter and in the refrigerator. Finally he settles to unpack his backpack to share with his mother.

- Transitions from one activity or setting to another or changing a familiar travel route
- Changes in familiar routines

> Andy, with his interpreter, took the pop cans from the teacher's lounge each day to recycle at a nearby store. The morning after a party in the gym, they were asked to take the cans from the gym also. As Andy started off on his normal route, his interpreter tried to get him to go to the gym, but Andy began to kick, bite his wrist, and hyperventilate. Since Andy had not processed the teacher's verbal directions, he was unprepared for the change.

4. Lack of information or misinterpreted information

Use the following "mental checklist" as a guide for pinpointing the exact cause of problems.

Figure 10.2. Checklist to identify the cause of a problem

The following five questions can be committed to memory and used as a quick mental checklist when a behavior signals a problem.

1. What is new, changed, or missing? (Related to people, time, space, or events)
2. What may have been misinterpreted or misunderstood?
   - The directions? Directions directed to others nearby?
   - A conversation? A conversation between others in another area?
   - Something read in the daily paper or a magazine?
   - Something heard on radio or TV?
   - A word? or concept? a rule?
3. Is some element of the instructional plan or task unclear? For example, does the individual *really understand (is it visually clear):*
   - What to do? Both sides of the picture—what can and cannot be done?
   - Why it is being done (the meaning, outcome, or purpose)?
   - How and where to do it?
   - Where to start? When to start?
   - What materials, people, or equipment are needed?
   - When it is finished?
   - What to do next?
   - When a favorite activity or interaction is scheduled?
   - When help or clarification is needed?
4. Is it a specific communication problem? Does the learner have an effective way to spontaneously:
   - Ask for help or clarification?
   - Get out of a boring or disliked situation?
   - Start or end an interaction?
   - Get a break, relief from overstimulation?
   - Specify choices? Needs?
5. Is some element of the environment confusing, irritating, disrupting or overwhelming (for example, heat, light, noise, textures, crowding, arrangement of materials, work too difficult, a medical problem)?
6. Is boredom and lack of stimulation the issue?

Step 3. Determine intervention priority, clarify, and adapt to resolve the problem

Whenever there is a problem, the potential for a crisis is present. Thus the interpreter must decide how to direct efforts to resolve the problem and prevent a crisis. The decision will depend on the type of problem, the setting of the problem, the individual's emotional state, and the interpreter's priorities—to prevent a behavioral crisis, to maintain the flow of the activity, or to capitalize on the problem situation to teach new skills.

The checklist in figure 10.2 illustrates the thinking process for identifying the intervention priority. The flow chart in figure 10.3 (page 144) illustrates the intervention process that matches the strategies to the level of stress.

Goal 1. To prevent a behavioral crisis

Become familiar with the information in chapter 25, pages 408-411, related to managing serious, potentially dangerous behavior.

Criteria. If the emotional state is accelerating rapidly (Stage 1b) and/or the individual is too upset to think or to hear and a crisis is imminent, (Stage 2c and d), then the *immediate priority is to prevent that crisis and keep people safe.*

Interpreter's goal. To defuse the stress, moving directly from Stage 1b or 2c directly to Stages 2e and 3, thus skipping the crisis at Stage 2d.

Strategies for immediate action. (Note that the following strategies are not necessarily sequential. Modifications are made to match the specific individual and the specific situation.)

- Use a calm, quiet, supportive attitude that silently communicates acceptance and confidence. ("You are okay. You will be able to handle this, and I will help you if you need it.")

Ignore the behavior, but acknowledge the message and tell the learner what to do right now to relax.

If the behavior that signaled the problem was ineffective or inappropriate, do not attend to, talk about, or call attention to it. Attention to an inappropriate behavior can:

—Serve as a reinforcer and increase the likelihood that it will be strengthened or repeated in other stressful situations; or

—Serve to increase the stress because it gives no direction for immediate action.

Figure 10.3. Making intervention decisions (Flow chart)

Decisions will be determined by the intensity of stress, as illustrated in the Profile of Stress (page 138)

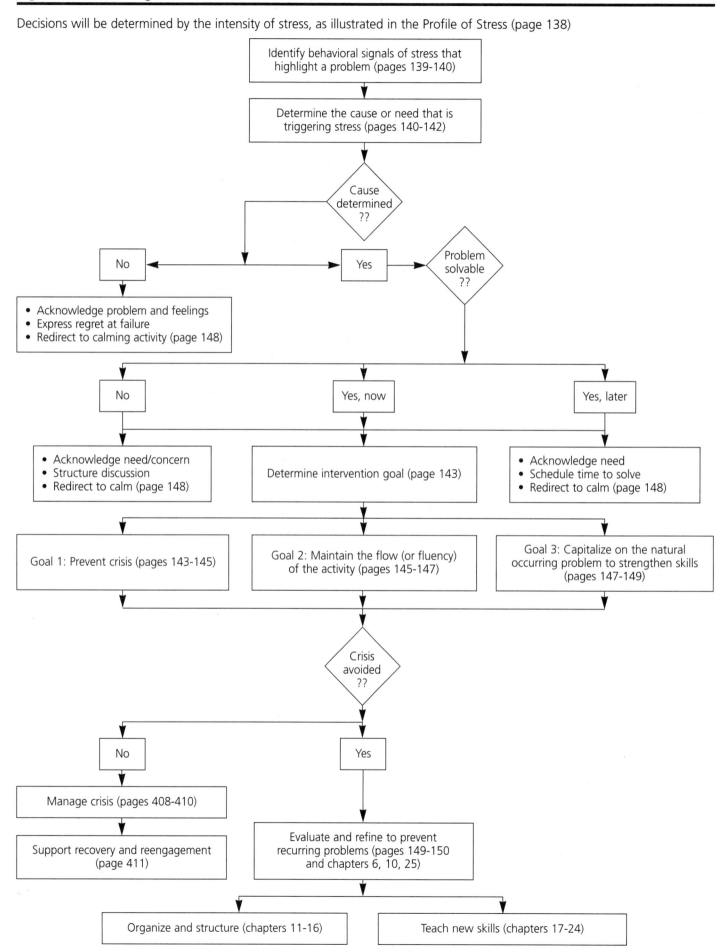

This is a modification of the reflective listening described in chapter 16, pages 220-221.

Acknowledge the problem and the feeling, and clarify a simple, clear course of action. ("Did the noise confuse you? Now you can go to your quiet place and relax yourself. Then, I will help you finish your work.")

> In the example on pages 53-54, Jeff thought he was going to miss seeing the movie and had his hands about the teacher's neck. The experienced and very calm teacher ignored his behavior and simply answered his unstated message: "First, do your math. Second, set up the projector and watch the movie. And third, take the projector to Mrs. Peters' room."

- Reduce the demands. When stress and emotions are high, the individual is not in a condition to listen, to learn, to work, or to communicate. The continuation or addition of a stressful requirement will increase the potential for a crisis. Do not require the individual to communicate, to explain, to apologize, or to make choices when stress and emotion are at Stage 2.

Refer to pages 194-200 for visual support strategies.

Stop talking; reduce the amount of auditory stimulation. Use a quiet voice and simple words, and provide printed words or line drawings to clarify the meaning of the words. *Often, the very simple act of changing the focus of attention from the individual to the marks on the paper will reduce tension and defuse a crisis.*

See chapter 23 for strategies for teaching self-control.

- Reinforce any effort or sign of self-control. At any slight pause or relaxation of tension, calmly and quietly say, "Good. You can calm yourself," or "Take a deep breath. . . . Good. . . . Now relax your shoulders. . . . Yes, you can relax yourself."

Goal 2. To maintain the flow of the task or activity

Criteria. When the problem occurs during the initial instruction of a new skill or routine, when an interruption will distract or disrupt others or when an interruption would call undue attention to the individual, then the priority is to provide only enough assistance to solve the problem immediately and maintain the flow of the routine or activity.

This priority is selected only during the Stage 1 levels of stress.

Interpreter's goal. To repair the situation as fluently and positively as possible

Strategies for immediate action.

When the problem occurs in a public place:

- Ignore the behavior and acknowledge the problem.

- Provide calm, clear directions and assistance to solve the problem quickly.

When the problem occurs during the initial presentation of a new skill or routine:

- Refine the instructional sequence quickly to highlight a natural cue; or

- Insert a more effective prompt; or

- Alter the arrangement of the space, materials, or information to prevent an error.

> Maria had quickly mastered all but one step of her new job, which was to fill small plastic containers, firmly press the cap on, then place the containers in order on a tray. While unsuccessfully trying to press the cap down with her fingers and between her palms, she began to lose her focus, move about in her seat, look about, and make whining sounds. As she raised her wrist to her mouth to bite, her interpreter quickly placed a small piece of paper on the work area. In the center of that paper, the interpreter had drawn a circle the size of the container. Without a word, the interpreter demonstrated placing the container on the circle and pressing the cap down, making a snapping sound. When Maria was ready to snap on the next cap, the interpreter touched the circle to direct the placement of the container. With the addition of minimal touch and gestural prompts on the next three containers, Maria had the routine mastered and no more prompting was needed.
>
> Two natural reinforcers provided the incentive to persist in this task: the snapping sound of the cap, and seeing the orderly lines of containers filling the tray. When the organization and structure matched the need, stress was reduced and learning was rapid.
>
> ---
>
> Maria was learning to ride the bus. On her second trip, she got on and moved past the driver without paying. Calmly, her interpreter said, "Oops, Maria, you need to pay. Come, I'll help you." As Maria returned, the interpreter gave her a token so she could pay quickly and not interrupt others. Later, the interpreter prepared a cue card, using simple line drawings to represent each step of the bus-riding sequence. The drawing that represents paying the fare had the money container and token highlighted. They used the card to review each step of the routine once or twice in a simulated setting and just before taking the next bus trip. The interpreter was alert and close by to provide assistance if needed.

See chapter 17 for a discussion of correction procedures.

When an error has already occurred:

- Quickly and quietly refine or add some element to repair or correct the situation so the routine or event can continue.

> Review the situation of Andy (page 142), who was kicking and hyperventilating in response to a change in his recycling routine. His interpreter quickly prepared a mini-schedule to highlight the changes in the routine, and Andy was able to continue successfully.
>
> ---
>
> Jeff, 7 years old, needed to put on his tennis shoes before going to PE. A new high school student was to assist him. After she told him to put on his shoes, he began to run around the classroom, climbing over tables and laughing. As the student tried to catch him, she was saying, "Stop, you

need to put on your shoes." The teacher, who knew that Jeff really liked PE, reasoned that he either did not understand the verbal directions or he did not know why he should put on his shoes. To cover either hypothesis, she took a scrap of paper to Jeff and, as he watched, she wrote quickly while saying, "1. Shoes on. 2. PE." Immediately, he put on his shoes and walked beside her to the gym—a natural reinforcement for following the visual direction quickly.

- Later: Evaluate and refine the instructional plan and/or the environmental situation to prevent recurrence.

- Review and practice the revised routine before encountering the situation again.

Goal 3. To capitalize on the problem situation to practice new skills

Criteria. When the stress is at a mild or moderate level with no crisis pending (Stages 1a to 1b) and it is not necessary to maintain the flow of the activity, then the priority is to capitalize on the natural and powerful opportunity to practice new communication, social, and problem-solving skills.

Interpreter's goal. To strengthen and generalize new skills

Strategies for immediate action.

- Acknowledge the problem and support active involvement in the solution.

  —Cue to use communication system or self-control and relaxation strategies.

  —Provide assistance as needed to ensure that those skills solve the problem quickly and effectively.

  —Verbally highlight the solution, the effort, and the accomplishment.

When Amy began to stretch and yawn—signals of fatigue and a wish to end an activity—her interpreter:

—Acknowledged the message of her behavior. "You look tired (the problem) and want to stop working" (the solution and natural reinforcer).

—Told her how she could solve the problem. "You can say, 'All done.'"

—Quickly, almost simultaneously, provided just enough assistance for Amy to touch the "all done" symbol on her communication board.

—Quickly and enthusiastically acknowledged her message. "You are *all done*. You can stop working and listen to tapes."

Sitting in the language circle, Kim began to scratch and pinch the child beside him. The teacher quickly interpreted, "Bob is too close. Tell him to move over." While speaking, the teacher placed Kim's hands on Bob's arm and gave a gentle push. Bob moved over.

The behavior was ignored, the message was acknowledged, and assistance was provided to actively involve Kim in solving his own problem. The teacher's message conveyed both the problem and a solution. Active involvement was reinforced because it ended the unpleasant closeness. At the same time, peers understood that Kim simply had a problem and needed assistance; he was not a bad, mean little boy to avoid.

When the reason for the problem cannot be determined:

- Acknowledge that there is a need, and express regret. "I'm sorry, I don't understand." Ask the learner to try another way to clarify the message (for example, "Can you show me with your communication book?").

- Ask the learner to point to the problem or take you to the problem.

- List some possible reasons on paper with words or line drawings, and say, "Point to the picture of the problem." The learner must have a way to indicate that none of the problems listed is the real problem. Therefore, include symbols to represent *yes, no,* and *none of those.*

If the message is still unclear:

- Say, "I'm sorry, I don't understand. Let's take a walk and get a drink. Then you can _____"; or, "I'm sorry. We can try to figure it out later. Now you can take a break" (or do some liked activity).

- *Do not try to distract until the learner knows that the problem was heard and that you regret that you cannot help.*

If the problem is something that cannot be resolved immediately:

- Acknowledge the message and clarify with a statement, such as:

—"You want pretzels. They are all gone. Let's put *pretzels* on the grocery list. Now, do you want a potato chip or a cracker?"

—"You want to see your mother. Remember, you see her on Saturday." Then write *See Mother* on the calendar and count the days. If the need continues to cause sadness or a problem, continue to refer to the calendar and cross off the days as they go by. In a situation such as this, it may help to suggest making a phone call, writing a letter, or starting a list of things to tell Mother on Saturday. Whatever the situation, clarify the solution visually

For a broader discussion and strategies for dealing with special communication and social problems, see pages 345-353.

for later reference. *The critical issue here is that the learner has a legitimate problem and concern and needs respectful assistance to deal with feelings.*

If the problem is related to a worry and concern about an unsolvable problem (such as famine, war, or the common cold):

- Acknowledge and share the concern, then structure the situation.

> One mother used a journal to resolve recurring and unsolvable problems. When her son was compulsively concerned about crime in the street, the subject was discussed very briefly, and she wrote the following explanation in the journal:
>
>> You are really worried about crime in the streets. That worries me, too. Neighborhood groups, legislators, the President, and the police are concerned, too. They are all working to solve crime in the street. Is it your responsibility? No.
>
> Later, whenever the concern was expressed, the young man was referred to the journal. Through this medium, he learned about language, reading, spelling, problem solving, and community and government responsibility.

See chapter 23, pages 364-366, for additional strategies for teaching problem solving.

The opportunities for capitalizing on naturally occurring problems are almost endless, limited only by the creativity and the flexibility of the interpreter and the stress level of the individual. Without the interpreter's assistance, these powerful opportunities would be lost.

Step 4. Make adaptations and teach new skills to prevent recurring problems

The tasks outlined in this step are addressed during the period of equilibrium between problems, when the individual with autism is most relaxed and open to new experiences and learning. This period is illustrated at Stage 4 on the profile (figure 10.1). It is a most creative and productive period for interpreters and the total support team. It is at this time when the various elements of the program are refined and new skills are introduced to prevent or to address problems in the future.

The basic tasks to address at this time are:

1. Update records

   The interpreter keeps anecdotal records of the problems, the context, and the immediate modifications. These records are shared with the support team. The notes can be brief but with enough detail to highlight the cause of the problems and the issues to address to prevent recurrence.

2. Make decisions

   The support team processes the information and collaborates to apply new insights to both prevent recurrence in the same or similar situations and to intervene more effectively.

   > Now that there is evidence that Andy (examples on pages 142 and 147) does not consistently process or remember verbal information, all his interpreters must remember to support verbal directions with visual reminders in order to prevent similar problems. In addition, Andy's communication system must include a better way to say, "Stop, I don't understand."
   >
   > _____
   >
   > When the support team knows that Kim (example on page 141) becomes disorganized when movement disrupts a routine, the information can be considered when evaluating other problems and when organizing and structuring other situations.
   >
   > _____
   >
   > Tony (example on page 23) covered his ears, fussed, and lost his focus for "no apparent reason." It was finally discovered that he could hear the sounds of a train long before others were aware of its coming. He was taught to place plugs in his ears as soon as he heard the noise and to place a sign on an easel that said, "The train is coming." Then he could refocus on the task at hand.

3. Restructure or refine elements of the space, time, and events that are confusing or unclear

   Clarify the daily calendar, prepare cue cards, . . .

4. Teach new skills or expand and strengthen old skills—relaxation and self-management procedures, communication skills, problem-solving skills, and others

Summary

This ongoing diagnostic/prescriptive process is the critical element of an effective intervention plan. When solving problems, the interpreter continually asks, "Why is the learner doing this in this way?" Once that is decided, the plan and/or the environment can be refined to match the specific needs of the learner at that specific time, and new skills can be taught to prevent recurring problems.

There is an important distinction between supporting to prevent and solve problems and overprotection. Overprotection is unproductive even though it is based on kind and honorable motives, a wish to be helpful, to prevent stress and feelings of rejection and failure. In autism, the individual who is not becoming more independent and capable is regressing, becoming more rigid, more dependent, and more isolated. Overprotection limits and reduces options because the individual never learns how to deal with stress, to solve problems, or to become more competent.

It is productive when learners with autism are provided the support and the skills to actively solve their own problems. Appropriate support and active involvement expands the world and increases options. Competence, confidence, and self-esteem are enhanced. This positive outcome is possible only when the support and teaching strategies are based on the learning strengths and deficits common in autism.

The strategies suggested in this chapter are expanded in later chapters and applied to many different situations. This evaluation process requires sensitivity, alertness, and quick thinking. It is an essential process that ensures the primary goals are met: to maintain equilibrium for effective learning and behavior, and to prevent escalating and costly learning and behavior problems.

11

Organize and Structure Events

Participation in a complex and confusing social and verbal world requires incredible effort—effort that is rarely successful for those with autism. When effort goes unrewarded or has unpleasant consequences, it is natural to stop trying. Psychologists call this phenomenon *learned helplessness*; it is safer not to try. One parent called it learned *hopelessness*. The conclusion that there is no way to understand and participate effectively in the world leads to defensive actions to avoid failure and punishment. Those who do not understand the world from the perspective or culture of autism often interpret the defensive efforts to avoid failure as laziness, noncompliance, or manipulation.

In chapters 11 through 16, several systematic processes are outlined for organizing and structuring the environment, the events, the space, and the time to clarify information for those who see this world from a different perspective (Mesibov et al. 1994). Organization and external structures compensate for the inability to scan an environment, analyze and select the relevant details, ignore the clutter, and elicit meaning and purpose. Organization and structure also reduce anxiety from distractions and overwhelming sensory stimulation while highlighting the critical important information. This systematic process provides a high degree of clarity that:

1. Increases the ability to focus on productive and independent activity in the natural community without constant verbal directions

2. Provides a familiar, predictable, and comfortable structure for adding new experiences, thus increasing flexibility and tolerance for change and expanding options

3. Ensures that all the critical goals (see figure 7.1, page 105) are addressed in the context of each naturally occurring activity

4. Increases motivation, success, competence, and confidence

Two facts to keep in mind:

1. It is not necessary to develop complex plans for every single event of the day, but it is important to plan systematically when:

    - Introducing new events

    - Planning instruction

    - Explaining changes in familiar routines and events

    - Evaluating and resolving problem situations

2. This planning process becomes more automatic and efficient with experience.

It is often surprising to see the difference in attitude and performance of those with autism when expectations are clearly defined and when the world makes sense. This positive effect increases the feelings of competence and confidence of all who contribute and support the effort.

Organize Events as Routines

An event is anything that occurs in a certain place during a particular interval of time. An event can be any variety of activities—a science class, recess, going to a parade, getting dressed, going to the dentist, or having a cup of coffee during a break at work—anything that a person could be involved with during a day. Each event can be conceptualized as a routine. Every day is filled with a sequence of these routines. Each involves a series of steps or skills flowing from the beginning to the end to achieve the purpose or critical effect of the event. There is a common set of components or parts that must be carried out in order to achieve the purpose or critical effect of each routine independently. Successful participation means that the critical effect or the purpose of the routine was accomplished (Brown et al. 1987).

Figure 11.1. Common components of routines

The essential components:

1. Initiate
2. Prepare
3. Perform essential steps
4. Terminate
5. Transition to next event

Extension/enrichment components:

6. Solve problems
7. Communicate and socialize
8. Make choices and decisions
9. Self-monitor

The traditional task-analysis planning strategy (which identifies all the essential motor actions necessary for completing a task) is not enough to ensure successful and independent participation. For example, a traditional task analysis for doing laundry would typically include:

1. Put dirty clothes in washer.
2. Add soap.
3. Close washer door.
4. Set dials.
5. Start washer.
6. When washer stops, open dryer door.
7. Open washer door.
8. Transfer wet clothes to dryer.

   . . . and so on, through the process—drying, folding, and putting away.

This type of planning does not ensure that the critical effect is achieved—that of clean, dry clothes folded in the drawer every time. One father highlights this fact as he describes the time his son returned folded, wet clothes to the drawer. The young man had not been taught the complete purpose or the final result of the routine, nor was he taught to monitor the quality of the work or what to do if there were problems, such as a defective heating element in the dryer (Hart 1989).

To achieve the critical effect of a laundry routine involves completing all the steps, from seeing the laundry basket full of dirty clothes to having clean, dry clothes folded and placed back in the appropriate drawers every time. For a party, the routine begins with knowing when it is time to get ready and ends when the party is over and the individual has returned home. A math class routine begins with the walk from the previous class and ends with the walk to the next class.

Most people automatically learn how to participate successfully in the many events of the day. It is never safe to assume that the learner with autism will automatically figure out how to carry out all the steps of a routine that are required for independence. Often, some problem occurs or an error is made that increases frustration or has unfortunate effects. These errors or social blunders are not only demoralizing, they are sometimes dangerous and can lead to an undeserved negative reputation and potential isolation.

> Gabriel, who was working in a local store, was befriended by two young children who came to the store frequently. One day the two children ran into the store with their mother and rushed to give their friend a big hug, one child hugging each leg. Gabriel stood very still until the children's mother came and rescued him. Tears were running down his face as he said, "I didn't know what to do."

The Process for Organizing Events

The process for organizing any activity or functional routine includes five parts:

1. Define the purpose or critical effect of the routine
2. Identify the sequence of steps or components needed to achieve the purpose
3. Identify the natural cues to initiate each step and the natural prompts to maintain performance
4. Identify and develop adaptations to support independence
5. Evaluate and refine to solve problems

These steps can be used quickly and informally to prepare the learner for participation in a new or changing activity. A more detailed and formal plan that is most likely to lead to independent participation is developed for instructional purposes.

The first three steps of the process are described in this chapter. In chapters 12 through 17, the intervention strategies used to develop the adaptations (Step 4) are described. Chapter 18 describes the process for developing and evaluating instructional plans for teaching routines.

See form 11.1 for an organizational method to complete this process. See figure 11.2 for a sample of a completed form.

Routine Planning

Adapted with permission from *Project QUEST Inservice Manual* (Falco et al. 1990)

Student: _____   Date: _____

Goal/Purpose of Routine: _____

Settings: _____

Component	Natural Cues/Prompts	Skills/Sequence of Steps	Adaptations
Initiate			
Prepare/Perform			
Terminate			
Transition			

(continued)

Student: _____   Date: _____

Component	Natural Cues/Prompts	Skills/Sequence of Steps	Adaptations
Solve Problems			
Communicate/ Socialize			
Make Choices			
Self-Monitor			

Figure 11.2. Sample: Routine Planning

This form is partially completed to show the first two steps in developing the support or instructional plan for an activity/routine. This is a transition routine that crosses four settings. It does not end until the learner is engaged in the next major activity. It was developed for an 11-year-old student who had difficulty following bus rules, going directly to his classroom, and starting the day's activities.

Adapted with permission from *Project QUEST Inservice Manual* (Falco et al. 1990)

Student: _____ **Date:** September 25

Goal/Purpose of Routine: Independently transition from home to school on bus and engage in the first school routine

Settings: Sidewalk in front of house, bus, from bus to front door of school, hallway, classroom

Component	Natural Cues/Prompts	Skills/Sequence of Steps	Adaptations
Initiate	1. Bus stops at house. Door is open.	1. Pick up backpack and move to bus.	
Prepare/Perform	2. At bus step. (Natural prompt: Driver waves checklist)	2. Enter and pick up checklist from driver.	
	3. In bus with checklist in hand.	3. Scan seats. Select a seat. Sit.	
	4. On seat.	4. Fasten seat belt. Sit quietly. (The bus ride itself is naturally reinforcing.)	
	5. Bus stops at school, door opens, kids get up and walk out door. (Natural prompt: Kid behind pushes to keep moving)	5. Pick up backpack and follow kids.	
	6. Line of kids to front door of school and entering school	6. Leave checklist with driver. Follow kids through school door.	
	7. Inside hall	7. Locate locker.	
	8. At locker—transition cue (TC) on door	8. Open locker. Stow coat, etc. Pick up transition cue (TC)	
Terminate	9. TC (transition cue) in hand (TC is an adapted prompt to remember destination.)	9. Take TC to calendar in classroom.	
	10. At calendar	10. Place TC in appropriate location. Review events on calendar. Pick up TC for first activity. (The calendar review process is naturally reinforcing.)	
	11. TC (transition cue) for first activity in hand	11. Move to first activity. Place TC in specified location	
Transition	(No additional steps to this transition routine required)	(The first activity should be a familiar and pleasant activity to serve as a natural reinforcer.)	

Student: _____ **Date:** _____

Component	Natural Cues/Prompts	Skills/Sequence of Steps	Adaptations
Solve Problems	12. Someone in favorite seat	12. Find another seat. Sign/gesture, "Can I sit here?"	
	13. Someone teasing	13. Laugh/sign: "You're funny!" and/or use relaxation/self-talk skills.	
	14. Can't find coat/bag to leave bus	14. Search for belongings. Ask for help	
	15. School door closed	15. Open door and walk in.	
	16. Locker won't open	16. Find appropriate helper.	
	17. Too much noise	17. Find ear plugs and insert.	
Communicate/ Socialize	18. Peers or staff greet (on bus/in school)	18. Return greetings, sign "Hi!" or "Good-bye."	
	19. Sitting beside peer on bus	19. Share sports magazine	
	20. Communicate to solve above problems	20. Use communication system to solve problems noted in items 12, 13, 14, 16, and 22	
Make Choices	21. Select seat partner	21. As in item 12, above	
	22. Select topic of conversation listed on cue card	22. Check topic cue card to select	
Self-Monitor	23. Monitor behavior on bus	23. Refer to checklist	
	24. Monitor stress level from bus to first activity in school	24. Use relaxation routine	

Step 1. Define the purpose or critical effect of the routine

What is the purpose or function of the event—the meaning, outcome or product? Why is this event important? What is the total critical effect?

A clear understanding of the purpose or effect of a routine:

- Provides motivation and clarifies the natural reinforcement for participation and effort

- Facilitates generalization and ensures that learning will be meaningful rather than rote

- Provides a base for evaluation to determine whether the total effect is achieved

Step 2. Identify the sequence of steps or components needed to achieve the purpose

Initiate

This component answers the questions: When do I begin? What is the first thing that must be done?

In figure 11.2, the initiating action is to pick up the backpack and step onto the bus. Often, the initiating action is to move to the appropriate location.

Prepare

What preparation is needed? What materials or supplies are needed? What needs to be done to get ready?

- One might need to collect a coat, backpack, and lunch before leaving for work or school. In a cooking routine, the preparatory steps involve washing hands and collecting ingredients and tools.

Perform core steps

What are the core (essential) steps to achieve the critical effect or outcome?

- One example of the core steps is given on page 153 in the traditional task analysis of a laundry routine. In an academic class, the core steps might include: Listen to teacher, read pages 5-13, write the answers to problems 1-10 on page 12. In a preschool language group activity, the core steps could be: Respond to attendance, sing four songs, listen to the teacher explain the day's schedule, and listen while the teacher reads a book.

- Motivation is increased and anxiety decreased when the learner is prepared for and understands the sequence of an activity. This understanding provides a foundation for moving from one step to another and for marking progress to anticipate the end.

Terminate

What must be done to terminate the event? What does *finished* look like?

- Identify those termination tasks, such as cleaning up the kitchen after a meal, paying the bill after selecting purchases, putting away the art supplies, or gathering coat and packages before leaving.

Solve Problems

What problems are likely to occur within the event? What solutions need to be taught or strengthened?

- Most people have learned from experience how to predict, prevent, or manage small problems—an empty toothpaste tube, something blocking the way, someone sitting in a favorite seat, or a desired food out of reach. Most people know what to do when small accidents occur—something gets spilled or torn, a finger is cut by a sheet of paper, or a tooth begins to ache. Those with autism have few resources for solving a problem in order to move on.

Communicate and interact

What communication and social skills are essential? What others are possible?

- Some routines require communication, cooperation, or other social skills to accomplish the purpose of the event. The goal of some other activities could be achieved without communicating or socializing, but the activity would be more natural or more enjoyable if visiting and sharing were possible. Identify both the communication and social skills required to accomplish the purpose of the event (part of the core skills) and those that would make the event more interesting.

Make choices and decisions

What choices or decisions are essential? What others are possible? Are some decisions or choices not possible? Are decisions based on specific, concrete rules, or do they require more subtle judgments?

- Is it possible to choose the activity, to decide when to do the activity, the sequence of doing the task, where to do it, where to sit, whom to work with, which materials to use? How can options be clarified—both the things that can be done and those that are not possible?

- Decisions will be difficult to make if they depend on social judgments, abstract rules, or rules with many exceptions. Adaptations will likely be needed. Decisions based on concrete and unchanging rules are much easier.

Making informed choices and decisions is a complex issue and the cause of considerable stress. Refer to Making Informed Choices (chapter 23, pages 366-369).

> Jose worked as a quality control manager in a graphics arts business. It was a job particularly suited to his excellent ability to attend to small visual details. The rule for accepting or rejecting a product was simple and concrete: If there are any paint spots or smears outside the design, reject the product.

Self-Monitor

Does the quality of the participation or product meet the predetermined standard? Does the speed of participation or work match that of others?

- Most people continually check to see how others are performing, to see whether they are keeping up, doing things in a similar way with a similar quality. Most people know if their behavior is out of line, and they attempt to match their participation to the cultural or setting expectations. The learner with autism is generally unaware of the performance of others unless specifically taught to attend to those subtle cues. The social expectations, as well as the speed and quality expectations, must be identified.

Transition to next event

What is the next task? What should occur during transition to the next task?

- To stop one event and move to another, especially when it requires movement to a different location, is one of the most difficult tasks for those with autism. The transition plan must be so clear that success can be achieved without continual verbal direction or undue anxiety.

Step 3. Identify the natural cues and prompts

What is the signal or natural cue for starting the routine? How do others know when to begin this routine? What triggers each action in the routine? What is the natural cue that the event is over? (What does *finished* look like?) What prompts are naturally available to everyone in the situation or setting?

Each step or action throughout most routines is triggered by some natural environmental signal. In many situations, natural prompts are also available to maintain independent performance. The natural cues and prompts are identified by watching others complete the routine. (What signals do other people use to initiate, prepare, perform, and terminate a routine?) Attention to these natural cues and prompts leads to independence from another person to give directions.

The natural cue to initiate action may be hearing a bell, seeing the bus arrive, or noticing the laundry basket full of dirty clothes. Sometimes a teacher tells all the students that it is time for a specific event. Perhaps the calendar or appointment book indicates the time. In a routine, the natural cue for one step is frequently the completion of the previous step. The cue for terminating a routine could be a timer or the fact that the materials are used up, everything is put together, clean, put away, filled up, or the clock indicates time to end. Achievement of the critical effect or purpose of the routine may indicate being finished (for example, groceries were purchased, the meal cooked and eaten).

Read more about the principles and strategies for capitalizing on natural cues and prompts in chapter 17.

Note the natural cues listed on the Routine Planning sample (page 157). A basic rule for using cues and prompts is to avoid adding artificial verbal cues and prompts unless they will always be naturally available to everyone in that situation. *The addition of artificial verbal cues and prompts lead to dependence on others.*

Summary

A well-planned activity or routine ensures that all the critical elements are addressed so the learner can be as successful and as independent as possible. Planning events as functional routines provides a pattern for preparing the learner for new and changing events, for developing adaptations and support systems, and for evaluating and refining troublesome situations to prevent future problems. In chapter 18, this process is extended to plan instruction and design adaptations and teach functional skills in the context of natural routines.

CHAPTER

12 | Organize and Structure Space

Homes, classrooms, work, and other community settings are often crowded, sometimes cluttered and noisy. They have an organization that is not readily apparent to one who perceives the world differently and cannot modulate sensory stimuli or make sense of random information. Most people can scan an area and locate the organizational markers, and most people know how to move around in an area to get themselves in the right places. Very young children automatically learn by trial and error that they cannot simply walk directly to their target if other people, toys, or furniture are in their way. Young children also automatically learn to search for things they want and to ask for help in finding them. This automatic learning cannot be assumed in autism. Planning movement through space is often very difficult. Many learners have particular problems organizing, locating, or moving their own bodies in large spaces.

When learners have difficulty scanning, selecting, and making sense of the relevant and important details in the environment, they try to keep the arrangement of details the same. An environment makes sense only if it is familiar. The problem of scanning an area and selecting the relevant information also applies to such problems as locating important information on crowded bulletin boards or chalkboards and deciding where to begin to work on a page, wash a window, or rake leaves.

> The janitor had set up a ladder in the hall to change light bulbs. As Jose walked to the bathroom, he bumped into the ladder, stopped, and screamed helplessly. He was either unaware that he could move his body around the ladder or he was unable to plan and execute the action.
>
> Each time Jason entered the classroom, he cruised about straightening the papers on the teacher's desk, the books on the shelf, and the charts and maps on the walls. Even in the middle of concentrated effort, he would jump up, dash across the room, and adjust a paper, book, or chart that had just gotten out of line.
>
> Review the example of Ben (page 141), who could not relax at home until everything had been returned to its exact place. Ben even went from person to person uncrossing their legs and placing their feet side by side on the floor (in response to the rule: Shoes are placed side by side in the closet).

The Process for Organizing Space

Like the guide for a person who is blind, the interpreter's role is to organize and structure the objects in space to clarify where things are done, where things are located, and how to move from one place to another. The interpreter also must address the sensory factors that could interfere with optimum functioning.

There are five basic steps for organizing space:

1. Assess to address unique sensory and spatial problems.
2. Identify the location of activities.
3. Organize and refine the structure of the space.
4. Locate and label materials and supplies.
5. Continue to evaluate and refine.

Step 1. Assess to address unique sensory and spatial problems

The Checklist for Assessing Environmental Demands (form 6.1, page 75) is one resource for identifying specific problems in an area. The following behaviors signal problems that might be solved by refining some element of the space:

- Random wandering and searching behavior
- Apparent distraction by details or materials in the space
- Distraction by activity in other areas
- Sudden confusion or disorientation during small or larger transitions
- Leaving an area before the end of an activity
- Moving into off-limit areas
- Distraction or apparent pain from some specific sensory stimulation (for example, covering ears or eyes, running to hide in a dark or quiet area)
- Not beginning a task (for example, the learner just stands or sits as if waiting for something to happen)
- Safety problems

Step 2. Identify the location of activities

What needs to be done? Where is the best place to do it? In general, the answers are the same for those with autism as for others of the same age. For example, homes have places to sleep, cook, eat, and relax. Schools have places for large- and small-group and independent work, eating, playing, or hanging out. The same can be said of most community environments.

The learner with autism often has a need for two other areas: a quiet space for relief from stimulation, and an individual work area.

The Quiet Space

Refer to the section on teaching self-monitoring and self-control (chapter 23, pages 358-360).

A quiet space is needed at home, school, work, and sometimes in other community settings. This is not the traditional time-out area where a person is placed as a consequence for bad behavior. Rather, it is a positive place where the learner goes to prevent loss of control—a place to find relief from sensory overload and regain composure and control.

The quiet space must be readily accessible and comfortable, in an area somewhat sheltered from the noise and visual stimulation of busy activity. It must be located and arranged for easy supervision—a small area in the classroom or at home, behind a bookcase, divider, or couch. In other settings, a specific spot beside a wall or under a tree in a park, a specific bench in a quiet corner of the mall, or a specific chair or room at a party or at work can be designated to serve as a quiet place.

This area may need some specific equipment, such as a mat, a beanbag chair, a mini-trampoline, or a rocking chair, that contributes a calming effect for the learner. The occupational therapist is an excellent resource for assessing the specific needs of an individual learner.

While working as a groundskeeper, Gabriel became very agitated as he worried about visits to his mother and the conversations of his coworkers. His interpreter designated a convenient location under a specific tree near a certain section of a wall where he could go to do his relaxation routine, then return to work.

When 4-year-old Anne begins to get stressed, she runs to a rocking chair, rocks fast for a few minutes, then returns independently to the group. George, 10 years old, crawls under a mat behind a divider where it is quiet and dark. He finds that the pressure of the mat is calming. Brad regains his composure and direction by returning to his special work area where his daily calendar and other visual support systems are located.

The Individual Work Area

The work area for some more capable learners is the same as the work area for peers—a school desk or work station. However, most learners need a specifically designed work area that combines the functions of a department-store information counter and a work station in a busy office. This work area serves several purposes:

- It becomes a *familiar space* where new concepts, skills, jobs, and information can be introduced without conflicting or distracting stimulation.

- It becomes an information focal point where supplies and visual systems (daily calendar, checklists, cue cards, work files, and other visual references) can be arranged to support a variety of independent or cooperative activities in that or other locations. For example, at some times, tutoring can occur in this area or a friend may be invited to work or play cooperatively without interrupting others. In some situations, the learner naturally moves from this area with supplies to work or participate in other locations.

The location and design of this area depends on the age and very specific needs of the learner and the demands of the setting. In general, the area should be located away from major traffic paths and noisy activity. But even when some learners have a visual barrier, they are so distracted by the noise of other activities that they constantly get up and look over or around the barrier. These learners need an area near the back of a room where they can survey the action with a quick glance, then return quickly to work.

A bulletin board or wall for mounting visual references and a shelf or shelves for supplies should be close by.

Tony wandered randomly about his home, constantly in trouble, becoming more and more frustrated, anxious, and stressed. When his family prepared a personal work station in their home that included his daily calendar, lists of jobs, and leisure options, he finally knew what he could do from moment to moment. When he was taught to follow the visual systems that included directions for his jobs, Tony relaxed and moved with purpose throughout the day. No longer was he unprepared for coming events. No longer did he need someone beside him every minute to tell him what to do or keep him out of trouble. His mother or father organized and explained the schedule to him each day, provided periodic support, and taught him new tasks to add variety and expand his skills.

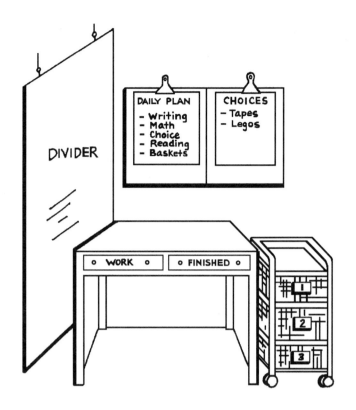

Examples of three work areas

Step 3. Organize and refine the structure of the space

Each of the various areas needs clearly defined boundaries to help maintain focus in an area until the end of an event and to facilitate travel from one area to another.

Boundaries are like frames that separate the material or activity inside the frame from the material or activity outside the frame. The most obvious way to define the boundaries of large areas is to use rugs, bookcases, dividers, or other existing furniture. For example, use a rug to define an area for playing with toys, move bookcases and dividers to block out some of the stimulation between areas, and arrange a couch or desks to highlight walkways and control the flow of traffic.

Once the various locations and boundaries are identified, post signs or symbols to designate which events occur in each area—play/leisure, work/vocational, cooking/eating, study, conference or group area, and supplies.

Sometimes, temporary markers are needed to define a specific work area or to remind a learner to stay in a specific area. Temporary markers have solved many different kinds of space problems. For example:

- A string, yarn, plastic tape, or strip of crepe paper taped across an opening serves as a reminder to stay in or out of an area.

- A small stop-sign propped on a chair was all one child needed to stay out of an area.

- Stakes and string can define an area of a garden for planting or weeding.

- A tape line across the middle of a work table can clarify a shared work area.

- A sticky-note placed in each corner of a table or at the left top and the right bottom corner of a window identifies starting and ending points for cleaning. The learner is taught to place the notes and to work from top to bottom and from left to right, removing the notes as each area is finished.

- A strip of crepe paper placed around an assignment on a chalkboard defines and isolates it from other material.

- A small piece of tape placed on the gym floor specifies where to stand during calisthenics.

- A mark on a specific chair (indoors) or sign post (outdoors) indicates where to stay while waiting for the bus.

- A tape line on the floor shows where to line up.

These temporary markers are simple to remove when it is time to leave an area or when they are no longer needed. Those who wander or run away are not always aware of natural boundary markers. To prevent harm, it is very important to clarify the boundaries and hazards in every new situation.

> The students in the third grade class were asked to copy a favorite poem onto paper and make a decorative frame around it for Mother's Day gifts. As the other children finished, Gabriel was still sitting with a blank piece of paper. His interpreter, who had just returned to the room, said, "Which poem are you going to copy?" Gabriel pointed to the poem. "Which border are you going to draw?" Again, he indicated his choice by pointing. Then the interpreter said, "Where are you going to start?" Gabriel made no response. After a brief pause, the interpreter placed a small x on the paper and said, "Start here." Gabriel immediately sat up and began to work.

Two groups of students were sharing the gym, one on each side of the center line. Matt was riding his tricycle all over the gym, disrupting both groups. To solve the problem, his interpreter, with paper and pencil in hand, knelt down beside Matt and began to draw as he said, "Matt, you can ride your tricycle on this side of the big black line. Can you ride on the other side of the line? No. You can ride on this side of the line." He took Matt to the center line, laid the drawing at the end of the line, and showed him specifically where he could and could not ride. From that time on, Matt rode only in the designated area.

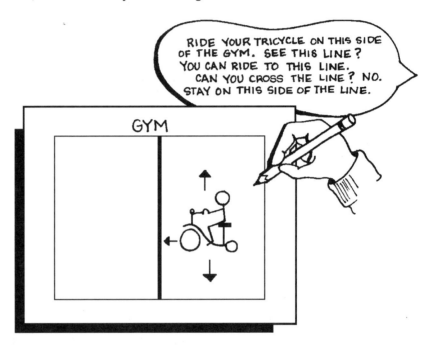

To prepare learners for managing themselves in the community, they must be made aware of natural cues and markers. Highlight or point out:

- The light over the checkout stand in the store
- The crowd-control ropes in post offices, banks, and airports that signal people to line up in order of arrival
- The lines painted on streets to define crosswalks

When learners know exactly what to do, what they cannot do, and where the boundaries are, they are generally cooperative and successful. In the following example, the interpreter was quick to use what was at hand to clarify the situation for Matt.

As the class of 3- and 4-year-old children left the bus for a picnic, the interpreter saw Matt break away and run toward the lake. She quickly followed and caught him at the edge of the lake, got down on her knees, took his hand, and said softly but clearly, "Matt, keep your toes behind this line." (She drew a line in the sand at the edge of the lake.) "You can put your fingers in the water, and you can play with these rocks in the water." (She pointed to rocks and placed one in the water.) "You can play with the sticks in the water." (She pointed to the sticks and placed one in the water.) "Can you put your toes in the water? No. Keep your toes behind this line. You can put your fingers in the water, the rocks in the water, and the sticks in the water; but your toes stay behind this line." (She pointed to and pressed on the toes of his shoes that were behind the line.) "Good! Your toes are behind the line." Then she moved away and watched closely. Two or three times she moved to him and played briefly in the water beside him as she complimented his ability to keep his feet behind the line. Matt enjoyed himself at the water's edge with his feet behind the line for more than 20 minutes until it was time for lunch.

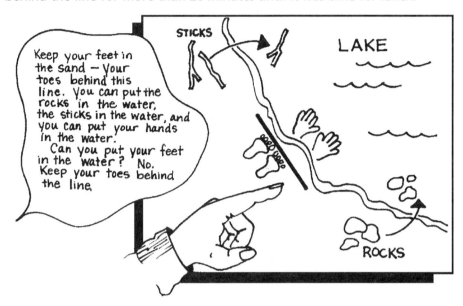

While this amount of verbal detail might seem excessive for a 4-year-old with limited verbal abilities, learners with autism need specific information and all the important and relevant details in order to know exactly what they are to do and not to do. Note that the verbal information was supported with visual references—the line in the sand, the pointing and modeling (placing fingers, rocks, and sticks in the water). *Reinforcement was provided in a quiet, natural manner that did not overstimulate or distract Matt from his appropriate play.*

Step 4. Locate and label materials and supplies

It is less stressful and easier to participate effectively when materials and supplies are arranged close to the area where they are to be used. Some learners with autism become disoriented and distracted during a search for needed materials. While there is a great deal of variation from one learner to another, many will not remember where something is stored if it is not in view—they forget to open a closet or cupboard door to look inside. The following suggestions have been helpful for many learners.

- Remove supplies that belong to or are used only by others, or label them clearly *(Teacher's things; Dad's things)*.

- Label storage containers, or use clear containers so contents are easy to identify.

- Remove cleaning supplies, medical supplies, and other potentially dangerous materials. Store them in safe and locked areas.

- Label shelves, drawers, and cupboard and closet doors to show where to find and return items.

- Organize a work table by taping three pieces of heavy paper on the table from left to right. Label the piece on the left *Supplies*, label the one in the middle *Work*, and label the paper on the right *Finished*. With these markers, the learner knows where to place a tub or box of supplies, where to do the work, and where to place a tub for the finished work. When the tub of supplies is empty and the completed work is in the *Finished* area, it is obvious that the work is completed.

- Develop simple maps to orient a learner to a new setting and as a reference for locating materials or moving from one room or building to another. Most very young children with autism can learn to use maps, a valuable lifelong skill that increases independence. Teach young learners to use maps of the room, building, and community. Some more advanced learners can make their own detailed maps and learn to use commercially prepared maps.

Involve the learner in making future changes in the setting. For example, the learner can help make decisions about a new location for furniture or supplies, help move the furniture and supplies, and help prepare and place signs and labels.

Step 5. Evaluate and refine

Interpreters continually evaluate the problems and refine the structure to resolve problems as quickly as possible. Once interpreters become aware of the range of problems and of simple strategies to clarify and structure space, they become very creative in resolving a learner's problems in space.

Summary

As the environment becomes more organized and meaningful, anxiety decreases and independence increases. Many of the problems in space are subtle and have simple solutions. Other students in a classroom also can benefit from this clarity.

Organize and Structure Events in Time

Most people have considerable control of their lives. To a large degree, people can choose what to do and when to do them. They also can choose not to do many things perceived as unpleasant or disliked. The ability to analyze and make sense of experiences and keep the information in sequential order allows most people to predict future experiences. This ability to predict and prepare for events and to plan and anticipate pleasant future events helps them deal with unpleasant or frustrating situations.

Those with autism generally do not have this kind of ability or control. Much that takes place in their lives is planned by others. Often they are coerced or taken into new or unpleasant activities and situations with little or no preparation. When they resist or try to avoid the confusion and stress that is present in these situations, their freedom and options are even more limited. These learners become increasingly inflexible. Severe anxiety and behavior problems occur when they must change a routine (for example, to wear new clothes, see a doctor, or move to a new home).

An individually designed calendar—a visual representation of events in time—compensates for many of these problems. When the calendar is based on a systematically organized schedule, it is one of the most important tools to address the problems of those who:

- Are fearful and resist changes and new situations
- Develop rigid, inflexible routines quickly
- Have difficulty predicting future events
- Have a limited number of reinforcing, liked activities.

The calendar, when reviewed consistently each morning, referenced throughout the day, and refined to match expanding skills, provides the natural structure to achieve critical goals (figure 7.1, page 105) to increase:

- Flexibility and tolerance for new and changing events
- Active participation, motivation, and persistence
- Language concepts related to time, space, events, and settings
- Ability to communicate preferences
- Ability to work and function independently
- Ability to make choices and decisions for self-management

This chapter provides guidelines for systematically organizing events in time—a prerequisite for designing the visual representation of those events, the calendar.

The relationship of severe behavior problems to schedules of events that do not match the individual's need for predictability is discussed in chapter 4.

Terminology

The terminology defined below is used in this and the following chapters with very specific meaning:

- *Scheduling* is a planning process that organizes a sequence of events to achieve a goal.

- A *schedule* is the product of that planning process. It is a plan or an arrangement of events to accomplish goals.

- A *calendar* is the visual representation of that plan, always available for frequent reference.

This distinction between a schedule and a calendar is made to emphasize the importance of the planning process involved in ordering the events in time to achieve goals and the importance of the calendar for communicating that sequence of events to the learner.

- A *mini-calendar* supplements a basic daily calendar and shows the sequence of specific activities scheduled to occur within small blocks of time.

- A *calendar system* is the combination and integration of all the elements that make up an effective calendar—one that will have an optimum effect.

Scheduling Principles

The process for developing schedules is based on two generally accepted rules of reinforcement. These rules state that:

1. If a reinforcing event occurs immediately as a direct result of effort and action (a response, behavior), it is more likely that the same effort and action will recur and be strengthened.

2. If a liked activity (a reinforcing event) immediately follows a disliked activity (a painful or frustrating event), it is likely that the disliked activity will increase its value and become a liked activity—a new reinforcing event (Premack and Collier 1962).

When these rules are applied as events are sequenced in time, there will be less need to use artificial food and verbal reinforcers. As with other behavioral principles, alternate or paradoxical effects can occur unless the principles are applied precisely. For example, *if a liked activity is always followed by a disliked activity, the liked activity will become disliked and lose its value as a reinforcer.* Therefore, simply alternating liked and disliked activities or randomly interspersing liked and disliked activities will not achieve the desired effect for these learners.

The Process

There are three steps for organizing and structuring events in time to ensure maximum effect:

1. Assess the reinforcing value of activities.

2. Organize the events to develop the schedule.

3. Evaluate and refine the schedule.

Step 1. Assess the reinforcing value of activities

Two procedures are helpful for assessing the reinforcing value of activities and the elements of activities that may trigger problems:

1. Preference Survey. This survey provides a format for identifying the activities that the learner likes to do, those that the learner would not choose but would willingly do if asked, and those activities that are resisted or that cause difficulty. The list includes both regularly occurring activities and those that occur periodically, whether optional or required. When completed, this survey provides a great number of activities that can add variety to the schedule.

   See form 6.6 (page 92) for a reproducible Preference Survey form. See figure 13.1 (page 172) and Case Study (page 423) for completed samples of this form.

2. Assessment of Daily Life Activities. This assessment pinpoints qualities and sequences of regularly scheduled activities that affect the learner's feelings and behavior. It addresses the importance of the activity as well as whether it is age-appropriate, too difficult or too easy; possible choices; and the number and types of problems that occur while participating in the activity. This information is important for modifying a schedule to solve a problem.

   See form 6.7 (page 93) for a reproducible Assessment of Daily Life Activities form. See figure 13.2 (page 173) for a completed sample of this form.

Step 2. Organize the events to develop the schedule

To develop an effective schedule, the events are systematically arranged to maximize their reinforcing qualities. The formula in figure 13.3, which is based on the two principles of reinforcement, guides the sequencing of events. This formula is used to develop the daily schedule and to develop mini-schedules for individual routines or short work sessions.

The major considerations to ensure maximum benefit are:

1. Begin and end the schedule with familiar and positive activities. This sets the stage for a pleasant experience and ends on a positive note, and the learner will be eager to return to or repeat the activity at another time.

2. Follow disliked activities with liked activities, to reinforce hard work and increase tolerance.

3. Follow liked activities with familiar and tolerated activities, to avoid losing the power of the reinforcing activities and to avoid resistance when ending the liked activity.

4. Follow familiar or tolerated activities with disliked activities.

In summary, when disliked activities are scheduled systematically and followed by a highly liked activity, the learner's tolerance and skills will increase. These once disliked activities *become tolerated and many will eventually become highly liked, new reinforcing activities.*

Caution: If a liked activity is always followed by a disliked activity, it will lose its value as a reinforcer!

The optimum effect of this schedule will be achieved when:

1. The schedule is flexible

2. The schedule includes variety

3. The learner knows what is on the schedule

4. The schedule is continually evaluated and refined

Figure 13.1. Sample: Preference Survey

Adapted from *Judevine® Training System* (Blackwell 1978)

Student: Becky   **Date:** July 12

LIKES What people, objects, or activities are liked a lot or selected during free time?	TOLERATES What is done when asked, but never done if not asked?	DISLIKES What people, objects, or activities are resisted, avoided or rejected?
Quiet spaces	Reading activities—class	Noise
Animal picture books	Math activities—class	Confusion
Puppets	Spelling and other classes	Cold
Familiar jobs: • Water plants • Straighten bookshelves • Wash sink • Feed fish • Empty waste baskets	Working with flash cards Writing activities and worksheets Language Master/computer Table game with one other person	Lunchroom Gym Recess Unstructured/creative activities
Play music tapes		Putting on outdoor clothing
Eat: • Crackers with jelly • Graham crackers with frosting		Playing active games Waiting/sitting and listening
Knead and role clay		Changes
Dress doll		
Stickers		
Puzzles (mazes and jigsaw)		
Drawing lines on paper		
Sitting beside Suzy		
Calendar review process		
Eating lunch/meals		
Walking outside		
Swinging		

Figure 13.2. Sample: Assessment of Daily Life Activities: Informant Interview

Adapted from Oregon Regional Autism Services

Student: _Becky_ **Date:** _December 15_

Directions: This form is used to structure an interview to determine the relationship of various conditions to problem behavior. First, parents and/or staff members make notes on a copy of the form prior to the interview. The interviewer then structures questions to clarify the details and to enlarge on the examples. When making comments, give details such as: types of problems, environmental conditions when problems occur, types of assistance, consequences, types of directions, and the possible perspective of the student when problems occur.

Time from/to	Activity Location/Supervisor and Group Size	Is this activity: Age-appropriate?	Meaningful?	Liked?	Does the individual have: Choice? Control?	Problems?	Comments Give details
8:15–8:25	calendar review classroom/1:1 with Judy	yes	yes	yes	some	no	Shows lots of interest. It is in a quiet corner of classroom with favorite person.
8:25–10:00	reading, math, spelling small-group and independent desk work, with Judy or Tom	yes	yes	generally OK	very little	restless sometimes	Desk work adapted, so works independently. Group work—pretty much follows along
10:00–10:20	recess in gym	yes	sometimes	no	could select activity	yes and no	Room is quiet and calm. If left alone, she walks along, trailing fingers on wall, staring at wall or hand. Attempts to involve her: screams, kicks, pulls away
10:20–11:40	in hall, to and from gym large group (2 classes), with Judy + 1 other staff	yes	maybe—the purpose is to get a break, release energy	generally	some	rarely	Same as earlier. Noisy, crowded. Has trouble holding and carrying bulky things.
11:40–11:50	classroom—academic as before	yes	usually	no	no	yes, always—screams, kicks, resists	
11:50–12:45	Prepare for lunch and recess outside. Gather lunch box and snow clothes to carry to lunchroom lunchroom	yes	yes	yes and no	no	yes	Likes to eat lunch. Doesn't like to sit near peers. Puts hands over eyes or gets under table.
etc.							

Figure 13.3. Formula for sequencing events in time
To capitalize on the reinforcing qualities of the activities

Adapted with permission from *Judevine® Training System* (Blackwell 1978)

Activity 1. Moderately liked activity—a pleasant beginning

Activity 2. Familiar and tolerated activity

Activity 3. Disliked activity

Activity 4. Most liked activity

Activity 5. Familiar or tolerated activity

Activity 6. Familiar or tolerated activity

Activity 7. Another disliked activity

Activity 8. A different highly liked activity

Activity 9. Familiar or tolerated activity

Activity 10. Continue to rotate as above

Final Activity. Pleasant and liked—a positive ending

Definitions

Activities can include functional routines (for example, cooking or dressing), recess, lunch, going home, free time, or a leisure activity, work or vocational task, social event, playing a game, or any priority IEP activity.

Liked activities are those that the learner would like to do all the time or that are highly motivating at specific times.

Familiar or tolerated activities are those that the individual is not likely to select during free time but would do willingly if asked or if they were scheduled. These activities may not be totally mastered, but they are familiar and not too difficult. With increasing practice and familiarity, these activities are likely to shift and *become valued and liked reinforcing activities*.

Disliked activities are those the learner resists and tries to avoid. Disliked activities are generally new, difficult, or confusing. A disliked activity needs further assessment to determine which element or elements of the activity are disliked.

Schedules Need to be Flexible

The amount of time spent in each activity depends on the learner's age, attention span, and whether the activity is liked, tolerated, or disliked. Three general rules apply:

1. Time spent on a difficult, stressful, or disliked activity should be brief. The activity must end at or just before the peak of effort and interest. Subtle, non-verbal signs of fatigue or frustration are signals for the interpreter to end or switch from the disliked activity to a liked activity before inappropriate or ineffective behavior occurs. For example, as the learner shows signs of rest-lessness, say, "Wow! You have worked hard. You can stop now and do _____ " (a liked activity).

   To avoid negative or paradoxical effects, *it is essential for a difficult or disliked activity to end before boredom or frustration interrupts attention and effort*. If a disliked activity ends after the learner begins to fidget or stops working, the individual will learn to fidget and stop working to end an activity. This negative reinforcement builds very strong negative behavior.

2. The reinforcing, liked activity should last as long or a bit longer than the difficult or disliked activity that precedes it. To help a learner willingly end a liked activity:

Refer to Application of Behavior Principles, chapter 17, pages 238-243.

To increase persistence and tolerance for working longer, refer to Guidelines for Using Contingencies, chapter 16, pages 214-220.

- Prepare the learner with a contingency statement and a timer or other concrete signal. As you set the timer, say, "When the bell rings, it will be time to put the tape player away and do ___" (a familiar tolerated activity).

- The learner must know and trust that the liked activity will be offered again. On the calendar or mini-calendar, indicate when the activity is scheduled again.

- *Avoid following a liked activity with a disliked activity.*

3. Decrease time demands when the learner's tolerance is low and the stress level is high. Recognize and respect the learner's variable tolerance and ability levels. Pushing beyond the learner's tolerance increases resistance, is likely to trigger problems, and decreases the learner's willingness to return to the activity another day.

Schedules Need to Have Variety

Variety increases motivation and flexibility and decreases the likelihood of developing rigid routines. Mothers often report that boredom is a major contributor to restlessness, anxiety, and a variety of repetitive behaviors. Alertness, interest, and effective behavior are increased when change and variety are well organized and structured systematically. Four strategies can guide the inclusion of variety into a schedule:

1. While the calendar and other basic structures remain the same, change at least one or perhaps several elements of the schedule each day. Provide a different activity, a different sequence of activities, different materials, different locations, different people, or a different time.

2. Balance the schedule to include activities that are inactive and active, fine motor and gross motor, quiet and noisy, as well as those that are liked and disliked. Also include individual, independent, cooperative, and small- or large-group activities.

3. To avoid resistance, do not repeat the same activity or routine in a single day or a single session unless it would be natural for others to repeat it. For example, it is normal to eat and wash hands several times a day, but generally it would not be natural to sweep the same floor twice in one day.

4. To avoid overwhelming the learner with too much confusing stimulation from new or changing events, introduce a new element within a familiar situation. For example, a familiar person introduces a new activity in a familiar setting, or a new person is introduced into a familiar activity in a familiar setting. An individual calendar provides a familiar situation for introducing variations and new activities.

Step 3. Evaluate and refine the schedule

Increasing tolerance leads to increasing practice time; and increasing practice time leads to increasing skills. To ensure progress, the reinforcing qualities of the natural activities must be continually assessed to reflect changing tolerances, skills, and preferences. The reproducible checklist on page 176 will guide the evaluation of a schedule to ensure that it is balanced and organized systematically.

Systematically add new, difficult, and disliked activities and expand the dimensions of activities. For example, if a once-disliked game has now become a reinforcing event, involve different people in playing the game, play the game in different settings, or add a different game in the familiar setting with familiar people. This expansion is essential for generalizing new skills and for increasing flexibility and the number of reinforcing events, people, and settings.

Balance

Over the course of a day, or week, the schedule includes:

1. **Skill development**
   - ☐ Developmental skills
   - ☐ Academic skills
   - ☐ Creative skills
   - ☐ Functional skills

2. **A balance of:**
   - ☐ Work
   - ☐ Play/leisure (seriousness and silliness)

3. **Experiences that are:**
   - ☐ Learner-directed
   - ☐ Interpreter-directed (parent or staff)

4. **Activity with others:**
   - ☐ Partnerships
   - ☐ Small-group
   - ☐ Large-group

5. **Opportunities for:**
   - ☐ Active involvement
   - ☐ Quiet recovery

6. **Work and/or leisure requiring:**
   - ☐ Quiet sitting
   - ☐ Movement
   - ☐ Strenuous exercise

7. **Opportunities to:**
   - ☐ Be independent
   - ☐ Help others
   - ☐ Receive help from peers

8. **Interactions with others of:**
   - ☐ Different ages
   - ☐ Different interests
   - ☐ Different abilities

9. **Instruction and practice in:**
   - ☐ Natural settings
   - ☐ Simulated settings

10. **Opportunities to pursue:**
    - ☐ Special interests and aptitudes
    - ☐ Special friendships

Structure

- ☐ Is the first activity familiar and pleasant?
- ☐ Is the last activity familiar and liked?
- ☐ Is there at least one familiar/tolerated activity before each disliked activity?
- ☐ Does the number of familiar/tolerated activities in one sequence vary from one to several?
- ☐ Is each disliked activity followed by a highly liked activity?
- ☐ Are new activities added frequently?
- ☐ Does each day's schedule include at least one change?

When evaluating a problem that may be resolved by refining the schedule, consider:

1. An event or a complex functional routine is composed of many small steps or mini-activities. Some may be difficult and disliked, others may be only tolerated, while others are easy and liked. Adaptations will be needed if too many elements of a routine are difficult, frustrating, or boring; that is, disliked. For example, visual adaptations may clarify and ease some of the difficult steps of the routine, or a break could be inserted into a routine to relieve frustration or tension. A break could be as simple as "taking five" to get a drink or look out the window for a few minutes before continuing the routine. If a routine is boring, but still an important task, incorporate a self-monitoring system, mini-calendar, or some concrete way to show progress toward completion.

2. In integrated settings, the learner's liked activities may be different from those of peers. Adaptations may be needed to ensure that reinforcing (liked) activities are sufficiently available.

To illustrate this situation, consider the sample Preference Survey on page 172 and the sample Assessment of Daily Life Activities on page 173, which were completed during the assessment of Becky's problems described below.

Becky was enrolled in a regular third grade class where she participated and worked very well in all the morning activities. At lunch time, stress was evident, and she screamed and resisted nearly all activities in the afternoon. When the afternoon schedule was analyzed, it was found that every activity was either disliked or barely tolerated. This was very surprising for the teacher, who assumed that all children liked lunch, recess, quiet time when the teacher read aloud to the group, and art and science activities.

It is easy to understand Becky's stress when the requirements of those afternoon activities were analyzed:

- Lunch time: Gather coat, boots, hat, gloves, and lunch box; walk in line to the lunch room; wait to enter; place belongings on the floor; find a table and eat; wait to be excused; put on outdoor clothes. Nearly every step was painful and disliked. The noise and echoes in the cafeteria also were stressful.

- Recess: Outdoor clothing was uncomfortable and restricted movement, the cold wind was painful on Becky's face, and the required play with peers was very confusing and disliked.

- After recess, quiet/reading time: Returning to the classroom required another struggle with clothing. Becky didn't understand the language of the story, and sitting quietly with no meaningful activity was difficult for her.

- Art and science classes: Changes, movement, and noise from independent activity and unfamiliar directions were confusing.

When Becky's schedule and activities were adapted to match her current needs, she was able to tolerate and participate successfully in most of the afternoon activities. The following adaptations were based on her preferences—quiet spaces, books, puppets, familiar jobs (watering plants, straightening book shelves, washing the sink):

- Lunch time: Leave outside clothing in the classroom; sit with familiar peers at the end of the lunch room instead of with the class in the middle of the room with conversations all around; ask permission to leave the lunchroom when finished eating; return to class and put on outside clothing in a quiet area. (Assistance will be provided, since this task is still difficult.)

- Recess: Before leaving for recess, choose two activities and write them on a cue card for reference on the playground. (Assistance will be provided for difficult cooperative play.) Return to the classroom early when the two activities are complete. Remove outside clothing in the quiet room, and then go to the library to straighten books.

- Quiet/reading time: Play quietly at desk with puppets or other liked material selected during calendar review time early in the day.

- Art and science classes: Refer to the mini-calendar for the art and science activities. (Intersperse some familiar jobs—watering plants, straightening bookshelves, washing the sink.)

Summary

See chapters 14 and 15 for considerations in designing and developing a calendar, a visual representation of events in time.

To prepare for changes and transitions, the learner needs information in a concrete and visual format that can be referenced frequently—a calendar that clarifies what will happen, when it will happen, what will happen next, and when preferred activities will occur. The value of a visual reference is not unique to autism. Most adults use some kind of calendar, appointment book, or reminder system to help them through busy days. A calendar that visually represents an individually designed schedule is a powerful and versatile adaptation for achieving many of the critical goals.

Design Visual Adaptations

The case for visual adaptations to compensate for deficits in autism was made in previous chapters that discussed the effects of the learning style. It is clear that learners with autism need information to function effectively—information that is visually clear and permanent for frequent reference and understanding. While systematic organization and structure of events, space, and time provide information to allow for more effective learning and independence, there is still a need to clarify ideas, concepts, sequences and processes. In chapters 14 through 16, strategies are presented for clarifying information visually to promote thinking, problem solving, self-management, interactions, and the ability to manipulate more abstract ideas.

In this chapter, a background is presented for making design decisions and constructing visual adaptations that will apply to many different situations. Chapter 15 contains a variety of visual systems for self-management and strategies for organizing information visually to highlight meaning so information can be used and applied. The concepts presented in chapter 15 also apply to the design and construction of visual communication systems that are presented in chapter 20.

Symbol Selection

Symbols are objects, emblems, words, signs, or conventional marks that represent something else. Visual information systems are based on symbols to represent real things and ideas. Typically, children learn about symbols and begin to use them during the first two years of life. They automatically learn that sounds, toys, and photographs can represent people and things. When these young children begin to imitate and pretend, it is obvious that they understand some fairly abstract symbols. For example, very young children will pick up a toy telephone, a block, or a banana and pretend to talk on a phone. They look at a photo of mother, point to the picture, and smile as they look at mother. A slightly older child sees a stop sign and shouts, "Stop!" while bracing for stopping.

The following progression, listed from the least abstract to the most abstract, is assumed to be the easiest to master for young children with learning differences:

1. Real objects (keys mean *ride in the car*, cup means *drink)*

2. Parts of real objects (a piece of chain represents the swing)

3. Miniatures of real objects, such as toys

4. Abstract objects, such as blocks

5. Photographs and magazine pictures

6. Abstract pictures (line drawings)

7. Printed and written words

Development in autism does not follow a typical step-by-step progression.
Learners with autism are very concrete and routine based, with little understanding of representational thinking. These learners do not automatically use objects to imitate and pretend. For example, one 4-year-old with autism had a toy school bus that was seen as a container—the child turned it upside down and carefully filled it with blocks. Never did he pretend it was a bus to drive about. Yet at the age of 3, he had learned to read some words, to read and write numbers, and to count to 100 without specific instruction.

It is difficult to know which symbols are understood or how a symbol is understood by an individual learner, because accurate and conventional meanings are not automatically associated or attached to everyday experiences.

Typical Problems in Understanding Symbols

Assume that a familiar object such as a medium-sized blue ball is chosen to represent recess time. From the perspective of a very literal learner, confusion can occur for any one or several of the following reasons:

- If a round, blue, bouncy object is a ball, and a ball is to throw, bounce, hit, kick, or catch, how can a football or a golf ball also be a ball?

- How can a ball or a photograph of a ball relate to a time period, such as recess, where various kinds of ball games might be played and many activities without balls also occur?

- If a ball is for throwing, bouncing, hitting, kicking, and catching, are those the only things one can do at recess time? A learner who tries to use the symbol literally may resist doing anything other than play ball during recess.

- If a ball takes on a broader meaning as a symbol for a period of time, it may lose its meaning as a toy for play. How is the learner to know when to play ball and when to simply go to recess?

Not only the type of symbol but the actual object selected to represent a time period can cause learned errors and confusion. If a drawing of a coat is used to represent going outside, it is likely that the learner will insist on wearing a coat whenever it is time to go outside, even in warm weather. This insistence is not related to retardation; neither is it a control issue or stubbornness. The learner is simply trying to follow the rule exactly as taught: This symbol means put on your coat, then go outside.

Real objects, photographs, magazine pictures, and colorful or comical drawings have a myriad of details that distract from the relevant details. Blemishes, labels, color, decoration, and people interfere with accurate and precise associations between the event and the symbol and with generalized use of the symbol in various situations.

> Colorful picture cards from a commercial language program were used for symbols on Matt's calendar. One day the picture of the sandwich, representing lunch time, was missing. When his interpreter replaced it with a picture of a sandwich from another set, Matt became upset. He kept saying, "Number 57," and he refused to go to lunch. In assessing the situation, the staff found an exact replica of the original picture and discovered that it had a tiny 57 printed in the top corner. Matt, who was fascinated by numbers, had selected the number as the relevant cue, ignoring the picture even though it was much larger and colorful.

Photographs of people in the setting are confusing to some learners. For example, a photograph of the learner sitting at his desk was confusing to one learner because the chair was always empty when he approached his desk. If a photograph shows the teacher leading a specific class and there is a substitute, the learner will be confused. (From the learner's perspective: "The picture says the teacher must be there. No one else can be in the teacher's place. This isn't right. What do I do now?")

A picture cut from a catalog or magazine is likely to have details that will distract the learner from the relevant cues in the picture. For example, a manufacturer's label in a photograph is likely to catch attention before the actual object in the picture.

> Jose learned to get ready for bed by looking at a sequence of drawings that showed him putting on and wearing his favorite blue pajamas with a star on the front. One evening, when those pajamas had been left at his grandmother's house, Jose refused to put on a different pair. When his mother drew another sequence of pictures that showed him in a different pair of pajamas, he put them on immediately.

Some learners are confused when line drawings made by different people are not exactly the same. In these cases, the new symbol must be retaught. For example, "This is a drawing of a desk and it means time to work. It looks a little different from the old picture, but it means the same thing."

See chapter 19 for strategies for teaching language concepts to address the problem of literal understanding.

Words can present problems for some learners. As with line drawings, some learners are confused by different handwriting and styles of print. Again, they must be taught that everyone writes a little differently but the words mean the same. A second problem relates to the very literal understanding of words.

Criteria for Symbol Selection

The gaps, discrepancies, and scattered skills common in autism not only cause confusion for learners but present a dilemma to those who select symbols for their first visual systems. The types of symbols selected for an individual will determine the effectiveness of the system.

Select a type of symbol that:

1. Is used spontaneously and meaningfully for at least a few basic purposes

   For example, a child who brings the car keys whenever he wants to go for a ride and who gets a glass to express a desire for a drink is likely to progress quickly with concrete objects as symbols.

2. Is free of previous associations that could confuse the meaning or limit generalization to a broader class of activities

3. Is generic; that is, free from detail that distracts from the relevant cues

4. Is attractive and interesting *to the learner*

5. Is matched to motor development and ability to manipulate

6. Will be easy to expand or shape to a more abstract level

Because they are so literal, concrete, and visual, most learners with autism progress rather quickly from the use of concrete objects to using line drawings and written words.

Concrete object symbols are generally required for very young learners with little or no concept that everything has a label or that an object can represent something else. At this early stage, the lesson is that everything has a name and a purpose; a round, bouncy object is a ball, and a ball means "Play ball."

See the activities in chapter 19, pages 271-273, for strategies to teach and expand symbol concepts.

Objects are most likely to match the motor skills of the toddler to 3-year-old. The transition from object symbols to line drawings is rather easy and can begin almost immediately by structuring simple, everyday play experiences.

Generic black-and-white line drawings have several unique qualities that make them particularly useful for learners with autism who:

- Have the motor dexterity and control to pick up and carry a card
- Line up toys, books, or papers and notice when they are out of line
- Look at magazines, newspapers, books, or product labels
- Are fascinated by lines or like to draw lines and pictures
- Read or write words
- Show interest in numbers, calendars, and clocks and read or write numbers

Generic black-and-white line drawings generally match the criteria for symbol selection (page 181). They are free of previous associations to confuse the meaning or to limit generalization to a broader class of activities. If designed correctly, they also are free of irrelevant elements and details that interfere with accurate associations, meanings, and generalizations (Groden and LaVasseur 1995).

Printed or written words have many of the same advantages as line drawings. As part of the natural language, they are easier for strangers, friends, and mentors to understand. Use of written words in visual systems increases reading comprehension and spelling skills.

Line drawings and words have several additional advantages. They are:

- Interesting and attractive

  Generally, learners are highly motivated by lines and print and by watching someone draw and print. (The learner with autism is not an art critic. Often simple stick figures and outlines are the most meaningful.)

- Relatively easy for literal learners to associate with the intended meaning, because these individuals make such quick associations

  For example, print the words *work time* under a simple outline of a desk while saying, "This is a picture of a desk. It means work time." If the drawing is immediately carried to the work area, it will likely be associated with work time after only a few experiences.

- Easy to draw to solve an immediate problem

- Easy to individualize to match a learner's need in a specific problem to highlight the most relevant cues

- Cheaper and more efficient to incorporate in systems than photographs

- Easy and quick to adapt, add to, or replace when different needs are identified or if the original symbol is soiled, torn, or lost

Some learners are more motivated by print than by object and photo symbols.

Matt, 5 years old, was not interested in his communication system or his calendar designed with photographs. His team followed a traditional rule of instruction: If the student makes errors or does not learn the lesson within a reasonable time, drop to a lower level of difficulty. The photos were replaced with miniature objects. When Matt continued to ignore his calendar, his support team sought consultation from a communication specialist who had considerable experience in autism.

This assessment showed that Matt was highly interested in line drawings and words and that he could read many words. Much to the surprise of his team, he began to use the systems once printed words and line drawings paired with words were incorporated.

In summary, every symbol, whether it is an object, line drawing, or printed word symbol, must be presented precisely to ensure that the correct associations are made. It is also necessary to be cautious in selecting the specific symbol to represent a specific activity in order to avoid learned errors and a need to reteach a rule.

Construction of Visual Systems

Consider the following criteria and construction strategies as design decisions are made. A visual system must be:

- Quick and easy to construct and use
- Flexible—easy to adapt to match changing needs and situations
- Sturdy to use, reuse, and carry around
- Inexpensive
- Visually clear and concrete, free of unnecessary details or decoration
- Effective and as age-appropriate and nonstigmatizing as possible

The issue of effectiveness is paramount. While it is important for an adaptation to be age-appropriate, if it is not effective, then it has no value.

Construction Strategies

The key to preparing a visual system is to have it ready as quickly as possible and to modify it as soon as a need is identified. When systems are not available immediately, are expensive, and require time to construct:

- Behavior problems may intensify and needs may change before the system is ready
- Systems are less likely to be refined as needs change
- Systems may be protected and preserved and less available to the learner for frequent day-to-day use

Specific decision requirements are described in chapter 15 for each type of visual system— calendar, checklist, and others.

Several design decisions are required before construction begins. The most important decisions relate to the type of symbols, the purpose of the system, how the symbols will be managed, and the amount of detail and information needed.

Materials

Interpreters always need writing materials close by. In one kindergarten class, all staff members carried pencils and pads of sticky-notes in their pockets. One mother made certain to keep a pencil and a pad of paper in the car, in her purse, and in every room of the house. In emergencies, use whatever is at hand to provide quick information that will clarify a situation—a paper towel, a lunch bag, a scrap of paper from the waste container, or marks in the sand or dirt (as in the illustration on page 167).

Formal or planned systems to achieve longer-term goals require more thought. Construction of visual materials can be burdensome if one person is totally responsible. If the following materials are available during planning sessions, the support-team members can do much of the construction work as the design needs are determined:

- File folders
- Unlined 3"x5" and 4"x6" file cards in white and a mix of colors
- Felt pens (especially black) and highlighters
- Masking tape, transparent tape, paper clips, stapler, ruler
- Utility or pen knife and scissors
- Hook-and-loop strips and circles
- Poster putty
- Self-adhesive labels of various sizes, shapes, and colors
- Envelopes of various kinds and sizes
- Plastic sandwich bags with locking tops
- A collection of boxes and containers of various sizes (shoe boxes with lids, plastic dishpans or tubs, margarine or yogurt containers, plastic freezer containers, plastic meat trays, egg cartons)
- Commercially available generic black-and-white drawings for communication systems; for example, rebus symbols by Mayer-Johnson (1992).

It is also helpful to have access to a computer with programs to develop grids, templates, flow charts, and generic picture symbols.

Constructing Object-Symbol Systems

Use of objects as symbols generally requires a format to represent blocks of time or the sequence of steps. A container is necessary to keep each symbol distinctly separated, and a larger container is needed for placing the symbols when the event or the step of the task is completed. Plastic tubs, baskets, or meat trays also can be used to represent time blocks. The type of symbol display will depend on the size of the symbols and the needs of the learner. Some learners will need higher or lower dividers between symbols for clear separation of time blocks, to accommodate motor dexterity, or to see the symbols easily.

Object systems can be constructed in a variety of ways.

- Tape together a series of shoe boxes or trays that are all the same size and large enough to hold the symbols easily. Each box represents a block of time. Prepare a larger box to hold the object symbols at the conclusion of each event or time block. Label this box *Finished,* and place it at the right end of the display. Paint over or cover the boxes to mask manufacturers' labels and irrelevant printed details that could distract the learner from the accurate name of the event. (From a learner's perspective: "Oh, it's Red Wing Shoes time.")
- Construct a wooden calendar box that has dividers to separate time blocks. Each section has its own hinged lid that can be closed at the end of each event or time block.
- Place objects in clear plastic bags with locking tops, and fasten the bags to a cord with clothespins or clips that are easy for the learner to manipulate.
- Fasten objects to a square of tagboard. Hang them in a sequence on small hooks or with clips. See page 272, Activity 4, for description of a strategy for making the transition from this type of object display to the use of line drawings.

The blocks of time on a calendar system can progress either from left to right or top to bottom.

Constructing Card-Symbol Systems

Line drawings and printed words (and photographs, if required) can be displayed on file cards. To display a sequence, mount the cards on a display board in some way that makes it easy to move or remove them. Use an adapted classroom card chart, or mount a series of envelopes on a bulletin board. Envelopes and display boards are easy and inexpensive to make from file folders.

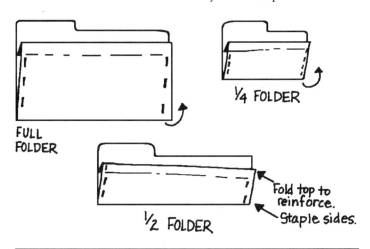

Making envelopes

- *Envelopes* are used as containers for transition cue cards for placing assigned and completed work sheets, check lists, cue cards, and any number of other purposes. Prepare a supply of envelopes made from file folders, and keep them on hand for quick system adaptations.

Construction: To make small envelopes for holding 3"x5" cards, cut a file folder in four parts. To hold larger cards, cut the folder in half. Use the whole folder to hold standard 8½"x11" sheets of paper.

- *Backgrounds* to display the card symbols in a sequence can be used for calendars, mini-calendars, job folders, and choice or activity option boards. These backgrounds can be adapted to hold any number of symbol cards and any type of card display.

Construction: To construct a display board for 3"x5" cards, split a file folder in half. Arrange short sequences of three or four cards on half a file (one strip.) For a longer sequence of six to eight cards, tape two strips together. If 4"x6" file cards are used, use two folders taped together. Tape or staple an envelope on the top and the bottom to hold transition cues or as containers for symbols at the end of an event. Attach the symbol cards to these backgrounds with hook-and-loop tape (as on Jason's calendar, page 186) or with paper clips (as on Jeff's calendar, on the same page).

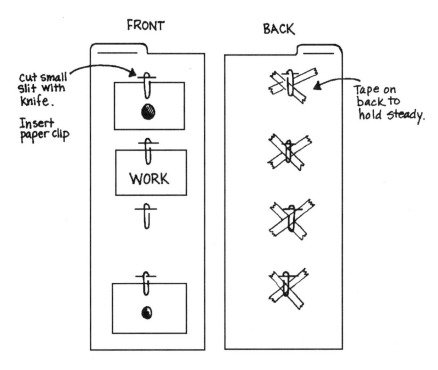

Making a display board from a file folder

Developing Grids or Templates

Develop and use grids and templates for mini-calendars, checklists, and choice and option lists when the format of a system remains the same but the content of the system changes each day. For example, although the activities on Matt's mini-calendar were changed each day, it was important to have a few communication symbols readily available. To save time, a template was made and a supply of these grids was always available for Matt's interpreter to complete each day.

A supply of picture strip grids—cartoon-strip formats with two to eight sections—makes it quick and easy to prepare checklists and stories when line drawings are required.

Evaluate and Refine

The design and construction elements of any visual self-management or information system are evaluated and refined from the time they are first introduced. Minor refinements are often all that is necessary, but at times it will become obvious that the total system needs revision; when:

- The system is rejected after introduction
- The learner fixates on some small detail of the system
- The learner is disorganized or disrupted by the organization of elements
- It is too burdensome or complicated for the learner to manipulate
- It is too complicated for the interpreter to adapt each day

To avoid frustration and to ensure progress to more independent use and increased options, the system must be refined as soon as the problem is identified.

Summary

The design decisions and specific elements of construction are described in chapter 15 as different types of visual self-management and information systems are introduced.

The design of visual systems will determine the rate of learning and effectiveness. Those with autism need concrete and literal information presented in clear, direct, and uncluttered ways. Concrete objects, generic black-and-white line drawings, and printed or written words present a minimum of conflicting stimulation. Since systems must be refined frequently, the construction must be simple and inexpensive.

Visual Instructional Strategies

The success or failure of many instructional or behavioral programs depends, to a large extent, on the ability to transfer information in a way the learner can understand. In general, learners need more details and information in a visual format than in an auditory format. There are many ways to organize information visually, and it is a very creative process for interpreters.

In this chapter, strategies are presented for developing visual self-management systems and for organizing information to clarify time, concepts, ideas, and processes. Six types of visual references and organizers will be discussed:

1. Calendars and mini-calendars

2. Transition cues

3. Checklists

4. Cue cards

5. Semantic maps

6. Stories

The chapter concludes with the introduction of imagery procedures. These visual strategies will be referred to in all chapters that deal with teaching new skills and solving behavior problems.

Once design decisions are made, refer to chapter 14 for construction strategies. The skills to use calendars, checklists and other visual self-management systems are taught in the context of natural routines as described in chapter 19.

Calendars and Mini-Calendars

Calendars and mini-calendars represent the sequence of events in time—perhaps the most important self-management tool for those with autism. A systematically structured schedule represented in a visual format for frequent reference is a necessary component for addressing many of the critical goals that compensate for the deficits of autism (figure 7.1, page 105).

Because young learners of the same age will likely have quite different abilities and needs, each of their calendars will be quite different. A child who is learning the concept of work, then play, may need to see the actual work (the beads to string and the blocks to stack), and then see a ball to represent play. A second child may understand that miniature objects represent a slightly longer sequence of activities (for example, group, work, play, work, lunch). A third child of the same age who can read words may be able to use 3"x5" cards with line drawings and printed words to represent the events scheduled for a whole day. Adult learners also will have varying needs; one may use line drawings to represent events, one event to a page, while another can use a typical appointment book.

A learner's first calendar should be quite simple. As the calendar and the calendar symbols take on meaning and the learner's interests and tolerance expand, frequent modifications will be required. The ultimate goal is for learners to independently use lists, appointment books, and standard wall calendars to manage time and life as adults.

Design Decisions

The calendar and its parts serve as natural cues for moving through the events of the day without verbal directions. The first task is to make design decisions that respect the learner's individual needs and most likely will lead to independent use. There are six design decisions:

1. The amount of time to display

    This decision depends on the learner's attention span and experience. Learners with a very short attention span and little or no understanding of sequences and cause/effect (this, then this) need short displays that initially represent three or four short activities in a five- or ten-minute block of time. As tolerance and understanding increase, the calendar is systematically expanded to represent a half or whole day. Often those with a longer attention span who have some understanding of cause/effect and sequence can manage a full day's display from the beginning.

    Weekly displays to supplement the shorter displays are introduced when learners are upset about not going to school on weekends. Standard wall calendars with ample writing space supplement the daily calendar as soon as learners show a need to know when special events will occur in the future.

SUNDAY	MONDAY	TUESDAY	WEDNESDAY	THURSDAY
5 No School Grandma's House	6 School Swimming	7 School Tia to Scouts To Store	8 School McDonald's	9 School

2. The types of symbols

    Review the discussion of symbol selection (pages 179-183) before making this decision.

3. The format for displaying symbols

    The format must ensure that the learner knows what to do first, what happens next, and how many more things must be done. Object and card systems can be displayed vertically or horizontally. Some learners find it easier to follow a sequence from left to right, while others more naturally move from the top down. Initially it is important to test out the most natural direction for a specific learner. With experience, most learners become more flexible and follow a list from top to bottom and a wall calendar from left to right and down the page.

4. The system to signify that an event is finished when the symbols are:

    *   Concrete objects: Objects are placed in a box labeled *Finished* as activities are completed.

    *   Line drawings or words on cards: The cards can be turned over or placed in an envelope or box labeled *Finished*.

    *   Line drawings or words on charts, checklists, or grids: Cross out or check off the symbol at the end of each activity.

    *   A single activity symbol on a notebook page: Turn over the page when the activity is completed. Secure the page with a clip or rubber band.

5. The amount of detail

Keep the calendar as simple as possible to allow for the greatest flexibility. It is easier to add detail when needed than to remove detail. *Do not add distracting decorative detail that draws attention from the relevant information.*

- A basic calendar that lists the sequence of time blocks labeled to represent the types of activities (music, work, choice, work, lunch) is good for a younger or less sophisticated learner who needs considerable flexibility and whose calendar is located in a specific location. A mini-calendar in each location provides the details to support this more general calendar.

Some less sophisticated and very literal learners may initially need space on the calendar to represent transitions.

- A detailed calendar that lists each event and the times for beginning and ending is useful for those who carry their calendars at all times. However, the increased detail reduces flexibility and can cause some problems. It is harder to adapt activity length to the learner's varying tolerance level if the specific time is listed. Listing the starting and ending times can also cause problems for those with compulsive time worries. A learner may become anxious if an event does not begin or end at the exact time. The learner can become a clock watcher or become very confused if the specifically stated time passes and the learner was not aware of it. If the learner needs to have the time displayed, this problem can sometimes be remedied by placing symbols around the time (<9:00>) and teaching that "It means *about 9:00—maybe a few minutes before, maybe a few minutes after.*"

6. Transition cues

A transition cue is an object or card that triggers the learner to go to a specific place independently without added verbal directions. The symbols on the calendar are obvious transition cues when carried to the location of an event. In the illustration, the ball serves as a reminder (a cue) to go to the gym.

- Transition cues to return to the calendar are important for those who have difficulty ending an activity and moving back to refer to the calendar. A mini-calendar or checklist for a specific block of time can include transition cues. The last event listed could be: *Check calendar.* A specific object (a block or a poker chip) or a symbol (3"x5" card with the learner's name printed on it) means to end the present activity and return to the calendar. Teach the learner to return the cue to an envelope or box that is labeled and attached to or placed near the calendar.

Jeff was just learning to use a calendar that incorporated labeled line drawings on 3"x5" cards. Transition cues were placed at the end of each mini-calendar so he always knew what to do at the conclusion of the specific time block. His interpreter always carried transition cues to the playground or elsewhere in the school. Initially, Jeff's interpreter met him at the bus each morning and gave him a cue card that directed him to his classroom to hang his coat. Once his coat was hung, the interpreter handed Jeff a cue card with his name on it that directed him to his calendar.

One day soon after the transition cues were introduced, Jeff was climbing on the playground equipment when it was time to return to class. When his interpreter gave him the transition cue, Jeff looked at it for a moment, and then slowly but independently climbed down and began to walk back to the classroom and his calendar.

Transition cues

7. The location and management of the calendar

Notebooks, clipboards, or appointment books are either carried by the learner throughout the day or located in an easily accessible place, such as on the learner's desk or work station. Object boxes and display boards are located in non-distracting locations and at a level that allows the learner to see the symbols easily. There are many creative ways to manage a calendar.

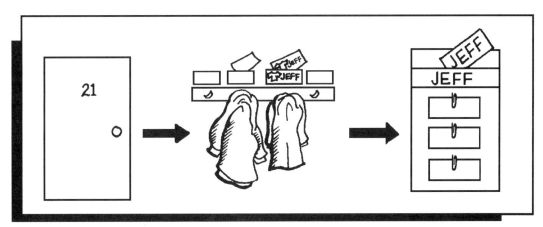

Sequence card to teach routine

One teacher arranged a transition center for three students with individual calendars. While each of the three calendars was different, the transition times were the same. The transition center was structured around a table that held all the calendars, with chairs for the three students and a single interpreter. The chairs allowed the students to feel centered to focus on their calendars. The interpreter was positioned at the student's eye level to make it easy to glance at each student, identify nonverbal signs of confusion, provide needed assistance, and cue interactions.

Tony and several of his peers needed daily calendars to help them keep track of the events in their third grade class. As the last students arrived in the classroom each morning, Mr. Garcia placed a large sheet of butcher paper on the table in the center of the room. As he began to write out the schedule with a black felt marker, Tony and others gathered around. Some students watched or listened quietly from their desks. Mr. Garcia noted all the changes, explained specific expectations, and answered questions about the day's activities. When finished, he placed the calendar on the bulletin board in front of the room near Tony's desk. It was Tony's job to cross off each event on the calendar as it was completed. In this way, a strategy that was essential for a few students also benefited others.

Variations and Expanded Applications
Mini-Calendars to Structure Changes within Small Time Blocks

A mini-calendar supplements a basic daily calendar and shows the sequence of specific activities scheduled to occur within a small time block such as a class, a therapy session, a trip, a party, or a period of work. These small calendars provide a visual reference that increases motivation and independence. The information allows the learner to:

- Prepare for each transition within a time block
- Measure passing time as each activity is completed
- Prepare for a larger transition at the end

A mini-calendar can be a simple, on-the-spot construction to deal with an unexpected situation, or it can be specifically planned and used routinely for periods of time that include several changes or to provide support during a new situation. *The last item on a mini-calendar is a transition cue so the learner knows what to do and where to be next.*

The design of these calendars depends on the learner's attention span and the type of symbols required:

- Actual materials placed in a sequence of boxes or tubs

  This type is useful for those who are using concrete objects and first learning to work, then play. When all materials are in the *Finished* box, it is time to play. A simple grid with four sections is used to help a young child transition from using real objects to using line drawings to represent the activities.

- Written as an agenda for group use

  This type is useful for regular classes when several students can use the reminder, circle time in early childhood or preschool classes, Sunday school classes, scout meetings, or therapy sessions. Write the mini-schedule on the chalkboard or a chart pad. To accommodate learners who need pictures, use tiny line drawings (rebus symbols) to represent important words or names.

- Constructed from file folders and 3"x5" cards for individual use

  The sequence of cards specifies activities to do during a specific time block. (See pages 183-186 for construction details.)

- Written on specifically designed grids

  This is useful for a regular class or a recurring event that includes many changes. See the illustration of Matt's clipboard on page 186.

Adaptations to Prepare for Planned Changes

Major schedule changes and new expectations will increase stress. This stress can be reduced with thoughtful preplanning.

Jose was dependent and possessive of Tom, his interpreter. If Tom was absent or involved with another person, Jose would become very upset. To resolve this problem, it was decided that Tom would begin sharing his time with other students. Tom used the familiar calendar routine to prepare Jose for this change. His calendar was a simple grid with each activity listed on a separate sticky-note. The notes for activities that occurred two or three times a week were placed on the edge of the calendar to reuse. Two days before the planned change, Tom placed a note on the edge of the calendar without comment. The note read: *Tom will work with Mary.* On the morning of the change, the note was moved onto the calendar and paired with the note that indicated what Jose was to do independently. During the regular calendar review session with Jose, Tom talked about the change. As he told Jose how he could get help during the period, Tom wrote out the procedure. Jose checked his calendar several times during the time Tom worked with Mary, but he managed this and future changes without incident.

Adaptations for Unplanned Changes

The calendar also provides a way to minimize the stress from unexpected interruptions and changes that occur each day. The learner has two needs: to know exactly what will happen, and to know when things will return to normal.

Unexpected changes generally involve a cancellation, substitution, or change in time, location, or people. The interpreter immediately takes the learner to the calendar to see how the change affects the expected routine of events. (If the calendar is not available when one of these changes occurs, the interpreter uses whatever is at hand to make the information visual.)

- Cancellations, substitutions, and changed times are visualized and explained while removing and replacing the calendar symbol or changing its location on the calendar.

- Changing locations, changing people, and changed behavioral expectations are highlighted on a sticky-note and placed on the symbol for the specific activity. Explain the change as the note is placed on the calendar. ("We usually go for a walk after dinner, but tonight Suzy and Tom are coming to visit. We will take a walk tomorrow night. While Suzy and Tom are here, you can read your sports magazine or listen to tapes.")

Adaptations to Increase Independence

Once the learner understands and uses the calendar system fairly independently, it is time to expand the complexity of the calendar system to:

- Increase the amount of work between reinforcing activities
- Add new, disliked activities
- Provide more opportunities for self-management
- Progress to more complex and abstract symbol systems
- Use more natural formats

See chapter 23, pages 366-369, for an overview of the issues involved in making choices and decisions successfully.

For example, involve the learner in making choices and decisions about the day—selecting leisure activities, selecting jobs, deciding when or where to do an activity, choosing the types of materials or the friends to involve in the activities.

- Expand the goals of the daily calendar review process or change the review format to solve a problem. Some older and more experienced learners have contact with an interpreter only once or twice a day, before and/or after work or school. If a longer review period is scheduled, it may be used to:

- Review the positive events of the previous day
- Expand problem-solving and self-management strategies related to real-life concerns
- Expand conversation and social skills
- Prepare for the coming day

> When Jose got off the bus each morning, he wandered randomly about the school and was either very late to class or upset because others had firmly directed him to class. His interpreter decided to preview Jose's calendar with him at the end of each school day. When Jose knew what was to happen first the next day (a liked activity), he went directly to class each morning.

Use of Contingencies

See chapter 16, page 214-220, for a discussion of ways to use contingencies effectively.

Contingency statements that call attention to the highly preferred activities shown on the calendar will increase persistence and independence.

Evaluate and Refine Calendar Systems

Evaluation of the calendar system and its use begins when it is introduced. Thoughtful evaluation is important to ensure that the system is adapted in a manner that matches the learner's expanding skills and increasing independence.

If the Learner Continues to Need Considerable Assistance

Some element or elements of the environment, the schedule, the format of the calendar, or the instructional sequence may be unclear. Note areas of confusion and difficulty. Where have errors occurred? Why? Where are prompts needed? Why? What could be modified or clarified? What may be misunderstood? Why? Sometimes another support-team member can provide a more objective perspective to pinpoint the elements that need revision.

Review sections related to organization of events (chapter 11), space (chapter 12), and time (chapter 13). Also read chapter 19 to pinpoint problems in the instructional sequence. After identifying a possible solution, refine the system quickly.

If the Learner Is Not Motivated to Use the Calendar

If the learner was never motivated to use the calendar system, review the previous section and make revisions to clarify the system or the instructional procedures. If the learner once used the calendar fairly independently and appeared to be motivated, consider the following reasons for the current lack of motivation or resistance:

1. The design of the calendar, the symbols, or the display may be too simple. Review the discussion of symbol selection (chapter 14, pages 179-183) and the example of Matt's problem (pages 182-183).

2. The scheduled activities are uninteresting or meaningless.
   - Reassess the reinforcing value of activities and the arrangement of the activities to take advantage of liked activities as reinforcers.
   - The activities may have been done too many times over a long period of time—they are too easy or not age-appropriate, and the learner is bored. Review the learner's goals and placement to be sure they are age-appropriate, and provide an appropriate level of stimulation.
   - Clarify the meaning and purpose of the activities. Make sure they are important and that there is a reason for doing them.

- Increase the number of changes and schedule variations. *When a schedule lacks variety, the learner memorizes the sequence, then has little reason to review the calendar.*

3. The location of the calendar is inconvenient and interrupts the flow of events. Perhaps a mini-calendar on a small clipboard or pocket card can be carried when a return to the basic calendar would be disruptive.

   - The location of the calendar calls undue or negative attention from peers. This can be a problem for more able learners who want to be like their peers. In this situation, make the calendar more "normal"; for example, place it in the front of a notebook or file folder, or include everyone in the process. (See the illustration of Tony, page 182.)

4. Verbal prompts have not been faded and the learner is simply moving through a turn-taking routine with the interpreter—a routine that has little or no meaning attached. Review procedures for prompting and fading prompts (pages 229-233). Again, it may take an objective team member to help pinpoint this problem and suggest modifications to increase meaning and independence.

A functional communication system and a calendar are the two most important lifelong tools for those with autism who have difficulty communicating, are confused by time and events, and resist changes, transitions, or new experiences. *It is not acceptable simply to stop using the calendar because the learner doesn't like it or doesn't "seem" to need it. The schedule or the calendar—or both—must be adapted quickly, so the activities are interesting, important, and varied and so the learner sees value in the calendar.* Keep in mind that the ultimate goal for those with autism is to use standard calendars, appointment books, and lists to manage their own activities as adults.

Teach learners to use the calendar in the context of functional routines. The systematic planning process described in chapters 13 through 15 ensures that critical goals will be addressed. With this structure, each event provides many opportunities for learning those subtle skills and lessons that others learn automatically.

Checklists

A checklist is a visual reference that highlights (cues) the steps of a routine, event, or task from initiation to termination and transition to the next routine. When a checklist is used during initial instruction or when introducing a new activity, it provides a structure to allow the learner to ultimately perform independently without verbal assistance. Creatively designed checklists can provide a format for:

- Clarifying or cuing communication and social strategies
- Marking progress toward completion; keeping the end in sight
- Monitoring productivity, speed, and quality of the performance
- Monitoring behavior—a major self-monitoring tool

Variations and Expanded Applications

Checklists can be prepared quickly to deal with unexpected problems, or they can be developed following assessment and development of a new routine. Checklists can take many forms, serve a variety of purposes, and incorporate any type of symbol.

1. Typed or written lists are the most common for those who can read.

   - Use a simple checklist to clarify the day's shopping trip.

- For a long checklist that will be used in the same form for many days, write on tagboard or a file folder and laminate it. Attach a clothespin or paper clip on the edge, and move it down as each step is completed.

- Prepare a checklist in story format with a single step on each page.

2. Picture symbol lists can take many forms and support routines as diverse as washing windows, preparing a snack, grooming, or playing a game.

- Pictures on 3"x5" cards held together on a ring can serve as a checklist. As each step of the sequence is completed, the page is flipped over and secured with a clip or rubber band.

- The picture strip shown below illustrates the steps for participating independently at the swimming pool.

3. Small objects placed in a specific order on a divided tray can clarify a sequence of steps and serve as a checklist.

- Soap, toothbrush, comb, and lotion lined up on a tray show the steps for a grooming routine.

- Materials for completing some assembly or packaging jobs, fastened in the required sequence on a card, tray, or file folder, provide a visual reference (checklist) for completing the job accurately and independently.

When Jose was 16 years old, he frequently missed school because his mother couldn't get him out of bed and ready for school each morning. He had been denied school bus service in the past because he didn't follow the rules, and his mother was unable to transport him. After analyzing Jose's situation, two checklists were prepared. One highlighted each step of the routine from the time the alarm clock sounded to the time Jose entered the door of the school bus. The second listed the bus rules translated into very specific behavioral expectations. The driver handed this second checklist to Jose as he entered the bus. (The first step was to greet the driver.) Jose held the checklist and referred to it during the ride. On arriving at school, he waited until other students had left the bus, then showed the checklist to the driver. The driver quickly rated the quality of his behavior and signed the checklist. Then Jose took the checklist to his teacher for congratulations.

The checklists were introduced to Jose with a story that clarified the problem and explained the checklists. Jose's teacher arrived at his home at 6:30 a.m. on two days to teach him to follow the two checklists. During this period, Jose's mother learned how to provide support to use the list. The bus driver was shown how to talk to Jose and how to rate his behavior. Jose was virtually independent and successful with the checklists after that initial instruction. Figures 15.1 and 15.2 illustrate these checklists and adaptations that support the travel routine on page 157.

Figure 15.1. Sample: Jose's checklist for preparing for school

This routine actually begins with a bedtime routine when Jose showers and selects and lays out his clothing for morning.

1. The alarm clock rings. Turn it off and stretch.
2. Get out of bed.
3. Go to the bathroom.
   Checklist mounted on the mirror directs bathroom tasks.
4. Return to bedroom. Get dressed.
5. Tell Mom, "Good morning."
6. Eat breakfast.
7. Brush teeth.
8. Make bed.

If everything is done before 7:10:
9. Set timer for 10 minutes and listen to tapes.
10. When timer rings, shut off tape player.
11. Put on coat and pick up backpack.
12. At 7:25, tell Mom, "Good-bye."
13. Go outside and stand on the yellow X on the sidewalk.
14. Watch and wait quietly for the bus to stop and the door to open.

Figure 15.2. Sample: Jose's checklist for riding the bus

This routine begins as Jose steps into the bus.

When the bus comes and the door is open, pick up backpack and step into the bus.

1. Greet the driver. Take checklist.
2. Locate an empty seat.
3. Sit down on the seat.
4. Fasten seat belt.
5. Hold backpack, take out *Sports Illustrated.*
6. Sit quietly and read magazine.

When the bus stops at school and the door is open:

7. Unfasten seat belt and follow kids to the door.
8. Stop and talk to the driver.

Report for Jose

Jose followed the rules.

- He did not yell or scream. He sat quietly.
- He did not run around the bus.
- He kept his seat belt fastened.

Driver

Cue Cards

Cue cards provide a visual reference to help the learner:

- Recall a word or phrase
- See the relationship of ideas or variations of meaning
- Recall a new or difficult step or skill to complete a routine or solve a problem
- Support choice and decision making and any number of other purposes
- Transition from one location to another

Some advantages of cue cards are:

- The visual information on a cue card is easier for the learner to process and less intrusive than verbal assistance from another person.
- A simple message can be delivered quickly to help solve a problem. Many learners cannot communicate effectively in stressful situations, but can remember to show a card to someone.
- When stress is high, a simple message that clarifies a solution to a problem can prevent a crisis. Shifting attention from direct eye contact to the cue card is calming.

Variations and Expanded Applications

Cue cards are very helpful for delivering messages such as, "Help please," "I need a break quickly," "Please move back," or "Write it down, please."

A short list of options can help a learner fit into social situations. For example, a few rules to fit a situation, several options for solving a common problem, or a list of conversation topics are helpful.

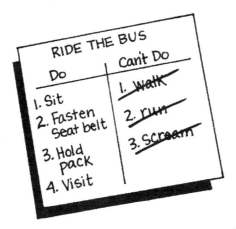

A T-chart format that clearly and briefly describes both the Do's and the Don'ts are invaluable for situations like trips or parties. *When learners understand what they are to do and not do, it is more likely that they will be able to function successfully.*

> When people crowded too close to Maria, she became agitated and anxious and sometimes bit or hit them. While standing in line at the theater one day, Maria began to fidget and her face flushed as people began to crowd close. Her mother recognized the subtle signals of agitation and handed Maria a small cue card as she said, "You can tell them to move back." On the card was written, "Please move back." Maria turned and touched the arm of the person behind her and held out the card as she said, "Please." As that person moved back, Maria relaxed and smiled softly.
>
> Situations were set up with other friends and other staff members to give Maria more opportunities to practice using this particular cue card until she could use it spontaneously.

Semantic Maps

Semantic maps—semantic webs or networks, tree charts, flow charts, and so on—provide a format to visualize all the elements or pieces of information that make up a concept, idea, story, sequence, or process to elicit meaning. These maps can show the relationship of old information to new information, identify categories, and correct misinterpretations. Two simple maps, using line drawings with words, are shown on the following page.

The use of semantic maps capitalizes on the visual, gestalt mode of processing common in autism, and compensates for the problems associated with literal interpretation and inability to organize information to elicit meaning, to process auditory information consistently, and to retrieve and think about several ideas at once.

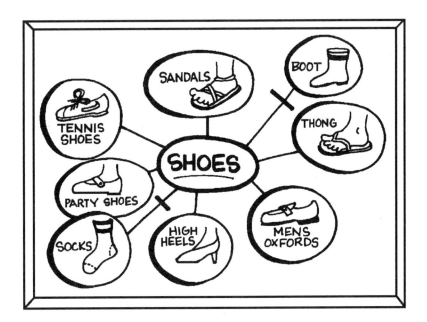

Variations and Expanded Applications

The maps can take innumerable forms to support a variety of needs (Pehrrson and Robinson 1985; Grossen and Carnine 1992). Maps can be adapted to use line drawings and printed words. They can be very simple or more complex to show the relationships between many details. Semantic maps can be used to:

- Improve reading and language comprehension
- Clarify concepts outside the learner's experience, as in history or geography
- Illustrate the elements of a decision process
- Visualize events in time past, present, and future
- Plan parties and organize work
- Clarify the various applications of a social rule

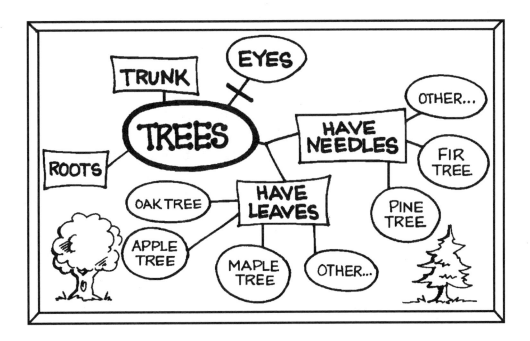

- Clarify cause/effect relationships, fact from fiction, opposing views
- Draw conclusions, predict outcomes, or develop a logical argument
- Solve a problem; generate and evaluate alternatives
- Identify family relationships as well as staff roles and responsibilities

Grossen and Carnine (1992) describe a procedure for teaching students with poor reading comprehension to use four types of text-structure maps and to identify the signal words in text to determine which type of map to use: a descriptive or thematic map, a sequential episodic map, a comparative and contrasting map, or a problem-and-solution map.

Stories

Stories provide a framework for teaching new skills and resolving a wide variety of problems.

- They can be used to introduce changes and new routines and to teach social rules and academic skills.
- They can be adapted for use by those of any cognitive ability and age.
- A story provides a permanent visual reference that is easy to review independently and in different settings.
- Both professional and nonprofessional interpreters can easily learn the strategies.
- Stories are designed and used to prevent problems. They are effective in integrated settings.

There are several types of story strategies. Three specific models are summarized below: experience stories, social stories, and imagery procedures that involve scripts or stories.

Experience Stories

These stories are adaptations of the language experience approach (LEA) to reading instruction (Allen and Allen 1966; Ashton-Warner 1963). The LEA approach is highly individualized. Based on the children's expressions of their own experiences—their words written down—LEA is an integrated language arts program that teaches language, reading comprehension, verbal expression, writing, and spelling in the context of a single experience.

See chapter 19, pages 262-292, for activities that expand the initial understanding of symbols and language concepts—those beginning language concepts that lead to reading, speaking, and communicating with meaning.

Those with autism can learn and expand those skills with modified LEA strategies (Shepherd 1983; Flowers 1990; Bock 1991). Very young learners begin to understand that experiences can be written down (symbolized).

Developing and Presenting Experience Stories

Initially, interpreters take the lead in developing stories and charts. Depending on the needs of a learner, line drawings or printed words are used. *Stories are written as the learner watches. Correct sentence forms and punctuation are used to prevent learning errors. The interpreter always speaks the words as they are written down.* The learner begins to add a few words to complete open-ended sentences and questions. As the learner gains understanding and confidence, new ideas or experiences are contributed spontaneously, either verbally or by taking the pen and drawing or writing them into the story.

Figure 15.3. Samples: Experience stories

Example 1. *A simple, beginning story written at home to share weekend experiences with the teacher*

Today is Monday, November 8.

Grandma and Grandpa brought ice cream.

I used the computer.

Example 2. *A group story to summarize the day*

Greg contributed the underlined words after the teacher had set up the sentence frame. As each child talked, the teacher wrote the child's name so Greg could associate the name to the child. Key words in the story were highlighted with tiny line drawings.

Today is Monday, October 10. The sun is shining.

Kim said, "Tony was sick today and went home."

Greg said, "For lunch today we (Kim, Katy, Caesar, Mary, and Greg) had <u>pizza</u>."

Katy said, "Today was Mary's birthday. She was excited."

Mary said, "Mother brought balloons and cupcakes."

Caesar said, "They were good."

Katy said, "We (all of us) felt sad that Tony missed the party."

Greg said, "In PE, we played with <u>scooter boards</u>."

Example 3. *A story about a picture of a boy holding a bat and a girl holding a ball*

The children have toys. The bat <u>belongs</u> to Peter. The ball <u>belongs</u> to Jane.

Example 4. *A story frame to answer questions about a picture*

The picture shows two people washing dishes. The view through a window shows that it is night. The answers are written in complete sentences that culminate in a story about the picture.

Who is in the picture? <u>This is a picture story about a boy and a girl.</u>

Where are the people? <u>They are standing at the sink in the kitchen.</u>

When did this happen? <u>It is dark outside, so it is night time.</u>

What are the people doing? <u>They are washing dishes.</u>

Why are they doing that? <u>The dishes were dirty after eating dinner.</u>

Example 5. *A story to summarize a graphing activity in math*

There are 19 children in our class.

Everybody eats lunch.

10 children buy school lunches.

4 children bring a lunch box.

5 children go home for lunch.

10 plus 4 plus 5 equals 19.

Variations and Expanded Applications

Experience stories can be developed to record individual experiences or to record the experiences of a group. Experience stories can supplement or replace a standard reading program for learners who are confused by phonetic or basal reading approaches. Other variations and applications include these:

- Stories are developed to review the experiences of the day in sequence, to share information between home and school, and to facilitate conversations.

For example, near the end of the school day, the learner and an interpreter review the day's experiences and prepare a brief story. The story is copied (on a photocopier or printed or written by the learner). One copy is placed in a notebook for later review at school, and the other is carried home to share with family. The learner is encouraged to read the story to parents and to respond to parents' questions by locating the answer in the story.

These stories must be positive and include interesting information. They must not be a summary of the day's behavior, especially if there were problems.

- To stimulate awareness of others and their perspective, write group stories. For example, a series of stories about the group might begin with one that describes each member (color of eyes, color of hair, whether hair is long or short, straight or curly hair, and so on) and requires a partner to get the information and report it for the story. Other stories could be about group members' favorite stories, TV shows, foods, or games. Others could target individual fears or worries. A more advanced story could summarize a common problem or situation that elicits different emotions, opinion, and perspective. Example 2, above, is a group story.

- Plan, Do, Review Charts are used to prepare for new events and changing routines, and to review, evaluate, and adapt an activity that will be repeated. An activity or routine is planned and written on a chart. The plan includes the steps of the event as well as some of the environmental cues and behavioral expectations. A chart can be referred to as many times as needed before the activity. Following the event, the chart is reviewed. Some actual experiences may be added, problems may be discussed, and possible solutions can be added for reference before repeating the activity.

- Expand language concepts, learn to interpret pictures, and answer WH questions, using story frames. See examples 3 and 4, above.

The use of LEA for increasing language and literacy is expanded in chapter 19.

- Clarify math, science, and other academic concepts by summarizing activity-based problems and experiments in the format of an experience story. See example 5, above.

In summary, experience stories can be adapted to prevent problems by clarifying information. They will also expand language, communication, and academic skills. Experience stories are written while the learner watches and learns to contribute more and more information.

Social Stories

Social stories as developed by Gray and Garand (1993) are based on the growing understanding of social cognition in autism (Baron-Cohen 1988; Dawson and Fernald 1987). These short stories describe relevant social and environmental cues, the perspective of others, and a solution or appropriate response.

If a learner is unable to gain meaningful information about the social environment, the first step for teaching any new social skill or solving a social problem is to provide a careful explanation of the social situation. "Traditional teaching involves interaction between teacher and student, creating a social situation whenever instruction occurs. . . . The use of traditional instruction to teach social behavior presents a student with a compounded challenge: understanding the lesson, and accurately interpreting the social cues used in its presentation. . . . Social stories . . . provide . . . direct access to social information" (Gray and Garand 1993, 2). Direct access occurs because the learner reviews the story independently; thus, after the first introduction there are no competing social cues to interpret. Improved behavior is often noted within a relatively short period of time.

Developing and Presenting Social Stories

An understanding of the learning style common in autism is necessary in order to plan a story that will avoid predictable misunderstandings and literal interpretations.

1. Identify the target problem. Then assess the situation to understand:

   - The learner's perspective and abilities

     Why is the learner doing this? What is misunderstood or interpreted literally? What does the learner believe about the situation?

   - The perspective of others

     How do others understand the situation? What are they doing and why?

   - Relevant environmental cues

     Does the environment contain confusing sensory stimulation? What are the natural cues that are relevant to the situation?

2. Write the story in a simple, clear format that is at a level slightly lower than the learner's comprehension level.

   - Write the story from the learner's perspective. For example, address the cause of the ineffective behaviors, fears, sensory intolerances, and misunderstandings.

   - Include at least two or three descriptive sentences to define the situation and the setting.

   - Include the answers to unasked questions *(who, why, what, where, when)*, as appropriate. Descriptions of facial expressions and the perspective and behavior of others add relevant information.

   - Include at least one sentence describing the perspective of others, to explain the reasons for their behavior.

   - Include no more than one directive statement to identify an appropriate response—a clear and positive statement (I can, I will, . . .).

   - Use literal and concrete statements. Avoid subjective and relative statements such as *too loud* or *too fast*. Provide concrete cues such as, "The noise will last about as long as it takes you to count to 30."

   - Be objective. Do not judge or assume potential feelings or reactions.

   - Be flexible, to account for the range of variables in the natural setting. For example, do not give specific names to the people in a story because the learner may assume that the story applies only when that specific person is present. Use the words *sometimes* or *usually,* because the words *always* and *never* will be overgeneralized. In fact, unless stated otherwise, a learner with autism will likely assume that a story is true for every setting, forever.

3. For a nonreader, prepare a book and supporting tapes if needed.

   - Place one concept or statement on a page.

   - In general, avoid the use of illustrations unless they represent a range of variables. Gray and Garand (1993) indicate that the details in illustrations are often misinterpreted or overgeneralized. Some learners would benefit from the use of simple, black-and-white line drawings that have very little detail.

4. Read the story as the learner listens and watches.

   - A nonreader follows the story with an audiotape or videotape with a signal for turning pages.

5. Have the learner read the story to you.

6. Thereafter, have the learner read the story independently once or twice each day.

7. Encourage the learner to share the story with others.

8. Cue the target response in the natural situation with one of the statements from the story. If others know the story, various people in various natural settings can provide the cues.

9. Monitor the responses and refine the story as problems are identified.

10. Fade the story by decreasing the number or frequency of reviews, by rewriting and dropping the directive sentence, or by changing the story to target a different situation.

11. Place the story in a notebook for review if the problem resurfaces.

See figure 15.4 for two social stories.

Variations and Expanded Applications

Stories can be developed and presented in a variety of ways to achieve a number of different goals.

- Curriculum stories can make academic lessons more functional.

- A checklist story has a single step of a routine on each page. Once the routine is familiar, the story can be intentionally sabotaged by omitting a page or placing the pages in the wrong order. These variations provide opportunities for the learner to recognize and correct a problem (an illogical sequence), to reorganize a sequence, and to discover that a sequence could be performed in different ways.

- Stories can clarify the meaning of a book, TV show, or movie. One young girl who had previously liked apples refused to eat them after seeing the movie, *Snow White*. A story helped her understand that *Snow White* is a fantasy, and it is safe to eat apples. Another young man who enjoyed historical documentaries and news reports on TV became confused about the use of the word *red*. The story in Figure 19.1 (page 275) was developed to clarify the range of meanings.

Social stories and experience stories have much in common. The major difference is that social stories specifically emphasize the perspective of others.

This summary of procedures for developing and presenting a social story is limited. For a more complete discussion of the strategies, see Gray and Garand 1993; Gray 1994a; Gray 1994b.

While there is, as yet, no empirical data to support the use of social stories, many learners have changed their behavior in a relatively short period after a story was presented. Before initiating a major behavior program to solve a serious problem, it would be logical to first develop a social story that provides the important and relevant details, so the learner understands what is happening, what response would be effective, and why it is important.

While this strategy seems almost too simple to be effective, one theme that has been repeated throughout this manual is that simple and subtle changes and adaptations often make a significant difference. One higher functioning young man said, "Now that I know, I can change."

Figure 15.4. Samples: Social stories

Example 1.

This story clearly outlines the social situation, the perspective of others, and the expectations.

The teacher says, "Everybody out!" when swimming time is finished. *(Highlights relevant cue)*

I can hear her say, "Everybody out!" *(Labels sensory perception)*

Most children stop playing in the water. *(Relevant cue)*

I will stop playing in the water. *(Directive)*

Some children may say, "Oh, no! I don't want to stop!" *(Perspective sentence to explain the behavior of others)*

But I will stop playing in the water. *(Directive)*

I will go to the side and climb out. *(Directive)*

The teacher may smile and say, "Good-bye" as she sees the children climbing out. *(Perspective sentence that explains how the teacher may respond)*

I will smile and say, "Good-bye." *(Directive)*

The children go to the dressing room. *(Relevant cue)*

I will go to the dressing room. *(Directive)*

. . . and so on.

Example 2.

This fairly complex story was prepared for a young man who previously had refused to go into the dentist's office, made loud noises, paced about the waiting room, and refused to sit in the chair or open his mouth. After reading the story for two days, he went to the dentist without incident.

My teeth are stained.

They need to be cleaned so I won't get a cavity.

A cavity would hurt.

I will go to the dentist after school on Friday.

The dentist's name is Dr. Jones.

Mother will be at the school with the car to drive to the dentist's office.

The dentist's office is at 1234 Main Street.

Mother and I will walk into the office.

Mother will tell the nurse at the desk, "Jose is here."

Mother and I will sit down and wait.

I may hear a high, shrill noise. The noise is made by an instrument for cleaning teeth.

Maybe there will be an aquarium to watch while I wait. Maybe not.

I can look at magazines while I wait.

I may look at one magazine, or maybe two or three.

When the nurse calls my name, it is time to see the dentist.

I put the magazine on the chair and follow the nurse.

. . . and so forth to explain the whole procedure.

Imagery

Imagery-based procedures rely on scripts or stories that describe actual or potentially stressful situations to teach coping strategies. The procedures used at the Groden Center in Providence, Rhode Island, are based on learning theory—behavioral and therapeutic approaches that research has proven effective. This approach assumes that internal behaviors such as thinking, feeling, and imaging (or imagining) follow the same laws of learning as do observable behaviors (covert conditioning). These procedures have been used successfully at the Groden Center since the early 1980s to help those with autism and other developmental disabilities function more effectively in the home and community. Imagery procedures have been used to address problems of those who simply lack effective social skills and those who have responded to anxiety with aggression, self-abuse, and severe tantrums. The clients at the Groden Center represent the full range of ability, from preschool children to adults who have moved from institutional to community settings. Over 44% of the Center's clients were able to relax themselves when cued verbally by a teacher or therapist. Another 31% learned to use the self-control procedures independently (Groden et al. 1994).

There are many advantages and reasons for using imagery procedures:

- Once learned, they can be used unobtrusively at any time and in any setting without additional materials, equipment, or reinforcers.

- Practice in imagery can be repeated as frequently as needed without disrupting or distracting others.

- The procedures are not limited by space or time restrictions. New environments and scenes can be created instantly in the imagination.

- Generalization is enhanced because the scenes representing the range of antecedents and reinforcers can be varied.

- Imagery is a preventive procedure. Potential problems can be anticipated and coping strategies can be rehearsed before ineffective and disruptive behavior occurs. As learners are increasingly successful and gain confidence in their ability to cope with problems in the community, their self-esteem increases.

See chapter 23 for discussion of applying these procedures to maintain self-control.

In summary, imagery procedures can be adapted and used to help those with autism learn to manage their anxiety and cope with life problems.

Several resources by Groden and others are listed on page 449. Especially helpful are works by Gorden and LeVasseur (1995) and Cautela and Groden (1978); as well as two videotapes developed at the Groden Center: *Breaking the Barriers I: Relaxation techniques for people with special needs* (1989), and *Breaking the Barriers II: Imagery procedures for people with special needs* (1991). A video guide for *Breaking the Barriers II* also is available (Groden et al. 1991).

The strategies presented in this chapter will be applied to a variety of situations in Part 5—Teach New Skills, and in Part 6—Manage Difficult Problems.

Summary

Visual supports, references, and organizers are a critical part of any program for those with autism. The potential for using visualization and imagery procedures to rehearse and learn new skills is exciting.

Organize and Structure Verbal Information

Most learners with autism who can hear have a very good—perhaps excellent—ability to receive or take in and store verbal information. However, auditory processing discrepancies can result in many learning and behavior problems. Because those with autism do not provide easily understood or consistent feedback to their parents and teachers, they receive less verbal input and fewer opportunities to learn the language and communicate. To reverse this cycle, learners need access to verbal information in a form they can understand. Hearing the language in natural contexts is a prerequisite for understanding and using the language for speaking, reading, and writing. Adaptations and many positive language experiences will most likely result in better understanding and meaningful use. The following sections provide basic strategies for talking to those with autism—strategies for organizing and structuring verbal information for more effective learning and behavior.

Basic Guidelines

When to Talk

In general, one talks to the learner with autism at the same times and for the same reasons as one talks with those who do not have autism. To ensure understanding, it is important to make some specific accommodations in the following situations:

1. During social interactions, to have fun and share experiences

2. When introducing new routines and explaining changes in familiar routines

3. At the beginning and the end of each day, to prepare for and review events

4. When providing feedback to solve problems and defuse stress

5. When providing positive feedback

6. When stress is at a low to moderate level

When to Stop Talking

Talking is not effective and, in fact, can create additional problems under the following conditions:

- When stress is at a high level

  The addition of extra and potentially confusing auditory stimulation is not useful when stress is high. In fact, it can create or trigger a crisis situation. While this problem is magnified in autism, it is not unlike the problem of most people who find it difficult to think or act effectively under intense stress.

- After the initial introduction of a new routine

  The learner is likely to become overly dependent on verbal directions and prompts unless the interpreter stops talking and incorporates visual and gestural cues and prompts early in the instructional process.

- After asking a question or giving a direction that requires a verbal or motor response

The learner needs extra time to process the auditory information and produce a response. Stop talking and wait expectantly for at least 30 seconds before repeating or rephrasing the question or direction.

Principles for Organizing Verbal Information

There are three guiding principles for organizing and structuring verbal information to increase understanding:

1. Provide an accurate and precise language model to prevent confusion and learned errors.

2. Speak softly and clearly to respect and accommodate the learner's extreme sensitivity to auditory stimulation.

3. Provide visual support to clarify and highlight important words.

Guidelines for Giving Directions

1. Get the learner's attention

- *To get attention in a one-to-one situation:*

  The speaker needs to be at the learner's eye level. Touch the learner's arm or shoulder gently but firmly while *quietly* saying something like, "Tony, look at the _____ (checklist or material) and listen. You need to know _____." Pause to give the learner time to shift attention. Attention may be in the form of brief eye contact or intermittent attention to the designated material. Tapping, touching, or moving the materials also may draw attention. *The moment attention is given, begin to deliver the message.*

  Note that attention is not requested simply for compliance, but to deliver a legitimate message. The learner is told exactly what to do and why it is important to do it. There is a reason for the request; there is no uncertainty.

  The attention may be brief and intermittent. Experience shows that if the learner stays nearby but looks away, it is likely that the words are heard and intermittent attention will be given to the materials either with direct or peripheral vision.

  A firm but gentle touch on the arm or shoulder often helps the learner to focus. If the learner is extremely sensitive to touch, an occupational therapist can assess the situation and provide suggestions to alleviate the stress and increase tolerance.

- *To get attention in a group situation:*

  The learner must understand the meaning of group directions. For example, words such as *everyone, anybody, class, you folks,* and so on, mean that the speaker is talking to *you and all the people in the room or area.* Sometimes the intended audience is implied and not directly stated. Statements such as, "Lunch time," "Line up," or "Look up here" are unlikely to get the learner's attention without specific instruction. The illustration on page 211 shows one strategy for teaching these words.

Also refer to the strategies for teaching language concepts in chapter 19.

2. Speak calmly and softly

There is evidence that a learner can attend to, understand, and respond to a calm, soft voice more easily than an excited, loud voice. Some learners respond well to whispered words. In a noisy or dangerous situation, it is natural and appropriate to speak louder and with more emphasis.

3. Speak naturally but clearly

- *Speak with normal tone and expression.* Do not use baby talk or an unnaturally high voice like that used with infants and toddlers. It is unfair to model a way of speaking that must be relearned later.

- *Speak at a normal rate,* like others in the natural environment.

  In order to understand the language of others in the natural environment, one must hear it as used in the normal environment. When introducing a new concept or a critical piece of information:

  —Pause briefly to separate the relevant words from ongoing conversations.

  —Speak a bit more slowly than usual.

  —Pair key words with visual references (words or line drawings).

- *Express a complete thought to clarify the message.*

  Ineffective: "Find coat," "Sit down," or "Let's go."

  > (Learner's perspective: Which coat? Find? Is it lost? Okay, the coat is over there—I found it.
  >
  > Sit down? Okay, but I don't know why I have to sit down here in the middle of the room.
  >
  > Go? Where? When? Why? This is too confusing. I'll just run around the room until I know what to do.)

  Effective: "Put on your red coat. Then we can walk to the park."

- *Speak literally and very specifically.*

  Ineffective: When directing a learner to identify pictures, an interpreter says, "Give me the cow."

(Learner's perspective: I don't see a cow, couldn't lift it if it were here. Guess I'll just sit here until she tells me to do something I can do.)

Effective: "Give me the *picture* of the cow."

Ineffective: "Put in" or "Put it away."

(Learner's perspective: Hmm, in? Put in? What's that mean? It? What's it? There are lots of things here. What do I put away? Where is away, anyway?)

Effective: "Pick up the toy trucks and put them in the box."

Most learners need to be taught to attend to more than one attribute or characteristic.

Ineffective: "Go and get a towel."

(Learner's perspective: Decisions, decisions. Which towel? There are big, little, fat, thin, striped, and flowered towels, red, pink, yellow, and white towels. Maybe I'll just sit here and rock.)

Effective: "Bring the big yellow towel."

- *Speak positively. Tell the learner what to do.*

Ineffective: "Don't get out of that chair."

(Learner's perspective: Oh dear, I have to stay in this chair always. Or, did he say get out of the chair? Okay, I'll stand up.)

Learners often do exactly what they were told not to do. It could be that some do not process the first part of the sentence and hear only the end. If so, they are actually complying to the command as best they can.

Effective: Say, "Sit in the chair"; or, better, "Sit in the chair until we finish eating."

Ineffective: "Don't kick."

(Learner's perspective: Don't kick? I can't even kick a ball? Yesterday, Dad told me to kick the ball. What does that have to do with now?)

Effective: Say, "You kick balls, not people. Now, keep your feet on the floor."

This illustration shows one way to help the learner visualize the word.

Ineffective: As the learner walked to the library, hitting the walls and doors, the interpreter said, "No! Stop hitting the walls. Keep your hands to yourself. That makes too much noise and bothers others."

> (Learner's perspective: No? Stop? What does that mean? I know what hands are, but how do I keep my hands to myself? What is the meaning of *bothers* or too *much noise?*)

The learner still will not know what to do even after processing all those words.

Effective: "Carry these books to the library"; or, "Walk quietly with your hands in your pockets."

To solve repeated disruptive behaviors such as this, refer to chapter 15, pages 204-207, and review the use of social stories to help the learner understand other people's perspective and the reason for certain rules.

- *Use only the words that carry meaning.*

Leave out words that don't carry information, such as polite forms and sarcasm. Verbalize basic information simply, briefly, and clearly.

Ineffective: "Would you _____?"; "I would like you to _____"; "It would be great if you would _____"; "Don't you know the dog is hungry?"

Effective: Say, "It is time to feed the dog. He will be hungry."

4. Exaggerate facial expressions

Model the expression of feelings as emotional situations are explained. *Do not discount or ignore feelings* even when the learner's expressions do not match the expressions of others in the same situation. Rather, provide a more typical model. For example, if the learner laughs hysterically when a friend is hurt, look sad and say something like, "Mary fell and hurt her knee. She feels bad. I feel sorry because her knee hurts." Use *natural facial expressions at other times* to avoid distracting attention from the words.

Ineffective: Look bright and happy when saying, "You're all right. Just get up. It doesn't really hurt."

Effective: Frown, look sad and concerned while explaining, "Oh, you fell and hurt your knee."

5. Support the words with visual cues

Illustrate key words, sequences, and outcomes while speaking. Draw pictures, write words, or point to the learner's visual communication system, if available. *Make critical information visual.*

Ineffective: "The book is on the table."

> (Learner's perspective: Which table? Which book? Am I supposed to do something with the book?)

Effective: Gesture toward the table and say, "Your math book is on that table. Put it in the book bag."

Ineffective: "You can eat at McDonald's on Monday evening."

> (Learner's perspective: Is this Monday? How many days until Monday?)

Effective: Move toward the calendar while saying, "You can eat at McDonald's on Monday evening. Let's write it on the calendar."

6. Ask only important questions

Ask questions only when there are real choices and when the answer is not known.

Ineffective: When the learner is expected to work now, the interpreter says politely, "Are you ready to work?"

> (Learner's perspective: Oh, good! I have a choice. I don't really like doing that work, and I still want to watch the leaves blowing in the trees. I'll just stay here.)

Since the demand was never clear, nagging or insistence on "compliance" is likely to be resisted.

Effective: "It will be time to work when the bell rings."

> (Learner's perspective: Okay, a few more minutes to watch the leaves, then back to the job.)

_____

Ineffective: After a field trip to the museum, the teacher says, "What did we just do?"

> (Learner's perspective: I just sat down; or, You were there. As long as you already know and it's hard for me to say the words, I'll just sit here until I really need to tell you something.)

Effective: "That was a great trip to the museum. Let's write a story about the things we saw."

> (Learner's perspective: Oh, good! Then I can share the story with my friend.)

7. Teach the meaning of rules and directions

If a direction is not followed, it is likely that it was not understood. Be prepared to teach and highlight the meaning of directions, both verbally and visually. Then provide assistance to carry out the directions quickly to ensure that the correct response is firmly associated with the directions.

Guidelines for Using Contingencies

A contingency is a contract that specifies and clarifies expectations. It defines the behavior to be performed and the reinforcer to be received. For example, an employee's contract states that for every 20 days of work, the employee will earn $X. The work rules state that after two hours of work, the employee will get a 15-minute break. This is not a bribe; it is a contract that motivates the employee to work. If the employer stops paying the wage, the employee loses trust and stops working. Notice that the contract and work rules are stated positively—they specify what is expected and what will be earned.

A contingency is a powerful verbal procedure that provides a structure for addressing a wide range of problems and critical goals. The power of a contingency depends on the wording, the timing, and the payoffs.

Figure 16.1. The value of contingencies

When used skillfully, a contingency will:
- Develop trust in the adult who states and honors the contract
- Provide a structure for understanding the language
- Teach sequencing and cause/effect relationships
- Increase motivation to work, to try, and to persist
- Provide the means to predict and prepare for coming events
- Clarify when work will be done
- Prepare for transitions
- Develop natural activity reinforcers
- Increase flexibility
- Decrease behavior problems

1. State the contingency positively and clearly

State the contingency like Grandma's rule, "Eat your peas, and then you can have dessert"—first the work, then the payoff.

A negative statement made when the interpreter has lost patience includes confusing emotional overtones that are more likely to trigger anxiety and less likely to motivate. A positive statement that reminds the learner of the reinforcer clarifies the situation and is motivating.

Ineffective: "You can't ride your bike until you are finished."

(Learner's perspective: Oh, no! Can't ride my bike? Will I ever ride my bike? What does *finished* mean? When will I ever be finished? Oh, no!)

Effective: "Do two more problems. Then you can ride your bike."

Ineffective: "You can ride your bike when the clothes are folded."

This kind of statement can lead to confusion or disappointment.

> (Learner's perspective: Oh, good! I get to ride my bike. Oh, no! I have to fold the clothes. I thought I could ride my bike.)

Effective: "When all the clothes in the dryer are folded, you can ride your bike."

Even more effective: "If you fold all the clothes before 5:00 o'clock, you can ride your bike."

This statement is positive and both verbally and visually clear. Stating the time clarifies the situation further so the learner will not be surprised by a sudden and unexpected loss of the reinforcer.

2. Support the contingency with visual and concrete markers

Find some way to clarify the amount of work and the payoff. Use visual markers to specify what *finished* looks like and to show progress toward the payoff. A timer or other signal also can specify that it is time for the payoff.

> Effective: Draw a circle around five problems on the worksheet as you say, "Do these five. Then you can look out the window." When the work is completed, set a timer and say, "When the timer rings, it will be time to finish the math paper, then go to lunch."

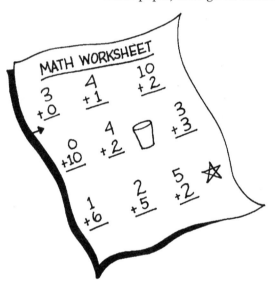

The timer is objective and concrete. It indicates when it is time to stop looking out the window and return to work. Also note that another contingency was developed to motivate and draw attention to the next reinforcing activity. In the illustration at the left, a math worksheet is marked to show a clear beginning and ending, as well as the location of a reinforcer to support the contingency.

Effective: As Mom takes away all but two pegs, she says, "Put in two more pegs. Then you can run." She helps her child get those two pegs in very quickly. This statement is appropriate for the very young child who is just learning about contingencies.

Effective: Give the learner three chips while saying, "Run around the gym three times. Here are three chips. Drop one chip in this box each time you go around. When the chips are gone, it will be time for lunch."

3. Offer a payoff that is valued

The power of a contingency depends on the reinforcing quality of the payoff. The Preference Survey (page 92) identifies the individual's liked activities to use as reinforcers. The scheduling formula in figure 13.3 (page 174) capitalizes on the preferred activities, to ensure that naturally reinforcing activities are always available. Artificial reinforcers, such as candy or toys that are unrelated to the natural activity, are rarely needed when contingencies clarify the work and a naturally occurring and preferred activity.

Ineffective: "If you work fast, you can earn more money."

(From the learner's perspective this statement has at least three problems:

- What's money for? Why would I want money?

  Money has little meaning to many learners. If the payoff is not valued, it is not likely to motivate.

- The term work *fast* is unclear; it does not clearly identify the amount of work or the time frame.

- An "if" statement is a bit like a question and suggests a choice. Use "if" statements only when there are real choices or options.

Effective: "Fold this one basket of towels before the timer rings. Then it will be time to bake cookies."

(Learner's perspective: Oh, boy! Baking cookies is fun! Let's get those towels folded!)

Effective: While stating the contingency, isolate one tiny bite of each food item on the plate, "First, eat one bite of potatoes and one bite of salad. Then you can play ball."

(Learner's perspective: Playing ball is fun. I'll hurry and eat those two bites. That's not much.)

The two isolated bites of food clarify *finished*. For this learner, the opportunity to play ball is highly valued.

4. State the contingency before inappropriate behavior occurs

A contingency statement that provides a reinforcer for stopping or ending an inappropriate behavior is a bribe and likely to reinforce an ineffective method of communication.

Ineffective: "When you stop screaming, you can listen to your tapes."

In this situation, screaming will likely be used in the future to communicate, "I want to listen to tapes."

Effective: Ignore the screaming altogether, and say, "You want to stop work. Say, 'Stop.' Then you can listen to your tapes." Quickly provide assistance to communicate *stop*. In this situation, the appropriate use of the communication system is reinforced and is more likely to be used to solve problems in the future.

Even more effective: At the first signal of boredom or frustration while the learner is still trying, say, "Only three more _____. Then you can listen to your tapes." Then provide assistance to finish quickly. This type of contingency statement is particularly effective for increasing persistence, attention span, and the number of reinforcers.

5. Payment must be prompt and made as stated

When first teaching the learner to understand contingencies, provide assistance to complete the work correctly and quickly, so the payoff is closely associated with the statement of contingency.

Always follow through; a contingency is a contract. The learner must be able to trust the interpreter's words. If the work is completed, the payment must be made. *A good statement sets up the motivation for success and a natural consequence if the learner does not follow through.*

Three situations illustrate the complexity of enforcing this rule:

- If a contingency was delivered with a negative statement, the interpreter may not want to follow through, since it could trigger a crisis.

    Ineffective: In the illustration below, the interpreter has a dilemma. Can the interpreter or the learner stay all night? Can the interpreter follow through to prevent negating trust and the meaning of the words? This statement and most other negative statements set up real power struggles and no-win situations.

    Effective: "When you wipe the table, you can go home." With this statement, the interpreter can provide assistance and emotional support to allow the learner to succeed. The learner receives the payoff even though the demands for independence were reduced.

- When some natural event gets in the way of the payoff, the interpreter has several options.

    Ineffective: The contingency was, "When you finish mowing the yard, we will go to the ice-cream shop." However, guests arrive just as the learner finishes mowing. The payoff is ignored, and the learner is told either that they cannot leave until the company leaves or that the trip is canceled. Any one of these consequences is seen as a broken promise.

    (Learner's perspective: I worked hard. I did my part. I can't trust them. I wish the company would leave. I'll ask them when they are leaving.)

    Effective: In the situation above, the interpreter says, "You worked hard and finished the mowing. I am sorry, we can't leave now, but we can go to the ice-cream shop tomorrow." The interpreter takes the learner to the calendar and reschedules the trip. "Now you can do _____" (another preferred activity).

(The learner's perspective: I can still go to the ice-cream shop, and now I can do _____, too! Oh, boy!)

Even more effective: In the same situation, say to the guests, "George mowed the lawn and I promised him a trip to the ice-cream shop. Will you join us?"

- When the learner does not do the work, the natural consequence is that the liked activity is not available.

In the situation above, the contingency did not state a time when the mowing must be completed in order to get the payment. If the learner does not do the work, the interpreter can say, "You have 15 minutes to finish mowing if you want to go to the ice-cream shop. I'll set the timer." If the mowing is not complete when the timer goes off, the interpreter says, "I'm sorry, the lawn is not finished, and now it's too late to go to the ice-cream shop." The consequence was natural, clear, and fair. If the trip was a valued activity, missing it is enough. Additional punishment, nagging, or criticism sets up a power struggle—another no-win situation. To reengage the learner in productive activity, provide a new contingency with reduced demands and a slightly less preferred activity.

- When a contingency motivates a learner to work faster than expected, an interpreter may be tempted to increase the demand in order to fill the scheduled amount of work time.

Increasing the demand is an unfair labor practice and will lead to distrust. The interpreter can do two things: congratulate the learner ("Wow! You did that so fast, you have more time to play"), and congratulate yourself for stating a highly motivating contingency.

6. Contingencies can be renegotiated

The amount of work required at any time must be flexible. More can be required on days when the learner is alert and processing quickly, less on days when the learner is ill or distracted. If tolerance is misjudged and it is obvious that the learner is struggling, becoming restless, but still trying, renegotiate to avoid a crisis or negative experience.

Effective: "You are trying very hard. Let me help you finish so you can _____"; or, "Do only one more, and then _____."

See the negative reinforcement principle in chapter 17, page 241, item 6.

Because the end was associated with trying hard or working hard, those valuable attributes will be strengthened. It is very reinforcing to end or avoid a difficult or painful situation.

7. Evaluate and refine

The benefits of contingencies will be lost if the learner does not do the work and receive the payoff. If success does not occur at a high rate, analyze the contingency statements, review the contingency rules, and rehearse until a clear and positive contingency can be produced automatically. It may be necessary to ask a support-team member to observe and provide constructive feedback to increase the success rate.

Parallel Talking

Parallel talking is the process for providing literal, clear, and descriptive language that includes simple but complete sentences related to the people, objects, and actions as they occur every day. The parallel-talking process is much like the reporting of a sportscaster who describes an athletic event so clearly that those at home can visualize the action. This procedure provides another way for those with autism to hear the language in natural contexts that will facilitate language and literacy learning.

This is a strategy used instinctively by parents of typically developing infants and toddlers as they move together through a day. But parents may stop talking to their child with autism because they get so little positive feedback for talking. Some of the considerations for using parallel talking include these:

1. Take advantage of natural daily routines that directly involve the learner—eating, dressing, riding in the car, buying groceries, and others. When the learner is engaged in some independent activity, pause in passing and provide a brief descriptive comment. Capture additional opportunities for the learner to stay nearby—to see and be involved in the action—when raking leaves, doing laundry, and other activities.

2. Label the people, objects, actions, and events as they occur. Identify the purpose or outcome of the action. Include descriptive words—colors, sizes, speeds. When appropriate, label facial expressions and the quality of voices (for example, "She is frowning, she may be confused"; "His voice sounds gruff when . . .").

3. Make no demands; ask for no responses; simply give accurate information and highlight critical elements. Questions, requests, and directions change the processing demands and raise anxiety.

4. Pause or break the stream of talk before giving a direction or asking a question. This break gives time for the learner to shift attention.

Reflective Listening

Reflective listening is used when a person has a problem and anxiety is accelerating—when stress is at a moderate to moderately high level (figure 10.1, page 138). This strategy:

• Recognizes that a problem exists

• Expresses concern and establishes a mutually respectful relationship

- Identifies and clarifies the problem
- Provides labels (the language) for the problem, the feelings, and the solutions
- Defuses frustration and anxiety
- Sets the stage for solving the problem

This strategy involves the following five steps:

1. Recognize and identify the subtle, nonverbal cues (behavioral signals) that indicate the presence of a problem, a need, emotion, or feeling that needs to be communicated. Some of the predictable behavioral signals of a problem are described on pages 139-140.

2. Quickly scan the environment for cues to interpret the cause of the problem. (See the checklist for identifying the cause of a problem, page 142.)

3. Tentatively verbalize the feeling and the problem. ("You look hot and thirsty. Do you need a drink?")

   - A hesitant statement is respectful and appropriate because an interpreter can never be totally certain of another person's feelings or needs.

   - Be as precise and descriptive as possible when labeling feelings and emotions. Use the range of feeling words to expand vocabulary (for example, *afraid, bored, disappointed, discouraged, worried, confused, frustrated, lonesome, surprised, . . .*).

4. Pause for acknowledgment. Acknowledgment may be made in a variety of ways; for example, the learner may make fleeting eye contact or become very still and the signs of stress may begin to decrease. If the statement did not accurately express the feeling or need, the stress will continue to escalate. In that case, make another effort to clarify the situation.

5. Suggest a way for the problem to be resolved, and provide assistance to solve it quickly. Because most problems can be solved by asking for help or for clarification, it is appropriate to provide a cue for how to communicate the message. (For example, tell the learner, "You can say, 'Want drink'" as you provide assistance to point to a glass.)

This reflective listening strategy can be modified to match specific situations. For example, reduce the number of words for a younger or less sophisticated learner, and use fewer words if the stress level increases.

See chapter 10 for a background for modifying and using this strategy to fit a variety of situations. Examples of reflective listening are provided in the examples on pages 147-149, goal 3.

Classes had been dismissed early for parent conferences. Jeff paced back and forth in front of the window as he waited for the bus. Every few minutes, he interrupted the teacher to say, "What time will the bus come?" The teacher responded by saying something like, "The bus will be here pretty soon. Just wait quietly." Finally, as Jeff asked the question with increasing agitation, the teacher asked, "Jeff, are you afraid the bus won't come to take you home?" Immediately, Jeff's face and shoulders relaxed as he said, "Yes." The teacher responded, "I talked to the bus driver. She knows that school is out early. She will come to take you home. You can sit in your chair and read these magazines until the bus comes." Jeff sat down at his desk and quietly looked at the magazines.

Summary

Learners with autism need clear and understandable information in order to participate successfully in the community. Interpreters who understand their needs and perspective have a broad range of strategies for providing support. Some of the informational needs can be addressed by evaluating and refining the organization and structure of environments, to highlight and clarify relevant cues within the settings and events. Visual systems such as calendars, checklists, cue cards, and stories provide the answers to unasked questions—the *who, what, when, where, why,* and *how* questions.

Because those with autism live in a verbal world, they must have a way to understand other people's words in order to learn and function effectively. For this understanding to occur, learners need access to the language. Not only must they hear the spoken language, but meaning must be attached to the messages. To facilitate this process, provide the learner with:

- A clear and precise model of the language
- Visual cues to highlight meaning
- On-the-spot interpretation
- Instruction

5

Teach New Skills

IN MY MIND

I TRY TO PRETEND I'M
NORMAL AS HUMANLY POSSIBLE
IN MY MIND

I TRY TO GO TO
TEACHING
IN MY MIND

TRY MY BEST
IN MY MIND

GO FOR MY LICENSE
IN MY MIND

GET MARRIED
IN MY MIND

HOPE MY DREAMS CAN
COME TRUE

—David Eastham
In *UNDERSTAND: Fifty Memowriter Poems*

Plan Instructional Sequences and Contexts

The quantity of details that have an impact on meaning is startling. It is a neurological miracle that most people organize and integrate information from experiences to learn concepts, rules, and routines without specific instruction. In autism, it is dangerous to assume that any concept or rule is clearly or completely understood without instruction.

When planning instruction for learners with autism, who are easily confused by the language and social rules, it is less risky to be too specific than to assume anything. The process for planning instruction is much like the process used by a manufacturer when packaging "The Amazing Machine," a complex and incredibly expensive piece of equipment that must be assembled by the purchaser. Each package contains a great deal of information and details *because the manufacturer does not know precisely what the customer will know*. The package includes:

1. All the parts

    *   The parts that go together are packaged together (a visual chunk) so they are not lost or attached to the wrong component (an association error).

    *   Sometimes a few extra tiny wires or screws are included that might be needed in some very specific or unexpected situations (to accommodate potential errors).

2. Visual references

    *   A checklist of parts—drawings of each part numbered and labeled

    *   A list of directions for assembly that clarifies what to do and what not to do

        —Diagrams and a step-by-step assembly sequence for each component

        —The directions for each component, visually chunked and framed

        —Directions for integrating each component to create the whole

        —Cautions and warnings

    *   An operator's manual

        —Step-by-step operating instructions

        —Photographs, diagrams, and checklists

        —Warnings, strategies for trouble-shooting and correction procedures

        —Optional uses or applications

        —A telephone number to call for help

The instructional sequence is much like the sequence of events that occurs after the customer decides to buy the "The Amazing Machine." There are three things that generally occur:

1. The packaged product is introduced to the customer (*the learner*) by the salesperson/trainer (*the teacher/interpreter*) in a showroom (*an individual presentation in a familiar setting free of outside-world distractions*). The salesperson opens the box, points out the parts, the various components, and the directions, and explains how the product works.

2. The salesperson/trainer goes with the customer and provides assistance and support during assembly and initial operation (*instruction in the natural environment*).

3. The salesperson/trainer provides group training to the team that will use the machine (*extra instruction in small groups to develop mentor support for the natural setting*).

The manufacturers of "The Amazing Machine" leave little to chance. They want a satisfied customer who can use The Machine independently to its fullest capacity.

The following section reviews the principles and strategies for using cues, prompts, and consequences to teach skills fluently so learners can function more independently, to their fullest capacity, and to prevent the paradoxical affects outlined in chapter 9.

The Basic Behavioral Sequence

Behavior happens naturally in a specific sequence:

1. Something happens that has an effect on a person.

2. That person responds.

3. That response affects the situation and results in a consequence.

The effect of the consequence determines whether that person will respond in the same way to the same situation in the future, whether the response will be altered, or whether a new response will be generated. If the consequence is positive or reinforcing in some way, the response is likely to be repeated. If the consequence is negative or punishing in some way, the response is more likely to be altered or a new response will be produced.

This basic behavioral sequence is summarized in figure 17.1.

Figure 17.1. Basic behavioral sequence

Cue → Response → Consequence

This simple sequence describes only one instance of behavior. But behavior is rarely so simple. Generally there are at least two people involved, and each interaction involves a chain of these sequences, as illustrated in figure 17.2.

Figure 17.2. Development of behavioral chains

This flow chart illustrates the behavioral chain that occurs when more than one person is involved and when the consequence of one response becomes the cue for the next response.

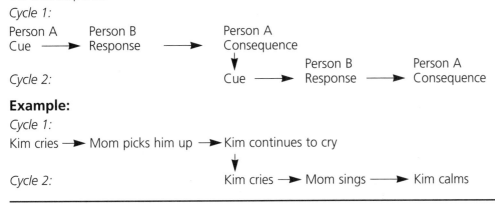

Cycle 1:

Person A Cue → Person B Response → Person A Consequence

Cycle 2:

Person A Consequence → Person B Cue → Person B Response → Person A Consequence

Example:

Cycle 1:

Kim cries → Mom picks him up → Kim continues to cry

Cycle 2:

Kim continues to cry → Kim cries → Mom sings → Kim calms

The instructional process changes the issue somewhat, because one person makes a deliberate attempt to build specific skills or alter the behavior of the other. In this situation, it is necessary to ensure that the cue, the correct response, and the reinforcing consequence are closely associated. To make sure this occurs, prompts are added and the consequences are manipulated, as illustrated in figure 17.3.

Figure 17.3. A basic instructional sequence

This flow chart illustrates the correct placement of the prompts and correction procedures. The chart also illustrates that the correct completion of each step of a functional routine (1) is naturally reinforcing or reinforced (R+), and (2) becomes the natural cue that leads to the next step.

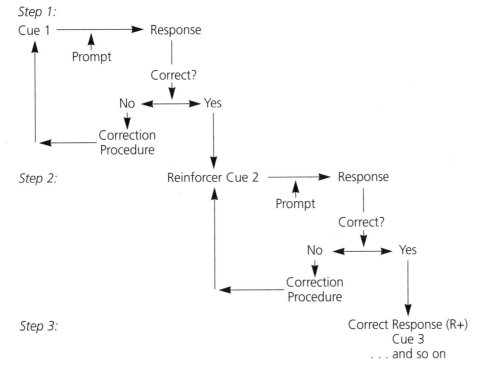

Step 1:

Cue 1 → Response
Prompt
Correct?
No ← → Yes
Correction Procedure

Step 2:

Reinforcer Cue 2 → Response
Prompt
Correct?
No ← → Yes
Correction Procedure

Step 3:

Correct Response (R+)
Cue 3
. . . and so on

Terminology and Guidelines

The clarity of instruction necessary for effective learning depends on the precise use of cues, prompts, responses, and consequences. A common understanding of the terminology and strategies is important for assessing learning and behavior problems and for teaching new skills efficiently.

Cues and Signals

A cue is an event or situation that stimulates or triggers a response. (A cue directs a person to do something.) *Antecedent, stimulus, event*, and other terms are sometimes used with the same meaning.

Types of Cues

- *Natural cues* are signals occurring naturally in the environment that trigger most people to respond in a certain way. For example, the heat from a hot stove is a cue to move away.

- *Artificial or adapted cues* are developed and added to the natural setting when there is no obvious natural cue. For example, a stop sign is an artificial cue placed at an intersection because too many people disregarded the subtle, natural cue—the knowledge of potential danger at every intersection.

Cues can take many different forms:

- Verbal cues

  A spoken direction can be natural (such as, "It's time to go") or artificial in an instructional situation ("Look at me" or, "Do this").

- Auditory cues

  A timer, a bell, or the sound of the bus stopping can trigger action.

- Visual cues

  A hand gesture, a frown, walk/wait lights, crumbs on the table, an appointment book, all are natural visual cues.

- Tactile/body-state cues

  Feelings of hunger, pain, cold, a pinprick, or sticky fingers serve as cues for action. Emotions such as fear and worry also can trigger actions.

- Other sensory cues

  The smell of smoke, a bitter taste, and similar sensations serve as cues.

Effective Use of Cues

One of the major problems in autism is the inability to scan an environment, identify the important relevant cues, and interpret the meaning of those cues. For effective use in an instructional sequence, a cue must be:

1. Natural—something that is always available in the environment when the specific response is required

   A full basket of dirty clothes is a natural cue to do laundry. Adapted cues such as checklists and cue cards are added when no natural cue is available.

See figure 11.2 (page 157) for a review of natural and adapted cues. Many strategies are provided in chapters 11 through 16 for organizing the environment to highlight natural cues and for developing visual adaptation to provide support when the natural cues are unavailable or not adequate.

2. Clear, so it stands out from the background and attracts the learner's attention

   A lighted sign, signifying that a checkout stand is open, triggers customers to line up.

3. Highlighted during initial instruction

   A traffic light is a natural environmental cue, but it may not be obvious to the naive learner because it does not stand out from the surrounding wires, signs, buildings, or shrubbery. One way to highlight this natural cue is to prepare photographs of three different traffic lights in different locations with different backgrounds. Each photo highlights a different-colored light (red, yellow, green). During the initial presentation of the photos, highlight the relevant cues by outlining the traffic signals with a black marking pen. Write a caption for each photo while providing a verbal label ("This is a picture of a traffic light. The red light is on. When the red light is on, it means we stop moving"). After a brief introduction of the picture stories, move to the natural setting and match the pictures to various light posts and continue instruction.

Prompts

A prompt is something added after the cue in order to get a correct response. It is the assistance needed to get it right *before* an error is made.

Types of Prompts

- *Natural prompts* are those that are always presented in a situation that requires a specific response. For example, when the customer does not attend and respond to the total amount of the purchase on the display (the natural cue), the cashier prompts payment by extending a hand with palm up, while saying, "One dollar please," or, "Cash or credit card?"

- *Artificial prompts* are added to the setting if there are no natural prompts available or the natural prompts are too subtle. Most artificial prompts need to be faded to allow the learner to become independent.

There are many forms of prompts:

- Physical prompts—prompts that involve the use of the interpreter's hands or body

  —Blocking prompts—blocking access or the opportunity to make an error; standing passively in the path to prevent the learner from going the wrong direction or placing a hand in position to block a throw and redirect to place an object in the appropriate location

  —Touch prompts—touching the learner's back, arm, shoulder, or hand as a signal to begin action or to direct the learner toward an appropriate location or material

  —Full or partial physical assistance—using hands to move the learner through the total task or intermittently through parts of the task

  —Hand-over-hand prompting involves moving the learner's hands through the routine

- Gestural prompts—pointing, tapping, or placing a hand beside the appropriate material or location, to direct or redirect attention to the task, cue cards, checklists, or specific directions

- Verbal prompts—restating a verbal cue (verbal directions), or making a statement to redirect, remind, or break down the steps of a task ("Remember, first do _____, then do _____"; "What's next?"; "Stand up, then pick up the _____")
- Within-stimulus prompting—a strategy to highlight the critical element of the cue (for example, outlining the critical element of a picture with a marking pen, or using a blue cleanser in a white sink so it is obvious when all parts of the sink have been washed)

Prompting Problems

Prompting presents many challenges because those with autism learn things exactly as taught. Some prompting strategies will have paradoxical effects:

- If a skill is taught as an interactive routine with the interpreter adding prompts in response to errors, it is likely that the learner will think that errors and prompts are a necessary part of the routine. For example, if a line is used to prompt straight columns when teaching a math problem, the learner is likely to continue adding the line even after the concept is learned.

See chapter 2, pages 28-29, for discussion of auditory processing problems.

- Confusion, frustration, and dependency may develop when prompts are delivered too quickly, before the learner has time to process a verbal direction and generate an independent response. This procedure is also likely to decrease motivation to try.

- When prompts are provided in a sequence from the least intrusive (gestural or verbal) to the most intrusive (full physical assist), the learner is allowed to make several errors and to experience several correction procedures and prompts. When the correct response is finally produced, the total sequence of errors, prompts, and correction procedures is reinforced. This establishes a long, cluttered, and interactive routine. Because the complete correct response and the reinforcement are not clearly associated with the original cue, meaning and generalization are not likely to occur and the learner becomes dependent on the interpreter to continue providing the prompts.

- Full physical assistance can lead to resistance, aggression, or efforts to escape. Efforts to avoid or stop the activity are often related to the overwhelming sensory stimulation of touch, close physical proximity, and/or panic from loss of personal control.

- Passivity occurs if physical assistance is provided when the learner is not attending or actively involved in the process.

Effective Use of Prompts

An effective prompt ensures a correct response and prevents errors during initial instruction. It also ensures that the original cue, the correct response, and the consequence are closely associated. When that association is made, meaningful skills are learned and used independently without someone constantly present to deliver prompts. The following strategies support that goal:

1. Effective prompts are subtle, delivered quietly, calmly, and without emotion to avoid highlighting. Calling attention to prompts may inadvertently tie them into the routine.

   Note: Cues are highlighted; prompts are subtle and unobtrusive.

Review figure 17.3, page 227, for the correct timing of a prompt.

2. Provide only the amount and type of assistance necessary to ensure a correct response during initial instruction.

- Allow enough time for the learner to process the cue and generate a response independently, but be prepared to prompt quickly to prevent an error. This requires careful observation and free hands (no clipboards).

- If the learner's attention wanders, redirect to the original cue and quickly provide the support needed for the learner to respond accurately.

- Time delay is a procedure that calls for the interpreter to gradually and systematically extend the time between the presentation of a cue and the prompt. Time delay is often recommended as a way to fade prompts. However, if a familiar and valued prompt is delivered after gradually longer periods of waiting, waiting is reinforced. Use this procedure with caution, because it may inadvertently teach the learner to wait for exceedingly long periods of time for delivery of a prompt. (Some have learned to wait comfortably for 20 to 30 minutes.)

3. Identify and capitalize on prompts that need no fading.

- Direct the learner's attention to the prompts that are naturally available in a specific situation (for example, looking to a peer's book to see which page to use, or observing a no-smoking sign or a barrier at cliffside).

- Embed prompts into the natural cue. These within-stimulus prompts highlight the relevant parts of the cue and may or may not require fading. (For example, in teaching to discriminate a capital E and F, highlight the third bar of the E.)

- Use gestures to direct attention to adapted visual references that can remain naturally in the environment (such as a checklist or sequence chart that specifies the steps of a routine, as illustrated in C, page 232).

- Verbal or physical prompts that call negative attention to the learner or divert attention from the natural cues must be faded quickly rather than gradually, to prevent the learner from becoming dependent on another person. If the instructional sequence is clear and supported with visual references, intrusive prompts are rarely needed.

4. Stop talking if the desired outcome of a routine is total independence. Provide verbal labels for actions and materials during the first one or two sessions (see *Parallel Talk*, page 220); *then stop talking*. Use touch or gestural blocking — prompts *that are natural to the situation.*

    While verbal prompts are often assumed to be the least intrusive and easiest to fade, generally this is not true in autism.

    - Inform the student early in the instructional process that prompts will be removed, and that the task will eventually be done alone or without the added prompt. ("I will help you this week. Then you will be able to do it alone. I will stay nearby if you need help"; or, "This line will help you keep the numbers in order now. In four days, you may be able to do the problem without the line.") Story strategies (pages 202-207) and picture sequences can support the message.

5. Do not prompt in exactly the same way more than once or twice in a row. Vary the type and the placement of prompts to avoid tying a specific prompt into the routine. *Anything that happens in exactly the same way more than once may become a routine.*

    - A touch prompt may be placed on the hand, wrist, arm, elbow, or shoulder (see B, page 232). A pointing gesture may take the form of a tap on some material, a touch to a specific section of the checklist, or a small, sweeping gesture to direct attention to an array or the location of a material.

6. Continually evaluate visual attention and active involvement, especially when using hand-over-hand or other physical prompts. If visual attention shifts from the task or the learner is passive and not putting out effort, quietly and gently hold the learner's hand motionless, as if the world had stopped. When the learner glances back to see why nothing is happening, the world starts again. This type of specificity requires the interpreter (1) to be in a position to see the direction of eye gaze, and (2) to maintain a state of awareness necessary to feel the active involvement of the learner's hands.

A particularly effective way to provide physical assistance or support for handwriting is illustrated in A, below. This hand placement, with your middle and fourth fingers placed under the learner's palm, allows for varied and minimal hand pressure while blocking erratic movements. If the learner's attention leaves the page, this hand placement allows you to gently and unobtrusively lift the hand to stop movements until attention returns to the task.

Be aware that peripheral vision may be more effective than central vision in many individuals who have autism.

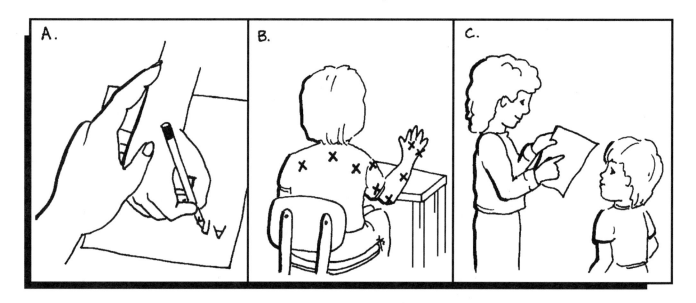

7. Avoid full physical assistance paired with positive verbal reinforcement. This strategy can lead to dependence as learners with autism learn the wrong lesson—that they are to passively allow their trainers to move them through the routines.

   • Biedeman et al. (1994) reported that hand-over-hand prompting in combination with positive verbal reinforcement is less effective than simply having the student observe (that is, using a modeling procedure).

Review chapter 10, pages 137-151.

8. Avoid repeated practice of an unsuccessful instructional sequence. If an error occurs more than once, clarify the instruction. Make adaptations quickly.

With foresight, most of the potential prompting problems can be prevented. An effective prompt provides direction toward a correct response or prevents an action that leads to an incorrect or ineffective response. This ensures that a natural cue, a correct response, and the reinforcing effect of the response are closely associated—"recorded together on the same tape."

See chapter 21, pages 326-333, for a discussion of FC.

Note: The physical support to facilitate communication (FC) by writing or typing serves a different purpose than a prompt. In FC, the physical assistance is a passive, resistive support rather than the active, directive support of the more typical physical prompt. The touch or physical support in FC provides a calming effect so the communicator can focus attention and effort and initiate action. The physical resistance slows down a response to avoid unintentional reflexive, impulsive, or perseverative movements *to ensure that the communicator deliberates and makes an intentional response. A facilitator does not provide directive support to get a correct or any specific response, as in a physical prompting procedure. The direction of the effort is left to the communicator.* The type of physical assistance in FC depends on the type of neurological or physical problem.

Responses

A response is a behavior or action that occurs as the result of a cue. In other words, a response is triggered by the effect of the cue.

Types of Responses

A response can be either a *reflexive, unintentional reaction* to the cue, or an *intentional, deliberate action.* A single behavior can be produced reflexively or deliberately.

Responses can be either *incorrect* or *correct.* A correct response is effective—a problem is solved, an important goal is accomplished, and it is within a reasonable range of cultural acceptability. An incorrect response is ineffective—it does not solve the problem, the problem becomes more complicated, important things are not accomplished, or the response is outside a reasonable range of cultural acceptability.

Response Problems

The purpose of instruction is to teach the learner how to solve problems effectively and to accomplish important goals with actions or responses that are within a reasonable range of cultural acceptability. There are several predictable response problems in autism:

- A tendency to repeat the same action over and over even when the response is followed by a painful or punishing consequence; a limited ability to spontaneously modify an ineffective response or to generate a new, alternative response

- A limited response repertoire that leaves the learner with only a few reflexive actions to use in response to many different problems

- Intentional and deliberate responses that often are delayed and appear labored, out of context, or dysfluent; rote responses that generally are produced quickly and fluently, often without the appropriate meaning attached

- An appearance of laziness, noncompliance, or lack of obvious effort to try

This seeming lack of motivation can be related to confusion (lack of instructional clarity or overwhelming sensory stimulation), an inability to initiate a deliberate verbal or motor response, discouragement, or boredom.

Teaching Effective Responses

The solutions to response problems correspond to the three basic intervention strategies introduced in chapter 9:

1. Systematically organize and structure space, time, and events to visually clarify unanswered questions *(who, what, where, when, why, how)*. (Chapters 11 through 14)

    • Provide visual references when introducing changes and new instruction, events, settings, and people. (Chapters 14 through 16)

2. Teach new skills.

    • Plan instructional sequences systematically to incorporate effective prompts and correction procedures that clarify and strengthen the association of cues, responses, and consequences.

    • Acknowledge and naturally reinforce efforts to initiate, to participate, and to persist in efforts. (Chapter 20)

    • Capitalize on naturally occurring problems to teach problem-solving skills and expand the repertoire of effective responses. (Chapters 18 through 23)

3. Continuously evaluate and refine the instructional sequence to ensure meaningful and fluent learning and to avoid repeated errors or dependency. (Chapter 10)

Consequences

A consequence is an event that occurs as a direct result or immediately following a response; it is a reaction to the action. The type and timing of a consequence affects learning and will influence the strength of a response and determine whether a response is likely to recur in the same form or be modified.

Types of Consequences

Consequences occur naturally in life as a logical result of actions or behavior. Natural and logical consequences can be either punishing or reinforcing. For example, when turning on the light switch immediately results in the flash of light, pressing the light switch is reinforced and likely to be repeated. When inattention immediately results in a fall, inattention is punished and the need to attend is emphasized. These natural and logical consequences are extremely powerful *when the cause/effect relationship between the behavior and the consequence is obvious and clearly understood.*

When natural consequences are not adequate in terms of clarity or timing to strengthen a behavior, parents and teachers add or manipulate events during instruction to increase the learning rate or to modify behavior (as illustrated in figure 17.3). For example, if the natural consequence is delayed and delivered only at specific times (such as a paycheck), the timing and amount of payoff for work must be adapted initially so a learner is paid immediately for small amounts of work. Similarly, the error message on a computer program may be so exciting (reinforcing) that a student quickly learns to make errors.

The type of consequence used during instruction will depend on the accuracy or effectiveness of the response. If the learner's response is correct, the instructor will see that the consequence is a positive reinforcer. If the response is incorrect, the instructor will ignore it in some way to ensure that it is not reinforced, and will provide a correction procedure. In a positive, proactive, and educative approach, as presented in this book, an error is not followed by a punishing consequence.

There are many times when consequences must be clarified or manipulated in some way during instruction to ensure that learning progresses and learned errors are prevented. This is especially true for those with autism who have difficulty analyzing and sequencing events in order to elicit accurate meanings and understand cause/effect relationships. This section on consequences includes discussion of the following issues:

- Punishers—types of punishers, a historical perspective of the use of aversives, the paradoxical effects of using punishment

- Reinforcers—types of reinforcers, reinforcement problems, and effective use of reinforcement

- Correction procedures—problems with ineffective procedures, and effective procedures that maintain fluent and accurate learning

- Natural consequences—problems commonly associated with natural consequences, and strategies for capitalizing on natural consequences

Punishers

As defined in the behavioral sense, punishment weakens behavior and reduces the likelihood that it will recur. For example, if a behavior is immediately followed by a disliked or painful event, it is less likely that the behavior will be repeated or be repeated in the same way. An event acts as a punisher only if the frequency, intensity, or duration of the behavior decreases. In theory, a behavior that is consistently punished eventually will be eliminated. Note that if a positive or effective behavior occurs just prior to a punishing event, it also will be weakened or eliminated.

Punishers may occur as a direct result or natural and logical consequence of an action or behavior. A punisher also may be added and manipulated in order to change or modify behavior. The type of artificial or added punishers used to eliminate a response or modify a behavior can range from taking away privileges or prized possessions, to assigning "time out," to saying, "No, that's not right." While it is more rare now than in the past, highly aversive punishments are still used in some programs that serve those with autism.

Some data does show that punishment quickly eliminates a behavior, at least for the short term. However, there are paradoxical effects that cloud the picture for the long term.

Historical Perspective

For centuries, parents and teachers have used punishments such as spankings, reprimands, and taking away valued objects or opportunities when children made mistakes or behaved badly. In most situations, children learned by trial and error to stop behaving in those ways. Most children understand the cause/effect relationship between the behavior and the punishment; they can reason and use judgment to generate a more appropriate answer or behavior. Most children also can communicate their confusion, ask for help and clarification, and explain or clarify their error or response.

Mild forms of punishment continue to be a part of many homes and schools because adults are reinforced as the child's behavior improves (at least momentarily; it may take longer to see the more positive effects of nonaversive procedures). Punishment also continues in use because it is generally supported by the culture and because many parents and professionals do not know of other strategies to use. Professionals and parents must make a decision about the use of punishment (aversive procedures) with children, with and without disabilities, because a different philosophy is required to use nonaversive strategies successfully.

In my experience, the use of punishment during instruction or to modify and eliminate inappropriate or ineffective behavior is never acceptable. This opinion is especially strong as related to those with autism who cannot consistently communicate to express needs, confusion, pain, a need for clarification, or to justify and defend themselves; cannot effectively analyze a situation to understand the cause/effect relationships and generate a more appropriate answer or behavior; and are confused by and misinterpret social and cultural rules.

My position in regard to the use of punishment was developed during more than 20 years of experience as teacher and consultant in public and private programs serving those with autism, in schools, treatment centers, and state institutions (psychiatric hospitals and training centers for those with developmental disorders). The research on the effects of punishment and the use of positive, proactive approaches supports this position (Carr et al. 1990; Datlow-Smith et al. 1994; Donnellan et al. 1988; G. Groden et al. 1993; LaVigna and Donnellan 1986; Meyer and Evans 1989; O'Neill et al. 1990; Schopler and Mesibov 1994).

Paradoxical Effects of Using Punishment

The use of punishing consequences with learners who have autism is counterproductive and has a negative effect on both those who must devise and deliver the consequences and the person being punished.

1. It is confusing and difficult for those with autism to learn to value, stay close to, and establish relationships with people who deliver punishment. Children, both with and without autism, learn best when they are relaxed and comfortable with their teachers, with whom they have an open and trusting relationship. It is very difficult, perhaps impossible, for a teacher to move successfully from a position of acceptance and calm support who highlights the positive, to the role of the harsh punisher who focuses on the negative.

2. Those with autism often learn to value the supposedly punishing event. Therefore, to obtain the desired effects, the intensity of the punisher must be increased. For example:

    *   Most people perceive a spanking as a punishing event to be avoided, thus decreasing the behavior that triggered the spanking. However, a spanking may reinforce and increase the frequency and intensity of a behavior if the learner needs attention and has no other way to get it, is comforted by the predictability of the consequence, or the spanking satisfies a sensory need and the learner is calmed by the physical pressure. Since the behavior still exists, the punisher tends to see it as a deliberate challenge and increases the intensity of the punishment.

    *   The commonly used time-out procedure to punish and eliminate inappropriate behavior frequently has paradoxical effects. The time-out environment is quiet and free of demands—a highly reinforcing environment for the learner who is confused and overwhelmed by stimulation. It is not uncommon for a behavior to decrease drastically when time-out is first instituted, and then increase in frequency and intensity after the learner discovers that a specific behavior provides access to a quiet, calm area. Teachers are reinforced for using time-out, because peace and quiet returns to the classroom. Since both parties are reinforced by time-out, the learner tends to be isolated for ever-increasing amounts of time, deprived of positive interactions and instruction.

    *   Learners often accommodate themselves to a punisher that is delivered in a highly consistent manner. When life is so unpredictable for those

with autism, whatever is predictable becomes valued. Again, both parties are caught in a cycle with increasing frequency and intensity of negative behavior and punishment.

3. The use of punishment assumes that the learner knows the correct response or is able to modify or generate and produce a new response by trial and error. Because this assumption is not necessarily true in autism, the same error is often repeated over and over. *It cannot be assumed that the individual with autism can analyze a problem and generate a better response or can shift flexibly from one response to another.* The following examples describe situations in which the learner never discovered the right answer but learned the wrong lessons.

> As a young child, Kim slapped his head when confused, frustrated, and upset. His behavior plan stipulated that his hands should be restrained for a brief period each time he slapped his head. While Kim never learned a better way to deal with frustrations, he very soon learned to slap his head, then hold his hands out for his parents or teacher to restrain. As an adult, he continued this unproductive routine whenever upset, even though restraint had not been a part of his program for many years.

> Annie, a very active child, cruised about the room, reaching and grabbing things, then dropping them to the floor. This was interpreted as disruptive and inappropriate behavior, and her teachers consistently slapped her hands, held them down, and said loudly, "No! Hands down!" Annie never learned to do any productive things with her hands while at school, but she did learn to keep her hands down. She walked about and sat with her hands at her sides. She didn't pick things up, and she never raised her hands to gesture. Several years later, a new teacher expressed concern to the autism specialist about Annie's passivity. To demonstrate, she offered Annie's favorite cookies to the students in class, saying, "If you want a cookie, raise your hand." Annie started to move her right hand upward, then drew it back as she remembered the rule, "Hands down." Everyone but Annie got a cookie.

4. Failure, criticism, and the harsh voices associated with punishers and repeated demands cause increasing confusion and anxiety that frequently lead directly to behavior problems. These situations have the same effect on most people.

> Tom's teacher drew a circle on the paper, pointed to it, and said, "What is this?" Tom responded, "Paper." The teacher slapped his hand down on the table and shouted, "No!" Startled, Tom jumped in his chair and placed his hands over his ears. Again the teacher pointed to the circle on the paper and repeated the question, and again Tom replied, "Paper." This sequence was repeated twice more. Tom became more tense and began to bite his wrist. The teacher moved the table away and placed Tom face down over his knees while holding the child's hands behind his back. After several minutes of time-out (restraint), the child was returned to the table and the question asked again. This time, Tom quickly imitated (echoed) the teacher's question, "What is this?"

> For several years, the consequence of Mike's every mistake was a loud, "No!" followed with a variety of repeated demands and physical assistance. As an adult, Mike screams and claps his hands over his ears whenever he hears the word *no*, even when it is directed to someone else in the room.

5. Punishing errors and negative behavior without identifying the function or message behind the behavior leads to escalating cycles of increasingly intense behavior. Review the discussion of behavior in chapter 4, and study the Profile of Stress in figure 10.1 (page 138). No amount of punishment will solve learning or behavior problems for the long term unless the basic issues ., or underlying needs are resolved.

6. Many severe behavior problems are a result of pain and medical problems. Refer to the discussion of medical issues in chapter 24 (pages 380-382).

7. Punishing errors decreases the motivation to try, and raises anxiety. The ability and effort to concentrate and to independently produce an effective and meaningful response are diminished. This leads to a cycle of dependency, with the learner dependent on the person who delivers the punishment.

8. Finally, and of critical importance, *those who are punished are seen as less than human by both those who punish and others in the environment who observe the punishment.*

In summary, it is ethically questionable and inefficient to add and manipulate punishers to eliminate behaviors that result from confusion, lack of skills, and medical problems. A punisher does not help the learner understand the problem or develop a better response or solution. Punishment is simply not a viable option. Those who have decided that punishment is not an alternative have chosen to assess and problem solve in highly creative ways to identify and address the real underlying issues.

Teaching is positive and a more efficient way to change behavior because it builds new concepts and effective skills to replace ineffective behavior. An instructional approach builds competence, confidence, and increases motivation. Instructional or manipulated consequences such as correction procedures and reinforcement ensure that learning continues fluently.

The information contained in this book leads to understanding the learning and behavior problems of those with autism, and provides a process for preventing or resolving those problems in a positive way that guides the learner to greater independence. This positive approach not only prevents many problems but makes punishing procedures irrelevant.

Reinforcers

To reinforce is to strengthen or to increase. In the instructional context, a reinforcer increases the rate of learning, increases the strength of new learning, and increases the likelihood that the behavior will recur. Reinforcement occurs by adding something pleasant or valued or by taking away something painful or disliked. Any behavior, correct or incorrect (effective or ineffective), that is immediately followed by something of value or ends something painful or disliked will be reinforced and strengthened.

A reinforcer may occur naturally as a direct and logical result of an action or effort, or it may be added or manipulated during instruction to achieve a desired effect.

Types of Reinforcers

Thus, there are two basic types of reinforcers:

- A *positive reinforcer* (R+) is something added or gained. The learner gets something of value as a direct result of effort (for example, good feelings as a result of achieving a goal or an opportunity to do something of value).

  Caution: Positive reinforcement strengthens an ineffective and inappropriate behavior as well as effective and appropriate behaviors. For example, if a child screams and is given candy, screaming will be strengthened and used again the next time the child wants candy.

- A *negative reinforcer* (R–) is something taken away or removed. The learner avoids a painful situation, or a disliked event was ended as a direct result of effort. For example, the act of turning off lights is reinforced because the irritating buzzing noise ends.

  Caution: Negative reinforcement strengthens ineffective as well as effective responses or behaviors. For example, if a child expresses displeasure by having a tantrum and the teacher responds by ending the disliked activity, the tantrum will be reinforced and will likely recur in other similar situations.

Both positive and negative reinforcement may occur naturally as a direct result of action or effort, or they may be artificially added or manipulated during instruction.

Reinforcement Problems

In general, learners with autism have a limited number of very specific and powerful reinforcers. They:

- Do not automatically learn to value the rewards that motivate most people in this culture

  For example, most people are automatically motivated to work and conform in order to get smiles, hugs, good grades, to win a competition, to gain recognition, or to earn money. Those with autism must be taught to value these things. They may never be reinforced by some of these things, such as receiving good grades or winning a competition.

- Become easily bored or satiated by overuse of artificial reinforcers, such as a specific food, toy, or activity

- Can become upset when a highly reinforcing activity ends or is withheld

Effective Use of Reinforcers

1. Identify effective reinforcers. An effective reinforcer is:

   - Naturally available as a direct result of a correct response or the learner's effort to produce a correct response

   - Easy for an interpreter to deliver quickly as a direct result of a correct response

   - Not available to the learner without a direct effort to produce a correct response.

To identify the things that are currently reinforcing, refer to the Preference Survey (page 92). To identify nontraditional reinforcers common in autism, consider the following questions:

   - What happens when there are no demands, when there is free time? Does the learner look out a window, flick a light switch, straighten the contents of the refrigerator or bookshelf, tear paper, read a specific magazine, click two sticks together?

- What special interests or sensory experiences are valued?

- Familiar and predictable events are reinforcing for those who live in an unpredictable world. Consider what familiar people, objects, and events provide predictability and comfort. The arrival of the mail? Mealtime? A walk after dinner? A specific TV show? Looking at a magazine with a friend at a specific time?

- What painful or disliked sensory experiences trigger efforts to escape or avoid? Certain noises, foods, activities, locations, people?

Recognize and use the natural and powerful reinforcers identified each time a learner asks for something, indicates a problem, or has a need.

> Kim pulls his father to the door and indicates a desire to go outside. *(A spontaneous and intentional communicative action that identifies a reinforcer)*
>
> His father says, "You want to go outside. I will help you open the door." *(Communication reinforced by acknowledging the message)*
>
> Kim cannot manage the doorknob, so his father provides assistance *(a prompt)* that involves his son's active participation and effort to turn the doorknob.
>
> Active participation, effort, and motor skills are reinforced the minute the door opens. Two critical goals and a functional motor skill are reinforced and strengthened. *(Spontaneous request, active participation, and opening a door)*
>
> If Kim's father had failed to identify and respond positively to the child's communicative effort (the original cue for the total routine), a natural opportunity and a powerful reinforcer would have been wasted.

Strategies for teaching routines are discussed further in chapter 18.

Review chapter 13 for strategies to develop reinforcers in the context of the daily schedule. See chapter 20 for strategies for developing reinforcing social relationships.

- The opportunity to complete a familiar routine is reinforcing. When a familiar routine is interrupted to insert and teach a new skill that would make the routine more efficient or effective, *the opportunity to continue and finish the routine provides enough reinforcement to strengthen the new skill* (Goetz et al. 1985).

- Provide instruction to systematically expand the number of reinforcing activities and relationships. For example, a daily schedule organized to capitalize on the reinforcing qualities of liked activities provides a context for developing new reinforcers.

2. Make certain that a reinforcer occurs only after effective responses. Ineffective behaviors are developed very quickly when a reinforcer is delivered with emotion or emphasis, as often occurs when a behavior is surprising or perhaps shocking. Ignore or unobtrusively and without emotion physically block the ineffective behaviors, and focus reinforcing attention to the co-occurring positive behaviors and responses.

> In the middle of an individual testing situation, Gabriel was unconsciously rubbing his eyebrow and lashes with his left hand. At one point, as he was computing a math problem with his right hand, he rolled his eyelid up. His interpreter shuddered and said with quick emphasis, "Gabriel, don't do that!" Gabriel was startled. He stopped, looked at the interpreter, then slowly smiled and began to roll his eyelid up with happy abandon. He

continued to watch the interpreter for a response. Immediately realizing what had happened, the interpreter calmly and without emotion continued the test, ignoring Gabriel's repeated manipulation of his eyelid. At one moment when his left hand lay quietly on the table, the interpreter nonchalantly rested her hand on his. Since she continued the test and reinforced his effort and work, he forgot about the eyelid and continued working.

3. During initial instruction of a new skill, the reinforcing event must occur immediately as a direct result of *every* effort or attempt to respond and every more accurate or correct response.

   - The goal is to *quickly and firmly associate the reinforcer with the correct response.* In autism, this association can occur very quickly as a result of one-trial learning.

4. When using an artificial reinforcer to strengthen a new and developing skill, change the rate of the reinforcement from continuous and quick delivery to a more varied, natural schedule. For example, delay the reinforcer for a few seconds, or provide it intermittently at unexpected intervals.

   - This variation occurs naturally in real-life situations. (Occasionally it takes a bit longer or requires a bit more effort to complete or accomplish a task.) In an artificial instructional setting, the timing is very important. A continuous rate of R+ will initially increase the rate of responses, but the strength and the quality of the response may begin to decrease as the R+ loses its value because it is so readily available (satiation).

   - The transition from a continuous to intermittent reinforcement schedule should occur fairly soon before a rigid and inflexible routine develops. For example, the learner may think that the R+ is an important part of the routine and be unable to move to the next step until the R+ is delivered. The intermittent schedule must begin before the reinforcer loses its value and the learner gets bored and begins to manipulate the situation. Intermittent reinforcement builds very strong behavior—both effective and ineffective behavior.

5. Artificial verbal reinforcement to strengthen effort and motivation must be unobtrusive so the effort continues without disruption.

Jose was learning to work independently for longer periods of time. At a moment when he was working, his assistant stopped by his desk and said with enthusiasm, "Wow! You really are working hard!" Jose looked up, startled, then jumped up and ran around the room.

   - *Avoid artificial verbal reinforcement of communication and social interactions.* These artificial statements interrupt the flow of the interaction and the powerful natural reinforcement inherent in having communication efforts acknowledged.

6. Negative reinforcement is effective when a learner is tired, frustrated, and having a bad day. An alert interpreter identifies a point when the learner has done at least some work and is still focused on the task. Then the interpreter says, "You have been working very hard. You can stop now and take a break." Working and attending are reinforced as the hard work ends. Again, timing is critical. Had the interpreter waited to end the task until after the learner lost interest or displayed inappropriate behavior, those inappropriate behaviors would have been positively reinforced.

7. Do not waste natural reinforcers. Capitalize on any expression of need or want.

    - If the interpreter ignores these communications, or solves the problem without requiring active involvement or effort, a powerful reinforcer is wasted and the learner has fewer opportunities to become more independent and competent.

    - *When a need is communicated with an inappropriate behavior, calmly ignore the behavior but acknowledge the need or message.* A reflective listening strategy (pages 220-221) provides a model for communicating the message and solving the problem. The active involvement in solving the specific problem is reinforced (as in the example of Kim, page 240).

8. Capitalize on intense interests to reinforce effort and new learning.

    - Attempts to ignore, discourage, or eliminate special interests is not only time consuming, but in most cases futile and perhaps unethical.

    - Teach new skills in the context of those special interests. One young boy learned to read, write, and do math while studying washers and dryers in magazines and catalogs. Temple Grandin (page 123) learned to do research and was stimulated to study and earn advanced degrees that led to a successful and satisfying career and friendships with others in her field.

Refer to the guidelines in figure 13.3 (page 174) for developing a reinforcing schedule.

    - Schedule opportunities to engage in special interests throughout the day as powerful reinforcement for extended periods of hard work.

9. Capitalize on the reinforcing qualities of stimulating or calming sensory activities.

    - As with intense interests, trying to eliminate sensory activities requires considerable time and seems both futile and disrespectful. When one young man was asked why he rocked and flapped his hands, he said that it felt good and helped him relax. Every person engages in some sensory activities in order to relax, whether chewing gum, smoking, stroking a beard, or jogging. The difference is, most people know when, where, and how long to engage in these personal behaviors.

- Analyze the reinforcing sensory properties of the specific behavior, and identify more productive activities that have similar qualities. For example, what is reinforcing about clicking the light switch on and off? The clicking noise? The flashing light? Perhaps a computer could be programmed to provide a clicking noise or a flashing light as part of a game or instructional program. One young man who was reinforced by the visual properties of shredding paper now shreds cheese at several local pizza parlors. Another young person now owns a paper-shredding machine and has contracts with several local businesses. There are many possibilities.

- Follow periods of work with opportunities to release energy. Prepare a specific and somewhat private space where rocking or jumping can occur without disrupting others or attracting undue attention.

See Scheduling Principles, chapter 13, pages 170-178.

It is important to highlight a stopping time (perhaps with a timer) and clarify the next activity on the schedule.

> As soon as Jeff returned home from school each day, he went directly to his bedroom, set the timer for 30 minutes, and began to jump up and down and flap his arms. When the timer went off, he stopped, went to the kitchen, opened his backpack, and shared his schoolwork with his mother. Because he knew when, where, and how long he could jump and flap, he was able to control the behavior during the school day; and because he knew when to stop and what to do next, he was able to move on to productive activity.

See chapter 16, pages 214-220, for discussion of contingencies.

10. Use powerful contingency statements, not bribes, to set up events that will reinforce effort.

Correction Procedures

A correction procedure is added as a consequence of an error or inappropriate response during instruction. The correction procedure provides assistance and gives the learner another chance to make an effective or correct response that will trigger a reinforcing event. A correction procedure facilitates the association of the correct response to the original cue so that learning can progress fluently.

See figure 17.3 (page 227) to review the correct placement of prompts and correction procedures.

The difference between a prompt and a correction procedure is subtle, but important. A prompt is added after the cue to prevent an error and elicit a correct response. A correction procedure is added after an error and directs attention back to the original cue, then provides assistance to produce a correct response.

Ineffective Correction Procedures

Ineffective correction procedures lead to further errors that become embedded into a routine. They disrupt the fluency of a routine and the direct association of the original cue, the correct response, and the reinforcing event. When teaching concepts, rules, social skills, and academic concepts, ineffective correction procedures clutter the meaning and the relationships.

Using Effective Correction Procedures

To ensure that learning proceeds fluently and new skills lead to greater independence, a correct response must be directly and firmly associated with the original cue.

1. Do not highlight an error. The attention and discussion may reinforce the ineffective response and unnecessarily increase stress. Signs of excitement, exasperation, frustration, reprimands, and nagging will highlight an error. Rather, *with a calm, supportive, and neutral attitude, tell the learner what to do.*

2. Direct attention back to the original cue, and provide support to start again.

- If an error occurs within the context of a functional routine, stop the action and help the learner return to the last natural cue (or to the checklist, sequence card, or other adapted cue) and proceed fluently through the sequence to the next cue.

- In some situations, it is not possible to go back and start over. For example, in learning to ride the bus, if the learner forgets to pay the fare, it would be disruptive to return to the street to the original cue. Calmly provide assistance to repair the situation, and continue the routine. Later, but before the next trip, review the sequence with visual cues and rehearse in a simulated setting. Immediately before the next trip, review the sequence highlighted on the cue card.

See chapter 10 for strategies for evaluating and refining the instructional sequences to correct problems.

3. Do not let the same errors occur over and over. Reorganize and refine the sequence, adapt the visual cues, and remain nearby to prompt and prevent another error.

Mother asked Amy to bring her red sweater so they could go to the park. When Amy returned with a yellow sweater, Mother said, "No, that's the yellow sweater. I asked for the red sweater. Go back and bring the right sweater."

Mother used too many words in a fairly negative (punishing) way and introduced an extraneous element—yellow. While Amy held and saw a yellow sweater, she heard the words *yellow* and *red* associated with it. Would she be able to analyze that complex sequence of words and make the correct associations? What was the original direction? Would she be motivated to repair the situation? Very likely, Amy would simply continue to stand where she was, or return to the bedroom and move about randomly because she didn't know exactly what to do.

In the following scenario, Mother used a more effective correction procedure. As she saw the error, Mother reinforced Amy's efforts to comply as she said, "Good! You brought a sweater. I'll help you get the red one." She took the sweater and guided Amy back to her bedroom. With the yellow sweater out of sight, they went to the shelf together. Mother touched the red sweater, pulled it out a bit (to highlight it), and restated the original cue, saying, "This is the red sweater. Bring the red sweater." Mother provided a bit of assistance to speed the process. When Amy had the red sweater in hand, Mother provided a quick reinforcement as she said, "Great! You have the red sweater. Now we can go to the park."

Maria was learning a new routine so she could be more independent in public rest rooms. The sequence of steps was represented with pictures on a card. On the third day of instruction, Maria had followed the cue card perfectly until she left the stall. Then she was distracted briefly by the shiny vent on the blow dryer. Just as she started to touch the blow dryer, the interpreter calmly and quietly took her hand and said, "Maria, stop. Try again." Leaving the stall door was the cue to move directly to the sink, so the interpreter guided her back to the stall, pointed to the picture of the sink on the cue card, and stayed nearby as Maria moved fluently to the sink. The opportunity to watch the water and soap bubbles on her hands was a natural reinforcer.

Had the interpreter verbally or physically prompted Maria to the sink from the dryer vent, the reinforcing effect of the soap and water would have strengthened both the ineffective wandering and compliance to an artificial verbal cue. Maria would have learned to wander about the rest room until someone else reminded her to wash and leave. To be truly independent, Maria had to experience fluent movement through the routine and associate the natural cues with the appropriate responses and natural reinforcements.

Natural Consequences

Natural consequences that occur as a direct result of an action or behavior provide a logical and powerful opportunity to learn important lessons and become more independent.

Problems with Natural Consequences

There are at least two problems that interfere with the potential learning in these situations:

1. Sympathetic and supportive interpreters attempt to protect learners from accidents and potentially negative situations. This overprotectiveness decreases opportunities to learn.

2. Learners with autism are not likely to spontaneously or automatically see the cause/effect relationships in these situations unless the relationships are highlighted.

Capitalizing on Natural Consequences

There are several strategies for capitalizing on natural consequences:

1. Avoid overprotection. Do not step in to prevent or fix things, but do provide a matter-of-fact warning when appropriate.

2. Use common sense. If the consequence will cause severe injury or irreparable damage, quietly provide assistance to prevent a catastrophe.

3. Highlight the cause/effect relationship of the natural consequence.

   - With a calm and friendly voice, use parallel talking to provide a simple explanation of the problem and the solution. ("Oops! You didn't see the edge of the table when you set the pitcher down. The pitcher fell off and broke. Let's clean it up.")

   - After the situation is repaired, use a friendly voice to highlight the cause/effect relationship and reinforce effort and responsibility. ("You set the pitcher too close to the edge of the table, and it fell off and broke. You took responsibility and picked up the broken pieces.")

   - Provide a visual reference—perhaps a story in the form of a cartoon strip.

4. Contingency statements provide a context for developing natural consequences. ("If your homework is finished by 7:00, you can watch TV.")

The most critical requirement for capitalizing on natural consequences is that the cause/effect relationship between the behavior and the consequence is clarified.

Summary

A well-designed instructional sequence specifies the natural cues and the target responses. The prompts and consequences are not necessarily predetermined because they must be used flexibly. Prompts are varied and as natural to the situation as possible to prevent dependence. Consequences are also flexible and capitalize on *the natural outcome of the effort and action*. The natural outcome of successful effort is logical, highly reinforcing, and promotes independence from another person to deliver artificial reinforcers. Artificial reinforcement is sometimes required but must be varied to:

1. Accommodate the learner's need at the time

2. Prevent disrupting the natural effort and flow of the situation

3. Prevent rigid expectations and routines

This flexibility necessitates a good knowledge of the guidelines for effective use.

If learners are to function effectively in many different situations, they must practice in many different situations and learn to attend to the natural cues, prompts, and consequences in those situations. When natural, everyday events do not provide enough opportunities to practice, situations must be engineered or set up.

Instructional plans are detailed and include elements of effective instruction and support that:

- Are positive and sensitive to feelings and self-image

- Are designed to promote success and prevent errors

- Involve active participation to plan, rehearse, do, and review

- Emphasize *why* specific skills or behaviors are important

- Include visual references and adaptations

- Lead to flexible applications in natural routines and contexts

- Capitalize on natural cues, prompts, and reinforcements

- Capitalize on strengths and interests

- Involve preparation for new and changing situations

- Incorporate practice in many different situations

- Involve peers as models, friends, and mentors, not as teachers

- Include continuous evaluation and timely revisions

- Avoid repetitive practice of rote responses and meaningless routines

- Avoid punishment

The following chapters illustrate many applications of these principles. Resources for a more comprehensive and technical discussion of behavioral principles include: Donnellan et al. 1988; LaVigna and Donnellan 1986; Meyer and Evans 1989; and Horner et al. 1988.

18 | Teach Functional Routines

Life is made up of a series of activities or events such as getting dressed, traveling, visiting with a friend, or working. Each of these events is actually a routine with a common sequence of steps that flows from beginning to end to achieve a goal. These are functional and practical routines that allow a person to take care of daily needs, arrive at a specific destination, relax and enjoy a friend, or earn money. Because those with autism learn routines quite easily, it is efficient to teach functional skills in the context of these important natural routines.

The number and variety of the routines that fill a lifetime make it impossible to predict which ones to teach. Even if they could be predicted with any degree of accuracy, there is not enough time to teach them all. Therefore, it is important to select and teach some pivotal processes and concepts that can apply to all routines.

This chapter begins with strategies for teaching children to use work systems—a pivotal skill that is expanded and applied to teaching all other routines (Mesibov et al. 1994). The basic elements for organizing these functional routines that include work systems were introduced in chapters 11 through 16, relating to organization and structure. The second part of this chapter presents strategies for refining instructional plans and for teaching functional routines. These strategies are designed to build independent, flexible, and meaningful skills and processes that can be expanded and applied to the broad range of home and community situations now and in the future.

Work Routines and Work Systems

Mary Anne Seaton wrote,

> The most positive [educational] experience [for my son] has been the introduction of "structured teaching"* (as defined by TEACCH) into his school program and home life. This process has allowed him to become independent in his activities throughout each day. Now, without someone standing over him and verbally directing him, he can feed the cats, wash and dry the clothes, prepare his lunch, recycle the pop cans, tolerate assistance with hygiene, go grocery shopping, and work in the community in four different jobs. . . . The nicest thing about his independence is his sense of pleasure and pride in doing all of these things and understanding what he is doing. . . . This . . . changed his life—and mine too.

Read Mary Anne's story on page 431.

Functional work routines are similar to other routines in that there are common elements and skills that can be applied to every routine regardless of the type of work, from washing windows, feeding the fish, and vacuuming the floor, to voca-

---

*Structured teaching concepts were developed at Division TEACCH, University of North Carolina (Mesibov et al. 1994).

tional jobs, school work, and leisure activities. A work system is composed of all the concepts and visual adaptations needed to support independence.

The initial instructional goal is to teach the processes and concepts for working independently—not to teach specific jobs or tasks. Growth to independence is a flexible three-stage process (see figure 18.1) that begins at a very early age. These basic work-related concepts and skills are introduced when visual references and small tasks are incorporated into 1:1 play routines. These first work routines capitalize on natural early-childhood manipulative materials and activities. The process for developing work systems and teaching these pivotal skills can be applied to older learners who are dependent on constant verbal cues, resist work, and have not learned to use visual adaptations.

Figure 18.1. Developing work-related concepts and skills

Adapted from Oregon Regional Autism Services

These three flexible stages will lead to independent performance in natural settings.

Stage 1. Establish basic work-related concepts and skills in 1:1 situations.

- Establish concepts of contingency and cause/effect (work, then play; first this, then this).
- Use visual references (mini-calendar and calendar).
- Establish a system for working (work from left to right and top to bottom; get task out, do it, put task away) and work-related concepts (begin and end/finish/all done).
- Understand basic rules (stay within a designated area. . .).
- Work and play in various contexts (on the floor, at a table).
- Make transitions (to and from the calendar to a work or play area; from one activity to another; from work to play and return to work).

Stage 2. Expand work-related concepts and skills to more situations.

- Expand skill in using visual references (checklists, cue cards, diagrams, jigs).
- Increase number of work sessions; increase length of tasks and sessions.
- Communicate need for assistance and clarification.
- Work and play (take breaks) in an increasing number of areas and with others.
- Increase tolerance for supervision, corrections, and interruptions.
- Establish basic self-monitoring strategies and a self-control routine.

Stage 3. Transfer work-related skills to the community.

- Use a broader range and more complex visual references (maps, cue cards).
- Expand tolerance for distractions and unfamiliar people and settings.
- Expand flexibility and tolerance for new and changing events and expectations.
- Tolerate corrections and supervision from different people.
- Manage more complex work and cooperative or assembly-line work.
- Extend stamina, routines, sequences, and concepts.
- Improve ability to communicate needs with an increasing number of people.
- Increase responsibility (set up own work area, get materials, help others).
- Expand self-monitoring and self-control skills to other settings.

Design the Work System

Work systems are highly individualized to match the learner's interests, preferences, abilities, deficits, and tolerances. Their design involves decisions about:

1. The type of system (how to give the directions and organize the materials)
2. The type of tasks, and
3. The variations to expand skills and concepts

The specificity of the details of a work system are much like those described in the analogy of The Amazing Machine (pages 225-226).

The System

System-design decisions include the types of symbols for giving directions, the organization of the task and task directions, the types of containers for organizing materials, and the organization of work areas. This organization must be so clear, literal, and logical that the learner can work without verbal or physical assistance after a brief instructional period.

The work area and the materials must be uncluttered and organized logically.

Refer to chapters 12, 13, and 14 for ideas and strategies. See the illustrations on page 164 for several types of work areas and work systems.

Seven questions will guide the planning process, but the final decisions are based on the needs of the specific learner. The quality of a work system can be evaluated by the visual clarity of the answers to those seven questions:

1. Where am I supposed to be?
   - The individual calendar provides this information.
   - See chapter 12 for strategies for clarifying space and boundaries.

2. What am I supposed to do? In what order?
   - A mini-calendar or sequence card displays symbols that match tasks organized in baskets, boxes, files, or drawers. Symbols for matching include shapes, colors, numbers, or written words.

3. Where do I start?
   - Color codes or an X indicate the starting place to work from left to right or top to bottom.

4. What do I do, right now, with this?
   - A checklist, sequenced picture strips, a jig, or a completed sample provides a model for beginning and completing a task.

5. How much of this must I do? What does *finished* look like?
   - The material is used up, the *finished* tasks are gathered in a *Finished* box, all the symbols on the mini-calendar are turned over or gone, all symbol cards for completed tasks are in an envelope or pocket marked *Finished,* or all the tasks listed have been crossed off.

6. What do I do next?
   - A transition cue placed at the bottom of the mini-calendar or the last item on the checklist indicates the next activity or a return to the calendar to see what is scheduled.

7. What do I do if there is a problem? If I get upset?
   - The individual communication system must include a way to request help or to ask for a break.

Selecting Tasks

When teaching independent work skills with a new system, the tasks must be familiar and easy. *If a learner does not have the skills to do the task independently, do not include it in an independent work session.* During initial phases of instruction, organize all tasks clearly and present all materials so the learner can begin and complete the task without problems. To maintain motivation and feelings of accomplishment, present initial tasks that are:

- Stable—Once together, they do not fall apart.

- Varied—Do not use the same task or materials more than once a day.

- Rotated systematically—Do not repeat a task day after day.

- Balanced—Vary the characteristics and demands of the tasks. For example, do not present all packaging tasks or sorting tasks.

- Logical—Do not require a learner to take apart a product that has just been assembled.

Variations

Once the system is familiar, the tasks are varied and expanded to teach more complex work concepts and skills. More functional tasks and new routines are incorporated into the system. A wide range of materials may be used to vary and expand the complexity of matching, sorting, sequencing, categorizing, assembly, and packaging tasks. Office, housekeeping, cooking, self-help, and functional academic tasks also may be incorporated into the system.

By changing the focus and the demands, familiar materials and tasks can be used to address critical goals and more advanced work skills.

- Sabotage tasks (initially in small ways) to provide more opportunities to communicate and solve problems.

- Incorporate interruptions to increase tolerance.

- Require the learner to share materials or space with a peer.

- Require the learner to check work quality and correct errors.

- Increase the amount of work to increase stamina.

- Have the learner set up the materials, using a checklist.

Once the work area, the visual support systems, and the tasks are developed, the basic instructional strategies are implemented. Evaluate continuously to refine the system as problems are identified and the learner's needs change.

A work system developed for a very young child is presented in figure 18.2.

Figure 18.2. Sample: Work system for a young child

These adaptations were made to Matt's play sessions when he was about 3 years old.

Interactive play sessions were structured (as described on pages 293-305). Matt had learned to enjoy interactions, to share the lead in interactions, and to play with a variety of materials. His productive play was still limited to a small carpeted area. He had difficulty moving in and out of the play area, and his behavior was disorganized and random when outside that area.

Phase 1. Establish basic work concepts and skills with a work system.

Prepare and present up to 3 containers for a 15-minute play session.

Do not schedule tasks for more than 3 minutes for a 3-year-old child.

End each work session while the child is still interested. Refer to scheduling principles (pages 170-175).

Begin and end each session with play.

Materials/Structure

- 3 small plastic dishpans (9"x12")
- Several familiar tasks to rotate, one task per container (pegboard with large pegs, shape box, puzzles with 3 or 4 pieces)
- A box large enough to hold 3 containers, labeled *Finished*

The initial procedure:

> After Matt had played for 5 to 10 minutes, the dishpan was placed on the floor near his left hand. While placing the pegs and pegboard in front of Matt, the interpreter modeled the task and said, "It's time to work. The pegs go in the holes." She helped Matt to complete the short task very quickly, and then said, "You are all done. Finished. Put them away." She placed the full pegboard into the basket and moved it off to the right as she said, "It's time to play. Work, then play." The play session continued as before until it was time to leave.

Variations:

Each day, something was changed or added to the routine:

- The *Finished* box for placing the completed containers
- The task—A different but familiar task, the length of task, the number of work tasks in the basket (from one to three)
- The number of containers per session, used one at a time, to practice making transitions from work to play and back to work
- A new task every 3 or 4 days
- A mini-calendar to preview the tasks and cross off as they were finished
- The location of the work area (moving from the floor to a small nearby table)
- The containers, always arranged to work from left to right
- A timer to end the play period
- A peer to complete a single task cooperatively

Phase 2. Work beside peers, using the work system

The group consisted of eight children including Matt, who had autism. After an initial instructional period, the group was supervised by one staff person for a 20-minute period. Matt first entered this group during the second week of school in September, after peers had already learned the routine. The interpreter monitored Matt's stress level carefully and offered breaks before problems occurred. During these breaks, Matt learned to go directly to a mini-trampoline and jump energetically for a few minutes, and then independently return to work. As his tolerance increased, he required fewer and fewer breaks.

(continued)

Figure 18.2. (continued)

Materials/Structure:

- All classroom manipulative materials were stored, one to a dishpan, on low shelves with a work table nearby.
- Each container was labeled with colored shapes, and the shelves were marked with the colored shapes to indicate where to return each container.
- A pocket mounted on the end of the shelves held laminated strips. Each strip had a different sequence of four colored shapes. A paper clip was placed on the strip to highlight the first colored shape symbol. These strips, or mini-calendars, structured the sequence of tasks and prevented inflexible routines.
- On top of the shelves were plain place mats labeled with each child's name. The word WORK was printed in the center and an X was printed on the left edge.

Procedure:

As the 3- and 4-year-old children arrived at preschool each day, their first task after hanging their coats was to work. The work routine had the following structure:

1. Initiate: Hang up coat.

    Matt's first task, after hanging up his coat, was to check his calendar and pick up his transition cue (3"x5" card with drawing of a table).

2. Prepare:
    - Move to work area.
    - Locate and put place mat on table.
    - Pick up mini-calendar (the strip of colored symbols).

3. Perform; conduct essential steps:
    - Check symbol for first task. Match to container.
    - Take container from shelf.
    - Place container on the left side of the place mat beside X.
    - Remove work and place on WORK area.
    - Complete work.
    - Return work to container.
    - Return container to appropriate location.
    - Slide clip down to next symbol.
    - Match next symbol to container.
    - Continue until all tasks are completed.

4. Terminate (Return last container to shelf).

5. Transition (Return mini-calendar (strip) *to pocket located on individual calendar*).

6. Solve problems (Need help, drop material, someone blocking access, peer sitting too close).

7. Communication/Interaction (Ask peer or adult for help, ask for break, ask peer to move).

8. Make choices (Location at table, opportunity to select basket work for free time).

Variations and adaptations made to accommodate Matt's needs:

1. The mini-schedule and the amount of work in the containers was controlled so the tasks were very short. Matt's containers were placed relatively close together on the shelf. Length of tasks and the location of containers were gradually extended.

2. Reflective listening strategies (pages 220-221), contingencies (pages 214-220), and assistance to complete tasks quickly kept Matt's stress at an optimum level.

3. Brief breaks to release tension were offered as needed. Breaks were taken in Matt's quiet area, with an opportunity to jump on the mini-trampoline.

(continued)

Figure 18.2. (continued)

Phase 3. Work independently at a work station

This phase was initiated two weeks after Phase 2.

Materials/Structure:

- A small desk in a quiet area of class room
- Shelf over the desk
- Materials and mini-calendars organized as in Phase 2
- 4 containers, placed on the shelf, containing familiar and easy tasks

Procedures:

This routine was initiated when indicated on Matt's individual calendar. The routine was identical to that listed in the essential steps for Phase 2.

Variations:

- Each day, materials were rotated and the sequence of symbols on the strip was changed.
- New toys and manipulative materials were introduced periodically in this setting.
- Functional classroom jobs were introduced and taught (watering flowers, helping to prepare the snack, feeding the fish). These jobs were illustrated with a sequence of line drawings in a cartoon-strip format. The job strip and the needed materials were placed in a container to be performed as indicated on the mini-calendar strip.

The Instructional Plan

An instructional plan for teaching a routine includes:

1. A description of the purpose of the routine

2. A list of each step of the routine, from the signal to initiate, through termination and transition to the next routine

3. Identification of the natural cues for each step and the natural prompts, if any

4. The adaptations (visual) to support the learner and lead to independence

5. Identification of the reinforcers that occur naturally in the context of the routine and a plan to include others as necessary

6. A plan for incorporating the variations (different settings, people, problems)

7. A plan for monitoring progress and problems

8. Evaluation and refining

Review chapter 11 for guidelines to complete the first three steps of the planning process. Also review the example of the routine in figure 11.2 (page 157). Guidelines for planning steps 4 through 7 are discussed below.

Note that only the natural prompts are specified in the plan. Added artificial prompts are not specified in advance because they will vary to match the situation or need at the time to prevent an error.

Design Adaptations to Support Independence

Adaptations are needed when the learner's abilities do not match the demands of the event. The support team may know the learner well enough to predict the steps or components of the routine that will most likely be troublesome. The Checklist for Assessing Environmental Demands (form 6.1, page 75) is helpful to address both the sensory demands of the environment and the processing and skill demands of the activity. Adaptations and support systems, usually visual references, need to be designed for use during initial instruction. Some learners will need a system to provide support through most of a routine, while others may need support in only one or two steps.

Adaptations most often needed to support participation are those that help the learner to:

1. Clarify the meaning or purpose of the routine

   Initiating a new event or routine with a clear description of its purpose is a key factor in continuing effort. This information can be provided via a checklist or sequence chart. The illustration below shows a recipe format that simply identifies the purpose of a cooking event—to make and eat scrambled eggs.

2. Recognize natural cues

   Line drawings, tape lines, or color coding are only three of the many ways cues can be highlighted.

3. Prepare, complete, and terminate the basic steps of a routine

   Cue cards and checklists are effective references.

4. Maintain appropriate behavior or work quality and speed

   Various visual and/or concrete self-monitoring systems can be devised that the learner can manage independently (including checklists, counters, and timers).

See chapter 23, pages 364-367, for strategies for teaching problem solving.

5. Solve potential problems

   Cue cards and additions to existing communication systems are often helpful. Generally, situations must be engineered to provide many opportunities to practice identifying and solving problems.

6. Communicate and interact effectively

   It is generally necessary to expand and adapt existing communication systems. Cue cards and sequences of line drawings (as in cartoon strips) are also helpful.

See chapter 23, pages 366-369, for more strategies for teaching choice-making skills.

7. Make decisions and choices

   Preparing a T-chart (see the illustration) is one way to clarify choices and decisions.

8. Identify the end or completion of a routine

   The physical arrangement of materials, checklist, or a sequence card can clarify the end of a routine.

9. Transition to the next event

   Checklists and maps can provide visual references to manage transitions. Transition cues are especially helpful.

Several problems can be addressed in a single, well-designed calendar, communication system, or checklist. Sometimes adaptations can carry over from one routine to another. Adaptations are inserted during the initial instruction of a new routine or task, and may not be needed once the routine is familiar. Other adaptations, such as communication systems, calendars, and cue cards, may always be required.

See figure 18.3 for a sample routine to help one young man participate in an art class. See figure 18.4 for a sample of the art project plan that supported his participation. The illustration below shows a notebook system that integrated several of his visual adaptations. Adaptations were added to complete the transition routine plan introduced in chapter 11 (page 157) and illustrated in figure 18.5.

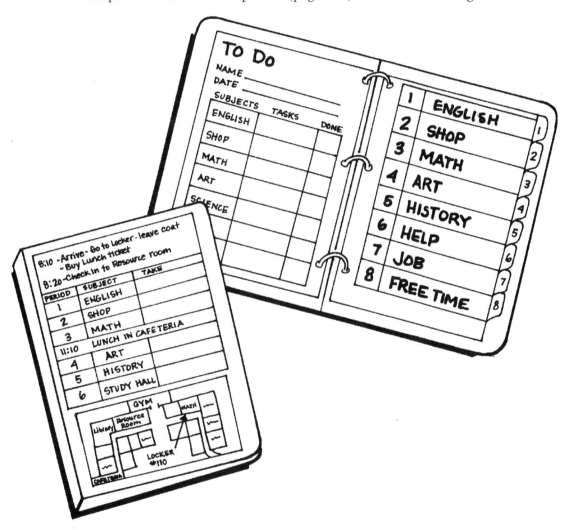

Figure 18.3. Sample: Routine Planning

This planning form illustrates an art class routine developed for a ninth grade student who could read and communicate verbally.

Routine Planning — FORM 11.1

Adapted with permission from *Project QUEST Inservice Manual* (Falco et al. 1990)

Student: _____ **Date:** _____

Goal/Purpose of Routine: _Participate effectively in 9th grade art class without constant verbal directions_

Settings: ___Art classroom_____

Component	Natural Cues/Prompts	Skills/Sequence of Steps	Adaptations
Initiate	1. Schedule indicates time for art class	1. Find classroom.	1. Set up notebook system: • Written schedule on cover; • Map of school with classrooms labeled also on cover; • List of conversation topics inside cover; • Cue card for solving problems inside cover

Prepare/Perform	2. In art class
	
	3. Project folder in hand
	
	4. Folder open
	
	5. Teacher asks for attention
	
	6. Folder open on desk with directions in view
		2. Get folder with project directions.
		
		3. Take folder to assigned work area. Open folder.
		4. Check folder, assemble and set up supplies.
		5. Sit appropriately and follow directions as teacher explains.
		6. Follow the sequence of listed steps to complete.
			2. Prepare folder that includes daily project directions, materials, and sequence of steps to completion. Folder is always placed in specified location.
			3. Assigned seat near stable, capable peer model/mentor.
			4. Art supplies, materials, storage area clearly labeled.
			5. Special instructional needs:
			  • Review directions with student individually after others begin working.
			  • Specify whether project to be done by end of class or carried over. If carried over, show how to mark stopping place on checklist.
			  • Model any new processes.
			  • Model and check for safe tool use
			  • Clarify pacing (Circle step number, and say, "By 10:20, finish this step").

Terminate	7. Teacher alerts class that bell will soon ring 8. Project completed or stopping place marked on checklist	7. Work quickly to finish project or complete the step. (If not completed, mark stopping place to complete next day.) 8. Follow termination procedure, put materials and project away. Clean area.	
Transition	20. Final bell rings 21. Folder/materials away	20. Check area and materials. Is folder put away? 21. Check schedule and map • Move to next class	

FORM 11.1 (page 2 of 2)

Student: _____ **Date:** _____

Component	Natural Cues/Prompts	Skills/Sequence of Steps	Adaptations

Solve Problems	9. Folder or materials not where supposed to be
	
	10. Materials gone
	
	11. Peer sitting in assigned work space
	12. Accident makes a mess
		9. Locate teacher, raise hand for attention, specify need.
		  • Check cue list for solving problems.
		  • Watch peers for cue to solution.
		10. Ask to borrow materials. Use "Please" and "Thank you."
		11. Say, "Can I share this space?"; or scan and locate different area.
		12. Clean up or ask for assistance.
			9-12. Skills listed on the cue card for solving problems are introduced and rehearsed (role played) in individual and/or small group sessions.

Communicate/ Socialize	13. Visit with or greet peers before/after class
	
	14. Need to borrow or share materials
	15. Comment or acknowledge peer's comments about work
		13. Use small talk; or, if time, check peer's interest and negotiate topic.
		14. As above in item 10.
		15. Acknowledge and/or give compliment about work.
		  • As leaving, say, "See you later" or other natural comment to teacher or peer.
			13-15. Use of communication cue card is introduced and rehearsed in individual or small group. Skills include:
			  • Small talk
			  • Negotiate topic. ("What do you want to talk about?" or, "I'd like to talk about . . .")
			  • Give and acknowledge compliments.
			  • Share and ask for materials

Make Choices	16. Choice of colors or materials 17. Choice of project (initially, not more than two options)	16-17. Scan and select in timely manner.	16. Options listed on direction sheet; samples to look at 17. Practice making choices in social skills group and in other natural routines.
Self-Monitor	18. Check quality/neatness of work and work area 19. Pace work to complete at specified time	18. Scan area periodically to clean up any mess. 19. Work steadily, following checklist. • Observe peer for pace of work	18-19. Note on Direction sheet (checklist) only if problem occurs.

Figure 18.4. Sample: Visual adaptation to support a school routine

These directions are part of the folder system supporting an art class routine.

Art activity: Silk screen painting—Christmas cards
Quantity: 5 Christmas cards
Materials needed: 5 sheets of paper, screen with frame, roller, ink, drying rack
Directions:

1. Get materials from silk-screen shelf.
   Choose color of paper.
   Choose different color of ink.
   Choose screen pattern with frame.
2. Put materials on your work area:
   Paper
   Ink and roller
   Screen and frame
   Rack
3. Listen and watch while the teacher demonstrates the project.
4. Insert paper in frame (as the teacher demonstrated).
5. Remove paper from the screen.
   Put it on the drying rack.
6. Roll roller in ink and then over screen from left to right.
7. Repeat steps 4, 5, and 6 until you have 5 cards finished.
8. Wash roller, screen, and your hands.
9. Put materials back on silk-screen shelf.
10. Get ready for the next class.
    Talk with friends until it's time to leave.

Identify the Natural Reinforcers

The effort to focus attention, initiate, and participate effectively requires a tremendous amount of energy (Cesaroni and Garber 1991). Unless the effort leads to a meaningful goal or has a reinforcing effect, the learning rate, motivation, and participation decreases. Each routine must be examined to identify the naturally occurring reinforcing events and to ensure that they occur at a rate to maintain motivation and highlight the critical effect of the effort.

Review the information on use of reinforcement (chapter 17, pages 238-243).

When the natural reinforcement does not occur at a rate to match ability to focus effort or is not powerful enough to maintain effort, the routine will need adaptations. Strategies for maintaining effort include inserting short, reinforcing breaks, use of contingency statements to refocus attention on progress toward a reinforcer, or providing encouragement and unexpected assistance to reach the goal faster. Any added reinforcement must be varied (to prevent dependence) and subtle (to prevent distracting attention from the natural cues and the fluency of the routine). In general, avoid using food and artificial verbal reinforcement. However, providing calm encouragement intermittently during a period of persistent effort, or an enthusiastic but naturally worded compliment at the conclusion of a particularly difficult step, can be very important. ("Wow! You worked hard and you got it done"; or, "Good job! Give me five!")

Figure 18.5. Sample: Routine Planning

This routine was developed for an 11-year-old student who had difficulty following bus rules, going directly to his classroom, and starting the day's activities.

This transition routine does not end until the learner is engaged in the next major activity.

Routine Planning **FORM 11.1**

Adapted with permission from *Project QUEST Inservice Manual* (Falco et al. 1990)

Student: ______________________ **Date:** September 25

Goal/Purpose of Routine: Independently transition from home to school on bus and engage in the first school routine

Settings: Sidewalk in front of house, bus, from bus to front door of school, hallway, classroom

Component	Natural Cues/Prompts	Skills/Sequence of Steps	Adaptations
Initiate	1. Bus stops at house. Door is open.	1. Pick up backpack and move to bus.	
Prepare/Perform	2. At bus step. (Natural prompt: Driver waves checklist) 3. In bus with checklist in hand. 4. On seat. 5. Bus stops at school, door opens, kids get up and walk out door. (Natural prompt: Kid behind pushes to keep moving) 6. Line of kids to front door of school and entering school 7. Inside hall 8. At locker—transition cue (TC) on door	2. Enter and pick up checklist from driver. 3. Scan seats. Select a seat. Sit. 4. Fasten seat belt. Sit quietly. (The bus ride itself is naturally reinforcing.) 5. Pick up backpack and follow kids. 6. Leave checklist with driver. Follow kids through school door. 7. Locate locker. 8. Open locker. Stow coat, etc. Pick up transition cue (TC)	2. Prepare checklist that includes: • Bus rules • Behavioral expectations • Steps of relaxation/self-talk routine 2a. Introduce and use as instruction begins 7. Locker highlighted with symbol for favorite professional sports team on door. (Symbol serves as natural reinforcement for getting to locker because student enjoys looking at it.) 8. Envelope fastened inside locker door holds transition cue (TC) to carry to calendar in classroom. (TC = Name written on 3"x5" card.)
Terminate	9. TC (transition cue) in hand (TC is an adapted prompt to remember destination.) 10. At calendar 11. TC (transition cue) for first activity in hand	9. Take TC to calendar in classroom. 10. Place TC in appropriate location. Review events on calendar. Pick up TC for first activity. (The calendar review process is naturally reinforcing.) 11. Move to first activity. Place TC in specified location	9. Envelope beside calendar with name on outside, to hold TC. • Individual calendar prepared - Calendar review process developed 10. Envelope on end of shelf beside first activity for TC. Note: First activity is a familiar and pleasant activity to serve as natural reinforcer. Once the routine is familiar, the opportunity to complete each step is generally reinforcing.
Transition	(No additional steps to this transition routine required)	(The first activity should be a familiar and pleasant activity to serve as a natural reinforcer.)	

FORM 11.1 (page 2 of 2)

Student: ______________________ **Date:** ______________

Component	Natural Cues/Prompts	Skills/Sequence of Steps	Adaptations
Solve Problems	12. Someone in favorite seat 13. Someone teasing 14. Can't find coat/bag to leave bus 15. School door closed 16. Locker won't open 17. Too much noise	12. Find another seat. Sign/gesture, "Can I sit here?" 13. Laugh/sign: "You're funny!" and/or use relaxation/self-talk skills. 14. Search for belongings. Ask for help 15. Open door and walk in. 16. Find appropriate helper. 17. Find ear plugs and insert.	12-16. Engineer opportunities to practice solving problems 13. Relaxation and self-talk, taught and expanded in individual and small-group settings 17. Obtain spongy ear plugs; rehearse use in all settings where noise is a problem
Communicate/ Socialize	18. Peers or staff greet (on bus/in school) 19. Sitting beside peer on bus 20. Communicate to solve above problems	18. Return greetings, sign "Hi!" or "Good-bye." 19. Share sports magazine 20. Use communication system to solve problems noted in items 12, 13, 14, 16, and 22	12-22. Communication skills introduced and strengthened in small groups • Backup communication system needed in settings where others do not sign
Make Choices	21. Select seat partner 22. Select topic of conversation listed on cue card	21. As in item 12, above 22. Check topic cue card to select	21. Be sure magazine or comic book is available 22. Prepare cue card to select topic of conversation
Self-Monitor	23. Monitor behavior on bus 24. Monitor stress level from bus to first activity in school	23. Refer to checklist 24. Use relaxation routine	

Plan the Variations

For strategies for teaching problem-solving skills, see pages 364-367; for making choices and decisions, see pages 366-369; and for social/communication skills, see chapter 22.

For true independence, instruction must be provided to manage the problems and varied situations that may occur as the routine is carried out in the natural setting. Determine which situations must be arranged to provide opportunities to practice solving problems, making choices, and socializing. If the routine will be used in multiple settings, schedule and set up these opportunities in all or a sample of those settings.

Prepare the Monitoring Plan

As an interpreter, you must have hands free to model and provide quick prompts and assistance during initial instruction. Record the data at the conclusion of the routine, noting problems and the refinements or adaptations made as problems were identified. After two or three days, schedule to collect data at least once a week. See page 94 for a data form for monitoring progress. This form can be adapted to monitor the variations by taping short sections of the grid to the edge of the data form. These sections list the steps included in the variation. They function as overlays to flip over or under as needed. Thus, all the data related to a routine is held together for easy review.

Evaluate and Refine

Evaluation is a continuous and ongoing process. Refinements must be made quickly to maintain success and motivation and avoid embedding prompts and errors into the routine.

As a routine or event is introduced and taught, continue to evaluate. When motivation is low, behavior problems increase, errors are frequent, or the learning rate is slow, look for small clues and patterns that indicate why this is occurring. Consider four possibilities:

1. Some element of the setting, the schedule, or the event is misunderstood, unclear, or interfering. For example, a sensory issue, a personal problem, or a worry may distract and interfere with effective participation. Review the Checklist for Assessing Environmental Demands (form 6.1, page 75) to assist in evaluating aspects of environments and tasks to identify the problem.

2. The purpose or outcome of the routine is either unclear or not valued.

3. The steps of the routine, the natural cues, or the adaptations are unclear or do not match the learner's need.

4. The activity is too easy, too boring, or too difficult. (Recall the discrepancies and variable abilities commonly present in autism.)

Use the Checklist for Evaluating the Routine Plan (form 18.1, page 260) to guide evaluation of the routine plan. Once the problem is identified, refine or adapt to clarify or resolve the situation quickly to prevent learned errors, frustration, or potential isolation and decreasing options.

☐   1.   Is the critical effect or purpose of the routine clearly defined?

☐   2.   Will the learner know when or how to initiate the routine?

☐   3.   Are core steps identified and in the correct sequence?

☐   4.   Are the self-regulatory steps built in?

         ☐   Prepare/get/set up needed materials?

         ☐   Monitor quality?

         ☐   Monitor tempo?

         ☐   Problem solve?

         ☐   Terminate?

         ☐   Transition?

☐   5.   Have enrichment components been identified and embedded?

         ☐   Communication?

         ☐   Make choices?

         ☐   Social interactions?

☐   6.   Are the natural cues for each step of the routine identified?

☐   7.   Are natural prompts identified to support fluent movement through the routine?

☐   8.   Is the natural reinforcement adequate? Will adaptations be needed to maintain motivation:

         ☐   During initial instruction?

         ☐   To maintain independence?

☐   9.   Are adaptations and support systems designed to:

         ☐   Highlight natural cues and prompts?

         ☐   Monitor progress through the routine from beginning to end?

         ☐   Make choices?

         ☐   Communicate?

         ☐   Socialize?

         ☐   Solve problems?

         ☐   Transition from this routine to the next?

☐   10.   Are the variations planned to support generalization?

☐   11.   Other considerations: _____

_____

_____

_____

_____

Kim's job was to stack the chairs following parties and assemblies in the gym. He learned the routine quickly, and he worked steadily so he could be at his next job on time. Soon Kim was doing so well that the supervisor periodically left him to work alone. One day, Kim pushed someone out of a chair as he worked. This apparent act of aggression led to a reprimand. A week or so later, when two people had lingered to visit following the assembly, Kim pushed them out of their seats. After these two unpredictable and seemingly unprovoked acts of aggression, school staff members expressed concern for the safety of others.

Pushing people from chairs is potentially dangerous and cannot continue. However, isolation without appropriate intervention leads to a larger problem—a cycle of increasing aggression and isolation. To intervene effectively, it is important to know why the action occurred. Following a functional analysis of the problem, there were two hypotheses: Kim felt rushed to get to his next job on time, and he had no way to deal with the situation when people were still seated in their chairs. The staff action plan to prevent recurrence included the following steps:

1. Modify and reteach the total routine—not only how to stack up the *empty* chairs, but how to solve potential problems when people are still sitting in their chairs.

2. Refine Kim's communication system to include a cue card with a message asking people to move to another area. Teach Kim to use the card for solving related problems (people standing in the way, one or a group of people remaining in chairs, and other situations), and teach him how to get their attention politely and to thank them.

3. Relieve time pressures. Provide assistance to work out a solution with the supervisor for the times Kim might be delayed.

4. Teach a self-control routine for stressful problem situations (see chapter 23).

Kim was able to keep his job. The school staff members learned that he was not aggressive by nature, and that his aggressive actions were motivated by information and skill deficits.

The following vignette illustrates the problems that occurred when:

1. The job was not adapted to the needs of a learner

2. The learner was not sufficiently prepared

3. Well-meaning staff members were not sufficiently trained to provide effective support

It also describes the modifications that were made to solve the problems.

On the first day of a new job in a local business, Maria screamed and threw her work materials when she got confused and frustrated. Another employee, a friend who had agreed to be a mentor for Maria, quickly came to provide assistance and give Maria a break to calm down. This happened several times during the first few days of the job. When her mentor could not come immediately, Maria would continue to scream until he arrived. By the end of the first week, the episodes were occurring several times a day and lasting longer. Her mentor felt he had failed, and there was concern that Maria might lose the job.

Explanations

1. It was very hard for Maria to communicate with words. When she was upset, she would forget to try to communicate and simply scream and throw whatever was in her hands as a reflex response to frustration and lack of more effective skills.

2. Because her friend came quickly each time and Maria was able to stop a frustrating job to take a break, Maria quickly learned (she was inadvertently taught) to scream and throw materials. This happened because three powerful reinforcers were provided each time she screamed and threw materials: quick and predictable access to her friend (positive reinforcement), a break (a favorite activity and a positive reinforcement), and an end to frustrating work (negative reinforcement).

3. When her mentor was sometimes delayed, the reinforcement was delivered intermittently or on a varied schedule, which actually strengthened the tendency to scream and taught Maria to scream persistently for a longer period of time.

The Interventions

A job coach with experience in autism evaluated the situation and developed an intervention plan that included the following adaptations:

1. The work area, the task sequence, and the materials were reorganized to reduce distractions. A logical work routine was clarified with visual references. Materials were arranged in a logical and convenient order that clarified the amount of work required before breaks. A simple, easy-to-use visual communication system was developed—a small card with two messages: *I need help* and *I need a break*.

2. Instruction was provided to teach Maria to use the new systems, refining the plan as a problem became apparent. While the coach varied his position and moved away from Maria's work station periodically, he remained watchful so he could prompt to prevent errors and predictably respond to her use of the communication card. The reorganized task reduced frustration, and the use of the communication card was acknowledged quickly. Seeing the work accomplished and break time coming closer became a major reinforcer.

On the days when Maria's tolerance was low and she seemed less able to focus or complete the allotted work, her work requirements before break were reduced. Her coach was attentive, and while Maria was still involved with her work he would say, "You are working so hard, you can take an extra break today." Thus, he reinforced her work effort by ending the frustrating work, and the opportunity to take the break prevented potentially ineffective behavior. She learned to return willingly and work productively because the work itself and the outcome of the work (earning money and seeing the work completed) were now reinforcing.

The next step toward independence was to extend Maria's ability to wait and to ask for and accept help from others. Four strategies were incorporated to address these important and realistic goals:

1. Vary the time between the presentation of the request card and the acknowledgment. Initially, the variation was short—only a few seconds. Later, the variation was longer, ranging from an immediate response up to a minute or so.

2. Provide acknowledgment from a distance. ("Maria, I see you need help. When I finish with Fred, I will help you.") The verbal acknowledgment reinforces the spontaneous request; waiting will be reinforced when the coach arrives at the work station to provide the assistance.

3. Provide an alternate, easy task to do while waiting. Provide instruction and a visual reference to cue and prompt, so Maria learns to shift from one activity to the other. To reinforce shifting tasks, verbally acknowledge Maria's independence. Develop a point system to provide a delayed reinforcer. Teach Maria to self-monitor and give herself points when she shifts independently.

4. Provide opportunities for Maria to become familiar with potential helpers and develop reinforcing relationships. For example, the coach can acknowledge her request for assistance: "Maria, I see you need help, but I need to stay with George. Carla can help you now." Carla responds quickly and helps Maria finish the work quickly so she can take her break.

Prepare the Learner

In most cases, a new routine is introduced in a calm and familiar setting when the following information is provided:

- Clarify the purpose and meaning of the routine with visual references—a story, a chart, a checklist. Highlight the value of the outcome or product at the completion of the routine.

- Draw attention to the natural cues and the sequence of actions highlighted by the visual reference (checklists and picture strips). Label objects and materials involved in the routine if appropriate.

- In many instances it is helpful to indicate:

  —When the routine will be initiated (clarify by placing a note on the individual calendar),

  —Where the routine will be performed, and

  —Whether ultimately the routine will be performed independently.

Provide Instruction

The following instructional sequence is designed to:

- Reduce the stress of a new experience
- Ensure that the routine takes on the intended meaning
- Avoid dependency on others to provide verbal cues or directions
- Increase the learning and generalization rate

Initial Instruction

Initial instruction generally occurs in the natural setting. The goal for this first phase of instruction is to complete the routine fluently without errors so the natural cues are closely associated with the correct responses. Movement through the following phases should be quite rapid to prevent boredom and to avoid developing rote routines.

Phase 1. Model the routine

Model the routine once. Provide a running commentary to describe the objects and actions. Make references to the checklist to highlight the natural cues for each step. Review the discussion of parallel talking (page 220). *This phase may not be necessary if the learner is already familiar with some parts of the routine. This phase would be omitted in teaching some personal care routines.*

Phase 2. Conduct the routine together

After modeling the routine once, engage the learner in the flow of the routine. Provide opportunities for active participation—to hold materials and to assist or complete some of the steps. Continue the commentary, highlighting the natural cues and visual references. Provide assistance to prevent errors.

- Naturally reinforce active participation and cooperation.
- Refine the routine or the adaptations if a problem is obvious at this stage.

Phase 3. The learner conducts the routine

After partially participating in the routine two or three times, say, "Now you know the routine. You can do it alone. I'll help you when you need it. I will stop talking so you can think."

- Stop the commentary and avoid verbal directions and prompts.
- Remain near to provide other subtle prompts (pages 229-232) and to prevent most errors. If an error should occur, use an effective correction procedure (pages 243-245).
- Remind the learner how to ask for help and how to use an adapted communication system, if appropriate.
- Vary the aspects of instruction that are not part of the task (that is, the prompts and the position of the instructor) as described on pages 243-245.
- Evaluate and quickly refine the routine, the adaptations, or the organization of the space if problems occur during this stage.

Expand Instruction to Increase Independence

This phase of instruction begins after the routine is quite familiar, *but not yet firm*. The goal of this phase is to increase flexibility and independence in the variety of situations or settings where the routine will be required to solve problems, make choices, monitor performance, communicate, and socialize within the context of the routine.

Refer to chapter 10 to review the process for solving instructional problems.

- Set up situations to practice skills needed to manage the range of potential problems, choices, or social opportunities. When the instruction for these new skills is embedded into a familiar routine, the motivation to complete the routine reinforces the effort (Haring et al. 1987; Goetz et al. 1985).

- Move away but stay close enough to cue and assist with the new demands until the learner is able to seek help when needed.

- Errors that occur at this stage provide a context for learning that everyone makes mistakes and mistakes can be corrected.

- Expand the routine and contexts systematically to include different people and the range of settings.

- Evaluate and refine or modify elements of the environment. Probe to determine whether adaptations or visual references need modifications.

Expanded Applications

While the same basic planning and instructional steps are involved in teaching most other functional routines, some adaptations are generally necessary to match the requirements of a specific routine and/or the needs of a specific learner. The following section describes some specific adaptations that may be required for teaching calendar use and specific work routines.

Calendar Routine

Use of an individual calendar involves a mini-routine that serves as a bridge between a completed routine and the next routine. The calendar symbols serve as natural cues for the initiation of the next routine. The calendar routine occurs during the transition component, beginning at the termination of one routine (activity) and ending with the initiation of the next routine. Once the individual schedule and calendar system are developed (as described in chapters 13-15), the instructional plan is developed.

1. Develop the calendar routine.
2. Design the variations.
3. Develop the visual supports.
4. Organize the daily review procedure.
5. Prepare the learner.

Basic Steps of the Calendar Routine

See figure 18.6, a calendar routine designed for Jeff. This routine was initiated each day when Jeff arrived in the kindergarten classroom. Note how the calendar routine is embedded between each of the daily activities.

Design the Variations

Several variations are considered in planning the calendar routine.

1. The learner needs to experience the total sequence of the routine several times rather quickly. Consider the following adaptations for the first day of instruction:

    - Schedule activities that are familiar and easy, to prevent stress associated with instruction of the new routine.

    - Select activities that can occur near the calendar.

    - Keep the activities short.

2. Identify and plan situations for making choices, solving problems, and socializing. Develop self-monitoring procedures to incorporate as appropriate.

3. Plan expansion steps that transfer calendar skills to other settings (for example, to move from the calendar to other rooms or buildings). Incorporate checklists and mini-calendars to provide support when the learner is away from the calendar for extended periods.

Develop the Visual Supports

The calendar is an adaptation, a visual reference to clarify events in time. Two other visual references may be needed during the instructional period to clarify the routine and achieve independence at a faster rate:

1. Transition cues to support movement to and from the calendar. Determine the type of transition cue and a plan for managing the cues.

See the example of Jeff's calendar (page 186). See page 191 for illustrations of cue cards and the sequence card to help Jeff initiate the calendar routine.

2. A sequence card to highlight the steps of the routine.

Organize the Daily Review Procedure

For the calendar system to have its intended effect, the learner must know what is scheduled each day. Each morning, review the calendar with the learner, noting changes and expectations for any new activities. Make this a friendly, positive, and interactive experience to begin the day. Initially this daily review takes only a few minutes, depending on the learner's attention span and the amount of time and detail included in the calendar.

Prepare the Learner. Before the initial instruction begins, introduce the calendar and the routine. While pointing to the various parts of the calendar system, say, "This is your calendar. See? Your name is here. These pictures *(objects, words)* show what you will do each day. Let's see what's on your schedule today. First, _____. Then, _____ and _____. Last, you will _____. Then, see this card? It tell you that it's time to go home on the bus. Okay, let's start at the beginning and see how it works. First, you will do _____" *(a liked activity)*. Continue instruction as described in the basic instructional guidelines (pages 264-265).

Personal Care Routines

While the basic instructional strategies are effective and will need little adaptation for teaching personal care routines, special attention is needed to prevent dependence on another person to deliver verbal directions and prompts. Two strategies are often helpful:

Figure 18.6. Sample: Calendar routine for Jeff

1. **Initiate**

   At the conclusion of the arrival routine when coat is hung up:
   - Pick up transition cue card from pocket mounted over coat hook.

2. **Prepare**
   - Carry card to calendar.
   - Place card in designated pocket.

3. **Perform essential steps**
   - Review calendar with interpreter.
   - Pick up symbol card for the first activity.
   - Carry card (transition cue) to the location of the activity.
   - Place card in designated location.
   - Follow the activity routine through to termination.
   - Pick up transition cue card to return to calendar.
   - Carry card to calendar.
   - Place transition cue in designated location.
   - Pick up symbol card for the second activity.
   - Continue as above throughout the day to the termination of the last activity.
   - Return last transition card to designated area near the calendar.

4. **Terminate**
   - Pick up the symbol indicating time to go home.
   - Carry to designated location near coat.

5. **Transition**
   - Place card in pocket.
   - Put on coat and pick up bag.
   - Leave room.
   - Begin travel routine.

6. **Solve problems**
   - Access to calendar is blocked, container for the symbol is missing, and access to next activity is blocked.

7. **Communicate/Socialize**
   - Ask for assistance or direction.
   - Peer greets and asks, "Where are you going?"

8. **Make choices**
   - Choose route to next activity, select activity for break time.

9. **Self-monitor**
   - Complete the calendar routine fast enough to get to the next activity on time.

1. Prepare social stories, diagrams, or checklists to clarify the steps of the routine and to clearly specify the expectation of independence. Refer to these visual references during the introductory and the initial instructional periods.

2. After one or two days of instruction, stop talking. Instead, use gestures or touch prompts. Point or gesture to direct attention to the appropriate step on the checklist.

School Routines

Develop functional routines and work systems to support performance in academic classes, to manage homework, and to participate in assemblies, athletic events, parties, and projects. Organize directions, materials, and work in baskets, folders, or notebook systems.

Summary

It is highly effective to teach functional skills in the context of total routines that incorporate both the basic steps and the extension or enrichment components. The basic guidelines for instruction can be adapted to a wide range of routines and learners. Even very young children can learn to use visual references that support functional routines. These visual references and work systems will remain constant and familiar, a context for adding change.

As early routines and skills are established, new activities and increasing demands are constantly added to expand competence. As each new element is added, it creates a measure of stress and uneven behavior much like dropping pebbles, one at a time, into a pool of calm water. Initially the water is agitated and disturbed, but the water soon accommodates itself to the disturbance. The center calms, the radiating waves spread out, and the water is calm once again. If too many pebbles are dropped at one time, the disturbance is greater, the pattern does not develop, and the water remains disturbed for a longer period of time.

CHAPTER

19

Teach Concepts

The impact of the autism learning style and perspective on the development of language, communication, and social skills cannot be overstated. Jim Sinclair, at age 27, wrote his personal story in which he explains his own learning and thinking problems and abilities:

> Being autistic does not mean being unable to learn. But it does mean there are differences in *how* learning happens. . . . [What I think is most] frequently overlooked is that autism involves differences in what is known *without* learning, . . . gaps between what is expected to be learned, and what is assumed to be already understood. Even when I can point to the gap and ask for information, . . . my questions are usually ignored, treated as jokes, or met with incredulity, suspicion, or hostility. . . . People become impatient when I don't understand things they think I'm "smart enough" to know already or to figure out for myself. . . . Assumptions that I know things which in fact I don't understand often lead directly to conclusions that I can't learn things which in fact I already know. . . . No one guessed how much I understood, because I couldn't say what I knew. And no one guessed the critical thing I didn't know, the one missing connection that so much else depended on: I didn't communicate by talking, not because I was incapable of learning to use language, but because I simply didn't know that was what talking was for. Learning how to talk follows from knowing *why* to talk—and until I learned that words have meanings, there was no reason to go to the trouble of learning to pronounce them as sounds. . . . I had no idea that this could be a way to exchange meaning with other minds (Sinclair 1992, 295-96).

While Jim describes only his own experience, it is likely that many others with autism, who are not able to explain their problems, share this experience to some degree. Many parents and teachers have reported that it is often the small missing detail or piece of information that makes the difference between understanding and not understanding. Until there is data to prove that Jim's explanation does not hold true for other learners, the strategies in this chapter are based on the following assumptions:

- One cannot assume that those with autism will automatically learn all the complexities of language meaning by trial and error, from simply hearing it in the context of the natural environment.

- Traditional language-development programs and strategies, while helpful, are not totally adequate because they assume that the child will learn some of the basic lessons without instruction.

- One never knows which concepts and rules are misunderstood or not fully understood until there is a problem. Learners are either unaware of their erroneous or limited understanding and perspective of an issue, or they cannot ask (or at least they rarely ask) the appropriate questions for clarification. Even if they do ask, often their message is ignored, or perhaps the form of the question is not understood.

Without full and accurate meaning, the language is interpreted and used literally and sometimes erroneously (or eccentrically), based on the perspective of the world shared by those with autism. These problems affect learning and functioning in many unexpected ways.

Two types of strategies are described in this chapter: informal strategies used as an ongoing part of natural daily life, and formal strategies used to systematically teach concepts so they can be used more flexibly in a broader range of situations.

Informal Strategies

Model Language Use

See chapter 16 for basic strategies for talking to those with autism to facilitate understanding.

Learners need to hear and understand the language before they can be expected to communicate with language. They must hear and understand the language in order to function effectively in the world where others are speaking. The following strategies provide the language model paired with visual references to clarify meaning. When language is enhanced, both communication and literacy will be enhanced (Koppenhaver et al. 1991).

Labeling Concepts (Four Activities)

Spoken and written words are symbols of real things and ideas that allow information to be shared. This is an abstract, complex, and fundamental concept that most young children learn without being taught, but one that must be taught to most learners with autism. Some of the fundamental language concepts that need emphasis are:

1. Everything has a name. You can speak and write the name words.

2. Everything can be represented in different ways. ("This is a _____. This is the word for _____. This is a picture of _____. This is a drawing of _____.")

3. A word or visual symbol can represent a single thing and relate to something bigger. ("This is a game. These are the parts of the game. This is a drawing of the game. A drawing of a game can mean, 'It's time to play the game.'")

4. Words are powerful. They help you get the things you want.

These basic concepts can be reinforced through the following four activities.

Activity 1. What's Its Name?

Purpose: To teach that everything has a name, and names can be written down

Materials: 3"x5" cards, black felt marker, tape

Setting: Natural home or school setting

Procedure: Move about the room with the learner, stopping at various places to name and label furniture, objects, or other features. Stop at the door and get down to the learner's eye level. Place your hand on the door and move it about while saying, "This is a door." As the learner watches, quickly print the word, *door,* on a 3"x5" card and say, "This is the word, *door.* Help me tape the word on the door." Provide assistance as needed. Depending on attention span, encourage the learner to touch, open, or close the door while describing the actions with the door.

Do not insist that the learner say the word, and *do not ask questions.* This is neither a test nor an exploratory experience. *It is not a time to risk a wrong answer and a misassociation.*

Activity 2. See What's New

Purpose: To teach that everything has a name, parts of things have names, and a thing with many parts can be represented by a single symbol

Materials: A single new game, toy, food, or material on a table; 3"x5" card; black felt marker

Setting: A one-to-one context in a natural setting

Sit with the learner, in a conversational position so it is easy to glance at each other. Have the learner sit facing away from any distracting activity in the room. If the learner still is distracted, move to a more private area.

Procedure: With the new material in view (for example, a new Candy Land game), use a hand gesture to indicate the whole object—not just a small detail of the object. Say, "This is a game. It is called Candy Land. See the words here, *Candy Land.*" Label the different parts of the game while demonstrating the spinner and the markers on the board. Use parallel talk as the learner explores the game. If the learner's attention span is sufficient, play the game. When it is time to leave, print the name of the game on the 3"x5" card (add a line drawing if needed), and say, "These words are *Candy Land.* When this card is on your calendar, it will mean it is time to play Candy Land." Have the learner carry the game to the shelf, and place the card in the box of calendar symbols. Schedule to play the game later in the day or early the next morning.

Introduce only one new material and its symbol at a time. While conversation is appropriate during the session, do not test or ask questions that might elicit a wrong response. This whole process can take only a few minutes.

Variation: Write a story about the material.

Activity 3. What's That In the Mirror?

Purpose: To teach that real people, things, and actions are reflected in mirrors; drawings and printed words represent real people, things, and events; and drawings and printed words remind us of things we have done

Materials: Full-length mirror, ball or other favorite toy, 3"x5" card, black felt marker, notebook

Setting: A quiet area or separate room with no distracting images that can be reflected in the mirror

Sit on the floor facing the learner.

Procedure: Play together with the ball. While playing, draw attention to the reflections in the mirror. Point back and forth between the mirror and the actual situation while saying, "See? That's a reflection of you. And there's the ball, and there I am. You can see us in the mirror, playing with the ball." Play for a few more minutes, pausing periodically to look and gesture to the mirror. Stop the play, and quickly draw and label stick figures and the ball. Say, "See? This is a picture of you, Jason. Here I am—Jan. And here's the ball." Label the picture and draw attention to the

"WE ARE ROLLING THE BALL"

words and their referents. Continue to play while periodically drawing attention to the mirror, the drawing, and the actual event. After the session, involve the learner in placing the story in a notebook to talk about later.

Variations: Use the drawing later to introduce the same game. "Look at this picture. There is a picture of you, me, and the ball. Let's play ball." Repeat the activity at different times with different objects. Draw pictures and write brief stories of other experiences in other settings without the mirror. Review the notebook periodically. Send copies of the picture stories home to share with parents. These stories form the early reading program.

Activity 4. Let's Make a Picture

Purpose: To teach that an object has a name and can tell us what to do; and that a drawing of an object also can tell us what to do

Materials: 3"x5" card, black felt marker, child-sized scissors, tape

Setting: Sitting at a table in a nondistracting area

Procedure:

Phase 1. With the learner watching, tape a small pair of scissors to a 3"x5" card and print *scissors* on the card while saying, "This is a pair of scissors. I am taping the scissors to the card. This is the word, *scissors*. It's time to cut with scissors." Help the learner carry the card with scissors attached to the cutting area and place them on the table. With another pair of scissors, assist the learner to cut. After a few minutes, say, "It's time to stop cutting." Put away the scissors and have the learner carry the card, with scissors still attached, back to place in the box of calendar symbols. Use the same symbol in the schedule during the next two days.

Phase 2. On the fourth day, trace around the scissors with the felt pen and remove them from the card while saying, "Now we have a picture of scissors. It is time to cut with scissors." Have the learner carry the card and scissors to the cutting area and place them on the table. Assist the learner to cut. At the end of cutting time, have the learner leave the scissors in the area and return the card to the storage box.

Variations: Repeat the procedure, using other objects.

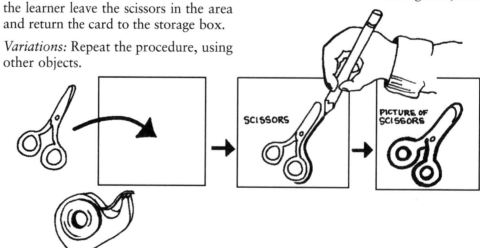

UNDERSTANDING THE NATURE OF AUTISM

The critical elements of the above strategies are:

1. The learner must see the object and hear the correct label at the same time to ensure that they are associated ("recorded on the same tape").

2. The verbal and printed label of the object or action must be quickly paired with the action or activity that illustrates its meaning or purpose.

3. Do not ask questions. These are not exploratory sessions, nor are they tests. This is the time to record clear and correct information uncluttered with irrelevant information. It is not a time for guessing and wrong answers.

Although these concepts are best taught in early childhood, some of the strategies can be modified to introduce new materials and concepts to older learners.

Formal Strategies

Target Concepts for Instruction

1. Identify the concepts and rules that need specific instruction from standardized or criterion-referenced checklists of basic language concepts.

   Teach most basic language concepts systematically to all young children with autism because they are not likely to learn the *full* meaning without instruction.

2. Pinpoint the misunderstood concepts that trigger problems in daily activities and events.

   Often a problem is related to a specific word or concept that has no meaning, limited meaning, or a distorted meaning for the learner. For example, words with multiple and nonspecific meanings (such as *hurt, normal, later, over, others*), homonyms, sarcasm, and idioms often lead to misunderstandings and increased anxiety that disrupt learning.

3. Identify the abstract concepts and the words that depend on the context for meaning while planning instruction in academic content areas and vocational or leisure pursuits.

Plan the Instruction for Generalization

The literalness of thinking and beliefs in autism are such that unless specified, a concept is assumed to have a single meaning *and there's nothing else to add*. For this reason, the instructional sequence is planned with exquisite detail. The process for planning described below is based on general case instruction (Albin and Horner 1988; Horner et al. 1988). The Concept Planning Guide (form 19.1, page 274) will direct this six-step process. See figure 19.1 (page 275) for a sample Concept Planning Guide.

Step 1. Define the concept.

Use the most literal and commonly accepted definitions for concepts (for example, Red is a color; or, Shoes cover feet).

Step 2. Define related concepts, variations, and contradictions.

This is the most critical step for planning instruction to ensure that the meaning is clear and inclusive. Information about related concepts, variations, and contradictions ensures that the instructional examples represent the range of variations. In teaching the concept of red, examples might be selected from each of the variations listed below. (Note: The italicized words highlight the need to specify that there are other possibilities.)

Concept: _____

Define the concept:	Instructional examples		Natural and/or simulated contexts for generalization	Visual references to clarify details and relationships
	Positive examples ("This is a _____")	Negative examples ("This is not a _____")		
Related concepts:				

Figure 19.1. Sample: Concept planning guide

The following illustrates the details that must be considered when selecting instructional examples and planning experiences in natural settings. This kind of planning is designed to prevent misperceptions and lead to broader and more flexible understandings necessary for generalization.

Concept Planning Guide

Concept: Red

Define the concept: Red is a color.	Instructional examples		Natural and/or simulated contexts for generalization	Visual references to clarify details and relationships
	Positive examples ("This is a ____")	Negative examples ("This is not a ____")		

Related concepts:
1. Many things are red:
  • Big things and little things
  • Metal, wood, cloth, paper...
  • Things that are hard, soft, rough...
  • Toys, tools, flowers, food...
2. There are variations of red:
  • Bright, light, dark, bluish, orange-red...
3. Some variations have different names:
  • Magenta, scarlet, cherry, fire engine...
4. Some things are almost red but not red:
  • Orange, pink, fuchsia, brown, purple...
5. Some things can be all red.
6. Some things are part red and other colors, too.
7. Sometimes <u>red</u> has different meanings:
  • Red hair, red cows...
  • Red faces—flushing that is not really red—might mean a person is embarrassed, sick, upset, hot, or sunburned.
  • Red lights and red signs sometimes mean <u>warning</u> or <u>stop</u>.
  • There are other meanings, too.
	• little red toy truck
	• red apples
	• big red sweater
	• child's red sock
	• new red crayon
	• long red pencil
	• red book
	<u>Later positive examples</u>
	• red and yellow striped apple
	• red-handled screwdriver
	• multicolored fabrics, ribbon, paper...
		(Note: Negative examples must be exactly like positive examples except for color.)
		• little yellow truck
		• green apple
		• big orange sweater
		• child's pink sock
		• new fuchsia crayon
			Highlight and talk about red things seen while:
			• Walking or driving down street
			• Doing laundry (matching, sorting)
			• Cooking, eating, buying food
			• Shopping
			• At paint stores and looking at paint samples
			• Looking at magazines and catalogs
			• Mixing paints for art projects
			• Doing preschool sorting or matching tasks
			• When referring to objects when giving directions ("Bring the red towel"; "Eat the red apple")
				• Create semantic maps.
				• Write experience stories.
				• Draw illustrations.
				• Keep a journal or notes during experiences.
				• Keep a concept notebook for saving visual references.

- Many things can be red, or they can be other colors.

  Crayons, paints, lips, cars, sweaters, balls, flowers, lights, cows, mosquito bites, apples, cars, lights, and *many other things*

- There are variations (or many shades) of red.

  Not pink, not orange, not brown, not purple, not . . .

- Some shades of red have different names.

  Red-orange, scarlet, cerise, cherry red, poppy red, fire engine red, and *many other names*

- Some things are part red.

  An apple can be red and other colors; scissors can have a red handle; fabrics and pictures can have some red and many other colors; other things can be part red, too.

- Big things and little things can be red, part red, or not red.

- The word *red* is used in *many different ways.*

  Red face, red hot, red tape, red light (meaning *stop* or *warning*); and *many other ways*

- There is a word that sounds like *red,* but it is spelled differently and means something else. The word is *read.* I *read* a book. (This does not mean that you colored a book red.)

Step 3. Identify instructional examples.

Because it is not possible or reasonable to present all the variations and contradictions, select examples for initial instruction that represent the range of attributes, meanings, and uses.

Select positive examples and negative examples. For example, *a big red sweater* represents the attributes of size, color, and clothing. A negative example, *a big orange sweater* that is an exact replica of the other sweater except in the attribute of color, is *not* red. These negative examples provide information to make fine discriminations.

Note that the word *not* is also an abstract word that must be taught. These instructional procedures help to clarify that concept as well.

Other negative examples for the color red might be a small, red, wooden truck and a replica that is brown; a child's all-red tennis shoe and a replica that is purple; or a new red crayon and a new pink crayon.

Positive examples that represent other variations might include a long, red licorice stick; a short, orange-red string; a small, soft, bluish-red ball; a sheet of red paper; a large, dark-red book; or a bright-red metal bucket.

Note that just these few examples represent the attributes of big/small, soft/hard, long/short, new/old, cloth, leather, plastic, metal, wood, paper, clothing, toys, tools, containers, and foods. They also include colors that are close to red but not red, and different shades of red.

Shortly after the initial instruction, introduce variations. Add a few objects to represent things that are part red—a red-handled wrench, a yellow and red apple, or a piece of printed fabric that has red in it.

Step 4. Identify natural environments for instruction and practice.

To ensure generalization to a broader range of situations, apply the concept in many different natural situations. Natural experiences for teaching and experiencing red might include:

- Visiting a paint store to see paint chips and color wheels
- Art projects that involve mixing colors
- Observing traffic signals on the street
- Visiting a fabric store, grocery store, auto dealership, toy store
- Sorting laundry, cooking, eating
- Looking at magazines and catalogs
- Performing preschool sorting, attribute, and other tasks
- And many, many more possibilities

Step 5. Plan and prepare visual references.

See chapter 15 for many examples of visual strategies. Specifically note information about semantic maps (pages 200-202) and the use of stories (pages 202-208).

Total communication strategies that simultaneously pair signs with speech are useful when teaching some basic language concepts because the shapes and the movement of the signs are highly graphic. While signs augment and support the instruction, they are transient and leave no permanent reference.

Permanent visual references that show the gestalt of a concept are most always important in autism. There are various ways of organizing ideas and details visually to match the specific qualities of the concept or event to the needs of a specific learner.

To extend the example of teaching red, the objects themselves are visual and appropriate for the initial introduction and instruction. Immediately following the initial instruction, summarize the information with a chart or semantic map that lists each item under the appropriate categories *RED* and *NOT RED*. Use a red and various not-red markers to enter the information. Expand this chart as new examples are discovered. Use a color wheel or mark a chart of paint strips to identify the shades of *red* and *not red*.

This visual was developed while summarizing a lesson to clarify the homonym blue/blew. The lesson activities involved going outside to feel the wind, coloring with a blue crayon, blowing bubbles, blowing out candles, and making sad faces while talking about feeling blue.

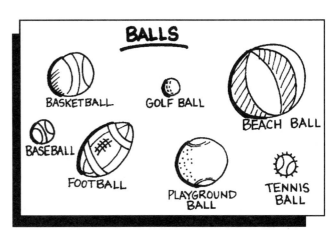

This chart illustrates the gestalt of the word ball—that the word refers to many different types of round and not-round (football) objects used to play games. Later lessons might include a ball of paper, a gumball, and perhaps the concept of ball used in reference to a dance.

Provide Instruction

Initial Instruction (One Activity)

For a young child, do not spend more than a few minutes on this first lesson.

Activity: Sorting (Concept Identification)

Purpose: To highlight the critical cues that discriminate this word/concept from other words/concepts; to ensure a clear and accurate association of the word/label with the concept; and to prepare the learner to identify and use the concept in natural daily activities

Materials: Positive and negative examples and materials to prepare a visual summary—paper, black felt markers. . .

In teaching some concepts, prepare charts or other visual references prior to the initial instruction. In the example of teaching the concept of red, prepare two containers large enough to contain the examples. Cover all extraneous printing or design, and attach a label to one of the containers that indicates *RED*.

Setting: A one-on-one context where distracting and conflicting stimulation can be controlled

Procedure: Model a sorting process while labeling the examples and placing them in the appropriate container. ("This is a red crayon"; "This is not red.") Sort and label quickly so the several examples and the concept are "recorded on the same tape." This is not an exploratory experience. End the first session by making a chart to summarize the basic information.

Rules to facilitate discriminations and prevent learned errors:

1. Attach the label of the attributes to the label of the objects (red balloon, a red toy car, a picture of the red book on a table). *These basic attribute/concept words are descriptive and clarify the item or the action; they are not a new label for the item.* The learner must see that the balloon is always a balloon, but this specific balloon is a red balloon; the red car is not a real car, but a toy; in the picture, it is the book that is red, not the table. This rule is particularly important for those who are exceptionally literal, who are not likely to learn this basic fact without instruction.

2. Avoid confusing the presentation. Do not label the negative examples other than to say, "This is not _____." The negative examples are simply *not* examples of the concept being taught. In the example of red, the focus is *only* on red. If the learner makes an error, say, "This is not red" and place the item in the correct container.

3. During initial instruction, do not ask test questions or guessing questions ("Is this red?"; "What color is this?"). There are at least three reasons for not asking questions during an introduction. First, this is a receptive language task; the purpose is to present a quantity of accurate information quickly. Second, asking a question changes the nature of the task to one that requires discrimination, decision making, and production of a verbal response. This causes delay, potential anxiety, and a shifting of focus from the relevant cues. Third, if the learner gives an incorrect answer, the presentation is no longer clean or clear of conflicting information. In teaching concepts, the rule is: no testing, no guessing. After many experiences with a new concept, create situations in natural contexts for the learner to demonstrate understanding (as when Amy was asked to bring the red sweater, page 244).

Expanded Instruction

Repeat the sorting activity on subsequent days until all attributes of the concept have been presented. Involve the learner in sorting the materials. Use touch, gesture, or blocking prompts to avoid errors. Simultaneously:

- Capitalize on situations that occur naturally or are set up to experience the concept in different contexts and settings.

- Organize and integrate the information from natural experiences with stories, logs, or journals.

- Prepare the learner for planned events by starting a story that describes the context for the coming experience. Keep writing material on hand when in the community, and note experiences immediately for later review. Complete the story at the conclusion of the event while reviewing the notes.

> The following story was written to prepare Maria for a trip to the mall to experience the concept red in a variety of natural situations. Tina, the interpreter, used a red felt marker to make line drawings of the red items. The word *red* was written with the red marker. When they returned from the trip, they reviewed the story and added additional information.
>
> Today Maria and Tina will go shopping. They will see many *red* things and other things that are not red. When the traffic light is *red,* they will stop and wait. At Shoppers Mall, they will buy *red* construction paper, *red* ribbons, and *red* socks. They will buy a hamburger and put *red* catsup on it. They will buy a drink. Will the drink be in a *red* container?

Variation to Correct or Expand the Meaning of a Concept

More experienced learners are likely to have a great deal of information about a concept, but it may be disorganized, distorted, or limited. Provide assistance in organization. First, assess the learner's present understanding of the concept. Then set up opportunities to experience the corrected or expanded meaning. Incorporate visual references. Place concept stories, charts, and semantic maps in notebooks for later reference and for listing additional meanings.

> The following story was written to clarify the various meanings of the word red for an older learner who was confused by the language in TV documentaries, news, and sports shows.
>
> **RED**
>
> Red is a color.
>
> Not all red colors look the same. Some reds look almost orange. Other reds look a bit purple.
>
> Most red colors are very bright and intense.
>
> Sometimes red is light. Sometimes red is not so bright.
>
> Insect bites, injuries, and sunburn make parts of the skin look red.
>
> Sometimes people use the word *red* in different ways.
>
> 1. The Red Sox is a baseball team from Boston.

2. "Is my face red" is an expression that means to feel embarrassed. When some people are embarrassed, blood rushes to the skin of their faces and makes them feel hot and look flushed (reddish).

3. When people think there are too many government rules, they say, "There is too much red tape."

4. "Red river" and "red tide" refer to pollutants or some kinds of algae that make the water look almost red.

5. People who are members of the Communist political party or who have Communist-like ideas are sometimes called *Reds.*

6. Some red signs and some red lights mean to *stop* and *wait.* Warning signs are sometimes red. Warnings tell us to stop and think and be careful so something bad won't happen.

7. Another word that sounds like red is spelled *read.* This word is used to say, "I read a book yesterday," or "I just read the thermometer. The temperature was 85 degrees."

8. The word *red* is used in other ways, too.

Teaching Rules

The strategies for planning and teaching concepts can be modified and applied to teaching most types of rules, be they social or academic. The considerations and the process for teaching rules is applied below to social rules because they are subtle, abstract, and have a great number of exceptions.

Some social and behavioral rules are ineffective because they fail to address the reason for the problem and do not specify what the learner should do. Two problems are particularly common in autism: seemingly simple rules are often interpreted literally and followed rigidly, and the rule is memorized without meaning and echoed. Note the potential problems in the following rules:

- *Keep your hands to yourself. Keep your hands down.* The literal learner will likely have questions and problems. How do you keep your hands to yourself? Where is down? When do you keep your hands to yourself? For how long? Some learners have virtually quit using their hands as they try to follow these rules literally.

- *Don't interrupt.* What is *interrupt?* Don't *ever* interrupt? What if there is an emergency?

- *Keep your feet on the floor.* How do you walk with your feet on the floor? Does this mean I cannot kick a football?

- *You can't hurt people.* What is hurt? (Feelings? Is there pain?) Each of these words is abstract. What hurts people? What is it that I do that hurts people? What could I do to solve my problem without hurting people?

To understand and follow social rules requires the ability to identify relevant and subtle social cues, understand another person's feelings and perspective and the impact of one's behavior on another, understand the meaning of abstract concepts, and modify a response or generate a new response based on changing conditions. These requirements are not learned automatically in autism, so instruction must be carefully planned.

Assess the Problem

Before planning begins, assess the problem with interviews and observations to identify the relevant cues and the possible reasons for the problem. Could it be a sensory problem? a misunderstanding? a limited concept or a skill/concept deficit? There could be at least six reasons why a learner might have a problem standing in line:

1. The individual fears being hurt by the bumping and shoving.

2. The individual is experiencing overwhelming sensory stimulation from the noise, touching, and closeness of others.

3. There is lack of understanding of the concepts *line up* and *stand in line*.

4. There seems to be no reason to stay in line.

5. Waiting is hard, and it is unclear how long to stand in line—once for a few seconds, or forever.

6. What do you do while standing in line?

In interviews, learners who are more experienced and verbal often can provide important clues to the problem. They also may be involved in developing the solutions and visual references (Gray and Garand 1993; Lovett 1985).

The following examples illustrate the importance of a good assessment before teaching a new rule.

> The vocational staff members at the sheltered training center were frustrated and nervous about working with Jason. At age 20, he had no functional communication system, would not stay seated at his work station, would run out of the room, and sometimes urinated in the work room. When staff members tried to get him back to the work station or keep him from leaving the room, he would become aggressive. It was decided that he needed to learn the rule, *Stay in your chair.* Staff members requested a full behavior assessment when the instruction was not effectively solving the problem.
>
> Observations showed that when Jason got out of the chair, staff members physically returned him to the chair, restating the rule. After this cycle was repeated several times, Jason urinated in the chair. During succeeding observations, Jason slugged the staff member who physically restrained him in the chair, and then he ran into the hall to the restroom to urinate. An interview with his mother revealed that at home he needed to use the bathroom frequently, and he managed his physical needs independently without asking permission. However, while he was at work, there were several reasons why he needed permission and supervision to use the bathroom. Jason was taught to use a communication card that read, *I need a restroom break.* Once staff members learned that Jason's behavior problems were logical and that he would use the communication system consistently, they all were more relaxed.
>
> ———
>
> The members of Jose's family were frustrated that he failed to follow their directions. His teacher was invited to observe Jose at home and show the family how to teach him to follow their rules and directions. To everyone's surprise, the observations showed that Jose followed his mother's directions 100% of the time. For example, when his mother

called the family to dinner and told Jose to sit at the table, he was in his chair before anyone else, stayed about two seconds, and then ran off. None of his family saw him sitting at the table. He was always in the right place to do what he was told; but if his parents were not present to help him immediately, he was gone. In this situation, teaching rules and directions would have been both frustrating and ineffective. Instead, his family had to learn how to acknowledge his good behavior and engage him quickly while he was following directions.

Develop the Instructional Plan

The planning process is similar to that for teaching concepts and consists of the following steps:

1. Define the problem.

   What is the reason for the rule? What is the impact of the problem behavior on others, and how does that impact the learner? Does the problem reduce interesting options? Is the behavior unsafe? What could happen if the rule is followed? (Perhaps others would want to be friends, injury and bad consequences might be avoided.) This information provides the meaning, motivation, and natural reinforcement for following the rule.

2. Define the rule.

Review Verbal Strategies, chapter 16.

   Develop a rule that clearly and positively states what the learner is to do and clarifies how to do it.

3. Identify the natural cues that indicate when and where the rule is applied.

4. Define some of the alternatives for when the rule does not apply.

5. Develop the visual references—charts, semantic maps, cue cards, self-monitoring checklists, social story, or others.

The Instructional Process

Introduce each new rule, with its visual references, in a familiar setting. Role play or rehearse as appropriate. Provide instruction in the context of natural routines.

Amy's grandmother had become frail and needed care. Amy's mother was responsible for providing the care every afternoon and evening. Nine-year-old Amy, who accompanied her to the elderly woman's home each day, had to entertain herself during this time. During the first week, Amy was noisy and ran about the house, tugging and pulling at her mother to go home. Her mother enlisted the help of Amy's teacher, and together they developed a plan to teach two rules: *Play quietly,* and *If you need help, come and take my hand.* The new plan included two major components:

1. Organize and structure the space and the events.

   A space near Grandma's room was organized for quiet play, with familiar and liked toys and activities—cutting, drawing, listening to tapes with earphones, rocking in the rocker. Play time was structured with a mini-calendar. The calendar and arrangement were similar to the one Amy used at school. The calendar also specified one or two short visits with Grandma.

2. Provide visual references.

A story was written to answer potential questions—why, what, when, where, how, and then what? The story included descriptions of the setting (odors, objects, and sounds) and what Mother and Grandma were doing and how they felt. It described the rules, the mini-calendar, and the things Amy could do quietly during her visits with Grandma (rub lotion on her hands, look at a book together). It also specified the things she could not do. The story was illustrated with a series of simple line drawings and an audiotape was prepared.

Mother introduced the story on Friday. As Mother read, Amy followed the line drawings. On Saturday and Sunday, the story was repeated and the audiotape was given to Amy to use with the pictures. On Saturday, Mother also introduced the mini-calendar and showed Amy how to use it.

While Amy was at school on Monday, her mother set up work and play areas at Grandma's house. After school, Amy carried a bag with her things to Grandma's. Amy greeted Grandma, and her mother showed her how to use her schedule and begin. Amy's first activity each day was to listen to the story tape to review the rules. Within a week, she was able to play quietly. Mother was careful to check in frequently to comment on Amy's responsibility and to admire her work. The activities were varied each day to prevent boredom. While problems occurred occasionally, Amy was generally independent and comfortable within this flexible routine.

Academic Instruction

The basic guidelines for planning instruction for teaching routines, concepts, and rules apply to other academic content as well. If academic instruction is to be useful and generalized, it must be specifically applied to functional contexts during instruction. The functional academic skills listed in figure 19.2 are a sample of those that must be addressed to increase learner independence.

Planning Academic Instruction

1. Organize units of instruction to show the gestalt.

Introduce the unit with semantic maps or flow charts of the concepts and major points, skills, and activities. Highlight the purpose or importance of the content. Provide visual references and daily study guides. (See figure 19.3; and refer to figure 18.4 on page 257, showing a visual project plan designed to support one young man in an art class.) Darch and Carnine (1986) describe the use of visual references as advanced organizers of content area material. Other techniques and strategies for organizing instruction in content areas are included in articles by Leverett and Diefendorf (1992). Also see Pehrsson and Denner (1989); and Isaacson (1988).

2. To promote generalization, use variety in practice. *Avoid rote and repetitive practice of single skills or concepts in isolation.*

Variations and examples that illustrate the range of applications are included in practice from the beginning of instruction. When a single application or example is practiced repetitively, it becomes a rote routine that stands alone and is difficult to expand and generalize. Figure 19.4 illustrates two math

Figure 19.2. Sample: Functional academic skills

Math
- Sorting
- Concepts of quantity, space, and size (big/little, long/short, one/many, full/empty, more/less, same/different, equal . . .)
- One-to-one correspondence and counting objects (not rote)
- Identifying numbers and symbols
- Math operations and calculator use to solve real problems
- Money management—budgeting
- Time and time management
- Measurement and functional fractions
- Other

Reading
- Personal data
- Signs/labels
- Lists
- Fill-in-the-blank forms
- Dials, gauges
- Schedules, tables, calendars
- Illustrated advertisements
- Bills, time cards, receipts
- Alphabetizing
- Map skills—community, state, other
- Technical documents
- Phone books, emergency/community resources
- TV guides
- Menus
- Other

Reading for personal management
- Meal planning, recipes
- Sorting junk mail from important mail
- Refrain from responding to credit card applications and offers
- Modified directions for medications
- Survival words
- Directions for household equipment

Recreational reading
- High interest books and magazines
- Reference materials, use of the library
- Directions for games, electronic equipment, computer programs, model kit assembly
- Other

Writing
- Personal data
- Signature
- Forms
- Lists
- Schedules
- Notes and letters
- Other

worksheets. These worksheets are designed to prevent developing rigid routines that interfere with generalization. If all the instructional examples are the same (as in Worksheet A), a learner will assume that the rule or principle applies only to one type of problem or situation. When a new application is introduced, the learner approaches the problem as if it requires a totally different rule. When variations or applications are introduced and practiced together (as in Worksheet B), the rate of learning to generalization is increased (Albin and Horner 1988).

Real-life problems and story problems of real-life situations also would be incorporated into practice at an early stage.

Figure 19.3. A study guide for content area classes

The first four sections of this study guide are completed prior to distributing it to the learner with autism (or to all students in the class). You may use a transparency of the guide to introduce the lesson, and again at the end of the class to summarize the concepts and review the homework assignment for all students.

Study Guide

Date _____

1. Today we will study about:

   •

   •

   •

   •

2. New words:

   •

   •

   •

3. We will do these activities:

   •

   •

   •

4. Materials needed:

5. Summary of concepts:

6. Homework assignment:

Figure 19.4. Use of variations to increase learning rate

Worksheet A—Addition and Carrying

7	9	5	3	6
+7	+3	+7	+8	+6

2	9	3	8	6
+6	+9	+7	+8	+8

5	8	1	7	4
+5	+4	+9	+6	+9

Worksheet B—Addition and Carrying

9	13	304	8	8 + 7 =
+1	+38	+ 7	6	
			+9	

7	82	11 + 9 =	746	77
+3	19		86	+44
	47		+ 9	
	+63			

---

3. Teach thinking skills, organizational skills, and study skills to support regular education academic programs. See chapter 23 (pages 355-370) for strategies for teaching self-management and problem-solving skills. A notebook organizational system is illustrated on page 250. Other resources include:

- *Cognitive Curriculum for Young Children with Autism (CCYC)* (Hayward et al. 1990). The authors directly address the deficits of autism in the areas of thinking, perceiving, and problem solving. In this cognitive approach, the students participate and collaborate in activities as the teacher models, demonstrates, and discusses the mental strategies involved in meaningful learning. This approach is described in *A Cognitive Approach to the Education of Young Children with Autism* (Butera and Haywood 1992).

- Buser and Reimer (1988) also report that cognitive strategies can be developed in the context of solving real-life problems.

- *Advanced Skills for School Success* (Archer and Gleason; 4 volumes, 1992-94). The authors describe four modules for grades 7-12: School Behaviors and Organization Skills, Completing Daily Assignments, Learning from Verbal Presentations and Participating in Discussions, and Effective Reading of Textbooks. This series includes many strategies and activities that can be modified to address the needs of learners with autism of various ages.

- *Teaching Organizational Skills to Students with Learning Disabilities* (Shields and Heron 1989). The authors describe several important strategies for teaching organizational skills.

4. Plan support.

- Interpreters are often needed to preteach abstract concepts and rules and to assist with hands-on activities and practice. An interpreter can teach and support study and organizational skills to manage homework and solve problems related to logistics and interpersonal problems.

- Enlist peers as models, mentors, and friends. One young man could not learn the exercise routines for PE until a peer stood beside him and modeled the movements. Recruit staff or community members who share the learner's special interests to be mentors (Grandin 1990).

5. Evaluate and refine to identify and resolve problems quickly.

- Monitor skill acquisition in cooperative learning situations. Ensure that the learner understands the meaning and purpose of each task. Many learners find that participation in cooperative groups is interesting, and these groups provide an important context for learning. However, many learners follow along with the group routine without acquiring meaningful academic concepts or skills.

- Individualize and clarify the goals and objectives and the testing and grading procedures for learners in integrated settings. Inform parents, staff members, and the learner, as appropriate, of the adaptions. Ensure that needed visual adaptations are available, used, and updated to match changing needs.

- Generally, a learning disabilities specialist or resource teacher is a good resource for solving problems and developing adaptations for those who learn differently.

Teach Reading, Writing, Spelling, and Language

An Integrated Visual Approach

Traditional developmental and basal reading approaches have been less than successful when used to teach the language arts to those with autism. A more successful approach is one that accommodates the learning strengths and deficits common in autism—a wholistic, visual approach taught in a meaningful context.

Koppenhaver and associates (1991) noted that literacy learning begins with language experiences in infancy and early childhood for those with developmental disabilities as well as for those developing in a more normal way. Many young children with and without autism learn to read at very early ages without formal instruction to match shapes, repeat the alphabet, and know the names of the letters. In fact, those with autism often learn to read words even though they may not be able to speak. However, instruction in a meaningful context is critical for the words to have meaning (Pehrsson and Robinson 1985).

The modified Language Experience Approach (LEA) as introduced in chapter 15 (pages 202-204) capitalizes on actual experiences and integrates reading, writing, spelling, and language instruction. This experiential, visual, and integrated approach has been quite successful for many learners (Bock 1991; Flowers 1990; Shepherd 1983). The LEA approach is highly individualized and can be modified to match the needs of those who are higher functioning and verbal as well as for those with limited or no verbal abilities. In fact, Shepherd reported that these LEA strategies were instrumental in teaching his son with autism to read, write, spell, and speak.

The context for writing stories can vary from one-to-one to small- or large-group settings. Stories can be written at the kitchen table, in a restaurant, at the park, in the classroom, or in the speech or play rooms. They can be written on a multitude of materials—note pads or cards, chart pads, chalkboards, on lined and unlined paper in a rainbow of colors and a variety of textures and patterns; and with pencils, pens, chalks, and markers of various colors. A Polaroid camera for instant pictures also may be useful.

Strategies for Initiating the LEA Program

Initially, the young learners with autism watch as the interpreter (parent or teacher) says the words and writes the story. The basic strategies for this first stage are described on pages 202-204. See pages 270-273 for examples of informal activities for teaching language concepts that incorporate the LEA approach. Once the learner understands that written words are meaningful, you can adapt the activities to increase the child's active involvement to contribute to the stories.

Strategies to Increase Active Involvement

Develop a basic routine for story writing that makes the experience comfortable and predictable. As with other routines, vary it to some degree nearly every day to prevent rigidity. At first, set a specific time and place to write stories. Each story might begin with the day and the date written at the top.

In my classes, the 3- to 5-year-old children sat in a circle at the chalkboard to begin and end the school day with an experience story. The opening activity was a story to prepare the children for the events of the day. The story illustrated here was developed in one session to prepare the class for a trip to the beach. The closing activity was a summary of the events of the day. These stories were copied on paper and sent home so the parents could have a meaningful conversation with their child and the child could see and hear the story several times.

The following strategies will ensure that the child with autism learns the correct language structures and begins to contribute to the story.

1. Model correct language, sentence structure, spelling, and punctuation to ensure that the learner with autism does not learn incorrect structures. This is a modification from the standard practice of writing the words exactly as the child speaks them.

2. Write with a questioning attitude. ("Is that right? Is that what happened? What else happened? Let's see, first, we . . .; You can fix it—here's the pencil.")

3. Use sentence starters and expectant pauses as cues to contribute. ("For lunch we had _____; Tony pulled the big red _____.") This strategy is particularly effective if a photograph is available to aid recall. If the learner is nonverbal or a response is delayed, make a quick line drawing, label it, and say, "You can show me what we had for lunch. For lunch we had _____." Help the learner point to the picture. Then quickly write the word in the story.

4. Periodically remind the learner that "It's your turn to talk" or "You will be able to talk later." If the learner is nonverbal, provide response cards.

5. Involve the learner in reading the story. Model reading while pointing to the words; then encourage and assist the learner to point during reading. Once the story has been reread a few times:

- Pause and wait expectantly to encourage the learner to read the next word or to indicate that the reading should continue. (Do not pause too long, or the flow of the story and attention may be lost.)

- Make mistakes and pause for corrections. The learner may need to learn a signal to indicate that an error was made.

- Have the learner locate words in the text to underline or circle.

6. In group situations, peers can model and provide assistance. For example, peers take turns contributing to the story. If a learner does not respond in turn, ask a peer to help. ("Mary, tell Tony what we had for lunch.") Once the story is written, it is read aloud with the individual students reading their contributions. The leader can ask peers to locate and circle specific words, to take turns leading the rereading, and to select the next leader.

Strategies to Expand Decoding and Language Skills

Avoid phonics instruction, at least until the fundamental concepts of language are firm. Approaches that break words apart and require analyzing and reassembling are very difficult for most learners. The gestalt of the word is lost when the focus is on the individual letters, and it is difficult to blend the sounds back into a whole word. Some children virtually change the way they speak; from using whole words naturally, they begin to speak in sounded-out words ("C-a-t and m-ou-se").

Approaches based on repetitive drills cause additional problems because the drills are memorized without understanding the purpose and meaning. Some learners enjoy the routine of the drills, but the routines become so rigid that the learner cannot use the sounds to decode words. Other learners dislike the meaningless drills and try to avoid them.

While the traditional phonics (auditory) approaches are confusing and cause problems for most learners with autism, the cognitive visual strategies are much more likely to be successful because they capitalize on the learners' prior knowledge. The cognitive visual strategies listed below are just a sample of those possible.

1. Develop a word bank. As learners demonstrate that they know a word, write it on a 3"x5" card, and place the card randomly in a file box. Say the names of the letters while writing the words, and then quickly say the whole word ("C-a-t, cat" or "C-a-t spells cat"). Use these cards for:

- Sorting activities. Sort by first letter or last letter or by blends or digraphs in different positions (bl, br, sh, th, . . .). Sort to make lists of word families (cart, mart, part, start, . . .). Read the lists aloud to highlight the common sounds.

- Using duplicate sets of word cards, play Concentration, Bingo, and similar games.

- Use the word bank often. Provide frequent experiences to search for a specific word.

- Introduce the alphabet when there are so many words in the bank that it is frustrating to search for a word. Provide alphabetized file dividers and a printed alphabet strip as a visual reference. The concept and value of the alphabet—the letters in a specific sequence—becomes immediately apparent. Model the filing and search processes. Use parallel talking to provide the language for thinking about the task.

2. Prepare small word strips of the words in the bank. Make them ½" to 1" high and only as long as the word. Make duplicate words, and gradually expand visual discrimination skills by using different types of paper (some with patterned backgrounds) and different ways of forming letters (a, A, . . .). Use these word strips to teach a number of skills:

   - Initially, select only a few words to use at any one time, but include three or four duplicates of each word. Place a handful of these word strips on the center of the table to sort into a divided tray. This process not only makes it faster to find words; it also expands the concepts of sorting, that upper- and lower-case letters mean the same thing, and that letters can be made in different ways. These word strips also can be used for fill-in-the-blank activities and for playing Word Bingo and other games.

   - Use the word strips to make new sentences, and help the students to learn that the position of the word in a sentence changes its meaning. This strategy also provides an opportunity to check for clarity of meaning. (Does the sentence make sense? The ball wants the girl/The girl wants the ball.)

   - Include punctuation marks on separate strips.

   - Play games with the sentences. For example, take turns forming simple but silly directions for the others to follow.

   - Prepare sentence-starter strips with spaces left for the learner to fill in the blanks with words from the word-strip bank.

3. Write stories and sentences on the computer. If commercial computer programs are used, make them interactive by having partners work together and take turns contributing parts of the story.

Strategies to Develop Writing Skills

Although fine motor skills develop early in some young learners, others have significant problems in this area. There are at least four issues to consider when developing instructional activities for teaching writing skills:

1. The visual motor integration process involved

2. Difficulties initiating and carrying out the motor actions fluently (that is, impulsivity and perseveration)

3. Understanding where to start on a paper

4. The motivation to practice

Some learners will grab the pencil during the story development process and change a word or add words. Others seem unable to grasp, hold, or manipulate a writing instrument. To address sensory motor and motor problems, consult with an occupational therapist. The idea that they could do the writing themselves is foreign to many learners. The process for transferring words from a model on another piece of paper or the chalkboard also can be a problem. The following strategies can help resolve some of these problems.

1. To copy print from a vertical plane to a horizontal plane over a distance (from chalkboard or chart to paper at a desk):

   - Tape a piece of paper to the chalkboard, and label the top and bottom while saying, "This is the top of the paper. This is the bottom of the paper." After writing a brief one-line story, remove the paper and place it on the student's desk for the student to copy. Comment about the location of "the top of the paper" when it is lying flat. Tape the learner's writing paper so the lines for printing are directly under the story line. (Note: The learner may believe that it is always necessary to label the top and bottom of the paper unless told otherwise.)

- When writing on the chalkboard, write the letters of each word quite close together (to see the gestalt), and leave a bit of extra space between words. Other strategies to facilitate copying from the board include underlining the sentences, leaving a bit more space between each line, and numbering the lines after writing the story.

- Keep the chalkboard story compact. If the letters, spaces, and lines are too far apart, it is harder to follow and to see the gestalt of the story. Draw a border around the story or material to be copied, to separate it from other material on the board. Try moving the learner's desk closer to the board; but if the desk is too close, it is harder to see the whole story and the learner must twist the head to follow the lines.

2. To initiate and support the writing process:

- Assure learners that the process will get easier, and that in time they will be able to write the stories without help.

- Provide subtle physical support like that described and illustrated on page 232, or similar to that used in facilitated communication (see page 327).

3. To identify a starting place:

- Place an X or a dot on the paper, and say, "Start here." Use parallel talk to provide the work system rules ("Top to bottom, left to right").

4. To increase motivation:

- Provide a purpose for the writing. Make a copy of the story to take home to share, write messages to request favorite things from someone in another area or room, or require a signature to check out materials or to check in and out of work or play centers.

5. To increase motivation to trace the letters:

- Fasten a piece of tracing paper over the story so an actual product is produced. This tracing can be taken home to share with family, placed in a book, or displayed on a bulletin board.

- Repetitive writing practice is boring and often resisted, but sometimes it is necessary. In these cases, change the focus. ("How many *readable* letters can you write in X amount of time? How many very good letters can you write on one line or a page?") These activities provide an opportunity to request assistance to check quality and to count the number of circled readable letters to enter in a graph.

- Perfectionism is often a roadblock for those with autism. They may want their writing or printing to look exactly like the teacher's or just like the book print. Model and teach the concept that some work simply needs to be readable and done quickly, while other work needs to be done carefully to look nice for a special purpose. Model making and correcting errors with positive self-talk.

Summary

If the goal is reading, writing, and spelling with meaning, it is taught meaningfully from the beginning. Strategies that expand language meaning and use also expand literacy. The opposite also is true. To reinforce concepts and motivation, always have writing material available for quick notes and stories. Keep copies of stories in notebooks. These books can provide a focus for conversations and sharing past experiences. Some learners have used the stories as a means of requesting to repeat an event.

Interpreters must remember that seemingly simple concepts that others learn automatically must be specifically highlighted for those with autism. When instruction is organized to include the details and visual references that accommodate these learners' literal perspective and learning style, the learning rate is surprisingly rapid. Small and subtle pieces of information can have a major impact on learning and performance. Teachers in regular classrooms need reassurance that the accommodations described in this chapter will benefit other students as well.

20 | Establish Basic Early Interaction Skills

Expanding social and communication skills is the most challenging and critical task for those who support individuals with autism. Communication skills are social skills; communication does not occur unless there are two people interacting in some way, taking turns, giving and receiving. The pervasiveness and complexity of the communication and social problems in autism can be both surprising and daunting. That a person can do some things so well and then have such incredible and unexpected gaps and deficits is nothing short of astounding. These discrepancies and variabilities are confusing and often lead to expectations that are either too high or too low. The impact of autism on developing social and communication skills is described more completely in chapter 3.

Because the drive to interact and communicate is neither strong nor automatic in autism, young learners need many opportunities to practice the interaction habit and experience the power of communication. Without a strong communication habit, the learner will not use communication consistently to solve problems, especially in stressful situations. *The ability to talk does not guarantee communication.* Learners with autism may be able to speak, point to or label pictures, repeat rules or facts, use signs, write, type, or use a computer; but spontaneous and meaningful communication will not occur without a strong communication habit and a realization that:

- People are interesting, helpful, and somewhat predictable.
- Others do not know what I know or need unless I tell them.
- I must find a communication partner and persist in getting that person's attention.
- I can send signals and messages to influence others.
- Communication pays off!

Develop Spontaneous Interaction Skills

The first steps toward spontaneous communication involve learning to:

- Tolerate people and the stimulation they provide
- Stay near and watch people for longer periods of time
- Initiate interactions and take turns giving and taking
- Share attention to a topic, object, or action
- Send signals that stimulate others to action
- Predict the actions of others, and understand cause/effect relationships (I do something/You do something)
- Watch others, and imitate both familiar and new actions

Structured Play-Based Strategies

The strategies discussed in this chapter are adapted from the work of Klinger and Dawson (1992); MacDonald (1989); Merzer and Chastain (1982); Pulice (1987); and Lussier et al. (1994). Read Tiegerman and Primavera (1984) for a report of their early work that supported the use of imitation to increase gaze behavior.

One of the most promising strategies for developing spontaneous interaction skills is based on those that are used naturally by parents as they play and care for their young normally developing infants and toddlers. For effective use in autism, these intuitive play strategies must become more systematized or structured to keep the stimulation at an optimum level for learning and to accommodate the chronological age and interests of the learner.

Structured-play strategies provide a context for achieving other goals as well as spontaneous communication. In the optimally stimulating and successful play situation, a learner will also:

- Develop emotional bonds and trusting relationships

- Play more creatively

- Become more flexible, use materials with more adaptability, and engage in less rigid routines

- Expand the number and complexity of interactions

- Try—and persist in trying

An individual structured-play program is designed after a comprehensive, functional assessment of cognitive, communication, social, sensory, and motor skills. See pages 72-73 for descriptions of several functional assessment procedures (Beckman and Lieber 1994; Lindner 1993; Wetherby and Prizant 1993).

Organize the Environment

Time Schedules

Schedule at least three 10- to 20-minute structured-play sessions a day in a calm and controlled environment at home or at school. One study showed that after 20 minutes of imitative play with their mothers each day for two weeks, children with autism played more creatively with their toys and attended to their mothers' faces significantly more than they had on the first day of study (Klinger and Dawson 1992).

Learners whose parents and other interpreters are trained to use the strategies at home and in school settings are likely to generalize their developing interaction skills to a broader range of people and situations. Several short periods of interactive play at home each day may be more valuable than a single longer session if there are disruptions, when the parent must be concerned with the care and safety of other children.

Arrange the Settings

- At school or clinic: The ideal space for structured play is a relatively small, safe area with clear boundaries, free of distractions and clutter so choices are limited. In this setting, any choice or action the learner makes can be accepted. This calm, controlled, and successful environment is most important during the early stages of intervention, when the learner needs immediate reinforcing responses to every initiation.

  A full-length mirror can stimulate imitative play and be useful for those children who find it less confusing to watch people indirectly; other children may be overly stimulated and distracted by a mirror.

- At home: Arrange a small play area in the corner of a bedroom or in a small area behind a couch or bookcase. In a larger room, define an area by a small rug, and use the area only when others are occupied elsewhere. The most important consideration is to avoid the distracting stimulation of TV and the activity of others, especially of other children who might want to join the session or to play with the special toys. While play with others is to be encouraged, the critical goal for these sessions is to learn how the social interaction game works.

Select and Arrange Materials

For initial sessions, select identical sets of small objects or toys that are most likely to interest the learner and that can be used to draw attention to:

- The interpreter's actions: Small noise- or music makers, sparkling or noisy things to shake, mechanical toys that make noises, small cars or trucks, push-toys that make noise, floppy stuffed animals and dolls, paper sacks, toy telephones, blocks, hammer-and-peg toys. . .
- The interpreter's face: Balloons, scarves, rings to peek through. . .

For later sessions, select toys that can be shared and that support or require:

- Interactions: Blocks, form boards, puzzles, balls, cars, trucks, puppets. . .
- Assistance: Interesting objects in clear containers with tight lids or fasteners, wind-up toys that are interesting but difficult to manipulate, bubbles and pinwheels that are difficult to blow. . .

Limit the number of toys at each session to avoid overstimulation and distraction. While only five or six different toys are required at any one time, rotate the materials every two or three sessions to avoid boredom, to broaden experiences, to increase flexibility, and to prevent unproductive routines.

Structure the Interactions

The success of structured interactive play is dependent upon the skill and attitude of the interpreter. See figure 20.1 for a description of the attitude and role of an effective interpreter.

Structure the Beginnings and Ends of Play Sessions

Structure each session to flow from a clear beginning to a clear end. Announce the time for play or represent it on the individual calendars. Use a transition cue, a toy, or picture card to guide the transition to the play area. End the session positively, while the child is actively involved. However, to extend the time in interactions, strive to engage the child in "one more turn" after the child indicates a desire to end the session (MacDonald 1989).

1. Set a timer to ring a few minutes before the specified ending time. When the timer rings, say, "It's time to stop playing. Let's put in two more pegs and then put away the toys."

2. When the child begins to show fatigue or an interest in leaving the area, say, "You want to stop playing. Let's roll the ball one more time and put away the toys." Work together to close the container and put the toys on the shelf.

3. If the child runs off before the session is clearly ended, gently but firmly return the child to the activity and say, "I see you want to be all done. Put the lid on the bubbles, and then you will be all done." Provide assistance to end the session quickly.

4. Highlight the actual end of the session and prepare for the next activity with a transition cue. Say, "Play time is finished. It's time for _____," while handing the child an object or a picture to show the next event. Have the child take the cue to the designated location.

Figure 20.1. Interpreter's attitude and role in structured interactive play sessions

1. Interpreters are alert and observant. They:
   - Provide an optimal level of stimulation—not too little or not too much
   - Are sensitive to subtle, nonverbal signs of interest, overstimulation, fatigue, or boredom
   - Watch for signs of developing rote routines
   - Watch for subtle, nonverbal behaviors that communicate feelings, preferences, and needs; they acknowledge and accommodate the messages conveyed by these behaviors

2. Interpreters are flexible, with the ability to adapt their interaction styles to match the learner's stimulation needs. They are:
   - Playful, animated
   - Relaxed, calm, and generally quiet (unhurried)
   - Expectant, respectful, interested, and encouraging

3. Interpreters are responsive and noncontrolling. They:
   - Set up interesting situations
   - Give the learner control to select activities and levels of interaction
   - Allow the learner to end or change topics (game or action with toy)
   - Respond naturally to reinforce all of the child's efforts to interact
   - Avoid artificial verbal statements (such as, "Good looking") that interrupt the flow of the conversation and interfere with the direct association of the learner's effort to the highly reinforcing natural responses
   - Make no demands; they know that demands for eye contact, compliance, or to play or talk "the right way" decrease spontaneity and willingness to initiate or engage

4. Interpreters share control. They follow the child's lead, then add variations to share the lead.

5. Interpreters are dependable, consistent, and clear. They:
   - Begin and end sessions and interactions in a positive and obvious way
   - Speak for the child, verbalizing the child's intentions and reflecting the child's feelings in clear, concrete language
   - Provide just enough assistance to guide and support expanding effort
   - Arrange the environment so the child can take the lead without concern for safety

6. Interpreters are systematic. They:
   - Evaluate and keep records of interactions, noting the types of toys and activities, the nature of the interactions, and any problems
   - Predict potential problems and make modifications to prevent learned errors and nonproductive routines
   - Refine, modify, and add variations in a timely and systematic way to increase and expand motivation and confidence and to maintain progress

They create an environment in which the learner and the interpreter have fun and feel so successful that both want to return for another interaction.

5. Clarify the beginning and ending of informal interactions that occur throughout the day in natural settings. Begin these brief, spontaneous interactions by joining the child, who is already involved in an activity. Ease into the play in some subtle way so as not to startle or interrupt. Touch the child's arm, smile, and say, "Hi." Watch a bit before joining into the activity. End the involvement before the child "takes off." Do not simply walk away from the interaction without acknowledgment; you would not leave a friend without some kind of a statement to give closure.

Core Strategies

Four strategies form a base that adds familiarity and predictability to the interaction. They allow the child to test and predict the adult's actions and keep the interaction at the child's level of understanding and tolerance. These core strategies are not necessarily used in any particular order or sequence. Rather, the adult moves from one strategy to another in response to small, nonverbal signals of interest, stress, or fatigue. The adult returns to a lower level to relieve stress, and periodically adds variations to prevent boredom and unproductive routines.

1. Imitate or match the child's actions. Do what the child does in a slightly exaggerated form, so the child is drawn to your actions rather than to the toys or objects.

2. Sit with your face within the child's natural line of vision, and exaggerate facial expressions while imitating. This calls the child's attention to your facial expression and increases the likelihood of accidental eye contact.

3. Pause before imitating to set up an opportunity for taking turns. This gives the child time to think and to vary his actions slightly to test his control over your behavior.

4. Imitate with slight variations of speed and rhythm or sounds, with the same or a different object. For example, if the child says, "Ma-ma-ma," you can say, "Ma-ma-mom." This variation provides a model for the next step. These variations increase the child's alertness and set the stage for the child to imitate the new behavior when ready.

Imitating repetitive and stereotypic behaviors is an effective strategy that allows the child to control the level of stimulation and ensures success. There is no evidence that the behaviors are reinforced and strengthened when the core strategies are followed. These core strategies, in fact, decrease repetitive behaviors as the child becomes more involved in a broader array of productive activity and when the optimum level of stimulation is maintained—not too little, not too much.

Caesar and Tom, the speech pathologist, are sitting on the rug with several toys between them. Tom has a duplicate set of toys within easy reach but slightly shielded from Caesar's view.

Tom waits expectantly.

Caesar flaps his hands.
Tom flaps his hands in the same way (matches Caesar's actions).

Caesar continues flapping, unaware of Tom's actions.
Tom continues flapping, but begins to exaggerate the action.

Caesar, still seemingly unaware of imitation, stops flapping and begins to rock.
Tom stops flapping and matches Caesar's rocking action.

Caesar continues rocking, then stops and starts to flap his hands.
Tom exaggerates rocking, stops, then exaggerates flapping.

Suddenly Caesar looks directly at Tom and stops moving.
Tom stops, and waits expectantly.

Caesar flaps his hands and stops.
Tom delays imitation for one or two seconds, then flaps for one or two seconds and stops.

Caesar flaps a bit, then stops and watches.
Tom continues to matching Caesar's actions with varied time delay.

Caesar, seemingly very excited, flaps his hands and shakes his entire body.
Tom matches the actions, time, and intensity of the actions.

Caesar stops, waits as if thinking, then hums and rocks, looking away.
Tom waits, then hums and rocks.

Caesar continues looking away, humming and rocking.
Tom continues matching, then suddenly stops and slaps his hands on his knees, leans forward, and waits expectantly (thus adding a new idea to recapture Caesar's interest and avoid routine).

Caesar looks quickly, stops rocking, watches, and waits.
Tom waits briefly, then rocks, stops, slaps his hands to his knees, and leans forward.

Caesar rocks, stops, and slaps his hands to his knees.
Tom matches Caesar's action.

The conversation (interaction) continues, with the interpreter adding small variations to keep interest high, avoid uninvolved routines, and add new ideas and expand the topic.

A timer signals the ending of the session. Tom provides assistance as he says, "It's time to stop. Put the toys in the basket. Then play time will be finished. . . . Good! The toys are in the basket. Now we will walk back to your class."

Variations for Expanding Interactions

Variations are used in conjunction with the core strategies to maintain the optimum level of stimulation and continued growth. The variations are little surprises—novel actions added to the natural flow of the interaction when the child is engaged and attentive. Some of the variations are set up before the session by arranging materials in certain ways or places.

These variations, or new ideas, demonstrate the next slightly higher step, a new dimension of the actions on the materials and more complex interactions. The variations also increase flexibility and tolerance for new and novel information. Remember that a variation is added as an option for the child to consider. If that option is ignored or the child shows stress or withdraws, return to the core strategies. Later in the session, reintroduce the same variations several times, making them more familiar to the learner.

1. Match the learner's actions, add variations, and wait. Introduce a different action with the same object at the same or slightly higher level of difficulty, or introduce a familiar action with a different object. Then wait. For example, if the child had been shaking a stuffed dog and saying, "Yeh-yeh-yeh," you might briefly shake, hug, and rock the dog while saying, "Yeh-yeh-yeh-ohh!"; or you might pick up and shake a rag doll while saying, "Yeh-yeh-yeh!"

2. Arrange the materials or activity so the child must do something—send some signal—to continue an action or to gain access to a desired activity. This strategy develops active dependency (Merzer and Chastain 1982) or interdependency—a realization that a communication partner is important and that there is a way to send a signal to get what you want or need. For example, place a highly desired object in view but out of reach, or stand between the desired object and the child. To obtain the object, the learner must touch or bump you. Interpret this nonintentional touch as a signal to get attention. ("You want me to get you the toy. Here it is.") Show the learner that a touch on the arm will get attention.

3. Introduce interesting objects or activities that cannot be done alone or that are too hard for the child to do independently. Set up the activities so the child has an opportunity to realize the task cannot be done alone. At that moment of realization, guide the child's hand to extend the object (thus teaching a natural gesture), and say, "Want help with the bubbles." While picking up the bubble bottle, say, "I will help you with the bubbles."

   While most children would naturally extend the object to the adult for help, a child with autism is most likely to do one of three things: simply stand there, get frustrated and throw the object, or drop the object and wander off. The adult must be alert to provide assistance at the most optimal point for the child to associate the need for help with a way to express the need. Receiving help quickly reinforces the effort and the action of requesting help.

   The verbal expression of intent must be literal and specific. *Help* is not the label of the object, but an abstract word that applies to a variety of objects and situations. Provide a clear statement of intention that specifies very literally the want or need ("You want help with the bubbles"). This strategy prevents confusion and a misconception that suddenly the bottle of bubbles is now labeled *help*. These verbalizations require no response from the child.

4. Set up a social or motor routine, and suggest a way for the child to signal a continuation of the activity. Hold the child on your lap and begin to bounce your legs, and then stop. If the child seems to enjoy the routine, continue for a bit, and then pause and say, "Stop." Wait briefly for any slight movement. Then say, "Want to bounce," and quickly begin to bounce. Add variations to the routine so the child must signal differently to specify which action is desired. To continue bouncing, the child must take your hands and give a little bounce; and to continue a rocking routine, the child must grasp your hands and lean back.

- To keep the child actively involved in the situations described above and to prevent a repetitive routine, move your hands to different locations (high, low, to one side or the other) so the child must search for your hands in order to send the signal. Otherwise, the child continues the same routine over and over again without involvement or thought, learning nothing.

- Gradually increase the requirement. For example, the child sends the signal. You acknowledge the signal ("OK, you want to bounce"), tense your body as if to start, then pause until the child looks to see why the action did not begin. The moment that eye contact is made, begin the action. *The child will need many experiences to understand that eyes can send messages.*

- Acknowledge a signal, and indicate whether or not the child's request is forthcoming by responding with exaggerated nonverbal cues. When the child sends the signal, smile broadly, nod your head to indicate yes, and immediately provide the action or object requested.

- Pretend not to hear or see the signal, so the child must do something to gain your attention and repeat the signal. This is a very important skill for those with autism, who generally do not persist in getting their messages understood.

These strategies also can be applied to the needs of older learners.

Tony, four years old, did not talk or use gestures to indicate his wishes. The following interactions occurred in his third session with Ann, his interpreter.

Ann sits between Tony and the toys, waiting expectantly.

Tony accidentally bumps into Ann as he tries to reach the bubbles. Ann says, "Tony wants bubbles. I will give you the bubbles." She hands him the bubble bottle, with the lid screwed on tightly.

Tony struggles intently with the lid.
Ann guides his hand to extend the bottle toward her, and interprets, "Tony needs help with bubbles." She opens the bottle quickly and waits with the bottle in her hand.

Tony stands on tiptoe, looks into the bottle, and reaches for the wand. As he reaches, Ann says, "Tony, you want to blow the bubbles," and hands him the wand.

When he is unable to blow bubbles, Tony looks directly at Ann. Ann says, "You want me to blow bubbles. OK." She takes the wand, fills it with liquid, and waits with the wand in front of her mouth.

Tony looks at her as if to say, "What's holding up the bubbles?" Ann immediately blows the bubbles.

Tony, excited, bounces on his toes as he breaks bubbles. When all are broken, he stands quietly in front of Ann, looking at the bottle. Ann says, "You want more bubbles," dips the wand, and pauses as above.

Tony again looks to see why she stopped.
Ann repeats the routine in the same way two more times, and then begins to add variations to keep him actively involved.

- She "accidentally" drops the wand several times in different places at or near her feet. She helps Tony pick up and return the wand to the bottle when he is ready for more. Each time, she pauses with the wand at her mouth until he looks at her.

- She blows the bubbles to land on his hand, then his shoe, as she says, "Bubbles on your hand" or "Bubbles on your foot." She asks, "Where do you want the bubbles?" When Tony twitches his hand, she blows them on his hand. The next time she asks, he moves his foot ever so slightly forward. Each time she says, "The bubbles are on your hand (foot)."

- She blows the bubbles up into the air in different directions, and as Tony dances and breaks the bubbles she says, "Bubbles, bubbles, Pop, Pop, Pop! Tony is popping the bubbles."

Tony looks out the window and starts to move in that direction. Ann takes his hand and says, "You are all done with the bubbles. Let's blow one more time. Then we will be finished." She blows one more bubble with Tony watching, then helps Tony put the lid on the bottle as she says, "We are finished. You can look out the window." (Ann provides a clear ending for the routine: You get it, you do it and you put it away.)

Saul, 17 years old, had just moved to another city and was having difficulty adapting to the new environment. The first days in the new school were very stressful. He had no communication system, he resisted most of the teacher's requests and assistance, and he became agitated whenever the teacher approached. Lena, the teacher, noticed that he carried several playing cards in his pocket, and that he repetitively bent the corners of a card back and forth. This activity seemed to calm him. She decided to join him in this familiar activity.

Saul is seated at his desk, folding the corners of his cards up and down.
With playing cards in hand, Lena sits down quietly at Saul's desk and waits.

Saul continues to fold the cards while staring out the window. Without comment, Lena begins to fold the corners of one of her cards, matching Saul's actions.

Saul stops and watches Lena briefly, then continues folding his card. Lena stops for about as long as Saul had, then starts folding again with slightly exaggerated movements.

This routine continues for a few minutes. Then Saul folds very quickly for about five seconds, stops, and watches to see what will happen. Lena waits briefly, then matches Saul's quick actions for about five seconds, and stops.

This phase lasts for several turns as Saul varies the activity to test the teacher's responses, folding faster and slower and for differing amounts of time.

Finally, after about 10 minutes, Lena touches Saul's hand briefly as she says, "I must go. This was fun." Then she gets up and walks away. Saul watches the teacher closely as she helps others. When she returns to her desk, Saul walks over and stands quietly beside her.

Lena says, "Hi," acknowledging his presence, and continues to work. After a few minutes, she looks at Saul and quietly says, "I will show you your calendar." She walks to the calendar. Saul follows her and watches quietly as she explains his calendar.

While their problems were not over, it was a beginning. Each day, Saul's calendar specified a talking time. Every day or two, the teacher offered one or two new materials or activities for Saul to choose, to broaden their conversation and keep it interesting. They looked at sports magazines and different kinds of cards, they sorted cards, and they played modified turn-taking card games. Occasionally, a peer was invited to join them. The communication specialist taught Saul to use a communication system that incorporated line drawings mounted on playing cards. Saul carried a card in his pocket to occupy his hands while waiting for events to begin.

Niko, 12 years old, had severe autism and cerebral palsy. (He could walk slowly and manipulate some fairly small objects.) He was nonverbal and strongly avoided people, demands, and new experiences. His only independent leisure activity was to sift things through his fingers. At recess, he sat on the ground and sifted the dirt. At home, he sifted the dirt in the house plants, the ashes in the fireplace, or the sugar and rice in the kitchen. His parents were tired.

Niko's support team had determined that he was reinforced by the visual aspects of sifting rather than the feel of the material. The team identified several activities that had the potential for similar visual stimulation: planting seeds, cleaning and raking flower beds, cooking (sifting flour, measuring salt, sorting beans, packaging soup mixes, shredding cheese), measuring soap into the washing machine, and making crafts with yarn and raffia.

A daily calendar and a structured work system were instituted in the classroom to support the addition of new materials and activities. Staff received extra training to understand how to use the new components of the program and how to encourage interactive relationships throughout the day. They learned to identify and respond to nonverbal signals, to talk less and use visual supports, to share control by setting up opportunities and waiting, and to join into Niko's own activities. The following sequences illustrate some of the early interactions between Niko and his interpreter, Kate.

Day 1: 10-minute interaction at recess

Niko is sitting in a sandy area of the playground sifting the sand. He is bent over so he can see the sand fall.
Kate joins him quietly, watches for a few minutes, then begins to sift. Occasionally, she labels the activity ("Sifting, sifting, sifting sand"). They progress to taking turns, with a few variations. After about 10 minutes, Kate says simply, "Sifting sand was fun. I have to go."

Day 2: 12-minute interaction at recess

Kate joins Niko as before, saying, "Hi." After reestablishing the interaction and taking turns, Kate slowly and tentatively adds the following variations to expand the topic:

- Kate makes a small pile of sand, then quickly smooths it out.
- She uses a small stick to make lines in the sand, then places the stick on the ground between them to share.

Niko tries both new variations after seeing them twice. Kate's talking is limited to a few simple, quiet, and brief commentaries to label their actions ("Sifting sand. . . We are sifting sand. . . Whee! Smooth it out. . . Drawing lines in the sand. . .").

They return to the classroom together. With Niko watching, Kate draws a picture of themselves sifting sand. She labels the picture, and they put it in a notebook.

Later that day, Kate takes Niko to visit a nearby construction site to see the dump trucks. She shows him a toy dump truck in her shopping bag. She sifts a bit of dirt into the truck to show him how it works. Then they put the truck away and return to school. They draw a picture of a dump truck on a card, and put it in the bag with the truck.

Day 3: 12-minute interaction at recess

When Kate joins Niko, she places the dump truck nearby and begins to sift sand, matching his actions. After a bit, she pulls the truck close and sifts sand into it. When the truck is full and running over, Niko reaches across and dumps it. Kate laughs and says, "You dumped the truck."

Niko returns to simple sifting sand. Kate matches his sifting for a bit, then fills the truck again. When it is almost full, she pushes it to Niko and waits.

Niko watches the truck, but continues to sift sand. Kate sifts sand, taking turns with Niko.

Niko stops, quickly dumps the truck, looks at Kate, and laughs. Kate laughs and says, "Wow! You dumped the truck."

The interaction continues until the recess bell rings. They walk together back to the classroom, where they draw a picture of themselves and the dump truck and put it in the notebook. The interactions progress in other activities in the classroom.

Day 4:

Niko waits for Kate at the door and walks beside her to the playground—a major accomplishment.

Not all days went smoothly. Sometimes Niko was distracted and irritable and not open to new ideas. Kate was patient, calm, and noncontrolling as she continued to introduce different elements and toys to the conversations. The time spent in simple sifting decreased as Niko became more interested in doing a variety of other activities. They enjoyed reviewing the notebook of experiences together. Niko began to point and comment as he had seen and heard Kate do in play (approximations of *wow, oops, oh,* and other exclamations). He began to refer to his daily calendar and to try more new things in the classroom. His parents, pleased by Niko's progress at school, incorporated the structure of a calendar and more interactive opportunities at home.

Expanded Applications

These strategies can be expanded and applied to a broad range of skills and to match the needs of a broad range of learners.

1. Add new materials—new topics for the interaction.

   - Select objects with similar sensory elements.

   - Rotate materials and objects frequently.

   - Provide structure to make choices and plans. At first, present a choice between items which you have preselected. Later, expand the choice so the learner selects the materials or topics before a session or event begins.

2. Shape and model more complex actions and language.

   - Model slightly more complex and longer utterances and actions. For example, to promote symbolic and pretend play, introduce different ways to play with a toy.

   - Add commentary to label objects, actions, intentions, and feelings. Provide comments that are specific and at the learner's level, with pauses and quiet time between.

   - Shape natural gestures so they are more specific, meaningful, and communicative. As the learner looks and reaches for the truck, shape the learner's hand to a point, and say, "Want that truck." Then quickly give the object.

   - Expand by drawing pictures and writing experience stories for later shared interactions.

   - Introduce new systems for expressing preferences, needs, and feelings, and for rejecting or avoiding choices (as described in the Picture Exchange System, pages 321-322).

3. Add new people and different settings.

   - Ask parents and other support-team members to apply the strategies during natural daily routines at home, at school, and in the community.

   - Invite a same-age peer to share in interactions—to play a game or to share in a construction or cooking project or a field trip. This peer can serve as a mentor or friend in the regular classroom or in a play group. Wooten and Mesibov (1986) describe reverse mainstreaming strategies. Review the information on pages 336-341 for strategies for using play groups to expand interaction and communication skills.

   - Support interactions between peers during recess and exploratory or free-play periods. Capitalize on free-play situations by setting up opportunities for sharing materials interactively and taking turns.

   - Establish social skill groups (see pages 342-345), and plan with the learner to both participate and take the lead.

During circle time in the kindergarten class, Angelo became restless and began to shake his hands. His teacher said, "That looks like fun. Let's all shake our hands." Everyone started shaking their hands in the same way. When the teacher said, "Stop," everyone stopped. In a moment, the teacher said, "Go," and they all started shaking hands again. Angelo grinned. After several rounds of this routine, the teacher said, "Shake, shake, shake, stop!" and firmly stopped her hands on her knees. "Now, stretch, shake your shoulders, and let's sing Old MacDonald." This was a quick and refreshing change of pace for the entire class and a very positive way for Angelo to learn to gain some control over his actions and to get some acceptance. At another time, the teacher asked Angelo and others to take turns leading the group in the activity.

Summary

Adults are responsible for a child's well-being. They must provide limits, boundaries, demands, and instruction so the child is safe and is given opportunities to learn acceptable behavior and self-control. For the most part, this system works well for the child who has a strong social interactive habit. However, the learner with autism withdraws and has no opportunity to become a better communicator when the stimulation is too overpowering; that is, when adults talk too much and dominate the conversations (play) with questions and demands.

When adults follow their own agendas and ignore the subtle, nonverbal behaviors that signal feelings, preferences, and needs, learners stop trying. Their early efforts are not expanded into more complex and effective communications.

Learners will spend more time with people when the demands and overwhelming stimulation are reduced, and when their interests, ideas, and efforts are valued. Under these conditions, learners will discover that people are interesting and helpful. However, it will take many, many successful interactions to develop the habits that support effective communication.

Interpreters must continuously evaluate and refine their actions, the settings, and the materials to encourage continued progress. Child-directed play strategies are critical for teaching spontaneous interaction skills, but there must always be a balance. The child must learn to share control; in some situations the adults make demands and take charge, and in other situations the child will have control.

CHAPTER

21

Expand Communication Skills and Options

Expansion of the ever-fragile interactive communication habit is a major challenge for children with autism and their teachers. Effective communication is such a complex skill that this expansion rarely occurs automatically. Spontaneous communication will not occur unless there is a clear understanding of the purpose and power of communication and an understanding of how social interactions work.

Watson and associates (1989) suggest that communication skills are expanded systematically across several dimensions to:

- Communicate for a larger number of reasons or purposes (functions); see figure 21.1

- Communicate with a larger number of people

- Understand and use words more flexibly with a broader range of meanings and accurate word/concept associations (semantic categories)

- Communicate in multiple ways (forms or systems); see figure 21.2, page 316

- Communicate in an increasing number of natural situations and settings (contexts)

New skills are generally introduced in nondistracting situations, but expansion occurs in natural contexts where natural cues and reinforcement are available to make the skills meaningful and spontaneous. Communication skills taught and practiced in the context of rote drills will be used repetitively without meaning.

Each child's program is individualized and grows from the child's spontaneous efforts, even though they may be tiny. Activities are planned and support is provided to ensure systematic movement in steady but small steps across the dimensions to match gradually changing skills and needs. Interpreters constantly evaluate and refine the environment to set up situations that capitalize naturally on the child's efforts. If a child spontaneously takes mother by the wrist and pulls her to the sink to indicate a need for a drink, expansion occurs as the child is taught systematically to indicate other needs by pulling mother to other locations. Next steps involve taking father or teacher by the wrist in other settings or situations to indicate other needs. Simultaneously, other dimensions are addressed by expanding the child's experiences in natural contexts to learn new concepts (words) and to provide opportunities to communicate different types of messages. In this system, language and communication skills are learned meaningfully, rather than through rote and repetitive drills.

While the content of language and communication instruction is similar for all children, the problems and the strategies will differ. This chapter addresses some of the problems that are unique to most children with autism. Echoed and repetitive speech, two difficult problems that disrupt effective communication and behavior, are discussed in the first section. The second part of the chapter summarizes the issues involved in teaching alternative communication systems that incorporate formal signs, pictures, and written words.

Teaching Spontaneous Communication to Autistic and Developmentally Handicapped Children (Watson et al. 1989) is an excellent resource for speech-language pathologists and teachers. The expansion process described and illustrated by the authors begins with an assessment of the learner's spontaneous communication skills—the skills used without cues or assistance. It includes many strategies and case examples to illustrate the systematic and highly successful approach developed at Division TEACCH, University of North Carolina at Chapel Hill.

Causes and Effects in Communication and Language (Warren and Reichle 1991) is another excellent resource.

Figure 21.1. Basic communication functions

Requests for:
Foods/objects
Action/activity
More, or to continue
Stop, or end action/activity
Bathroom
Assistance
Attention
Affection
Social interaction
Information/clarification
Permission

Response to:
Directions
Yes/no and WH questions

Protest/Reject:
Action/event
Object/food
Removal or denial of object/activity
Changes of routine or environment

Comment:
On self or other person
On objects/people/events (present)
On objects/people/events (not present)

Express:
Pleasure
Pain
Fear
Surprise
Confusion
Frustration/stress
Choices
Other

Echolalia

Echolalia—repeating words and sentences produced by others—is a special problem in autism. Echolalia is a natural step in the normal progression of language development. In autism, learners appear to get stuck or stay in this step for prolonged periods. There are two basic types of echolalia: immediate and delayed. While there are similarities between the two types, assessment and intervention strategies are somewhat different. Both immediate and delayed echolalia show variations in:

- The exactness of the repetition
- The degree of comprehension of the repetition
- The presence or absence of intention

The articulation and intonation of the echoed words in both types of echolalia match that of the original production almost exactly (Prizant 1988).

Immediate Echolalia

Immediate echolalia occurs just after or very soon after the original words. The echoed words may or may not be used interactively. This type of echolalia serves several different functions. Often it is used to fill a conversational turn, to rehearse or process the meaning of the words, or to affirm that the message was heard—although perhaps not understood.

Immediate echolalia most commonly follows a question or a demand that the learner does not fully understand, but the learner knows a response is expected. The learner repeats the question—a strategy similar to that used by many people when they need time to think or when they are puzzled by the words and need more information. The difference is in the intensity and the inflexibility of the repetition. Other people can move flexibly from one strategy to another until they fully understand the words and can generate an appropriate response. The learner with autism may have only the one strategy—to echo the chunk of meaningless words over and over. The learner continues until the interpreter either leaves in exasperation or sets up the situation to clarify and guide the learner to an appropriate response.

Strategies for Dealing with Immediate Echolalia

1. Pause following a question or demand so the learner has time to generate an appropriate response.

2. Provide visual references to highlight the meaning of questions and demands (for example, line drawings of the critical words, or stick figures labeled to represent the learner and the interpreter with their words written in bubbles as in a cartoon).

3. Respond to echoed questions literally to model an appropriate response.

   Interpreter: Do you want a cookie?

   Learner: Do you want a cookie?

   Interpreter: **Yes,** I want a cookie, **please.**

   (The interpreter quickly takes a cookie and eats a bite before restating the question.)

   Do **you** want a cookie?

   (Note the emphasis on the critical words.)

4. When the confusion seems to be caused by not understanding the pronouns, highlight the relationship expressed by the pronoun. For example, say, "I, Jan, want a cookie. Do you, Tony, want a cookie?" As the pronoun and the name are paired, touch the person indicated. A full hand touch to the person's chest is very concrete and distinct from the kind of touch used to get attention.

5. Highlight natural cues or add adapted cues and prompts.

   - Quickly write out the appropriate response ("Yes, I want a cookie," or "Yes, please"). Prepare cue cards for some simple responses, and keep them ready to use quickly in other natural situations.

Caution: *These verbal and touch cues can add a confusing dimension that may lead to incorrect associations. Refer to the use of cues and prompts, pages 228-233.*

- Whisper or say the correct response, as if talking for the learner, while touching the learner's chest ("Yes, I, Tony, want a cookie"). Then hand the learner a cookie.

- Once the question is presented, quickly whisper the first part of an appropriate response with exaggerated mouth movements; then pause for the learner to complete the response ("Yes, ple . . ."). Gradually fade to simply mouthing the beginning sound of the first word.

6. Teach the meanings of different kinds of questions and directions and the types of responses that match different types of questions. For example, teach that the answer to a *why* question begins with *because*. Use visual references to illustrate the concepts.

7. Teach sentence frames with an open slot and set up situations to practice filling in words to fit the immediate situation. ("I need _____"; "I don't understand _____.")

8. Set up and practice many different situations within the context of group instruction so others can model appropriate responses.

9. Teach rejection responses in natural situations. ("No, I don't want a cookie"; "No, thank you.")

10. Avoid teaching rapid and rigid rote responses to questions and directions. If the response was not taught with meaning attached, the learner will not be able to apply it flexibly to different situations. If the learner was taught to respond quickly, the response will be echoed without meaning. The learner with autism must have time to process verbal requests or questions and generate a response to fit the specific situation.

Delayed Echolalia

In delayed echolalia, the words and phrases are echoed days, weeks, or even years after they were originally heard. Often, echoed words were first heard spoken with a great deal of emphasis and emotional content, and now are repeated much like a toddler learns and repeats his parent's swear words at the appropriate emotional times but without understanding the meaning. This is the situation in autism as TV commercials, correction procedures, rules, commands, warnings, or swear words are echoed. Some learners may repeat complete conversations, including the words of both partners. For example, during free time one young boy sat alone in the language circle, echoing the complete language lesson—both the teacher's script and the responses of the children.

Delayed echolalia is used for a variety of reasons and to serve several functions, among them: to request, protest, provide information, initiate conversations, and answer questions; and for self-regulation and rehearsal. Higher-functioning learners often intersperse fragments of borrowed phrases into their own creative utterances. In delayed echolalia, *no matter how ordinary or how intellectual the words sound, the words themselves are generally repeated without a clear or complete understanding of the conventional meaning.*

Delayed echolalia can best be understood in the context of the gestalt learning style common to autism. Words are taken in and stored in unanalyzed chunks that include many bits and pieces of sensory and emotional details from the original situation. A chunk of words is triggered by some common element of the current situation, but the words themselves lack meaning or have a different meaning to the individual with autism than to most other people. In the example of Tony and the cat (page 39), the chunk of words, "The cat jumped off the balcony," was associated with the emotional state of those in the original situation—tension, concern, and excitement—rather than the fact that the cat jumped off the balcony. Thus, that specific chunk of words is triggered whenever Tony is in a situation that includes similar emotional content.

The implications of delayed echolalia are far-reaching. People are misled and arrive at inaccurate conclusions when well-articulated and fluent talk about an intense interest or a concrete fantasy is combined with delayed echolalia.

- Too often, it is assumed that these learners are able to function in all areas with the same degree of skill as they can articulate echoed phrases and concrete information about special interests. When the learners cannot meet those expectations, they are seen as lazy, noncompliant, willful, or spiteful. Family and support staff may become frustrated and angry when they respond from their misperceptions rather than from the learner's perspective.

- Echoed phrases are sometimes misinterpreted as evidence of psychotic behavior, hallucinations, or delusions.

Strategies for Dealing with Delayed Echolalia

1. Quickly assess whether the words are borrowed. Generally, but not always, the echoed words are fluent, well articulated, and include the intonation and emphasis used by the first speaker. Original, self-generated utterances are frequently slower, more labored, and delivered in a flat, expressionless voice.

2. Consider the immediate situation and determine the purpose or meaning of the borrowed utterance; then use a reflective listening strategy. One girl repeated the Oreo cookie commercial when she wanted a snack—not necessarily a cookie. Her interpreter said, "You feel hungry and want a snack? You can say, 'I'm hungry. I want some pretzels.'" Provide visual references, either in the form of a cue card, a cartoon strip, or a semantic map that illustrates the sentence frame and a variety of available snack foods for filling in the blank.

3. *Do not make assumptions.* The learner with autism frequently does not understand the full meaning of all the words articulated.

4. When checking for understanding:

   - Avoid asking, "Do you understand?" or "Tell me, what did I just say?" *Even when the learner repeats a direction or indicates understanding, one cannot assume that the message is truly understood.* As one mother explained, "I cannot trust what she says. I can only tell if she understands from what she does. If she truly understands, she does it. If she doesn't understand, she doesn't do it."

   - Do use visual references or ask a more open-ended question. ("What are you going to do?"; "How are you going to do that?"; "Show me what you will do.")

5. Ensure that the correct meanings are associated with words and phrases by reviewing experiences and writing stories to highlight the important elements.

> In the example of Tony and the cat, the interpreter reviewed the highlights of the day by writing an experience story to correct the misinterpretation. The story was illustrated with simple line drawings.
>
> We were driving to Grandmother's house. The trip took two days. We stopped at the Acme Motel to stay overnight. When we got into the motel room, Mary opened the balcony door, and Johnny opened the cat's cage. Blackie, the cat, ran out of the cage and jumped off the balcony. We were surprised, excited, and worried. We had to go find

Blackie. Now, when I am surprised or worried, I can say, "Wow! Look what happened!" or "What happened?" or "What do we do now?" or "Wait a minute!"

6. Keep a log of echoed words and phrases with their meanings and a brief description of the situation when they were first heard. Keep track of the different ways the phrase is used. For example, is it used to initiate a conversation, to comment, to indicate displeasure? (One young man said, "I'll kill you," whenever he didn't want to do something. His mother indicated this began when he heard the phrase in a TV show.) Keep the log up-to-date, and use it as a reference for new interpreters.

7. Teach more effective ways to communicate messages in the context of natural and simulated situations. When problems occur, use cue cards as references.

8. When assessing the meaning of language, check with parents and others who know the learner very well. This is especially important for psychologists, counselors, and behavior specialists. *A diagnosis or intervention cannot be determined on an assumption that the learner understands and uses the words with the typical, conventional meaning.*

For a broader understanding of echolalia as representing a gestalt or holistic processing style, read Language Acquisition and Communicative Behavior in Autism: Toward an Understanding of the "Whole" of It *by Barry Prizant (1983).*

In summary, echoed or borrowed words carry meaning that must be interpreted by others. *Do not punish or try to eliminate echolalia.* The use of these verbal routines is an important and normal stage in language development. The learner with autism needs help to understand word meanings and to use the language more flexibly in order to move on.

Repetitive Questions and Conversations

Questions about time, events, worries, and special interests often continue, seemingly without end. The learner often shows considerable tension and concern as if genuinely worried about something. On other occasions, the learner will accept only specific answers to the repeated questions. The same questions will be asked of each person in a room, one after the other. If the learner's questions are ignored, the individual may become even more insistent and upset. Stress can accelerate when the same answers are not provided, when the same answers are provided, or when the questions are ignored.

Strategies for Dealing with Repetitive Questions and Conversations

The first step is to determine the function or purpose of the questions or conversations. There are at least four, perhaps more, reasons for repetitive questions and conversations. The learner:

1. Needs information but doesn't know how to ask the right questions

2. Wants a social interaction but doesn't know how to initiate, extend, or terminate an interaction

3. Has a genuine concern about major unsolvable problems

4. Is locked or stuck into a repetitive action and doesn't know how to stop it

When specific information is needed, but the learner doesn't know how to ask the right question

1. Provide a concrete and literal answer with visual references as appropriate. For example, answers to questions about time are paired with a concrete and visual way to mark the passage of time:

- Mark the occasion on the calendar and count the days.
- Refer to the daily calendar of events and clarify. ("First, _____, then _____.")
- Place three blocks on the table and say, "In 15 minutes it will be time to leave." To show the passage of time, remove a block after each five-minute period.

> To calm her son who was concerned that his mother was still talking to a friend when it was time to go to lunch, one mother held up three fingers and said, "I must talk about three more things. Then it will be time for lunch." As she finished talking about each item, she lowered a finger. When all three fingers were down, she ended the conversation and left with her son.

2. If the same question continues several times, it may be an indication that the learner wants other information but is not able to frame the right question. Stress is likely to build if the interpreter probes with a series of questions. Switch from a face-to-face verbal conversation to a visual conversation on paper. Sit at a table beside the learner, and write down the learner's first question and the answer that you gave. Move the paper closer to the learner, write the repeated question, and change the answer slightly to provide different information; or, ask a slightly different question ("Do you want to know about _____?"). Then put down the pencil. Shifting the focus to the paper seems to reduce the stimulation and stress. Altering or broadening the answer with more details seems to help identify the real issue. In some situations, both partners verbalize their answers, but the interpreter still writes it all down. In other situations, both stop talking and each writes his own questions and responses. It may take considerable time to arrive at the real need, but the stress level is considerably reduced. One resource teacher used this strategy at school; but instead of staying near the learner while he wrote his response, she moved away until he quit writing, and then she returned to write her response. When the pressures are reduced, many learners can find ways to state their needs more clearly.

3. Teach the learner to use sentence frames or cue cards to communicate. ("Let's write this down so I can understand.") The communication notebook shown here was useful to Jose, who could not recall the words to get information.

4. When the questions continue after you have made a genuine effort to provide the needed information, say, "I'm sorry, I don't understand. Let's take a break, and we can try again later." Set a specific time to try again. Only then, offer something to relieve the stress, change the focus, and divert attention—a drink of juice, or time to bounce on a mini-trampoline or rock in the chair.

Jose's communication notebook

When repetitive questions are used to initiate or keep a social interaction going

1. Respond to the question as you would to initiations of any friend. *It is important to attend in some way to all initiations,* to show respect and to strengthen the social/communication habit.

   - Stop and discuss the topic for a few minutes. Then say, "Now I would like to talk about _____. We can talk about earthquakes again after dinner"; or, "I am busy, but I have time to listen to two things about earthquakes." Keep track, holding up one finger and then the next. Then say, "That's two things. We can talk more at 2:00."

2. Consciously initiate more frequent informal interactions with the learner. These interactions provide important practice and are a sign of increasing social interest.

3. Clarify social interaction times on the daily calendar so the learner can see when the next opportunity will occur.

4. Structure the scheduled talking and interaction sessions to expand communication options. Add variations, model new strategies, and provide sensitive feedback. The variations increase skill and flexibility and decrease the amount of time for repetitive questions and conversations. For example, with a person who is very interested and knowledgeable about the weather, try these variations:

   - "We can talk about the weather for five minutes. Then I get to choose the topic." End promptly at the appointed time. If necessary use a timer.

   - "You can talk about the weather for four minutes, but tell me one new thing about the weather. Then it's my turn." Keep a log of new information about weather and another log of other topics.

   - "What do you want to talk about first: the garden, the weather, or the ball game?" When it is understood that there will be opportunities to talk about interests, *learners are likely to choose other topics.*

5. Teach a process for negotiating conversation topics. ("I want to talk about _____. What do you want to talk about?")

6. Provide a cue card to clarify conversation rules, topics, and questions.

   Interpreter: What do you want to talk about?

   Learner: The weather

   On a small card or sheet of paper, write:

   1.

   2.

   3.

   As you write the numbers, say to the learner, "First, say three things about the weather." As the learner talks, check off the numbers or write the three statements. Then point to the question, and wait quietly or softly cue the learner to read the words so you can prepare a new topic.

   Provide honest interest and reassurance. The learner needs self-confidence (I am valuable, my interests are valued, and people like to talk to me). The learner also needs to know that people want to hear new information, like to share talking time, and want to talk about other things, too. The goal is to expand confidence, knowledge, and conversation skills. Visual systems help the learner manage conversations more satisfactorily.

When the learner is genuinely concerned about major or unsolvable problems

Stressful and repetitive questions about major problems are most obvious in the highly verbal learners who watch TV or read the news about natural disasters, starving people, wars, crime, and conflicting medical or nutritional research. Even Disney movies can be frightening if the learner does not automatically understand the difference between fantasy and fact. Some learners become upset and ask repeated questions about religious issues after hearing forceful or dramatic sermons.

1. Assess to determine the learner's existing knowledge of the situation, the terminology and concepts, and the misperceptions. Then clarify and provide basic information and reassurance. For example, locate the site of a disaster on a map, figure how far away it is, and identify those who are responsible for taking care of the people or the problem (the President, the police, the Red Cross, others). Define fact or fantasy, propaganda, rumor, and theories. Discuss research and the fact that "Nobody knows exactly." Keep the explanation concrete and as literal as possible. Use visual references.

2. Schedule times to talk about worries. Develop a routine that clarifies the activity that will follow talking time and allows for some time at the end of each session to talk about other things.

3. Identify a specific place to talk about worries. ("We only talk about worries when we sit in these chairs.") Do not schedule the worry time at the dining table or in the bedroom; meal and bed times must not trigger worry.

4. End the discussions at the stated time with a satisfying or calming phrase that signals the end of worry talk, provides some reassurance, and reminds the learner of the next activity. Select calming phrases that fit the concern, and use them routinely. ("That's about all we can do"; "It's pretty amazing!"; "Well, the facts are not all in yet"; "That's just make-believe"; "The common cold is not dangerous"; "It's a real tragedy"; "We'll have to leave it to the Red Cross.")

5. Keep a log of worries, and list the group or person responsible for taking care of each problem. Clarify that big problems take a lot of time to fix. Anxiety may be relieved by participating in food and clothing drives for the homeless or joining in organized walks to raise money for other relief efforts.

6. If the worry continues, say, "You can ask two more questions about _____. Then it will be time for _____. You can talk about it again at 8:15." Hold up two fingers or draw two circles to keep track of the two questions. Then move away and make a note on the calendar for the next talking time.

7. Develop a worry-management routine that begins with thought stopping and relaxation techniques (see pages 356-362). When developing the routine, include some of the strategies listed above, such as identifying an appropriate source of information and using positive self-talk. Imagery procedures (pages 207-208) and cognitive picture rehearsal (pages 362-363) can lead to greater independence.

In summary, to manage repetitive talking, the learner needs information, strategies, options, and respectful assistance. Teach rules, sentence frames, and coping or calming statements. Provide visual references that can be used independently.

Alternative and Augmentative Communication Systems

All people need to be able to communicate in every setting. They need not only a consistent and dependable primary communication system, but also backup systems. Those who cannot speak need an alternative communication system. Those who can speak need an augmentative system to support or augment their speech when it is difficult to understand or when it is limited or not available for use. For example, extreme stress can make speech difficult to produce consistently; others have difficulty recalling words or initiating speech.

There are still many adolescents and adults with autism who have no consistent and effective communication system. They manage fairly well in familiar settings with trusted and sensitive interpreters, but they are at a distinct disadvantage when they are alone in new situations. Those without effective and dependable communication systems have more severe anxiety and behavior problems and fewer opportunities and options to participate in society.

Speech is only one of several natural ways to communicate; well over half of communication is nonverbal. Most people use gestures, facial expressions, and body language to convey messages and support their speech. Many young children with autism are learning to communicate more effectively now that:

- The communication and processing deficits in autism are more clearly understood

- Early diagnosis and appropriate early intervention are available

- Alternative and augmentative communication (AAC) systems are more commonly available

It is not possible to predict the potential achievement of this first generation of children with these opportunities. It is clear, however, that when people with autism learn to communicate in some way, they tend to be more relaxed and more involved—prerequisites for learning the language and learning to speak meaningfully.

Figure 21.2. Forms of communication

Motoric: Using direct manipulation of another person or object to send a message
(Pulling mother to the sink to request a drink)

Gestural: Using hand, head, or body actions to convey messages
(Pointing or nodding to indicate *yes* or *no*, pushing something away to reject, touching a person's arm to ask for attention, and making other gestures)

Object: Using real objects, miniatures, or parts of objects as symbols to convey needs
(Handing mother a cup to request a drink)

Pictorial: Using photographs or generic line drawings to communicate

Vocal/verbal: Using sounds to communicate
(Saying, "Ah-ah-ah" to draw attention, producing different sounds for different needs, or using conventional spoken words)

Written: Pointing to printed messages; writing or typing messages

Signed: Using conventional gestures and hand movements developed as a formal communication system for the deaf

Because speech is the most efficient form of communication, understood by more people, speech development continues to be a goal. But it is important to remember that speech does not automatically ensure communication. The highest priority and ultimate goal is for every learner to have some way to communicate effectively in every setting and situation. The ability to communicate, by whatever means, opens many doors and increases the options for a more satisfying and productive life. Those with autism, like most other people, are lifelong learners. With support, they will continue to expand their communication skills and their options throughout life.

Considerations for Making Decisions

When making decisions about AAC systems and planning instruction to expand communication options for those with autism, consider that:

See pages 72-73 for a list of some assessment resources and strategies. Also see pages 95-99 for conducting and interpreting standardized tests.

1. Skill development does not follow the normal or expected sequence. Probe a broad range of skills in the context of a number of natural and simulated situations to identify the learner's strengths and the gaps. A learner may have low test scores and appear to have very limited potential but have the ability to read and spell.

2. The drive to communicate is weak, even in those who are very verbal but not necessarily effective communicators. Instructional experiences must be exceptionally clear, meaningful, and positive so the communication habit is continually and naturally reinforced. *Whatever type of AAC system is selected, it must be introduced in the context of making spontaneous requests.* This ensures that the effort to communicate receives a powerful and natural reinforcer.

3. *Contrary to earlier belief, basic skills such as attending, eye contact, motor and verbal imitation, symbol matching, or labeling skills are not prerequisite for communication training.* Rather, these basic skills are learned far more meaningfully in the context of communication training.

An AAC specialist and an autism specialist are important resources for solving problems when planning and implementing an AAC system.

Select a Primary Communication System

System selection depends on the learner's spontaneous skills, interests, and motor abilities. All alternative systems have some limitations. Picture/word systems must be carried about and have a limited amount of space for symbols. Signed communication requires an interpreter, and it takes a long time to learn a comprehensive sign vocabulary. Written or typed communication requires the presence of writing materials, a typewriter, or a computer. Interpreters need additional training to support the use of AAC systems. Before making decisions, review the discussion of symbol selection in chapter 14. Some of the considerations are summarized in Beukelman and Mirenda (1992).

Picture systems are appropriate for those who show interest in pictures—for very young children as well as for older learners who are functioning at a very concrete level. Pictures provide permanent visual references and are an aid for those who have difficulty recalling a word from memory. For many learners, adding printed labels to pictures facilitates transition to written words.

Written/printed word systems are more interesting and motivating for some learners with autism, even those who seem to be quite limited. The ability to read and profit from these systems seems to have little relationship to scores on intelligence tests or "apparent" ability. Typing or writing messages provides unlimited vocabulary options, but it can be very slow.

See discussion of facilitated communication and written communication strategies on pages 326-333.

For further discussion of signing, see pages 322-326.

- Written or printed word dictionaries are useful tools for augmenting speech for very verbal learners who have difficulty recalling words and initiating communication.

Sign systems also have value for many learners—the very young as well as more experienced learners. Signs are easy to shape and prompt. They provide visual, tactile, auditory, and proprioceptive feedback as the signs are shaped. Auditory feedback is also provided when the interpreter simultaneously verbalizes the signed messages. The sensory feedback received during the act of producing signs tends to stimulate language learning and speech in some learners. While signing is very confusing for some individuals, it is beneficial for others.

Like those without autism, many learners incorporate, or can learn to incorporate, a variety of systems for different situations. They may use gestures to communicate some messages, but in other situations they may use objects, pictures, sounds, or written words. Before establishing a primary communication system, conduct an extensive assessment that includes systematic experimentation with a variety of systems and formats. When the primary system is determined, it may be feasible to incorporate a more expensive higher-tech system. However, *a learner must be encouraged to continue speaking when speech is available and to use gestures, cue cards, and other back-up systems to augment that primary system. This will ensure that messages are clearly communicated when a higher-tech system needs repair or revision or when interpreters or facilitators are not available.*

Design a System

There are many ways to arrange and display pictures and words for communication purposes. They range from handmade picture, letter, or word boards to extremely high-tech systems with speech output. For discussion of issues to consider in the design, see Beukelman and Mirenda (1992).

High-technology systems can be expensive, so generally a learner's first system is handmade to specifically match the individual's abilities to scan and direct attention, understand the picture/word symbols, and physically manipulate the system. A system is effective and will be used when it is:

1. Portable, durable, easy to manage, and always available

A simple belt-loop system supported one learner whose interpreter was absent.

Systems that require boards, books, clipboards, or computers must be compact, sturdy, and easy to carry. Systems used by small children must be especially sturdy, and perhaps waterproof. A system must be large enough for easy use; but if it is too large or too complicated, it will get in the way, become a burden, and will be avoided. A system must be easy to transport everywhere and at all times—in a pocket, purse, fanny pack, or fastened to the belt or around the neck. If the system is not constantly available, it will not be used and the learner will not learn the power of communication in all settings.

2. Easy to use and capable of delivering a clear message as quickly as possible

A single picture can be labeled with the word or with a sentence to clarify the meaning for an unfamiliar communication partner. Speed is enhanced when the learner needs to touch only one letter, word, or picture to deliver a complete message. In *Silent Words and Forever Friends* (1990, 230), author Margaret Eastham describes the messages that were programmed into a Sharp Memowriter so that her son, David, could send a message by touching only one key. Some of those messages were:

A = I WANT TO BE ALONE

H = MY HEAD HURTS

J = I FEEL JUMPY, EXCITED

X = COULD WE GO FOR A WALK?

1 = I AM SORRY

3 = I AM FRUSTRATED

3. Easy to adapt and/or expand

Review chapter 14 for design and construction suggestions.

A system must be updated and adapted as the learner's needs and skills change. If the system does not keep pace with the learner's ever-changing needs, it will not be used.

- Initially, a very young learner may be overwhelmed with more than two or three symbols, while others may be bored and refuse to use a simple display. The ability to manage larger numbers of symbols develops with time and practice.

- Separate vocabulary boards or books can be prepared to match the needs of a particular situation. These are useful for learners who cannot speak as well as for those who are verbal.

- Collections of simple, clear, black-and-white line drawings are available commercially (Carlson 1988; Mayer-Johnson 1992).

An ongoing evaluation process is needed to identify problems and modify or refine the system as soon as a need arises.

Select Vocabulary

Refer to the section on identifying reinforcers (pages 238-243).

Vocabulary for initial picture, word, or sign systems is selected for its *reinforcing value to the learner*. Initial vocabulary needs to allow learners to access/request their most valued objects, food, drink, or actions. Support-team members who spend the most time with the individual learner already may know which foods, objects, or actions are highly reinforcing. To identify a broader range of reinforcers to expand the system, place an assortment of things on a table and see what the learner selects.

Other considerations for selecting initial vocabulary include these:

- While the word *bathroom* has significance for mother, teacher, or an older learner, it is not likely to be highly valued by a young child.

See pages 324-325 for strategies for teaching point = this.

- Generic words such as *eat, drink,* and *play* represent a broader range of objects, actions, and concepts; but they are confusing for the literal learner who associates a single meaning with a single word. Because space is limited on picture/word board systems and it takes a long time to learn a large sign vocabulary, a generic word plus a point that means *this* (for example, "Eat *this*") is highly communicative and quickly expands the opportunities to be understood in many natural situations.

Additional vocabulary depends on age, interests, and the types of problems the learner is likely to encounter each day in various settings. The following messages can be added as the need arises:

- Vocabulary for requesting help, indicating preferences, and for rejecting or protesting (*Help, Yes/No, Stop, All done,* and *Need break*) are high priorities and will reduce many behavior problems.

- Often, a learner who does not have the answer will sit passively, making no effort to communicate. The phrase, "I don't know," provides an active alternative response.

- Phrases on a word board that are helpful for the learner with autism include: "I don't understand," "Draw a picture," and "Write it down." To assist in making choices, a learner needs a way to say, "I don't want any of those."

Guidelines for Instruction

Teaching the spontaneous use of communication systems requires a planning and instructional process similar to that described in chapter 20 for teaching spontaneous interactions. These basic instructional guidelines can be modified and applied to teaching most AAC systems, including a sign system, or to match the individual needs of a specific learner.

The goals: To make a spontaneous request and learn the basic concept of a social/communicative exchange ("I give you something, you give me something")

The setting: The initial introduction of a new system or vocabulary occurs in the structured and familiar 1:1 play, work, or therapy setting at home or in school. The exact location, session structure, and materials will depend on the vocabulary displayed on the system and the learner's age and ability.

Arrange the area so that you control the materials and choices, which are in view and available to the learner. Initially, present only a single object or action that is most highly reinforcing. With only one option, there is little opportunity for error and a greater likelihood that the correct associations will occur.

Position yourself so you can see where the learner is looking and you can easily guide, support, or shape the learner's hand. Conversations normally occur in a face-to-face position so that natural and spontaneous eye contact can occur easily.

Initiate Instruction

Teach communication skills in the context of turn-taking interactions. The power of the system is taught in the context of choice and capitalizes on the learner's natural gesture—reaching to grab. As a young child reaches to touch or grab a highly desired item, the child's hand is shaped to point to a specific picture/word, shaped to form the sign, or assisted to pick up the symbol and place it in the interpreter's hand. The interpreter simultaneously verbalizes the learner's intent and immediately delivers the requested item, thus reinforcing the association of the action, the symbol, and the meaningful consequences. To ensure that the correct associations are made and to avoid dependence and passivity, in the initial instruction:

Review cuing and prompting procedures (pages 228-232).

- Avoid the use of verbal cues, prompts, and reinforcers (such as "What do you want?"; "Do you want the chip?"; or "Good pointing!"). Instead, set up the reinforcing situation and wait expectantly for the learner to express intention by reaching to grab.

- Avoid passive physical assistance, which leads to passivity and the development of meaningless motor routines. Assistance that is provided as the learner is looking at the object and directing physical effort to reach an object is more likely to result in a spontaneous and meaningful communication habit. Having a request fulfilled immediately after the communication effort strengthens the effort to communicate. However, if the requested object or action is delivered while the learner is looking away, looking away will be reinforced. If the learner's attention drifts away before the natural reinforcer is delivered, stop all movement and say, "I don't understand. Show me again."

An older learner may need more information prior to initial instruction. For example, the introduction of a new system or a new vocabulary word might include:

1. A brief explanation

   ("This is a picture board. You can use it to tell me what you want. This is a picture of _____"; or, "This is a new trampoline. Here is a picture of the trampoline on your board. Touch the picture when you want to jump on the trampoline.") Avoid trial-and-error strategies that can lead to wrong associations.

2. A brief demonstration with commentary to model its use and power

3. An opportunity to practice using the system with assistance

The following scenario illustrates one procedure to ensure that the learner:

1. Spontaneously initiates the action

2. Actively participates in expressing intention

3. Hears a verbal interpretation of its intent

4. Quickly receives the requested object to reinforce the association between the action and the result

> Angie, the interpreter, is sitting across the table from Simon. Several small crackers and a sparkling toy—both highly liked by Simon—are between them. The picture board also is on the table, and Angie's hands are resting on the table ready to provide assistance quickly. After a brief introduction of the board and the materials, Angie picks up the picture board, holds it close to the crackers, and says, "I want cracker," while pointing to the symbol of the cracker. Immediately she picks up a cracker and eats it. Then she replaces the picture board on the table and waits.
>
> Simon reaches toward the crackers.
>
> Angie places the picture symbol over the crackers to block further hand movement, and says, "You want crackers. You can ask for crackers." She taps on the board and touches the cracker symbol to draw attention.
>
> Simon shifts his gaze to the picture.
>
> Quickly Angie guides and shapes his hand to point to the picture as she says, "Simon wants a cracker. You can have a cracker. Here!" She quickly slides a cracker across the table.
>
> The procedure is repeated with varied gestures and touch prompts. Periodically, Angie takes a turn and models making choices between the two items.

Expand Instruction

Schedule several short, highly structured sessions each day to introduce and integrate new vocabulary into the system. Simultaneously set up or engineer many opportunities to use familiar vocabulary in the context of all natural routines of the day to communicate with more people in more settings.

- Initially, take the responsibility for ensuring that the communication system is always available. When it is understood that the system provides power, the learner will take more of the responsibility.

- Avoid repetitive, rote symbol-labeling activities and testing strategies such as, "Touch *jump*; . . . Touch *help*." The ability to label a symbol does not ensure that it will be used communicatively. The system must be used communicatively to express and obtain wishes, needs, and ideas in order to build a strong communication habit. Testing for understanding is best done in natural contexts.

Picture Exchange Communication System

The Picture Exchange Communication System (PECS) developed at the Delaware Autistic Program has been used as an initial mode of communication for children as young as two years of age (Bondy and Frost 1994). The PECS is used to teach the child to locate a communication partner, present a picture of a desired item, and get the item in exchange for the picture. There are no prerequisite skills for initiating this system. This social communication exchange is based on child-selected reinforcers. The child spontaneously and intentionally initiates the exchange to request a highly desired item. The exchange is completed when the communication partner gives the highly reinforcing item to the child.

Advantages of the PECS are:

- The exchange is obviously intentional and easy to understand

- The child is taught to take the initiative—to seek a partner and deliver the message

- The communication is meaningful and highly reinforcing

This procedure prevents some of the most difficult problems that often occur when teaching children with autism to use picture/word communication systems, as illustrated in the following examples.

> At snack time, Mary gazed out the window as she repetitively tapped the picture of *juice*. Interpreters were left to wonder whether this was an intentional act or simply a rote routine.
>
> When Mark wanted his favorite toy, he ran to his communication board and tapped on the picture. When he got no response, he fell to the floor in a major tantrum. He didn't know that he needed a communication partner.

There are six phases of PECS training:

1. Teach the basic exchange with physical assistance.

   The child extends the picture and places it in the trainer's hand. No verbal cues, prompts, or reinforcers are used. (During initial instruction, physical assistance is provided by a second adult standing behind the child.)

2. Expand spontaneity to locate a partner, orient, and persist in getting attention.

3. Discriminate between two or more pictures, and expand vocabulary to 12 to 20 words.

4. Build sentence structure with an "I want" picture/word card to request items present and not present.

At the end of this phase, the communication system contains 20 to 50 pictures (generally, pictographic line drawings on ¾" or 1" square cards), and the child is communicating with a variety of partners.

5. Respond to "What do you want?"

    By the end of this phase, the child spontaneously requests desired items and actions and answers the question, "What do you want?" in all daily activities.

6. Comment in response to a question, "What do you see?" with an "I see" card.

    By the end of this phase, the communication system contains 30 to 50 pictures and two sentence-starter cards.

Beyond Phase 6, vocabulary, language concepts, and sentence structures are expanded to more people and settings. Children typically progress through Phases 1 and 2 within a matter of days. Phase 3 training can take from several days to several months. Phases 4 and 5 are mastered in a few weeks.

When started on PECS as preschoolers, speech was acquired by a large percentage of the children who had no form of functional or socially appropriate communication skills (Bondy and Frost 1994).

In a typical case described by Bondy and Frost, a child entered PECS training at age 36 months with no speech and no intentional communication. After four months of training, he began to use speech while moving the pictures. Within a few months, his vocabulary grew to more than 100 pictures. After 11 months of training, he used only speech to communicate. Bondy and Frost indicate that the rate of progress varies, but nearly all children who eventually developed speech used the picture exchange system as their only mode of communication for a while.

Sign Language Systems

Early in the 1970s, the use of sign language as a communication option for those with autism seemed to be encouraging. Some children learned to communicate for the first time, and a few began to speak after first learning to sign. For several years, nearly every child with autism received sign language training.

By the end of the decade, it was apparent that sign language was not helpful to every person with autism. Some children became very confused, while others learned only a few signs as rote motor routines or echoed the signs of others but never generated their own signs. But other children did benefit from sign language training, especially when teachers used Total Communication strategies (that is, simultaneous use of signs and words to teach language). Those benefits ranged from learning to sign only a few words, to learning to speak. Some learned to:

- Ask for help and request a few favorite things
- Make requests and answer yes/no questions
- Think and self-cue with signs
- Understand basic concepts at an increased rate, because the signs for many pronouns, space, time, and action words are visually descriptive
- Articulate multiple-syllable words more clearly
- Speak as they signed, later dropping the use of signs

In some cases, signing served as an alternative to repetitive/stereotypic finger and hand movements—an unexpected benefit!

At the age of 7, Maria was unable to speak. She did not use gestures or attempt to interact. After learning a few signs, she became more aware of others. She spontaneously initiated those signs to request specific foods and toys and to request help. One morning, after several weeks of sign language training, she pulled her teacher by the wrist to her new friend who had hurt his finger. Maria signed "Help" and pointed to her friend. She had learned to seek a partner and spontaneously pair a sign and gesture to seek help for another person—an amazing feat!

Matt, whose speech was unreliable, learned many signs. When he needed to say something, he watched his hands as he signed the words; then he spoke the words.

While many teachers continue to use Total Communication strategies during instruction, other AAC systems have replaced signing as an expressive system in many cases because:

- It takes a long time to learn a functional sign vocabulary
- Teaching sign language to a learner with autism is different from teaching signs to those who are deaf
- Interpreters must be trained and available in all settings

Because of the potential benefits, signed communication needs serious consideration when making program decisions for a young learner. If it is decided that a signing system is an appropriate option, the support team must make a major commitment. Training must be systematic over a long period of time. *Signed Speech® Language Program for Nonverbal Students* (Schaeffer, et al. 1994) is an important reference to guide the team.

Select the Sign System

Several manual sign language systems have been developed for those who are deaf. Some are highly symbolic and based on large or global concepts, while others are based on the English language.

A system such as described in *Signing Exact English* (Gustafson et al. 1980) is useful for those with autism because it is structured to match the spoken and written language that is seen and heard every day. When matched with the spoken language, this system avoids confusion for these very literal learners. The system:

- Serves as a bridge to move from signing to speech, reading, and writing
- Facilitates receptive language development and provides experience to understand the language spoken by others
- Serves as a visual reference to highlight word meanings, articulation, and sentence structure, and to clarify the meaning of prefixes, suffixes, tenses, and other forms

It is important to select a system with potential for expansion, because it is not possible to predict which young learners will advance to speech, reading, and writing.

Select Vocabulary

Review the guidelines for selecting vocabulary presented on pages 318-319.

The first signs will be less confusing and easier to discriminate and learn if:

- The movement of the sign is modified to match the movement of natural gestures

  For example, modify the sign for *no* to match or flow with the natural motion of pushing away to reject or with the natural back-and-forth motion of a head shake.

- The number of movements are modified to match the rhythm of the syllables in the word

- The first few signs have different shapes, locations, and movements

  For example, teach *candy, cracker,* and *ball.* (The sign for *candy* is a movement of the index finger on the cheek, the sign for *cracker* is a chopping movement of the fingers to the opposite elbow, and the sign for *ball* is fingertips together as if holding a ball.)

Guidelines for Teaching Signs

The procedure for teaching signs is similar to that for teaching picture/word systems, except that the shaping of the sign is more direct and does not interrupt the flow and energy of the natural gesture that shows intent. The first lesson is to assign a meaning to the pointing gesture *(point = this)*. The interpreter uses a basic sequence of seven strategies:

1. Set up as described on page 319.

2. Model with slightly exaggerated movements, and say, "I want *this* candy." Touch the candy while saying *this*. Take a piece of candy and eat it.

3. Wait and watch for the learner to reach toward the candy.

4. Quickly shape and guide the learner's hand to *point* to the targeted object.

5. Verbalize and sign the learner's intent. ("Jose wants *this* candy.")

6. Immediately give access to the desired candy (natural reinforcement).

7. Repeat with variations.

   - Take turns, and share the foods and toys naturally, just as you would share in any social situation.

   - Vary the placement of the objects, the seating arrangements (various sides of the table, on a rug. . .), but continue to sit opposite the learner to make eye contact natural and to be in a position to shape both hands for two-handed signs.

   Refer to prompting procedures, pages 229-233.

   - Vary the physical shaping procedure so the learner doesn't begin to think that you will always be there to provide hand-shaping. After some experience with a new sign, use touch prompts. Give reassurance that soon the learner will be able to make the sign alone.

   - Ensure that the learner's dominant hand is shaped to make the sign. (In general, the dominant hand will be the reaching hand. Sometimes this is confusing when the interpreter is sitting in a face-to-face position.)

   - *Avoid passive physical assistance and the addition of verbal cues and prompts.*

   - *Avoid teaching signs by imitation;* this leads to echolalic signing.

   - Verbalize the intent of the message in simple but complete sentences.

Strategies to Prevent or Repair Typical Problems

Instructional decisions are designed to make sense from the literal perspective of the learner with autism.

1. Echolalic signing

   Prevent echolalic signing by teaching signs as a spontaneous expressive language task. Shape the natural gesture (reaching to grasp) into the sign, and avoid teaching signs as a visual/motor imitation task. If the learner begins to echo signs, quietly and gently lower the learner's hands and say, "It is my time to talk." If the problem persists, use a card with "My turn" written on it, or place a block in front of the person whose turn it is to talk.

2. All signs mean *want*.

   Occasionally, learners will run through their entire repertoire of signs as if searching for the magic motor movement that will satisfy a present need. If a sign is sometimes used meaningfully in appropriate situations, it is likely that the sign is correctly associated with the object label. Because signs cannot be learned fast enough to address each and every need that arises during a day, old signs are echoed to indicate, "I need this, but I don't have the words. Perhaps one of these motor routines will work." This situation is a bit like delayed verbal echolalia: when no better or specific response is available, the individual uses one that worked in similar situations.

   See pages 309-311 to review the discussion of delayed echolalia.

   If a sign is never used meaningfully in appropriate situations, but becomes part of a rote routine of signs, it is likely that the specific association of the sign, object, or label was never clear. Instead, hand movements became "magical" routines associated with the concept of *want*. ("When I want something, I do these things with my hands.") This sometimes occurs when the initial vocabulary is composed of generic words (*eat, play, more*). These very literal learners generally believe that everything has only one label and that a single word can refer to only a single concept or entity. How can a generic word such as *eat* refer to so many things—the act of eating as well as a label for hamburger, cracker, cereal, pickles?

Several strategies are needed to address these problems:

1. Teach that a pointing gesture means *this*. When the learner reaches to grasp an object, shape that hand to point to the object, and verbalize the intention: "Tony wants *this* (specific object)." Emphasize the word *this*. Note that the correct label is added but not emphasized at this first stage. This procedure not only provides the correct label for future use, but ensures that the learner will not erroneously believe that everything is now labeled *this*. Systematically expand the concept within the sentence frame to teach the signs *want this, want this X, I want this X,* verbalizing the full sentence as above. If using generic words, such as *eat*, teach in the following sequence: *this, eat this, want eat this, want eat this X, I want eat this X.*

   It may take several weeks to achieve total understanding and independence. As all interpreters use the sentence frame to respond to requests in all settings by pairing the *point = this* with the noun, the learner has a model for requesting many different objects, each with its own name. Once the sentence frame is understood and the sign, verbal label, and object are presented together enough times, some will learn new signs almost spontaneously. Other learners may not progress to that level, but they will have a logical and effective way to request many objects and actions in many different situations.

2. Teach the concepts and meanings of generic words. Provide many opportunities to sort and categorize (for example, things to eat and things you do not eat).

The concept of *more* is especially confusing because it is abstract and used in a variety of very different situations—more food, more time, more space. The word *more* is used only when something has been used up or gone. (The time for playing with the toy is used up, or all the milk in the cup is gone.) If the interpreter asks, "Do you want more?" the learner may think, "No I don't want *more*, I want *milk*." Clarify the meaning by saying, "The milk is all gone. Do you want more milk?" As with other generic terms, it is important to be specific; *milk* is still *milk*—it does not have a new label.

Strategies to Stimulate Speech

Pairing the signs with the speech during instruction offers a language-rich environment that automatically stimulates speech production in some learners. Scheduling separate talking times also may increase the potential for speech. During these periods, tell the learner, "This is talking time, time to use voices." For the very young, this is a time for vocal and word play. More formal strategies for stimulating speech are appropriate for more experienced learners. *However, avoid traditional physical prompting strategies to stimulate sound and speech production*, because the learner with autism is likely to learn the motor movements of the prompts as part of a routine. For example, one child learned to hold his lips together with his fingers as he said, "Mmmm," after the therapist held his lips together during instruction. If prompts are needed, make them as natural as possible. *Vary all prompts; any prompt that is used in the same way more than once is likely to be learned as a part of a routine.*

If the learner begins to verbalize while signing, accept it as a natural phenomenon. Undue excitement could interrupt the natural and meaningful situation. When speech becomes easier to use than the signs, the learner will automatically and gradually stop signing. Some will continue to use the signs in stressful situations or as a way to support thinking, rehearsal, and self-regulation. Encourage this by asking, "Can you show me what you need?"

In summary, the total communication process for teaching signs and language may overwhelm or confuse some learners with autism. For others, hearing the word, seeing the object, and feeling the movement of the sign simultaneously tends to tie it all together into a meaningful chunk that can lead to a better understanding of the language and communication, and possibly to speech. See Schaeffer et al. (1994) for additional strategies and considerations.

Facilitated Communication

Parents and professionals with many years of experience in autism have developed a healthy skepticism about new cures or procedures. They have learned that most, but not all, new ideas have merit and may benefit some individuals with autism, but not every individual. They also know that it is important to explore new ideas with an open mind.

In 1990, interest and emotions mounted as the media reported that Facilitated Communication (FC) can help those with autism communicate (Biklen 1990). The excitement has waned, and many stopped using FC when the research failed to support its validity.

As with other strategies, procedures, or therapies, however, FC has opened doors for some individuals. Many parents have reported the positive effects of FC for their child and their family. These parent reports cannot be discounted or denied. My reasons for including information about FC in this manual reflect the opinions of Beukelman and Mirenda, who said, "We believe that people with autism deserve to communicate successfully, even if we are unable to understand exactly how the technique helps them do so. We have included (this material) in the hopes that additional information concerning efficacy will be generated by people who utilize the technique" (Beukelman and Mirenda 1992, 288).

What Is Facilitated Communication?

For discussion of the attitudes and strategies for using FC, see Biklen 1993; Schubert 1992; Crossley 1992; and Crossley and Remington-Gurney 1992.

FC is a strategy for providing emotional and physical support to help an individual express needs and ideas by spelling on an alphabet board or by writing or typing on a typewriter or computer. FC is not a communication system, but is a way of supporting written communication.

Emotional support gives learners confidence, first to try, and then to persist in their efforts to communicate. Physical support to the hand, arm, or shoulder helps learners to focus and to control extraneous repetitive and impulsive movements. In effect, the facilitation slows and inhibits the movements so the communicator must put forth considerable and deliberate effort to move toward a specific letter. In some cases, the facilitator must support the communicator's hand and index finger to point while inhibiting the forward movement.

Communicating with facilitation is a very slow process. Facilitation looks easy when viewed by those unfamiliar with autism; but, in fact, it is very difficult and demanding in terms of time, energy, and physical control. It also demands that the facilitator is constantly alert and ready to make many quick and difficult decisions—some with serious implications (Sabin and Donnellan 1993).

Facilitation is not new; refer to Biklen (1990, 1993) for history. Several families and speech-language pathologists, working alone, discovered that specific physical and emotional support allowed some severely impaired individuals to communicate by typing on a computer (Swezey 1985; Schawlow and Schawlow 1985; Eastham and Eastham 1990).

Commonly Asked Questions

Media attention to some outstanding success stories and to allegations of abuse have engaged emotions and raised many questions about FC and its value. Traditional research methods have not verified that the learner is actually doing the writing, but suggest that the facilitator is directing or influencing the messages. Others who support FC and have seen many positive outcomes suggest that the research methods are faulty. The controversy surrounding FC is explored in a balanced and reasonable way in the Fall 1994 issue of *Journal of the Association for Persons with Severe Handicaps* (JASH). In that issue, see Halle et al. 1994; Green and Shane 1994; Biklen and Duchan 1994; Horner 1994; Kaiser 1994; Whitehurst and Crone 1994; and Williams 1994b.

The following answers to frequently asked questions provide a perspective for making decisions about FC.

What is a successful strategy?

A strategy can be considered successful if it enables a person to do something that had not been achieved with other strategies. With facilitation, some individuals have articulated complex ideas and thoughts in written conversations, stories, and poetry. Facilitation can be considered effective when:

- A learner can type out meaningful single-word responses or phrases to answer open-ended questions or to complete open-ended sentences

- The person can type or write meaningful phrases and questions about things that were not possible with previous AAC systems

- Behaviors change or when people whose intelligence was once disregarded begin to concentrate their thoughts and effort and become more interactive and more effectively assertive

- A person who talked softly to no one in particular now takes the facilitator to a computer to express a preference or opinion, to ask a question, or to ask for help to clarify a misunderstanding

Facilitation has been of less value to others whose speech is echolalic and highly repetitive. It has not been useful for those who can already communicate fairly easily with speech.

> At age 22, Tony had very limited ability to use a picture communication system. He was considered severely retarded and aggressive. During his first FC session, he was able to type answers to a few simple questions. After a few months of infrequent facilitation sessions, his mother engaged a facilitator to work with him at home. At the end of the first session, the facilitator asked Tony if he had anything he wanted to say. Tony typed, *NXTYM.TOTYP.* He had asked his first question to find out when the facilitator would return: *Next time to type.* That is success, even if the words are misspelled!
>
> It is highly unlikely that the facilitator would have thought to type that specific string of letters if he had exerted influence over Tony's message.

What is the range of success?

As with most therapies and strategies, the range of success is broad depending on the individual abilities of the communicator and the skill of the facilitator.

Is it logical? Does it match the individual's deficits and strengths?

Neurological and motor problems were described by Kanner (1943) in his first descriptions of the syndrome. Some of the movement problems documented in the autism literature include: movements similar to those found in Parkinson's disease, poverty of movement, delay in initiation of movement, delay in stopping or changing movements, and rapid fatigue with prolonged tasks (Attwood 1993). Many parents and teachers have long suspected that much of the seeming noncompliance and apparent laziness observed in autism were related to an inability to initiate and maintain motor responses. Recent research has documented abnormalities of the cerebellum in those with autism (Courchesne et al. 1994). "We have known for a long time that the cerebellum is involved with sensory motor coordination and the promotion of efficient and skilled movement" (Attwood 1993, 20).

Several individuals with autism have reported that they must be constantly vigilante and spend extraordinary effort to control repetitive motor behaviors. "Producing speech (. . . or any other kind of motor behavior) requires keeping track of all the body parts involved, and coordinating all their movements. Producing any behavior in response to any perception requires monitoring and coordinating all the inputs and outputs at once, and doing it fast enough to keep up with changing inputs that may call for changing outputs. . . . Do you have to find your legs before you can walk?" (Sinclair 1992, 295). Other references related to movement disorders include Hill and Leary (1993); and Wing and Attwood (1987).

Speech-language pathologists routinely use touch and physical support when teaching new motor movements to clients with a variety of neurological disorders. FC was "designed to accommodate specific movement disorders. For example, touch is used to initiate the response, a technique well known for helping people with Parkinsonism" (Attwood 1993, 20).

Developmental discrepancies—strengths and deficits within and across skill areas—are well documented in autism. The ability to read and spell without specific instruction is not surprising; in general, those with autism have excellent abilities to take in and remember visual detail. Hyperlexia—the ability to read and spell at a high level without formal instruction—is fairly common in autism (Goldberg 1987; Bryson et al. 1994; O'Conner and Hermelin 1994). There have been multiple reports of individuals who learned to read without instruction. A review of the emergent literacy research suggests that "written language learning, like oral language, proceeds from birth. . . . All children, including those with [developmental disabilities], learn written language as a by-product of functional, everyday activities involving printed and oral language" (Koppenhaver et al. 1991, 42).

Who is likely to benefit?

Individuals who have made the most progress using FC are those who are nonverbal or who have limited verbal ability, those who are slow to initiate other responses, and those who show interest in TV, magazines, signs, and other printed material. Persons who have made the fewest gains are those who use repetitive or echoed speech. Scores on standardized intelligence tests are not a relevant predictor.

Can you believe everything they type?

Can you believe everything you read in papers and magazines or hear on television or radio? Have you ever said something that was misleading and needed clarification? In general, those with autism are honest and naive and tend not to lie. The major problem is that most people with autism see the world from a different and very literal perspective. They do not always know when they don't understand something completely. For example, some learners are not clear whether a certain piece of information was reported on the radio or discussed in class, or really happened to them. Media reports, movies, and television offer a mix of fact, fantasy, and fiction that is often misunderstood. (At one time I participated in therapy sessions with a group of streetwise girls who had emotional and behavior disorders. After several months, it was almost impossible to tell which experiences had been reported by others and which had been actually experienced by the young woman with autism.)

The situations that have caused the most concern in relation to FC are those involving allegations of abuse. To keep a calm perspective, one must remember that abuse happens to those with or without disabilities, and abusers are from all walks of life. There is no reason to think that those with autism would be immune from such tragedies. Some allegations are confirmed, and some are unconfirmed. Recent attention to the false-memory syndrome is evidence that allegations and confirmations are problems that are not unique to autism.

Will a facilitator always be needed?

Some individuals gradually will need less support, and others will learn to type independently. It is likely that more individuals will become independent as facilitators receive broader training and experience. However, total independence will depend on the reason FC was needed initially. For example, facilitation may have been needed because of low or variable muscle tone, difficulty in isolating the pointing finger, perseveration, poor eye-hand coordination, tremors, or difficulty focusing attention. Individuals with these problems probably will continue to need support to type.

Who is really speaking?

Obviously, there is potential for facilitators to lead, direct, or express their own thoughts through the learner in some way. There are also several simple and unobtrusive ways to assess the ownership of the words. One way to track ownership is to keep a log of typical errors or unique word uses, sentence structures, and expressions. Determine whether these patterns are similar to ones that a specific facilitator might use. Have similar ideas been expressed by the facilitator on previous occasions?

When a learner writes about information that the facilitator has no way of knowing or little reason to suggest, it is obvious that the learner is writing an original message.

> When Angelo arrived at school in an irritable mood, the facilitator asked him what was wrong. He typed: SOMETIMES THE JOY IS GONE. The interpreter was excited about this very poetic statement and shared it with Angelo's mother. Mother chuckled as she explained that he liked to hold a bottle of Joy detergent in front of his eyes and spin around. On this particular morning, the bottle was gone; it had been emptied and placed in the garbage the night before, and Angelo was upset.
>
> ---
>
> Tony was sitting on the couch with a special facilitator, watching and commenting (with FC) about a football game on TV. His mother and a friend were across the room visiting quietly. Suddenly, Tony typed, SISSY COLORS. The interpreter was puzzled and said, "Sissy colors? I don't understand." His mother looked up, startled, and said, "Sissy colors? Don't you want a new yellow bedspread?" Tony typed, NO SISSY COLORS. This young man who rarely verbalized and was considered by many to be severely intellectually impaired had heard his mother's discussion about redecorating his bedroom, and he chose to express his opinion. A facilitator would have had little reason to attend to the conversation occurring across the room and even less reason to guide such a comment.

How much emphasis should be directed to FC?

Facilitating communication through typing and writing is a single but important strategy for at least some learners, and it should be available to them in multiple settings. The most critical issue is for the learner to communicate with confidence as early as possible with some system. Facilitated typing or writing should be explored just as other systems are explored and included as one part of a comprehensive communication program.

Do some learners stop talking after using FC?

If speech is labored and unavailable for expressing ideas fully and typing is easier and more effective, it would be natural to use typing. We all communicate in the easiest way possible; some communicate by phone, others write letters or send E-mail. The computer is replacing handwriting in many situations. A learner who chooses to type instead of speak still needs a backup system to provide support when a facilitator is not available.

Guidelines for making decisions about the use of FC are being developed by many state agencies. Two papers are available to discuss some of the concerns and political issues involved; see Lehr (1994); and Shevin (1994). Refer to Sabin and Donnellan (1993) for a discussion of other ethical considerations.

Ethical Considerations

Facilitator Training

In FC, the facilitator's role is complex and demanding. In addition to providing emotional and physical support, the facilitator also acts as a major decision maker and negotiator of meaning during interactions (Sabin and Donnellan 1993). With such an important role, the training to prepare facilitators must be comprehensive to match the actual demands of the task. Training should include a supervised practicum and follow-up, especially to discuss ethical issues related to decision making. Training competencies are being developed, and more comprehensive training for facilitators is offered at several reputable centers. See the list of resources, page 438.

Fading Support

The goal of FC is ultimate independence, and some individuals with autism are achieving that goal. However, if the underlying neurological/motor problems persist, independence may be a distant goal. An occupational therapist can offer suggestions for selecting the most effective equipment, for arranging the height of chair or table to provide physical stability, and for strategies to increase muscle tone.

The following strategies may contribute to greater independence:

- Use only the amount of physical assistance needed. The need may vary within the session and across sessions. Often an increasing amount of support is needed when the learner is tired or in an unfamiliar situation. Systematically vary the elements of the physical support in subtle ways. To be effective, the support must be comfortable for the learner.

- Provide opportunities to establish trusting relationships with many facilitators.

- Inform learners that some people can type alone and that they will probably be able to type alone too, but it will take practice.

Interpretation of Writing

Some messages are quite clear; others leave much to interpretation. An understanding of the communicator's perspective and cognitive style provides a base for interpreting the meaning of both written and verbal communications. An interpreter must avoid leading questions that may confuse the communicator. For example, many communicators with autism are overly compliant and likely to give affirmative answers to questions whether or not they are fully understood. To clarify the meaning of messages, ask such questions as, "Is that what you meant?"; "Do you mean _____?"; "Let's clarify"; "Can you tell me in a different way?"; "Can you tell me more?"; "Is it OK to ask your teacher to help me understand?"; "Did this happen to you, or to someone else?" Check the meaning of any unusual message with parents or other facilitators, because it may relate to an experience in another setting.

Confidentiality

At what point is confidentiality breached when a facilitator asks others for assistance in interpreting meaning, or talks for the communicator, or shares a particularly wise or cute message with others? Questions that show respect and provide an opportunity for the communicator to give permission for their messages to be shared include: "I'm going to talk for you. Is that OK?"; and "Can I tell them about the _____?"

Recordkeeping

It is important to keep records to show progress, to evaluate the facilitation procedures, and to resolve potential questions. Again, confidentiality must be considered. Several strategies for keeping records to verify authorship are discussed in articles by Biklen et al. (1995), Olney (1995), and Vicker (1993).

Multiple Facilitators

Once a learner begins to communicate with facilitation, it is only ethical that someone is always available to provide the support. Otherwise, the learner is left without a voice. One program identifies at least two people in each setting to share the facilitation, so that one is available at all times. Another advantage of multiple facilitators is that the learner becomes more flexible and less dependent on a single person.

Implications for Early Education

Written communication, with or without facilitation, has always been an important alternative communication option for these highly visual, gestalt learners. Responsible decision making dictates that options must be kept open, for a child can grow up before all the research questions are answered. Therefore, include the following components as a natural part of a balanced and structured early childhood program regardless of a child's apparent intellectual potential:

Refer to the following sections for strategies:

- *Visual instructional strategies: chapter 14*

- *Teaching concepts, rules, and academic content: chapter 19*

- *Informal strategies for teaching language concepts and expanding symbol concepts: chapter 19, pages 270-273*

1. Provide many natural opportunities each day to hear and see the language written down.

2. Introduce keyboards, typewriters, and computers. Computers are highly reinforcing to most learners; use them as tools to expand communication. Structure fun and meaningful turn-taking games, and exchange messages so learners understand that communication can occur in various ways and can be fun.

Unstructured random play with a computer may not be productive, and it has the potential for developing meaningless and repetitive visual/motor routines. The computer's error messages are often very reinforcing, providing the motivation to practice errors.

3. Provide physical support under the wrist or hand when a learner is slow to initiate a response, point to pictures or words while sharing a story book or magazine, or specify messages on picture communication systems.

4. Use a gentle but firm touch to the arm or shoulder to calm and direct attention.

5. Hold the learner's hand back to slow down and prevent impulsive movements. This gives the learner time to survey and consider the options and make real choices. Illustration A on page 232 shows one way to support the hand.

> Although Matt liked to print letters, he made them impulsively, stacking them on top of each other while he looked around the room. His teacher sat to the front on his dominant side so she could support his writing hand and know when he was looking directly at his work. The physical support was provided by placing two fingers under the palm of his writing hand. Each time Matt looked away, the teacher lifted his hand an inch or so from the paper and held it there gently and quietly. When Matt's eyes returned to the paper, the teacher lowered his hand so he could begin to write again.

See chapter 10 for strategies to continually evaluate to identify problems and refine the elements of the environment to support success and competence.

6. Capitalize on all natural opportunities to communicate and provide the assistance to maintain success and develop the learner's self-esteem, confidence, and willingness to persist.

In summary, written communication is a valid option for many learners with autism. FC strategies appear to provide the support needed to allow some individuals to communicate more fully than ever before and to reveal previously unexpected abilities. Learners who have never developed a dependable communication system should have the opportunity to try FC as part of a balanced program, regardless of their assumed potential. Whether or not the validity of FC is confirmed, attitudes have changed as a result of its use. Individuals who previously were seen as hopelessly without potential for learning are suddenly seen in a different light. Once they spell their first word, they are given respect and new opportunities. The facilitation and the change in attitude and support allows some learners to become more interactive. For some, FC opens the door to speech (Schawlow and Schawlow 1985).

Since the introduction of FC, the world has changed for those with autism. It will never again be quite so easy to disregard their potential.

Summary

The interpreter has a major role in expanding the communication habit and options. The interpreter's primary role is *to ensure that the system is always available and used consistently.* To expand the communication habit in other settings and situations, the interpreter:

1. Identifies subtle behavioral signals of needs, confusion, and problems that can be solved with communication

2. Cues and/or coaches the learner to use multiple ways to send messages effectively

3. Verbalizes the learner's intentions as expressed through the alternative communication system

When the message is heard, the learner:

- Can associate the activity of using the system to the meaning of the message

- Knows that the message was sent and received

- Has a model for communicating the message; the message is stored in the receptive language bank for future use

4. Uses appropriate prompting strategies to ensure spontaneity and independence

5. Models the use of the system to have fun, to play turn-taking games, to share experiences, to augment verbal instructions, and to facilitate interactions with peers

6. Works closely with the support team to evaluate, refine, and share information; as a team member, keeps an open mind to explore the potential value of new communication options and strategies such as FC

Everyone needs a dependable system for expressing ideas and needs and to have fun. Ultimately, *accessibility is the key issue,* even if it means the individual looks a little different. Just as the person who is visually impaired has a cane and a guide dog, the person with autism has a communication system and an interpreter.

Expand Communication and Social Competence

Most individuals with autism want to fit in. They want to be socially involved and have various kinds of successful relationships with others. But many of these individuals are baffled by the way others think, talk, and manage social situations—by the way they use words, change topics, and make decisions so quickly. To compound the problem, people with autism commonly hold false perceptions that have a unique impact on their communication and social skills.

Figure 22.1. Some false perceptions that are common in autism

- Every word has a single meaning.
- A rule applies only to a single situation;
  or,
  A rule applies in the same way always and forever.
- Everyone believes the same things I believe.
- If I know something, everyone else knows it, too.
- In a group, the speaker is talking only to me;
  or,
  In a group, the speaker is not talking to me.
- If someone says it, it's true.
- I should do exactly what I'm told, in exactly the way I'm told or taught.
- If I don't know exactly what to do, I should do nothing.

An understanding of these false beliefs, along with a brief review of the specific learning strengths and deficits common in autism (pages 131-133), will provide clues for interpreting the cause of social difficulties.

We cannot assume that a learner fully or accurately understands a particular problem, situation, or expectation—social or otherwise. For example, when one young man finally understood why it was important not to interrupt and learned how and when to enter a conversation politely, he did stop interrupting—but he continued to carry on long dissertations about electronic speakers and microphones, unaware of his listeners' boredom.

To increase social competence, it is necessary to plan interventions carefully. The first steps are to identify the details that the learner:

- May currently misunderstand
- May misunderstand during instruction
- May misunderstand later as new skills are applied to different situations

Systematic analysis and instruction will increase social awareness and competence. But because it is not possible to teach everything, we must decide which skills to teach; that is, which skills might be pivotal and have impact on a broad range of situations (Koegel and Frea 1993).

Regardless of how comprehensive instruction may be, some problems will remain with literal thinking, predicting and understanding the perspective of others, making judgments, and making considered and safe decisions. Therefore, an interpreter must be available on some regular basis to provide practical assistance, to help the learner make sense of the social world, and to assist in solving problems and sometimes developing adaptations that provide support in confusing or high-risk situations. The support team, and especially the family, must consider both the risks and the value of increasing independence, and they must ensure that appropriate support is available.

Social problems are manifested differently in each individual, and the instructional and support needs will vary depending on age, verbal ability (or skill with an alternative system), past experiences, level of cognitive development, and the demands of individual environments.

See figure 22.2 for a sample of the complex array of communication and social skills required for effective participation in different situations. Many of these skills are learned almost automatically by most people, but those with autism need specific information and instruction to manage them.

Communication and social skills are best learned in the context of natural routines. Some opportunities can be set up within natural routines to make choices, solve problems, and use functional communication skills. However, the natural activities of the day do not offer enough opportunities either to teach those lessons that others learn without instruction or to practice the complex skills to establish strong social and communication habits.

More opportunities are needed to provide the systematic instruction and additional practice for the more subtle skills such as sharing, cooperating, providing assistance, negotiating, and resolving conflicts. Because these skills cannot be learned in isolation, it is necessary to plan additional contexts. Reverse mainstreaming (Wooten and Mesibov 1986) has been a successful first step when a learner is served in a special classroom. For those integrated in regular classrooms, it is necessary to organize and structure many peer interaction opportunities and provide support to ensure success. In structured small groups, peers can model and provide more natural practice.

Structured play groups provide a natural context for learners younger than 8. For learners who are 9 or older, social-skill groups offer a setting for a more systematic, cognitive approach that can lead to greater independence. After leaving the school structure, young-adult learners need social support groups to maintain social contacts and transfer skills to a wide variety of situations (Mesibov 1986).

Guidelines for Planning Group Instruction and Practice

Five elements of successful group instruction require thoughtful planning: membership, rules, routines, leadership, and strategies to promote generalization of new skills.

Membership

An effective instructional group has an even number of members to allow for work, play, or interactions with partners. There can be two or as many as six or eight members, depending on age, abilities, and goals of the learner. Members are selected for their ability to share ideas and model socially acceptable social and communication skills. While peers who have mild communication or interaction

Figure 22.2. Skills for social and communication competence

Skills for giving and receiving information
- Locate partner; initiate interaction appropriately.
- Acknowledge and respond to others who want to talk to you.
- Manage conversations:
  —Take/maintain/relinquish turns.
  —Stay on topic, or suggest a new topic.
  —Check for and repair breakdown in understanding.
  —Terminate the conversation politely.
  —Recognize when others want to terminate.
  —Enter an ongoing conversation politely.
- Keep a conversation going:
  —Engage in chit-chat, "hanging out."
  —Identify/negotiate topics.
  —Express messages clearly.
  —Ask for clarification.
  —Give and follow directions.
  —Ask and answer questions to expand the topic.
  —Persuade.
- Delivery:
  —Use appropriate eye contact.
  —Check body language, posture, distance.
  —Check vocal quality, intonation.
  —Check speed.
  —Use courtesy and good manners.
  —Check whether assertive and persistent, or passive, aggressive, or dominating.
- Identify meanings. Are they:
  —Nonliteral (Idioms, sarcasm, jokes, . . .)?
  —Fact, or opinion?
  —Real, or pretend/fantasy?
  —True or false?
- Active listening:
  In individual conversations or small groups:
  —Use eye contact, and give attention to speaker.
  —Identify meaning of nonverbal messages (facial expressions, body language).
  —Identify meaning of verbal messages; generate responses to messages.
  In class:
  —Identify instructions and main points; make notes.
  —Use reflective listening.

Understanding the perspectives of others:
- Who is speaking? Whom does that person see? To whom is that person speaking?
- Who is in the audience? What does the audience see and hear?
- What do other people know? Do they always know what you know?
- What might others feel, think, or believe?
- Who did it? Did it happen to you? To someone else? Did you read about it or see it on TV?

(continued)

Figure 22.2. (continued)

Skills for peer-group participation:
- Get attention.
- Take turns; share and cooperate.
- Assist, and ask peers for assistance.
- Give compliments; say, "Thank you."
- Watch and imitate peers play and/or communicate.
- Follow group directions.
- Solve conflicts.

Skills for making and keeping friends:
- Identify mutual interests.
- Invite, accept, or reject invitations politely.
- Learn to play a variety of games.
- Plan events for mutual enjoyment.
- Keep in contact (make phone calls, send messages via modem/FAX).
- Offer and provide assistance.
- Provide feedback indicating pleasure and displeasure.
- Cooperate and negotiate.
- Observe social and sexual rules.

Skills for self-management:
- Solve problems.
- Make choices.
- Plan to achieve a goal (social, work, other).
- Make phone calls (at home; from pay phones).
- Seek assistance regarding medical, business, and personal needs.
- Follow workplace and community social rules.
- Obtain and accept assistance.
- Tolerate correction.
- Monitor your own feelings and behavior.
- Manage stress; maintain self-control.

problems can be effective models, those who are streetwise and who model inappropriate behavior present problems for learners who lack social judgment and reasoning ability.

- Membership should reflect a balance of interaction styles and skill levels. It is difficult to have fun if all are withdrawn or inhibited, if all want to dominate, or if all have the same strengths and deficits.

- Peers without autism often need advance preparation to understand how to be helpful without providing unnatural or too much support.

Group Rules

A few simple rules are necessary to facilitate interactions and involvement and to establish and maintain a positive and productive session. For example:

1. If you need help, ask your partner.

2. Everyone gets a chance to talk.

3. When someone else is talking, watch and listen.

Young learners will need support to learn basic group participation skills—to watch and listen to the teacher, to do what the teacher says, and to wait and take turns. They also need to understand the language of group directions and rules.

Group Routine

The considerations for planning a group session are the same as for planning other events and routines. All of the components of a routine must be clarified. See figure 11.1 (page 153) for a list of the components and figure 11.2 (page 157) for a sample plan.

The primary goals for the first few sessions are to establish a familiar routine and to nurture a working and supportive relationship between the members. The formula for scheduling activities to capitalize on their reinforcing qualities (see figure 13.3, page 174) applies to this situation as well.

- A session begins with discussion of the session schedule (with visual references) and an easy and enjoyable activity or routine to help the members focus on each other.

- The hard work comes in the middle of the session. A central activity or project provides the structure and common focus for the hard work of interacting. The type of activity depends on the age and skills of the group members and the goals for the group.

- The session ends with another easy and enjoyable activity that enables the members to leave calmly but eager to return. For example, summarize the session activities and concepts in a group experience story. A group relaxation and visualization period provides closure and helps members to leave the session relaxed and ready for the next event.

Beginning and ending each session with the same or similar activities develops a comfortable and familiar routine within which the learner can tolerate the hard and demanding interactions. The group experiences must be interesting and fun, and all members must feel successful when they leave.

Group Leadership

The effective group leader is a facilitator, a coach (Little 1989). The facilitator sets up situations, then coaches the action. In setting up the situation, the coach selects the partners for balance (that is, determines the lineup).

In the role as coach, the facilitator:

1. Explains the activity and the rules (the game plan)
2. Uses diagrams and charts
3. Suggests strategies—ways to solve a problem
4. Demonstrates and models
5. Observes and coaches the practice sessions from the sidelines
6. Reviews, provides feedback, and prepares for the next session

In summary, the leader encourages the members to talk and interact with each other. The leader:

- Does not dominate the attention by asking questions to elicit specific responses
- Encourages the members to respond naturally in ways that reinforce a partner ("Tommy said he wanted the yellow truck. Can you hand it to him?"; or, "Tommy is helping you button your paint shirt. You can say, 'Thank you, Tommy.'")

- Avoids unnatural and intrusive verbal reinforcement (such as, "I like the way you said 'Thank you'"; "Good talking"; "Good playing")

This type of verbal reinforcement interrupts the focus and flow of the activity and the relationship. It also disrupts and clutters the natural reinforcement delivered by the peer as a direct result of efforts to interact, to request, or to suggest.

Strategies for Generalization

Develop a plan to share the group goals and new skills with other interpreters so they may support them in other natural contexts. This may be done with a newsletter, a schedule of planned activities and goals, or a group experience story written at the conclusion of each session. Incorporating self-monitoring cards or checklists also contributes to generalization. Parents and other interpreters need to know of any specific or sensitive topics that came up in the sessions.

Resources for Planning

Borba, M., and C. Borba. *Self-esteem—A Classroom Affair: 101 Ways to Help Children Like Themselves*. San Francisco: Harper & Row, 1978.

Canfield, J., and H. C. Wells. *100 Ways to Enhance Self-Concepts in the Classroom*. Englewood Cliffs, NJ: Prentice Hall, 1976.

Chastain, L. D. *A Handbook on the Use of Songs to Teach Autistic and Other Severely Handicapped Children*. Goodhue, MN: White Oak Press, 1986.

Cihak, M. K., and B. Jackson-Herson. *Games Children Should Play*. Glenview, IL: Scott, Foresman, 1980.

Crary, E. *Kids Can Cooperate: A Practical Guide to Teaching Problem Solving*. Seattle: Parenting Press, 1984.

Gajewski, N., and P. Mayo. *SSS: Social Skill Strategies. Books A and B: A Curriculum for Adolescents*. Eau Claire, WI: Thinking Publications, 1989.

Grant, J. O., B. B. Lazarus, and H. Peyton. The use of dialogue journals with students with exceptionalities. *Teaching Exceptional Children*. Summer 1992: 22-24.

Mayo, P., and N. Gajewski. *Transfer Activities*. Eau Claire, WI: Thinking Publications, 1987.

Mayo, P., and P. Waldo. *Scripting: Social Communication for Adolescents*. (Scripts for role playing.) Eau Claire, WI: Thinking Publications, 1986.

Musselwhite, C. R. *Adaptive Play for Special Needs Children*. San Diego: College-Hill Press, 1986.

Orlick, T. *The Cooperative Sports and Game Book*. New York: Pantheon, 1978.

_____. *The Second Cooperative Sports and Game Book*. New York: Pantheon, 1982.

Schwartz, L. *What Would You Do?* Santa Barbara, CA: The Learning Works, 1990.

Shure, M. B. *I Can Problem Solve: An Interpersonal Cognitive Problem-solving Program for Intermediate Elementary Grades*. Champaign, IL: Research Press, 1992.

_____. *I Can Problem Solve: An Interpersonal Cognitive Problem-solving Program for Kindergarten/Primary Grades*. Champaign, IL: Research Press, 1992.

_____. *I Can Problem Solve: An Interpersonal Cognitive Problem-solving Program for Preschool*. Champaign, IL: Research Press, 1992.

Trovato, C. A. *Teaching Kids to Care*. New York: The Instructor, 1987.

Vernon, A. *Thinking, Feeling, Behaving: An Emotional Education Curriculum for Adolescents, Grades 7-12*. Champaign, IL: Research Press, 1989.

_____. *Thinking, Feeling, Behaving: An Emotional Education Curriculum for Children, Grades 1-6*. Champaign, IL: Research Press, 1989.

Early Childhood Play Groups

As soon as a very young child learns to value interactions with an adult and learns to tolerate structured play with a peer, expand those skills in the context of a play group.

Goals

Some of the goals for structured play groups are listed in figure 22.2: Skills for peer group participation (see page 338). Sensory and motor skills, symbolic play, and a variety of other developmental goals also can be addressed in play contexts (Musselwhite 1986).

Organization and Sructure

A group of four children is ideal for three-year-olds. As tolerance and skills expand, so can the number of children in the group. An even number of children is needed so everyone can have a partner. Two or three 15-minute sessions a week is a minimum amount of time to provide continuity for very young children. Older children can benefit from fewer but longer sessions. For an optimum level of stimulation so the learner can maintain equilibrium, balance the new with the familiar. If the peers are unfamiliar, plan a familiar setting, interpreter, materials, and activities.

Setting

Provide a relatively small, safe area with limited distractions and well-defined boundaries. A small table with chairs, shelves for materials, and a small rug will define the spaces within the play setting.

Materials and Activities

Materials and activities are those that age-appropriate peers enjoy in the natural setting. Adapt the rules for using the materials so that sharing and cooperation is required. For example, have two children share a puzzle or pegboard. Give each partner half the pieces, and require the partners to take turns to complete the activity. Organize snack time so that one partner holds the jar of peanut butter while the other spreads it on the cracker, and one holds the glass while the other pours.

Strategies

The group rules, routines, and leadership role provide the supportive structure for using a wide variety of strategies. In the role of coach, the interpreter provides suggestions and cues to keep the interactions positive.

Strategies include modeling, parallel talking, and reflective listening. Visual strategies include the use of a chart or mini-calendar to clarify the session schedule of activities, use of cue cards during the activities, and stories to summarize the session activities or lessons.

Social-Skills Groups

The social-skills group is an important context for learners between ages 9 and 21, when the more cognitive aspects of thinking, reasoning, and problem solving must be established. In this context, learners begin to understand the perspective of others. The social-skills group provides a safe place to rehearse new ways of interacting and opportunities to develop friendships and mentor relationships.

Goals

The broad range of skills listed in figure 22.2 can be introduced at a basic level for younger elementary students and expanded to address the needs of the adolescent. Other goals can relate to developing friendships that can carry over to school, church, 4-H, scout, and other community groups.

Organization and Structure

Groups generally meet weekly for at least 30 minutes (or one school period) as a natural part of the regular school program. A limit of six to eight students in each group provides enough time for all to express themselves. The most effective models are those who are not perfect—individuals who have some problems, but can still provide appropriate models. Without some prior training, high-achieving peers may dominate and inhibit others in the group. Review the guidelines for selecting members (pages 336, 338).

Setting

The setting is similar to that for play groups, with enough space for larger students to role play and engage in various projects.

Materials and Activities

Provide butcher paper or chart pads and pens to record ideas and decisions. Other materials will depend on the scheduled activity. A video camera, player, and monitor are useful for recording and reviewing role-play sessions or for observing commercially prepared instructional tapes.

Select activities from the basic social-skills curriculum and resources such as those listed on page 340, but adapt them to encourage cooperation, joint efforts, and negotiation.

Strategies

Visual and verbal strategies that are effective with higher-functioning verbal learners and can be adapted for individuals who communicate in different ways include:

- Basic verbal strategies: giving directions, using contingencies (pages 210-220)
- Reflective listening (page 220)
- Checklists, cue cards (pages 196-199)
- Semantic mapping (pages 200-202)
- Problem-solving and cause/effect formats (pages 364-366)
- Social stories (pages 200-207)
- Self-instruction
- Group planning and rehearsal (pages 336-340)
- Coaching (pages 339-340)

- Modeling with commentary and visual references
- Role playing with scripts and feedback
- Videotaping actual or simulated situations for discussion and feedback
- Imagery procedures and cognitive picture rehearsal (pages 207-208; 362-363)
- Relaxation procedures (pages 357-360)

Most people, including those with autism, do not like to remember or think or talk about their social failures. Often they withdraw or resist discussions or assistance that they perceive to be criticism. It may be more effective, and certainly it is more sensitive and respectful, to focus group discussions, role playing, stories, and other activities around a fictional person who has similar problems.

Some direct-instruction social-skills programs are useful resources; but without modification, the learner with autism is likely to memorize the rules, the scripts, and the responses with little understanding.

Strategies for Expanded Applications and Transfer

- Vary the activities as naturally occurring school problems dictate so that skills are relevant.

- Inform parents and other teachers of the learner's objectives and new strategies so they can provide cues and support in natural situations.

- Provide cue cards, self-monitoring, and self-reinforcement systems to use in the natural setting.

- Begin sessions with opportunities to share failures and successes that occurred since the last meeting. Koegel and associates (1994) describe some systematic ways to teach self-monitoring and self-management skills.

- As group members become more experienced, they can rotate responsibilities for the session. With support (and sometimes using prerehearsal and cue cards), they can take turns planning and directing the activities, managing the group discussion, and taking responsibility for other tasks.

- Most learners will continue to need an ongoing social-skills group, while peers may need or want to participate only briefly. Changing membership can be a positive experience in that it allows learners to become acquainted with more people. One way to preserve the continuity of the group is to require a commitment for a series of six or eight group meetings. Schedule a new series after a two- or three-week break, thus giving peers opportunities to either make a new commitment or drop out. Begin each new series with getting-acquainted activities to establish group cohesiveness and trust.

Social-Support Groups

Support groups are common and productive for people with various kinds of physical or emotional needs. They provide a place where problems are understood and new coping strategies are learned. Those with autism also need a place where it is not necessary to be on guard constantly to control every action and "act normal."

Goals

The primary goals of social-support groups are to strengthen and expand previously learned skills, to learn new skills, and to have enjoyable social experiences. Too often, those with autism are isolated without social contacts after leaving school.

Organization and Structure

Leadership can be shared by parents and professionals from local autism programs or parent groups. Some responsibilities can be shared by the group members if support is available. For example, committees can be established for making calls to remind the membership of meetings, make arrangements for special events, and plan refreshments for each meeting. (Some individuals come to the group because of the food.) Committee work can be a valuable means of developing self-esteem, responsibility, and leadership skills.

Membership in the group is open; any adult with autism is welcome to join. Peers without disabilities are recruited to provide support and structure for enjoyable experiences or to be partners in team activities and committees. University students in psychology, social work, or education, who are preparing to work with those who have disabilities, may be excellent peer partners, mentors, and friends. Sinclair (1992, 299) notes that mentors are needed to provide structure so interesting things can happen.

Schedule a series of six to eight meetings or a series that coincides with a school or university term. A series with a clear beginning and end provides a natural time for changing membership while giving the group time to develop relationships and a sense of group cohesiveness. Schedule several series each year.

Adult groups generally have evening or weekend meetings, two or three times a month. Meetings can last for one or two hours to allow time for planning special events, to rehearse the skills needed for successful participation in special events, and to allow for refreshments and social interactions.

Activities

Goals are addressed in the context of planning and participating in special group events, outings, and projects. A group might plan to eat at a favorite restaurant, go camping or hiking, attend a sporting event, or participate in a community improvement project or drive.

- Plan a fair or festival for members to display hobbies and collections related to their special interests. This project provides an opportunity to find others with common interests that can be shared outside the group.

- Hold game nights to learn a variety of games. Both physical and table games can provide a vehicle for interactions in other social settings. Often, game rules need to be adapted to compensate for physical problems or the lack of competitiveness.

Strategies

To ensure that all aspects of an event are considered in the planning, refer to pages 153-160, where strategies are detailed for organizing an event as a total routine. The strategies discussed on pages 336-340 are incorporated into the following steps for planning social events:

- Establish a familiar group routine.

- Identify and visually clarify the elements of an event so that all the participants will have a common experience that can be shared and discussed later. Without this preparation, the members are likely to have little to share after the event is over, even though they all participated. After a trip to the bowling alley, one person may know how many holes are in the ceiling tile, another may know the number of balls of each size and color, one may have been concerned that the bowling shoes were not arranged neatly on the shelf, another may have the snack-shop menu memorized, and still another may have been so overwhelmed that she kept her ears covered and was aware of only the noise of the pins falling over.

- Identify the social expectations of the event. Discuss, rehearse, and role play appropriate strategies for managing those expectations successfully.

- Develop individual visual adaptations. A cue card may support one learner at a restaurant, or a card setting forth modifications to the game rules may allow another learner to participate and have fun. Ear plugs may provide comfort to those with highly sensitive hearing.

- Members may have more fun at a party if they are assigned specific jobs, such as passing a tray of food, pouring the coffee, managing a guest book, or organizing guests' coats. Many individuals can benefit from cue cards to remind them of things to talk about. Others may feel more secure with something to share that can focus an interaction—some photographs, a magazine, or a small but tricky puzzle. Augmentative communication systems must be available.

- Before the event, discuss and rehearse the sequence of the event and the expectations. Following the event, review and share experiences, and identify and discuss problems and new solutions. The group may want to repeat an event simply because it was fun.

Guidelines for Planning Individual Support Sessions

The individual instruction or counseling sessions described in this manual are not to be confused with traditional psychoanalytic therapies or 1:1 sessions based on clinical behavior-modification principles that manipulate the antecedents and consequences. Rather, a more effective approach for those with autism involves cognitive strategies that *actively involve the learner* in analyzing and solving real problems and that address the misperceptions (page 335) that confound emotional and relationship problems. Cognitive strategies are practical, and they address issues in a concrete and forthright manner that ensures understanding and increases motivation and self-esteem.

Ideally, these sessions are conducted by a sensitive and skillful interpreter who understands the impact of autism on thinking and behavior. The interpreter might be a teacher, speech-language pathologist, occupational therapist, school counselor, or counselor in private practice.

Goals

In addition to addressing many of the skills listed in figure 22.2 (pages 337-338), other complex and sensitive issues can be targeted.

1. Understanding the subtleties of social relationships

   How do you know whom you can trust? What do you do when someone teases? Tells you to eat garbage? Tells you to take something that is not yours?

   > Sam, age 17, had a number of questions: What is a friend? What is a friend who is a girl? When is a girl a girlfriend? What is a girlfriend? What does a girlfriend expect? What is a date—June 26th, or dates you eat? Why do people kiss? (His perspective was that kissing is not sanitary. "If the girl is really nice and likes me, she won't want to kiss me and give me her germs.") Sam decided that he didn't want a girlfriend if it meant she would touch, hug, or kiss him and expect him to touch, hug, and kiss her. (See pages 349-353 for discussion of decisions related to sex education and sexuality.)

2. Coping with everyday problems to make choices, solve problems, and manage stress to maintain self-control

3. Understanding and dealing with feelings and complex social problems, such as intense worries and grief and loss related to death and major changes

   > One young person wondered: What does it feel like to be sad? Where do you feel sad? What makes you feel sad? How does feeling sad look? He told his interpreter, "I knew I should feel sad, but I just watched others feeling sad."

Structure and Strategies

The support team may identify a need for more formal, regularly scheduled individual support to manage confidential emotional and social issues.

More formal individual sessions that address these complex and highly sensitive issues require a certain structure to ensure that learners will achieve their goals. The interpreter or counselor assigned to lead these sessions needs the background and experience to:

- Establish rapport and a trusting relationship that supports the learner who is facing these most difficult and sensitive issues

- Establish a familiar routine within the session—a routine that allows the learner to:

  —Relax and remain open to think about abstract concepts

  —Figure out how the details fit together

  —See the consequences of any actions

  —Solve problems and practice new ways to interact

- Identify the critical issues, details, and misperceptions

  The interpreter must be able to see the problem from the learner's perspective and help the learner see the world from the perspective of others. This requires creative sleuthing and sensitive questioning. Often, it is the smallest detail that triggers major problems; and it may be the smallest adjustment or bit of information that makes a major difference toward solving a problem.

- Establish a cooperative relationship with parents and teachers in order to:

  —Target important problems and obtain some of the critical facts about those problems

  —Provide feedback so others can offer consistent support and help the learner transfer new skills and insights to the real world

- Use visual strategies to:

  —Augment verbal information and serve as reference for later use

  —Organize details and show relationships

  —Reduce the effort required to hold the ideas together in order to think about them

  —Reduce stress and anxiety from emotions that are too intense

- Allow the learner to use alternative ways to express ideas

> Tom, 15 years old, had been expelled from school after getting angry and pushing over a bookcase. The interpreter visited this young man at his home. Tom was relatively open and friendly until the conversation turned to his problem at school. Then he moved to the couch and curled up in a fetal position with his eyes closed. With a yellow tablet and pencil in hand, the interpreter moved calmly to sit on the floor beside the couch. "Is this the way it happened?" she asked, as she sketched a sequence of line drawings to illustrate her explanation of the problem. Tom opened his eyes and watched her draw the pictures as she talked softly. Soon he reached for the pencil to make his own drawing as he said, "No, it was like this." When the pressure of face-to-face discussion was removed, and with an alternative way to express himself, he and the interpreter were able to identify the real problems.

- Some learners are able to process and express ideas more clearly in writing, especially when they are confused and under stress.

> Jeff, 11 years old, was in a regular school program with an interpreter. When in stress, Jeff could express himself better by writing out his thoughts in response to his interpreter's written statements. This script was written during a counseling session that occurred right after a major tantrum when Jeff did not follow his teacher's directions. The punctuation and spelling are his.
>
> Mrs. K: Jeff, here is a rule. Do whatever the teacher says. When the teacher tells you to do something, you need to do it.
>
> Jeff: What if I felt inside that I don't want to do it. But I know what I'm so post to do but it happen sometimes. Mrs. K. Its or right I know you know.
>
> Mrs. K: One of the things you learn to do in school is follow directions, so we'll keep working on you following directions without having a tantrum.

Jeff: Please I know OK. Remember in you r sometimes I could of got out of control and I won't mean to do it. You don't have to get stern no more because every time its my behaver its an acciedent never on purpose. You can give me a hug sometimes it really happens and its not your dream.

Mrs. K: I know it's an accident Jeff. But when I tell you to do something and I show you how to do it and I make sure you understand, what are you going to do?

Jeff: Remember its just how the way it is. But sometimes Jeff will do it if its that it wont make me feel like I wont do it.

Mrs. K: Jeff, will you follow the teacher's directions?

Jeff: Only if I feel in side Yes it I'll do it.

Mrs. K: Answer yes or no.

Jeff: It just depends If I want to do it or not. It just depend on what its like OK. Sometimes I don't want you doing something I don't want you to do It makes feel like saying NO I don't want to do it OK Its just that you don't know whats going on OK You don't have to get stern because you know why it's just that it depends on how its like OK The only reason why it happens is because you have to know why it happens and guess what you want to be stern. That's the problem. . . .

Building Social Skills through Pragmatic Analysis: Assessment and Treatment Implications for Children with Autism by Frankel and associates (1987) is a good resource for counselors.

This type of thinking is typical in autism—an inability to identify the real problem and an inability to simply agree or to make a promise that will end the lecture. To Jeff, a promise meant *every time and forever*—a promise he could not keep because, "It just depends on what its like . . . its just how the way it is."

This type of script is most helpful in assessing misunderstandings and false beliefs before planning interventions.

Grief and Loss

People experience a sense of loss about many things—death, lost jobs, friends who move away, personal moves to new communities or houses or schools, a family illness or divorce. Most people are involved in the process enough to understand when a major change or loss is imminent, and they can prepare themselves. When losses occur, they have many ways to work through their feelings, primarily through remembering and sharing with friends.

Those with autism have little control over their lives, and often they don't receive information that would prepare them for these changes or losses. They tend to be left out of the family preparation and grieving process because they appear to be disinterested and devoid of feelings. Their inability to communicate feelings and ask questions contributes to the problem. People move in and out of their lives with little explanation, and they fail to understand why things happen.

For the verbal learner, the first sign of a problem may be when the learner asks repeated questions about the loss. For the learner with limited verbal ability, the first sign may be withdrawal or some form of agitation, resistance, or general "out-of-sorts" behavior. These signs may not occur for many weeks or even months after the loss occurred.

Strategies

Review the information in chapter 15 on use of experience stories and social stories (pages 202-207).

In assessing behavior problems, one important question relates to losses. Has the individual experienced losses or major changes in the past year—moves, deaths, divorce of parents, sister off to college, or a favorite staff member or support person no longer present? The learner needs direct and literal preparation for potential changes. During and after the change, the individual needs sensitive, concrete, and literal explanations and opportunities to share memories. Experience stories and social stories provide contexts for preparing for changes and for sharing in the grieving process.

A month after his grandfather died, Jose began to ask people, "When will Grandpa be back?" He approached his parents, his teacher, the school secretary, even strangers to get information. When he got a different answer from each person, he became more and more upset. It was finally decided that Jose needed to talk about his grandfather, and that he needed to know whom to approach and when he could approach those people. His calendar was revised to include two 10-minute periods (morning and afternoon) when he would visit the school counselor. The counselor and Jose's mother coordinated their messages so that both would give him the same information. His mother sent snapshots of the grandfather to school so Jose could share them with the counselor and place them in an album. As Jose worked through his grief, other topics of conversation were offered. Gradually, Jose needed less time to talk about his grandfather.

Social and Sexual Issues

See Ousley and Mesibov (1991) for a review of sexual attitudes and knowledge of higher-functioning adolescents and adults. Some of the common thinking and perspective problems are described by Dewey (1991).

Social awareness generally increases during adolescence in young people with autism, just as it does in the general population. Many higher-functioning young people are attracted to members of the opposite sex, and they suffer intensely when their awkward attempts to establish relationships are rejected. In general, those with autism want someone to be a friend to go places with, someone who shares and provides comfort, encouragement, and an occasional hug. Many males seem to show little drive for the more physical aspects of a sexual relationship. Attempts to have more serious relationships often end because the person with autism is unable to empathize, reciprocate, or provide emotional support to a partner. Some young learners do actually "fall in love" and feel sadness and pain when their naive efforts are rebuffed (DesLauriers 1978). Some who express a desire for marriage and children indicate, on further questioning, that it is because "that's what others do." Until proven otherwise, it can be assumed that those without verbal skills have similar social needs, desires, and problems.

The deficits of autism that are particularly problematic in the area of social and sexual relationships include:

- Difficulty maintaining or regaining self-control

- Poor or no ability to discriminate socially appropriate and inappropriate words and actions, coupled with a general lack of social judgment
- A general lack of empathy and awareness of the perspective and needs of others (Hobson 1992)
- Difficulty understanding the consequences of behavior and the effect of that behavior on others
- Difficulty identifying and understanding nonverbal messages, while verbal messages are understood literally or misinterpreted

The implications of these problems are compelling reasons for thoughtful decision making. The world is not tolerant of young people who masturbate on the bus or who appear in public unclothed. Those who interpret a friendly greeting as a romantic invitation are likely to be arrested for harassment or stalking if they make continued attempts to establish a relationship. Naive and compliant young individuals are in danger of exploitation or abuse if their trust is misplaced. A young person with poor self-control, without empathy or sensitivity to the feelings of others, could unintentionally hurt a partner in efforts to achieve self-gratification. Realistically, masturbation may be the only sexual outlet for many adults with autism (Melone and Lettick 1983).

Other viewpoints are expressed in *Sex Education and Social Awareness Building for Autistic Children and Youth: Some Viewpoints and Considerations and Responses* by Elgar and associates (1985).

In making program decisions in this sensitive area, the safest course is to involve the total support team, including the parents and the learner when appropriate. Parents know their child's problems from experience in a variety of situations, and they must live with and support the decisions. The professional members of the team have greater access to information and resources, and they can provide balance from their experiences with many other individuals and family situations. As the team considers the Criterion of the Least Dangerous Assumption (see pages 103-104) and the family's values, they can make decisions that balance the risks with the individual's needs and abilities.

Considerations and Strategies

Decisions will depend on the individual learner's interests, abilities, living situation, opportunities, support system, and family values.

1. Because learning is literal and relatively inflexible, attempt to project into the future and decide, "Will this behavior or skill still be socially acceptable at age 6? At 12? At 21? At 45?" If it is not, then begin at a very young age to replace or expand limited skills. Teach only those skills that will continue to be appropriate at age 50.

   - Tantrums, screaming, and hitting are fairly common ways for two-year-olds to solve problems, but a 12-year-old or an adult who continues this kind of behavior to problem solve is isolated and restrained.

   - Nudity is cute in a three-year-old, but not at age 21.

   - A young child who is taught to like hugging and begins to nuzzle up to teachers, volunteers, peers, and acquaintances is seen as sweet and friendly. However, indiscriminate hugging is not appropriate and may be dangerous for an adolescent or adult.

   - Often, little boys are taught to drop their pants while standing up to urinate. Most boys quickly learn to manage the process like Dad and big brother. Unless taught otherwise, an adult with autism will continue to drop his pants even in public restrooms—a signal to others that he is a naive and vulnerable person.

2. Teach skills that have immediate and literal relevance and that deal with the real issues. Be guided by the old story about the child who asked his father, "Where did I come from?" When father finished the story of the birds and bees, the child said, "Oh, I thought we came from Boston."

> A young man had invited a new friend, a young woman, to visit him at his group home. When she arrived, he took her into his bedroom and closed the door. The staff question: Should he have a quick sex-education course? The team decision: To teach him to plan appropriate activities for entertaining guests, and then evaluate. With help to plan the visits, this young man entertained female guests in the living room, where they watched TV, shared magazines, listened to music, danced, and ate snacks. They did not indicate or suggest that they wanted more private personal time. Lesson: Begin with the simple and concrete solutions, then evaluate and refine if the situation changes.

3. Some basic concepts and rules are best taught in early childhood, then expanded and modified over time.

   - Identifying body parts

     Use correct anatomical terms. This is an important lifelong skill needed to get appropriate medical care and for discussing hygiene and social/sexual instruction.

   - Private and public behavior—the basic rules that guide appropriate behavior

     It is important to teach the exceptions that match the immediate need, and to systematically modify or add to the exceptions as needs change. (Keep clothing on except when bathing, changing clothing, trying on clothes in the store, swimming, for doctor examinations, and . . .)

   - Value a variety of social reinforcers

     Teach the learner to value compliments and a high-five salute for additional reinforcers. An arm around the shoulder or a pat on the arm, shoulder, or back can be satisfying, but save hugging for close family members or old family friends. Also teach the concepts for these discriminations.

Sex Education

Ford (1987) discusses a variety of issues related to structuring information for sex education.

1. Identify appropriate skills and instructional resources from sex-education materials written for those with developmental delays. Adapt the curriculum to match the autism learning style.

   - Individualize the instruction, and deliver it in a 1:1 context. This allows the instruction to be modified to fit the learner's specific need and avoids confusion.

   - Use instructional procedures to ensure that the learner understands the correct and relevant information and does not learn unintended lessons. One young man was taught condom use with a banana as a model. Later, he told his instructor that he had had sex. He was asked if he had used a condom, and he replied, "No, I didn't have a banana."

Review use of social stories, pages 204-207.

- Teach private and personal care and hygiene skills in the context of total routines. Incorporate visual adaptations, checklists, cue cards, and other visual references so the learner is less dependent on the verbal instructions of others to manage private personal needs. This policy is as important for toilet training as it is for teaching young women to manage their menstrual needs independently.

- Use written and taped stories to provide clear information for understanding the purpose of a new skill or strategy. Include all the relevant details needed for generalizing the skill to different situations. Stories provide opportunities for the learner to review and rehearse the skills privately at home.

2. Train staff to provide effective instruction and responsible guidance, and to understand the ethical implications of their actions. Monitor staff members frequently to avoid situations that have the potential for exploitation, confusion, frustration, or disappointment. Hugging, patting, or flirting can arouse sexual feelings that individuals with autism have little skill in understanding or controlling (Melone and Lettick 1983).

   - To avoid confusion and to protect both staff and client, personal assistance and instruction in private matters should be provided by staff of the same sex. A woman—staff member or client—should not be required to enter a men's restroom, nor should a man be required to enter a woman's restroom to provide or receive assistance. This is not always possible, but it should be given thoughtful consideration for individuals as young as six or seven years of age. Exceptions to this policy should be made only in extraordinary situations, and should be explained to the learner to avoid misunderstandings.

Masturbation

Masturbation is an issue that needs thoughtful management to prevent serious problems during puberty and adulthood. Whatever management decisions are made, it is important to deal with the situation calmly and in a matter-of-fact way. Emotional expressions of shock, distaste or "badness" will call undue attention to the behavior and likely will serve as a reinforcer. Boredom, lack of physical exertion and strenuous activity, ill-fitting clothing, infections, and inadequate hygiene can intensify the frequency of occurrences.

The basic goals are to teach learners when and where they can masturbate, and to avoid turning masturbation into a problem. Instruction begins as soon as a young child begins to masturbate outside the bedroom. The child is calmly redirected to the bedroom with the statement that masturbation is done there. It is much easier to teach a young child this important rule than to wait until adolescence when problems may have developed and the consequences of poor judgment are more serious.

Strategies

1. Organize and structure the learner's time.

   - Provide a balanced schedule of activities so the learner is alert and physically, socially, or intellectually active most of the time. Limit the amount of uninterrupted quiet time spent in public areas such as the living room or classroom. Structure these quiet times, and interrupt periodically with activities, toys, materials, or social opportunities.

- Instruct the learner that private places are where private things are done. Specify private places—the bathroom *at home* and the learner's bedroom. Some learners need a reminder that you can do other than private things in those rooms, and that others also use the bathroom. Make sure the learner understands that masturbation in public restrooms is not a safe option.

- Schedule some private, uninterrupted bedroom time on a regular basis. Give this block of time a name—perhaps simply *private time*. As with any other activity or routine, private time needs a clear beginning and a clear ending. The beginning can be specified on a daily calendar. A mini-calendar can list optional activities for the private time. An alarm clock or timer provides an impersonal and concrete way to end this period and make the transition from private to public time.

- Parents can help the young child end this private period by checking the calendar to see what's next. A routine is helpful for some older learners. The routine could begin by managing basic hygiene needs—perhaps with a shower—and continue with an enjoyable activity such as listening to music. ("After your shower, it will be time to play your new CD.") Checking the calendar before the beginning of private time prepares the learner to move on to the next activity.

2. Teach new skills and routines for private times.

   Be aware that anxiety and frustration are an ongoing part of the autism syndrome. There is little indication that anxiety and frustration will be relieved for long by sexual gratification alone. Caution is advised if it is suggested that the learner needs instruction to masturbate more effectively. Confusion and even more frustration are the likely result for those who learn skills exactly as taught. For example, if another person is present to teach the behavior, the learner may assume that another person should always be part of the behavior.

3. Evaluate and refine to address changing needs.

   - Examine for signs of irritation or infection. Check the fit of clothing.

   - Review the schedule of activities and the materials. Is the learner bored? Does the learner need more variety, more challenging activities and materials, more strenuous physical activity, or more frequent social interactions?

   - Perhaps one of the rules needs to be modified or clarified, or a new rule may be needed.

Summary

Communication and interactions present the most stressful and demanding challenges for those with autism and those who support them. Individuals with autism do feel emotions that they do not express in the typical ways. Many want social contacts and interactions. However, it cannot be assumed that they want those contacts for the typical reasons, or that without instruction they will know how to manage interactions in a way that satisfies both partners.

Even with these limitations, more young people with autism are marrying today than ever before. With more effective instruction during their school years and with the sensitive support of mentors and interpreters to help clarify the world and fill the gaps, even more individuals with autism will be able to lead satisfying lives in the future.

A statement by Jim Sinclair has much to help us understand the nature and the needs of those with autism as we make decisions that will affect their lives:

> In some ways I am terribly ill-equipped to survive in this world, like an extraterrestrial stranded without an orientation manual. . . . But my personhood is intact. My selfhood is undamaged. I find great value and meaning in my life, and I have no wish to be cured of being myself. . . . Grant me the dignity of meeting me on my own terms. Recognize that we are equally alien to each other, that my ways of being are not merely damaged versions of yours. Question your assumptions. Define your terms. Work with me to build more bridges between us. (Sinclair 1992, 302)

CHAPTER

23

Teach Self-Control and Self-Management Strategies

The six critical goals to address the deficits of autism are:

1. To value people, and to interact and communicate spontaneously
2. To learn the language and to communicate effectively
3. To tolerate change and accept new experiences; to be more flexible
4. To focus on and participate in instruction
5. To do things independently, using visual references
6. To monitor and manage stress

Instruction to achieve each of these goals begins in early childhood and continues throughout life as needs change. Self-control and self-management are dependent upon refining and expanding all six of these goals. Increasing competence in these areas makes the world more understandable and less stressful. When stress and anxiety increase, skills are likely to fade, leaving learners vulnerable and in need of greater support.

Intervention and instruction involve three specific tasks:

Review chapter 10, pages 137-151, for strategies to identify and defuse stress; and chapters 11-16 for strategies to organize and structure events, space, and time.

1. Evaluate continuously to identify the signals of stress, identify the problems or causes of the stress, and intervene by providing understandable information and assistance to solve the problem to defuse stress.

2. Organize and structure the events, the space, and the time so information is visually clear (to answer the unasked questions, *who, what, when, where, how, how long,* and *what's next)*. This clarity prevents potential and recurring problems (Mesibov et al. 1994).

3. Teach new skills such as those listed in figure 23.1.

For procedures to plan and initiate instruction and embed new communication, social, self-control, and self-management skills into natural routines, see Koegel et al. 1994; Gray and Garand 1993; Groden and LaVasseur 1995; and *Video Guide to Breaking the Barriers II (Groden et al. 1991)*.

Figure 23.1. Skills required for self-management and maintaining self-control

- Identify stressful feelings and learn to relax.
- Take a break to regain or maintain control.
- Use self-control routines to maintain control in the natural setting.
- Gain control over repetitive behaviors.
- Solve problems.
- Make informed choices.

Many of the self-control procedures described in this section are commonly used by counselors to help people manage and cope with emotional problems, pain, and the stresses of everyday life. The strategies also are used in therapy to control compulsive behaviors such as smoking, overeating, and panic attacks. While these self-control procedures would seem to be beyond the abilities of those with autism, they are in fact very effective with more able verbal learners as well as those who are seemingly less capable. Instruction and support to develop self-control and self-management strategies can begin as early as age 3. The degree of independence in using the strategies will vary; some can learn to cue themselves independently, while others will continue to need someone or something (such as a cue card) to provide a signal to initiate and use the strategies (Cautela and Groden 1978; Groden et al. 1991, 1994; and *Video Guide to Breaking the Barriers II* by Groden et al. 1991).

Identify Stressful Feelings

The ability to identify one's own feelings of overwhelming stress, tension, panic, fear, or excitement is a first step toward self-control. The sensory and learning differences in autism have a significant impact on this ability. Information provided by some adults with autism indicates that they do not automatically learn the concept of *feelings*, nor can they automatically recognize what is causing the overwhelming panic or excitement (Cesaroni and Garber 1991; Sinclair 1992).

Strategies

The following strategies and experiences can increase the ability to identify feelings of tension and stress.

1. Use reflective listening when the behavioral signals of tension and accelerating emotions are identified. For example, when a learner covers her ears and begins to rock as several people are talking and giving directions, the interpreter tentatively says, "There are too many people talking, and you feel tense and confused"; or, when a learner sees peers going to lunch and begins to pace and hyperventilate, the interpreter reflects, "You look worried. Are you afraid you will miss lunch?" This model for associating the label of the emotions to the cause of the problem is also a first step for solving problems.

2. Use parallel talking in natural situations to highlight the facial expressions and body language that show how others feel. ("When the ball hit Tommy, it scared him and hurt his arm. He is crying. Sometime people cry when they are scared or hurt. When people cry, their eyes are almost shut and tears come out of their eyes and run down their faces. Some people make loud noises when they cry, but others make only a little noise. Tommy is making loud noises. When Tommy feels better and relaxes, he will stop crying.") While the amount of detail depends on the learner's attention span, it is just such detail that those with autism miss. Some of the detail may be added later as an experience story is written and illustrated with line drawings to highlight the critical elements.

3. Model feelings and emotions by exaggerating facial expressions and parallel talking through actual problems. ("I really goofed. I feel so frustrated. I forgot to _____.")

4. Provide practice through role play, stories, art activities, puppet play, and other activities in individual and group contexts.

5. Highlight the critical cues and concepts during instruction to identify and manage feelings and emotions provided in typical early-childhood classes.

6. Use progressive muscle relaxation training to teach the learner to discriminate between feelings of tension and relaxation.

Relaxation Training

The strategies described in this section are adapted from the following sources:

Cautela, J. R., and J. Groden. *Relaxation: A Comprehensive Manual for Adults, Children, and Children with Special Needs.* Champaign, IL: Research Press, 1978.

Groden, J., J. R. Cautela, and G. Groden. *Breaking the Barriers I: Relaxation Techniques for People with Special Needs.* Champaign, IL: Research Press, 1989.

This videotape, which was developed at the Groden Center, demonstrates instructional procedures and various applications.

Refer to these resources for detailed strategies before initiating instruction.

Progressive Muscle Relaxation (PMR) is a strategy for identifying and relaxing tension in the various muscle groups. The ability to reduce tension is the foundation for self-control and self-management. Unless one can relax enough to focus and think, it is impossible to solve problems or make choices. PMR is used in a variety of ways:

• To reduce general anxiety before and during a stressful situation

• As an alternative to stereotypic or repetitive motor behavior

 For example, hand flapping cannot occur when the hands are relaxed.

• As an incompatible alternative to aggressive or tantrum behavior

 One cannot scream or kick if the mouth and legs are relaxed.

PMR is useful for anyone who has a high level of stress. Interpreters who learn the relaxation strategies can provide a calming model during instruction and in highly stressful or crisis situations. Frequently, relaxation skills are combined with imagery-based procedures to establish self-control routines. These routines serve to break the chain of accelerating stress and are useful for maintaining or regaining control.

Strategies

While PMR is generally introduced and taught in individual sessions, the skills can be initiated in a group. Some learners have difficulty mastering the relaxation responses until a peer sits beside them to model the procedure while the interpreter verbalizes the steps. Biofeedback procedures benefit some learners. *Caution is advised if a seizure disorder is present.*

Initial lessons teach the concepts and the feelings of *tighten* and *relax*, first the arms and then the legs. These concepts are not taught as visual-imitation tasks. because learners could come to depend on the presence of a visual model. Rather, in teaching the concept of *tighten your arm*, the interpreter might hold out a pencil. As the learner grasps the pencil, the interpreter pulls it gently, stretching the learner's arm out and up while saying, "Tight." The interpreter stops pulling and lets the learner's arm slowly bend to a relaxing position, while saying, "Relax." Reinforcement involves stroking and softly saying, "Good! Your arm is nice and relaxed." (At first, other reinforcers also may be needed.) Once the learner understands how it feels when the arm, neck, or leg is tight and tense, the word *tight* is no longer used. In real life, the tightness or tension of the muscle is the natural cue to relax.

Remember that individuals with autism learn and use skills exactly as taught. If they always lie down on a mat during relaxation training, they will not automatically be able to relax themselves while walking, sitting, or working in various settings. If a pencil is always used, or always used in the same way to prompt tightening of the arm muscles, the learner probably will come to believe that *tight* is somehow related to the pencil rather than to the feeling of tension. Therefore, as in all other instruction, variations must be systematic. Vary the position (sitting, standing, walking, lying down), the location (inside and outdoors), the cues and prompts, the consequences, the instructor, and the number of other people present.

> The following situations were observed at the Groden Center in Providence, Rhode Island.
>
> ———————
>
> On returning to their group home after delivering presents to their mothers on Mother's Day, the six adolescent boys with autism were having difficulty settling down. Most of the boys were excited from the afternoon visits, but Jason was upset because his mother had not been home. To complicate matters, Dr. Groden dropped in unexpectedly with a stranger. As the excitement and stress escalated, Dr. Groden suggested that they go into the living room and relax. Immediately, the six young men moved to the living room while staff and guests remained in the dining room. Jason sat in a rocking chair, rocking furiously. Gabriel, one of the more verbal boys, led the group through the relaxation exercise. Some of the boys closed their eyes, and all became quiet and calm. Even Jason stopped rocking. At the conclusion of the session, one of the boys said softly, "Tell us a nice picture," so Gabriel led them through a visual-imagery story about walking on the beach. When the story ended, the boys sat almost motionless for a few moments, then calmly moved away and became involved in various activities.
>
> ———————
>
> As Dr. Groden and I were touring the Center, we entered a room where Kim was folding towels for gym classes. He was visibly upset, folding and unfolding a towel, rocking energetically back and forth, hyperventilating, and making harsh throat noises. From the door, about eight feet away from Kim, Dr. Groden held out her hand and softly said, "Stop. What do you need to do?" Kim looked at her, stopped, and took a deep breath. As Kim let out his breath, Dr. Groden said, "Good! You know what to do." She waited quietly for a moment or two as Kim continued to relax himself. Then she moved toward him as she said, "Good! You can relax yourself." She helped him to reorganize and reengage in his work; and as Dr. Groden and I left a moment later, Kim was working steadily and calmly.

Take a Break to Regain or Maintain Control

Most people automatically know when their stress is so high that they must get out of a situation quickly, and they automatically know how to reduce that stress. They think about something else that is pleasant, leave the area, or do any one of a variety of other acceptable options. But those with autism must be taught positive ways to escape overwhelming stress before they lose control. Taking a break to relieve stress is one self-control routine. Even very young children can learn to take breaks independently.

Taking a break to relieve stress is a positive skill that is taught and reinforced in order to prevent a behavior problem. This break is very different from a time-out that occurs after losing control.

Strategies

Organize the instruction as for teaching any other routine. Before beginning instruction:

1. Prepare a quiet space in a nearby area that is easy to monitor.

2. Prepare or provide a very simple and quick way to communicate the need for a break. Even those who can ordinarily talk need a backup system to use when under stress. One method is to make "break tickets."

3. Prepare a visual representation of the routine—a checklist, story, or series of line drawings.

The general components of a break routine are:

1. Initiate

   Recognize the natural cue to initiate a break. Recognizing feelings of overwhelming stress is a self-monitoring task.

2. Prepare

   Locate a break ticket and walk to interpreter.

3. Perform the essential steps

   - Touch the interpreter's arm to get attention.

   - Give the break ticket to the interpreter.

   - Go to the quiet area.

   - Use a relaxation strategy. (This may involve rocking in a rocking chair, jumping on a mini-trampoline, or using PMR and deep breathing.)

   - Self-monitor ("Am I relaxed?").

4. Terminate

   When relaxed, end the break and return to the appropriate area to reengage.

5. Solve problems

   Teach strategies for identifying and solving potential problems when the learner is in a location where the quiet area is not accessible, when an interpreter is not available, when the learner doesn't know what to do to reengage after break, or when other unexpected complications occur.

   Introduce the routine with the visual representations. Use parallel talk. Ensure that the learner knows the location of the quiet area and how to use the area to relax. Review the routine in imagery once or twice a day until it is familiar. Instruction occurs in the natural context of high-stress situations. The first few times the learner uses the routine, provide assistance and parallel talk; and gradually fade the prompts. During initial instruction, honor each request for a break.

Typically, three problems occur during the instructional process: the learner does not terminate the break when relaxed, leaves the break area before becoming completely relaxed, or repeatedly asks to take a break whether or not stress is present.

If the learner does not terminate the break when relaxed

Evaluate the environment and expectations.

- Is the area uncluttered and calm, containing only the material to support relaxation? This is a place to do a specific task—relax—with specific objects or materials. It is not a place to make choices or to play. If a learner needs music to relax, a relaxation tape is in the tape player and other tapes are stored away from the area.

- Are the expectations clear and at the right level? Does the learner know how to end the break, what to do next, how to move from the area to the next activity? Is there a visual reference available to clarify the next steps?

- Can the learner identify relaxed feelings?

- Does the learner have difficulty ending one task and beginning another in other situations? Arrange a concrete signal for ending the break. Set a timer (or teach the learner to set a timer) for a reasonable period of time—the time it usually takes the learner to relax.

If the learner leaves the break area before becoming completely relaxed

Use the timer. If the learner is not relaxed when the timer rings, reset the timer and say, "You are still upset. I'll set the timer for another five minutes."

Clarify the concept and feelings of being relaxed. Use visual references.

If the learner repeatedly asks to take a break without the appearance of stress

Rejoice! It is a sign that the individual has learned the routine and understands the power of the communication. However, it also is a sign that more work is needed.

- Ensure that the natural setting is interesting, relatively unstressful, and reinforcing—a place where the learner wants to be.

- Structure and visually clarify the number of break options. For example, if assessment of the situation shows that the child is overly stressed on an average of three times in a two-hour period but has requested as many as seven breaks in that length of time, provide seven break tickets for a two-hour period. Then systematically vary and reduce the number of tickets. If the learner maintains control and has some tickets left at the end of the specified time period, trade them for a privilege or something pleasant.

Teach a Self-Control Routine to Solve Problems

A more advanced self-control routine involves a series of complex skills used to maintain control in order to solve problems in the natural setting. The sequence of skills generally includes self-monitoring, relaxation, thought stopping, assertive responses, self-instruction, and self-reinforcement. These routines are introduced, then practiced in imagery as learners visualize themselves calmly solving problems in stressful situations.

Strategies

The instructional considerations that follow are adapted from these sources:

Groden, J., and P. LaVasseur. Cognitive Picture Rehearsal: A Visual System to Teach Self-Control. In *Teaching Children with Autism: Methods to Enhance Learning, Communication, and Socialization.* Edited by K. A. Quill. Albany, NY: Delmar, 1995.

Groden, J., J. R. Cautela, and G. Groden. *Breaking the Barriers II: Imagery Procedures for People with Special Needs.* Videotape. Champaign, IL: Research Press, 1991.

Groden, J., J. R. Cautela, P. LaVasseur, G. Groden, and M. Bausman. *Video Guide to Breaking the Barriers II.* Champaign, IL: Research Press, 1991.

Stories or scripts used to introduce self-control routines are based on functional analysis of problem situations. (See chapter 25, pages 395-399.) These stories identify the conditions in the immediate or distant environments that trigger stress, an appropriate alternative response, and several reinforcers. The stories are developed to match the learners' language and attention abilities. They are highly descriptive to help learners imagine or see themselves in the scenes. Sensory details are included with such statements as, "I hear the sound of the _____"; "I smell the _____"; "I feel the _____." For those who do not like to imagine themselves in a problem situation, the story is developed to describe someone else with similar characteristics and problems. This procedure, called *covert modeling,* allows the individual to imagine someone else responding with the target behavior and experiencing a rewarding consequence.

The number of scenes in a story are limited. Generally, the routine can be represented in seven scenes:

Scene 1: The problem or trigger for the stress

Prepare several scenes to describe the range of situations in which the stressful problem occurs. Rotate these scenes during instruction, to ensure generalization of the new skills to a variety of settings.

Scene 2: The feelings that describe the target behavior

("My shoulders feel tight, I feel hot, and I start to breathe faster.")

Scene 3: Thought stopping

Thought stopping is an imagery procedure that allows a person to gain control of unwanted and unproductive thoughts. It is used frequently in therapy for those with panic disorders and addictive behaviors. As the individual imagines the undesirable behavior (for example, feelings of panic or fear), he imagines himself shouting, "STOP!" As this quick and sharp statement is imagined, the negative thoughts are disrupted.

Scene 4. The relaxation response that clearly describes what the individual is to do (for example, take a deep breath and relax the neck and shoulders)

Scene 5. A pleasant consequence to reinforce the relaxation response and thought stopping

Scene 6. Strategies and skills to solve or deal with the problem effectively—the new skills to be increased

This scene redirects attention from the problem and feelings of stress, to focus on the solution. The solution might include:

- Self-instruction to initiate positive action ("How shall I start? First, I'll do _____; then I can do _____.")

- A coping statement that relieves the pressure ("If I forget a step, I can go back"; "If I do it wrong, I can fix it"; "If I need help, I can ask ____.")
- An assertive response that acknowledges the problem ("I'll try to do better next time"; "I'll write that down so I'll remember"; "I understand. I can do that now.")

Scene 7: A pleasant scene to reinforce the positive direction—the new skills to be increased

Once the story is developed, the scenes are represented visually for use during instruction. The story may be represented in print, with one scene described on each page of a small book. It also can be represented with line drawings.

Cognitive Picture Rehearsal

Cognitive picture rehearsal involves the presentation of the script with a picture to represent each scene. These pictures help the learner to imagine the scene more clearly. This format is most helpful for those who learn more efficiently with a visual display, who have difficulty attending to a verbal presentation, or who are unable to provide verbal feedback. Pictures are designed to match the learners need; but in general, "The more abstract the picture, the greater the generalization. Black-and-white line drawings without background can often convey enough information for learning to take place, yet not be so specific that they inhibit generalization" (Groden and LeVasseur 1995, 26).

Pictures can be presented in a variety of ways: flash-card style, laid out on a table from left to right, in storybook form, in a cartoon-strip format with one scene to a frame, or carried in a credit-card folder.

Self-control routines are introduced individually in a quiet, distraction-free area. Visual imagery typically involves a verbal presentation: the individual listens with closed eyes and imagines the scenes as they are described. The individual then repeats the scene aloud (or in sign) with eyes remaining closed while continuing to imagine. The interpreter asks questions to monitor the learner's participation. ("Do you taste the ice cream? Raise your finger when you taste the cold chocolate ice cream.") This procedure is modified when visual references are used; the turning of the page or switching from one picture to the next shows participation.

The scripts are rehearsed at least twice a day. When the learner is familiar with the script, it may be taped so the scenes can be rehearsed independently in other settings. Scripts are constantly evaluated and adapted as the situations change. Occasionally, a learner will suggest additional sensory details that make the story more personally vivid.

> Matt was having trouble at the library, where one of his jobs was to shelve books. He worked independently on most days; but when there was a large stack of books to return, he worried that he would not finish before quitting time. When this panic occurred, he was unable to work steadily or efficiently. He might drop a book several times or begin to hyperventilate or rock repetitively. One day, he was so worried that he pushed a patron who was in his way.
>
> Following an assessment of the situation, Matt was taught a self-control routine containing basic elements that could be varied to apply to different situations.

- I see a big stack of books. I think I'll never get done.

- My shoulders feel tight and tense. I am breathing hard.

- I say, "STOP!" I take a deep breath. I relax my neck and shoulders.

- I say, "That feels good. Now I can deal with this."

- I think about having a tall, cool, glass of soda pop at quitting time.

- If I don't get all the books put back today, I can do them tomorrow.

- If someone is in my way, I can say, "Excuse me," and then wait for the person to move.

- I will sort the books and get started, one book at a time.

- There! That's not so bad. I'm making progress.

- I will stay relaxed. I'll have that glass of soda pop after work.

After being taught the basic routine and the variations, Matt was given an audiotape to listen to each day before going to work and again at break time if he felt the need.

Managing Repetitive Behavior

Review the effects of negative reinforcement (pages 239, 241).

Repetitive and stereotypic (R/S) behaviors (rocking, finger flicking, jumping up and down) occur more often in the presence of problems, stress, and excitement. These behaviors can occur automatically when the individuals with autism are not attending to and consciously controlling their behavior (Cesaroni and Garber 1991; Sinclair 1992). In general, when skills increase and more time is spent in interesting and productive activity, the R/S behaviors decrease. While R/S behaviors are generally reflexive and nonintentional, sometimes they are used intentionally to avoid or escape demands if they have been negatively reinforced by reduced demands.

While there is nothing bad or wrong about the R/S behaviors, they do make the individual stand out and look different or less competent to those who are not familiar with autism. In some situations, an individual will perseverate in the behavior and need someone to break the repetitive cycle. Assessment and intervention considerations for unconventional (repetitive) verbal behavior are discussed in Prizant and Rydell (1993).

Strategies

Use the following strategies to avoid making the problem worse and to help the learner gain control:

1. Develop a balanced schedule that includes:

   - Frequent opportunities to move about and engage in strenuous exercise (Levinson and Reid 1993; Kern et al. 1984; McGimsey and Favell 1988)

   - A balance of activities that are liked and disliked, familiar and new

   - A balance of active and quiet activities

   - Frequent opportunities for attention and social interactions

   - A minimum amount of unscheduled or unstructured time (for example, waiting)

2. Ignore the behavior, but attend to the message (the function) of the behavior. End activities at the earliest signs of restlessness, boredom, and fatigue. Use a contingency statement such as, "You need a break? Do one more problem, and then it will be time for a break"; or cue the individual to ask for help or for a break. Teach more effective "functionally equivilant" ways to communicate the need for help, breaks, and needs (Carr 1988).

3. Teach the learner that the behavior is OK, but there is a time and place to do it.

4. Teach the learner a self-control routine to ask for and take a break. Some individuals who are highly anxious or easily overstimulated need a private space identified in each new setting.

5. Identify the reinforcing element of the behavior, and provide other more productive or less obvious activities that provide the same type of reinforcement. One young man, who was visually reinforced by the long strings of moving paper as he shredded the family newspapers, now grates cheese at a pizza parlor.

6. In preschool classes, use group activities to strengthen language concepts related to self-control. Be sure an interpreter is available to ensure that the correct actions are associated with the words. For example:

   - Fast/slow: Instruct the children to walk, clap, or jump fast or slow; move to fast and slow drum beats or rhythms.

   - Tight/relaxed: Chant, "Get ready, 1-2-3; tighten your fists, 4-5-6; relax, 7-8-9-10; stretch your arms and take a deep breath."

   - Stop and go: While walking, running, clapping, jumping, or stomping feet, shout (or whisper) directives at random intervals: "Ready, set, GO! . . . STOP! 1-2-3, GO!"

   - Use relays, balance-beam activities, and obstacle courses that require alertness and control. These include walking with a bean bag on the head, carrying a ball on a spoon, and stepping over objects on a beam. Balance beams need to be at least 8" to 10" from the floor or higher to motivate the learner to stay alert and in control. Allow for natural consequences of inattention, but have mats and spotters nearby to prevent injury.

Solving Problems

Because those with autism do not automatically learn to solve problems, they are at a loss to know what to do when the unexpected occurs. The stress and panic that accompanies the inability to manage a situation leads to withdrawal, panic, and severe behavior problems. One of the major self-management skills is to learn how to solve at least some problems independently and to recognize when help is needed.

Strategies

Recognizing that each individual's problems, knowledge, and abilities are different, the instructional plan should address the following issues in some concrete and literal way:

1. The full meaning of the abstract idea or concept of *problem* may be unclear, and many things may not be recognized as problems. Teach the concept of *problem*. Provide a clear and literal definition with examples of different types of past problems and some that may be encountered in the future.

2. The nature and severity of a problem may be unclear. The learner is as likely to consider all problems as either life threatening or trivial. Use semantic maps, flow charts, or cue cards to teach a process for evaluating the severity of a problem and a process for dealing with the various types of problems.

- For problems that need to be solved quickly, those that are dangerous, or those that stop progress: Teach a self-control routine to focus attention and behavior on the critical issues. Teach relaxation and self-control routines.

- For problems that can be solved later—those for which there is time to think and plan: Teach a process for brainstorming to generate new solutions, for evaluating those solutions, and for selecting a solution to try. Once a solution is selected, rehearse it with stories or scripts.

3. It may be unclear whether the problem can be solved without assistance, or whether help is needed. Teach a self-control routine that can guide the learner's actions.

- Specify and rehearse strategies for locating a helper, initiating a request for help, and communicating the problem clearly. Expand the learner's communication system to address these needs.

- Provide practice in self-instruction. Model self-instruction strategies in the context of solving real problems, puzzles, or mazes. Provide a self-instruction cue card that clarifies the steps. (What is the problem? How/where do I start? What do I do first?) Include coping statements and self-reinforcement.

4. Capitalize on visual references. In addition to semantic maps and flow charts, consider preparing:

- A problem/solution checklist or chart much like in a technical manual

- T-charts to visualize the cost/benefit analysis of options

- Visual references for alternative solutions

- Small self-monitoring/self-reinforcing checklists on cards to carry throughout the day

  These cards can serve as cues to use the procedures and for recording successful use. The opportunity to record successes is generally a reinforcing event. When checklists are shared with the interpreter, the skills are reviewed and reinforced again.

5. Plan the instruction, and teach for generalization and flexibility.

   - Use the same process to solve many different kinds of problems.

   - Incorporate literal description of the setting, highlight the natural cues, and vary the practice in a broad range of natural and simulated situations.

   - A social-group setting offers many opportunities to identify potential problems, generate alternative solutions, and rehearse in a safe and supportive environment. For references for activities and strategies, see Shure 1992a, 1992b; Buser and Reimer 1988; Pehrsson and Denner 1989.

   - Set up or sabotage some part of a natural routine to create opportunities to practice and receive support and quick feedback in the natural setting.

   - Practice in imagery with visual references.

See figure 23.2, a flow chart that illustrates the numerous components and the complexity of planning involved in teaching independent problem solving. The process begins in early childhood by teaching concepts such as *problem, hurt, safety,* and others; and the process for identifying and solving small problems as they occur. (Milk is spilled; the interpreter says, "That's a problem. Let's clean it up.") A similar flow chart can serve as a visual reference to clarify the gestalt of solving problems for adolescence. With a long-term approach, more independence can be achieved in adulthood.

Making Informed Choices

The ability to make informed choices is a complex and high-level skill that has many implications for those with autism, who have a limited number of preferences, resist trying new things, are repetitive, and indicate preferences in unexpected ways that are difficult to interpret. Many behavior problems are related to making choices or indicating choices.

An informed choice implies that all the options are understood and that the mode of indicating the preference is, first, understood; and second, motorically and communicatively possible. The following questions highlight some of the problems in autism.

- Can a lack of protest imply informed consent, or merely simple resignation?

- Is habitual or repetitive behavior an active and informed choice? For example, if a person always chooses the object on the right, always chooses vanilla ice cream, or always chooses to rock in the rocking chair when offered several leisure options, can it be assumed that the person fully understands the options?

- If an individual does not do a job, can it be assumed that the person is noncompliant and chooses not to work? Perhaps some part of the task is unclear, or the job is not one that is preferred, or the person prefers not to do that work in that way at that time.

Figure 23.2. Sequence of concepts and processes involved in solving problems

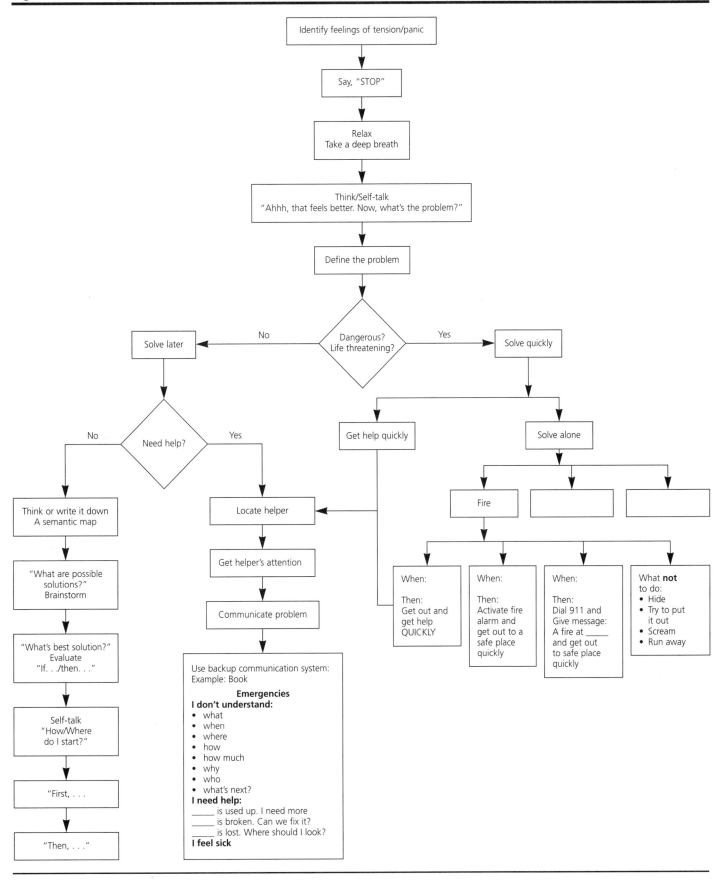

- If someone flails about, hits, and refuses to get dressed, has that person chosen to be stubborn and contrary? Perhaps the message is, "I don't like these clothes, I prefer to wear a different outfit"; or, "I would like to brush my teeth before getting dressed."

- When asked, "Do you agree to the conditions of a behavior contract?" and the individual says, "Yes" and signs the contract, can it be assumed that this is informed consent? Is the individual really saying, "Yes, I choose for you to do these things to me," or, "Yes, I agree; these are the best strategies for you to use to get me to do what you want"? Does the person have a way to indicate a desire not to change that behavior? Perhaps the individual signs the contract simply because it is expected.

It cannot be assumed that an informed choice was made in any of the above situations. One cannot assume that those with autism understand the language concepts, have enough experience with the options to have a preference, understand the consequences of a specific choice, or have a clear way to indicate either a protest or a different choice. Rarely is a learner given the opportunity or the means to indicate, "None of these" or "I don't understand."

Strategies

Skills for making informed choices must be taught. Instruction begins in early childhood by providing two options and an opportunity to choose. Instruction for developing choice-making skills involves the following issues and strategies:

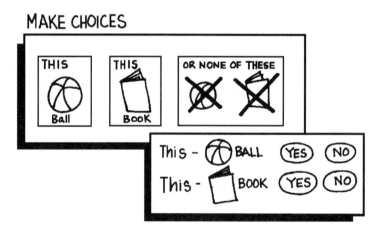

1. Increase the learner's flexibility and willingness to try new things. Provide experiences from which to develop preferences.

   - Teach the concept of *try* in a contingency format. ("Try a touch of this; then _____"; "Try it on, and then you can take it off.")

   - Reintroduce new options often over several days or weeks. As familiarity increases, tolerance also increases. Then real choices can be made.

2. Identify the communicative intent of behaviors and the early signals of preferences and feelings.

3. Teach more understandable ways to communicate preferences and to reject, end, or avoid options ("I want/don't want this"; "I like/don't like that").

4. Teach the concepts *choose, finish, now, later, more,* and others that relate to preferences and making choices.

5. Provide many opportunities and experiences to select food, clothing, toys, activities, partners, and working conditions in the context of natural routines.

Other Considerations

The Importance of Choice-Making Skills, an article by Shevin and Klein (1984), is a good resource.

The support-team members have a responsibility to identify the risks of options and balance those risks with the learner's ability to deal with the consequences.

Do not give a choice unless there is a *real* choice.

- At first, offer only options that are both possible and safe. Gradually offer riskier choices as the learner develops competence.

- Avoid overwhelming the learner with too many options. Initially, limit the options to only two or three.

- Avoid overwhelming the learner with too many options *when the learner is frustrated or stressed*. Decision making is demanding; communicating the decision is even more difficult and likely to accelerate stress to the point of losing control.

- Avoid pressure to make immediate choices. If a decision must be made quickly, provide a concrete means for measuring time, and remain quiet or move away while the learner is considering the options.

- Sometimes a learner may need time to touch, look at, and think about all the options. At other times, the learner may need a way to communicate, "I don't want any of these." Make quick line drawings to represent each option as it is presented. Include a symbol to represent "None of these."

- When the learner is required to make critical choices and decisions that could have long-term implications, use a T-chart and provide assistance to do a cost/benefit analysis.

- Allow for changes of opinion. All people change their minds sometimes. However, when it is necessary to live with a choice, be sympathetic but calm. ("I understand you don't like the licorice ice cream, but we don't have money to buy another flavor just now. You can eat the licorice ice cream, or you can drop it in the garbage. Next time, you can make a different choice.")

Integrate Self-Management Systems

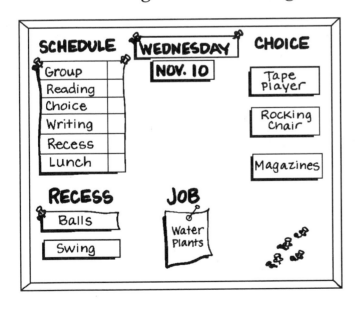

A learner may have a daily calendar, several mini-calendars, and several checklists, cue cards, and stories. To avoid confusing the learner and the interpreter, these systems must be organized. They may be displayed together on a bulletin board or arranged within the individual work area. Pockets or hangers for folders and cue cards also can be placed on a bulletin board. See page 255 for an illustration of an integrated system for a more sophisticated learner who carries a notebook. Stories and semantic maps also can be organized in notebooks for later reference.

Summary

Persons with autism can learn to manage stress and maintain self-control when:

1. Given appropriate instruction and visual support systems

2. The environment is stimulating and structured to match needs

3. An interpreter is available to evaluate and modify the environment or provide assistance when needed.

6

Manage Difficult Problems

UPSETS

GOD I NEED A FEARFUL
FEASIBLE FIT
SAL* SAYS NOT
MOM AGREES
YELLING WOULD HELP
HITTING HEAD WOULD
BRING RELIEF
DAVE REALLY BETTER AFTER
ONLY RELEASE IS TOO
MUCH TROUBLE

—David Eastham
In *Silent Words and Forever Friends*

---

*Sal was a former teacher.

CHAPTER
24

Managing Specific Problems

Behavior problems are often the first concerns expressed by parents and teachers of those with autism. Problem behaviors normally begin before the second birthday. This is the stage when toddlers can move about but have not yet figured out how the world works. The problems of typically developing children are similar to those with autism, but the differences in the form and intensity of the behavior and differences in ability to process information from the world requires a more systematic approach when the child has autism. Schopler and Mesibov (1994) offer a useful overview in their book, *Behavioral Issues in Autism*.

One of the major goals in writing this book is to provide a process for addressing the issues related to behavior problems. The first step in this process is to understand the background of the problem and to identify the perspective, the misperceptions, and the skill deficits that caused the problem. Once the causes are identified, appropriate strategies become more apparent. Strategies are related to the three intervention tasks presented in chapter 9:

1. Organize and structure the environment to clarify information and eliminate some of the factors that contribute to the problem.

2. Teach new concepts, skills, and rules.

3. Continuously evaluate and refine to address changing needs.

> By the time Adam was three years old, his parents were extremely frustrated by his screaming. Adam screeched and screamed many times a day, and nothing seemed to make him stop. During the assessment of his problem, it was discovered that Adam screamed when he was confused, sick, or upset because he couldn't have or do something he wanted. He also screamed when excited and when he wanted to play. For the most part, he would stop screaming when his problems were addressed; but when he was excited and when he wanted to play, he was totally out of control and the screaming accelerated. Previous behavior programs were designed to eliminate screaming in all situations because it was such a problem in some situations. Not only were those programs unsuccessful, but Adam's parents hesitated to punish the screaming because he had no other way to communicate his problems.
>
> The strategies for addressing this problem were based on the decision that screaming is not a bad behavior. In fact, it is a positive behavior in the correct place and at the correct time (for example, when playing outside, when in danger, or when at a sporting event). An intervention program was designed that focused on positive goals to teach Adam:
>
> - When and where to scream
>
> - How to communicate his problems
>
> - How to manage his excitement
>
> - How to initiate social interactions with others

The intervention plan was detailed and contained many elements, including progressive muscle relaxation, a visual calendar so Adam would know when events would occur, and a communication component. The initial strategy was effective, and the results were enjoyed by Adam and his parents.

The garage was organized to ensure a safe place. When Adam screamed, his mother or father said, "Adam, you can scream in the garage. Let's go to the garage." Once in the garage, parent and child screamed together. After a few minutes of screaming, the parent said, "Okay, STOP!" and a few seconds later signaled, "Okay, SCREAM!" Both began to scream again. After repeating the sequence several times, the parent said, "We can scream one more time. Then it will be time to stop screaming and go inside to play with the _____."

Variations were added after two or three trips to the garage. For example, the parent would change the focus slightly and say:

- "Adam, you want to play. Let's go play."
- "When you want to play, you can touch my arm and say, 'Play.'"
- "You want to play. Do you want to scream or play ball?"
- "I know you want to play, but I'm busy. You can go to the garage and scream alone."

When the focus of the intervention changed in a positive way, Adam's parents were able to relax and have fun with him, knowing that they were teaching him some new skills.

Children with autism have not only the typical problems of most children, but also more severe problems in five specific situations: eating and mealtimes, sleeping and bedtimes, obtaining medical care, encounters with the law, and managing major transitions. The process for addressing these special problems is the same as for any problem.

Eating Problems

There are three basic types of eating problems among children with autism:

1. Refusing to eat, or eating very limited amounts or types of foods
2. Problems with chewing, swallowing, gagging, and regurgitating
3. Eating things that are not food (pica)

In some cases, an eating problem may be present at birth. In other situations, the problem may begin from some small incident and expand to life-threatening proportions.

Assess the Problem

Before developing any intervention, keep a record of all foods and nonfoods eaten each day. Include fruit juices, milk, vitamin supplements, and other consumables. Especially note the little between-meal bites and snacks. This information, along with a record of weight and growth, will help to determine the extent of any nutritional problem and may indicate possible links to sensory differences. Record answers to these questions:

1. How did the problem begin? Has the situation always been a problem, or did it begin suddenly, seemingly for no reason? Could it be related to a misperception, an unusual association, or a learned error? For example, did it begin:

   - During a bout with the flu or a bad cold? If the act of swallowing with a painfully sore throat was closely associated with the act of swallowing, it might trigger continuing refusals to eat even when the throat is no longer sore.

   - After seeing someone else vomit or gag?

   - After a coughing or choking episode received a quick and dramatic response?

   - After hearing news reports or a story about the dangers of certain foods? One young man totally quit eating any foods containing fats or cholesterol after hearing a news report of research.

2. Could the eating problem be related to physical problems? Allergies? Cravings related to metabolic or nutritional factors? Dental problems, sores, or injuries in the mouth? Neurological or motor problems related to chewing and swallowing? Indigestion, "nervous stomach," or blockages of some type?

   A medical evaluation is especially important for such problems as regurgitation, weight loss, frequent illnesses, or a drastic change in behavior.

3. Is the situation a sensory problem involving the texture, color, odor, or flavor of foods?

Pica can be related to some of the above issues, especially sensory factors and cravings from metabolic disorders. It has been associated with other factors as well. To assess problems related to pica, consider the following questions:

1. Did a quick and dramatic response follow attempts to eat objects from the floor? Most toddlers soon stop putting things into their mouths after several corrections; but in children with autism, the attention from corrections may reinforce the activity.

2. Is the situation a discrimination problem or a skill deficit? Does the individual understand the concept of *food* and *nonfood*? Does this orderly person know what to do with garbage and things found on the floor and ground?

3. Are nutritious and liked foods available on a schedule that matches the individual's changing needs? For example, during growth spurts, most children require more food, more frequently.

Effective intervention sometimes involves the collaboration of all team members, including an autism specialist, an occupational therapist, a pediatrician, and possibly a nutritionist. Medical problems must receive immediate attention; but medical treatment alone may not totally resolve a particular problem. Whatever the initial cause may have been, the problem may have developed into a strong habit or routine that will require a multifaceted intervention.

Organize and Structure

Organize and structuring the environment to match the needs identified during the assessment.

- The location of meals and snacks may need to be changed to one with fewer distractions.

- The eating schedule may need to be changed. Smaller, more frequent meals may be needed.

- Food or snack storage and availability may need to be adapted.
- Visual and verbal adaptations will be needed to support new instruction and clarify misperceptions.
- Trash containers may be needed in all settings.

Teach New Concepts, Rules, and Routines

One major goal of intervention is to avoid making problems worse. Review chapter 17 to ensure that the cues, prompts, and reinforcers are used correctly.

Incorporate some of the following strategies to teach appropriate eating and meal-time behavior and prevent future problems:

Ignore the behavior

Do not talk about the problem in the presence of the learner. Do not threaten, bribe, punish, or unnaturally reinforce eating. Avoid using food for reinforcement.

Unless specifically ordered by a doctor, do not force feed. Force feeding associates the activity of eating with punishment. Treat eating as a natural part of life, without expressing excitement or concern. Overreaction calls undue attention to the problem and inadvertently reinforces and increases inappropriate behavior. *This does not mean that the problem is ignored; it simply means that we do not give the problem power by highlighting it with excitement and attention.*

Teach eating routines and rules

- Schedule several short eating periods—perhaps 5 to 10 minutes every hour or two. Indicate these periods on the individual calendar, and follow eating time with pleasant, liked activities. Offering small amounts of food at frequent intervals may be helpful in treating gagging and regurgitation.
- Establish rules, such as: We always sit down to eat. We try new things.
- Vary the eating locations—a specific table, a picnic on a blanket, a party on the playground, . . .
- A mealtime rule related to staying at the table or eating area until everyone has finished eating can backfire and result in a long-term punishing routine for the whole family. A better strategy involves a rule, such as: We start the meal together. This type of flexible rule *is respectful to the learner's attention span and tolerance for waiting.* Begin at a successful level, and gradually expand the child's ability to stay at the table successfully.

   The importance of this type of rule varies from one family to another. Each family must set priorities. It may be more productive to calmly feed the individual early, and teach the learner what to do quietly while the rest of the family eats. This is particularly effective when there are other children in the family who need their share of attention and a calm family mealtime.

- Some young learners must be taught a very basic eating routine to prevent stuffing, gorging, choking, or gagging—problems that make eating a punishing experience. Teach the child to "Take a bite, chew, swallow; take a bite, . . ."; or, "Pick up your spoon, scoop some food, put it in your mouth, put your spoon down, chew, swallow."
- Consult with an occupational therapist if neurological problems make chewing and swallowing difficult.

Develop a routine for introducing new foods

- Systematically offer foods that are new or disliked, tolerated, and favorites. Initially, select new foods that are similar to highly liked foods. Gradually add foods that have slightly different textures, flavors, odors, or colors. *This is not a time for the learner to choose which foods to eat first. Rather, offer foods in an order that capitalizes on the reinforcing qualities of the liked foods.*

- Keep portions small. Offer one or two very small tastes of a new food, then three or four small bites of familiar foods. It is far better to start small and have success than to start big and have failures. If the learner's tolerance is misjudged, reduce demands. For example, isolate one or two tiny bites on the plate, and state a contingency. ("One bite, and then _____.")

- At the beginning of each mealtime, review a printed menu or list to highlight the foods available. This visual reference will teach food labels, provide a familiar structure for introducing new foods, and make it very clear that both new foods and familiar foods will be offered.

- Systematically make a new food more familiar. Introduce a new food for several days before offering a taste. Select a food with qualities similar to the most liked foods; then use some of the following activities:

—Involve the learner in buying the food.

—Show the new food, label it, and talk about it.

—Prepare a symbol for the food (a line drawing or word), and place it with other symbols of foods that will be added to the menu later.

—Involve the learner in preparing the food.

—Model tasting the food. Use exaggerated expressions of pleasure. Offer a taste, but do not insist that it be taken.

—Use stories with line drawings that show the learner eating a tiny bite of the new food followed by a favorite food.

—After a few days of these experiences, put the new food on the menu.

—Schedule food-of-the-week activities. This strategy allows the child to have enough experiences over several days with the new food to develop real familiarity and develop preferences.

Keep these activities as routine and as natural as possible to prevent learned errors. Use stories or cartoon strips to incorporate concepts. ("Mary likes applesauce a lot. I don't like applesauce very well, so I eat only a little bit. Here is a little applesauce. You might like it a lot, so you can ask for more.")

Provide clear and accurate information about food research and good nutrition

Clarify food misperceptions from television, comics, stories, and cartoons; and be sure the learner discriminates between fact and fantasy. End discussions of concerns by saying, "Well, the research is contradictory"; or, "It's only a pretend story. It didn't really happen."

Give access to nutritious snacks midway between meals

Adolescent boys in particular need a lot of food. In a few situations, free access to nutritious snacks resolved the problem of eating nonfood items.

Teach new discriminations between foods and nonfoods

Pica is a serious, potentially life-threatening problem. It must be dealt with directly with supervision to prevent the problem, and by teaching appropriate alternative behaviors. Isolating or restricting the learner to a sterile environment can trigger different and often more severe behavior problems.

Categorize different types of foods according to the major food groups. Emphasize that food is stored in cupboards and refrigerators, and litter is placed in the garbage. As soon as a toddler begins to pick up lint or dirt from the floor, teach the child to place it in the garbage.

Use visual references

Use stories, imagery, cartoon formats, T-charts, menus, and other visual references to support these lessons.

Eating problems can be dealt with only after determining the reasons for the problem. While each situation is unique, strategies involve some common themes. *Seek medical assistance promptly if a young child begins to lose weight or actually stops eating.*

Sleeping Problems

Families often find themselves caught in rigid nighttime routines that leave them exhausted. Too often, the child sleeps with the parents or a parent sleeps in the child's bed. This situation develops because it is the only way to get any sleep and to ensure the safety of a night-roaming child. These night routines are extremely hard to change, and without specific intervention they will be lifelong problems.

Lack of sleep is the parent's problem; those with autism seem to need very little sleep. Two intervention goals are needed: to teach these children to stay safely and quietly in their own rooms at night while others are asleep, and to avoid making problems worse by developing other unproductive routines.

Assess the Problem

Answer these questions:

1. Why does this learner not sleep or stay in the bedroom at night?

    • Is it loneliness? fear? restlessness? an inability to stay occupied? hunger?

    • Could it be a need to go to the bathroom at night? This is a particularly complicating factor. If a bathroom problem is not adequately addressed, it can lead to urinating in corners or smearing feces.

    • Is it a sensory problem—the sound of a furnace fan, the outside lights reflecting through moving tree branches or venetian blinds? Could it be the sound or feel of the child's own heartbeat or breathing in the silence? Is it the feel or odors of bedclothes or the bed?

    • Does the child *truly* understand what to do in the bedroom at night? Or has the child developed the concept that sleep occurs only in a bed in which others are sleeping?

    Together, parents and other members of the support team can assess and determine the reasons for the problem. Whenever possible, ask the learner, who may be able to provide the critical piece of information. Effective intervention certainly will involve organizing and structuring the environment to maintain safety and address sensory problems.

2. What safety factors must be addressed in the intervention plan?

    Those with autism have little sense of danger. When they are in panic or determined, they have an uncanny ability to open locks or climb to the top of cupboards and out windows. Wandering about the house without supervision can lead to other dangerous situations, such as turning on the stove or other appliances, leaving the house, or getting into matches, dangerous chemicals, or hazardous equipment. To prevent these kinds of problems, the child must learn to stay safely and happily in the bedroom.

Examine the child's bedroom to identify potentially dangerous situations that must be modified for safety—windows, plug-ins, light fixtures, mirrors, locks, and other elements. The types of necessary modifications will depend on the age, abilities, and interests of the individual.

Organize and Structure

1. Structure the environment for safety. The following modifications have helped other parents keep their child safe while they slept:

   - Replace glass windows with acrylic plastic. Place heavy screens or guards on the outside of windows. Install childproof locks on windows.

   - Place alarms and childproof locks on outside doors.

   - Install infrared alarms at the doorway to the child's bedroom and to the kitchen and other areas where there are dangerous materials.

   - Place a lock on the outside of the child's bedroom door. While this is an uncomfortable decision, it is necessary in some situations. Parents have developed a variety of ways to prevent panic and fear in their children while ensuring their safety. A Dutch door with the bottom half locked and the top open might be enough for some children.

> At four years of age, Jeff was very active and required only a few hours of sleep each night. As one part of their intervention plan, his parents decided they must lock his bedroom door. When he was in the room alone with the door shut, however, Jeff panicked, screamed, and threw himself at the door. Jeff's father installed a small opening in the original door. The opening was large enough to see out, but not to climb through. The parents hung a colorful and interesting picture on the wall opposite the opening to provide a view, and they kept the hall light on all night.
>
> Initially, Jeff's parents taught him to enjoy the room at various times of the day. First, they developed a mini-schedule similar to one he used at school, and they arranged a series of activities for him to do in the room. They played peek games through the opening, first with one parent in the room with him and the other parent on the outside of the door. Sometimes Jeff was outside with one parent and the other parent was inside. After several months, when all the components of the intervention plan were in place, Jeff learned to stay quietly in his room at night.

   - Install an electronic monitoring system such as those used to monitor babies.

   - Install recessed light fixtures with unbreakable covers. Remove plug-ins, or disconnect the power to those in the room. Install protective covers for heaters, heater fans, and thermostats.

   - Remove mirrors, glass from picture frames, and other breakable objects or potentially dangerous items.

2. Structure to address sensory factors.

Consult an occupational therapist for help in identifying and resolving sensory problems.

The following modifications have helped some learners sleep better and allowed their families to sleep as well:

- Consider a different type of bed. A water bed, hammock, bean-bag chair, or a mummy-type sleeping bag could provide the type of pressure or movement that calms and promotes sleep.

- Sleeping garments, pillows, and bed linens also may need modification. Sleeping garments need to be soft, without harsh nylon labels or seams. Lycra tops and leggings that fit smoothly and tightly may be soothing. Sleeping under heavy blankets or pads may be helpful.

- Eliminate fan and heater noises if at all possible. To mask other sounds, install some type of safe sound system, and play soothing music throughout the night. Tapes of nature sounds or white noise may be helpful.

- Use battery-operated night lights or soft, indirect lights to mask shadows or wavering lights from outside. Replace venetian blinds with attractive hardboard window covers inside the windows.

Teach New Skills

1. Teach a new nighttime routine.

   Develop the components of a nighttime routine, allowing transition from the family areas to the bedroom. Schedule a bath, story, and other relaxing activities. A few crackers or juice may be offered for a snack.

2. Teach the child to use a nighttime calendar and work system similar to one used in other settings. Plan activities that are pleasantly neutral, easy, and not overly stimulating. Vary the activities to prevent boredom. Schedule specific times to lie down and cover up, listen to a relaxation tape, and go to sleep. This structure will provide comfort.

3. Establish a system for communicating a need to use the bathroom.

4. Teach a method for determining the passing of time—how much longer it will be until morning. Provide a watch or clock, and mark the face to show where the little hand will be when it is time to get up.

Evaluate and Refine

Be alert for any new problems. The schedule and system need constant variations to prevent boredom and to match changing needs.

Medical Problems

Physical problems and medications are often associated with behavior problems. Some severe behavior problems are triggered by allergies, infections, and a variety of other physical conditions.

Assess Medical Care

It is important to seek and work with physicians and dentists who are either knowledgeable and experienced in providing care for those with autism, or who are open and willing to seek resources, work closely with families, and consult with support-team members. The willingness to consult with autism experts is particularly important in situations involving prescription drugs, because those with autism respond idiosyncratically to many drugs. For information about the physical/medical aspects of autism, see Gillberg 1990; Gillberg and Coleman 1992; Harty 1990; Handen 1993; and Tsai 1994.

Once doctors are selected, develop a plan so care can be more efficient and effective.

Figure 24.1. Some behavioral symptoms and underlying medical conditions

The following problems did not respond to behavior modification but were corrected when underlying medical conditions were treated

Sources: Personal conversations; Marsella and Marsella 1991

- Hitting or banging the head, nose, ears, and sinus area—Related to allergies, ear and sinus infections, migraine headaches; in one situation, to trigeminal neuralgia, a painful condition affecting the nerves of the face
- Touching teeth to windows and walls, jamming things into the mouth, tantrums while eating and swallowing food without chewing—Related to tooth abscess, cavities, gum injuries
- Breaking things that made noise (vacuum cleaner, toilet, kitchen mixer, stereo, . . .)—Related to impacted and abscessed wisdom teeth
- Tearing and wetting pants, slapping or hitting the lower abdomen—Related to bladder infections, premenstrual discomfort
- Sticking foot in the toilet bowl, reluctance or refusing to walk—Related to overly long toenails, blisters, boils on the ball of the foot
- A myriad of other aggressive, self-injurious, or unusual behaviors—Related to seizure disorders, digestive problems, or drug reactions

Organize and Structure

1. Prepare the medical professional and office staff with information about autism and about the particular patient. Provide medical records, and explain predictable problems and strategies for developing rapport and reducing anxiety.

   - Make an appointment to meet briefly with clinic staff members. Ask to attend a regular staff meeting.

   - Show photographs of this new patient who is not too different from other people.

   - Provide information about the confusion and anxiety related to sensory and communication problems common in autism. Provide specific information about the individual—how this particular patient communicates and expresses confusion and anxiety.

   - Enlist staff members' ideas for ways to make medical care easier for the learner. If possible, set up a series of field trips to familiarize the learner with staff personnel, the environment, and the anticipated procedures. Schedule visits at times when the patient load is light and when the learner is not stressed by illness.

   - Provide strategies to help doctors and staff members develop rapport and communicate effectively to the patient.

     —Talk calmly in a low voice.

     —Explain procedures with words, drawings, cue cards, simple checklists, and other visual references.

—Provide concrete ways to mark the amount of time to endure a procedure. ("This will be over by the time we count to 20"; or, "This will hurt only as long as it takes us to sing 'Twinkle, Twinkle, Little Star.'"

2. Keep medical records. A diagnosis depends as much on past medical history as on an examination (Dalldorf 1983). Parents need to develop notebooks of medical reports, immunizations, and laboratory tests. Forms for keeping these records can be obtained from most health departments and medical offices.

Also keep records of behavioral symptoms that indicated medical problems in the past. Record current symptoms, indicate the conditions that are generally present when those symptoms occur, and write details on how the current episode may be different from previous episodes.

- Is the face flushed? Do the eyes look dull? Are they focused, or do they dart about?

- Is the nose runny or stuffy? Have others been ill?

- Has medication changed? If so, did behavior change immediately or soon after?

- Does the episode seem to be related to diet?

- What has seemed to help or relieve the problem? (One child who had impacted teeth stopped screaming and banging her face after jamming a Popsicle to the back of her mouth.)

- When and how does an outburst begin? Does it occur at the same time every day (before meals, after meals, after strenuous exercise)?

- Does the problem start gradually, or is there a sudden change in behavior?

- Has it happened before? If so, when? Is the occurrence seasonal or cyclical?

- Is it related to sensory conditions (flickering lights, specific kinds of noise, . . .)?

- Can the behavior be interrupted, or does the learner seem locked into it?

- If the problem involves self-injury, what is the target—the eyes, nose, ears, stomach, mouth, other areas of the body?

Insist that all interpreters monitor and record behavior before and after changing medications.

A trusting relationship between the parents and medical staff can make access to good medical care more efficient.

Jeff had headaches and chronic ear infections. The behavioral symptom of these problems was banging on his forehead and ears. His tolerance for others was very low at these times, and he could lash out at those who talked too loud or came too close. It was difficult for Jeff to tolerate a visit to the doctor during these episodes. His mother and his doctor had worked together on these problems for some time and had developed the following plan:

- When it was obvious that Jeff had a headache, he was routinely given aspirin.

- His mother checked his temperature morning and night. The moment his fever began to climb, she called the doctor, who phoned a prescription to the pharmacy.

3. Prepare the learner. In reality, little can be done to change the structure of medical facilities, except to prepare adequately beforehand.

- Take familiar and favorite materials to use while waiting.

- Plan for relief from potential sensory discomfort. Ear plugs may relieve unusual or painful noises, and eye shields may protect from bright overhead lights.

- A soft and familiar gown or shirt may be more comfortable than harsh fabric or disposable gowns. A cotton flannel sheet may be less irritating than paper on the examination table.

4. Structure the trip so it ends with a pleasant activity—*not as a reward for good behavior, but simply as something pleasant to think about and anticipate.* If the pleasant activity is contingent on good behavior, the fear that it can be lost may raise stress. If the "reward" is lost in the first moments of the examination, there is no power—or hope—left. Disappointment at the loss of something pleasant can trigger serious problems.

Teach New Skills

1. Teach the concept of *hurt* or *pain.*

2. Modify the communication system to include terms related to medical care.

- Teach a way to express pain and to show the location of pain or discomfort. The word *hurt* paired with pointing can indicate *hurt here* or *hurt this.* Some young children may not be able to identify the source of pain because of differences in sensory processing.

- Provide a way to signal a need for relief. Most people can tell a dentist to stop a minute for relief, or tell a nurse or doctor when the end of endurance is near. Perhaps a hand signal or a cue card could be used to indicate, "Stop. I need a minute to rest." This communication strategy needs rehearsal before the appointment and with the doctor and nurse prior to the potentially stressful procedure. A measure of control and trust can reduce feelings of panic.

3. Teach a new routine for going to the doctor or dentist, using the guidelines in chapter 18, pages 263-265. Before developing the routine, assess the environment to identify sensory elements that need to be addressed. Consult with the nurse to ensure that critical procedures and equipment are correctly labeled and described. Use a social story or cognitive picture rehearsal for introducing and rehearsing the routine before making the first trips to the office or hospital. Rehearse in the natural setting before illness occurs.

Evaluate and Refine

Interventions, environments, and routines need continuous evaluation to identify possible problems. Address all issues related to developmental changes, new medical staff or procedures, new offices, and new fears and sensitivities.

Involvement with the Law

Naiveté, overcompliance, and an inability to effectively reason and make social judgments can lead to a variety of problems that involve the law. Some of the problems are a result of victimization—doing things others say to do. Other problems involve trespassing and inappropriate approaches to people. In some cases, stereotypic behavior is frightening to those who are uninformed about autism, and this situation can lead to police reports. Child protection agencies also may become involved if there are reports of suspected abuse.

Generally, police officers, social workers, and others who are charged with protecting people have little or no training to understand autism. Strategies for questioning or for gaining the trust and cooperation of those with autism are often contrary to the strategies and procedures for handling others.

Organize and Structure

Get to know the local police, and enlist the aid of an officer with some authority as an advocate. Become acquainted with neighbors and local business people. This is easier in small towns than in large cities, but it is particularly important if the learner tends to wander away or hang out with a group of peers. Learners also need to know the local officers so they do not panic when approached by police. Teach them that police can be trusted to help.

1. Set up opportunities for the learner to meet and develop rapport with some police officers, neighbors, and local business people. Provide these people with basic information about autism and specific information about this learner, so problems can be prevented or resolved more effectively. You may use or adapt information from *Guidelines for Interviewing and Communicating with Individuals Who Have Autism,* the reproducible instructional sheets on pages 385-386.

   Some community police departments have established trading-card programs. Officers carry trading cards, similar to sports trading cards, with photographs of themselves in uniform and brief biographical statements. The cards are distributed personally to local residents, especially to students and senior citizens; and students are encouraged to collect cards of the total force. This is a promising practice for making local residents more familiar with community helpers.

2. Ensure that learners carry personal information for emergencies and small business cards to indicate that they have autism. Include emergency phone numbers and brief information about a few basic strategies that are calming and will help others communicate with learners. A Med-Alert bracelet or necklace also is useful for this purpose. Some learners could carry personal trading cards to hand out when meeting new neighbors or community helpers.

Teach New Skills

Teach critical skills in the context of natural routines. Those with autism must learn to manage themselves in the community, and to use public transportation in order to access goods, services, and leisure activities.

Some of the critical concepts and skills to be more independent and avoid problems with the law include:

- Respect for boundaries and other people's property

  This involves teaching both concepts and rules. Visual references are essential components.

- Social skills regarding how to approach people and use appropriate public and private behavior

- Communication skills

  Learners must know how to provide information in an emergency; and how to ask for help from appropriate people.

Guidelines for Interviewing and Communicating with Individuals Who Have Autism

Autism is a neurological condition that causes sensory and communication problems. Some people with autism can talk, but have difficulty expressing ideas and answering questions. Others cannot talk at all, but can answer questions by pointing to pictures or words. Many can read, and some can write their answers.

These people may be overwhelmed and distracted by noise, lights, crowding, and being rushed. They are easily confused, highly anxious, and often in a state of near-panic. Individuals with autism are typically naive, honest, and compliant. They also are perfectionists. If they do not understand some part of a question or expectation, they likely will not respond at all. If they seem noncompliant, it is likely that they do not totally understand the expectations.

Other problems affect the reliability of information.

- People with autism need a longer time to process the words they hear and to generate a response.
- They understand many words very literally. For example, if told to sit down, they might drop to the floor exactly where they are instead of finding a chair.
- They memorize words quickly and may echo them back. Sometimes they answer questions with "tapes" of things they heard many years ago. Often they do not truly understand the full meaning of the words they echo. Their echoed tapes may or may not fit the present situation and can be misleading. Sometimes these tapes give the impression of being hallucinations or fantasy.
- Time is confusing to those with autism. They may not be able to report an accurate sequence of events. They tend to have excellent memory for details, but the information may be presented in the wrong context or sequence. They may tell of incidents that occurred years ago as if they had happened today.
- Leading questions and questions requiring reasoning or judgment will be very difficult for them to answer.
- Time pressures—being rushed or pushed to move or respond quickly—will increase their stress.

Interview Strategies

The following strategies can reduce stress and make an interview more productive.

1. Prior to the interview, find out:
   - How does this client communicate?
   - What might trigger a problem?
   - What might be calming?
2. Arrange to have a familiar, trusted person in sight. If appropriate, that person could serve as an interpreter. Otherwise, enlist the assistance of someone who knows autism well.
3. Conduct the interview in a calm, distraction-free room. Sit next to the person, rather than across a table or desk. Eye contact and face-to-face contact tends to increase confusion and stress.
4. Talk softly, and remain calm. Use concrete and literal language to ask a question. Leave out unnecessary words. Jokes or sarcasm will likely be confusing and misunderstood.
5. Take the time to establish trust and let the client know what to expect of this meeting. Make a list of the meeting agenda. Involve the client in keeping track of time by crossing off items as completed. Include some brief break periods in the schedule.

(continued)

6. Have writing materials available. Often, the client can think and process information better when the spoken words are illustrated visually.

   - As you talk, write out the key words or make line drawings to illustrate key people, objects, or sequences of events. Print labels on those drawings to compensate for questionable artistic ability.
   - Represent time blocks and sequences of events visually, using a cartoon-strip format with a square for each time block or event. Numbering each square or adding dates may be helpful. Verify the sequence by asking questions.
   - Write out or draw optional answers so the client can respond by pointing. Space the pictures or words far enough apart so it is easy to know which answer is being selected. While drawing, ask, "Is it _____, or _____, or _____? Point to the picture to show me what it is."
   - Prepare a 3"x5" index card with the words:

       YES   NO   I DON'T KNOW (or NONE OF THESE)

       Use this card for answering yes/no questions.
   - If none of the options seem satisfactory, give paper and pencil to the client and say, "Show me the way it was" or, "You fix it the right way."

7. Avoid questions that begin with *"Why?"; "What do you think?"* and *"How."* Be sure that *"when"* and *"where"* questions are very concrete and include the visual options described above.

8. Questions such as, "Did it happen this way?" are likely to receive the automatic response, "Yes." This is the time to have optional answers available ("I don't know" or "None of those").

9. Provide extra time—perhaps 30 seconds or so—before repeating a question. Try writing out the question and remaining quiet while the person thinks. Give the client the pencil and suggest writing the answer.

10. Relax, and understand that this interview may take a long time or may need to be completed in another session or, perhaps, two.

In summary, people with autism become very confused and may panic when:
- They do not understand exactly what to do
- They are rushed or pressed for a quick answer
- People use harsh voices and keep repeating the same questions
- People talk too loud, too fast, or use too many words
- People get too close, force them to have eye contact, or say, "Look at me"
- People grab and try to restrain them

People with autism are more cooperative and able to give better information when:
- They are relaxed and when expectations are understood
- Questions are concrete and clear
- Spoken words are paired with pictures or written words
- Optional answers are made visual; and "I don't know," "Something else," and other options are included
- They are asked to "Show me _____"
- Anatomically correct dolls are used *without leading questions*

- Concepts of rules and laws—what they mean, why they are important, and exactly how to obey a law

  The concept of punishment for disobeying laws must be taught in very literal ways, as opposed to scary and threatening ways. What is punishing for most people may be an exciting adventure for one with autism.

Evaluate and Refine

Instruction begins in early childhood, and continuous evaluation and refinements are necessary to match changing needs and skills.

Interviewing Individuals with Autism

When individuals with autism must provide information or interact with strangers, especially in unfamiliar settings, their anxiety is so great that they will not be able to function at optimum levels. Interviews or interactions under these stressful conditions generally are not productive and may result in inaccurate information, no information, or a severe behavior outburst. The guidelines presented on pages 385-386 will make these interactions less stressful and more productive for the individual with autism and for the professional or paraprofessional involved.

Managing Major Life Transitions

The need to prepare learners for transitions, changes, and new and unexpected events is emphasized throughout this book. It is equally important to prepare new staff members to provide appropriate support in the new situation. The information and strategies presented in this section can be applied to any type of change—a move to a new community, home, or school; changing employment; a stay in the hospital; a move from one classroom to another; or joining scouts, 4-H, church or recreational programs, and other community groups.

Assess and Plan

Use Form 6.1, *Checklist for Assessing Environmental Demands* (page 75) to identify the demands of the setting and the sensory factors that may have an impact on the learner's ability to function effectively. Set up meetings among interpreters who know the learner best and staff members and potential interpreters to plan together for the transition.

Prepare the Learner for the Transition

1. Arrange at least one visit to the new setting before the move. Locate the areas for eating and sleeping, the bathrooms, quiet time; and identify where to go for help. Introduce the critical support staff members and perhaps a peer who might be a mentor/friend.

   - Videotape or photograph this first visit. Review it often before the move.

   - Prepare a floor plan or map of the new area. Label the major spaces.

   - Draw pictures or write stories about the new situation. Compile a list of expectations.

   - Prepare a directory of the new staff members and interpreters. Include their photographs, and describe their jobs and roles. Highlight the primary interpreters.

   - Preview a typical schedule and rules.

- Discuss special privileges and opportunities that will be available in the new situation.

- Be sure the learner understands that familiar and favorite belongings also will be moved.

2. Develop a plan for saying good-byes and for keeping in touch with favorite support people after the move:

    - Prepare a calendar that clarifies the dates of visits or phone calls.

    - Videotape the old setting, or prepare a photo album for talking about and sharing memories of old friends and experiences. Leaving old friends is a true loss that must be dealt with as other grief experiences. Even in autism, where emotions and feelings are not as obvious or understandable, unresolved grief experiences can result in depression, anxiety, and problem behaviors.

Review the issues related to grief and loss (pages 348-349).

Teach New Skills

While some transitions happen too quickly to make much preparation, others can be anticipated months in advance. When detailed plans are possible, teach:

- New transportation routes and maps of the area
- Work organizations or systems that match those of the new setting
- Expectations and rules of the new setting
- The history and resources of a new community
- Background information about a vocation
- Strategies for adapting different teaching styles
- Strategies for maintaining contact with old friends
- Strategies for dealing with anxiety and accessing resources in the new setting

Prepare New Staff to Provide Appropriate Support

1. If those in the new setting have no experience with autism, provide information about the autism thinking style and strategies for interpreters. (See chapters 2 and 10; and the guidelines on pages 385-386.) This information will be helpful to support people as they develop rapport and establish relationships.

2. Arrange to attend a staff meeting to introduce the learner. If the learner cannot participate in the meeting, show photographs or pictures. If appropriate, have the learner share photographs or information about special interests and skills. Knowledge of special strengths and abilities as well as specific problems provides a balanced perspective for new interpreters.

    - See form 24.1 (pages 390-391) for an interview outline. Use this format for obtaining information from parents and previous interpreters, and for organizing information to share with new interpreters.

    - See form 24.2 (pages 392) for a quick-reference outline that can be used by new or substitute staff members to summarize basic and critical information. Keep this form in a confidential but easily accessed location.

3. Arrange for new support persons to visit the old setting to observe:

    - How the learner operates in a familiar environment
    - The types of adaptations and visual systems that are used
    - How others relate and provide support to the learner

One mother prepared a booklet to introduce her son to the staff at his new preschool. The booklet, titled "I Am Robby," featured his photograph and a number of sections that were written as if he were speaking:

My family and my life to now. I am Robby. I'm almost four years old. I live with my mom and dad, and I have no brothers or sisters. I have a dog named Ramsey.

(This section also included a brief description of Robby's typical activities and previous school programs and support services.)

How I communicate. At home, I have an object/photo schedule. At school, I understand the sequence of events in the same way. I understand the sign "No," and I am beginning to sign. I'm just now learning that I can get my needs met through my own actions and words. . . .

(This section included photographs of his communication systems and two or three schedules.)

This is how I tell you what I want or need. If I'm thirsty, I will hand you a glass. Please keep one handy. You can show me a container. If I want a drink, I may not react at all; but if I don't want it, I may push away the container.

(This section included a series of line drawings showing familiar signs.)

These are my favorite activities: . . .

These are my favorite foods: . . .

Sleep. I like to go to sleep with my sheepskin while listening to restful music.

Discipline. Please don't slap my hand or spank me. These actions may encourage me to solve problems by hitting.

I like to do my work system.

(This section included types of work and drawings to illustrate the structure.)

These are the ways I learn best: . . .

These are things I just can't abide! Large, noisy, or crowded places are confusing and make me very active and boisterous. I may make loud, monotone sounds to help drown out the noise.

These are things I can tolerate: If I have to remain seated, I calmly accept restraints such as a car seat, a highchair with tray, or a buckle strap in a grocery cart. For walks, I'll tolerate a wrist strap to keep me from running off.

Ways to calm me: . . .

When typical major life transitions are addressed in a systematic way, learners can make these changes with more confidence. With more confidence, they project increased competence. People who project competence are accepted and integrated into new groups and have more options for interesting lives.

Summary

While problems cannot be avoided, effective solutions can be developed through efforts to understand the impact of autism on the learner, understand the background of the problem, and understand the basic strategies. Interpreters who maintain sensitive, evaluative attitudes will be able to adapt and refine to prevent most severe problems.

Use this form to obtain important information from parents or previous staff. Expand and clarify answers with examples.

Student's name _____ **Date** _____

Interviewer _____ **Phone** _____

Interviewee _____ **Phone** _____

☐ Parent ☐ Guardian ☐ Other _____

1. Communication Abilities

Does the student have a special communication system? Describe. _____

_____

How does the student communicate wants and needs?

- Food _____
- Activity _____
- Break _____
- Assistance _____
- Feelings _____
- Need for bathroom _____
- Other _____

_____

Does the student misinterpret things other people say? Interpret things literally? Describe.

_____

List the student's pet phrases with specific meaning. _____

_____

How does stress affect the student's ability to communicate? _____

_____

What behavioral symptoms does this student show when stressed and anxious? List early warning signals.

_____

2. Problems

What problems can be expected? Describe.

- Sensory problems or sensitivities that trigger anxiety or efforts to escape? _____

_____

- Compulsive behaviors? _____

(continued)

- Problems with change and the unexpected? _____

- What activities, foods, events, or strategies are especially disliked? _____

- List triggers that accelerate stress or potential crises. _____

What situations are particularly upsetting? _____

_____

When the student is under stress, what is calming? _____

_____

What is the best way to give information or direction? _____

_____

Has the student ever required physical restraint or movement? If so, please give details about:

- Situations and environments _____

- Emergencies _____

How long did it take for the student to relax? _____

3. Establishing rapport and cooperation

What are the student's special interests and abilities? _____

What are special food and activity preferences? _____

Please give details of strategies that have been especially helpful. _____

Does the student use an individual calendar or work system? If so, describe. _____

What things are particularly comforting that should always be available? (These are the things that the individual should never have to work for or fear that they will be taken away.)

_____

_____

4. Other specific concerns and suggestions

_____

_____

_____

_____

_____

_____

Summary of basic and critical information for new or substitute staff members

Keep this form in a prominent but confidential location. Review periodically to keep information current.

Quick Reference for (name) _____

Date _____   **Birth date** _____   **Age** _____

Teacher _____

Parent _____   **Phone** _____

Communication

Primary system _____

Alternative system _____

How does the student let you know:

- Wants/Needs _____
- Object/Activity _____
- Assistance _____
- Need for break/Stop _____
- Feelings _____
  _____
- When confused/frustrated _____
- Sick _____
- Need for bathroom _____

How can you provide information?
(Check all that apply)

☐ Visual references ☐ Signs ☐ Writing

☐ Pictures ☐ Objects ☐ Gestures

Describe _____
_____
_____

Preferred Activities/Foods

Highly preferred/interesting (Include repetitive, stereo-typic, or compulsive interests)
_____
_____
_____

ALWAYS keep available _____
_____

Specific help needed (bathroom, eating, other)
_____
_____
_____

Sensitivities/Dislikes/Triggers

_____
_____
_____

Warning signals and emergency procedures
(medical and behavioral)
_____
_____
_____

Notes
_____
_____
_____
_____

Copyright © 1996 by Marvin M. Janzen and Janice E. Janzen, trustees of the Marvin M. and Janice E. Janzen Family Trust / All rights reserved.
Published by Therapy Skill Builders™, a division of The Psychological Corporation / 1-800-228-0752 / ISBN 0761643796

Assess and Plan Interventions for Severe Behavior Problems

The processes and strategies developed in the preceding chapters comprise functional, proactive approaches for preventing severe behavior problems. These strategies are summarized in figure 25.1.

All of these strategies are nonintrusive and nonaversive (Carr et al. 1990). They do not include the addition of painful or punishing consequences for behavior that occurs as a result of boredom, confusion, stress, medical problems, or lack of skill. Experience and a growing body of research supports this positive educational approach as a practical way to reduce the frequency and the intensity of problem behaviors while increasing competence and independence. "We must go beyond the use of single interventions and develop comprehensive, multicomponent plans of support that are responsive to the unique demands of each person and setting and are guided continually by functional assessment data" (Lucyshyn et al. 1995, 28).

In general, the only time an aversive procedure such as restraint might be considered is to prevent life-threatening self-injury (eye gouging, severe head banging, severe biting) or to prevent injury to another person. Even then, *restraint would be used only as an emergency procedure, to be followed immediately by a comprehensive functional assessment of the problem and the implementation of a positive, proactive approach to prevent recurrence.*

Just as in the population as a whole, those with autism will occasionally lose control. Learners with autism will continue to face challenges that reduce tolerance and intensify stress simply because of difficulties or discrepancies in their ability to:

- Understand the culture
- Understand and use the language
- Predict future events from past experiences
- Tolerate sensory stimuli
- Generate solutions to problems

Medical or physical problems also provide challenges that decrease tolerance and increase stress.

Interpreters must know how to react to the rapidly accelerating stress to prevent a crisis and possible injury. The information in this chapter extends the decision-making and management process described in chapter 10 by including assessment and intervention strategies for the most severe behavior problems. The chapter concludes with a case study to illustrate the assessment and intervention planning process. With this information, teachers and other support personnel can assess the situation and resolve many of the problems themselves.

There are times, however, when families and other interpreters are too close to the situation to be objective—too emotionally involved or worn out from their past efforts. Then it is important to call an outside consultant to provide a fresh, more objective perspective. This is particularly true if the behavior is life-threatening or dangerous to others. It is also important to engage an outside consultant if the problem has persisted and the individual is in danger of being moved to a more restrictive setting.

Figure 25.1. Proactive and reactive strategies

These functional, nonaversive strategies are incorporated into multicomponent intervention plans to maintain effective behavior and optimal independence.

See the table of contents for a page reference for each strategy listed below.

Proactive Strategies To prevent problems		Reactive Strategies In response to problems
Organize and Structure Provide support to match need	**Teach New Skills** To prevent recurring problems	Interpreter available and trained to:

• *Space*
  —Clarified visually
  —Free of overwhelming sensory elements
  —Materials clearly labeled and located
  —Uncluttered and safe
• *Activities*
  —Organized as routines
  —Meaningful
  —Varied/balanced
  —Clarified visually
  —At an appropriate level to prevent boredom or failure
• *Time*
  —Schedule balanced
  —Flexible
  —Clarified visually
• *Sensory conditions*
  —Noise/light/crowding
  —Movement/temperature
• *Information/expectations*
  —Complete and visually clear
• *Support system*
  —Interpreter(s) always available
  —Mentors and friends to model
  —Visual calendars and work systems available and used
• *Success/failure rate*
  —High success rate
• *Changes and new experiences*
  —Systematic preparation
  —Clarified visually
  —Adequate support
	• *Communication skills*
	• *Social skills*
	• *Relaxation/self-control*
	• *Self-management/self-monitoring*
	• *Functional routines and skills*
	• *Skills to manage change*
	• *Skills to accept new situations*
	• *Skills to use visual references*
	• *Instructional Strategies:*
	  —Cues, prompts, correction procedures, and reinforcement based on learning style
		• *Predict and prevent problems*
		  —Identify behavioral signs of problems
		  —Interpret cause and acknowledge need
		  —Provide assistance to prevent or resolve problems quickly
		• *Manage crises with safe, supportive, and nonaversive strategies*
		  —Model calm, quiet, reassuring behavior
		  —Give space; stay an arm's length away
		  —Minimize talking and auditory stimulation
		  —Reduce demands
		  —Calmly, clearly, simply, tell learner what to do
		  —Support any sign of relaxation and control
		  —Avoid demands for eye contact or explanations
		  —Avoid restraint procedures:
		    • Unless there is imminent and critical danger to self or others
		    • Unless trained in nonaversive procedures
		    • Unless help is available

Evaluate and refine in a timely manner, to address ever-changing needs		

Any consultant, psychologist, autism specialist, or behavior consultant involved in conducting a functional assessment of serious behavior problems must have a current understanding of the impact of autism on communication and behavior. The consultant also should have experience with positive, nonaversive strategies for developing an effective and productive intervention plan.

The Functional Assessment

Assessment Goals

A functional assessment or analysis of a severe behavior problem identifies the relationship of the behavior to environmental conditions and the needs of the learner. Potentially dangerous behaviors increase when the individual has problems without the skills or resources to solve them. Thus, in assessing problem behaviors, the goal is to:

1. Identify and understand the background of the problems

   - When, where, and why did the behavior occur?

   - Why does this person respond to problems in this specific way?

   - Why does the individual want to escape or avoid this situation?

   - Why does the behavior seem like noncompliance? Why aren't instructions followed?

   - What might the learner say in this situation, if he could?

   - Why must this person get attention in this way?

Saul, a large adolescent boy with severe autism who was unable to speak, was in serious trouble. He was about to be placed in an institution because he was so aggressive. Several teachers and teaching assistants had bruises from being hit. So far, there were no major injuries, but the program administrator was rightfully concerned. An ex-police officer was hired as an assistant to make sure that nobody was hurt, and a consultant was called in to assess the situation. During the assessment, it was reported that Saul would hit when upset, and sometimes he hit without warning and for no apparent reason. One situation occurred during an observation as Saul and his assistant were walking down the street. Saul seemed to be relaxed, but suddenly he hit his assistant hard in the chest with a backhand movement. Later, while discussing the situation, one hypothesis was put forward: Could it be possible that Saul was trying to initiate a social interaction or make a comment? It had been observed that his assistant never talked to him except to give directions. A trial intervention was instituted that included teaching Saul two basic communication strategies: to get attention by touching his assistant's arm, and to point to interesting things. The assistant was trained to attend to any of Saul's efforts to initiate an interaction, to quickly block and shape a potential hit into a touch, and to parallel talk. ("If you want to tell me something, you can touch my arm.") Saul also was given strategies for initiating other conversations about things they saw. These strategies eliminated the backhanded hitting and provided strong justification for teaching appropriate communication skills to relieve stress in other situations.

2. Identify the components of an effective intervention plan. What needs to be modified or taught that will help the individual deal with problems more efficiently and effectively?

- What specific skills does this person need to learn in order to prevent or solve problems independently?

- What will parents and other interpreters need to do differently to prevent or decrease the frequency and intensity of the problem or to manage the problem more effectively?

- What environmental conditions need modifications to reduce stress and clarify information?

Assessment Process

The functional assessment of a severe behavior problem depends on three major activities:

1. A detailed record review

2. Interviews with those most knowledgeable about the situation

   In many cases, an interview with the learner also might provide information to pinpoint the exact cause of the problem.

3. Observations of the learner in various situations where the problem does and does not occur

To achieve the assessment goals, consider the following elements and questions:

- Space

  Are there sensory elements that may overwhelm and reduce tolerance or trigger problems (noise, light, crowding, disorganization, clutter, odors, and others)?

- Activities

  Are activities meaningful? Balanced between easy/liked, difficult/disliked, active/inactive? Varied to prevent boredom? Are they age-appropriate? Is there a calendar to clarify the schedule of activities?

- Success rate and expectations

  Is there too much failure, too little challenge, or too little support? Are expectations clear? Does the learner always know what to do?

- Peers

  Do peers tease, undermine, or set up problems? Do they model inappropriate behavior, or are they good models, relating positively? How could they be used to support effective behavior?

- Staff members

  Do staff members identify and deal effectively with early signals of problems? Do they use calm voices and have good rapport with the learner? Are interactions positive or negative?

- Social interactions

  Do interpreters and friends periodically initiate friendly interactions that have no demands or require specific correct responses? Are social opportunities scheduled regularly? What does the learner have to do to get a social interaction? Are interactions generally positive or negative? Does the learner have enough quiet time alone?

- Physical factors

  Could allergies, infections, medications, or dental or medical problems be a contributing factor?

- Worries and compulsions

  Is the learner concerned or worried about conditions in the world (famines, wars, environmental disasters), community, or the home? One young man was so concerned about his father's drug problem that he was unable to maintain focus on the demands of school.

Assessment Tools

There are many different forms and formats for conducting a functional analysis of severe behavior problems (O'Neill et al. 1990; G. Groden et al. 1993; Meyer and Evans 1989). The following tools and procedures are specifically designed to elicit the detailed information required for understanding the relationship of the problem behavior to environmental conditions.

To understand the background of the problem and the environmental conditions that trigger or maintain the problem

- *Functional Analysis: Problem Review Worksheet* (form 25.1, pages 400-402)

  This worksheet is designed to obtain a history of the behavior and determine which of the many factors known to be associated with severe behavior problems might be implicated in this specific situation. The interview format has been used to help staff think through the problem to identify possible reasons and potential solutions and to identify the need for further evaluation.

- *Checklist for Assessing Environmental Demands* (form 6.1, page 75)

  This checklist provides a systematic process for understanding the sensory and instructional demands of the environment that affect tolerance and stress levels or that could trigger severe behavior problems.

- *What Happened (Flow Chart)* (form 6.2, page 76)

  This form is adapted from a procedure developed at the Judevine Center. It provides a format for recording the frequency and duration of behaviors within the natural context. At the same time, it allows for recording unidentified skills and strengths. Some of the most valuable information is collected by an observer who becomes open to the gestalt of a setting and situation and records the learner's responses to the flow of simultaneously occurring sensory, instructional, and social events. This flow of events is recorded without evaluation, as quickly as possible. Following the observation, the material is reviewed to decipher abbreviations, fill in missing information, highlight important relationships, and pull out objective frequency and duration data.

- *Preference Survey* (form 6.6, page 92)

  Many behavior problems occur when a learner must engage in long sequences of activities that are nonpreferred, difficult, or stressful. Therefore, it is necessary to understand not only the preferred or reinforcing activities, but to understand which are disliked or only tolerated. This survey, also adapted from one used at the Judevine Center, does more than simply identify reinforcers; it also identifies the activities, people, or other elements of the environment that are disliked or only tolerated. The information from this survey provides the foundation for developing effective schedules and contingencies to increase tolerance and flexibility. Information elicited from this

For a more complete discussion of forms 6.1, 6.2, 6.3, 6.6, and 6.7, see pages 72-74.

form is used to evaluate the data obtained from the *Assessment of Daily Life Activities* (form 6.7). For completed samples of the Preference Survey, see page 172, and Case Study, page 423.

- *Assessment of Daily Life Activities* (form 6.7, page 93)

  This form provides a format for analyzing the reinforcing or punishing qualities of the daily schedule and highlights the elements of activities that may trigger a problem.

To understand how the behavior looks and the message behind the behavior

- *Functional Communication Assessment: Informant Interview* (form 6.3, pages 77-86)

  This form is discussed more completely on page 72. Assessment of functional communication is one of the most important tools for understanding behavior problems—the behaviors that signal emotions, needs, and ideas. Not only is this tool helpful for assessing the communicative behavior of those who are not verbal, but *it is also invaluable for assessing the breakdown of communication resulting from stress in those who are verbal and higher-functioning.*

- *Incident Report* (form 25.2, pages 403-404)
- *Brief Incident Report* (form 25.3, page 405)

  These forms are used to track incidents of severe behavior. They are designed to serve two functions:

  1. To satisfy the legal requirement for an incident report following a behavioral outburst with potential liability

  2. To assess the environmental conditions that triggered the problem and to identify the communicative intent of the behavior

  When one of these forms is completed in detail following an incidence, it provides the data for understanding the situation from the perspective of the individual with autism.

To understand physical conditions that may be associated with behavior problems

Signs of physical problems, cyclic behavior, and sudden changes of behavior (including problems related to sleeping, eating, or self-abuse) will be highlighted in the incidence reports, observations, and interview reports.

In summary, there are many different ways to structure a functional assessment. The procedures described above elicit the detailed information that is so important for developing intervention plans to prevent future problems and manage those that may occur.

Summarize the Data

A functional assessment yields an abundance of detailed information to be organized and interpreted from the perspective of the individual with autism. The *Functional Analysis Summary* (form 25.4, page 406) is an effective tool for organizing the data to show the relationships of the environmental conditions, the triggers, behavior signals, and the communicative function of the behavior. After seeing the data in this visual format, interpreters can quickly grasp the problem and begin to generate logical strategies and modifications for the intervention plan. For a completed sample of this form, see Case Study, page 424.

Intervention Planning

Develop the Proactive Plan

The summary information leads naturally to a positive plan for supporting effective learning and behavior. The *Intervention Planning Worksheet* (form 25.5, page 407) is based on the Profile of Stress (see figure 10.1, page 138). This worksheet provides a key for matching intervention efforts to the learner's fluctuating needs. For a completed sample of the *Intervention Planning Worksheet*, see Case Study, page 425.

Refer to the following sections for intervention strategies: Stage 1: chapter 10, pages 137-151; Stage 2: pages 408-410; Stage 3: page 411; Stage 4: chapters 17-23.

This planning worksheet illustrates that the learner's behavior and the interpreter's goal and strategies are different at each of the four stages. For example, the goal at Stage 1 is to identify and solve problems to defuse anxiety and move directly to Stage 3, thus avoiding a crisis. *Stage 2 is not a teachable moment; it is the time to implement the crisis management plan described below. At this level of stress, the learner is unable to think and hear clearly or to use good communication skills.* Stage 3 is a vulnerable period when stress could easily re-escalate. The most productive period is during Stage 4, when the demands of the environment match the competence and tolerances of the learner.

The things that happen during this stage of equilibrium will influence the frequency, duration, and intensity of future problems. The interpreter's role at Stage 4 is to teach new skills, expand flexibility, and continually evaluate to identify problems and refine elements of the environment.

Functional Analysis: Problem Review Worksheet (Interview Format)

Adapted with permission from Oregon Regional Autism Services

Student: _____ Date: _____

Informant: _____ Interviewer: _____

1. Description of the Social/Behavior Problem	Data/Description	Need More Information
What actions are involved in the behavior?		
What are the warning signs or behaviors that lead up to the behavior of concern?		
How long is the behavioral episode?		
How intense is it?		
How often does it occur?		
How long has the behavior been a problem?		
What is the intervention history?		
Other:		

2. Student Characteristics	Description	Need More Information
Are there any physiological symptoms closely associated with the behavior? (Does student show signs of allergies, headaches, seizures, fever, other conditions?)		
Is student on medication?		
What related elements seem to go along with this behavior (such as signs of pain, discomfort, changes in mood)?		
Does student have an effective communication system?		
Does student have a way to say, "My head aches"; "I'm tired"; "I'm scared"; "That surprised me"; "I don't like that"; "I like _____"; "I want _____"?		
What are student's learning strengths and weaknesses?		
What are student's likes and dislikes?		
What activities are very hard for this student?		
What activities are very easy for this student?		
What is student's response time? Is there a processing delay?		
What are student's personality traits (active/inactive, introvert/extrovert, fearful/trusting, flexible/rigid, anxious and tense, etc.)?		
Other:		

(continued)

	Description/Comments	Possible Factor Y/N/?
3. Antecedents—The context—instructional or environmental conditions that precede (set off or trigger) the behavior of concern		
A. Environmental setting:		
Where does the behavior occur?		
Where doesn't the behavior occur?		
What are the environmental conditions in the setting where it occurs? (Too hot or cold, crowded, cluttered, noises, lighting, other factors)		
Have there been changes in the environment just prior to or simultaneous with the behavior?		
Does the student have a way to say, "I'm hot"; "He's too close to me"; "It's too noisy"; etc.?		
B. Time factors:		
Does the behavior occur in a cyclical pattern? (Good day, bad day)		
Time of day when it occurs?		
How long has the student been engaged in the task?		
Does the student know the schedule and what is to happen next?		
Does the student know or have a way to ask about how long until time to stop or take a break?		
Is the student prepared for endings and beginnings? ("It's almost time to clean up. Then it will be time for _____.")		
C. Others in the environment:		
Number of adults (staff/student ratio):		
Do adults talk to the student and give information?		
Are the behavioral expectations, directions, and consequences clear?		
Do adults recognize and acknowledge the student's nonverbal and verbal attempts to communicate?		
Do they talk about the student's problems where the student can hear?		
What is the nature of their interactions? (positive, reinforcing, negative, challenging, consistent, etc.)		
Number of students in the environment?		
Are peers good models?		
Do other peers tease or intimidate student?		
Are peers close to, bumping, or touching student?		
Does student have a way to greet others? Express humor? Seek attention and interaction? Protect self? Say, "Bug off"; "I like you"?		
Does the problem behavior often occur in the presence of any particular adult or student? Describe.		

(continued)

	Description/Comments	Possible Factor Y/N/?
3. Antecedents (continued)		
D. Task/Activity factors:		
Does the behavior usually occur while student is engaged in any specific task or activity?		
Is the task too hard? Is student making many errors?		
Is the correction procedure clear?		
Are the consequences for making errors punishing?		
Is the task too easy?		
Does the task have meaning for the student?		
Has the student done the task or used the same materials for too long in the same way? (Is the student bored?)		
Is there a clear task or activity?		
Is it a liked or disliked activity?		
How long has the student been engaged in the task (or in free time)?		
What was the preceding task? Was it a liked or disliked activity?		
Were there sudden changes in the activity?		
What activity was scheduled to follow? Was it a liked or disliked activity?		
Does the behavior occur during transition periods?		
Are there clear directions during transitions?		
Does the student have a way to say, "I need help; "I don't understand"; "I need a break"; "This is too hard"; "But I've done this a million times"?		
Does the student have any choices or options for activities?		
4. Consequences—What did people do immediately after the behavior of concern?		
What occurs immediately after the behavior of concern:		
• Teacher interaction/attention		
• Peer attention		
• Excitement and turmoil in room		
• Acquisition of wants (food, objects, activities)		
• Removal of instructional or activity demands		
• People move away		
• Isolation/time alone		
• Sensory stimulation		
• Other		
Are the consequences intermittent?		
Does the student appear to be more upset as a result of the consequence?		
Does the student appear to enjoy the consequence?		

Incident Report

Adapted with permission from Oregon Regional Autism Services

Note: The information in this report is confidential. It will satisfy liability concerns and will provide data for developing effective and ethical intervention plans.

Student: _____ **Date:** _____

School: _____ **Teacher:** _____

1. **Activity:** _____

   Location: _____ Date/Day of week: _____

   Time incident began: _____ Ended: _____

   Staff members present when incident occurred:

   Name: _____ Address: _____

   Name: _____ Address: _____

   Others (nonstaff members) present when incident occurred:

   Name: _____ Address: _____

   Name: _____ Address: _____

2. **Describe what was happening just before the behavior occurred.**
   Describe the environment—noise, crowding, and other conditions.

   What was the student supposed to be doing?

   What was the student doing?

   What were others doing?

(continued)

3. **Describe in detail what the student did and what happened during the incident.**

   Was anyone called to assist? ☐ No ☐ Yes If yes:

   Name: _____ Address: _____

   Was anyone injured? ☐ No ☐ Yes If yes:

   Name: _____ Address: _____

   Describe:

4. **Describe what happened to the student immediately after the incident. Include any consequences.**

   If student was injured, describe injury and any treatment (what and by whom).

5. **Additional information for team evaluation and planning**
   (To be completed by the staff person most directly involved in the incident)

   Why do you think the incident occurred—why the person behaved in this way? (From the perspective of the student, could something have been misunderstood or confusing? If so, describe.)

   What recommendations do you have for preventing a recurrence or for managing the problem if it occurs again?

   Additional comments (Use extra sheets if necessary)

6. **Reported by:**

   Name: _____

   Address: _____ Phone: _____

Brief Incident Report

Adapted with permission from Oregon Regional Autism Services

Student: _____**Date:** _____**Time began:** _____**Ended:** _____

What happened?

What happened just before?

What happened right after?

Student's point of view?

Reported by: _____Phone:_____

Address: _____

Functional Analysis Summary

Adapted with permission from Oregon Regional Autism Services

Student: _____   Date: _____

Environmental Events that Affect Tolerance (Allergies, weather, worries, sensory conditions)	Antecedents or Triggers	Escalating Chains of Behavior (From earliest signals of stress to most intense behavior)	Communicative Function (The problem from the learner's perspective)

Notes:

Intervention Planning Worksheet

Adapted with permission from Oregon Regional Autism Services

Student: _____   Date: _____

Stage 1. Escalation	**Stage 2.** Crisis level	**Stage 3.** De-escalation	**Stage 4.** Equilibrium
Intervention goal: Defuse stress, return to equilibrium	**Intervention goal:** Prevent escalation, keep people safe, support deescalation	**Intervention goal:** Support self-control, reengage	**Intervention goal:** Evaluate/refine, organize/structure and teach skills
Behavior signals:	**Behavior signals:**	**Behavior signals:**	**Behavior signals:**
Strategies:	**Strategies:**	**Strategies:**	**Strategies:**
			Evaluate and refine:
			Organize and structure:
			Skills to teach, strengthen, or generalize:
Avoid:	**Avoid:**	**Avoid:**	**Avoid:**
			Plan staff/family training and support:

Crisis Management

The strategies and principles listed in this section are general guidelines for managing an emergency situation. If a learner has shown the potential to become seriously out of control in a way that could cause injury to self or others, interpreters must be trained in safe and effective nonaversive physical management strategies. A specific crisis management plan must be developed, based on a comprehensive functional assessment.

The crisis plan is developed by the total support team, including the parents and a program administrator or case manager. The team may need additional information from consultants. An occupational therapist could assess sensory problems and make recommendations for strategies that might be calming. An autism specialist could focus attention on the effects of the autism learning style (misperceptions and lack of skills) in different situations. The school counselor, a resource teacher, behavior specialist, or psychologist also could provide insights and balance.

The crisis plan will include:

Review the Profile of Stress and the four stages of stress (figure 10.1, page 138).

1. The behavioral signals that precede and follow a loss of control

   The signals exhibited during stress stages 1, 2, and 3 are identified during the functional assessment.

2. A plan to prevent injury in all settings, to maintain a safe environment and keep others safe

   Team members review these plans in a trouble-shooting "What if _____?" format to ensure that all situations are covered. General guidelines include:

   • A description of what to do at stages 1 and 3 to defuse anxiety, prevent crisis, and permit the learner to regain self-control

   • A description of the things to do at Stage 2 to prevent injury and help the learner regain control

   • A description of the things to avoid doing at all stages that have the potential for triggering a crisis

3. A training plan for interpreters and others in the environment

   • Interpreters need training and opportunities to practice with feedback.

   • Siblings, students, roommates, co-workers, and others in the environment need training to keep themselves safe. Schedule crisis drills and training sessions. Tell siblings and peers that the learner sometimes gets confused and anxious, and when that happens they can help by being very quiet and not watching. Train them to carry out the crisis drill quickly when they are given a signal.

4. A recordkeeping and monitoring plan to review progress, identify potential problems, and modify elements of the plan to match the learner's changing need

5. A staff support plan

A crisis plan is a situational plan, not a teaching plan.

Guidelines for Managing a Crisis

Generally, the danger of a crisis increases as anxiety and panic increase. Therefore, the goals of any crisis management plan are, first, to defuse anxiety and panic; and second, to keep people safe.

Anxiety and panic increase when:

- Others panic and show fear or excitement

  Model calm, quiet, reassuring behavior. Relax your shoulders, your face, your eyes, and take a deep breath. Keep your arms and hands relaxed and in view but ready to use if needed to block or deflect a thrown object or a hit.

- Personal space is invaded

  Step back with one foot and stay at least an arm's length away. Do not move in closer. This supportive stance honors personal space, reduces the overwhelming feeling of being blocked into a corner, and offers an escape route. This position also offers the interpreter protection from a hit or a kick. Be alert, but move slowly and in a relaxed manner. Periodically break the direct face-to-face gaze.

- People talk too much or too loud

  Minimize talking, keep your voice calm, and use an even rhythm. Match the volume of your voice to the distance (that is, talk softly if close to the learner, raise your voice if you are at a distance). *Identify a single interpreter to manage the crisis and do the talking. Others in the room will attend to other matters unless signaled to assist. Those assisting do not talk.*

- Pushed to give eye contact or to verbalize

  Reduce demands during periods of elevated stress. Do not say, "Look at me"; eye contact may only confuse the learner. Do not force a choice or say, "Tell me what is wrong"; talking is stressful even under calm conditions. Insistence on a verbal response is likely to trigger increased anxiety and complicate the situation. Repeated demands are strongly associated with an increase in severe behavior problems.

- Threatened with the loss of a powerful reinforcer

  Clearly, calmly, simply, tell the learner what to do. Provide visual supports. *Threats are unproductive; they simply give additional reason for stress. A threat does not clarify the situation or provide clear instruction. The learner still has no solution—only more problems.*

- Physically restrained or engaged in a physical struggle

  Do not attempt physical restraint or engage in a physical struggle unless there is *imminent* physical danger to the learner or to others. *Without proper training, do not attempt to restrain a person alone unless the person is considerably smaller. Caution: A smaller learner, although easier to restrain, is also easier to injure.*

  If restraining a young learner, do it from the back to avoid panic from the overwhelming stimulation of physical closeness. Try to get the child in a sitting position in front of you, so you both are sitting down. (It may be a long time before the child can be released.) Hold the child firmly and securely enough so you will not be hurt and so it cannot become a struggle, but gently enough so the child will not be hurt. Some young children are soothed by gentle rocking motions or soft singing. As the child relaxes, periodically say something soothing. ("Good. You are relaxing"; "It will be okay, I will help you.")

  See page 411 for strategies to support re-engagement.

  The child is ready to be released when you can feel the child's total relaxation. Release will reinforce the relaxed attitude. When the child has been totally relaxed for five or so minutes, state a contingency to set a direction for reengagement.

Do not ask, "Are you ready to get up?" or "Are you relaxed?" The response generally will be, "Yes." If released before totally relaxed, the child's tension and stress are likely to accelerate and require another struggle and further restraint.

Proper restraint is not a punishing consequence; it is a safety measure. Do it quietly, calmly, with a matter-of-fact, supportive attitude.

With older learners, plan ahead. If there is potential for injury to self or others, arrange for backup assistance—the principal or a neighbor who can come quickly to assist if needed.

Staff members and parents need hands-on training from certified trainers in nonaversive, physical management procedures. Contact state or local Developmental Disabilities offices for references. Procedures may need some modifications to accommodate the autism learning style.

Guidelines for Defusing Anxiety

Five additional strategies are helpful to defuse anxiety and the potential for a crisis:

Review Reflective Listening, pages 220-221.)

1. Listen to what the learner says. It may provide a clue to the need or problem.

2. Use reflective listening strategies. Acknowledge the feelings and the cause of the problem if it can be identified. Clarify the situation simply or, in some way, calmly show support. ("We can work it out"; "I'll help you to _____"; "Let's write it down.")

3. Tell the learner something specific to do. Cue the learner's individualized relaxation routine, or tell the person to do something very simple that is incompatible with hitting or kicking. ("Put your hands in your pockets," or "Sit down," or "Hold this pillow.") If the person does this simple thing, give reinforcement for listening and responding.

   Do not say, "Don't hit" or "Stop yelling." In many cases, these statements are said in a harsh voice, which is another trigger for increased anxiety. *The learner does not know what else to do at that moment. Tell the learner what to do.*

4. Reinforce the learner's every effort to self-control. The primary goals are to calm down and to regain control. Verbally reinforce calming down and self-control. If the learner puts his hands in his pockets as requested, say, "Good! You can control yourself." When a learner who had been screaming stops for breath, say, "Good! You took a deep breath. You can calm yourself. Let's take another deep breath," as you model deep breathing. Use a calm, even, quiet voice, and time the reinforcement to the calming—not the out-of-control behavior.

5. Introduce a surprise. In some *rare moments* of crisis when it seems the learner may be caught in a perseverative cycle of behavior, it may help to do something dramatic to startle or break that cycle.

> One young man was rocking back and forth, waving his arms about in a threatening manner and shouting, "Don't hit! Don't hit!" over and over again. When the recommended strategies failed to break this repetitive cycle, his teacher suddenly turned away and said cheerfully, "I'm leaving." She said to the other students, "Let's go to recess quickly." They all got up and left the room. *(They were in a safe place, and supervision was available: An assistant was working quietly in one corner of the room.)* Later, the assistant reported that the learner looked a little stunned, then moved quietly to sit at his desk with his head down on his arms. When the class returned, he was relaxed and ready to join in the normal activities.

Guidelines for Reengagement

The time following a major crisis is a highly vulnerable period. Generally the learner is exhausted, so a new crisis could be triggered easily. The following strategies can facilitate movement through the Stage 3 level of stress and a return to the normal routine that occurs during the stage of equilibrium.

1. Independence comes from learning to calm oneself independently. The interpreter sets the stage and remains calm, quiet, and supportive.

   Move away and keep busy with writing or some quiet activity while monitoring the situation with peripheral vision. This strategy gives the learner space to relax, without the stress of being watched intently. It also provides time for you to relax and make notes for reporting the incident.

2. Avoid nagging about the ineffective behavior or what should have occurred. Also avoid asking questions ("Why did you ____?" or "What upset you?") and asking for apologies. *This is not a time to teach cause/effect or problem solving.* In fact, any of those strategies may lead to reescalation. Address these issues during the stage of equilibrium.

3. Do not attempt to reengage until the learner is totally relaxed.

4. Structure the transition back to natural activity.

   - Use cue cards or other visual references.

   - Set the timer and say, "In five minutes, we will check your schedule to see what is next."

   - Say, "I'll help you finish your job, and then you can have a break"; or, "First get a drink, and then check your calendar."

5. Avoid having the learner return to a difficult or disliked task. Provide support until the learner has completed one or two familiar and relatively easy tasks successfully.

Most crises can be defused with these strategies. The key is to model a calm and quiet demeanor, and acknowledge the feelings and the problems. *Avoid overreacting; overreactions often accelerate the problem.*

In general, behavioral crises are not premeditated or manipulated to punish you directly. The learner is confused and anxious and doesn't know what else to do to solve the problem or to relieve anxiety. *However, a learner whose needs continue to be disregarded may learn that severe aggression or self-injury is the only way to get relief from demands and overwhelming stress.*

Recordkeeping Plan

Most school and community programs have liability insurance that requires reports of any serious behavioral outbursts that had potential for injury. Also, the support team needs not only the basic descriptions of these incidents, but objective and subjective information to use in modifying an intervention plan to prevent recurring problems. The team needs information to:

1. Understand the reason or reasons for the behavior

2. Identify the elements of the environment that need to be restructured or refined

3. Identify skill deficits—those language, social, communication, and self-control skills to solve problems more effectively

4. Identify potential medical problems

Staff needs training and time to include the appropriate information in the incident forms. Use form 25.2 (pages 403-404) when the incident caused (or might have caused) an injury. Use form 25.3 (page 405) when there was no physical struggle.

Summary data

Include names, dates, environment, and times (the time the episode started and the time it ended).

What was happening just before the problem occurred?

What was the learner doing? Were there demands, questions, corrections? What were others doing? What were the sensory conditions (noise, crowding, rushing)? Was the activity structured or unstructured, liked/easy or disliked/difficult? Was the activity just beginning, or had it been going on for some time? Were there any warnings—agitation, making noises, changes in breathing pattern, or others?

What was happening during the incident?

What did the learner do, with what, and to whom? How was the situation handled? Were additional support people called? This statement clearly but briefly describes the actual behaviors so someone who was not there will be able to know and understand what occurred. (Words such as *noncompliant, attention-getting, angry,* and *deliberately* are not helpful.)

What happened immediately after the incident?

What did the learner do? (Smile, scream, run, . . .) Was the learner exhausted after the incident? Did the learner sleep? If so, for how long? What did interpreters and peers do? Indicate the intensity of the reactions. Were there consequences? Describe any property damage or injury and treatment.

Why do you think the behavior occurred?

From the learner's perspective, what might have been confusing or misunderstood, or what might have triggered the problem? Was the learner trying to initiate a social interaction or trying to request, protest, or reject something? Describe what you might have done or said if you had been in the learner's position.

Interpreter Support Plan

High-anxiety situations are always exhausting and emotionally draining for everyone involved. While most of the attention and concern is focused on the vulnerable person, the learner, the interpreter who defuses or manages the crisis also needs support.

At Home, Alone

Each parent must develop a routine to follow after any highly stressful period. The routine includes plans for:

1. A safe, comfortable place to settle the child with things to keep the child occupied for a short period of time. It is helpful for parents and teachers to work together to develop a plan that has common elements in both the home and the school setting (for example, a visual calendar or checklist, and relaxation routines).

2. Engagement in a low-key, relaxing activity—a coffee break in front of the TV, a call to a supportive friend, screaming into a pillow, a shower, or a structured relaxation or visualization routine.

In School, Vocational, or Group-Home Setting

The interpreter who is actively involved in the incident needs a break—a brief time alone or an opportunity to debrief and talk about the situation *to a member of the learner's support team*. This break might include time to complete the incident report while the details are still fresh.

Caution: This highly personal and confidential information must be handled discreetly. Do not share the dramatic details with others over coffee in the staff room. While it is reinforcing for others to sympathize and comment about the interpreter's courage, patience, and skill displayed while handling this situation, it does nothing for the learner's reputation. Sharing the information indiscriminately is not only unethical, but it will make it more difficult to recruit mentors and advocates if staff members have heard only fearful stories.

Summary

Behavior problems are a symptom of an environment that does not match the needs, the skills, or the tolerance levels of a learner. When the problem is understood from the context of autism, it is possible to both predict and clarify information to prevent most problems. It is impossible to prevent all problems; but this understanding and these strategies make it possible to effectively manage a crisis.

The following case study summarizes not only this chapter, but also the processes and strategies presented throughout this book.

Tony - A Case Study

Summary Report

Functional Assessment, Consultation, and Training

Student: Tony

Date: April 15

Functional Assessment of Problem Behavior

1. Interview Tony's support team (parents, foster parents, vocational staff, and local autism consultant) to:

   - Establish baseline and identify concerns (form 25.1)

   - Identify preferences (See attached Preference Survey, page 423)

   - Identify elements of Tony's environments that contribute to problems (form 6.7)

   - Identify Tony's current functional communication abilities (form 6.3)

2. Direct observation:

   - At home and vocational site

   - During 1:1 testing: Selected subtests of the Adolescent/Adult Psychoeducational Profile (AAPEP)

3. Review incident reports

4. Provide six hours of consultation and training to the support team:

   - Explain the impact of autism on communication and behavior

   - Provide strategies for identifying stress and attempts to communicate

   - Provide strategies for identifying and interpreting the cause of problems

   - Match interventions to stress level; teaching use of visual references

   - Provide strategies for reviewing and fine-tuning the intervention plan

Background

Tony is a tall, slender, 20-year-old male with severe autism who is in transition from school to a vocational site. In addition to severe communication and social problems, he has coordination and other motor problems and migraine headaches. He continues to have back pain from surgery to repair a curvature of the spine.

Although Tony has been considered to be severely retarded, there is evidence that he can read with meaning (at least to some degree). He rarely initiates interactions with others or persists in getting the attention of a communication partner. On occasion, however, he has been heard to make meaningful comments in a very soft voice, to no one in particular. Most of the time, his messages are not heard and thus are not acknowledged. Occasionally he uses a Wolf (an electronic communication system), but in general he has no consistent system for communicating in various settings.

Tony was referred for a functional assessment and assistance because he is in danger of losing his vocational placement due to behavior and safety concerns. Tony lives with a foster family and visits frequently with his parents; all were involved in the assessment and training.

The following concerns were identified by the support team.

Behaviors of concern:

- Self-abuse: Slapping face and head, biting hand, throwing himself on floor

- Aggression: Hitting others, hitting or striking at objects

- Emotional responses: Laughing or giggling unrelated to situation, crying, extreme mood shifts, and rapid acceleration of problem behavior

Transition concerns:

- People: Responses to his current foster mother's absences and visits from parents and former foster family

- Safety: Fire drills (in home and vocational site), staff injury from hitting

- Changes: Activity schedules, routines, travel to and from home and work site

Communication concerns:

- How to communicate effectively with Tony

- How to develop a system for Tony to communicate with others

Assessment Summary

I. Learning Style—Strengths and Deficits

General activities and abilities:

- Tony sorts by size, shape, color, food, animals, and other basic categories.

- He can follow a familiar routine in a familiar place with a familiar person. He can perform a few routines (such as assembly tasks) independently. Tony continues to need assistance with many personal care routines.

- He has difficulty following familiar routines with a new person, even when the setting is familiar.

- He has difficulty with unexpected schedule changes.

- Tony follows visual directions when given one or two clear demonstrations.

Disorganization/Distractions:

- Tony is confused by clutter in the immediate physical environment.

- He is confused when materials needed for a task are disorganized or cluttered.

- He is overwhelmed when several people talk at once, even when those conversations are soft, a distance away, and unrelated to him.

- Tony has a tendency to "hyperscan" the environment. He is constantly watching and alert to where people are and what they are doing.

- He is easily distracted by unexpected movement of people within the environment.

Programming note: Tony worked and responded best when he could see the entire area about him. When he could look up briefly to watch the surrounding movements, he was able to return to the task in front of him without prompts or reminders. When people moved or activities changed outside his visual range, he became anxious, resisted tasks, and began to slap his face and bite his hand. When placed with his back to the activity, he turned around when he heard or saw movement from the corner of his eye, and then was not able to reorient to the task behind him. *Arrange his work space so he can see what people are doing.*

Cause/Effect:

When Tony did not understand what was expected or what was going to happen (when to begin or end a task and what would happen next), he became agitated and anxious. Verbal information was not enough to clarify and reduce his anxiety.

Visual references paired with verbal explanations reduced his anxiety, and transitions were easier.

Tony quickly learned new task routines when:

- The materials were clearly organized to work from left to right

- A simple visual model (reference) clarified the sequence of steps, and the end of the task and the finished product were clearly indicated by a "Finished" box or container.

When the sequence of the task was clear, Tony quickly learned to anticipate the activity and persisted in attempts to complete the task and correct errors.

Programming note: Tony is a perfectionist. When the task was clear, he recognized and corrected his own mistakes. However, when *verbal* demands, prompts, or reinforcement were provided in this process, he slapped his face, rocked, made loud noises, and bit his wrist. This behavior escalated with each *verbal* request or warning. *Prompt with quiet gestures; use line drawings and photographs with written labels or short phrases.*

Understanding the language and communication of others:

- Tony displayed a significant processing delay (the time needed to process information he heard and generate a response).

- He was more confused by lengthy or complex verbal directions when anything (person, task, materials, schedule, or location) was unfamiliar and he was expected to generate a verbal or motor response.

- When Tony was anxious or confused, repeated verbal demands or prompts given by even one familiar person caused escalating behavior problems. Escalation was more rapid when two or more people tried to help by giving more verbal directions or diversions.

- He was able to understand and follow clear, one- or two-step familiar commands or directions within familiar situations.

- Pointing without talking was helpful to direct or refocus his attention.

- He was able to follow clear visual instructions and models (line drawings, pictures, demonstrations).

II. Summary of Functional Communication

Expression of wants and needs:

- Tony scans the environment for a familiar person or preferred item. If he can locate the item, he simply gets it without interacting with another person.

- If the item cannot be located, he takes the wrist of a nearby adult and attempts to guide that person toward the item.

- If something is not where he expects it to be, he gets upset, begins to rock, slap his face, and bite his wrist.

Expression of protest or refusal (activity, object/food; something not allowed, taken away, or changed):

- Tony softly verbalizes, "No." Often, this is not heard by others and is rarely repeated.

- He may walk away from the person or activity.

- He may push away an object.

- If a staff member insists on compliance, speaks loudly, or rushes him, he hits himself, bites his hand, or hits and tries to push the person away.

Request for attention or affection:

- Tony approaches the preferred person, "nuzzles" the person's cheek or hair, and whispers softly. He may sit next to the preferred person and lean into the person's shoulder or side.

Expression of dislike/confusion:

- Tony vocalizes and slaps the side of his face. If the person near him pauses, waits, and clarifies quietly with a gesture or visual cue, often

Tony will stop after two or more slaps. However, if the person says, "No slapping" and repeats the demand or tries to hurry him to compliance, the behavior escalates.

Expression of extreme confusion:

- Tony slaps his face, vocalizes loudly, talks to himself (often using echoed phrases), paces, and may remove his glasses. At these times, if approached too rapidly or given verbal corrections or verbal demands to stop, he may strike out or drop to the floor.

Expression of pain or fear:

- He says, "Ow," "Uh-oh," screams, yells, or cries. When in pain (with backache or headache), he winces and presses his sinuses or back, or lies down.

- When afraid, he becomes tense, stares, yells loudly, and may stomp his feet.

- When startled, he may quickly hit the person nearest him (a reflexive response).

III. Summary of Conditions that Affect Behavior

See attached Functional Analysis Summary (page 424).

Tony's problem behaviors occur in a fairly predictable pattern or chain that begins with an appropriate verbalization, then escalates rapidly if the situation is not clarified or his need is not addressed.

Environmental events that reduce tolerance:

- Physical problems: Headaches, backaches
- Sensory problems: Noise, too many people talking, too much movement, disorganization, and clutter
- Changes and transitions: Routines, places, people, schedules, expectations
- Lack of clarity: Missing information that causes confusion

Situations that trigger problem behavior (antecedents):

- Demands:

  —When unexpected

  —To change from a highly preferred to a disliked activity/task

  —From a new person, whether the task is familiar or unfamiliar

  —Rapid, repeated demands or corrections from a familiar or unfamiliar person

  —Repeated demands and verbal assistance from more than one person at the same time

  —To return to or do more of an activity that he thought was finished

- Changes and transitions when tolerance is low
- Being rushed
- Being stopped in the middle of a routine, especially when required to start it over
- Physical restraint, especially if two or more people keep talking

- Being told, "No hitting" or, "It's not okay to hit"
- Time out (unless taken quietly by a familiar person before stress intensifies)

Escalating chain of behavior, and staff role at each stage:

Stages correspond with those illustrated on the Profile of Stress; see attached Intervention Planning Worksheet (page 425).

Stage 1a:

Tony's signals:

- Verbalizes softly: "Uh-oh," "No," "Knock it off"
- Pauses or stops moving
- Flushes
- Touches head or face where he slaps
- Places hands together, then stretches arms over his head

Staff/interpreter role:

Identify the signal, clarify the problem, and help Tony solve the problem

Stage 1b - 2c:

Tony's signals:

- Verbalizes in louder voice: "Oh-oh-oh"; echoes, "Knock it off, Tony"; or, "Don't hit me"
- Holds head
- Hits or slaps head or face two or three times, then pauses
- Puts hand to mouth as if to bite
- Cries, screams

Staff/interpreter role:

Model calm; reduce stimulation and demands; cue or assist to a safe, quiet space

Stage 2d:

- Bites hand
- Hits nearby person
- Butts head into other person or wall
- Lies on floor, hitting head on floor
- Pulls off clothes (only rarely)

Staff/interpreter role:

Keep people safe, model calm, quietly reinforce efforts to become calm

IV. Critical Goals and Strategies

Autism is a neurological disorder that affects how a person makes sense of and responds to information—the things they hear, see, smell, taste, and feel. The following critical goals are lifelong concerns for all with autism. Focusing on these goals will help family and staff members develop the support systems required to reduce Tony's anxiety and confusion and enable him to function more effectively at home, work, and in the community. As these strategies are implemented, behavior problems will decrease.

Goal 1: To increase flexibility and tolerance for change; to develop willingness to try new things

1. Inflexibility, rigidity, and fear are a result of too little information. A person must have all the information possible in order to predict a particular situation and be able to plan ahead. Because Tony understands some of what he hears, people tend to think that he understands everything they say. This is not true. He needs information about events in a visual format so he can see "the whole thing." Then he can refer to the visual aid and know what, when, and where things will occur. Tony needs:

    *   Daily, weekly, and monthly calendars, and brief mini-calendars to clarify expectations for specific activities and changes

    *   Cue cards and checklists with line drawings and printed words. Use these visual aids while quietly giving him verbal information—the answers to questions he cannot ask *(who, what, when, where, why, how, how much, how long, what's next).*

2. Plan Tony's routines and schedules so that small changes occur systematically and regularly. He can learn to tolerate these changes because they will be supported by visual information. The systems for giving information will remain familiar; therefore, he will learn that change is okay.

    *   Develop Tony's daily schedule of activities to capitalize on the reinforcing qualities of preferred activities. See the attached Preference Survey (page 423).

        (Note: There was not enough training time to show how to implement this strategy. We suggest that additional training be scheduled.)

Goal 2: To be independent of constant verbal and physical directions and prompts

1. Provide visual references, as discussed above, to clarify the expectations and to cue the steps of an activity or routine. Introduce new information with these visual references. Demonstrate new skills. Prompt by pointing to the appropriate location on the visual reference or the materials. Avoid verbal prompts and repeated verbal directions. Avoid hand-over-hand and full physical assistance.

2. Organize the environment so it is logical and uncluttered. Arrange Tony's work space so he can scan the entire room without turning away from his work.

    *   Label material and storage areas. Show Tony where things are and how to return things to their appropriate spaces.

    *   Organize his work space so he can work systematically from left to right.

    *   Clarify the beginnings and ends of tasks, activities, and events.

As Tony learns to make sense of his environment and he is given enough information, he will be able to function more independently.

Goal 3: To communicate intentionally and effectively

We recommend that a speech-language pathologist and/or communication specialist be engaged to provide training and support for staff members and family as they implement these recommendations. A more comprehensive assessment of Tony's language and communication needs also may be required.

1. The Wolf communication device is familiar, and Tony uses it periodically when it is present. Expand the system with new vocabulary and make it available to him at all times. He will need more instruction to use the system more independently. Those who support Tony will need specific training in how to communicate with him by using the Wolf.

2. Tony must learn how to find a communication partner and persist in getting that person's attention before he delivers a message.

3. Tony needs backup communication systems for times when he wants to talk about something that hasn't been programmed into the Wolf, when the Wolf is unavailable, or when he is too stressed to remember how to communicate. Teach him to use "break cards" and signals of distress that mean "Help me quickly."

4. Provide sports magazines and photo albums of Tony's favorite people, activities, and places so he can visit and share with friends at work or at home. He needs to know when he will have opportunities to socialize and visit with friends. Specify these times on his daily schedule.

5. Because Tony can read with meaning (at least to some degree), facilitated communication is an option that needs to be explored.

Goal 4: Learn relaxation and self-control strategies

Your local autism specialist has access to the following resources for accomplishing this most important goal:

> Cautela, J. R., and J. Groden. *Relaxation: A Comprehensive Manual for Adults, Children, and Children with Special Needs.* Champaign, IL: Research Press, 1978.
>
> Groden, J., J. R. Cautela, and G. Groden. *Breaking the Barriers I: Relaxation Techniques for People with Special Needs.* Videotape. Champaign, IL.: Research Press, 1989.
>
> _____. *Breaking the Barriers II: Imagery Procedures for People with Special Needs.* Videotape. Champaign, IL.: Research Press, 1991.

V. Other Recommendations

1. *Share information with all staff members.* Duplicate the attached Functional Analysis Summary and the Intervention Planning Worksheet (pages 424-425). Share them with all members of Tony's support team. Use these forms as guides for matching interventions with specific needs, to prevent the frequency, intensity, and duration of behavioral crises.

   Train all staff members in safe, nonaversive, physical management procedures and sequences for carrying out the crisis management plan.

2. *Identify one person to be in charge.* Tony must always know who is in charge—the person who is available to clarify information and provide comfort and support. To avoid inflexible dependence on a single person, systematically change the one in charge. Each morning, Tony needs to meet the one in charge. If that person is changed during the day, inform

Tony immediately. Perhaps the one in charge could wear a distinctive name tag or pin so Tony could quickly scan the area and locate support. If a second person is needed to assist during a crisis, *that person should not talk or give distracting information.*

3. *Plan the visits with Tony's former foster family.* Determine whether Tony wants and needs the visits or if only his former family wants the visit. If the visits are for Tony, they should be carefully scheduled and planned. Some of the following strategies also can make visits with his natural family more successful.

   - Plan for the visits to occur at his current foster home or a familiar nearby location.

   - Arrange for Tony's current foster mother to be present to follow through with familiar support.

   - Schedule relatively brief visits—perhaps no more than 30 minutes.

   - Prepare Tony before the visit. Write the event on his daily schedule.

   - Provide a mini-calendar so Tony will know what he will do during the visit—perhaps share photo albums, go for a walk, go to a restaurant for a snack, or do other familiar, low-key activities. He also needs to know what he will do after they leave.

   If the visits are primarily for the comfort of Tony's former foster parents, perhaps they could meet more frequently alone with Tony's natural mother, instead of with Tony, to share memories and catch up on his current life.

4. Support Tony's team. Tony's autism will not be cured. His stability will depend on the sensitivity and skill of those who support him. While the above strategies and skills will decrease problems and increase Tony's abilities, at times Tony will be overwhelmed with too much stimulation, confusion, and changes. New problems will arise. His team needs to be very well trained, and they will need to meet frequently to solve problems and coordinate information and strategies. They also need to meet frequently to support one other. It is helpful if the team members can consult periodically with a specialist in autism who has broad experience with others like Tony. Such a consultant brings perspective and new ideas and can help the team members to assess, clarify, and solve problems before they reach critical levels. We suggest that Mark continue to work with Tony's team.

In summary, Tony is a great person and we have enjoyed this opportunity to get to know him. The members of his team are to be commended for their commitment. If there are any questions about this report, feel free to contact us.

Autism Consultants: _____

Date: _____

Adapted with permission from *Judevine® Training System* (Blackwell 1978)

Student: Tony   **Date:** April 15

LIKES What people, objects, or activities are liked a lot or selected during free time?	TOLERATES What is done when asked, but never done if not asked?	DISLIKES What people, objects, or activities are resisted, avoided or rejected?

<u>People</u>
• Parents and foster parents
• Peers: Nick and Dawn
• Vocational trainers, especially Bonnie
 	
<u>Activities</u>
• Playing chase games
• Walking and eating at the mall
• Going for walks
• Listening to music
• Watching others
• Watching all sports, especially football
• Attending sports events with family, friend
• Looking at photo albums
• Looking at sports magazines
• Eating (lunch breaks; all meals)
• Watching TV
  Game shows
  Cartoons
  Star Trek
  Sports shows
 	
<u>Sensory</u>
• Touching soft blankets
• Touching women's hair
• Baths/showers
 	
<u>Foods</u>
• Pizza
• Grilled-cheese sandwiches
• Hamburgers
• Pancakes
• Finger foods
• Popcorn
• Spaghetti
	<u>People</u>
	• New people at a distance
	• New or nonpreferred people on his own terms
	
	<u>Activities</u>
	• Brushing teeth
	• Washing hair
	• Putting things away
	• Assistance with dressing
	• Familiar work (once, but not repeated later)
	
	<u>Sensory</u>
	• Walking on bumpy ground
	
	<u>Foods</u>
	• Sweets
		<u>People</u>
		• People "getting in his face"
		• New people moving in too soon or too close
		
		<u>Activities</u>
		• Mother leaving after visit
		• Losing control of himself
		• Too many requests or demands
		• Waiting
		• Events that last longer than expected; lunch delayed
		• New jobs, activities, routines
		
		<u>Transitions</u>
		• Bus between work and home
		• Between work/lunch/work
		• Ending interactions with favorite people before he is ready
		
		<u>Sensory</u>
		• Loud sounds, loud voices
		• Overlapping conversations
		• Wool next to his skin

Functional Analysis Summary

Adapted with permission from Oregon Regional Autism Services

Student: Tony   **Date:** April 15

Environmental Events that Affect Tolerance (Allergies, weather, worries, sensory conditions)	Antecedents or Triggers	Escalating Chains of Behavior (From earliest signals of stress to most intense behavior)	Communicative Function (The problem from the learner's perspective)

Tolerance decreased by:
• Migraine headaches
• Back pain from surgery
• Fatigue
• Working too long in one place
• Working too long at a single task
• Boredom
• Too many people talking at once
• Movement and noise of transitions
• Background noises that are out of view
• Changes—new routines, places, people, or expectations
• Disorganization and clutter of space and materials
	• Demands:
	  —When unexpected
	  —Made in a loud voice
	  —To change from preferred to disliked activity
	  —From an unfamiliar person
	  —Rapid, repeated demands or corrections
	  —Repeated demands from more than one person at the same time
	  —To return to or do more of a task that he thought was finished
	• An unexpected change
	• Being startled or afraid
	• Being rushed
	• Being stopped in the middle of a routine, then required to start over
	• Physical restraint by two or more people (especially if all are talking)
	• When told, "No hitting," or "It's not okay to hit"
	• Time out (unless taken quietly by a familiar person before stress intensifies)
		Stage 1a:
		• Soft verbalizations: "Uh-oh," "No," "Knock it off"
		• Pauses/stops moving/watches
		• Flushes
		• Touches head or face where he slaps
		• Hands together, then stretches arms over his head
		
		Stage 1b – 2c:
		• Louder verbalizations: "Oh-oh-oh"; echoes, "Knock it off, Tony," "Don't hit me"
		• Holds his head
		• Hits or slaps his head two or three times, then pauses
		• Puts hand to mouth as if to bite
		• Cries or screams
		
		Stage 2d:
		• Bites hand
		• Hits nearby person
		• Butts head into other person or wall
		• Lies on floor, hitting head on floor
		• Pulls off clothes (only rarely)
			• I am confused.
			• Don't rush me.
			• Be quiet, I can't think.
			• Where did it go? I can't find it.
			• My (head, back) hurt.
			• I need a break.
			• I don't want to (or, I want to stop).

Notes:
- Tony worked best when he could see what others in the area were doing.
- He has significant information-processing delay.
- He is a perfectionist. If expectations were clear, he recognized and corrected his own mistakes. If prompted verbally during this process, he slapped his face and bit his hand (escalated with each prompt or reprimand).
- Tony responded well to quiet gestural or pointing prompts and line drawings or photos with written labels or short phrases.

Intervention Planning Worksheet

Adapted with permission from Oregon Regional Autism Services

Student: Tony   **Date:** April 15

Stage 1. Escalation	Stage 2. Crisis level	Stage 3. De-escalation	Stage 4. Equilibrium
Intervention goal: Defuse stress, return to equilibrium	**Intervention goal:** Prevent escalation, keep people safe, support deescalation	**Intervention goal:** Support self-control, reengage	**Intervention goal:** Evaluate/refine, organize/structure and teach skills

Stage 1. Escalation	Stage 2. Crisis level	Stage 3. De-escalation	Stage 4. Equilibrium

Behavior signals:
• Noises/Words: Squeals, "Uh-uh-uh," "Knock it off"
• Pauses/Stops moving
• Touches head where he slaps
• Stretches arms over head
• Flushes
• Rapid breathing/hyperventilation
• Puts hand to mouth as if to bite
Strategies:
Talk softly; acknowledge feelings/problem.
If "stuck" or looking confused:
• Say, "Are you 'stuck'?"; "Do you need help?"; "Let me show you"; "Start here"; then model or point to visual references.
• Or: Cue to check schedule.
• Or: Quickly draw and talk simply to clarify.
If faced with change or unexpected event:
• Say, "That surprised (or worries) you," and pause; then visually clarify.
• Or: Refer to calendar and modify to clarify.
If bored, tired, sick:
• Say, "You look _____. (bored, tired, sick).
  Do you need a break?"
• Clarify contingency ("Do this much, then break") with a quick drawing.
If Tony wants something he can't have:
• Say, "I know you want _____, but that belongs to _____."
• Or: "You can have/do it on _____"; then mark the calendar.
• Or: "I'm sorry. I know you want to go to the Cotton Bowl, but _____"; then offer diversion.
If overloaded with too much noise/confusion:
• Say, "It's too noisy. Do you need a break?"; then provide a break.
If you do not understand the problem:
• Say, "Can you show me in your book?"
• Or: "I'm sorry. I don't understand"; then offer diversion.
If acceleration continues:
• Cue to go to safe area before he loses control.
Avoid:
• **Do not** ignore or try to divert until attempt is made to understand and solve the problem.
• **Do not** demand, push, or rush Tony beyond his tolerance level.
	Behavior signals:
	• "Oh-oh-oh" as he slaps head
	• Echoes, "Knock it off, Tony" or "Don't hit me"
	• Holds head
	• Hits head two or three times, then pauses
	• Bites hand
	• Cries/screams
	• Hits nearby person
	• Butts head into wall or other person
	• Lies on floor, hitting head on floor
	• Pulls off clothes (only rarely)
	Note: These behaviors will intensify if stress and pressure continue.
	Strategies:
	Model calm, and:
	Stop talking; or use a few calm, quiet words to tell Tony what to do:
	• "Put your hands in your pockets."
	• "Relax, take a deep breath."
	Model soft, slow, deep breathing.
	Move back to avoid crowding him, turn slightly sideways, keep your hands relaxed.
	If he is not in a safe place:
	• Cue others to move away.
	  —or,
	• With one other, well-trained person, physically assist him to a safe place. Do this in a calm and nonthreatening manner. If at all possible, say, "We will help you to a safe place" before starting to move him.
	If he stops screaming or takes a deep breath:
	• Softly say, "Good! You took a deep breath. You can calm yourself!"
	Avoid:
	• Do not make demands.
	• Do not push, rush, confuse, or crowd him with two or three people giving directions.
	• Do not say, "It's not okay to _____" or, "Stop hitting (or, biting)." Instead, give positive directions. Tell him what to do.
	Remember:
	This is not a teaching time or a time to threaten or bribe. It is a time:
	• To keep people safe
	• To reduce demands, be calm and supportive, and talk only a little
		Behavior signals:
		Calming, watchful
		Strategies:
		Calmly and periodically, reinforce Tony's efforts to regain control and relax. Give him hope.
		• "We'll solve the problem"; "You will learn to _____."
		Give cue or contingency so he will know how to resume normal activity.
		• "First a drink, then do _____ then it will be time for a break"; "When the timer rings, we will check your schedule."
		• As you talk, prepare a cue card to highlight these sequences.
		If returning to a task that triggered the problem:
		• Reduce the demands or ensure that the end of the task is visually clear.
		• Provide assistance to help Tony focus and make progress.
		Watch carefully for signs of increasing stress.
		• Use contingency and help end job quickly to take break before he loses control.
		Avoid:
		• Do not rush him to return to the task before he is totally relaxed.
		• Do not lecture, blame, or push for an apology.
		• Do not punish. Punishment will not help him know what to do the next time he has a problem.
		Also to do:
		While he is relaxing:
		• Write a flow log of his calming behavior. (Use "What Happened?" Flow Chart, form 6.2.)
		• Make notes; later, record the incident.
		• Relax yourself.
			Behavior signals:
			Stable, calm
			Strategies:
			Evaluate and refine:
			• The crisis management plan
			• The schedule:
			  Activities appropriate? Balanced? Flexible to match fluctuating tolerance?
			• Visual systems (communication, work systems, calendar)
			• Staff support plan
			Organize and structure:
			• The work area with visuals:
			  —To clarify the space, boundaries, and materials
			  —To reduce clutter
			  —To answer what, when, where, how, how long, and what's next
			  —To arrange so the entire room is in view
			• A quiet break area
			Skills to teach, strengthen, or generalize:
			• Communication skills to persist in getting attention
			• System to express:
			  —"I don't understand"
			  —"Don't rush me"
			  —"It's too noisy; I can't think"
			  —"Where did it go? I can't find it"
			  —"My head (back) hurts"
			  —"I need a break"
			  —"I don't want to"
			  —"I want to stop"
			• To recognize stressful feelings; then ask for and take a break
			  —Relaxation and self-control strategies
			• To use visual work systems
			Remember: Problem behaviors are a symptom of: misunderstandings, lack of ability to communicate needs, boredom, lack of skills, too much noise or crowding, head or back pain, or panic reactions. They are not intentional or deliberate efforts to hurt or humiliate.

In Conclusion

While those with autism present major challenges, they also provide major rewards for anyone who takes the opportunity to understand their unique perspective. The ability to understand and deal effectively with the challenges forces us to be creative and flexible. Those who live with and support the person with autism will never stop learning!

Our interventions will be successful only if we understand the world, or the situation, from the perspective of the individual with autism. We must thank David Eastham and other adults with autism who have so eloquently described their own experiences and given us insight into the nature of autism, their struggles, their fears, and their dreams.

UNDERSTAND

I WANT PEOPLE TO UNDERSTAND
I KNOW ITS HARD TO DO
I THINK THEY CAN IF THEY TRY
UNDERSTAND WON'T YOU?

UNDERSTANDING IS SO HARD
I LONG TO SEE IT REAL
I JUST HOPE, REALLY HOPE,
ITS NOT A LOST IDEAL

—David Eastham
In *UNDERSTAND: Fifty Memowriter Poems*

Appendixes

Family Stories

These stories were written by parents to give others a glimpse into life with autism. They illustrate some of the problems, the frustrations, and the rewards of having a child with autism.

Dean's Story
—*Written by his mother, Elaine Piper-Vardas*

The day had begun sunny and warm. Dean was dressed in his blue pajamas. His hair was long and brown and curled softly around his face. Dean was particularly relaxed and calm as he looked at me from across the room. This morning would mark our final moments as mother and son in a home we had shared together since his birth. Soon Dean's new parents would arrive. His clothes and a few personal possessions were packed into their large, old station wagon. The image of them driving away is burned into my memory forever.

Dean was born March 26, 1970. A year later, he was diagnosed as mentally retarded. A few years later, Dean's father and I divorced. The diagnosis of autism came many years later, when Dean was 9. After many months and long hours of counseling and training, the stark reality set in. As a single working mom, I could not provide the stable home my son needed. The continued turnover of baby sitters and the inability to find trained, reliable day-care providers made matters worse. Few people wanted to take care of this child with his bizarre behaviors. I felt alone and scared. As the years passed, Dean's behavior worsened from constant screaming into head-banging on the floor and self-abuse. Now I felt afraid. What would his future bring? Who would take care of him as he grew into adulthood? How would I be able to protect him? Who would serve as his advocate in matters of health, education, and family? I realized that I could not care for Dean alone and would need outside help.

I immersed myself into (developmental disabilities) organizations and worked to establish (a 24-hour special needs care facility for developmentally disabled children). I explained to Sister Marian Kathleen the difficulty Dean was having. She told me about a foster family she knew. Within two weeks of that conversation, Dean was off to a new life with (his new) family.

Dean was 5 years old. The year was 1975. It was the year we both put our emotional heads through walls. Dean did not understand this change in his life. For the next three months, I was not allowed to see Dean. It was a long and tortured time for us. For me, it was a time of agonizing self-punishment. I wanted Dean to have a family—a full-time mother and father with a stable home to support his needs. But I also wanted to be a mother. Then, when I was allowed to visit my son, he ignored me. I remember well that first visit and the sense of devastating rejection. While driving home after that first visit, I cried so hard that I ran into another car. For years, I felt guilt and self-doubt, believing that I had somehow failed. It took Dean many months to accept his new home. It took me many years before I would be able to recognize the wisdom of my decision.

His new foster mother was a great mother. She gave him love, stability, and a family with six children. Their lives were always full of happenings. Dean lived in a real world. He was not protected from chaos. (He went) off to visit (other families), off to Disneyland, off to spend the weekend with Mom. (His new mother) and I became great friends and I learned to respect her quiet authority and her genuine love for others. The three of us would go on long drives. Dean always loved the open road and a big hamburger at the end of each journey. We spent weekends at the beach several times each year. There were many adventures for Dean, all of which have helped him to develop into the person he is today. He can participate in large groups and go to the mall, out to eat, and to sporting events. He loves a good party. (Just watch out for your wine glass!)

For my part, I had to back away from full-time parenting into the role of advocate. I channeled those parenting energies into organizations and committees that benefit people with disabilities. At one point, I was president of the Autism Council of Oregon.

When Dean was 13 years old, he spent several weeks at the hospital, recovering from spinal rod surgery. Because (his foster mother) was not able to stay with him during this time, I stayed with Dean in the hospital during his recovery. I relished playing the role of caregiver to my son. His foster mother and I grew to respect and love one another, we laughed and cried together. It was during these times that I came to realize that it would take more than one heart, one pair of hands, one person to provide Dean with a good life.

As Dean grew older, it was obvious that his foster family could not continue to care for him. At 21 years old, he was 5'8" and weighed 130 pounds. His outbursts were not as frequent; but because of his size, they required more care and physical strength. He required someone to bathe and dress him, brush his teeth, and prepare his meals. He wouldn't be able to get himself out of a house fire. All this and more made caring for Dean a challenge. So we began the search for a new foster home. The agony of wondering whether we would ever find Dean "the right home" took its toll on all of us. It was a difficult and delicate issue because of limited resources, the pressure to make a selection, and the need to respect that gut feeling about which place would be best for my son. Finally (a new family was selected and they agreed) to become Dean's new foster parents.

Just as before, the transition was a nightmare. Difficulty in funding accelerated the transition beyond Dean's ability to accept the changes. He was completely out of control—mad, frustrated, and angry. He seriously abused himself and others. [Note: Dean ultimately spent a week in the psychiatric wing of the local Health Sciences Center for evaluation and to adjust to medication.] Dean showed his strength to survive. His character and life's experiences helped him during a desperate and difficult time.

(At his new home), Dean is respected as an autistic person. (His new mother) keeps herself informed through autism seminars and specialized training which has helped her to create a positive, loving environment. He is always part of the decision-making process and is helped to understand what is expected of him and what will occur. Each stage of change is explained. (His new father's) patience and intuitive skills have helped to accomplish much in Dean's life. (Dean has learned many new skills, he is more social, and is communicating more.) This is a positive and loving family environment. Dean again has a stable, loving home.

Burleigh's Story
—Written by his mother, Mary Anne Seaton

Several things come to mind as I look back at how we have survived these years and how Burleigh has endured them. First, I remember clearly the day (that I first heard that my son had autism). I even remember what I was wearing, the room that we went to, and my first opportunity to see a child who displayed characteristics similar to my child's. I remember how very kind and gentle you both were. But most important, I remember you all saying, "There is no cure; but if you work very hard, you can make a difference for your child." Those words and your caring attitude toward me were the beginning of turning my life around and setting the direction for Burleigh and our family.

Second, having the opportunity to learn how Burleigh's disability affects him clearly changed our lives. Without that information, we would not have survived. It allowed us to come to grips with who Burleigh is and to start accepting him. In addition to learning all I could about autism, I had the opportunity to become involved in the state systems that serve people with disabilities and their families. By my learning about how the systems work and what role they should play in helping people, we were able to get better services for Burleigh.

Third, over the past eight years, several people have been involved with our family by assisting us at home with Burleigh. They made it possible for Burleigh to continue to live at home. One of those people, however, has had the most impact on our lives. At first, he was a paid assistant to Burleigh in the home and school, and later he became his teacher. But most important, he became Burleigh's friend. One of the things that I am reminded of frequently by parents is that their children with autism don't have friends, and that people who are a part of their lives come in and go out without any closure. Burleigh has been fortunate. His friend continues to take him places—to visit his (own) parents (whom we now call Burleigh's extended family), to walk down by the waterfront, or to just hang out together. They have a special bond. One that Bill (Burleigh's father) and I cannot replace.

Fourth, Burleigh has had some good educational experiences. The most positive experience has been the introduction of "structured teaching" (as defined by TEACCH) into his school program and home life. This process has allowed him to become independent in his activities throughout each day. Now, without someone standing over him and verbally directing him, he can feed the cats, wash and dry the clothes, prepare his lunch, recycle the pop cans, tolerate assistance with hygiene, go grocery shopping, and work in the community in four different jobs. He also takes great pleasure in setting up and putting away his work. But probably the nicest thing about his independence is his sense of pleasure and pride in doing all of these things and understanding what he is doing. This process, called structured teaching, changed Burleigh's life—and mine, too. Things that we could never get Burleigh to do, he will now do without resistance. I get excited each day I see him working. He likes what he is doing.

Charlie's Story
—Written by his mother, Christine Marshall

Charlie is a 17-year-old high-functioning young man with autism. Taking time to reflect back over those 17 years helps me recognize how far we have come. I thought that child-rearing would allow me to put into practice all the wonderful knowledge I'd gleaned while getting my master's degree in education and during numerous years of teaching elementary school. I am having a difficult time finding examples of anything in my training or experience that prepared me for coping with a child who did not respond the way those children in the textbooks and classes responded.

Charlie was not diagnosed as autistic until he was 8 years old. I knew he was unique in the first year. Charlie was diagnosed as microcephalic (small head in comparison to the rest of body size) in his early years. This led to testing for mental retardation and other developmental delays, all of which came out negative. Yes, he was slow in some areas, but not to a significant degree. What made a difference in these early years was the involvement of patient grandparents and getting him accepted into an exceptional preschool program. Charlie was reading at age 3. I think this was due to grandparents who could sit for hours and play language games and be willing to play these games over and over. (They played "name this object," then talked to Charlie about the object; made words with magnetic letters, and again talked about the words.)

[The question of whether to have Charlie begin] school was one of the few areas where I felt being a teacher made it easier [for me to decide to hold him] back for a year. Although he could read, the social-emotional areas were delayed. I had seen too many parents push children into school because they could read, while not attending to deficits in other areas of development.

During elementary school, getting Charlie labeled was a very positive step for everyone. Teachers who felt he was weird had more patience, adults around him were more accepting of his odd behavior, and his parents now had articles to read about his uniqueness. During this time, the greatest help came from a pediatrician who was able to problem solve and research ways to get Charlie diagnosed; use of Cascade Regional Services to help develop ways to work with Charlie in the classroom; and teachers who were willing to work with him.

In spite of services available, parents need to communicate constantly with schools about what is going on with their child's program. An example of miscommunication: At the end of Charlie's elementary career, arrangements were made for a smooth transition to middle school. His schedule was to be hand-selected, and all teachers who would work with him would be given an inservice on autism. At the beginning of the school year, I checked with the school about his schedule and inservice, and discovered that nothing had been done. I continue to be Charlie's most reliable advocate.

Middle school provided the biggest problem, with puberty and homework getting the most attention. Much time was spent helping him see he could work at home and at school on what he thought was too much work. The school was aware of Charlie's autism, and teachers were chosen who could best work with him.

I found I really needed to be aware of his schedule, his classroom expectations, and his homework, because he was not going to share that information. Finding one person in the building to coordinate information, meet with the Regional people, and keep parents informed is a real must. In both high school and middle school, this role was filled by the resource-room teacher.

High school has presented some of the biggest rewards as well as challenges. Charlie adapted well to the change, thanks in large part to the resource teacher who arranges his schedule and informs Charlie's teachers about his disability and how it may affect his work. Charlie is now seeing himself as being able to succeed in a classroom. The challenge has been dealing with a few problems that developed along with puberty. At 16, everything was moving forward much better than ever expected. Then, a most annoying problem was diagnosed—obsessive-compulsive disorder (OCD). In Charlie's case, the disorder manifested itself with excessive hand washing and the need to straighten things over and over. The last two years have been spent trying several different drugs to help alleviate some of the symptoms. Chlomipramine, the first drug, worked wonders. We had a much more social child who said he even felt more social. The drug also helped with the OCD. However, after several months Charles developed a rapid heart rate, and we had to discontinue using Chlomipramine. We tried several other drugs and have chosen to leave him on Prozac until a new drug becomes available. Prozac has helped with Charlie's anxiety and OCD, but it hasn't provided all the positive changes of the first drug.

Now we are looking ahead to high school graduation and the future. Fortunately, there are still some services to help with the transition. For me, one day at a time is all I can handle; the future still seems a little overwhelming to ponder for long.

Brad's Story
—Written by his mother, Linda Benson

"Whatever do they have to smile and laugh about?" This was the question asked by my friend, another mother of a child with autism, as we attended our first meeting of Parents with Handicapped Children in 1971. At that point in our grieving lives, little seemed humorous. Indeed, I have a vast litany of horror stories from the early days.

Brad could have horrible nosebleeds. I became quite expert at stopping these. One, however, I couldn't stop. No one knew then he had autism. Of course, this child would not allow the doctor to treat him. A battle began between Brad and all the adults we could gather. The young doctor began swearing at me and screaming that I must be the worst mother he'd ever seen because I couldn't control my child. When the ordeal ended, I came to the lobby to pay my bill and cringed as the people there stared at this terrible mother.

Perhaps this helped build my character. However, I was a pretty nice person before having Brad, so why did I need this? As the years have ticked by, we have come to enjoy this young man, now 24 years old. He has made us laugh, and experiences with him have made us laugh. Imagine that!—actually enjoying having an autistic adult in the home. His innocence has brought on therapeutic belly-laughs from his family. We so enjoy his literalness. We enjoy his unique abilities. (When other kids) come into the house, they say, "Hi, Brad. What years was *Lassie* on the air?" They all want him on their team for *Encore* and *Trivia*. When Brad's friend (also with autism) comes over, the other kids try to trick him on sports scores, but they never can. We all like to show off our talents, and those with autism are no different.

Since I have lived with autism for half my life and have been involved with other families, I feel capable of making some observations. It's work, it's time consuming, it's often overwhelming to have a child with autism. However, parents do better if they attend workshops to learn and get inspiration to try new things. I believe it is true that moms who are tough—not abusive, not mean, but tough—do better in the long run. If you know autism, your child, your rights, and the limits of what you will and will not tolerate, you will be further ahead than the mom who withdraws and lets her child run the show. To get where we are today has not been easy. Many mistakes have been made. I was tough on Brad in the early years, for I truly believe my job is to make my son socially acceptable. Being tough paid off. When Brad goes to movies, sporting events, concerts, plays, and out to eat, he acts appropriately.

Early intervention is the key. (Because there was no early intervention when Brad was young), I arranged our schedule by keeping the other kids up late and getting them up early so they would want a nap. Brad, who seemed to need no sleep, and I were then free to work for three hours every afternoon. We acted out prepositions, dramatized words, etc. He learned much from one-on-one experiences.

I remember not going through the years of discontent my friends did. I learned I had better things to do. I remember wondering why they worried about what color to paint the bathroom—not that one shouldn't paint the bathroom occasionally. I began to learn balance. I remember being thrown out of a store. I learned to hold my head up high. I remember kneading bread with a fury. I learned to have useful outlets for my anger. I remember being upset with the school. I learned diplomacy. Brad now works part time in the office at our business. His coworkers enjoy him and even ask him out to lunch. We "buy" other friends for Brad. I learned reality. Parents of garden-type kids often call me when things go wrong with their children. They see me as less judgmental than their other peers. I learned to listen.

Our mothers' group took as much delight in bragging about this one being able to walk across the backs of a line of folding chairs; another one knowing all the scores of past ball games; one son being able to recite who produced, directed, and starred in any movie or TV show and the year it was made; one who could build marvelous block towers that defied the laws of gravity; and another who was able to pump the swing as high as it would go while he took off one shoe, scratched his foot, and put the shoe back on. Other mothers had such mundane brags—the honor roll or a hat trick in hockey. Their stories paled by comparison to ours.

Brad still wrings his hands, occasionally loses control, and is obviously disabled. There has been no miraculous cure. He can offer no insights into the world of autism. He never admitted to being autistic until *Rain Man* was made. Brad saw much of Raymond in himself. It was a status symbol to be like Dustin Hoffman.

He has worked hard to be like other people, and he grows more independent each day. We love our son. It sounds corny, but when things get rough, I always go to my bedroom and read the sign someone sent me: "Bloom where you are planted." I've tried. Hope you do, too.

[Note: In telephone conversations, Linda expressed her concern about the move to full integration for all students with autism, especially when it is seen by administrators as a means of saving money. If integration cannot be appropriately supported with staff training, it will be of little benefit and is likely to lead to behavior problems that disrupt the education of other students. Linda also wanted to emphasize that those with autism:

- Need extra time to process the things they hear, because the processing delay is a significant problem.

- Must be kept busy. Boredom and unstructured "down-time" lead to problems.

- Need opportunities to learn factual information about the world. A computer is a great tool for this.]

One Mother's Hopes

—Written by Valda Fields, mother of a 13-year-old young man with autism

I hope my son learns the skills that he needs to function at home, at school, in the work place, and in the community.

I wish that school districts had the resources to provide a better functional education, beginning at the middle-school level.

I hope my son learns appropriate social skills to help him at home, at school, in the work place, and in the community.

I wish that an effective social-skills program existed for individuals with autism.

I hope my son will have an appropriate place to live when he leaves my home.

I wish there were more community-living options available for individuals with developmental disabilities.

I hope my son learns to enjoy community activities with people who are not family members.

I wish that more people would persevere in their relationships with individuals who have autism, so that lasting friendships could result.

I hope my son learns problem-solving skills needed to successfully function at home, at school, at work, and in the community.

I wish I could foresee the problems that he will encounter, so that training could begin now.

I hope my son's program achieves an adequate "mix" of academic and functional skills.

I wish that we could better see the fine line between the two.

I hope that my son's innocence and naiveté don't make him a victim as an adult.

I wish that we could bottle this innocence and naiveté and pass it out generously. If we could, the world would be a much better place in which to live.

APPENDIX

B | Resources

Organizations

The Autism Society of America (ASA)
7910 Woodmont Avenue, Suite 650
Bethesda, MD 20814
Phone: (301) 657-0881—(800) 3-AUTISM

> With both parent and professional members, ASA was organized in 1965 to promote information and public awareness about autism. The organization operates through a network of more than 190 state and local chapters in 48 states. ASA maintains an active advocacy and lobbying effort, sponsors an annual national conference, and publishes *The Advocate* six times a year. This newsletter provides current information about medical and educational research, political advocacy issues, and stories about families and individuals coping with autism.

> *State or local ASA chapters.* These local parent/professional groups are important sources of family support and information about regional resources. Local groups play a critical advocacy role to ensure appropriate services in a community. They may sponsor workshops, conferences, lending libraries, or newsletters. Check the phone book and newspapers, or call a local information and referral service.

The Autism National Committee (AUTCOM)
7 Teresa Circle
Arlington, MA 02174

> AUTCOM was founded in 1990 to advance and protect the civil rights of people with autism/PDD and related disorders of communication and behavior. The organization publishes a quarterly newsletter, *The Communicator*.

Autism Training Centers

There are numerous private and public centers across the country that offer effective training to parents and professionals as well as services to those with autism and their families. The following centers are listed here because their philosophy of autism and autism services is consistent with that proposed in this book. I visited each of these programs and was impressed with the quality of their professional and parent training programs and the skill and sensitivity shown to their clients with autism.

The Groden Center
86 Mt. Hope Avenue
Providence, RI 02906
Phone: (401) 274-6310
Contact: June Groden, Director

> This private, nonprofit Center pioneered the work in relaxation and self-control training for those with autism. The Center provides an on-site program as well as support to individuals who are integrated into local school and community living and supported employment programs. The Groden Center offers workshops and training in relaxation and self-control procedures to parents and professionals in other states and countries.

The Judevine Center for Autism
9455 Rott Road
St. Louis, MO 63127
Phone: (314) 849-4440
FAX: (314) 849-2721
Contact: Lois Blackwell, Director

> This private, nonprofit research and treatment center offers a multitude of services to those with autism and their families in home, local school, and community settings across the state. While the Center previously maintained specialized classrooms for those with autism, it now has only a few diagnostic classrooms that also are used as practicum sites for parent and professional training. The Judevine Center offers assessment, consultation, and training to those from other states and countries.

Division TEACCH
University of North Carolina
310 Medical School, Wing E
Chapel Hill, NC 27599-7180
Phone: (919) 966-2173
Contact: Gary Mesibov, Director

> The TEACCH Program (The Division for the Treatment and Education of Autistic and Related Communication Handicapped Children), established in 1972, is the first statewide, comprehensive, community-based program dedicated to improving the understanding of and services to those with autism and related disabilities. In addition to the local services provided by six regional centers in North Carolina, the TEACCH Program offers assessment, consultation, and training to parents and professionals from other states and countries.

Autism Resource Centers

Autism Research Institute (ARI)
  (Formerly: The Institute for Child Behavior Research)
4182 Adams Avenue
San Diego, CA 92116
Phone: (619) 281-7165
Contact: Bernard Rimland, Director

> The Autism Research Institute maintains one of the largest data banks on individuals with autism, evaluates various forms of treatment. ARI is a source of information about auditory integration training and facilitated communication. It also disseminates information about biomedical and educational research via information sheets and publication of a quarterly newsletter, *The Autism Research Review International*.

The Indiana Resource Center for Autism at Indiana University
Institute for the Study of Developmental Disabilities
2853 East 10th Street
Bloomington, IN 47405
Phone: (812) 855-6508
Contact: Cathy Pratt, Ph.D., Director

> This Center offers short papers on specific issues, pamphlets, manuals, and videotapes. For a catalog of publications, write to the above address.

The Autism Services Center
P.O. Box 507
Huntington, WV 25710-0507
Phone: (304) 525-8014

> This is an information and referral center that includes the National Autism Hotline.

The Center for Neurodevelopmental Studies
5430 W. Glenn Drive
Glendale, AZ 85301-2628
Phone: (602) 915-0345
Contact: Lorna King, Director

> This Center distributes information about and offers training in sensory integrative therapy and provides therapy services to children with autism and related disorders.

National Information Center for Children and Youth with Disabilities (NICHCY)
Phone: (800) 695-0285 (Voice/TT)

> An information clearinghouse, NICHCY provides free information on disabilities and disability-related issues. The organization provides personal responses to questions, referrals to other organizations, and information searches; and maintains data bases and a library.

The Geneva Centre
111 Merton Street
Toronto, Ontario, Canada M4S 3A7
Phone: (416) 322-7877

> This resource center sells a wide range of printed material and videotapes related to autism and related disorders. The Centre maintains a computerized resource library of current information. Write for the Catalogue of Autism Resources.

Facilitated Communication Institute
Syracuse University
370 Huntington Hall
Syracuse, NY 13244
Phone: (315) 443-1870

> This Center distributes information about facilitated communication, conducts research, and offers workshops to train communication facilitators.

MAAP Services, Inc.
P.O. Box 524
Crown Point, IN 46307-0524
Phone: (219) 662-1311
Contact: Susan Moreno

> MAAP Services, Inc., gathers and disseminates information about those with autism who are "More Able," and distributes a newsletter for sharing information about higher-functioning individuals.

Autism Publications

The Advocate
Autism Society of America
7910 Woodmont Avenue, Suite 650
Bethesda, MD 20814

> Newsletter published six times a year

Autism Research Review International
Autism Research Institute
4182 Adams Avenue
San Diego, CA 92116

> Published quarterly

Journal of Autism and Developmental Disorders
Plenum Publishing Corporation
233 Spring Street
New York, NY 10013

> Published quarterly

Focus on Autism and Other Developmental Disabilities
PRO-ED, Inc.
8700 Shoal Creek Blvd.
Austin, TX 78758

> Published bimonthly

The Communicator
Autism National Committee
7 Teresa Circle
Arlington, MA 02174

> Newsletter published quarterly

Our Voice
Autism Network International (ANI)
P.O. Box 448
Syracuse, NY 13210-0448
Contact: Jim Sinclair

> Newsletter of the Autism Network International (ANI), an independent organization
> and newsletter run entirely by and for individuals with autism/PDD

Glossary

adaptations. Modifications or alterations of the curriculum, the support systems, the environments, or the teaching strategies to match individual needs (strengths and deficits). The adaptations ensure that the student can participate actively and as independently as possible.

assessment. The act of determining the value of one's efforts. This term refers to the process of determining skills and deficits for educational planning.

behavior. Observable actions and responses to environmental stimuli. These actions and responses are also influenced by internal factors such as understanding, feelings, and emotions related to the stimuli.

behavioral signals. *See,* **signals.**

calendar. A visual representation of scheduled activities. In this book, a distinction between a schedule and a calendar is made to emphasize the importance of the planning process involved in ordering the events in time to achieve goals and the importance of the calendar for communicating that sequence of events to the learner. A **mini-calendar** supplements a basic daily calendar and shows the sequence of steps or specific activities scheduled to occur within a small block of time. *See also,* **scheduling.**

calendar system. The combination and integration of all the elements that make up an effective calendar—one that will have an optimum effect. For example, it includes the systematic ordering of activities, the physical design of the calendar, transition cues to move from one location to another, etc. See chapters 13–15.

central nervous system (CNS). The structure that consists of the brain, the spinal cord, and related systems that controls all aspects of learning, thinking, and movement.

chunk. A substantial amount of something. In this context, it refers to the gestalt processing style that results in one-trial learning—when all the information present in the environment at one time is recorded together in chunks. These chunks include both relevant and irrelevant material.

clutter. A disordered heap; litter. In this context, the word refers to irrelevant or unrelated environmental events or details that compete with the relevant information so that critical associations cannot be made. Sounds of crackling paper, of people breathing, of a truck starting up, the odors of nearby people, the touch of a prompt, or the feel of a scratchy shirt label on the neck may overpower or clutter the important details of a demonstration or verbal direction.

cognitive picture rehearsal. An application of imagery procedures. It incorporates a visual display to help a person visualize the scenes associated with a problem situation.

cognitive processes. The neurological processes involved in knowing, thinking, reasoning, and solving problems.

communication. An interactive process that conveys information and ideas from one person to another. Communication is a social skill that has the potential for influencing others and gaining some control over one's environment.

consequence. Something that occurs as a direct result of action or effort. Consequences can be pleasant and reinforcing or unpleasant and punishing. Some consequences occur naturally. (When you touch a hot stove, you get burned.)

contingency. A contract that specifies and clarifies expectations. It defines the expected behavior (work or effort) and the reinforcement (payoff). Contingencies are generally stated in an *if/then* or *when/then* format.

conventional signals. Words, gestures, signs, or behaviors that are understood by everyone in the same cultural group. Whether the signal is verbal or nonverbal, most people in that group could easily interpret it. **Nonconventional signals** are signals not commonly used or understood in the culture. For example, flicking fingers, flapping arms, or biting wrists can be used to signal a variety of problems, but they do not carry a commonly understood meaning.

covert conditioning. An imagery procedure. In this context, it is based on the work of J. Cautela, and assumes that thinking, feeling, and imagining follow the same principles of learning as observable behaviors. **Covert positive reinforcement** occurs when a person imagines the target behavior that results in a positive consequence. The imagined positive consequence strengthens the behavior or increases the likelihood of it recurring. **Covert modeling** is the act of imagining another person performing the target behavior and visualizing that it resulted in a positive consequence.

covert modeling. *See,* covert conditioning.

covert positive reinforcement. *See,* covert conditioning.

criterion. A standard for judging mastery or level of accuracy. For example, mastery is assumed if a skill occurs with a specified degree of accuracy or within a specified amount of time.

delayed echolalia. *See,* echolalia.

developmental goals. Goals relating to the sequence of normal development of language, cognitive, social, motor, and academic skills. The progression to the next step depends on mastering a lower step; for example, discrimination of shapes and sounds leads to recognition of letters, letter names, letter sounds, and then to reading. Those with autism skip many steps of the developmental sequences.

echolalia. The repetition of speech produced by others. The echoed words or phrases can include the same words and exact inflections as originally heard, or they may be slightly modified. **Immediate echolalia** refers to echoed words spoken immediately or a very brief time after they were heard. **Delayed echolalia** refers to echoed "tapes" that are repeated at a much later time—days or even years later.

evaluation. A process for determining the significance of symptoms, as in a diagnostic study of a physical or mental condition. In this context, the term refers to the process for determining the presence of autism; the evaluation will determine how or if a child's symptoms are like, or not like, those of others with autism.

forms of communication. The means or method of communication—gestures, pictures, signs, spoken or written words, and other methods.

functional analysis of behavior. *See,* functional assessment.

functional assessment. A process for documenting an individual's actual ability to function in the natural environment. A **functional analysis of behavior** is the procedure for identifying the relationship between aspects of the environment and behavior. These functional procedures provide information for understanding the reasons for problems, for setting practical (functional) goals, and for identifying support needs.

functional goals. Goals that lead directly to increased independence in the real world, such as cooking, doing laundry, managing a bank account or leisure time. **Nonfunctional goals** are those related to developmental sequences, such as walking a balance beam or cutting with scissors on a line, that have no direct relevance to increased independence.

functional routines. The set or sequence of steps or procedures directed to achievement of a practical purpose; for example, a routine for washing dishes or for going to a movie.

functions of communication. The purpose or reasons to communicate; for example, to request, protest, comment, . . .

generalize, generalization. Terms used to describe the ability to learn a skill or a rule in one situation and be able to use or apply it flexibly to other similar but different situations. The term **overgeneralize** refers to the tendency of those with autism to use a skill in all settings just as it was taught, without modifications that reflect the differences in a situation.

gestalt, holistic. Terms used to describe the distinctive processing mode common in autism. Information is taken in (recorded) and stored quickly in whole units or "chunks," without analysis for meaning. These 'chunks' are stored directly in the long-term-memory system.

glitch. A defect, error, or malfunction, as in a machine. A brief or sudden interruption or surge in electric power.

holistic. *See,* **gestalt.**

hyperlexia. An ability to learn to read at advanced levels without instruction.

imagery-based procedures. Procedures that promote learning by thinking, imagining or visualizing one's self, or a model, performing a behavior that results in a pleasant consequence. *See also,* **visual imagery.**

immediate echolalia. *See,* **echolalia.**

instructional sequence. A systematic teaching plan that specifies the materials, settings, variations, adaptations, and teaching strategies to ensure effective learning.

integrated systems. Refers to the organization or consolidation of all the visual information systems to clarify meaning and avoid confusion.

intentional communication. Behavior that is done with a purpose and the knowledge of potential effect. **Unintentional communication** is reflexive behavior, done automatically without the knowledge of potential effect.

interpreter. One who can explain or provide the meaning; a person who can clarify the meaning of events, words, and experiences. In the context of autism, the interpreter must also take on the role of guide who provides assistance to reach a destination or goal, who shows and comments upon, supplies advice or counsel, highlights important details, attracts the eye, and provides quick reference.

joint attention. When an infant and caregiver coordinate their attention about an object of mutual interest. This involves shifting their attention from each other to an object and back. Joint attention is sometimes called **referential looking.**

language. A set of symbols with meanings and rules for use that are commonly understood and used by all in a cultural group for the purpose of communication.

learning style. A distinctive manner or way of taking in and processing information in order to learn, to think, to remember and to function in the world.

mini-calendar. *See,* **calendar.**

natural cue. An object or event that is always present or always occurs as part of the natural environment, that stimulates or triggers a response or action. (A full laundry basket is a signal that it is time to do the laundry; the sound of the cash register ringing up the total is a signal to pay.)

natural prompt. Something that calls attention to a missed cue or that assures a correct response. (If payment is not made at the expected time, the checker holds out a hand and says, "That will be $10.00." If a person in line does not move up, the person behind says, "Hey, move along.")

nonconventional signals. *See,* **conventional signals.**

overgeneralize. *See,* **generalize.**

perseveration. The redundant repetition of a word, thought, or action without the ability to stop or move on. For example, when a person steps through the door, then rocks back and forth, seemingly unable to follow through with the other foot; or, when one erases a mistake until the paper is worn through.

perspective. A point of view based on location, experiences, prior knowledge, beliefs, etc.

pragmatics. The practical aspects of using language to communicate in a natural context. It includes the rules about eye contact between speaker and listener, how close to stand, taking turns, selecting topics of conversation, and other requirements to ensure that satisfactory communication occurs. Many of these rules have a cultural base.

problem. Any situation or event that one does not understand, that causes uncertainty and requires a solution.

progressive muscle relaxation. A type of therapy procedure for reducing stress. A person is taught to identify feelings and location of tension and to consciously relax the muscle groups that are tense. For example, the feelings of tension in the neck and shoulders cues the person to consciously relax the neck and shoulder muscles.

proprioceptive. Stimuli from the nerve receptors located in the muscles, tendons, and inner ear that provide a sense of the position of one's body in space.

punishment. An unpleasant event that occurs as a direct consequence of a behavior, which decreases the strength of the behavior or the likelihood that it will be repeated.

rebus. A symbol or line drawing, a representation, that illustrates or suggests a word or phrase.

referential looking. *See,* **joint attention.**

reflexive. Actions that occur quickly, automatically, and without thought as an immediate response to some type of stimulation or emotion; for example, the fight-or-flight responses that occur as a result of panic, surprise, or pain.

reinforcement. A pleasant event that occurs immediately as a direct result of an action that increases the strength of the action or the likelihood that the action will be repeated.

representations. Symbols that take on the meaning of a real object or idea. For example, signs and words are symbols that represent real things. An understanding of symbols allows a person to use words (symbols) in thinking.

response cost. A type of punishing procedure that involves the loss of something valued (a reinforcer) as a direct result of an action (behavior), thus decreasing the likelihood that the behavior will reoccur. Response cost involves the giving up of something already in possession; it is not simply that reinforcement is withheld. (A child who draws on the wall must give up crayons; a person who is caught speeding must give up money.)

response. An action or behavior that is triggered by a preceding cue or stimulus (object, action, or event).

savant. A person who exhibits unusual gifts and abilities in a few areas (or a single area) that contrast sharply with abilities in other areas.

schedule. *See,* **scheduling.**

scheduling. A planning process that organizes a sequence of events to achieve a goal. A **schedule** is the product of that planning process—a plan or an arrangement of events to accomplish goals. A **calendar** is the visual representation of that schedule.

semantic categories. The type of meaning a word has when used to communicate an idea or concept. An example of the category *object wanted* is, "Want ball." An example of the category *action* is, "I jumped."

semantic maps. Diagrams or flow charts that show the meaningful relationships between elements of concepts, processes, or events.

sensory channels. The pathways for receiving information from the environment (for example, eyes: visual channel; ears: auditory channel; nose: olfactory channel).

signals. Objects or events that trigger or cue a response or action; for example, traffic lights. **Behavioral signals** are actions that indicate an emotional state. (Flushing and hyperventilation may be a signal of increasing stress.) *See also,* **conventional signals.**

social cognition. The thinking, understanding, and reasoning skills involved in or required for social interactions; knowing about others and their perspectives.

social stimuli. The sensory stimulation provided by people and interactions. The amount and the type of stimulation presented by people is highly unpredictable. The stimulation includes expressive and changing facial features (especially the eyes and mouth), loud and often high-pitched talking, odors, unexpected movements, and touches.

standardized tests. Assessment tools that measure one individual's performance against the performance of many other individuals who have taken the test under the same precise conditions. Standardized tests involve highly specific directions and provide age/grade-level or intelligence (IQ) scores.

support systems. The adaptations and assistance required to ensure increasing independence. (One learner's support system may include a daily calendar, transition cues, a 1:1 interpreter for some classes, and a consulting occupational therapist.)

syndrome. A condition characterized by a cluster of co-occurring symptoms that has a specific effect on a group of individuals; for example, fetal alcohol syndrome, Down syndrome, autism).

synergistic effects. The concept that the total effect produced by the interaction or integration of multiple elements is greater than the sum of the effect of each element alone. For example, it is the interacting or synergistic effects of all the learning style elements that complicates the picture in autism. The extreme strengths and the extreme deficits cause paradoxical effects.

theory of mind. Terminology used to describe the concept of thinking about thinking; thinking about what we know and think, and what others know and think.

transition cue. An object that serves as a reminder of the targeted destination. (The car keys held in the hand trigger or cue moving to the car; a 3"x5" card with a drawing of the gym serves as a reminder to continue moving to the gym.)

unintentional communication. *See,* **intentional communication.**

visual adaptations; visual support systems. Written schedules, lists, charts, picture sequences, and other visuals that convey meaningful information in a permanent format for later reference. **Visual adaptations** allow the person with autism to function more independently without constant verbal directions. These visual adaptations serve the same purpose for those with autism as a hearing aid and sign language serve for the person who is deaf. A person who is blind gets information from reading Braille or from an interpreter.

visual imagery. An instructional strategy that involves the ability to imagine scenes, feelings, and actions. A traditional counseling strategy.

work system. The visual organization of directions, materials, and environments to clarify expectations. This clear visual organization promotes independence from another person to provide verbal cues and prompts.

References

Akerley, M. S. 1984. Developmental changes in families with autistic children: A parent's perspective. In *The effects of autism on the family*, edited by E. Schopler and G. M. Mesibov, 85-98. New York: Plenum Press.

Albin, R. W., and R. H. Horner. 1988. Generalization with precision. In *Generalization and maintenance: Life-style changes in applied settings*, edited by R. H. Horner, G. Dunlap, and R. L. Koegel, 99-120. Baltimore: Paul H. Brookes.

Allen, R. V., and C. Allen. 1966. *Language experiences in reading.* Chicago: Encyclopaedia Britannica Press.

Amenta, C. A., III. 1994. Auditory integration therapy: Where's the science? In *1994 Autism Society of America conference proceedings.* 229-237. Arlington, TX: Future Education.

American Psychiatric Association (APA). 1994. *Diagnostic and statistical manual of mental disorders (DSM-IV).* 4th ed. Washington, DC: American Psychiatric Association.

Archer, A., and M. Gleason. 1992-94. *Advanced skills for school success, modules 1-4 for grades 7-12.* 4 vols. North Billerica, MA: Curriculum Associates.

Ashton-Warner, S. 1963. *Teacher.* New York: Simon and Schuster.

Attwood, A. J. 1993. Movement disorders and autism: a rationale for the use of facilitated communication and an alternative model for training staff and students. In *1993 International Conference Proceedings: Autism, a world of options.* International Conference on Autism, Toronto. Arlington, TX: Future Education.

Ayres, J. A. 1979. *Sensory integration and the child.* Los Angeles: Western Psychological Services.

Baron-Cohen, S. 1988. Social and pragmatic deficits in autism: Cognitive or affective? *Journal of Autism and Developmental Disorders* 18:379-402.

Beckman, P. J., and J. Lieber. 1994. The social strategy rating scale: An approach to evaluating social competence. *Journal of Early Intervention* 18(1):1-11.

Beukelman, D. R., and P. Mirenda. 1992. *Augmentative and alternative communication: Management of severe communication disorders in children and adults,* 285-289. Baltimore: Paul H. Brookes.

Biedeman, G., V. Davey, C. Ryder, and D. Franchi. 1944. The negative effects of positive reinforcement in teaching children with developmental delay. *Exceptional Children* 60(5):458-465.

Biklen, D. 1990. *Communication unbound: Autism and praxis.* Harvard Educational Review 60(3):219-314.

_____. 1993. *Communication unbound: How facilitated communication is challenging traditional views of autism and ability/disability.* New York: Teachers College Press.

Biklen, D. and J. D. Duchan. 1994. "I Am Intelligent": The social construction of mental retardation. *Journal of the Association for Persons with Severe Handicaps (JASH)* 19(3):173-184.

Biklen, D., N. Saha, and C. Kliewer. 1995. How teachers confirm the authorship of facilitated communication: A portfolio approach. *Journal of the Association for Persons with Severe Handicaps (JASH)* 20(1):45-56.

Bissell, J., J. Fisher, C. Owens, and P. Polcyn. 1988. *Sensory motor handbook: A guide for implementing and modifying activities in the classroom.* Torrance, CA: Sensory Integration International.

Blackwell, L. 1978. *Judevine® Training System: Competency-based training for parents and professionals.* St. Louis: Judevine Center for Autism.

Blanche, E., T. Botticelli, and M. Hallway. 1995. *Combining neurodevelopmental treatment and sensory integration principles.* Tucson, AZ: Therapy Skill Builders, a division of The Psychological Corporation.

Board of Education of the Hendrick Hudson Central School District vs *Rowley.* 1982. 458 U.S. 176 (June 28). U.S. Supreme Court Decision.

Bock, M. A. 1991. A modified language experience approach for children with autism. *Focus on Autistic Behavior* 6(5):1-15.

Bondy, A. S., and L. A. Frost. 1994. The picture exchange system. *Focus on Autistic Behavior* 9(3):1-19.

Borba, M., and C. Borba. 1978. *Self-esteem: A classroom affair—101 ways to help children like themselves.* San Francisco: Harper & Row.

Bristol, M. M., and E. Schopler. 1983. Stress and coping in families of autistic adolescents. In *Autism in adolescents and adults*, edited by E. Schopler and G. B. Mesibov, 251-276. New York: Plenum Press.

Brown, F., I. Evans, K. Weed, and V. Owen. 1987. Delineating functional competencies: A component model. *Journal of the Association for Persons with Severe Handicaps (JASH)* 12(2):117-124.

Bryson, S. E., R. Landry, and I. M. Smith. 1994. A case study of literacy and socioemotional development in a mute autistic female. *Journal of Autism and Developmental Disabilities* 24(2):225-231.

Buser, K. P., and D. Reimer. 1988. Developing cognitive strategies through problem solving. *Teaching Exceptional Children.* Winter:22-25.

Butera, G., and H. C. Haywood. 1992. A cognitive approach to the education of young children with autism. *Focus on Autistic Behavior* 6(6):1-14.

Canfield, J., and H. C. Wells. 1976. *100 Ways to enhance self-concepts in the classroom.* Englewood Cliffs, NJ: Prentice Hall.

Carlson, F. 1988. *Picsyms categorical dictionary.* Little Rock, AR: Baggeboda Press.

Carr, E. G. 1988. Functional equivalence as a mechanism of response generalization. In *Generalization and maintenance: Life-style changes in applied settings*, edited by R. H. Horner, G. Dunlap, and R. L. Koegel, 211-241. Baltimore: Paul H. Brookes.

Carr, E. G., S. Robinson, and L. W. Palumbo. 1990. The wrong issue: Aversive versus non-aversive treatment—The right issue: Functional versus nonfunctional treatment. In *Aversive and nonaversive treatment: The great debate in developmental disabilities*, edited by A. Repp and R. Singh, 361-379. DeKalb, IL: Sycamore Press.

Cautela, J. R., and J. Groden. 1978. *Relaxation: A comprehensive manual for adults, children, and children with special needs.* Champaign, IL: Research Press.

Cesaroni, L., and M. Garber. 1991. Exploring the experience of autism through firsthand accounts. *Journal of Autism and Developmental Disorders* 21(3):303-313.

Chastain, L. D. 1986. *A handbook on the use of songs to teach autistic and other severely handicapped children.* Goodhue, MN: White Oak Press.

Cihak, M. K., and B. Jackson-Herson. 1980. *Games children should play.* Glenview, IL: Scott, Foresman.

Coleman, M. 1990. Autism: Non-drug biological treatments. In *Diagnosis and treatment of autism*, edited by C. Gillman. New York: Plenum Press.

Coling, M. C. 1991. *Developing integrated programs: A transdisciplinary approach for early intervention.* Tucson, AZ: Therapy Skill Builders.

Courchesne, E., N. A. Akshoomoff, B. Egaas, A. J. Lincoln, O. Saitoh, L. Schreibman, J. Townsend, and R. Yeung-Courchesne. 1994. Role of cerebellar and parietal dysfunction in the social and cognitive deficits in patients with infantile autism. In *Autism Society of America conference proceedings,* 19-21. Arlington, TX: Future Education.

Crary, E. 1984. *Kids can cooperate: A practical guide to teaching problem solving.* Seattle: Parenting Press.

Crossley, R. 1992. Getting the words out: Case studies in facilitated communication training. *Topics in Language Disorders* 12(4):46-59.

Crossley, R., and J. Remington-Gurney. 1992. Getting the words out: Facilitated communication training. *Topics in Language Disorders* 12(4):29-45.

Dalldorf, J. S. 1983. Medical needs of the autistic adolescent. In *Autism in adolescents and adults,* edited by E. Schopler and G. B. Mesibov, 149-158. New York: Plenum Press.

Darch, C., and D. Carnine. 1986. Teaching content area material to learning disabled students. *Exceptional Children* 53(3):240-245.

Datlow-Smith, M. 1990. *Autism and life in the community: Chapter 1, Overview of autism.* 1-12. Baltimore: Paul H. Brookes.

Datlow-Smith, M., R. G. Belcher, and P. D. Juhrs. 1994. *A guide to successful employment for individuals with autism.* Baltimore: Paul H. Brookes.

Dawson, G., and M. Fernald. 1987. Perspective-taking ability and its relationship to the social behavior of autistic children. *Journal of Autism and Developmental Disorders* 17:487-498.

DeMyer, M. K., and P. Goldberg. 1983. Family needs of the autistic adolescent. In *Autism in adolescents and adults,* edited by E. Schopler and G. B. Mesibov, 225-250. New York: Plenum Press.

DesLauriers, A. M. 1978. The cognitive-affective dilemma in early infantile autism: The case of Clarence. *Journal of Autism and Developmental Disorders* 8:219-228.

Dewey, M., 1991. Living with Asperger's syndrome. In *Autism and Asperger's syndrome,* edited by U. Frith, 184-192. Cambridge, England: Press Syndicate of the University of Cambridge.

_____. 1992. Autistic eccentricity. In *High-functioning individuals with autism,* edited by E. Schopler and G. B. Mesibov, 281-288. New York: Plenum Press.

Dewey, M., and M. Everard. 1974. The near-normal autistic adolescent. *Journal of Autism and Developmental Disorders* 4:348-356.

Donnellan, A. M. 1984. The criterion of the least dangerous assumption. *Behavioral Disorders* 9(2):141-150.

___. 1985. *Classic readings in autism.* New York: Teachers College Press.

Donnellan, A. M., G. W. LaVigna, N. Negri-Shoultz, and L. L. Fassbender. 1988. *Progress without punishment: Effective approaches for learners with behavior problems.* New York: Teachers College Press.

Eastham, D. W. 1985. *UNDERSTAND: Fifty Memowriter Poems.* Ottawa: Oliver-Pate.

Eastham, M. W., and D. Eastham. 1990. *Silent words and forever friends.* Ottawa: Oliver-Pate.

Elgar, S. D., B. Knoll, D. Toriskey, C. Toriskey, J. Money, A. L. Lettick, J. A. Cardamone, and G. B. Mesibov. 1985. Sex education and sexual awareness building for autistic children and youth: Some viewpoints and considerations and response. *Journal of Autism and Developmental Disabilities* 15(2):214-227.

Everard, M. P. 1976. Mildly autistic young people and their problems. Paper presented at the International Symposium on Autism, St. Gallen, Switzerland.

Falco, R., J. Janzen, J. Arick, K. Wilgus, and M. DeBoer. 1990. *Project QUEST inservice manual: Functional assessment of student needs and functional instruction for communication, social interactions, self-management, and choice.* Portland, OR: Department of Special and Counselor Education, Portland State University.

Fisher, A. G., E. A. Murray, and A. C. Bundy. 1991. *Sensory integration: Theory and practice.* Philadelphia: F. A. Davis.

Flowers, T. 1990. From my classroom: Teaching reading for information. *The Advocate* 22(1):10.

Ford, A. 1987. Sex education for individuals with autism: Structuring information and opportunities. In *Handbook of autism and pervasive developmental disorders,* edited by D. J. Cohen, A. M. Donnellan, and R. Paul, 430-439. New York: John Wiley & Sons.

Frankel, R. M., M. Leary, and B. Kilman. 1987. Building social skills through pragmatic analysis: Assessment and treatment implications for children with autism. In *Handbook of autism and developmental disabilities,* edited by D. Cohen, A. M. Donnellan, and R. Paul, 333-359. Silver Spring, MD: V. H. Winston and Sons.

Frith, U. 1989. *Autism: Explaining the enigma.* Oxford, England: Blackwell.

_____. 1991. *Autism and Asperger syndrome.* Cambridge, England: Press Syndicate of the University of Cambridge.

Fullerton, A. 1994. *Higher functioning adolescents and young adults with autism: A teacher' guide.* Portland, OR: Department of Special and Counselor Education, Portland State University.

Gajewski, N., and P. Mayo. 1989a. *SSS: Social skill strategies. Book A: A curriculum for adolescents.* Eau Claire, WI: Thinking Publications.

_____. 1989b. *SSS: Social skill strategies, Book B: A curriculum for adolescents.* Eau Claire, WI: Thinking Publications.

Gerlach, E. K. 1993. *Autism treatment guide.* Eugene, OR: Four Leaf Press.

Gillberg, C. 1986. Onset at age 14 of a typical autistic syndrome. A case report of a girl with herpes simplex encephalitis. *Journal of Autism and Developmental Disorders* 16:369-375.

_____. 1990. *Diagnosis and treatment of autism.* New York: Plenum Press.

Gillberg, C., and M. Coleman. 1992. *Biology of the autistic syndromes.* 2d ed. London: MacKeith Press.

Goetz, L., G. Sailor, and W. Sailor. 1985. Using a behavior chain interruption strategy to teach communication skills to students with severe disabilities. *Journal of the Association for Persons with Severe Handicaps (JASH)* 10(1):21-30.

Goldberg, T. E. 1987. On hermetic reading abilities. *Journal of Autism and Developmental Disabilities* 17(1):29-44.

Grandin, T. 1990. Needs of high-functioning teenagers and adults with autism: Tips from a recovered autistic. *Focus on Autistic Behavior* 5(1):1-15. Austin, TX: PRO-ED.

_____. 1992. An insider's view of autism. In *High-functioning individuals with autism,* edited by E. Schopler and G. B. Mesibov, 105-126. New York: Plenum Press.

Grandin, T. and M. Scariano. 1986. *Emergence labelled autistic.* Novato, CA: Arena Press.

Grant, J. O., B. B. Lazarus, and H. Peyton. 1992. The use of dialogue journals with students with exceptionalities. *Teaching Exceptional Children.* Summer:22-24.

Gray, C. 1992. *The curriculum system—Success as an educational outcome: Educating students with autism and other developmental disabilities for life in the community.* 2d ed. Jenison, MI: Jenison Public Schools.

_____. 1994a. *Comic strip conversations.* Jenison, MI: Jenison Public Schools

_____. 1994b. Social assistance. In *Higher-functioning adolescents and adults with autism: A teacher's guide*, edited by A. Fullerton, 105-133. Portland, OR: Department of Special and Counselor Education, Portland State University.

Gray, C. A., and J. D. Garand. 1993. Social stories: Improving responses of students with autism with accurate social information. *Focus on Autistic Behavior* 8(1):1-10. Austin, TX: PRO-ED.

Green, G., and H. C. Shane. 1994. Science, reason, and facilitated communication. *Journal of the Association for Persons with Severe Handicaps (JASH)* 19(3):151-172.

Groden, G., S. Stevenson, and J. Groden. 1993. *Understanding challenging behavior: A step-by-step behavior analysis guide.* Providence, RI: Manisses Communications Group.

Groden, J., and P. LeVasseur. 1995. Cognitive picture rehearsal: A visual system to teach self-control. In *Teaching children with autism: Methods to enhance learning, communication, and socialization*, edited by K. A. Quill. Albany, NY: Delmar Publishing Company.

Groden, J., J. R. Cautela, and G. Groden. 1989. *Breaking the barriers I: Relaxation techniques for people with special needs.* Videotape. Champaign, IL: Research Press.

_____. 1991. *Breaking the barriers II: Imagery procedures for people with special needs.* Videotape. Champaign: IL: Research Press.

Groden, J., J. R. Cautela, P. LaVasseur, G. Groden, and M. Bausman. 1991. *Video guide to Breaking the Barriers II.* Champaign, IL: Research Press.

Groden, J., J. R. Cautela, S. Prince, and J. Berryman. 1994. The impact of stress and anxiety on individuals with autism and developmental disabilities. In *Behavioral issues in autism*, edited by E. Schopler and G. B. Mesibov, 177-194. New York: Plenum Press.

Grossen, B. and D. Carnine. 1992. Translating research on text structure into classroom practice. *Teaching Exceptional Children* Summer:48-53.

Gustafson, G., D. Pfetzing, and E. Zawolkow. 1980. *Signing exact English.* 4th ed. Los Alamitos, CA: Modern Signs Press.

Halle, J. W., J. Chadsey-Rusch, and J. Reichle. 1994. Editorial introduction to the special topic on facilitated communication. *Journal of the Association for Persons with Severe Handicaps (JASH)* 19(3):149-150.

Handen, B. L. 1993. Pharmacotherapy in mental retardation and autism. *School Psychology Review* 22(2):162-183.

Hardy, P. M. 1985. Anxiety and panic disorder in autism. Paper presented at the Annual Meeting and Conference of the National Society of Autistic Children, Los Angeles, CA.

Haring, T., J. Neetz, C. Peck, and M. Semel. 1987. Effects of four modified incidental teaching procedures to create opportunities for communication. *Journal of the Association for Persons with Severe Handicaps (JASH)* 12(3):218-226.

Hart, C. 1989. *Without reason: A family copes with two generations of autism.* New York: Signet Books.

Harty, J. R. 1990. Pharmacotherapy in infantile autism. *Focus on Autistic Behavior* 5:2.

Hayword, H. C., P. Brooks, and S. Burns. 1990. *Cognitive curriculum for young children with autism (CCYC).* Watertown, MA: Charlesbridge.

Hill, D., and M. Leary. 1993. *Movement disturbance: A clue to hidden competencies in persons diagnosed with autism and other developmental disabilities.* Madison, WI: DRI Press.

Hobson, R. P. 1992. Social perception in high-level autism. In *High-functioning individuals with autism*, edited by E. Shopler and G. B. Mesibov, 157-184. New York: Plenum Press.

Horner, R. H. 1994. Facilitated communication: Keeping it practical. *Journal of the Association for Persons with Severe Handicaps (JASH)* 19(3):185-186.

Horner, R. H., G. Dunlap, and R. L. Koegel. 1988. *Generalization and maintenance: Lifestyle changes in applied settings.* Baltimore: Paul H. Brookes.

Isaacson, S., editor. 1988. Special focus: Teaching written expression. In *Teaching Exceptional Children.* Winter:32-39.

Note: This special focus section includes short descriptions of: The directed reading and writing procedure (DRAW), by J. P. Cox and E. Wood; The self-instructional strategy training procedure (SIST), by K. R. Harris and S. Graham; Computers and Writing Instruction (SCAN procedure), by C. A. MacArthur.

Kaiser, A. P. 1994. Invited Commentary: The controversy surrounding facilitated communication: Some alternative meanings. *Journal of the Association for Persons with Severe Handicaps (JASH)* 19(3):187-190.

Kanner, L. 1943. Autistic disturbances of affective content. *Nervous Child* 2:217-250.

Kasari, C., M. D. Sigman, P. Mundy, and N. Yirmiya. 1990. Affective sharing in the context of joint attention. *Journal of Autism and Developmental Disorders* 20:87-100.

Kern L., R. L. Koegel, and G. Dunlap. 1984. The influence of vigorous versus mild exercise on autistic stereotyped behavior. *Journal of Autism and Developmental Disabilities* 14(1):57-67.

Klinger, L. G., and G. Dawson. 1992. Facilitating early social and communicative development in children with autism. In *Volume 1: Causes and effects in communication and language intervention,* edited by S. F. Warren and J. Reichle, 157-186. Baltimore: Paul H. Brookes.

Koegel, R. L., and W. D. Frea. 1993. Treatment of social behavior in autism through the modification of pivotal social skills. *Journal of Applied Behavior Analysis* 26(3):369-377.

Koegel, R. L., W. D. Frea, and A. V. Surratt. 1994. Self-management of problematic social behavior. In *Behavioral issues in autism,* edited by E. Schopler and G. B. Mesibov, 545-565. New York: Plenum Press.

Koppenhaver, D. A., P. P. Coleman, S. L. Kalman, and D. E. Yoder. 1991. The implications of emergent literacy research for children with developmental disabilities. *American Journal of Speech-Language Pathology* 1(1):38-44.

LaVigna, G. W., and A. M. Donnellan. 1986. *Alternatives to punishment: Solving behavior problems with non-aversive strategies.* New York: Irvington Publishers.

Lehr, S. 1994. Designing usable guidelines and policies for facilitated communication. *Facilitated Communication Digest* 2:3.

Leverett, R. G., and A. O. Diefendorf. 1992. Students with language deficiencies: Suggestions for frustrated teachers. *Teaching Exceptional Children* Summer:30-35.

Levinson, L., and G. Reid. 1993. The effects of exercise intensity on the stereotypic behaviors of individuals with autism. *Adapted Physical Activity Quarterly* 10:255-268.

Levy, S. 1988. *Identifying high functioning children with autism.* Bloomington, IN: Indiana Resource Center for Autism, Institute for the Study of Developmental Disabilities, Indiana University.

Lindner, T. W. 1993. *Transdisciplinary play-based assessment: A functional approach to working with young children,* rev. ed. Baltimore: Paul H. Brookes.

Little, J. Unpublished. Being an effective coach for communication. Paper presented at the Annual Autism Conference, Eugene, Oregon, 1989.

Lord, C. 1991. Followup of two-year-olds referred for possible autism. Paper presented to the biannual meeting of the Society for Research and Child Development, Seattle.

Lovett, H. 1985. *Cognitive counseling and persons with special needs.* New York: Praeger.

Lucyshyn, J., D. Olson, and R. Horner. 1995. Building an ecology of support: A case study of one young woman with severe problem behaviors living in the community. *Journal of the Association for Persons with Severe Handicaps* 20(1):16-30.

Lussier, B. J., D. B. Crimmins, and D. Alberti. 1994. Effect of three adult interaction styles on infant engagement. *Journal of Early Intervention* 18(1):12-24.

MacDonald, J. D. 1989. *Becoming partners with children: From play to conversation.* San Antonio, TX: Special Press.

Marsella, A., and B. Marsella. 1991. The medical side of behavior. *The Advocate: Newsletter of the Autism Society of America.* Spring issue.

Mayer-Johnson. 1992. *The picture communication symbols book, III.* Solana Beach, CA: Mayer Johnson Co.

Mayo, P., and N. Gajewski. 1987. *Transfer activities.* Eau Claire, WI: Thinking Publications.

Mayo, P., and P. Waldo. 1986. *Scripting: Social communication for adolescents.* Scripts for role playing. Eau Claire, WI: Thinking Publications.

McGimsey, J. F., and J. E. Favell. 1988. The effects of increased physical exercise on disruptive behavior in retarded persons. *Journal of Autism and Developmental Disabilities* 18(2):167-179.

Melone, M. B., and A. Lettick. 1983. Sex education at Benhaven. In *Autism in adolescents and adults,* edited by E. Schopler and G. Mesibov, 169-186. New York: Plenum Press.

Merzer, S., and L. Chastain. 1982. Social skills: Assessment and interventions. In *Iowa Monograph: Autism—Programmatic Considerations,* edited by C. Smith, J. Grimes, and J. Freilinger. Des Moines: State of Iowa Department of Public Instruction.

Mesibov, G. B. 1986. A cognitive program for teaching social behaviors to verbal autistic adolescents and adults. In *Social behavior in autism,* edited by E. Schopler and G. B. Mesibov. New York: Plenum Press.

_____. 1992. Treatment issues with high-functioning adolescents and adults with autism. In *High-functioning individuals with autism,* edited by E. Schopler and G. B. Mesibov, 143-156. New York: Plenum Press.

Mesibov, G. B., E. Schopler, and K. A. Hearsey. 1994. Structured teaching. In *Behavioral issues in autism,* edited by E. Schopler and G. B. Mesibov, 195-210. New York: Plenum Press.

Mesibov, G., E. Schopler, B. Schaffer, and R. Landrus. 1988. *Adolescent and adult psychoeducational profile (AAPEP). Manual and test kit.* Austin, TX: PRO-ED.

Meyer, L. M., and I. M. Evans. 1989. *Non-aversive intervention for behavior problems: A manual for community and residential settings.* Baltimore: Paul H. Brookes.

Minshew, N. J. 1992. Neurological localization in autism. In *High-functioning individuals with autism,* edited by E. Schopler and G. Mesibov, 65-89. New York: Plenum Press.

Moreno, S. 1991. *High-functioning individuals with autism: Advice and information for parents and others who care.* MAAP Services, Inc. (3701 W. 108th Place, Crown Point, IN 46307; 219-662-1311).

____. 1992. A parent's view of more able people with autism. In *High-functioning individuals with autism,* edited by E. Schopler and G. Mesibov, 91-104. New York: Plenum Press.

Musselwhite, C. R. 1986. *Adaptive play for special needs children.* San Diego: College-Hill Press.

Neel, R. S. 1989. *IMPACT: Functional curriculum handbook for students with moderate to severe disabilities.* Baltimore: Paul H. Brookes.

O'Conner, N., and B. Hermelin. 1994. Two autistic savant readers. *Journal of Autism and Developmental Disabilities* 24(4):501-515.

Olney, M. 1995. Reading between the lines: A case study on facilitated communication. *Journal of the Association for Persons with Severe Handicaps* 20(1):57-65.

O'Neill, R. E., R. H. Horner, R. W. Albin, K. Storey, and J. R. Sprague. 1990. *Functional analysis of problem behavior: A practical assessment guide.* Sycamore, IL: Sycamore Press.

Orlick, T. 1978. *The cooperative sports and games book.* New York: Pantheon.

_____. 1982. *The second cooperative sports and games book.* New York: Pantheon.

Ornitz, E. M. 1987. Neurophysiologic studies of infantile autism. In *Handbook of autism and pervasive developmental disorders*, edited by D. Cohen, A. M. Donnellan, and R. Paul, 148-165. Silver Spring, MD: V. H. Winston and Sons.

Ousley, O. Y., and G. B. Mesibov. 1991. Sexual attitudes and knowledge of high-functioning adolescents and adults with autism. *Journal of Autism and Developmental Disabilities* 21(4):471-481.

Pehrsson, R. S., and P. R. Denner. 1989. *Semantic organizers: A study strategy for special needs learners.* Rockville, MD: Aspen.

Pehrsson, R. S., and H. A. Robinson. 1985. *The semantic organizer approach to writing and reading instruction.* Rockville, MD: Aspen.

Peschel, E. 1994. Autism and PDD (autism spectrum disorders) in the context of other neurobiological disorders: Recent findings from the neuroscience revolution. In *Autism Society of America Conference Proceedings* 7-9. Arlington, TX: Future Education.

Premack, D., and G. Collier. 1962. Analysis of nonreinforcement variables affecting response probability. In *Psychological Monographs: General and Applied* 76:5. Washington, DC: American Psychological Association.

Prizant, B. M. 1983. Language acquisition and communicative behavior in autism: Toward an understanding of the "whole" of it. *Journal of Speech and Hearing Disorders* 48:296-307.

_____. 1988. Communication problems in the autistic client. In *Handbook of speech-language pathology and audiology*, edited by N. J. Lass, L. V. McReynolds, J. L. Northern, and D. E. Yoder, 1014-1039. Philadelphia: B. C. Becker.

Prizant, B. M., and P. J. Rydell. 1993. Assessment and intervention considerations for unconventional verbal behavior. In *Communicative alternatives to challenging behavior: Integrating functional assessment and intervention strategies,* edited by J. Reichle and D. P. Wacker, 237-262. Baltimore: Paul H. Brookes.

Pruitting, C., and D. Kirchner. 1987. A clinical appraisal of the pragmatic aspects of language. *Journal of Speech and Hearing Disorders* 52(5):105-119.

Pulice, P. 1987. *Autism and attachment: An attachment-based intervention guide for children with autism and other pervasive developmental disorders.* Minneapolis: Minneapolis Children's Medical Center.

Quill, K. A. 1993. Methods to enhance learning in students with autism. In *1993 International Conference Proceedings: Autism, a world of options.* International Conference on Autism, Toronto. Arlington, TX: Future Education.

Raaz, N. 1982. Working with parents of students with autism. In *Autism—Programmatic considerations: A monograph of the Iowa State Department of Public Instruction*, edited by C. Smith, J. Grimes, and J. Freilinger. Des Moines: Iowa State Department of Public Instruction.

Rimland, B. P. 1991. *ARI recommendations on treatments for autistic and other mentally and neurologically handicapped children.* ARI Publication 49. San Diego: Autism Research Institute.

_____. 1994. Recovery from autism is possible. *Autism Research Review International* 8:2-3.

Rimland, B., and S. Edelson. 1994. The effects of auditory integration training on autism. *American Journal of Speech-Language Pathologists* 5(5):16-24.

Sabin, L. A., and A. M. Donnellan. 1993. A qualitative study of the process of facilitated communication. *Journal of the Association for Persons with Severe Handicaps (JASH)* 18(3):200-211.

Schaeffer, B., A. Raphael, and G. Kollinzas. 1994. *Signed Speech® language program for nonverbal students.* Seattle: Educational Achievement Systems.

Schawlow, A. T., and A. L. Schawlow. 1985. Our autistic son. In *Integrating severely and moderately handicapped learners: Strategies that work,* edited by M. Brady and P. Gunter. Springfield, IL: Charles Thomas.

Schopler, E., and G. B. Mesibov. 1992. *High-functioning individuals with autism.* New York: Plenum Press.

_____. 1994. *Behavioral issues in autism.* New York: Plenum Press.

Schopler, G., R. J. Reichler, A. Bashford, M. Lansing, and L. M. Marcus. 1990. *Psychoeducational profile—Revised (PEP-R). Manual and test kit.* Austin, TX: PRO-ED.

Schubert, A., editor. 1992. *Facilitated communication resource guide.* Brookline, MA: Adriana Foundation.

Schwartz, L. 1990. *What would you do?* Santa Barbara, CA: The Learning Works.

Shea, V., and G. B. Mesibov. 1985. Brief report: The relationship of learning disabilities and higher-level autism. *Journal of Autism and Developmental Disorders* 15(4):425-435.

Shepherd, T. R. 1983. Using experience language (LEA variation) to teach an autistic-like child with visual disorder to read (and write and talk). Paper presented at the Conference of the Great Lakes Regional International Reading Association, October 1983. Available through: U.S. Department of Education, National Institute of Education, Educational Resources Information Center (ERIC).

Shevin, M. 1994. An exercise in silencing: The New York OMRDD model guidelines on facilitated communication. *Facilitated Communication Digest* 2(3):3-10.

Shevin, M., and N. K. Klein. 1984. The importance of choice-making skills for students with severe disabilities. *Journal of the Association for Persons with Severe Handicaps (JASH)* 9(3):159-166.

Shields, J. M., and T. E. Heron. 1989. Teaching organizational skills to students with learning disabilities. *Teaching Exceptional Children* Winter:8-13.

Shure, M. B. 1992a. *I can problem solve: An interpersonal cognitive problem-solving program for intermediate elementary grades.* Champaign, IL: Research Press.

_____. 1992b. *I can problem solve: An interpersonal cognitive problem-solving program for kindergarten/primary ages.* Champaign, IL: Research Press.

_____. 1992c. *I can problem solve: An interpersonal cognitive problem-solving program for preschool ages.* Champaign, IL: Research Press.

Sinclair, J. 1992. Bridging the gaps: An inside-out view of autism (Or, Do you know what I don't know?) In *High-functioning individuals with autism,* edited by E. Schopler and G. B. Mesibov, 294-301. New York: Plenum Press.

Stehli, A. 1991. *The sound of a miracle.* New York: Doubleday.

Swezey, S. 1985. Never too late. *The Advocate: The Newsletter of the Autism Society of America.* November/December.

Tiegerman, E., and L. H. Primavera. 1984. Imitating the autistic child: Facilitating communicative gaze behavior. *Journal of Autism and Developmental Disorders* 14(1):27-38.

Trovato, C. A. 1987. *Teaching kids to care.* New York: The Instructor.

Tsai, L. 1994. Neurotransmitters and psychopharmacology in autism. In *Autism Society of America Conference Proceedings* 23-25. Arlington, TX: Future Education.

Tsai, L. Y. 1992. Diagnostic issues in high-functioning autism. In *High-functioning individuals with autism,* edited by E. Schopler and G. Mesibov, 11-40. New York: Plenum Press.

Turnbull, A. P., and H. R. Turnbull, III. 1990. *Families, professionals, and exceptionality: A special partnership.* 2d ed. Columbus: Merrill.

Van Bourgondien, M. E., and G. B. Mesibov. 1987. Humor in high-functioning autistic adults. *Journal of Autism and Developmental Disorders* 17(3):417-424.

Vernon, A. 1989a. *Thinking, feeling, behaving: An emotional education curriculum for adolescents, grades 7-12.* Champaign, IL: Research Press.

_____. 1989b. *Thinking, feeling, behaving: An emotional education curriculum for children, grades 1-6.* Champaign, IL: Research Press.

Vicker, B. 1988. *The high-functioning person with autism also has a communication problem.* Bloomington: Indiana Resource Center for Autism, Institute for the Study of Developmental Disabilities, Indiana University.

_____. 1993. Tracking facilitated communication and auditory desensitization training in Indiana: Hopes and outcomes. In *1993 International Conference Proceedings: Autism, a world of options.* International Conference on Autism, Toronto. Arlington, TX: Future Education.

Warren, S. F., and J. Reichle, eds. 1991. *Causes and effects in communication and language.* Baltimore: Paul H. Brookes.

Watson, L. R., C. Lord, B. Schaffer, and E. Schopler. 1989. *Teaching spontaneous communication to autistic and developmentally handicapped children.* New York: Irvington.

Webster's New Collegiate Dictionary. 1977. Springfield, MA: G. & C. Merriam.

Wetherby, A. M., and B. M. Prizant. 1993. Profiling communication and symbolic abilities in young children. *Journal of Childhood Communication Disorders* 15(1):23-32.

Whitehurst, G. J., and D. A. Crone. 1994. Invited commentary: Social constructivism, positivism, and facilitated communication. *Journal of the Association for Persons with Severe Handicaps (JASH)* 19(3):191-195.

Williams, D. 1992. *Nobody nowhere: The extraordinary autobiography of an autistic.* New York: Avon Books.

_____. 1994a. *Somebody somewhere: Breaking free from the world of autism.* New York: Random House.

_____. 1994b. In the real world. *Journal of the Association for Persons with Severe Handicaps (JASH)* 19(3):196-199.

Wing, L. 1980. Foreword. In *Autism: New directions in research and education*, edited by C. Webster, M. Konstantareas, J. Oxman, and J. Mack. Elmsford, NY: Pergamon Press.

_____. 1992. Manifestations of social problems in high-functioning autistic people. In *High-functioning individuals with autism*, edited by E. Schopler and G. Mesibov, 129-142. New York: Plenum Press.

Wing, L., and A. Attwood. 1987. Syndromes of autism and atypical development. In *The handbook of autism and pervasive developmental disorders*, edited by D. Cohen, A. Donnellan, and R. Paul, 3-19. Silver Spring, MD: V. H. Winston & Sons.

Wooten, M., and G. B. Mesibov. 1986. Social skills training for elementary school autistic children with normal peers. In *Social behavior in autism*, edited by E. Schopler and G. B. Mesibov, 305-319. New York: Plenum Press.

Yirmiya, N., M. D. Sigman, C. Kasari, and P. Mundy. 1992. Empathy and cognition in high-functioning children with autism. *Child Development* 63:150-160.